LUTHERAN QUARTERLY BOOKS

Editor

Paul Rorem, Princeton Theological Seminary

Associate Editors

Timothy J. Wengert, The Lutheran Theological Seminary at Philadelphia and Steven Paulson, Luther Seminary, St. Paul

Lutheran Quarterly Books will advance the same aims as *Lutheran Quarterly* itself, aims repeated by Theodore G. Tappert when he was editor fifty years ago and renewed by Oliver K. Olson when he revived the publication in 1987. The original four aims continue to grace the front matter and to guide the contents of every issue, and can now also indicate the goals of *Lutheran Quarterly Books:* "to provide a forum (1) for the discussion of Christian faith and life on the basis of the Lutheran confession; (2) for the application of the principles of the Lutheran church to the changing problems of religion and society; (3) for the fostering of world Lutheranism; and (4) for the promotion of understanding between Lutherans and other Christians."

For further information, see www.lutheranquarterly.com.

The symbol and motto of *Lutheran Quarterly,* VDMA for *Verbum Domini Manet in Aeternum* (1 Peter 1:25), was adopted as a motto by Luther's sovereign, Frederick the Wise, and his successors. The original "Protestant" princes walking out of the imperial Diet of Speyer 1529, unruly peasants following Thomas Muentzer, and from 1531 to 1547 the coins, medals, flags, and guns of the Smalcaldic League all bore the most famous Reformation slogan, the first Evangelical confession: the Word of the Lord remains forever.

Living by Faith: Justification and Sanctification by Oswald Bayer (2003).

Harvesting Martin Luther's Reflections on Theology, Ethics, and the Church, essays from *Lutheran Quarterly* edited by Timothy J. Wengert, with foreword by David C. Steinmetz (2004).

A More Radical Gospel: Essays on Eschatology, Authority, Atonement, and Ecumenism by Gerhard O. Forde, edited by Mark Mattes and Steven Paulson (2004).

The Role of Justification in Contemporary Theology, by Mark C. Mattes (2004).

The Captivation of the Will: Luther vs. Erasmus on Freedom and Bondage, by Gerhard O. Forde (2005).

Luther's Liturgical Music: Principles and Implications, by Robin A. Leaver (2006).

Bound Choice, Election, and Wittenberg Theological Method: From Martin Luther to the Formula of Concord by Robert Kolb (2005).

A Formula for Parish Practice: Using the Formula of Concord in Congregations by Timothy J. Wengert (2006).

The Preached God: Proclamation in Word and Sacrament by Gerhard O. Forde, edited by Mark Mattes and Steven Paulson (2007).

Luther's Liturgical Music

Principles and Implications

Robin A. Leaver, R.A.

WILLIAM B. EERDMANS PUBLISHING COMPANY
GRAND RAPIDS, MICHIGAN / CAMBRIDGE, U.K.

© 2007 Robin A. Leaver

Published 2007 by
Wm. B. Eerdmans Publishing Co.
2140 Oak Industrial Drive N.E., Grand Rapids, Michigan 49505 /
P.O. Box 163, Cambridge CB3 9PU U.K.

Printed in the United States of America

12 11 10 09 08 07   7 6 5 4 3 2 1

Library of Congress Cataloging-in-Publication Data

Leaver, Robin A.
    Luther's liturgical music: principles and implications /
    Robin A. Leaver.
        p.   cm. — (Lutheran quarterly books)
    Includes bibliographical references (p.   ) and index.
    ISBN 978-0-8028-3221-4 (pbk.: alk. paper)
    1. Church music — Lutheran Church — 16th century.
    2. Church music — Germany — 16th century. 3. Luther, Martin, 1483-1546.
    Hymns.   I. Title

ML3168.L43   2007
781.71 410092 — dc22

                                                                    2006035021

www.eerdmans.com

Contents

Preface

In one sense this book has had a long gestation period, though most of it has been written in recent years. A good many of the chapters, in earlier manifestations, have appeared in a variety of publications, as is recorded in detail in the Postscript. The earliest was first published in 1983 and the latest in 2006. Some originated as conference papers, others as commissioned articles. None appears here without revision, sometimes substantial, or without additional material.

My interest in Luther began while I was studying theology in the early sixties. Being involved with church music from an early age, the combination of music and theology in Luther's writings was intriguing, stimulating, and irresistible, especially in my native England. The general view of Luther that I grew up with was of a Reformer whose prophetic actions created Protestantism, but whose theology was suspect and therefore not to be investigated in much depth! This is hardly surprising in a general Anglican context that had evolved in different directions from sixteenth-century Lutheranism. It was out of my dissatisfaction with this *status quo* that I began researching Luther's writings for myself. Out of this grew an extended essay on Luther's theology of justification. Martin Franzmann — who had been Professor of New Testament at Concordia Seminary, St. Louis, and was then tutor at the Lutheran Westfield House in Cambridge — encouraged me to expand it for publication.

This I did, and when the manuscript was completed he was instrumental in the negotiations that led to its publication by Concordia Publishing House in St. Louis and London. The book was published as *Luther on Justification* (1975), with a preface written by the English Luther scholar Gordon Rupp, Professor of Ecclesiastical History at Cambridge University. Some years later at Latimer House, Oxford, I was privileged to be a colleague of another English Luther scholar, James Atkinson, formerly Professor of Biblical Studies and Director of the Centre for Reformation Studies at Sheffield University. Although none had a direct influence on the content of this volume, I am nevertheless indebted to these three professors who personally encouraged my study of Luther, and thereby indirectly but significantly have conditioned much that appears here.

Reference to the Postscript will reveal that a number of the following chapters have appeared within the pages of the journal *Lutheran Quarterly.* This is due to its editor, Paul Rorem, who since the early 1990s has been constantly asking me for contributions. Sometimes he had heard about a paper I had given and wanted the substance to be repeated in the journal. At other times he would approach me with specific requests, as in the case of the series of articles on Luther's catechism hymns. A few years ago, when this series, *Lutheran Quarterly Books,* was being conceived, he made the suggestion that perhaps I would think about bringing my *Lutheran Quarterly* articles on Luther, together with others, to be published in the series. Up until then I had not thought about creating such a book. Therefore, if anyone other than me is responsible for this book seeing light of day, it has to be Paul Rorem! I am extremely grateful to him not only for making the suggestion in the first place but also for his superb editorial oversight, answering all kinds of questions, checking translations, and so forth.

When planning the book I realized that what I had already written needed to be prefaced by some substantial background chapters. The first section, Chapters 1-3, was therefore specifically written for this book, Chapter 2 and part of Chapter 3 being published in *Lutheran Quarterly* in anticipation of the publication of the complete volume.

I am greatly indebted to others for their assistance and help, being particularly grateful to Leofranc Holford-Strevens, who at my request graciously provided the translation of Gerson's poem in praise of music that appears as Appendix 2. I could not have completed the manuscript without the wisdom, experience, insight and collaborative research of the following: Mark Bangert, Lutheran School of Theology, Chicago; Jill Burnett Cumming, Drew University; Stephen Crist, Emory University; M. Patrick Graham, Director of Pitts Theology Library, Emory University; Scott Hendrix, Princeton Theological Seminary; Robert Kolb, Concordia Seminary, St. Louis; Michael Marissen, Swarthmore College; Kate Skrebutenas, Speer Library, Princeton Seminary; Knud Svensen, Aarhus, Denmark; Martin Treu, Director of the Lutherhalle, Wittenberg; Timothy Wengert, The Lutheran Theological Seminary at Philadelphia; and Daniel Zager, Eastman School of Music. I am particularly indebted to my former graduate assistant J. Mark Dunn for creating the musical examples. Without the assistance — and forbearance — of my wife, Sherry Vellucci, I would still be working on the manuscript. Errors and misstatements are, of course, to be laid at my door rather than at those of my advisors.

Now that the writing of this book is complete I have a better understanding of two comments of Luther found in the *Tischreden:* "He who does not know writing thinks it requires no effort. Three fingers write, but the entire body is at work" (WA TR No. 6438); and, "Music is a very fine art. The notes make the words live" (WA TR No. 2545).

ROBIN A. LEAVER

Abbreviations

AWA	*Archiv zu Weimarer Ausgabe der Werke Martin Luthers.* Cologne: Böhlau, 1984- .
AWA 4	Markus Jenny, ed. *Luther's Geistliche Lieder und Kirchen gesänge: Vollständige Neuedition in Ergänzung zu Band der Weimarer Ausgabe.* Cologne: Böhlau, 1985.
BC-W/K	Robert Kolb and Timothy J. Wengert, eds. *The Book of Concord: The Confessions of the Evangelical Lutheran Church.* Minneapolis: Fortress, 2000.
BSLK	*Die Bekenntnisschriften der evangelisch-lutherischen Kirche.* 11th edition. Göttingen: Vandenhoeck & Ruprecht, 1992.
BWV	Wolfgang Schmieder, ed. *Thematisch-systematisches Verzeichnis der musikalischen Werke von Johann Sebastian Bach: Bach-Werk-Verzeichnis.* 2nd edition. Wiesbaden: Breitkopf & Härtel, 1990.
CW	*Christian Worship: A Lutheran Hymnal.* Milwaukee: Northwestern, 1993. Hymnal of the Wisconsin Evangelical Lutheran Synod.
DKL	*Das deutsche Kirchenlied.* Dates with superior numbers (e.g., DKL 1524[13]) are references to the bibliography: *Das deutsche Kirchenlied I/1: Verzeichnis der Drucke.* Edited by Konrad Ameln, Markus Jenny, and Walther Lipphardt. Kassel: Bärenreiter, 1975. Other references (e.g., DKL A327) are to specific melodies: *Das deutsche Kirchenlied: Kritische Gesamtausgabe der Melodien. Abteilung III: Die Melodien aus gedruckten Quellen bis 1680.* Edited by Joachim Stalmann et al. Kassel: Bärenreiter, 1993- .
ELH	*Evangelical Lutheran Hymnary.* St. Louis: Morning Star, 1996. Hymnal of the Evangelical Lutheran Synod (Mankato, Minn.).

HEK	*Handbuch der deutschen evangelischen Kirchenmusik nach der Quellen.* Edited by Konrad Ameln et al. Göttingen: Vandenhoeck & Ruprecht, 1932-.
JbLH	*Jahrbuch für Liturgik und Hymnologie.* 1955-.
LBW	*Lutheran Book of Worship.* Minneapolis: Augsburg, 1978.
LH	*The Lutheran Hymnal.* St. Louis: Concordia, 1941.
L-J	*Luther-Jahrbuch.* 1919-.
Lossius	Lucas Lossius. *Psalmodia, hoc est, Cantica sacra veteris ecclesiae selecta.* Wittenberg: Rhau, 1561; facsimile, Stuttgart: Cornetto, 1996.
LU	*Liber usualis with Introduction and Rubrics in English.* Tournai: Desclée, 1934 and later reprints.
LW	*Luther's Works: American Edition.* 55 volumes. St. Louis: Concordia and Philadelphia: Fortress, 1955-1986.
LWor	*Lutheran Worship.* St. Louis: Concordia, 1982. Hymnal of the Lutheran Church–Missouri Synod.
MGG	Musik in Geschichte und Gegenwart.
New Grove 2	*The New Grove Dictionary of Music and Musicians.* 2nd edition. Edited by Stanley Sadie and John Tyrrell. New York: Grove, 2001.
OER	*The Oxford Encyclopedia of the Reformation.* 4 volumes. Edited by Hans J. Hillerbrand. New York: Oxford University Press, 1996.
RMD	Georg Rhau. *Musikdrucke aus den Jahren 1538 bis 1545 in Praktischer neuausgabe.* Kassel: Bärenreiter, 1955-.
WA	*Luthers Werke: Kritische Gesamtausgabe.* 65 volumes. Weimar: Böhlau, 1883-1993.
WA BR	*Luthers Werke: Kritische Gesamtausgabe. Briefwechsel.* 18 volumes. Weimar: Böhlau, 1930-1985.
WA TR	*Luthers Werke: Kritische Gesamtausgabe. Tischreden.* 6 volumes. Weimar: Böhlau, 1912-1921.
WGA	*Johann Walter Sämtlicher Werke.* Edited by Otto Schroeder. Kassel: Bärenreiter, 1953-70.
WLS	*What Luther Says: An Anthology.* Translated and edited by Ewald M. Plass. St. Louis: Concordia, 1959.
Zahn	Johannes Zahn. *Die Melodien der deutschen evangelischen Kirchenlieder.* 6 volumes. Gütersloh: Bertelsmann, 1889-1893; reprint Hildesheim: Olms, 1963.

N.B.: References to chant are to LU for Catholic use and to Lossius for Lutheran use.

Tables, Figures, and Musical Examples

Tables

PART I

Background & Principles

CHAPTER 1

Introduction

Among sixteenth-century Reformers Luther, together with his Wittenberg colleagues, was positive with regard to the role of music within evangelical worship, whereas many others, such as Calvin and his Genevan followers, were more cautious, limiting music to the simple unaccompanied unison of the gathered congregation, and a few, notably Zwingli and those who emulated the worship patterns of Zurich, were negative toward music, banishing it completely from the Reformed sanctuary.

English-language Luther studies in general have tended to ignore or give scant attention to his role as a liturgical reformer; indeed, he has been frequently characterized as an inept cut-and-paste reviser.[1] Since music is frequently subsumed under liturgical matters, it too tends to suffer a similar fate. For example, the collection of essays *The Cambridge Companion to Martin Luther* contains no study of Luther's liturgical reforms, his hymns, or his understanding of music.[2] The volume is therefore out of step with European Luther studies, as represented, for example, by the collection of essays issued to mark the 500th anniversary of the Reformer's birth that includes studies of Luther's liturgical reforms in general, his liturgical collects in particular, as well as his role as an editor of hymnals; and the recently-published *Luther Handbuch*, which has a chapter on Luther and music.[3] One of the reasons for this neglect in the English-speaking world is the Reformed orientation of a significant number of authors and editors of Luther studies, a tradition that historically has ceded to music only a limited role in worship. This in turn has contributed to the pervasive contemporary view of worship music as an optional extra, useful for creating a desired mood but with no essential theological meaning or significance. But Luther, together with the clergy and musicians who contributed to the distinctive Lutheran tradition of church music that was the outgrowth of his theology and reforms, thought differently. Luther's positive approach to music has been described and evaluated in print in virtually every succeeding generation — mostly, naturally enough, by German-speaking Lutherans — though to begin with such discussions occurred within a wider context than simply "Luther and Music."[4] For example, Johann Aurifaber's *Tischreden* (Eisleben: Gaubisch, 1566), a collection of verbatim reports of the Reformer's conversations at table and elsewhere, includes a section headed "Von der Musica." Other examples include Christoph Frick, *Music-Büchlein Oder Nützlicher Bericht Von dem Uhrsprung/Gebrauche und Erhaltung Christlicher Music* (Lüneberg: Stern, 1631),[5] and Wolfgang Caspar Printz, *Historische Beschreibung der Edelen Sing- und Kling-Kunst* (Dresden: Mieth, 1690), both of which include Luther's views on music set within a broad historical context. Many of the earlier treatments of Luther's approach to music are found in studies of his creativity as an author and composer of hymns, such as those by Cyriacus Spangenburg (1569-70), Johann Adolf Liebner (1791), August Jakob Rambach (1813), Justin Heinrich Knecht (1817), Friedrich Adolf Beck (1825), and August Gebauer (1828).[6]

Throughout the nineteenth century there was a growing tendency to treat Luther's understanding and use of music in a more independent manner. These were the years when the German Lutheran churches were beginning to recover their distinctive liturgical traditions that had been all but erased by the combined influences of rationalism and Pietism in the previous century. But this interest in Luther was not confined to Germany. In England in the later eighteenth century interest in Lutheran hymnody and music was fostered by the succession of Hanoverian kings and the music of Handel, and in the nineteenth century Anglo-German connections were reinforced by the marriage of Queen Victoria to Albert of Saxe-Coburg and Mendelssohn's frequent visits to England. In North America the ties with Germany were even stronger because of the successive waves of German immigrants who made the New World their home. Thus articles on Luther and music, and/or quotations of Luther's views of music, were published in the following representative nineteenth-century journals:

> Germany: *Berliner allgemeine musikalische Zeitung* 2 (1825); *Berliner musikalische Zeitung* 3 (1846); *Allgemeine musikalische Zeitung* 1 [new series] (Leipzig, 1866).
> France: *Revue musicale* 3 (Paris, 1830).
> USA: *The Euterpeiad, or Musical Intelligencer* 1 (Boston, 1820), 3 (1822); *The Message Bird — Journal of the Fine Arts — The Musical World* 1

(New York, 1849); *Dwight's Journal of Music* 3 (Boston, 1853), 5 (1854), 15 (1859), 18 (1861), 33 (1873).

England: *The Musical World* 7 (London, 1837), 13 (1839), 32 (1854), 34/43 (1856), 37/43 (1859); *The Musical Times* 1 (London, 1845).

In the later nineteenth and early twentieth centuries various studies appeared, notably those of Johannes Rautenstrauch (1907), Karl Anton (1916), Hermann Abert (1924), Hans Joachim Moser (1925), Friedrich Blume (1931), and Christhard Mahrenholz (1937).[7] In the restoration period following the Second World War, when a significant number of new church music institutions were created,[8] new studies of Luther and music were circulated, such as those by Karl Honemeyer (1941), Christoph Wetzel (1954), Walter Blankenburg (1957), Oskar Söhngen (1961), and Winfried Kurzschenkel (1971).[9]

During the same period a succession of studies on Luther and music was published in America, written by such authors as Ulrich S. Leupold (1940), Walter E. Buszin (1946), Paul Nettl (1948), Robert M. Stevenson (1951), and Theodore Hoelty-Nickel (1960).[10] Of these, Buszin's study proved to be the most influential, being frequently cited in later literature.[11] More recently Carl Schalk has produced a similar study (1988),[12] which is to some degree dependent on the translations of Buszin, and there have been numerous shorter articles, of which those by Daniel Reuning (1984) and Edward Foley (1987) are representative examples,[13] as well as accounts in standard reference works, such as my own in the second edition of the *New Grove Dictionary of Music and Musicians* (2001).[14]

With all this literature it might be argued that there is hardly the need for yet another study of Luther and music. However, even though there is a general consensus, these previous studies are not uniformly the same. Therefore new interpretations need to be evaluated; older research, especially where it was based on misconceptions, requires correction; and neglected areas of study demand attention.

Recent Research

Among the new developments is the minority view of a few scholars that the general consensus regarding Luther's knowledge and use of music is misleading. The similar view presented in numerous studies, such as those by Anton, Söhngen, Buszin, and Schalk, among others, is based on numerous statements regarding music that are to be found throughout Luther's extensive literary output. The statements are topically arranged and discussed, presenting the view that music was fundamentally important to the Reformer, both in terms of its intrinsic nature as well as its theological significance. Some recent writers, however, have argued that such interpretations of Luther are suspect, and perhaps reveal more about the authors' concerns with contemporary matters rather than with Luther's views in the sixteenth century. Karl Honemeyer regards Thomas Müntzer as more significant than Luther with regard to liturgical music, a view that was first raised in his 1941 University of Münster dissertation,[15] and continued in subsequent published writings.[16] Joyce Irwin's doctoral dissertation on Müntzer[17] strongly reflects Honemeyer's point of view, and provides the background for her dismissive comments with regard to Luther and music in the "Prelude" to her book *Neither Voice nor Heart Alone* (1993).[18] Matthias Silesius Viertel has doubted whether Luther actually gave to music a proclamatory function, as many have claimed.[19] Some have argued that since Luther's statements on music form but a small proportion of his total literary output, it is a distortion to give disproportionate attention to them.

Such deconstructionist viewpoints have not received widespread endorsement and the general scholarly consensus continues to reiterate established conclusions concerning Luther's references and allusions to music.[20] Even though it will be argued in this study that Luther's approach to music is more significant than recent critics have suggested, nevertheless, some of these alternative views raise some really important issues. For example, there has been a tendency to imply, by selective citation, that all of Luther's references to music are positive. As some of the recent critics have pointed out, this is manifestly a false impression, since a significant number of his references to music are extremely critical, as the following representative citations demonstrate:

> Therefore, let the works go, no matter how great they may be, prayers, chants, yammering, and yapping; for it is certain that nobody will ever get to God through all these things.[21]

> Christ's Mass was most simple, without any display of vestments, gestures, chants, or other ceremonies.[22]

> [The Pope directs] how one can serve God and do good works through tonsures, cowls, orders, fasting, begging, eating milk, eggs, meat, butter, singing, organs, censing, bell-ringing, celebrating, buying indulgences, and the like, all of which God does not know.[23]

We . . . have no great need of organ music, bells, and rote recitation.[24]

Reason . . . is as blind as a bat and says that we must fast, pray, sing, and do the works of the law. It continues to fool around in this manner with works, until it has gone so far astray and thinks we serve God by building churches, ringing bells, burning incense, reciting by rote, singing, wearing hoods, having tonsures, burning candles, and by other countless foolish acts of which the world is full, indeed more than full.[25]

[St. Paul] perceives with great clarity what great fools they all are who want to become pious through works, and he will not give one penny for all the tonsures of priests, monks, bishops, and popes nor for cowls, incensing, ringing of bells, burning of candles, singing, organs, and reciting prayers with all their external performance.[26]

In particular it seems that Luther was especially critical of organs, since his references to them are frequently negative. For example, commenting on 1 Corinthians 14, Luther wrote:

If now (as Paul says) some unbeliever were to enter into the midst of these men and heard them braying, mumbling, and bellowing, and saw that they were neither preaching nor praying, but rather, as their custom is, were sounding forth like those pipe organs (with which they have so brilliantly associated themselves, each one set in a row just like his neighbor), would this unbeliever not be perfectly justified in asking, "Have you gone mad?" [1 Cor. 14:23]. What else are these monks but the tubes and pipes Paul referred to as giving no distinct note but rather blasting out into the air [1 Cor. 14:7]?[27]

Similarly, speaking of people who pray superficial prayers, Luther wrote:

These people utter this prayer with their lips, but contradict it with their hearts. They are like lead organ pipes which fairly drawl or shout out their sounds in church, yet lack both words and meaning. Perhaps these organs represent and symbolize these singers and petitioners.[28]

The context of most of these statements, however, reveals that the criticisms were not of music *per se* but of its use, or rather abuse, in unreformed liturgies, which for Luther was a theological issue. His critical references to the sound of the organ may have had more to do with the imperfect development of the instruments he had heard — that they had not yet reached the refinement of later times — rather than with any objection to organs on principle. For example, the Italian Antonio de Beatis traveled from Italy through Germany in 1517-1518 and his journal suggests that organs in southern German-speaking areas were generally superior to those further north. He wrote:

> In the chief church [in Innsbruck] there is an organ which, while not particularly large is most beautiful, with many stops which produce the purest tone representing trumpets, fifes, flutes, cornets, crumhorns, bagpipes, drums and the . . . songs of various birds . . . ; indeed, of all the many other organs we saw in the course of our whole journey, this was pronounced the most perfect.[29]

On the other hand, given the association of Paul Hofheimer, Austrian court organist, with the court of Frederick the Wise in Torgau, Luther must have heard some good organs and accomplished organ playing. Despite the criticisms cited above, organ music was not eliminated from Wittenberg churches but given specific liturgical functions.[30] Further, Luther's relationship with Johannes Weinmann, organist in Wittenberg, and his respect for Wolff Heinz, organist in Halle, as well as his connections with other organists, confirm that he understood that organs and organ music could be put to positive use within evangelical worship.[31] Similarly, comments found elsewhere in his writings make it clear that vocal and instrumental music were not to be banished from evangelical churches.

What was at issue, according to Luther, was not music itself but how it was used. If it was performed merely in fulfilment of the demands of unreformed ecclesiastical law then it was to be condemned, but if it was performed in response to the gospel then it was to be commended: "After faith we can do no greater work than to praise, preach, sing, and in every way laud and magnify God's glory, honor, and name."[32] Therefore, when he created his evangelical Mass, he only eliminated the offertory and canon and left almost everything else unchanged, including monodic chant and polyphony, but with the proviso that the Gospel should be preached, so that the celebration would not be interpreted as a function of Law.[33] The issue was not the use of music in the liturgy but rather its misuse. As he was thinking towards reforming the Mass he wrote:

> The first step is to let the old practice continue. Let the Mass be celebrated with consecrated vestments, with chants and all the usual ceremonies, in

Latin, recognizing the fact that these are merely external matters which do not endanger the consciences of men. But besides that, through the sermon keep the consciences free, so the congregation may learn that these things are done not because they have to be done that way or because it would be heresy to do them differently, as the nonsensical laws of the pope insist.[34]

Later, as the reforming movement was being intensified around 1530, he expanded on this positive appreciation of the musical portions of the evangelical Mass that had been taken over from unreformed use:

I believe that many hymns were included and retained in the Mass which deal with thanking and praising [God] in a wonderful and excellent way, as for example, the Gloria in Excelsis, the Alleluia, the Creed,[35] the Preface, the Sanctus, the Benedictus, and the Agnus Dei. In these various parts you find nothing about a sacrifice but only praise and thanks. Therefore, we have also kept them in our Mass. Particularly the Agnus Dei, above all songs, serves well for the sacrament, for it clearly sings about and praises Christ for having borne our sins and in beautiful, brief words powerfully and sweetly teaches the remembrance of Christ. In short, God has wonderfully arranged it so that essentially the priest reads secretly the evil parts of the Mass which deal with sacrifice and works, and this is called the secret Mass; but whatever is publicly sung by the choir or the multitude is essentially a good thing and a hymn of praise. It is as if God were actually saying in this way that he wants to preserve his Christians from the secret Mass so that their ears might not hear such an abomination; and so let the clergymen torment themselves with their own abomination.[36]

The introduction of the Reformation into other areas followed the same pattern. Thus for the reforms being introduced into Leipzig in 1539 Luther advised: "It would be good to keep the whole liturgy *with its music,* omitting only the Canon."[37] But his concern was for the people, in participating in liturgical music, that their minds and hearts should be in harmony with what was expressed through their mouths: "We must take care . . . lest the people sing only with their lips, like sounding pipes or harps [1 Cor. 14:7], and without understanding"[38]; "Heart and mind must be cheerful and willing if one is to sing. Therefore, God abrogated the service that was rendered so indolently and reluctantly."[39]

While it is true that, purely on a statistical count, Luther's comments on music comprise but a small proportion of his total output, this does not diminish their importance. In addition to the specific references to music there are many allusions to musical matters that are made in passing that are not always noticed. Instances include recollections of familiar chants, references to his musical experiences as a boy, examples of various aspects of music that are used to illustrate theological points, and so forth, examples that are explored here in Chapters 2 and 3.

Old Research and Misconceptions

Older studies of Luther and music — especially those in English — are frustrating to use for a number of reasons. First, since their publication there have been other books and articles that have either corrected the information or have demonstrated that subsequent research has come to different conclusions. Second, much of recent Luther research has, not surprisingly, been published in German, and there is the need to present the fruits of these studies in English. Third, modern standards of annotation were not necessarily followed by earlier writers, such as Friedrich Blume in the first edition of *Die evangelische Kirchenmusik* (1931), and Paul Nettl in his *Luther and Music* (1948)[40]; while their information is detailed and informative, the sources are not always specified but only hinted at, which means that the reader has to spend a good deal of time in the attempt to discover the exact source of the information. When the source is discovered it is frequently found, especially in Nettl, that the citation has been truncated, sometimes severely, without ellipsis markings, and in some cases may not even refer to the issue being discussed.

Another problem of the older literature is the tendency to cite from more than one edition of Luther's works, and from editions no longer in current use. An example is Walter Buszin's otherwise excellent summary that first appeared in the *Musical Quarterly* over half a century ago; he used either the Erlangen or the St. Louis editions but not the Weimar edition that is now standard for Luther studies.[41] Since Buszin wrote his article on Luther and music the American edition of Luther's works in English translation — though still not a complete edition — has been published. There is therefore the need to review the literature on Luther and music from the perspective of these two primary editions of Luther's works that are standard in this country, the Weimar and American editions, to locate sources that are common to both, and to identify those that can be conveniently found only in the Weimar edition, rather than in any of the earlier editions of the writings of the Reformer.[42]

Not all the problems, however, can be resolved by using the Weimar edition. While it is *the* authoritative edition of Luther's works, its editors did not always get things right the first time they published a work of the Reformer; hence the various appendices and alternative versions in the later volumes of the edition. One of the most important documents concerning Luther's understanding of music is his Latin preface to Rhau's *Symphoniae iuncundae atque adea breves quattuor vocum,* published in 1538. Much confusion has been created by various German translations of the document. The accepted chronology, followed by the editors of the Weimar edition, posits that the first translation was by Johann Walter, published as a preface to his [Walter's] second and longer poem in praise of music, *Lob und Preis der Himmlischen Kunst Musica* (Wittenberg, 1564); the Weimar edition included the 1538 Latin text in parallel with Walter's German text of 1564.[43] A second German version appeared as a preface to Wolfgang Figulus's *Cantionem sacrum . . . primi tomi decas prima* (Nuremberg, 1575). A third translation was made by Johann Jakob Greiff and published in the last volume (Vol. 22) of the Leipzig edition of Luther's works, issued in 1734.[44]

The Walter and Figulus versions are characterized by differences in content, sometimes substantial, when they are compared with the Latin text, including both omissions and expansions. This led August Jakob Rambach, at the beginning of the nineteenth century, to raise the question that perhaps Luther originally wrote in German, which might mean that what was considered to be Walter's German translation was in fact Luther's original text. However, having raised the possibility within the main text of his book, in an appendix Rambach expressed his later judgment that in his view the Latin version was the original.[45]

In eighteenth- and nineteenth-century editions of Luther's works one or another of these three German versions was included. In the course of time these various documents, instead of being considered different versions of the presumed original Latin text, came to be viewed as different and independent expressions of Luther's views on music, so that one of the early translations was cited as being from the Latin preface to Rhau's 1538 anthology, *Symphoniae juncundae,* and the other was presented as a different preface emanating from the same year. For example, Karl Anton gives the text of Walter's translation, under the heading, "'Symphoniae juncundae' Wittenberg, Rhau, 1538," then follows it with Greiff's 1734 translation under the heading, "D. Martin Luther's Vorrede auf die Harmonie vom Leyden Christe."[46] The error was created by Hugo Holstein towards the end of the nineteenth century,[47] who made the mistake of regarding Greiff's translation as another independent document from Luther's pen.[48] Had Holstein checked more thoroughly he would have discovered that the preface to *Selectae Harmoniae Quatuor Vocum De Passione Domine* (Wittenberg: Rhau, 1538) has a different content and was in fact authored by Philipp Melanchthon rather than Luther.[49]

Walter Buszin, clearly influenced by Anton, included a translation of Luther's 1538 *Encomion musices*, translated from the Latin as found in the Erlangen edition of Luther's works, but described as the preface to "a collection of part-songs based on the suffering and death of Christ."[50] He then followed it with an excerpted translation of Walter's 1564 German version, identifying it as Luther's preface to Rhau's *Symphonia iucundae* (1538), that is, as another independent work.[51] Carl Schalk makes a brief citation from the translation of the Latin text found in Volume 53 of the American edition of *Luther's Works*, then adds in a footnote, "For another translation of this passage, see Buszin," but does not explain that this other translation is not of Luther's Latin but of Walter's German version.

In his research regarding Johann Walter, Walter Blankenburg reexamined the two sixteenth-century German versions of Luther's words and came to a conclusion that was similar to August Jakob Rambach's original thoughts on the matter, except that instead of regarding the 1564 German version as Luther's possible original text, Blankenburg demonstrated that the preface that Figulus published in 1575, rather than being an alternative German translation, was indeed Luther's original draft that he then translated into Latin in 1538. The Latin text parallels the "Figulus" version more closely than the "Walter" version, and, apart from a few sentences that appear only in the "Figulus" version, the differences are mainly slight expansions and alternative formulations of the same thoughts.[52] Thus the misconception of Holstein, perpetuated by Anton and Buszin among others, has now been clarified, and instead of a garbled form of the documentary evidence we now have a much clearer picture of the development of Luther's thought, since the German draft of his published Latin "Encomium" has thus been identified. There are significant implications of this discovery which are explored further in Chapter 3.

The "Secular" Music Mythology

Another persistent area of misunderstanding and misinterpretation concerns Luther's use of "secular" melodies. Again and again statements have been made that imply that Luther made extensive use of popular music. In support of the use of such music he is even quoted as asking the rhetorical question "Why should the devil have all the good tunes?" — words that cannot be found anywhere in his voluminous writings.[53] Certainly, Luther was aware of such tunes, especially their form and style, but not to the extent that is frequently suggested by those who seek to justify their own use of secular styles and forms in contemporary worship.

When Luther began writing religious songs — presuming that the earliest extant example was his first — he produced what amounts to a broadside ballad, a narrative song in the style of the secular Hofweise, the court song. It was headed "Eyn new lied von den zween Merterern Christi, zu Brussel von den Sophisten zu Louen verbrant" (A new song of the two martyrs of Christ, burnt in Brussels by the Sophists of Louvain).[54] The execution of the two Augustinian brothers took place at the beginning of July 1523. When the news reached Luther in Wittenberg, probably at the beginning of the following month, August 1523, he was deeply moved by the fact that their principal offense was that they were charged with being "Lutherans," thus implicating him in their deaths. One of his responses was to write a song, *Ein neues lied,* which followed the secular practice of disseminating news in ballad form. The common tradition is clearly seen when the opening lines of Luther's first stanza are compared with the opening stanza of a typical secular narrative song dating from approximately the same period:

Luther (1523)
Ein neues lied wir heben an,
des walt Gott, unser Herre,
zu singen, was Gott hat getan
zu seinem Lob und Ehre
Zu Brussel in der Nederland. . . .

The Battle of Pavia song (1525)
Was wöll wir aber heben an
ein neues lied zu singen,
Wol von dem könig aus Frankenreich,
Mailand wolt er bezwingen.
Das gschach da man zelt
tousend-fünf-hundert jar. . . .[55]

The verbal correspondences are obvious: "ein neues lied," "wir . . . heben an," "zu singen"; as are the references to specific people and places.

By accepting the discipline of the Hofweise, with its "barform" melody (repeated stollen [A] and abgesang [B] resulting in an AAB form) (see Example 1.1), Luther ensured that most of the Wittenberg congregational hymns he and his colleagues would write in the weeks and months ahead, would be largely written in this secular style (notice the similarity of the first line with Luther's later melody *Ein feste Burg;* Example 1.2 A and B). Thus of the eight Wittenberg broadside hymns that were collected together and issued in Nuremberg in 1523/24, under the title *Etliche Cristliche lyder Lobgesang/und Psalm,* seven conformed to the barform of the Hofweise. But the secular influence on these eight hymn texts was primarily textual rather than musical.

Example 1.1. Luther's *Ein neues lied wir heben an* (1523). Zahn No. 7245. DKL Ea12.

Example 1.2. Comparison of Similar Melodic Incipits

The Hofweise could be seen as a development of the Meistersänger tradition, as exemplified by the Nuremberg cobbler-poet Hans Sachs, who had extensive experience in writing religious verse and composing corresponding melodies, frequently in barform, years before he came under the influence of Luther.[56] After adopting the Reformation ideals of Luther Sachs began writing original hymns and metrical versions of the Psalms reflecting the "new faith." Sachs also created parodies or rewritten versions of preexisting religious lyrics — non-liturgical folk songs. Thus overt Catholic doctrines were eliminated and replaced by Luther's understanding of faith and theology, but were sung to the associated melodies of the original texts. For example, in 1524 two broadsheets were issued in Nuremberg, each one containing an old

Example 1.3. **Comparison of Variants of the "Rosina" Melody**

Marian hymn "verendert und Christlich Corrigiert" (altered and Christianly corrected), that is, instead of being directed to the Virgin Mary, as were the originals, these hymns of Sachs were addressed to Christ.[57]

Hans Sachs also wrote *contrafacta*, that is, parodies of secular songs that reinterpreted the original texts as specifically religious songs, again to be sung to the associated secular melodies. One example is the amorous song, *Rosina wo was dein gestalt*, which Sachs re-wrote as *O Christ wo was dein gestalt*. It is headed: "Das lied Rosina . . . Christlich verendert, von der erkenntnis Christi" (The song *Rosina* . . . Christianly altered according to the understanding of Christ). The associated secular melody first appeared in print in Arnt von Aich's *LXXV hubscher lieder*, published in Cologne sometime between 1512 and 1520 (see Example 1.3A), a collection that includes other secular melodies later associated with religious texts. The secular melody *Rosina* had wide currency in north Europe in the sixteenth century, circulating orally before appearing in print. A Dutch version of the amorous song was published in Antwerp in 1544 (see Example 1.3B), but this was after the melody had already been published in the *Souterliedekens* (Antwerp: Cock, 1540), assigned to a versification of Psalm 35. The German version of the secular song also appeared in Arnold von Bruck's *Hundert vnd fünff guter newer Liedlein* (Nuremberg: Ott, 1544). The melodic form is almost identical with that of Cologne, issued some thirty years earlier, and is therefore the form that was employed with Sachs's religious text throughout Germany, where the hymnals that included the parodied text only referred to the melody without supplying the specific musical notation (see Example 1.3C). Sachs's *O Christe wo*

Example 1.4. *O Gott Vater du hast gewalt* (1533). Zahn No. 8283. DKL Ee16. [facsimile from Wittenberg Gesangbuch 1533]

war dein gestalt is not frequently found in High German hymnals — an exception is the Zwickau *Enchiridion* of 1528 — but seems to have enjoyed some popularity in Low German hymnals issued in the north of the country, for example in such hymnals as Rostock (1531) and Magdeburg (1534). It was also translated into Danish, appearing in hymnals issued in Rostock (1529), Malmø (1533), and Copenhagen (1553). It occurs again in Hans Thomissøn's *Den danske psalmebog* (Copenhagen: Benedicht, 1569), where it appears in a variant form (see Example 1.3D).

Another *contrafactum* by Sachs, *O Gott Vater du hast gewalt* (1525) is headed: "Das lied, Ach Jupiter herst du gewalt, Christlich verendert" (The song, *Ach Jupiter herst du gewalt*, Christianly altered). Like the *Rosina* melody, the *Ach Jupiter* melody is also found in the collection of Arnt von Aich, issued in Cologne ca. 1512-1520. Sachs intended that his parodied text should be sung to the associated secular melody; however, the 1533 Wittenberg hymnal includes two other melodies for Sachs's text.[58] It is interesting to note that the first line of the first of the two related melodies is identical with the opening of Luther's *Ein neues lied* (apart from the gathering note in place of the *anacrusis* at the beginning of Luther's melody) (see Example 1.2C). The nature of the text gave rise to the use of two related tunes (or double tune). The

Example 1.5. Luther's *Vom Himmel hoch* Melodies

A=Pre-existing Melody (1535). Zahn No. 344a. DKL Ee.18.

B=Luther's Composed Melody (1539). Zahn No. 346. DKL Ei.1.

text of the original secular song is built on an acrostic in which the first letters of each of the twelve stanzas spell out the name of the author: Adam von Fulda.[59] The original song is a dialogue between the author and Jupiter. In Sachs's hands the text becomes a dialogue between the "Sinner" and "Christ"; hence each of the two voices is represented by its own melody in the Wittenberg hymnal of 1533 (see Example 1.4).[60] What is significant here is that the double tune of the 1533 Wittenberg hymnal was newly-composed and specifically designed to replace the secular melody.

Hans Sachs, of course, was not the only author of such *contrafacta*,[61] but what is significant is that, while Luther did adapt and rewrite early vernacular religious folk songs, he produced only one *contrafactum*, and it exhibits a somewhat different technique than the *contrafacta* of Sachs and others. This is his *Vom Himmel hoch, da komm ich her* (1535), a song that originated within the Luther family circle rather than as a hymn for congregational use, though it was later sung as a congregational hymn. The text begins as a parody of the secular riddle song *Ich komm aus fremden landen her* and Luther originally intended that his new text should be sung to the associated melody of the secular song. *Vom Himmel hoch* was therefore assigned to this secular tune in the Wittemberg hymnal of 1535,[62] and also, in variant forms, in some later hymnals.[63] But Luther was clearly not convinced that this was the best melody for his text (perhaps because of its repetitious A^1BA^2B form; see Example 1.5A), because he replaced it with a composition of his own, the melody that thereafter became inseparably connected with his *Vom Himmel hoch* (see Example 1.5B). Thus the only example of Luther's use of a secular melody (as opposed to religious folk-song melodies) was somewhat short-lived in that he specifically rejected it and replaced it with his specially composed melody.

Notwithstanding this significant evidence, the perception persists that Luther frequently used popular melodies for his hymns for congregational worship. Although such a view is usually expressed in popular literature, it can also be found in works of serious scholarship. Walter Blankenburg concludes that it was "Luther's wish that secular love songs be adapted for the [worship] service,"[64] and Rebecca Oettinger concurs: "For Luther and his followers, even the most worldly ballad could offer up a melody that would spread the Word."[65] But as the above discussion suggests, the conclusion that Luther was totally open to the use of melodies associated with overtly secular texts in evangelical worship cannot be supported either by a specific statement of the Reformer, or deduced from his practice as a writer of hymns and songs. It is a construct drawn mostly, by analogy, from the activities of his colleagues rather than Luther himself, and it overlooks Luther's specific statement in his 1524 preface commending Walther's polyphonic settings of the new chorales:

> These songs were arranged in four [or five] parts to give the young — who should at any rate be trained in music and other fine arts — something to wean them away from love ballads and carnal songs and to teach them something of value in their place, thus combining the good with the pleasing, as is proper for youth.[66]

Of course it could be argued that *contrafacta* by his colleagues achieve Luther's goal by replacing the original suspect texts with something more wholesome, but Walter's settings are far from this category of popular songs. Luther's view of love-ballads cited above severely tempers the widely held view that Luther uncritically supported the use of such popular music. While it is clear that he had a detailed knowledge of many popular folk melodies, a few of which are to be found in the Wittenberg hymnals issued during his lifetime, the following chapters will amply demonstrate that most of the music Luther provided and promoted for evangelical worship was based not on worldly ballads but rather on the chant of the church.

Neglected Areas of Research

If the fairly extensive literature on Luther and music is reviewed then it will be observed that there has been a tendency to emphasize one or the other of two approaches. On the one hand, there has been a stress on Luther's theology of music, expounded by way of systematic citation and commentary on the primary passages of Luther's writings that deal with music, often with scant attention, it must be admitted, to the context of these citations. On the other hand, there have been a good many studies where the emphasis has been on Luther's hymns, their creation, textually and musically, and only secondarily on the underlying theology. But Luther's declared aim with his hymns was to put the "Word of God into song,"[67] which meant that from the very beginning Luther's understanding of these communal worship songs was that they were essentially theological expressions in musical form.[68] Thus there is a strong link between hymnody and catechesis, a theme that is explored here in Chapters 4-11.

One of the weaknesses of some of the studies of Luther's hymns is that they are considered as individual entities within the total corpus of the Reformer's hymnody with little attention being paid to important contextual matters. The hymns, while being individual statements of theology, were intended to be sung corporately. Thus their liturgical functions need to be clearly identified and understood. Similarly, there has been the tendency to isolate congregational hymns from other forms of liturgical music. But this is to forget that in Wittenberg these hymns were effectively introduced to the wider congregation by a choir singing the polyphonic settings of Johann Walter published in the Wittenberg hymnal of 1524.[69] These are matters that form the substance of the discussions in Chapters 12 and 13.

With the stress on Luther's hymns there has been the consequential minimizing of Luther's concern for, and continued use of, liturgical monodic chant. While there have been many studies of Luther's hymns, his other forms of liturgical music have generally been neglected. Such overlooked areas of research include the essential musical nature of the *Deutsche Messe*, Luther's reformed use of Latin Responsories, his adaptation of the form of the Latin Sequence to create new vernacular liturgical chants, and his provision of biblical canticles in successive editions of Wittenberg hymnals. These form the substance of the discussions of Chapters 12-16.

The consequence of the neglect of these other areas of Luther's liturgical music, which until recently have not been given the prominence they deserve, is that the resulting image of the impact of his theology of music, as well as the practical outworking of this theology in liturgico-musical forms, have not necessarily been fully understood. Therefore Chapters 14, 17-18 attempt to redress something of the balance to give, hopefully, a more rounded picture of the impact Luther had on his own and subsequent generations.

Even though this book attempts to present a balanced view of Luther and music, it is by no means exhaustive. The stress here is on Luther's liturgical music, especially on areas that have tended to be undervalued or ignored in previous studies. There is much more that could and should be said. For example, I am acutely aware that we still have to come to terms with all the allusions to music in Luther's writings. Certainly the principal passages which deal with music are reasonably well known but there are many other places where Luther makes oblique rather than direct references to music when he is discussing other matters. I have attempted to draw attention to at least some of these instances in this book, but I am convinced that additional research will reveal more about Luther's understanding of music in the places where, at face value, he seems to be making an inconsequential connection, but closer inspection reveals that he is expressing something more profound. Hopefully the material presented in this book may stimulate further research along these lines.

CHAPTER 2

Luther as Musician

Music played an important part in Luther's life. His categorical statement is simple and straightforward: "Music I have always loved."[1] There are therefore a good many references to music, direct and indirect, in his literary output, some formally written as lectures, books, pamphlets, and letters, while others originated orally from church pulpits or from his own dining table, being transcribed by friends, colleagues, and students. When anyone has this much to say about music it usually means that the person has some close involvement in the art. This is certainly true for Luther. His sayings and allusions concerning music need to be set against the context of his own experience of the art, in theory and practice, which encompassed almost the totality of his lifespan, as will be explored in this chapter. At the same time attention will be given to the nature of Luther's musicianship, since some have suggested that he was more of a dilettante amateur than a competent and accomplished musician.

Pupil

Luther's introduction to music undoubtedly came from his parents. In 1535 he wrote a preface to a book by Urban Regius in which he recollected that his mother loved to sing the song *Mir und Dir ist Niemand huld,/das ist unser eigene Schuld* (Me and you no one loves, but that is our own fault).[2] In 1540 he reminisced that his father advised that one should avoid the intoxication of drink and instead sing and rejoice.[3] When he was about six months old the Luther family moved from Eisleben, the place of his birth, to Mansfeld. It was here that he entered the Latin school some years later, probably at the normal entry-level age of seven, on 12 March 1491, St. George's Day — St. George being the patron saint of the church and its adjacent school.[4] The Mansfeld school was a Trivialschule, so-called from its threefold *trivium* curriculum: grammar, logic, and rhetoric.[5] The primary purpose of the education was to promote the understanding and use of the Latin language, especially as found in the Mass and Daily Office.[6] The Latin of liturgical texts such as the Creed, Lord's Prayer, Ave Maria, and so on, was committed to memory by singing. Music therefore formed an important part of the learning process, with a stress on notation and sight-singing.[7] In the upper class the boys were expected to sing in St. George's Church on Sundays and major festivals; therefore they must have had at least some instruction in the rudiments of chant and basic music theory.

> The daily instruction in music was also religious instruction. Here one learned the hymns, versicles and responses, Psalms and psalm tones. Instruction in singing was an introduction to the liturgy of the church and its chant, and simultaneously was also religious formation [Lebensäußerung]. . . . The pupils took part in processions and sang in the choir. The church-going of the pupils on Sundays and weekdays and participation in the church choir were inextricably bound with the school and its education.[8]

Thus in Mansfeld Luther's understanding and experience of liturgical music had their beginnings.

Early in 1497, he was sent to Magdeburg, where he almost certainly attended the Latin cathedral school and lived with the Brethren of the Common Life, a quasi-monastic community that promoted a simple practical spirituality.[9] Although little is known about his education in Magdeburg it no doubt was a continuation of what had been begun in Mansfeld: Latin grammar, with some logic, rhetoric and a good proportion of music, which would have included singing within the liturgical services of the cathedral. In the ten years before 1498, when Luther moved on to the Latin school in Eisenach, he came to experience the essential corpus of liturgical music sung throughout the church year. Later in life he would frequently refer to individual chants he first learned at school, such as "the *Sanctus* in the Mass is a song for the boys."[10] Such comments are varied and found in every period of his literary output, as the following representative quotations demonstrate. Many references, in general and in particular, are to chants associated with the Mass and the Daily Office:

[The angels] sing *Gloria in excelsis Deo* to our Lord God; and you also sing the praise of the great mercy manifested in the fact that you have become God's children and heirs, coheirs with His dear Son, partakers of the Holy Spirit and of all gifts. . . . We preach Christ and are happy in the knowledge that He is our Savior, and we sing a *Gloria in excelsis Deo* to Him. . . .[11]

If the flesh did not hamper us and we were true Christians, we could sing nothing throughout our entire life but the *Magnificat*, the *Confitemini*,[12] the *Gloria in Excelsis,* the *Sanctus,* etc.[13]

These words, too, "And the Word became flesh," were held in reverence. They were sung daily in every Mass in a slow tempo and were set to a special melody, different from that for the other words. And when the congregation came to the words "from the Virgin Mary, and was made man," everyone genuflected and removed his hat. It would still be proper and appropriate to kneel at the words "and was made man," to sing them with long notes as formerly, to listen with happy hearts to the message that the Divine Majesty abased Himself and became like us poor bags of worms, and to thank God for the ineffable mercy and compassion reflected in the incarnation of the Deity.[14]

For . . . we sing in the sequence: "With the Holy Spirit shedding dew, Gabriel singled out the almond tree that was to produce the divine blossom."[15]

The church sings . . . of the Holy Spirit: *Veni pater pauperum,* "Come, O Father of the wretched."[16] . . . Therefore we sing in the article of the Creed concerning the Holy Spirit: "Who spoke by the prophets."[17]

[Speaking of birds:] Their singing of Lauds and of Matins to their Lord early in the morning before they eat is . . . excellent and . . . pleasant. . . . [They] sing a lovely, long *Benedicite* and leave their cares to our Lord God, even when they have young that have to be fed.[18]

Quadraginta annis proximus, "For forty years I was very close" [Psalm 95:10], which is chanted in the church, has been taken from the Roman Psalter.[19]

But this is the nature of faith. When the sun is shining and the sky is clear, we find satisfaction in the consolations set before us and sing *Te deum laudamus,* "We Praise Thee, O God, etc.," and *Benedicam Dominum omni tempore,* "I will bless the Lord at all times" (Psalm 34:1).[20]

In the hymn, *Verbum supernum,* the church sings how "he gave his disciples flesh and blood under the two kinds in order to feed the whole man, who is twofold in nature." If the church is right in singing this then they certainly ought to give both kinds to all Christians. Not only the priests, but the laity also are men and twofold in nature and the hymn sings of this food as whole food for the whole man.[21]

The best [Easter] hymns are *Rex Christe, factor omnium* and *Inventor rutili.*[22]

In a number of cases the references are to chants associated with funeral rites, which is understandable since the boys of the school customarily sang at funerals. The following quotations are again representative:

For myself I do not like to hear the [musical] notes in a [funeral] responsory or other song changed from what I was accustomed to in my youth.[23]

For a day of wrath [dies irae] is that day. This passage has been used frequently in all the churches, whenever the priests chanted funeral Masses, and they have applied it to the day of the Last Judgment.[24]

In addition to this there is the authority of the church, which chants, "Free them from the lion's mouth, lest hell engulf them" . . . and I do not believe the words of the church are empty words.[25]

If you listen to the Law, it will tell you: "In the midst of life we are in death," according to that ancient and pious hymn in the church. But this has reference to the Law alone. The Gospel, however, and faith invert the hymn and sing thus: "In the midst of death we are in life." . . .[26]

Similarly, Luther would have first encountered in the Latin schools of Mansfeld and Magdeburg the liturgical sources he later translated into German hymns:

Veni Redemptor gentium	*Nun komm der Heiden Heiland* (1523)
A solis ortus[27]	*Christum wir sollen loben schon* (1524)

Jesus Christus nostra salus	*Jesus Christus, unser Heiland, der von uns* (1524)[28]
Media vita	*Mitten wir im Leben sind* (1524)
Veni creator spiritus	*Komm Gott, Schöpfer, Heiliger Geist* (1524)
Veni sancte spiritus[29]	*Komm, Heiliger Geist, Herre Gott* (1524)
Da pacem Domine	*Verleih uns Frieden gnädiglich* (1529/33)
Hostis Herodes impie	*Was fürcht'st du, Feind Herodes, sehr* (1541)
O lux beata trinitas	*Der du bist drei in Einigkeit* (1543)

In the case of two of these Latin sources (*Media vita* and *Veni sancte spiritus*) they were also sung in late medieval German versions (*En mitten in des lebens zeyt*, and *Chum heiligergeist, herre got*, respectively) that Luther must have known, since he utilized a number of their lines and phrases in his vernacular versions.[30] Again it is highly likely that he first encountered them while attending the Latin schools in Mansfeld and Magdeburg, as well as other vernacular spiritual songs he later revised, expanded or recast:

Christ lag in Todesbanden (1524) — an expansion of *Christ ist erstanden;* and partially based in the Easter sequence: *Victimae paschali laudes.*

Gelobet seist du, Jesu Christ (1524) — expansion

Gott der Vater wohn uns bei (1524) — modeled on medieval pilgrim songs

Gott sei gelobet und gebenediet (1524) — revision[31]

Komm heiliger Geist, Herre Gott (1524) — expansion (see *Veni sancte spiritus* above)

Mitten wir im Leben sind (1524) — revision and expansion (see *Media vita* above)

Nun bitten wir den Heiligen Geist (1524) — revision and expansion[32]

Wir glauben all an einen Gott (1524) — substantially rewritten; virtually a new hymn[33]

Christ ist erstanden (1529) — revision[34]

Nun laßt den Leib begraben (1542) — slight revision and an additional stanza[35]

Unser große Sünde und schwere Missetat — (1544) an evangelical reinterpretation of the polemic song, *O du armer Judas*[36]

After only a year in Magdeburg Luther, now aged 14,[37] was sent to Eisenach, where he attended the Georgenschule, another Trivialschule, in which the education he had received in Mansfeld and Magdeburg was continued. Here there were many family connections, as he observed in a letter to Georg Spalatin, dated 14 January 1520:

Nearly all my kinfolk are at Eisenach, and I am known there and recognized by them even today, since I went to school there for four years, and there is no other town in which I am better known.[38]

In Eisenach he continued to be involved in the extra-curricula singing for bread, a practice he refers to from time to time:

They say, and rightly so, that the pope too was once a schoolboy. Therefore do not look down on the fellows who come to your door, saying, "Bread for the love of God," and singing for a morsel of bread. . . . I too was such a crumb collector once, begging from door to door, especially in my beloved city of Eisenach — though afterward my dear father lovingly and faithfully kept me at the University of Erfurt. . . . Nevertheless, I was once a crumb collector. . . .[39]

Whereas such singing in Mansfeld and Magdeburg would have been primarily monodic, certainly in his earlier years, Luther himself reports that a feature of this extra-curricular singing in Eisenach was that it was polyphonic:

[This is what] formerly happened to me in my boyhood and to my companions with whom I used to gather contributions for our support during our student days. For when at the time of the celebration of Christ's birthday in the church we were singing *in four voices* from door to door in the villages the usual songs about the boy Jesus who was born in Bethlehem. . . .[40]

There is here therefore the suggestion that Luther's musical skills were significantly developed during his Eisenach years, a probability underscored by other pieces of evidence. According to Johann Mathesius, one of Luther's early biographers, it was Luther's "singing and devout prayers in church," that persuaded a pious matron to provide him with food and lodging in Eisenach.[41] During his time in the town Luther was among the inner circle of students that were associated with one of the priests, Johannes Braun, a connection that was continued by correspondence and other means for at least the next twenty years.[42] In letters that only came to light at the beginning of the twentieth century, it is revealed that in Braun's circle of pupils in Eisenach music-making was a frequent activity, especially monodic songs and polyphonic motets.[43] The clear implication is that by the time he matriculated at Erfurt university in the spring of 1501, when he was 18, Luther's musical accomplishments, both in theory and practice, had significantly progressed beyond the rudimentary.

Student

Erfurt university at the end of the fifteenth century was second to none in Germany. The medieval pattern of education was that the *trivium* (grammar, logic and rhetoric) of the Latin school was augmented by the *quadrivium* (arithmetic, geometry, music and astronomy) of the baccalaureate curriculum of the university, thus together encompassing the *septem artes liberales* (seven liberal arts).[44] The Erfurt university statutes of 1412, reaffirmed in 1449, directed that baccalaureate students should study the *Musica speculativa secundum Boetium* of Johannes de Muris[45] for at least a month, a requirement that presumably continued in effect until the reform of 1519.[46] Luther may well have also studied other writings of music theory, such as those by Jean Gerson and Johannes Tinctoris. But it is clear that around the time Luther attended the university (1501-1505), music was not confined to theoretical studies since a good number of his contemporaries or near-contemporaries in Erfurt, who were later associated with the Reformation movement, were also known for their musical skills which must have been evident during their student days.[47]

Johannes Weinmann (ca. 1477-1542) matriculated in 1498 and was associated with the university until 1509 when he transferred to Wittenberg University. In 1506 he became the organist of the Schlosskirche, Wittenberg, and then the organist of the Stadtkirche, Wittenberg, in 1519, a position he held until his death in 1542.[48] His only known composition is a four-part setting of Luther's *Vater unser im Himmelreich,* published in Georg Rhau's *Newe Deudsche Geistliche Gesenge* (Wittenberg, 1544). As successively organist of the two principal churches in Wittenberg Weinmann would have worked closely with Luther.[49]

Georg Spalatin (1484-1545) also matriculated in 1498 and in 1502 went to Wittenberg for his master's degree, returning to Erfurt as a private tutor in 1504 while continuing law studies. He later returned to Wittenberg where he became Frederick the Wise's private secretary and the university librarian, and was closely associated with the reforms of Luther and Melanchthon.[50] Although there is no direct evidence for Spalatin's musicianship it is highly significant that Luther wrote to him towards the end of 1523 suggesting that he should put biblical Psalms into German verse, "so that the Word of God even by means of song may live among the people."[51] This seems to imply that Spalatin had the necessary musical sensibilities for the task, even though he apparently did not accede to Luther's request.

Justus Jonas (1493-1555) matriculated in 1501 and continued at the university until 1505, and was therefore a fellow student with Luther. He first studied law at Erfurt — as did Luther after completing his bachelor's degree — then at Wittenberg from 1511, returning in 1514 to teach law at Erfurt. He simultaneously studied theology, being ordained in 1516 and receiving his doctorate in both law and theology in 1518. In 1521 he was called to Wittenberg university to teach canon law and between 1523 and 1533 he was dean of the theological faculty. He must have also been a cultured musician because in 1521 it was suggested that he become the Kantor of the Schlosskirche, Wittenberg.[52] He was a poet, the author of a number of hymn texts — including *Wo Gott, der Herr, nicht bei uns hält*, his version of Psalm 124 written in 1524 — and almost certainly composed many of their associated melodies. Jonas became one of Luther's closest colleagues in the Reformation movement.[53] For example, he took a leading role in preparing the 1533 Wittenberg church order, which dealt with many musical matters, and, with organist Wolff Heinz — one of the circle of Luther's musical colleagues (see further below) — he was responsible for drawing up the liturgical orders with their associated chants for Halle in the early 1540s.[54]

Wolfgang Dachstein (1487-1553), who has been characterized as "the first evangelical organist,"[55] matriculated in 1503 and studied theology. By 1520 he had taken Dominican orders and in 1521 became the organist of the Thomaskirche, Straßburg. He was involved in the Straßburg Reformation from its beginnings and, with Matthias Greiter, introduced Luther's hymns into the Straßburg area as well as composing new melodies, such as his alternative melody for Luther's *Aus tiefer Not schrei ich zu dir* (1524),[56] thereby initiating, with Greiter, the distinctive Straßburg tradition of congregational song.

Georg Rhau (1488-1548) matriculated in 1508, transferring to Wittenberg university in 1512. From 1518 he was Thomaskantor in Leipzig, where he also lectured on music theory at the university. After teaching music in other schools he returned in 1523 to Wittenberg, where he became a printer/publisher and an important coworker with Luther, issuing many editions of Luther's writings, as well as a significant series of musical publications, both studies of music theory as well as anthologies of music for church and school.[57]

Johannes Spangenberg (1484-1550) matriculated in 1509, having previously studied philosophy, theology, and music in Göttingen and Einbeck. An ardent supporter of Luther, Spangenberg held important pastorates in Nordhausen (1524-1546) and Eisleben (1546-1550). He issued a number of books on music theory and compiled the most extensive collection of Lutheran liturgical music issued during Luther's lifetime, the *Cantiones ecclesiasticae/ Kirchengesenge Deudsche* (Magdeburg, 1545), a double volume in which the first part included the necessary chants with Latin texts for all the Sundays and celebrations of the church year, and the second part comprised chants and hymns with German texts and was structured the same as the first part.[58] The first part was in effect an outworking of the principles of Luther's *Formula missae* of 1523 and the second similarly followed the implications of Luther's *Deutsche Messe* of 1526.[59]

That all these men studied in Erfurt around the same time as Luther strongly suggests that music was particularly fostered among the students. For Luther it meant that his musical experiences were considerably extended beyond those of his school years. They would have included the study of polyphony *(musica figuralis)* and composition *(musica poetica,* to use the slightly later term, coined in Wittenberg[60]), although it is possible that these had begun in his final years in Eisenach.[61] Students sang simple, homophonic settings of the poetry of Virgil, Ovid, and Horace, and were encouraged to write their own verses following classical models and to compose musical settings for them.[62] Such exercises must have made a deep impression on Luther since Mathesius reports that years later Luther and his friends sang a setting of the last words of Dido, *Dulces exuviae,* from Virgil's *Aeneid,* which may have been Luther's composition;[63] and around the time that the *Deutsche Messe* was being prepared Walter reports that when he asked Luther who taught him the skill of setting words to music he replied: "The poet Virgil taught me this, who is also able to apply his poetry and vocabulary so artfully to the story he is writing. So should *music* arrange all its *notes* and songs in accord with the text."[64]

During his time at the university in Erfurt Luther must have also extended his knowledge of popular *Volkslieder,* which he had begun to learn at his mother's knee, a repertory that continued to fascinate him in later life, as is witnessed by his passing references to individual songs, such as *Den thornier von den vollen,*[65] *Der Papst ruft Kaiser und König an,*[66] *Der scheffer in der obermuhle,*[67] *Es fur ein paur gen holtze,*[68] *Hab dir meine Tochter,*[69] among others. Luther also used such melodies, either substantially unaltered or reworked in some way, for some of his hymns: such as *In Gottes Namen faren wir*[70] which became the melody for *Dies sind die heiligen Zehn Gebot* (1524);[71] *Ich gleich sie einem Rosenstock*[72] that provided a model for the melody *Nun freuet euch, lieben Christen gmein* (1523);[73] or *Ich kumm aus frembden landen her*[74] the text of which was partially parodied to become *Vom Himmel hoch ich komme her* (1535), and supplied the first melody to which Luther's Christmas hymn was sung[75] before he composed the later melody that is now universally associated with the text (1539).[76]

Crotus Rubeanus, humanist and satirical poet — one of the authors of the *Epistolae virorem obscurem* (1515-1517) — was another of Luther's fellow students in Erfurt. Crotus was later rector of the university and as such, in 1521, welcomed Luther, who was on his way to make his appearance at the Diet of Worms,[77] although he never accepted Luther's later Reformation stance. On 16 October 1519 Crotus wrote to Luther reminiscing of their time together in Erfurt: "With the closest intimacy we together devoted our toil at Erfurt to the noble arts in the days of our youth";[78] and in a later letter (dated 28 April 1520) declared, "You were the musician and erudite philosopher of our old circle [of students]."[79] This suggests that Luther's musical abilities were second to none. His skill as a lutenist was undoubtedly advanced during his student days in Erfurt, so much so that an eyewitness of the musical evening that preceded his entry into the monastery commented on his skill in playing the instrument. Significantly, that eyewitness was Justus Jonas (see above), who passed on the account to an anonymous scribe. The manuscript narrative in German was written on the verso of the title page of a 1530 imprint of the *Confessio Augustana*, in Göttingen University Library. Appended in Latin is the following declaration: "Jonas related this narrative to me [unidentified] in the home of Christopher Seßen, the treasurer of Zerbst, at a light breakfast on 28 January 1538":[80]

> It happened some thirty-two years ago . . . in Erfurt. . . . Luther sold all his law books secretly and ordered a grand banquet, an evening repast in Porta Celi [the name of a burse at Erfurt], invited several scholars, some virtuous, chaste young ladies and women, and dined with them in an unusually cheerful spirit, playing on the lute *(which he by now was able to do quite well)*. All were in happy mood. When the time for departure had arrived, all thanked him heartily, but they did not know what Luther had in mind, and left in happy spirits. Martin Luther, however, went immediately into the Augustinian monastery at Erfurt during the night, for he had also made arrangements for that, and became a monk.[81]

Similarly Matthäus Ratzeberger[82] recorded that, around the time Luther entered the monastery, his friends recognized his musical accomplishments and declared that he was "ein guter Musicus," a good musician.[83]

Monk

Towards the end of 1505, after a probationary period, Luther became a monk in a ceremony that had a specific musical content. Immediately following Luther's declaration that he was ready to accept the way of life of a monk the whole community joined in singing *Magne pater Augustine,* the office hymn for St. Augustine's day (28 August), which was also in effect the hymn of the Augustinian order.[84] As a monk he was completely immersed in the daily pattern of worship of the monastic community, which involved extensive singing of Gregorian chant. He was now exposed to the full extent of the daily offices throughout the church year; as a schoolboy he had taken part in the chanting of the offices of Matins and Lauds, but now as a monk he had to sing all the Offices every day, with their specific antiphons, hymns, responsories, and so on, appropriate to the time and season, as well as singing through the whole of the Psalter every week. Similarly, after his ordination (1506-7) his experience of the chants of the Mass was intensified because now he had to sing the biblical lections and other parts of the liturgy assigned to the priest, considerably more chant than he had learned as a schoolboy.[85] Luther celebrated his first Mass on Cantate Sunday (the fourth Sunday after Easter) — which began with the Introit that must have had special significance for him: *Cantate Domino canticum novum* (Sing to the Lord a new song)[86] — and among the invited guests was Johannes Braun, the Eisenach priest who had encouraged Luther in his music-making, and perhaps some of his former fellow pupils from the Braun circle also attended since he gave them an open invitation through the Eisenach priest.[87]

As Luther was fastidious about not making an error in reciting the text of the Latin Mass,[88] we can be quite sure that he was equally as exacting with regard to memorizing the associated chants, since a mistake in the melodic line might have caused him to make a verbal slip. There is evidence from a later time that he was meticulous in correcting wrong notes[89] and critical of ill-disciplined performance,[90] which would suggest he was just as scrupulous during these earlier years.[91] In celebrating Mass Luther, like many German priests of the time, was carefully observant of the specific details as well as the devotional nature of the rite; thus he was appalled by the perfunctory and spiritually barren way the Mass was celebrated by Italian priests in Rome in 1510,[92] in much the same way that an Italian priest a few years later was impressed by the superior attentiveness of Germans at Mass when compared to their Italian counterparts.[93] Care in celebrating Mass underlines a later reminiscence when Luther recalled an occasion during his Erfurt monastery days. He was vested at the altar of a village church when the sexton surprised him by accompanying parts of the Mass, such as Kyrie, Gloria, and Creed,[94] on a lute. When the sexton began Luther could hardly keep from laughing: "For I was not accustomed to such 'organ'[95] playing and had to adjust my Gloria to his Kyrie."[96] It is understandable that a lutenist monk, experienced in Gregorian chant and fascinated by music, should recall such an event.[97]

Luther's trip to Rome (1510), the furthest he traveled in his life, took him through such important cities as Nuremberg, Ulm, Memmingen, Milan, Florence, and Sienna, and returning through Mantua, Innsbruck and Augsburg. Many of these cities had cathedrals or large churches where there were significant musical foundations and thus Luther was undoubtedly exposed to a wide variety of music. In Milan and Rome he almost certainly heard the music of Josquin (1440-1521) (see further below), who had served in the churches of both cities and whose compositions continued in the repertory of these ecclesiastical foundations.[98] In Innsbruck, where the music of Josquin was frequently performed in the court of Maximilian, he probably heard the impressive organ in St. Jakob's church,[99] and his experience in the massive cathedral in Ulm and in St. Peter's, Rome, drew from him the later comment that though such buildings were fine for music their acoustic was not good for preaching.[100]

Professor

Luther's spiritual advisor, Johann von Staupitz — vicar-general of the Augustinian order in Saxony, Rhenish-Swabia, Cologne, and Bavaria, and dean of the theological faculty of the newly-founded Wittenberg university[101] — suggested that he should teach theology in Wittenberg. But before he could do so he would have to complete his doctorate, so in 1508 Luther was sent to the Augustinian priory in Wittenberg and began to study for his doctor's degree, which was conferred in October 1512. He did not begin teaching until a year later, during the winter semester 1513-1514, and his first lectures were on the Psalms, the songs of the Old Testament: *Dictata super psalterium* (1513-1515).[102] He then lectured on Romans (1515-1516), Galatians (1516-1517), and Hebrews (1517-1518), before returning to the Psalms: *Operationes in psalmos* (1518-1521).[103] These lectures were given during the period when he was simultaneously coming to terms with his own personal beliefs and emerging in public as a Reformer.

His protest concerning indulgences brought him under enormous pressure but he continued to find solace in music. Mathesius reports that in the period immediately following the papal ban (1521) he was found alone in the garden of the Augustinian cloister in Wittenberg singing with a great sense of joy. When asked if he had heard some special news he replied, "Nothing, except our Lord Christ, who will come in power from the right hand of his Father to subjugate his church, he will see to it."[104] Unfortunately, it is not recorded what he was singing.

Wittenberg University was founded by the Duke of Ernestine Saxony, Elector Frederick the Wise, in 1502. Frederick had a keen interest in music and created his Hofkapelle of musicians in 1491 to supply liturgical music in his ducal residences in Altenburg, Wittenberg, and Torgau, wherever he was "in residence."[105] His first Kapellmeister was Adam von Fulda, who served until his death in 1505, when Conrad Rupsch, one of the singers of the Hofkapelle, succeeded him. The Duke had contact with leading Franco-Flemish composers, among them Pierre de la Rue and Alexander Agricola; around 1500 Paul Hofhaimer was teaching the four organists of the Saxon court; and Adam Rener was appointed court-composer in 1507. In Wittenberg the duke's court chapel of All Saints also served as the university church and at the same time as he was consolidating his new university he was also intensifying the music ministry of his court chapel/university church. The "large choir" of the Allerheiligenstift, the body of clergy and musicians responsible for daily worship, numbered thirty-one in 1508 (the year Luther arrived in Wittenberg): twelve canons, four vicars, seven chaplains, and eight choirboys.[106] The same year a new set of partbooks was begun, manuscripts of polyphonic settings of liturgical texts by such prominent composers as Josquin, Isaac, Obrecht, among others; by 1520 the Allerheiligenstift had doubled in size.[107] The repertory sung at the daily masses and offices was extensive and included many polyphonic settings of propers, more than was usual than in similar contemporary foundations. This expansion of the liturgical music of the Castle Church occurred during Luther's first years in Wittenberg, and therefore was the immediate background against which the polyphonic liturgical music evolved in Wittenberg and elsewhere in the following decades and thus provided the foundation for the Lutheran tradition of liturgical music.[108]

That there was an overlap between the liturgical functions of the Allerheiligenstift and the university is seen in the double responsibilities of some of its members. For example, Ulrich von Dienstedt was the Cantor of the Stift and professor of canon law between 1507 and 1525. Thus when Justus Jonas was appointed a professor of canon law in 1521 it was first suggested that he should also become the Cantor of the Stift; but as this would have meant displacing Dienstedt, he was instead made provost (Probst), effectively the leader of the Stift. Jonas had been one of Luther's circle of student colleagues in Erfurt who shared his musical interests, and this experience of being responsible for the liturgical observances of the Stift was later put to good use when he was involved in devising reformed liturgical rites, and the role of music within them, in consultation with Luther. In 1521, shortly before he took up his appointment in Wittenberg, Jonas was still in Erfurt when Luther passed through on his way to Worms. It is significant that Jonas then joined

Luther and accompanied him to the Diet; on the journey Luther's music-making was observed and drew comment. The account is recorded not by one of Luther's friends but by one of his most severe Catholic critics, Johannes Cochlaeus. In his *Commentaria de actis et scriptis Martini Lutheri Saxonis* (Maintz, 1549; most of it written by 1535), he records the following concerning the journey to Worms:

> In the inns they [Luther's party, including Jonas, Schurff, and Amsdorf] found many a toast, cheerful drinking-parties, music, and enjoyments; to such an extent that Luther drew all eyes to himself in some places by playing songs on a lute, as though he were a kind of Orpheus, but a shaven and cowled one, and for that reason more to be marveled at.[109]

Cochlaeus was more than a Catholic theologian and polemicist: he had taught music theory at Cologne — where he was the teacher of Heinrich Glarean, one of the most influential music theorists of the sixteenth century. Cochlaeus also published two textbooks: *Musica* (Cologne, 1504; 3rd ed., 1515), and *Tetrachordum musices* (Nuremberg, 1511; 7th ed., 1526). It is not surprising, therefore, that Cochlaeus should make this musical observation, especially if it would serve his purpose of denigrating Luther by recording that he was scandalized that a monk should sing folk-songs in common inns. By using the term "testudo" ("a curved string instrument" = lute) rather than "lyra" ("lyre" = harp) — Orpheus's instrument — Cochlaeus was almost certainly underscoring the offence of a monk becoming a musical entertainer by revealing that Luther played the "low-class," popular instrument, rather than the "high-class," refined instrument, the harp, favored by humanists.[110]

The double appointments of the university faculty in the Allerheiligenstift is reflected in some of the matriculated students who also served as singers, such as the fourteen students who in 1509 were granted free places at the university in return for their participation in choral polyphony.[111] According to the university statutes of 1514 the study of music at Wittenberg at the master's level, as in Erfurt, was focused on *"Musica Muris,"* that is, the *Musica speculativa secundum Boetium* of Johannes de Muris.[112] But music in the university almost certainly would have included the study of the treatise *De musica,* written in 1490 by Adam von Fulda, the duke's former Kapellmeister, who had taught music in the university in its early years and would have undoubtedly used his own (unpublished) text.[113] On one occasion Luther was heard to express a Latin saying that can be found in Adam von Fulda's treatise: *in fine videbitur, cuius toni* — "at the end it will be seen which Tone [it is]."[114] The context for the statement in von Fulda's treatise deals with Gregorian chant and explains how to establish the Tone (mode) of a particular chant by going to the end of the *Gloria Patri,* where the vowels from *seculorum amen (euouae)* will be found with the notation of the particular ending, from which the specific Tone can be established. This is then followed by *in fine videbitur, cuius toni* which is quoted as an established proverb.[115] Thus when Luther used it, it may be that he was simply quoting a widely known saying;[116] on the other hand, it may mean that at this time it was especially well-known in Wittenberg circles, because of von Fulda's treatise, in which case it would be a witness to Luther's awareness both of von Fulda's *De musica* and of the specific teaching of music at Wittenberg University.

As the university was consolidating its humanist curriculum other texts of music theory came to be studied. Michael Koswick's *Compendaria musicae artis editio* (Leipzig: Stöckel, 1516) was probably used in Wittenberg (Koswick matriculated there in 1525). This was a concise summary of earlier works, notably those by Cochlaeus and Wollick, and addressed chant, the church modes, intonation formulae, and counterpoint, in which he moved in new directions for two- and three-voice composition. Andreas Ornithoparchus [Vogelhofer] almost certainly taught in Wittenberg for a short time from 1516 and thus his *Musicae activae micrologus* (Leipzig: Schumann, 1517)[117] had some currency at the university.[118] In contrast to earlier theoretical writers, Ornithoparchus stressed *musica practica* rather than *musica theoretica,* and among the composers whose music he commended are Josquin, de la Rue, Isaac, and Heinrich Finck.

In the first decades of the sixteenth century the teaching of music at the new humanist university of Wittenberg was already moving away from the late medieval tradition of focusing primarily on music as a theoretical science, a subdivision of mathematics, towards an understanding of music as a practical art in which theory is expressed in practice. Although Luther was busy with other things, he could not have been unaware of the teaching of music in the university, in the same way that he could not have been uninfluenced by the extensive liturgical music, vocal and instrumental, of the Allerheiligenstift. But the Reformation debate was heating up. Luther was summoned to appear at the Diet of Worms in 1521, and when he would not recant was taken to Wartburg castle for his own safety. Here, isolated from Wittenberg, he translated the New Testament, wrote other important works, and took solace in the songs of birds.[119]

In Wittenberg Andreas Bodenstein von Karlstadt was taking a more radical position than Luther. Karlstadt — who had also been a student at Erfurt university around the same time as Luther — Archdeacon of the Allerheiligenstift (from 1511) and professor of theology at the university, conducted the first evangelical mass (significantly truncated) in Wittenberg at Christmas 1521, a few weeks later was the first priest to marry, and wrote against images, which created civil unrest in the town. But before all this, in the late summer of 1521, in Luther's absence, he published *De cantu Gregoriano disputatio* (Disputation on Gregorian Chant), 53 theses consisting of a radical critique of music within the liturgy.[120] Karlstadt's basic position was that all music associated with the unreformed Latin mass and offices, the worship of the fallen church, was rendered invalid by the newly recovered spiritual content of the gospel: outward liturgico-musical forms were therefore detrimental to the essence of the gospel. For example (Thesis 11): "In this age deacons are judged by the melodiousness of their voices; formerly they were judged by the honesty of their lives."[121] Karlstadt argues that chants, "these mumblings," were instituted by "the church of which Gregory was head" and "not by the church of which Christ is the head" (Theses 37 and 38).[122] Similarly, polyphonic liturgical music accompanied by organs, trumpets and flutes cannot be condoned (Theses 17-18).[123] Karlstadt's concluding thesis (Thesis 53) echoes the sermons of the early, pre-Gregorian, Fathers of the church: "If, therefore, you wish chant to remain in the church, you should desire none except that which is one, so that there may be one God, one baptism, one faith, and one chant [= unaccompanied unison]."[124] In these theses Karlstadt, on the one hand, sets himself against the practice of the Allerheiligenstift, in which Gregorian chant forms and polyphonic vocal music (with the use of instruments) were regularly heard, and, on the other hand, argues against the sensibilities of Luther, who continued to value both traditional chant and the more recent expressions of polyphony in worship. While Karlstadt may have swayed popular opinion with regard to images he did not convince most of his colleagues of the Allerheiligenstift, or, more to the point, Duke Frederick the Wise, on the question of music because both chant and polyphony continued in the ducal chapel/university church of All Saints.

Reformer

Luther returned to Wittenberg in March 1522 and immediately preached his eight "Invocavit" sermons to quell the turbulence Karlstadt had created.[125] Over the next year or so he was actively involved in setting the church in Wittenberg to rights, which included writing expositions of the Lord's Supper directed against Karlstadt, who was excluded from the affairs of university and town. Karlstadt's radicalism had contributed to the significant decline in students attending Wittenberg university during the time that Luther was away in the Wartburg. Thus another of Luther's responses to the consequences of Karlstadt's teaching was to write his educational manifesto *To the Councilmen of All the Cities in Germany That They Establish and Maintain Christian Schools,* published in February 1524. It dealt with principles rather than offering a detailed curriculum — Melanchthon supplied that somewhat later — but Luther did make a point of stating that it should include music.[126] Later in the same year Luther collaborated with Johann Walter in the latter's set of partbooks, *Geystliche gesangk Buchleyn* — usually referred to as the *Chorgesangbuch* — published by Klug in Wittenberg (1524). Luther supplied the preface and Walter the polyphonic settings of the new German hymns that Luther and his colleagues had been writing during the winter of 1523-24, as well as a number of settings of Latin liturgical texts.[127] Walter was first a singer in the duke's Hofkapelle, then court composer in 1520 in succession to Rener, who apparently died that year. Walter had recently been in effect the acting-Hofkapellmeister when Rupsch withdrew from the practicalities of the office on espousing (temporarily) Karlstadt's radicalism. In the preface Luther declared that the aim of this anthology was both educational and aesthetic — and at the same time took the opportunity for an oblique sideswipe at Karlstadt's views:

> These songs were arranged in four [or five] parts to give the young — who should at any rate be trained in music and other fine arts — something to wean them away from love ballads and carnal songs and to teach them something of value in their place, thus combining the good with the pleasing, as is proper for youth. Nor am I of the opinion that the Gospel should destroy and blight all the arts, as some of the pseudo-religious claim. But I would like to see all the arts, especially music, used in the service of Him who gave and made them.[128]

In the same way that his 1524 treatise on the establishment and maintenance of Christian schools is somewhat ambiguous with regard to the dividing line between what should be taught in schools and universities, Luther's reference to "youth" in his preface to the *Chorgesangbuch* is not completely clear. Certainly later editions of the anthology of polyphonic settings were clearly published for use in schools, but at this stage the educational strategy was still being evolved. Thus by "youth" Luther probably did not mean schoolboys — who should have been too young to have known "love ballads and carnal songs" — so much as university students. The members of the Allerheiligenstift, including student singers from the university together with musicians from the ducal

Hofkapelle, would have been the first to have performed these compositions by Walter before they were committed to print. The Stift and Kapelle together therefore supplied a working musical laboratory, connected to both church and university, in which the new compositions could be tested and tried. But all too quickly these musical assets in Wittenberg were dispersed.

Frederick the Wise died on 5 May 1525 and was succeeded by his brother, Johann the Steadfast, who disbanded both the Hofkapelle and the Allerheiligenstift on the grounds that they were too costly to be continued. In consternation Luther wrote to the Duke on 20 June 1526:

> Finally, gracious Lord, I request that Your Electoral Grace will not permit the Kantorei [= Hofkapelle] to pass out of existence, especially since its current members have been trained for such work; in addition, the art [of music] is worthy of being supported and maintained by princes and lords, much more so than many other endeavors and enterprises for which there is not nearly so much need — in Wittenberg as you know well. The goods and possessions of the monasteries could be well used to take care of these people. God would derive pleasure from such a transfer.[129]

As part of a concerted effort, Melanchthon also wrote in similar terms to Johann the Steadfast on the same day, 20 June 1526, a letter that also indicates that Walter's polyphonic settings were frequently sung in Wittenberg:

> Johann Walter, the composer of the Kantorei [= Hofkapelle] . . . has composed songs that are sung a great deal at present. We have need of such people, not only in order that the good music that has been used might not be buried, but also that new and better music be written. I consider retaining the services of such people a good work from which God derives pleasure. Thus far have people in many places maintained music-groups for unnecessary pomp and other unbecoming purposes. Why should the noble art of music not remain active now for God's sake, since it is used for the service and glory of God?[130]

Luther commented adversely on these cost-cutting actions that diminished the experience of music:

> Some notables have cut and saved our gracious Lord [Johann the Steadfast] the [annual] sum of 3,000 gulden by doing away with his musical organizations, while at the same time squander 30,000 gulden [on other things]. Kings and princes must support music. Monarchs should work

to preserve and promote the arts. Private citizens who love the arts, are not able to do so.

> Duke George [of Saxony], the Landgrave of Hesse, and our [former] Elector Frederick [the Wise] maintained music, as does the Emperor, Ferdinand of Bavaria [but not, by implication, Duke Johann of Saxony]. One reads of David who supported male and female singers.[131]

The disbanding of these musical establishments had serious consequences for the university as well as for church reform. When the Allerheiligenstift was dissolved the choral stipends for university students were naturally withdrawn.[132] The cumulative loss stimulated Luther and his colleagues to accelerate their educational program for schools to become centers for learning music as well as for music leadership in the churches. Walter effectively became the first Lutheran cantor in the Latin school in Torgau, near Wittenberg, where, in collaboration with Luther and Melanchthon, he worked on the chant and polyphonic repertory for school and church.[133] Georg Rhau in Wittenberg published later editions of Walter's *Chorgesangbuch*, as well as other anthologies of liturgical music by a variety of composers, music to be learned in the schools and performed in the churches. Rhau — who had taught music in Leipzig, Eisleben, and Hildburghausen before taking up his printing and publishing career in Wittenberg — also published a significant series of textbooks of music theory for use in the reconstituted Latin schools (see Table 2.1).[134] Rhau had published his own music textbook while he was in Leipzig: *Enchiridion musices* (Leipzig: Johann Rhau, 1517), which was devoted to chant *(musica choralis)*. It was reprinted the following year (Leipzig: Schumann, 1518), and a second part dealing with practical issues *(musica mensuralis)* was published two years later under the title *Enchiridion musicae practicae* (Leipzig: Schumann, 1520). As part of the intensification of teaching the practical aspects of music in schools on the part of the Wittenberg Reformers, Rhau republished the two parts of his treatise in one volume in 1531, being reissued five times by 1553.[135] Another earlier work that Rhau had used in Leipzig was Venceslaus Philomathes, *Musicorum libri quatuor* (Vienna, 1512; repr. Leipzig, 1518), which he reissued as *Liber musicorum quatuor* in Wittenberg in 1534. Rhau also issued a significant series of theoretical works by the Magdeburg musician Martin Agricola: *Ein kurtz deudsche Musica* (1528; 3rd edition issued as *Musica choralis deudsch* in 1533), *Musica instrumentalis deudsch* (1529, reprinted 1530, 1532, 1542; revised 1545), *Musica figuralis deudsch* (1532), *Musica choralis deudsch* (1533), *Rudimenta musices* (1539). But the most influential textbook was that by Nicolaus Listenius, *Rudimenta musicae*, first published by Rhau in 1533.[136] Listenius's

Table 2.1 Books of Music Theory Associated with Wittenberg University

Only first editions, notable reprints in other cities, and substantial revisions are listed.

Author	Title	Place and Publisher	Year
Venceslaus Philomathes	*Musicorum libri quatuor*	Vienna: Singren	1512
Andreas Ornithoparchus	*Musicae activae micrologus*	Leipzig: Schumann	1517
Georg Rhau	*Enchiridion musices*	Leipzig: J. Rhau	1517
Georg Rhau	*Enchiridion musices*	Leipzig: Schumann	1518
Georg Rhau	*Enchiridion musicae practicae*	Leipzig: Schumann	1520
Venceslaus Philomathes	*Musicorum libri quatuor*	Leipzig: G. Rhau	1518
Martin Agricola	*Ein kurtz deudsche Musica*	Wittenberg: G. Rhau	1528
Martin Agricola	*Musica instrumentalis deudsch*	Wittenberg: G. Rhau	1529
Martin Agricola	*Musica figuralis deudsch*	Wittenberg: G. Rhau	1532
Johannes Spangenberg	*Prosodia*	Wittenberg: G. Rhau	1532
Martin Agricola	*Musica choralis deudsch*	Wittenberg: G. Rhau	1533
Nicolaus Listenius	*Rudimenta musicae*	Wittenberg: G. Rhau	1533
Venceslaus Philomathes	*Liber musicorum quatuor*	Wittenberg: G. Rhau	1534
Johannes Spangenberg	Quaestiones musicae	Wittenberg: G. Rhau	1536
Martin Agricala	*Rudimenta musices*	Wittenberg: G. Rhau	1539
Martin Agricola	*Musica instrumentalis deudsch*	Wittenberg: G. Rhau	1545
Heinrich Faber	*Compendiolum musicae*	Brunswick	1548
Adrianus Petit Coclico	*Compendium musices*	Nuremberg: Berg & Neuber	1552
Hermann Finck	*Practica musica*	Wittenberg: Rhau's heirs	1556
Lucas Lossius	*Erotomata musicae practicae*	Nuremberg: Berg & Neuber	1563

textbook, essentially a practical treatise on singing, clearly represented the Wittenberg approach to the teaching of music since its author was a university alumnus, matriculating in 1529 and receiving his master's degree in 1531. The work was extremely popular in Lutheran schools, being issued in more than 40 editions before 1583.[137] Rhau also published a number of titles by Johannes Spangenberg: *Prosodia* (1532) in which the rules of prosody were illustrated by four-part songs; *Quaestiones musicae in usum scholae Northusionae,* a catechetical work on the elements of music and chant, that first appeared in 1536 and by 1592 had been issued in 25 editions. Spangenberg was also editor of the most extensive collection of Latin and German chants for the church year issued during Luther's lifetime (see above), chants that were customarily sung by school choirs in the churches.

There is an important manuscript that witnesses to the teaching of music in the university in the 1540s, the notebook of Georg Donat, who matriculated in 1542. These lecture notes are heavily dependent on Agricola, *Ein kurtz deudsche Musica* (1528), Listenius, *Rudimenta musicae* (1533), and Spangenberg, *Quaestiones musicae* (1536), and emphasized various areas of composition.[138]

Other Wittenberg students became teachers and produced their own theoretical textbooks. Heinrich Faber (ca. 1500-1552) matriculated in 1542 (MA 1545) and became the rector of the cathedral school in Naumberg before returning to Wittenberg to lecture on music in 1551.[139] His *Compendiolum musicae pro incipientibus* (Brunswick, 1548) was perhaps the most popular textbook on singing in use in Lutheran schools; it was reprinted numerous times, recommended by no less than 49 different school ordinances issued between 1559 and 1613, and provided a model for many others on which to base their own textbooks.[140] Adrianus Petit Coclico (ca. 1500-1562), who claimed to be a pupil of Josquin, arrived in Wittenberg in 1545 and taught music there for a few years. His *Compendium musices* (Nuremberg: Berg & Neuber, 1552)[141] was written for above-average students who wanted to develop advanced singing techniques and composition. Hermann Finck (1527-1558), organist and great-nephew of the composer Heinrich Finck, matriculated in 1545 and taught music at the university from 1554 until his death. His *Practica musica* (Wittenberg: Rhaus Erben [heirs of Georg Rhau], 1556) is an extended work in five books with many complete musical examples: chant, polyphony, canons, modes, and performance practice. Finck relies heavily on the theoretical works of Wittenberg theorists such as Rhau, Listenius, and Faber.[142] Jan Blahaslav (1523-1571), from Bohemia-Moravia, studied in Wittenberg in 1545-1546, when he became acquainted with both Luther and Melanchthon. His *Musica* (Olomouc, Moravia, 1558; revised 1569), the first book of music theory written in Czech, owes much to the treatises of Listenius, Coclico, and Finck.[143] "Jan Josquin," the pseudonym of (most likely) Václav Solín (1527-1566), an associate of Blahaslav, also appears to have studied in Wittenberg. He too wrote in Czech and like Blahaslav's treatise his *Muzika* (Prostějov, Moravia, 1561) owes much to such Wittenberg theorists as Rhau, Listenius, and Faber.[144] Lucas Lossius (1508-1582) matriculated in 1530, was closely associated with both Luther and Melanchthon, and later became the reforming corrector of the Latin school in Lüneburg. He edited an extensive anthology of chant ordered according to the church year, to be sung by schoolboys in the services of the church: *Psalmodia, hoc est, Cantica sacra veteris ecclesiae selecta*, first published in Nuremberg in 1553, revised and reissued in Wittenberg in five editions between 1561 and 1595.[145] Lossius also produced his own musical textbook, *Erotomata musicae practicae* (Nuremberg: Berg & Neuber, 1563),[146] which was almost as widely used as the treatise of

Listenius, which continued to serve the needs of the primary classes while Lossius's was used in the upper classes of the schools.[147]

All this was in accord with Luther's deep concern for the role of music in schools where it was both an art to be learned and appreciated, and also a vehicle for praise and spiritual formation:

> Necessity demands that music be kept in the schools. A schoolmaster must know how to sing; otherwise I do not look at him. And before a youth is ordained into the ministry, he should practice music in school.[148]

Similarly:

> In addition, if the schoolteacher is a godly man and teaches the boys to understand, to sing, and to practice God's word and the true faith and holds them to Christian discipline, then, as we said earlier, the schools are truly young and eternal councils, which perhaps do more good than many other great councils [of the church].[149]

From the late 1520s there was an intensification of the teaching of music in Wittenberg university, with a significant shift from an emphasis on *musica speculativa* to *musica practica*. The many eminent Wittenberg teachers of music were abreast of modern theories of composition, and the music performed was similarly up-to-date. But practical music in the schools was the primary goal, for they supplied the choirs to lead congregations in worship, and from which university students could be drawn. Thus music formed an important part of the studies at Wittenberg because eventually some of these students in their turn would become teachers of music in the schools. This was a clearly defined policy that owes much to the leadership of Luther, but he was fully supported by such colleagues as Melanchthon, Bugenhagen, and Jonas, who wrote prefaces to musical publications and/or compiled Lutheran church orders in which the role of music was carefully prescribed. All of the theoretical books mentioned above promoted singing, the continuation of older chant forms, the understanding of the ecclesiastical modes, and the development and promotion of polyphony — in many respects the exact opposite of what Karlstadt had proposed.[150]

Given this emphasis on music one would have expected that there would have been a professor of music at the university; instead, the succession of impressive teachers conducted their musical instruction in private. It was certainly Luther's wish that there should be a professor of music (see below),[151] but every attempt to create and endow such a position was thwarted by Johann Friedrich the Magnanimous, who had succeeded to the dukedom on the death of his father, Johann the Steadfast, in 1532. The humanist-composer Sixt Dietrich was in Wittenberg in 1540-41 when an attempt was made to create a professorship for him, but the duke refused to spend the required annual sum of 100 gulden.[152] Similarly, in 1545-46 twenty students of Coclico signed a petition to the elector that their teacher be made a public professor of the university, an action that had the support of the university officials. But again, Duke Johann Friedrich refused to supply the necessary stipend.[153] Luther's position was clearly spelled out in a letter to the duke, dated 20 March 1541, which includes a thinly-veiled reference to the dissolution of the Allerheiligenstift and Hofkapelle by the duke's father some fifteen years earlier — the letter was probably written in support of Sixt Dietrich becoming what would have been the university's first professor of music:

> We have to this day great need for a capable musician (in Wittenberg). However, since no funds were available, we have disdained to trouble Your Electoral Grace with many petitions. Now that it has been decided to expend the funds supplied by Licentiate Blanken, it seems to me a good idea to use some of these to engage a first-rate musician. For there was a time when we, like others, were supplied with such as could sing by the papacy. Now that the day has come in which we must train our own singers, we are not in a position to do so [for the lack of a leading music teacher].[154]

Husband, Father, and Friend

Luther's marriage in 1525 was viewed with disdain by his opponents; that a monk should marry a nun was proof of Luther's apostasy. One of the negative responses came from Hieronymous Emser who satirized the wedding in Latin poetry that purports to express Lutheran views:

> Our masters are permitted every sacrilege, and shout down all honest
>   people
>   *with a song of joy!*
> They can trample rights and laws; they can slander kings, the Pope,
>   and the Emperor
>   *with a song of joy! . . .*
> We will destroy the enclosures of the cloister, we will plunder the
>   sacred vessels, which will supply our expenses

> *with a song of joy!*
> Go cowl, farewell cap, farewell Prior, Custodian, Abbot, together with
>   obedience
> *with a song of joy! . . .*
> Io, Io, Io, Io! Let us rejoice with a song of joy, sweet Lutherans,
>   *with a song of joy!*[155]

The poem with its basic 8.8.7. meter and repeated refrain implies that is was
set to music; indeed Cochlaeus reports that Emser "embellished the poem
with a harmony for four voices."[156] That Emser attacked Luther in a musical
form suggests that he knew of Luther's reputation as a musician and therefore
it was an added insult to the Wittenberg Reformer. In 1504 Emser had lectured on humanism at Erfurt university and Luther was among his hearers.
Later, at the 1519 Leipzig disputation between Johannes Eck and Luther,
Emser became personally acquainted with Luther. Thus Emser was in a position to have been aware of Luther's musical sensitivities and therefore used a
musical form to antagonize him and his followers; indeed, the refrain *Cum
jubilo* may well be a caustic reference to Luther's new hymns that had already
been widely published in Wittenberg, Erfurt, Augsburg, Nuremberg, Strassburg, and Worms between 1524 and 1525.

Even before he was married Luther was sure that if he had any children
he would want them to be taught music: "For my part if I had children and
could manage it, I would have them study not only languages and history, but
also singing and music together with the whole of mathematics."[157] Here he
makes it plain that he would want any children of his to have a balanced experience of music, both practical (singing) and theoretical (music as a subdivision of mathematics). When in the course of time he and Katharine von Bora
became the parents of three sons and three daughters,[158] their children were
encouraged to perform and study music. For example, we hear of him encouraging his beloved Magdalena to sing a folk song she had learned;[159] on
other occasions he sang various chants with his sons Martin and Paul;[160] and
he sent his eldest son Johannes, even though he already held a bachelor's degree at the age of sixteen, to study with composer Johann Walter in Torgau. In
a letter to Walter's colleague, Marcus Crodel, rector of the Latin school in
Torgau, dated 26 August 1542, he wrote:

> As you and I have agreed, my Marcus, I am sending my son Johannes to
> you so that you may add him to the boys who are to be drilled in grammar
> and music. . . . If I see success with this son, then soon, if I live, you will also
> have my two other sons [Martin and Paul]. . . . Farewell in the Lord, and

tell Johann Walter that I pray for his well-being, and that I commend my son to him for learning music. For I, of course, produce theologians, but I would also like to produce grammarians and musicians.[161]

Luther, however, was not content to make music only with his children; he would do so with anyone — and there were often many — who came into his home and shared his table. Ratzeberger records the following incident that dates from the early years of the reforming movement:

> Dr. Luther at the beginning of his struggle against papal abuses . . . had to withstand in private great attacks by Satan, that often happened when he was in his study reading and writing, disturbing him in many ways. At one time Lucas Edemberger (preceptor of Duke Johann Ernst of Saxony [Frederick the Wise's nephew]) came with his company, all good musicians, including Georg Rhau, to visit him. He found that Luther was shut up in his study and that he had been there for some time without eating or drinking and would not respond to anyone. Lucas thought that this could not be right and so came and stood [outside the door], knocked, but there was no answer. So he looked via the keyhole through the door into the room and saw Luther lying face-down on the floor, unconscious with arms outstretched. He opened the door by force, roused him and brought him out somewhat disheveled, gave him a little something to eat, tidied him up, and stood him among his companions to make music. Dr. Luther gradually regained consciousness, his melancholy and sadness left him, and before long he began to sing with them. He thus became full of joy and diligently begged them to visit him often, especially when they desired to make music. They should not allow themselves to be turned away; for he would want to join them, because he believed that immediately he heard music then his attacks and melancholy would be terminated.[162]

This experience confirmed his need to join with others to make music on a regular basis, a policy he hinted at in the *Smalcald Articles* (1537)[163] and encouraged others to follow. For example, he wrote to Matthias Weller, organist in Freiberg, Saxony, 7 October 1534:

> Dear Matthias, do not dwell on your own thoughts, but listen to what other people have to say to you. . . . Listen, then, to what we are saying to you in God's name. . . . When you are sad, therefore, and melancholy threatens to get the upper hand, say: "Arise! I must play a song unto the Lord Christ a song on my regal [small portable reed organ] (be it the *Te*

Deum laudamus or the *Benedictus*), for Scripture teaches me that it pleases him to hear a joyful song and the music of stringed instruments." Then begin striking the keys and singing in accompaniment, as David and Elisha did [1 Samuel 16:23; 2 Kings 3:15], until your sad thoughts vanish. . . . Act like that man who, whenever his wife began to nag and snap at him, drew out his flute from under his belt and played merrily until she was exhausted and let him alone.[164] So you too must turn to your regal or gather some good companions about you and sing with them until you learn how to defy the devil.[165]

There are numerous references to his singing at table in the writings of his colleagues, among them Johann Mathesius, a close associate of Luther between 1540 and 1542, who records such music-making during this period. For example, "the Doctor sang from time to time during and after meals, for he was also a lutenist, [and] I have sung with him";[166] "Now when Doctor Luther was weary and exhausted by work, he was joyful at table when from time to time a Kantorei [group of singers] was created."[167] Similarly the composer Johann Walter reported:

I know and bear true witness that the holy man of God, *Luther,* the Prophet and Apostle to the German *nation,* had a great love for *music* in *plainsong* and *polyphony* [*Choral* und *Figural*]. Many precious hours have I sung with him, and have often seen how the dear man became so merry and joyful in spirit from singing, that he could hardly become tired and weary of singing and speaking so splendidly about *music.*[168]

Sometimes the singers included his colleagues, such as Rhau and Melanchthon,[169] as well as students, such as Johann Zink.[170] While such singing brought him joy he would not tolerate misplaced levity: "'Music doesn't sound right when there is laughter in connection with it, for music is intended to cheer the spirit. The mouth gets no pleasure from it. If one sings diligently, the soul, which is located in the body, plays and derives special pleasure from it.' This he [Luther] said when we laughed during the singing [at table]."[171] Similarly, he was concerned that the music performed should be sung to the best of their combined abilities. Thus he wrote to an unidentified composer, 18 January 1535:

We sing as well as we can here at table and afterward. If we make a few blunders, it is really not your fault but our ability, which is still very slight even if we have sung over [the piece] two or three times. . . . Therefore you composers must pardon us if we make blunders in your songs, for we would much rather do them well than badly.[172]

Nevertheless, if he found any faults in the part books they were using he would immediately correct them, as Ratzeberger reports: "It is noteworthy that from time to time when he found false notation in a new song [they were singing], he immediately took it away and saw that it was correctly set and rectified."[173] He also had a concern for correct pitch: "No one should try to sing such a song in a higher key, for he will surely become hoarse and make a botch of it before he reaches five notes."[174]

The repertory of musical performances at Luther's table was distinctly liturgical. Ratzeberger reports:

> Moreover Luther was also accustomed immediately after the evening meal time to fetch from his study his part books[175] and with his table companions, who delighted in music, made music together with them. He was particularly pleased when it was a good composition by an old master of a responsory or a hymn of the season, and especially took great pleasure in every Gregorian chant and chorale. . . . He was especially pleased to sing along when it was a hymn or responsory of the season with the music composed on a Gregorian chant, and would sing with his young sons Martin and Paul, at table after eating, the responsory of the season, such as at Christmas *Verbum caro factus est, In principio erat verbum;* at Easter *Christus resurgens ex mortuis, Vita sanctorum, Victimae paschali laudes.* At the appropriate time he would sing such [chant] responsories with his sons, and in polyphonic settings he sang the Alto part.[176]

His former student in Wittenberg, Erasmus Alber, reported that Luther had a good singing voice: "He was a good musician and also had a fine, clear, pure voice, both for singing and speaking."[177]

Connoisseur

Luther was clearly fascinated by polyphonic music. For example, in the preface to Rhau's *Symphoniae iuncundae atque adea breves quattuor vocum,* published in 1538, he wrote:

> It is possible to taste with wonder (yet not to comprehend) God's absolute and perfect wisdom in his wondrous work of music. Here is it most

remarkable that one single voice continues to sing the Tenor [the *cantus firmus*], while at the same time many other voices play around it, exulting and adorning it in exuberant strains and, as it were, leading it forth in a divine roundelay, so that those who are the least bit moved know nothing more amazing in this world. But any who remain unaffected are unmusical indeed and deserve to hear a certain filth poet or the music of pigs.[178]

Many of Luther's friends and acquaintances were musicians or composers with whom he could discuss technical matters regarding how a piece had been composed and what the implications for performance might be. Some have already been noticed, but they include the following.[179] Johannes Weinmann, whom Luther almost certainly knew as a student in Erfurt, was successively organist of the castle and town churches in Wittenberg. Luther must have known Adam Rener, the court composer between 1507 and 1520, almost certainly the primary editor of the partbooks compiled for use by the Allerheiligenstift, whose compositions were included in Rhau's musical anthologies. Rener's successor, Johann Walter, became one of Luther's closest friends and supporters. Walter with Kapellmeister Conrad Rupsch collaborated with Luther in creating the music for the *Deutsche Messe* in 1525,[180] and it seems likely that Rupsch, as the leading musician of the Hofkapelle, would have been involved in the first performances of Walter's polyphonic settings and therefore may well have also played a significant part in the production of the *Chorgesangbuch* of 1524, together with Walter and Luther. Georg Rhau, another of Luther's closest friends as well as the printer/publisher of music, was also an accomplished composer whose *Missa de Sancto Spirito* was written for the opening Mass in St. Thomas's Church, Leipzig, before the disputation between Luther and Eck in 1519. Luther corresponded with Matthias Weller, organist in Freiberg, Saxony, in the mid-1530s.[181] Georg Forster, a chorister in the Heidelberg Hofkapelle, who later studied in Wittenberg between 1534 and 1539, was a frequent guest at Luther's table, and the Reformer encouraged him to compose sacred pieces,[182] many of which were issued in various Rhau imprints from 1538. Luther almost certainly had some input with regard to the selection of the pieces that Forster included in the first two parts of his *Frische teutsche Liedlin* (Nuremberg, 1539-1540), an anthology of settings of mostly secular strophic songs by leading composers such as Isaac, Hofhaimer, Senfl, and Othmayr, among many others. Sixt Dietrich was already an established composer by the time he taught music in Wittenberg in 1540, when Luther supported the bid for him to become professor of music. In a letter, dated 29 May 1543, Dietrich reviewed his experience in Wittenberg and observed that "D[r]. M. Luther has an especially great love for music, and I have sung much and often with him."[183] Rhau published Dietrich's *Novum ac insigne opus musicum 36 antiphonarium* (1541) and *Novum opus musicum tres tomus sacrorum hymnorum* (1545). Lucas Edemberger was a teacher who also sang with Luther[184] and was apparently a minor composer, although Luther did not think too highly of his compositional talents.[185] Similarly Luther was somewhat critical of Georg Planck, organist in Zeitz, when he played in public.[186] Wolff Heinz, organist in Halle, on the other hand, was warmly regarded in the personal, handwritten dedication on the flyleaf of the German Bible that Luther gave him in 1541.[187] Luther also wrote a personal dedication, a comment on Psalm 27:14, in the copy of the second edition of his larger Galatians commentary (1538) that he presented to Leonard Paminger, composer and rector of the Nikolausschule in Passau.[188] Significantly the compositions of a number of these musicians are represented in Rhau's *Neue deutsche geistliche Gesänge* (1544) — Dietrich, Förster, Heinz, Weinmann — which might imply that Luther had some input into the compilation of this anthology.

In addition there were other composers with whom Luther had little or no personal contact but whose compositions he regarded highly. For example, on New Year's Day 1537, it is reported that "after singing excellent songs [motets?] with much admiration, following a meal, Doctor Martin said with a sigh, 'Ah, how many fine musicians have died within the past ten years: Josquin, Pierre de la Rue, [Heinrich] Finck, and other distinguished [composers].'"[189] The named composers were generally recognized as the finest of their generation, especially Josquin, whose names recur again and again as superlative musicians worthy of emulation in the theoretical treatises on music employed in, or emanating from, Wittenberg (see above). The manuscript partbooks of the Allerheiligenstift contained seven polyphonic masses by Josquin, and compositions of the three composers mentioned by Luther were included in the publications issued by Rhau, such as motets by Josquin and la Rue in *Symphoniae iuncundae* (1538), and numerous hymn settings by Heinrich Finck in *Sacrorum hymnorum liber primus* (1542). Compositions of these three composers occur in the Torgau manuscripts compiled under the direction of Johann Walter.[190] Similarly, in Nuremberg, where there were close ties with Wittenberg, the works of these composers were also highly regarded, such as the eight masses by Josquin and the five by la Rue found in the Nuremberg publications, *Liber quindecum missarum* (Nuremberg: Petrius, 1539) and *Missae tredecim quatuor vocum* (Nuremberg: Formschneider, 1539).

For Luther two composers were accorded great respect, one he knew by reputation and the other by personal contact: Josquin and Ludwig Senfl (whose name was not included in Luther's 1537 list of deceased composers since he was then still alive). Luther almost certainly became aware of Senfl through Frederick the Wise's Hofkapelle. Senfl was a member of the Hofkapelle of Maximilian I, the Holy Roman Emperor, based in Vienna.[191] Around 1493 Elector Frederick the Wise had been offered the position of Emperor but had declined in favor of Maximilian. Thus politically Frederick was seen as king-maker and therefore retained a position of power and influence in German affairs, second only to Maximilian. With the founding of Wittenberg university as a humanist institution and the expansion of the Allerheiligenstift Frederick emphasized his significance by demonstrating that he could be compared only with Maximilian, an ardent supporter of humanism and the arts. Similarly, when Frederick set up his Saxon Hofkapelle at the end of the fifteenth century he did so in reference to Maximilian's Hofkapelle. It is possible that Luther met Senfl, a member of Maximilian's Hofkapelle, in Innsbruck on his return from Rome in 1510.[192] Adam Rener, then another member of Maximilian's Hofkapelle, became Frederick's court composer in 1507 and thus became a primary conduit by which the music of Maximilian's Hofkapelle was known in Wittenberg.

Maximilian was present at the Diet of Augsburg in 1518 and was attended by his Hofkapelle, including Senfl. Towards the end of the Diet Luther appeared before Cardinal Cajetan and while in Augsburg Luther's host was Conrad Peutinger, city secretary and privy counselor to Maximilian. Peutinger, a humanist scholar interested in church reform, became a close friend of Luther during these years, although, like Senfl, he never openly espoused Lutheran views. When Luther appeared at the Diet of Worms in 1521 — which Senfl also attended — Peutinger advised Frederick the Wise on how to secure Luther's safety and worked behind the scenes in the attempt to prevent Luther's condemnation.[193] It would seem likely that Luther and Senfl were in contact with each other in Augsburg in 1518, probably in Peutinger's home. For the next two years Senfl, then based in Augsburg, edited an anthology of liturgical music that contained numerous works by Josquin, Isaac, and himself, as well as representative pieces by other composers, such as Obrecht and la Rue. The work was issued as *Liber selectarum cantionum* by the Augsburg publishers Grim and Wirsung,[194] who also issued several titles by Luther between 1521 and 1523.[195] The *Liber selectarum cantionum* was a prestigious publication, a massive choirbook of 274 folios, measuring 44.5 × 28.5 cm., decorated with woodcuts. Peutinger contributed a significant introduction to the work in which he made one of the earliest references to the connection between music and rhetoric.[196] A fundamental question is: Did Luther perhaps own or at least know of the *Liber selectarum cantionum*, edited by Senfl and introduced by Peutinger? It was a collection intended for use in ecclesiastical musical foundations rather than possession by individuals.

Table 2.2. Compositions of Josquin and Senfl in
Liber selectarum cantionum (1520)

2	*Praeter rerum seriem*	Josquin	Christmas sequence
4	*O virgo prudentissima*	Josquin	
6	*Benedicta es caelorum regina*	Josquin	Annunciation sequence
9	*Miserere mei Deus*	Josquin	Psalm 50/51
10	*Inviolata integra et casta es Maria*	Josquin	Sequence
13	*Stabat mater dolorosa*	Josquin	Sequence
18	*De profundis clamavi ad te*	Josquin	Psalm 129/130
8	*Sancte pater divumque decus*	Senfl	
16	*Gaude maria virgo*	Senfl	Annunciation responsory
22	*Discubuit hiesus*	Senfl	Luke 22:14, 19
23	*Usquequo domine*	Senfl	Psalm 12
24	*Beati omnes quitiment*	Senfl	Psalm 127/128
25	*Salve sancta parens*	Senfl	Hymn

However, given Luther's public visibility at the time, coupled with his personal contact with both Peutinger and Senfl, together with his known interest in music, it seems highly likely that either Peutinger or Senfl (or both together) presented Luther with the anthology.[197] But even if they did not, the *Liber selectarum cantionum* was the kind of publication that Frederick would have wanted for his Allerheiligenstift and Hofkapelle, especially as it represented the music of Maximilian's Hofkapelle.[198] It therefore seems highly likely that one way or another Luther was aware of the contents of Senfl's *Liber selectarum cantionum,* a publication that did much to promote Senfl's reputation as a composer as well as prepare the way for the renaissance of Josquin's music in Germany that began in the later 1530s. Of the 25 compositions, seven were by (or in one case attributed to) Josquin and six by Senfl (see Table 2.2). The motets by Josquin included in Senfl's *Liber* became the most widely known and disseminated of all Josquin's works. Luther's connection with Peutinger and Senfl, together with Josquin's music that he almost certainly heard on his visit to Rome, and his exposure to the Josquin masses that were sung by the Allerheiligenstift, suggests that his knowledge of Josquin's music was quite extensive and significantly pre-dates the German Josquin renaissance of the later 1530s. Thus towards the end of 1531 he spoke of Josquin, "all of whose compositions flow freely, gently, and cheerfully, [and] are not forced or cramped by rules like the song of the finch."[199]

In 1523 Senfl became composer to the Hofkapelle of Duke Wilhelm of

Bavaria in Munich. He thus was part of the Bavarian retinue that attended the 1530 Diet of Augsburg, when the articles of the Lutheran *Confessio* were presented. Senfl's setting of Psalm 132/133, *Ecce quam bonum* was sung at the beginning of the Diet, highly appropriate given the divisions the Diet had to address: "Behold how good it is when brothers dwell together in unity." Luther was politically *persona non grata* so was unable to attend, although he did stay nearby in Coburg Castle and maintained a close connection with all that was going on by correspondence.[200] Someone must have informed Luther about Senfl's motet that had opened the proceedings since Luther was moved to write to him the warm, personal letter, dated 4 October 1530:

> Even though my name is detested, so much that I am forced to fear that this letter I am sending may not be safely received and read by you, excellent Louis, yet the love for music, with which I see you adorned and gifted by God, has conquered this fear. This love also has given me hope that my letter will not bring danger to you. . . . Because they encourage and honor music so much, I, at least, nevertheless very much praise and respect above all others your dukes of Bavaria, much as they are unfavorably inclined toward me. . . . I ask if you would have copied and sent to me, if you have it, a copy of that song: *In pace in idipsum* [Psalm 4:8].[201] For this Tenor melody [the chant Luther wanted set polyphonically] has delighted me from youth on, and does so even more now that I understand the words. I have never seen this antiphon arranged for more voices. I do not wish, however, to impose on you the work of arranging [composing]; rather I assume that you have available an arrangement from some other source. Indeed, I hope that the end of my life is at hand; the world hates me and cannot bear me, and I, in turn, loathe and detest the world; therefore may the best and [most] faithful shepherd take my soul to him. And so I have already started to sing this antiphon and am eager to hear it arranged. In case you should not have or know it, I am enclosing it here with the [musical] notes; if you wish you can arrange it — perhaps after my death.[202]

Senfl acceded to Luther's request and not only sent him a polyphonic motet of *In pace in idipsum*[203] but also another on the text *Non moriar, sed vivam et narrabo opera Domini* [Psalm 118:17: "I shall not die but live and declare the works of the Lord"] (see Example 2.1).[204] This text, which became in effect Luther's motto, was a great comfort to the Wittenberg Reformer, isolated as he was in Coburg away from the action in Augsburg. He arranged for the text of the antiphon, together with its chant notation, to be inscribed on the wall of his room in Coburg Castle (see Example 2.2).[205] Since Luther did not men-

Example 2.1. Motet: Senfl, *Non moriar, sed vivam*

Example 2.2. Antiphon: *Non moriar, sed vivam et narrabo opera Domini*

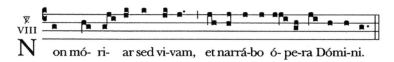

Non mó- ri- ar sed vi-vam, et narrá-bo ó- pe-ra Dómi-ni.

tion the antiphon from Psalm 118 in his letter to Senfl in October 1530, either he must have written another letter at a later time, or someone else informed the composer of Luther's attachment to the text and its associated chant. That Senfl should write a motet on this antiphon that was so important to Luther at this time is a measure of the respect he had for the Reformer.[206] Luther expressed his gratitude for this musical generosity by sending Senfl a box of books in 1531.[207]

In 1537 Hans Ott in Nuremberg published an anthology of polyphonic music, in four to six voices, *Novum et insigne opus musicum,* one of a number of publications with strong links with composers affiliated with the Bavarian court, notably Senfl. Given the Bavarian court connection and the fact that a high proportion of the compositions in the 1537 collection are by Senfl, he was either its primary editor or at least closely involved in its compilation. As in the 1520 collection edited by Senfl, the compositions of Josquin figure prominently and in Ott's preface are accorded high praise:

> All will easily recognize Josquin as the most celebrated hero of the art of music, for he possesses something that is truly inimitable and divine. Nor will a grateful and honest posterity begrudge him this praise.[208]

All except one (Psalm 129/130) of the Josquin motets, together with two by Isaac, found in the *Liber selectarum cantionum* of 1520 edited by Senfl also appear in Ott's 1537 collection (see Table 2.2), as well as others by Josquin.

Luther must have known Ott's partbooks and may well have owned a set, since comments he made on motets found in this anthology were recorded by his friends. On 26 December 1538 two of the motets were performed in Luther's home: *Haec dicit Dominus* by Josquin and *Sancta trinitas, unus Deus* by Antoine de Févin (ca. 1470–ca. 1512), both for six voices. Luther made the following comment on the Josquin motet:

> It beautifully comprehends the difference between Law and Gospel, death and life. Two voices make the plaintive lament *Circumdederunt me gemitus mortis etc,* against which four voices sing *Haec dicit Dominus, de manu mortis liberabo populum meum etc.* It is a very good and comforting composition.[209]

Two voices *(Quintus* and *Sextus)* sing the chant melody (the Invitatory of the Office of the Dead) in strict canon accompanied by the other four voices singing the freely-composed setting of the Latin text *Haec dicit Dominus.* The motet is a contrafactum of Josquin's French chanson-motet *Nimphes, nappés*

Example 2.3. Motet: Josquin, *Nimphes, nappés*

(a four-line stanza), an expression of grief that appropriately juxtaposes the funerary chant, the different texts serving as glosses on each other (see Example 2.3).[210] However, in Ott's collection the French chanson text is replaced by the Latin text thus making the motet appropriate for liturgical use in Germany. It appears that the Latin text was added by Conrad Rupsch, the former Kapellmeister of Frederick the Wise and collaborator with Luther on the *Deutsche Messe*.[211] The account in the *Tischreden* is introduced thus: "On 26 December was sung the six-voiced *Haec dicit Dominus*, composed by Conrad

Rupsch, which sings of the agony of death."²¹² The *Tischreden* scribe — Anthony Lauterbach, who was probably one of the singers — was following the composer ascription, "Chunradus Rupsch," given with the motet in the Ott part books. However, the index in the Tenor part book of Ott's anthology correctly ascribes the motet to "Iosquin." Luther knew that the composer was Josquin, rather than Rupsch, as Mathesius records when the motet was sung at Luther's table, sometime around 1540:

> In between the singing he expressed good things. "Josquin," he said, "is the master of the notes [Noten Meister], which must express what he desires; the other masters of singing [Sangmeister] must do what the notes dictate. He most certainly possessed a great spirit, like Bezalel [see Exodus 31:2-6], especially when he ingeniously and beautifully intertwines together *Haec dicit Dominus* with *Circumdederunt me gemitus mortis.*"²¹³

The inclusion of Rupsch's edited version of the Josquin motet implies a Wittenberg connection with the editorial process that resulted in Ott's *Novum et insigne opus musicum,* and also that Luther's knowledge of the motet almost certainly pre-dates the 1537 publication.

The second motet from Ott's collection sung on 26 December 1538 was by Antoine de Févin, though no composer ascription is given either in the partbooks themselves, or in the index of the Tenor partbook:

> They sang *Sancta trinitas,* partially in six-part harmony, but two of the parts were not authentic. He [Luther] said: "Someone wanted to improve on the original, forgoing simplicity as a result. For those four parts are a marvel of sweetness and simplicity. For simplicity in all the arts is delightful. . . . Therefore one should in each and every case leave the composition alone and not destroy his [the composer's] voice."²¹⁴

Sometime around 1527, the year he became the Hapsburg Kapellmeister in succession to Heinrich Finck, Arnold von Bruck (ca. 1500-1554) added two additional voice parts *(Quintus* and *Sextus)* to Févin's four-part motet *Sancta trinitas,*²¹⁵ that had first appeared in print in *Motetti de la corona I,* published by Ottaviano Petrucci in Fossombrone, Italy, in 1514. The six-part version is the third item in Ott's collection, being preceded and succeeded by motets by Josquin.

It is significant that with regard to the performances of these two motets from Ott's 1537 collection Luther was able to make some perceptive and revealing remarks about them. He recognized the two-part canon set against the freer four-part writing in *Haec dicit Dominus,* knew about the two additional voices in *Sancta trinitas* and saw that the six-part version obscured the beauty and simplicity of the original four-part composition.

Luther's attention to compositional detail prompts such questions as: Does Luther's appreciation of the music of Josquin mean that he understood the composer's use of rhetoric and theological symbolism in his music?[216] Was Luther aware of the way that la Rue symbolizes the unity of the Trinity by a three-voice canon in his motet *Pater de coelis,* found in Ott's 1537 collection?[217] Given his frequent comments on the connection between music and theology,[218] it seems highly likely that Luther was aware of at least some of such compositional devices found in these works and others like them.

Luther's detailed knowledge of such polyphonic works may well have links with his proficiency on the lute. A substantial portion of the pieces found in German lute intabulations of the period, both in manuscript and published, are drawn from vocal models. For example, in a manuscript probably copied in the Bavarian court in Munich, sometime between 1533 and 1544 (Bayerische Staatsbibliothek, *Mus. Ms. 1512*), there are lute versions of the vocal polyphony of Hofhaimer, Isaac, Senfl, and Stoltzer, among others. Similarly, in Hans Neusidler's *Ein newgeordent künstlich Lautenbuch,* 2 vols. (Nuremberg: Petreius, 1536), there are lute intabulations of vocal polyphony by such composers as Adam von Fulda, Alexander Agricola, Sixt Dietrich, Isaac, Hofhaimer, Josquin, Senfl, Stoltzer, and others.[219] There is therefore the possibility that Luther played such lute transcriptions as well as singing the vocal polyphony with his family, friends and colleagues.

Composer

Luther understood enough about composition to be able to write modest pieces in several parts. As mentioned earlier, there is a report that he composed a setting of the last words of Dido, *Dulces exuviae,* from the *Aeneid,*[220] and there are other references to his compositional efforts. While in Coburg castle during the period of the Diet of Augsburg in 1530 he corresponded with numerous people. One of these correspondents was Johann Agricola, then in Augsburg for the Diet. In one of his Coburg letters to Agricola Luther speaks of his composing and/or arranging at that time. Luther's letter to Agricola is dated 15 May 1530:

> I am herewith sending you a song for you to practice. Being unable to read or write for four days,[221] spiritually exhausted,[222] I chanced to find a

piece of paper on which was written this old song arranged for three voices. I cleansed, corrected, and improved it, added a fourth voice, and also quickly prepared a text for the music.

Luther then asked Agricola to authenticate the composition as coming from the Bavarian Hofkapelle, then in Augsburg, and that it was composed to celebrate the arrival of Charles V, Holy Roman Emperor, and Ferdinand of Bavaria. The composition should be returned to Luther who would use it to tease Georg Rörer, who was then deacon in Wittenberg, later a close associate of Luther in proofreading and editing many of the Reformer's writings. Rörer had been the liturgist for the first celebration of Luther's *Deutsche Messe* in Wittenberg late in 1525 who prided himself on his musical sensibilities. Luther wanted to play this trick on him "in order that once and for all this great music critic be deprived of his self-appointed and egotistic judgment in matters of music."[223]

Here is an example of Luther's ironic humor, which makes it difficult to know how much of this is tongue-in-cheek. Did he really find the scrap of paper inscribed with a three-part composition? Did he really add a fourth voice — a *vox vagans?* Did he really create a text for it? The likelihood is that he composed the whole thing himself, and that it was in the nature of a musical pun. But it is not clear who was the butt of the joke. At face value it was Rörer who apparently had musical pretensions, but was Luther teasing Agricola in some way? Nevertheless the letter does indicate that Luther was involved in composition, if only in a playful way.

There is a four-part faburden of Tone I (Dorian), published by Klug in 1546, with the German text of Psalm 64, that has been viewed as a composition of Luther,[224] but was almost certainly the work of Johann Walter.[225] On the other hand, the modest setting of Psalm 118:17, *Non moriar sed vivam* — the same text and Tone VIII chant melody that Senfl had employed in the motet he sent to Luther after the 1530 Diet of Augsburg — appears to be genuine. It was first published in Wittenberg in 1545 as the "Epilogum" to Joachim Greff's drama *Lazarus:* "*Non moriar sed vivam D. Martin Lutheri IIII vocum.* . . . Folget [now follows] *Non moriar sed vivam D.M.L.*"[226] (See Example 2.4.) That it was published in Wittenberg before Luther's death and that his authorship of the piece is stated twice in the introductory sentences establishes its authenticity. Luther was, however, aware of the limitations of his compositional abilities and certainly would not have compared his motet to that of Senfl:

> After some fine and beautiful motets by Senfl had been sung, D.[octor] M.[artin] L.[uther] was amazed, accorded them much praise, and said: "I would not be able to compose such a motet, even if I would tear myself to

Example 2.4. Motet: Luther, *Non moriar sed vivam* (Tenor)

pieces in the attempt, just as he [Senfl] would not be able to preach a Psalm as I can.[227]

Luther's modest composition (Example 2.5) on the same text and chant melody as Senfl's motet probably means that it was composed sometime before the latter (Example 2.1), the most likely time being while he was at Coburg castle in 1530, when the text was particularly important to him, when he was composing musical jokes in connection with Agricola and Rörer, and when he wrote his important letter to Senfl in which he reveals much of his theological thinking about music.

Luther's polyphonic skill may have been limited but in his understanding of how to compose melodies he had few rivals. What we know as the Lutheran chorale was in many respects the creation of Luther,[228] so much so that the title pages of many sixteenth-century hymnals include words such as "containing hymns by Martin Luther and others." He recognized the intrinsic qualities of some of the older melodies which he retained unaltered in the Wittenberg hymnals; others he modified with such simple sophistication that in effect they became new tunes; and, of course, he created new melodies that have clearly stood the test of time.

Example 2.5. Motet: Luther, *Non moriar, sed vivam*

Among the older unaltered melodies associated with Latin (or macaronic) texts found in the various Wittenberg hymnals, edited by Luther and issued by Klug between 1529 and 1543, are:

Dies est laetitiae/
    Der tag, der ist so freudenreich   Hypolydian (Mode VI)   Zahn No. 7870; DKL Eg17A

Christe qui lux es et dies/
    Christe, der du bist tag und licht   Dorian (Mode I)   Zahn No. 343; DKL B12B

In dulci jubilo   Hypolydian (Mode VI)   Zahn No. 4947; DKL Ee12

Similarly, among older, essentially unaltered, melodies associated with vernacular religious songs he included the following:

Nun bitten wir den Heiligen Geist	Hypolydian (Mode VI)	Zahn No. 2029; DKL Eg17A
Wir glauben all an einen Gott	Dorian (Mode I)	Zahn No. 7971; DKL Ec18
Christ ist erstanden	Dorian (Mode I)	Zahn No. 8584; DKL C11B
Gelobet seist du, Jesu Christ	Mixolydian (Mode VII)	Zahn No. 1947; DKL Ec10
Dies sind die heiligen zehn Gebot	Mixolydian (Mode VII)	Zahn No. 1951; DKL Ea1

These melodies, of course, retained their modal identity, but when he modified existing melodies and created new ones, while he still used some of the older modes — such as Phrygian (Mode III) for *Aus tiefer Not schrei ich zu dir*[229] — most of these tunes tend to be either Dorian (Mode I) or Ionian (one of the four additional modes systematized by Glarean in 1547),[230] the equivalents of modern minor and major tonality. For example Luther created no less than three different Dorian melodies from the same basic source, the Latin hymn melody *Veni redemptor gentium*:[231] the three melodies are *Nun komm der Heiden Heiland*,[232] *Verleih uns Frieden gnädiglich*,[233] and *Erhalt uns, Herr, bei deinem Wort*[234] (see Example 13.2). Although the three melodies have a common origin it is remarkable how Luther was nevertheless able to give to each one its own distinctive characteristics.

Many of his composed melodies tend to fall within the Ionian mode,[235] for example:

Ein neues Lied wir haben an (1523)	Zahn No. 7245; DKL Ea12
Ein feste Burg ist unser Gott (1529)	Zahn No. 7377a; DKL B31
Sie ist mir lieb die werte Magd (1535)	Zahn No. 8289; DKL Ek1
Vom Himmel hoch da komm ich her (1539)	Zahn No. 346; DKL Ei1

To these can be added the following which, though essentially Lydian (Mode V), share many characteristics with Luther's Ionian melodies:

Jesaia dem Propheten (1526)	Zahn No. 8534; DKL D19[236]
Vater unser in Himmelreich (c. 1538)	Zahn No. 2562; AWA 4, 35A[237]

In the creation of these melodies Luther was being both forward-looking, pointing towards modern major tonality, but also backward-looking, exploiting the skills of the composers of the Hofweise (court-song) and Meistersang traditions.[238]

In the late nineteenth and early twentieth centuries there was the tendency to minimize Luther's composition of melodies, suggesting that they were not "original" but mostly the work of others. For example, in 1886 Wilhelm Bäumker went to some lengths to demonstrate that the melody of *Ein feste Burg ist unser Gott* was a cut-and-paste compilation of Gregorian fragments.[239] But Bäumker was writing at a time when ideas of artistic creativity were absolute, and therefore the reuse of earlier material was considered to effectively diminish the stature of the creator. We now know more about how the sixteenth century viewed what it meant "to compose" — literally "to put together" — and, as Ameln has pointed out, Bäumker "failed to explain how, out of a mosaic-like combining of melodic fragments, melodies of such unity and magnificent impression could have grown."[240]

More recent scholarship tends to understand the context of Luther's time with clearer vision and to give more weight to the opinions of his contemporaries who are uniform in their praise of his abilities. Composer Johann Walter had no doubts about Luther's abilities as a creator of melodies:

> Let it be seen, heard, and understood, how the Holy Spirit himself collaborates, both with . . . *authors* of Latin [chant] and with Herr Luther, who until now has written most of the German *chants* [deutschen Choral Gesänge] and set them to music. Therefore, it may be observed in the German *Sanctus* (Jesaia dem Propheten das geschah, etc.) and in other places, how carefully he fitted all the notes so masterfully and so well to the text, according to the right *accent* and *concent*.[241]

Here Walter is confirming Luther's abilities as well as the Reformer's long-held conviction that there is an intimate connection between text and tone, such as his statement: "The [musical] notes make the text live."[242] Luther was not the first to create a "German Mass," and one of the reasons why he hesitated was that, in his view, any vernacular liturgical forms would need to be supplied with appropriate melodies. Thomas Müntzer had already issued his *Deutsch Euangelisch Messze* (Eilenburg, 1524), in which the German texts were supplied with the unaltered notation of the Latin originals,[243] when Luther wrote his treatise *Against the Heavenly Prophets* (1525). In this work Luther was critical of Müntzer, though he does not name him, in his use of Latin chant melodies which are not adjusted to accommodate the different characteristics of the German language:

> I would gladly have a German mass today. I am also occupied with it. But I would very much like it to have a true German character. For to translate the Latin text and retain the Latin tone or notes has my sanction,

though it does not sound polished or well done. Both text and [musical] notes, accent and melody, and manner of rendering ought to grow out of the true mother tongue and its inflection, otherwise all of it becomes an imitation, in the manner of apes.[244]

As will be explored in later chapters, while Luther stressed that music has a proclamatory function as bearer of the Word of God, he neither undervalued music nor gave it merely a subservient, functional role. For Luther music in worship was too important to be used unthinkingly or superficially: it had to be creatively crafted, nuanced and aesthetically expressive. The composer Johann Walter expressed that, in his opinion, Luther not only understood how music should be created in close connection with the sound and sense of its associated text, he also had the ability to actually compose such music. Walter was not alone in that opinion. For example, Cyriacus Spangenberg — son of Luther's long-standing friend Johann Spangenberg, and a guest in Luther's household between 1542 and 1546 — wrote the following in the preface to his *Cithera Lutheri* (Erfurt 1569):

> Of all the Mastersingers since the time of the apostles, Luther is the best and most artistic. . . . Everything flows and comes from him, most beautiful and artistic, full of spirit and doctrine. . . . The meaning is clear and intelligible; the melody and sound beautiful and heartfelt. In sum, everything is admirable and delightful, with marrow and strength that heartens and comforts, and truly no one is his equal, much less his master.[245]

Conclusion

Earlier twentieth-century writers on Luther's musicianship tended to classify him as an enthusiastic amateur, a dilettante who pursued music as a hobby.[246] But more recent scholarship suggests that such discussions of Luther's musicianship in terms of amateurism and professionalism are anachronistic, a reading back of later concerns into the period of the Renaissance-Reformation, resulting more in the nature of a caricature rather than a characterization.[247] This chapter has sought to demonstrate that Luther's musicianship was anything but superficial and is the essential starting-point for any discussion of his musical understanding of theology or of his liturgical use of music. Attempts to portray such concepts and activities from the perspective of Luther as a mere dabbler in musical matters are in danger of distorting the true significance of these principles and accomplishments. As Paul Henry Lang, writing more than sixty years ago, concluded:

> In the center of the new musical movement which accompanied the Reformation stands the great figure of Martin Luther. He does not occupy this position because of his generalship of the Protestant movement, and nothing is more unjust than to consider him a sort of enthusiastic and good-natured dilettante.[248]

Music was the constant accompaniment of Luther's life. He never ceased to wonder at its profound effects on him as a performer and listener, and he was certain that the finest music he had heard in this life would be surpassed in the life to come. Towards the end of his life (December 1538), after various motets had been sung, he observed: "If our Lord God has given us such noble gifts in the latrine of this life, what [music] will there be in eternal life where everything is perfect and joyful?"[249] It is reported that the last thing he uttered before retiring to his bed for the last time was the words from Psalm 31:5: "Into thy hands, O Lord, I commend my spirit, for you have redeemed me, O God of truth." According to Johannes Bugenhagen Luther repeated these words three times, but gave the text in German;[250] according to Justus Jonas and others Luther uttered the text in Latin: "*In manus tuas commendo spiritum meum, Redemisti me Domine DEVS veritatis.*"[251] These are among the words that Jesus uttered from the cross (Luke 23:46), but they were also words that Luther had sung almost every day for much of his life: the words of the short Respond following the Scripture reading at Compline. It is significant that Bugenhagen informs us that Luther repeated them three times, since the principal text occurs three times in the Compline Respond,[252] which suggests that this was the last thing he sang this side of eternity.

After his death, as his body was being transported back to Wittenberg from Eisleben where he had died, the people in Halle appropriately marked his passing by singing one of the hymns he created: *Aus tiefer Not schrei ich zu dir.*[253]

Luther's Theological Understanding of Music

Luther's comments on music are many and varied. One, however, he repeated at different times and in different contexts: "Music is next to theology."[1] His letter to composer Ludwig Senfl, dated 4 October 1530, contains his most extended statement:

> I plainly judge, and do not hesitate to affirm, that except for theology there is no art that could be put on the same level with music, since except for theology [music] alone produces what otherwise only theology can do, namely, a calm and joyful disposition. . . . This is the reason why the prophets did not make use of any art except music; when setting forth their theology they did it not as geometry, not as arithmetic, not as astronomy, but as music, so that they held theology and music most tightly connected, and proclaimed truth through Psalms and songs.[2]

It is this distinctive statement — "music is next to theology" — that distinguishes Luther from his predecessors, as well as from many of his contemporaries, and has therefore been continuously quoted and commented upon. But it is a dictum that should not be considered in isolation: in order to understand what Luther meant, it needs to be set against the context of medieval views concerning music, compared with his other comments about music, and examined with regard to the way in which music was incorporated into his theological thinking.

Evolving Views of Music: From Medieval to Reformation

In one sense it could be argued that Luther's view of music being close to theology is merely the logical conclusion of the medieval understanding of the nature and purpose of music. In summarizing medieval music documents, Herbert Schueller concludes: "Ultimately . . . the purpose of music is affirmed as the praise and glorification of God. Always and everywhere this aim was proclaimed: to sing the praise of God, the eternal *alleluia,* is music's primary function."[3] For example, the anonymous ninth- (or tenth-) century author of *Scholia enchiriadis* makes the following comment concerning the *quadrivium* (music, arithmetic, geometry, and astronomy):[4]

> These four disciplines are not arts of human devising, but are investigations, such as they are, of divine works; and they lead noble minds, by wonderful arguments, to a better understanding of the work of creation. It is inexcusable to come by these means to know God and his eternal divinity, and then not to glorify him or give thanks.[5]

Luther would have readily endorsed the view that the primary function of each of the four disciplines of the *quadrivium* was the evocation of the praise and glory of God, but he would not have accepted the equality of the disciplines implied by the anonymous author of the *Scholia enchiriadis.* As his letter to Ludwig Senfl makes clear, Luther went far beyond his predecessors by insisting that in matters concerning expressions of theology — the praise and glory of God — music takes precedence over the other disciplines of the *quadrivium:* "This is the reason why the prophets did not make use of any art except music; when setting forth their theology they did it not as geometry, not as arithmetic, not as astronomy, but as music."[6]

Having been an Augustinian monk, Luther would have been aware of the writings of Augustine that deal with music, notably Book 10 of the *Confessions,* wherein Augustine describes the influence of music on his recovery of the Christian faith he had earlier rejected, and Chapter 6 of *De musica,* written after this conversion experience. But Luther would also have been aware of the musical treatises of Boethius, de Muris, Gerson, and Tinctoris,[7] among others, which he studied as a student at the university of Erfurt.[8] But even if he was not aware of all of the names of such music theorists he would nevertheless have been familiar with the substance of their treatises since all of these authors by and large shared the same basic perspectives.

The Invention of Music

Many of these treatises began with some reference to *De inventione et vsv mvsice* (the invention and use of music).[9] On the question of the invention of music there was a fundamental conflict between the Judeo-Christian biblical tradition and Greek philosophic perceptions of history. On the one hand, Genesis 4:21 states, according to the Vulgate: *"Iubal ipse fuit pater canentium cithara et organo"* (Jubal is the father of those who play the harp and organ). On the other hand, according to Greek tradition it was Pythagoras who, on hearing the different pitches made by blacksmiths hammering metal, deduced the basic proportions of musical sound.[10] The earliest music theorists simply state the dilemma without attempting to resolve the conflict: "Moses says Jubal . . . but the Greeks say Pythagoras."[11] Between the fifth and thirteenth centuries most theorists cite Pythagoras rather than Jubal as the "inventor" of music, after which there was marked shift in the reverse direction, citing the primacy of Jubal.[12] In one earlier source, Jubal is ignored and preference given to Pythagoras, but the Greek thinker is not credited with inventing music. The source is the manuscript known as *Carmina cantabrigiensia* (Cambridge Songs), copied in eleventh-century England, but its individual stanzas originated in Germany and elsewhere in Europe.[13] One of the songs (No. 12) does represent a reconciliation between biblical and extrabiblical claims regarding the origins of music, by first asserting the priority of God's creation before recounting the discovery of Pythagoras:

Giver of life, creator of all,
God, shaper of nature,
enclosing the whirling globe
of the world beneath his powerful palm,
is magnificently resplendent
in his creation for ever.
He bade many of old, not yet
followers of the truth,
to go searching through the
trackless byways of unprovable
wisdom, to prepare a way
for us through their blundering.
Among them clever Pythagoras
was renowned
for the keenness of his mind;
. . .

Thus, as this foresighted man
on a certain day
passed by a smithy,
he perceived the blacksmiths
striking hammers
with unequal weight
and with different sound,
and thus recognizing
that some formless power
of tones lay hidden,
he for the first time made known
a beautiful art by adding form.[14]

There is here the concept that the origin of music is hidden within the secrets of God's creation, but it is not an explicit statement of the kind one finds frequently in Luther's writings. However, the fact that this concept could be found in medieval documents suggests that such sources must have had at least some influence on the beginnings of Luther's theological understanding of music.

When thinking about the origins of music Luther had a more fundamental approach compared to that of his medieval predecessors. For him it was beside the point to discuss the primacy of either Jubal or Pythagoras, since neither invented music. While Luther does mention Pythagoras from time to time in his writings, the contexts for most of these references are non-musical, and the few that are musical refer to the "harmony of the spheres" rather than the origin of music.[15] But what is really surprising is his treatment of Jubal in the extended lectures on Genesis he gave in Wittenberg between 1535 and 1545. It is remarkable, given Luther's musical interests, that on Genesis 4:21 — "But the name of his brother was Jubal; he was the father of such as play the harp and wind instruments" — he only offers a comment on the first half of the verse and is completely silent on the second half, which deals with Jubal and instrumental music. He simply states, "The origin of this name [Jubal] is the same as that of the preceding one [Jabal, in the previous verse], for it denotes 'brought,' 'raised.'"[16] Luther is more concerned here with the fact that these people were the descendants of Cain rather than Abel. They are therefore not of the "true church" and were attempting to make a name for themselves by increasing the number of their descendants:

Moreover, these two names [Jabal and Jubal] include the wish that the family might be increased. For Cain's descendants aimed at surpassing the others in numbers. Over against the true church they no doubt laid great stress on that blessing as clear proof that they had not been cast off by God but were themselves also the people of God.[17]

Luther expands on this thought in his comment on the following verse (Genesis 4:22), and while he does refer to the invention of musical instruments, it is ascribed to the Cainites in general rather than to Jubal in particular. He also makes the point that the Cainites would not have been able to have invented their musical instruments without the stable environment provided by the family of Abel. Luther wrote:

> They imagine that Cain's descendants were compelled to engage in other occupations because for them the earth was cursed, and that for this reason they gained their livelihood by another method. Some became shepherds; others, workers in bronze; still others devoted themselves to music, in order to obtain from the descendants of Adam grain and other products of the earth which they needed for their support. But if the Cainites had been so hard pressed by hunger, they would have forgotten their harp and the other musical instruments in their poverty. There is no room for music among people who suffer hunger and thirst. The fact that they invented [instrumental] music and devoted their efforts to developing other arts is proof that they had a plentiful supply of everything needed for sustenance. They had turned to these endeavors and were not satisfied with their simple manner of life, as were the children of Adam, because they wanted to be masters and were trying to win high praise and honor as clever men. Nevertheless, I believe that there were some among them who went over to the true church and adopted Adam's faith.[18]

Earlier in these lectures Luther had expressed the view that in the true church, that is, Adam and his descendants, the singing of hymns to God — of necessity unaccompanied — was the keynote of its worship. Thus on Genesis 2:24, "Therefore a man will leave father and mother and will cling to his wife," he comments:

> Accordingly, if Adam had continued in his innocence, the children that were born would have married. . . . At times they would have come to their father Adam to sing a hymn and praise God, and then they would have returned to their own homes.[19]

Although he does not spell out all the details, his meaning is clear. Luther envisages that music had a fundamental place in the worship of the "true church" before the Fall, and that it was the simple combination of human voices singing praise to God. After the Fall, the descendants of Abel continued such vocal singing in the true worship of God, whereas the descendants of Cain employed instruments in their misdirected worship. Nevertheless, Luther appears to suggest that instrumental worship was introduced into the "true church" by some of the descendants of Cain who chose to worship with the descendants of Abel: "I believe that there were some among them who went over to the true church and adopted Adam's faith."[20] Thus for Luther the question of the origin of music cannot be answered simply in terms of history, chronology, or human progenitors; indeed, the question cannot be understood, let alone answered, without recourse to theology, since music *per se* was not invented by humans but rather created by God.[21]

Repeatedly in his writings Luther states that music is the *donum Dei*, the gift from God, and therefore is only secondarily a human art or science. Interestingly these statements mostly cluster chronologically around the later 1530s[22] and therefore coincide with his lectures on Genesis:

> Music is a gift of God.[23]

> I would certainly like to praise music with all my heart as the excellent gift of God which it is and to commend it to everyone . . . the gift of language combined with the gift of song was only given to man to let him know that he should praise God with both word and music.[24]

> Music is an outstanding gift of God and next to theology.[25]

> Music is God's greatest gift.[26]

> Music is an endowment and gift of God, not a gift of men.[27]

> Music, or the notes . . . are a wonderful creation and gift of God.[28]

For Luther, therefore, music is a God-given benefit to humankind: it may be developed and refined in new ways,[29] but the raw material of music — physical vibrations in the air, the proportions and relationships of different pitches, and so forth — is absolutely and fundamentally the gift of God in creation.

The Use of Music

In his understanding of the *inventio* of music Luther is distinctly different from his medieval predecessors but in his expression of the *usus* of music he is much closer to their opinions. In his *Complexus viginti effectuum nobilis artis musices* (ca. 1475)[30] Johannes Tinctoris expounds and illustrates twenty aphorisms on the use of music:

Music delights God.
Music embellishes the praises of God.
Music intensifies the joys of the blessed [the saints].
Music joins the church militant to the [church] triumphant.
Music prepares for the reception of the Lord's blessing.
Music encourages souls to piety.
Music drives away sadness.
Music releases the anxiety of the heart.
Music puts the devil to flight.
Music creates rapture.
Music elevates the earth-bound mind.
Music revokes the evil will.
Music delights humans.
Music heals the sick.
Music tempers work.
Music incites the soul to [spiritual?] combat.
Music encourages love.
Music increases the joy of conviviality.
Music glorifies those skilled in it.
Music makes [our] spirits glad.[31]

Music therefore is more than occasional entertainment for the human spirit; it exercises a moral influence that diminishes the negative effects of evil, promotes the positive aspects of goodness, and creates a sense of therapeutic well-being for individuals as well as for groups as they perform or hear it.

The French theologian Jean Gerson (1363-1429) made a significant impact on Luther especially during his early theological studies,[32] but the Reformer continued to refer to Gerson throughout his life.[33] What is not always appreciated is that Gerson was also the author of a significant number of treatises on music.[34] Gerson included his poem in praise of music in the second part of *De canticis* (written between 1424 and 1426): *Carmen de laude musicae*. The poem had a certain resonance in Wittenberg, since it was cited at some length in Adam von Fulda's *De musica*,[35] a treatise written in 1490 and used by the author in his teaching in the university at the beginning of the sixteenth century.[36] Thus Luther's known interest in and knowledge of the writings of Gerson, together with the Wittenberg awareness of Gerson's poem within von Fulda's treatise, make it a strong possibility that Luther knew of it. Many of the lines of Gerson's poem read like expansions of Tinctoris's aphorisms:

New music that comes about through the impulse of divine love
cannot be adequately exalted by any praise;
it refreshes the spirit, drives away cares, and soothes ennui,
and is a congenial companion to the travelers whom it bears along

. . .

Bodies are organs consonant with spirits, the world is
a single choir with which the mind loves to play.
With the harmony of the world the evil will, at discord with itself,
becomes concordant with the whole under God's direction.

. . .

Moreover, music is beneficial in healing bodies,
in that it rejoices, soothes, and relieves the spirit.

. . .

Furthermore, every people's own music changes ways of behavior.

. . .

one kind of music expands the heart and bears it along, another
    constrains it.

. . .

The shepherd's pipe soothes the beasts, herds, and flocks,
nor does the apparition of the wolf frighten them.
Then they graze the pastures free from care, and that rustic sound
diminishes the tiresomeness of feeding them for the herdsman.

. . .

The terrible trumpet sharpens the spirited breasts of horses
for war; the rider's wrath is roused.
When a woman weaves, or lulls the child in the cradle to sleep,
in her want of education she sings stupid songs.
The heavenly host sings the celebratory songs of Jesus' birth
"Peace to man on earth, lofty glory to God."
The rustic cultivating the fields makes merry in shouting;
the traveler sings and thereby lightens his journey.
Everyone eases his craft and its hard toil
with whatever kind of sound he can, even if it be somewhat harsh.

The devout voice placates God's wrath, and pleases the kindly citizens
[of heaven];
it sings together with the choirs of angels.[37]

Luther wrote a vernacular poem in praise of music that in many respects echoes the aphorisms of Tinctoris and Gerson. It first appeared in print as the preface to Johann Walter's similar but much longer poem *Lob und Preis der löblichen Kunst Musica* (Wittenberg: Rhau, 1538).[38] There is, however, reason to believe that it was written some years earlier. It is headed "Vorhede auff all gute Gesangbücher" — which is usually rendered in English as "A Preface for All Good Hymnals."[39] But Walter's publication was not a hymnal, which implies that Luther's poem was not originally intended to introduce Walter's verse; Markus Jenny suggests a no longer extant Wittenberg hymnal published sometime between 1535 and 1538.[40] But "Gesangbücher" in the 1538 published title of the poem does not necessarily mean "hymnals" in the modern sense; it could quite easily mean the more general category "songbooks." There is good reason for translating it this way because of the document into which Luther entered in his own hand this vernacular poem in praise of music. The source was discovered in the nineteenth century, and Luther's manuscript of rhymed couplets was published in facsimile in 1842. Luther wrote his poem into the alto part book of a set of five (in vellum bindings), published in 1534, once owned by Luther's colleague Veit Dietrich, whose name was inscribed on one of the outer leaves. The location of the part-books in 1842 was given as "Archiv zu Nürnberg," but their later whereabouts are unknown.[41] These five part-books published in 1534 must have been Arnold von Bruck's *Hundert und ainundzweintzig newe lieder* (Nuremberg: Formschneider, 1534).[42] This suggests that Luther wrote his rhymed "preface" with polyphonic, choral compositions in mind rather than monophonic congregational hymnody. It also implies that Luther penned his poem sometime before 1538, perhaps as early as 1534/35, confirming that it was not originally written as the preface to Walter's poem of 1538. Although the part-books are no longer extant the editors of the Weimar edition reproduced the 1842 facsimile of the two pages of Luther's handwritten poem in praise of music.[43]

The manuscript version of the poem is not exactly the same as the published text of 1538, the differences being mostly alternative spellings and punctuation. But more important are the corrections that Luther made in this manuscript. These would seem to indicate that Luther was copying from an existing draft, and in the process he occasionally made transcription errors that had to be corrected, but in one or two cases he appears to have modified the text as he copied the lines into the part-book.[44] The poem comprises 40 lines (8 syllables per line, 20 rhymed couplets):

Frau Musica[45]	Lady Music
1 Fur allen freuden auff erden	Of all the joys upon the earth
Kan niemand keine feiner werden	none has for us a greater worth
Denn die ich geb mit meim singen	than what I give with my singing
Und mit manchem süssen klingen.	and with others sweetly ringing.
5 Hie kan nicht sein ein böser mut	Here cannot be an evil mood
Wo da singen gesellen gut,	where there are singing fellows good,
Hie bleibt kein zorn, zank, hass,	Here is no grudge, hate, rage,
noch neid;	or row;
Weichen mus alles hertzeleid	softened is all grief and sorrow;
Geitz, sorg und was sonst hart und leit	greed, grief and animosity
10 Fert hin mit aller traurigkeit.	depart with all melancholy.
Auch[46] ist ein jeder des wol und frey,	Thus is ev'ryone well and free,
Das solche freud kein sünde sey,	since in such joy no sin can be.
Sonder auch Gott viel bas gefelt	But it gives God more joy and mirth
Denn alle freud der gantzen welt.	than all the pleasures of the earth.
15 Dem Teuffel sie sein werck zerstörrt	The devil's works are confounded;
Und verhindert viel[47] böser mörd.	Evil murders are avoided.
Das zeugt David des Königs that,	Witness King David's actions good,
Der dem Saul offt gewehret hat	who often quelled Saul's evil mood
Mit gutem süssem harfenspiel,	by sweetly playing on the lyre
20 Das er nicht inn grossen mord fiel.	and thus escaped his murderous ire.
Zum Göttlichen Wort und warheit	By truth divine and God's own Word
Macht sie das hertz still und bereit.	the heart is stilled and is prepared;
Solchs hat Eliseus bekant	such did Elisha once propound
Da er den geist durchs harffen fand.[48]	when harping he the Spirit found.
25 Die beste zeit im jar ist mein,	The best time of the year is mine
Da singen alle Vögelein.	when all the birds are singing fine.
Himel und erden ist der[49] vol,	The heav'ns and the earth are filled
Viel gut gesang da lautet wol.[50]	with much good singing, clear, and
	skilled.
Voran die liebe Nachtigal	Above all, the precious nightingale
30 Macht alles frölich uberal	Makes all now joyful overall
Mit jrem lieblichem gesang,	with her delightful songs and lays
Des mus sie haben jmmer danck,	for which she must be thanked always,
Vielmehr der liebe Herre Gott,	But more so to God, our Maker,
Der sie also geschaffen hat,	who carefully created her

35 Zu sein die rechte Sengerin,	to be his own beloved songstress
Der musicen ein Meisterin.	and of *musica* a mistress.
Denn singt und springt sie tag und nacht,	Thus day and night she always sings,
Seines lobs sie nichts müde macht,	Untiring praise to God she brings.
Den ehrt und lobt auch mein gesang	I too will sing my laud and praise,
40 Und sagt im ein[51] ewigen danck.[52]	Eternal thanks will I thus raise.[53]

Although written as a complete whole, in terms of its subject matter the poem has two clearly distinguished sections. The first, lines 1-24, is strongly reminiscent of the earlier writings of Gerson and Tinctoris, among others, with its statements concerning music's positive influence over human hearts and minds, complete with references to the biblical examples of David, Saul, and Elisha. However, his reference to the effectiveness of God's Word when conveyed in musical form is not found in quite the same way in the writings of his medieval predecessors. The second section, lines 25-40, is more personal and independent, with references to birdsong, especially that of the nightingale, and to God as the ultimate creator of music, since God created birds as singing creatures. References to birds and music were, of course, not new. As early as the second century Theophilus could observe that "as for music . . . [some] say that Orpheus discovered it in the sweet song of birds," and two hundred years later Augustine referred to the "sweet song of the nightingale" as the model for good singing among humans.[54] For Luther, however, this was not a simple theoretical matter but one of personal experience: throughout his writings there are many references to his solace in birdsong, especially during times of crisis and pressure, such as when he was exiled in Wartburg after the Diet of Worms, 1521-22, and again in Coburg castle during the Diet of Augsburg in 1530.[55] The nightingale reference in the Reformer's poem — which also occurs in the German draft of his preface to Rhau's *Symphoniae iucundae* in 1538 (see below) — also has the possibility of being a veiled reference to himself, since it was Hans Sachs who in 1523 characterized Luther's proclamation of the Gospel as the singing of the "Wittenberg Nightingale that one can now hear everywhere."[56] Indeed, Sachs's poetry might have been a major inspiration for Luther to write his own rhymed couplets that stand in the general Meistersänger tradition, of which Sachs was then the leading contemporary example. Luther may also have been influenced by Martin Agricola's *Musica instrumentalis deudsch*, published by Georg Rhau in Wittenberg in 1529, reprinted in 1530 and 1532, a treatise on musical instruments and how they should be played, written entirely in rhymed couplets.

Luther's poem in praise of music not only appeared in print as the preface to Walter's poem published in 1538, but was also included near the end of the 1543 edition of the Wittenberg hymnal,[57] and near the beginning of the tenor part book of Rhau's *Neue Deudsche Geistliche Gesenge* of 1544.[58] It was therefore fairly widely known during Luther's later years and clearly influenced the thinking of others with regard to music. But before this impact can be assessed another document of Luther's, closely related to his vernacular poem, needs to be investigated.

The same year that Rhau published Walter's poem, *Lob und Preis der löblichen Kunst Musica*, 1538, he also published two significant anthologies of music: *Selectae Harmoniae Quatuor Vocum De Passione Domine* and *Symphoniae iuncundae atque adea breves quattuor vocum*, the former with a preface by Philipp Melanchthon and the latter with a preface by Luther. Luther's Latin preface is in some respects an expanded version of his "Frau Musica" poem, in prose rather than verse.

Walter Blankenburg, while researching the life and works of composer Johann Walter, came to the realization that the German version of the preface that Wolfgang Figulus published in 1575, rather than being a translation of the Latin text, was in fact Luther's vernacular draft on which he based his own Latin version that was published by Rhau in 1538.[59] With this identification it means that it is now possible to trace the changes in Luther's thinking by comparing the German draft with the later Latin version.

The title in the German draft, "To all lovers of the free Art of Music, I Doctor Luther wish grace and peace from God the Father and our Lord Christ, etc.," was abbreviated in the published Latin to become the simpler, "Martin Luther to the Devotees of Music Greetings in Christ."[60] Luther's German draft begins thus:

> I would certainly have all Christians value and treasure my beloved music, that God has given to humans, yes, to love and retain it for it is such an excellent treasure, though I do not know how to speak about it adequately.

In the Latin version this is expanded to become:

> I would certainly like to praise music with all my heart as the excellent gift of God which it is and to commend it to everyone. But I am so overwhelmed by the diversity and magnitude of its virtue and benefits that I can find neither beginning nor end or method for my discourse. As much as I want to commend it, my praise is bound to be wanting and inadequate. For who can comprehend it all? And even if you wanted to encompass all of it, you would appear to have grasped nothing at all. First then, looking at mu-

sic itself, you will find that from the beginning of the world it has been instilled and implanted in all creatures, individually and collectively.

The German draft continues with the following sentence:

There is nothing on earth that is without its sound and its harmony, yes even the air, which is invisible and imperceptible, makes sound when a stick is struck through it.

In the Latin this becomes a more extended statement:

For nothing is without sound or harmony. Even the air, which of itself is invisible and imperceptible to all our senses, and which, since it lacks both voice and speech, is the least musical of all things, becomes sonorous, audible, and comprehensible when it is set in motion. Wondrous mysteries are here suggested by the Spirit, but this is not the place to dwell on them.[61]

The next section appears only in the German draft:

This noble art has its image in all creatures. Ah, with what delightful music the Almighty Lord has blessed his song-master, the dear nightingale, together with his young scholars and many thousands of birds in the air, that each kind has its own mode and melody, its delightful sweet voice and fantastic coloratura, that no one on earth can comprehend.

Then in both versions there follows a reference to the Psalmist David:

German: This dear David saw with great wonder and spirit, for so he says in Psalm 104[:12]: "By them the birds of the heaven sit and sing under their branches."

Latin: Music is still more wonderful in living things, especially birds, so that David, the most musical of all the kings and minstrel of God, in deepest wonder and spiritual exultation praised the astounding art and ease of the song of birds when he said in Psalm 103 [= 104:12], "By them the birds of the heaven have their habitation; they sing among the branches."

There are here strong connections with Luther's "Frau Musica" poem, especially lines 25-36; the German version is particularly close, with its specific reference to the song of the nightingale:

The best time of the year is mine
when all the birds are singing fine.
The heav'ns and the earth are filled
with much good singing, clear, and skilled.
Above all, the precious nightingale
Makes all now joyful overall
with her delightful songs and lays
for which she must be thanked always.
But more so to God, our Maker,
who carefully created her
to be his own beloved songstress
and of *musica* a mistress.

In both versions of his prose encomium of music, Luther then refers to the inability of philosophers to adequately explain the mysteries of music, the Latin version being somewhat longer than the German. In the German draft Luther thereafter continues:

> In short, noble music is next to God's Word, the highest treasure on earth: it governs all thought, perception, heart, and mind.

In Latin this is significantly expanded to become:

> Here it must suffice to discuss the benefit of this great art. But even that transcends the greatest eloquence of the most eloquent, because of the infinite variety of its forms and benefits. We can mention only one point (which experience confirms), namely, that next to the Word of God, music deserves the highest praise. She is a mistress and governess of those human emotions — to pass over the animals — which as masters govern men or more often overwhelm them. No greater commendation than this can be found — at least not by us.

The two versions then continue:

> *German:* Whether you wish to make a sad person joyful, an insolent uncouth person civilized, a fearful person courageous, an assertive person meek, and so forth, what could be better than to use this lofty, beloved, and noble art? The Holy Ghost himself honors it and holds it in high regard, as he witnesses that the evil spirit left Saul when David played on the harp [1 Samuel 16:23]. Similarly, when the prophet wanted to prophesy a minstrel was brought to play the harp for him [2 Kings 3:15].

Latin: For whether you wish to comfort the sad, to terrify the happy, to encourage the despairing, to humble the proud, to calm the passionate, or to appease those full of hate — and who could number all these masters of the human heart, namely, the emotions, inclinations, and affections that impel men to evil or good? — what more effective means than music could you find? The Holy Ghost himself honors her as an instrument for his proper work when in his Holy Scriptures he asserts that through her his gifts were instilled in the prophets, namely, the inclination to all virtues, as can be seen in Elisha [2 Kings 3:15]. On the other hand, she serves to cast out Satan, the instigator of all sins, as is shown in Saul, the king of Israel [1 Samuel 16:23].

Again there are emphatic echoes of Luther's German poem in praise of music, especially lines 15-24:

> The devil's works are confounded;
> Evil murders are avoided.
> Witness King David's actions good,
> who often quelled Saul's evil mood
> by sweetly playing on the lyre
> and thus escaped his murderous ire.
> By truth divine and God's own Word
> the heart is stilled and is prepared;
> such did Elisha once propound
> when harping he the Spirit found.

In the German draft of the preface Luther draws the following conclusion:

Thus it was not without reason that the dear fathers and prophets wanted music to always be in the church in the form of many songs and Psalms. And it is this cherished gift alone given to humans that they thereby should remember and use it to laud and praise God.

But in the Latin version Luther is more expansive and includes comments on the proclamatory function of music, as well as the richness of its different sounds:

Thus it was not without reason that the fathers and prophets wanted nothing else to be associated as closely with the Word of God as music. Therefore, we have so many hymns and Psalms where message and music join to move the listener's soul, while in other living beings and instruments music remains a language without words. After all, the gift of language combined with the gift of song was only given to man to let him know that he should praise God with both word and music, namely, by proclaiming [the Word of God] through and by providing sweet melodies with words. For even a comparison between different men will show how rich and manifold our glorious Creator proves himself in distributing the gifts of music, how much men differ from each other in voice and manner of speaking so that one amazingly excels the other. No two men can be found with exactly the same voice and manner of speaking, although they often seem to imitate each other, the one as it were being the ape of the other.

This leads Luther, in his German draft and published Latin version, to reflect on the wonder of polyphonic music in which the voices weave around each other, after which he ends with an exhortation not to misuse this gift of God. The German draft thus concludes:

> Therefore let us recognize the Creator in this costly creation and not misuse it to serve the devil, but therewith to laud and praise the Lord God. But misuse, such as drunkenness, carousing, wantonness, and lewdness, the things that are attested yet within the devil's kingdom, is hostile to God, nature and every good thing that God has made. Herewith I commend you all to the Lord God. Wittenberg 1538.

The published Latin version is more obviously directed at the young people who would be singing the compositions found in Rhau's *Symphoniae iuncundae:*

> But the subject is much too great for me briefly to describe all its benefits. And you, my young friend, let this noble, wholesome, and cheerful creation of God be commended to you. By it you may escape shameful desires and bad company. At the same time you may by this creation accustom yourself to recognize and praise the Creator. Take special care to shun perverted minds who prostitute this lovely gift of nature and of art with their erotic rantings; and be quite assured that none but the devil goads them on to defy their very nature which would and should praise God its Maker with this gift, so that these bastards purloin the gift of God and use it to worship the foe of God, the enemy of nature and of this lovely art. Farewell in the Lord.

Luther's two documents — his poem in praise of music and his prose preface in both German and Latin versions — expounding the good influences of music on human hearts and minds, reflect to some degree the views expressed by Gerson, Tinctoris, and other medieval writers on music, yet at the same time, they are distinctive in the way music is presented as the gift of God, which by its nature is a bearer of the Word of God and therefore is second only to theology.

Luther's German poem in praise of music clearly inspired others who followed his example,[62] such as Valentin Voigt's *Lob des Gesanges* inscribed in a manuscript sometime between 1536 and 1557,[63] and both published poems of Johann Walter, *Lob und Preis der löblichen Kunst Musica* (1538) and *Lob und Preis der himmlichen Kunst Musica* (1564).[64] While the rhymed couplets of Martin Agricola's *Musica instrumentalis deudsch* (1529) may have influenced Luther's poetic encomium of music, the imagery of Luther's verse appears to have had some impact on Agricola's substantially re-written version of his treatise, issued by Rhau in Wittenberg in 1545. In the earlier edition Agricola speaks of "Musica" in feminine terms, such as "holdseligen Junckfraulein" or "schöne Junckfraw" ("revered" or "beautiful maiden"),[65] but in the later revision he uses the title of Luther's poem published in 1538, "Frau Musica,"[66] or alongside "Musica" or "diesem Frewlein" in the text puts "F.M." (= Frau Musica) in the margin.[67] Further, the same woodcut of "Fraw Musica" — by Lucas Cranach the Younger (see Fig. 3.1) — that Rhau printed alongside Luther's poem in 1544 appears as the frontispiece in Agricola's 1545 publication, with the same heading.[68] This depiction of Frau Musica, sitting on a grassy bank, playing a lute and surrounded by other musical instruments, clearly inspired the later woodcut by Jakob Lucius, the Elder, that appears as the frontispiece of Walter's *Lob und Preis der himmlichen Kunst Musica* (1564) (see Fig. 3.2). There are differences — Frau Musica is standing rather than sitting and is inside a building rather than in the open air — but she is similarly surrounded by other musical instruments, plays a lute, and the fingers of each hand are almost identical in the two woodcuts, and the rakish angle of her hat is the same in both representations. But the woodcut had been used before. The Wittenberg publisher of Walter's 1564 poem, Lorenz Schwenck, had first used it as one of a series of woodcuts accompanying some German verses on the seven arts. The woodcut appears in the undated publication under the heading "Musica," with rhymed couplets that echo both Luther's and Walter's poems (see Fig. 3.2):

All gute Künst Gott geben hat/	God has given all good arts
Zu mehren sein grosse wunderthat	To adorn his mighty acts

Figure 3.1. *Fraw Musica,* by Lucas Cranach the Younger (1544)

Figure 3.2. *Frau Musica,* by Jakob Lucius the Elder (1564)

. . .	. . .
Durch mich Gott lobt der Engel schär.	Through me [Musica] all angels God's praises redound;
Sein ehr vnd preis erschallet klar.	His honor and glory now clearly resound.
Im Himel durch dein Cherubim/	In heaven sings his Cherubim,
Mit heller stim singt Seraphim.	And, with bright voice, the Seraphim.
Der heilig Dauid ein Prophet/	The holy David, also a prophet,
Mit seiner Harffen loben thet.	With his harp did praise beget;
Des lieben Vaters gütigkeit/	The goodness of the Father dear
In seinem Son vnd Geist bereit.	Known in his Son and Spirit here
. . .	. . .
Die vögelin in dem Holtze fein/	The little birds in the woods around
Mit meiner stim erschallen rein.	With my voice make a perfect sound.[69]

There were also later Latin poems that in content were influenced by Luther's German "Frau Musica" poem as well as by his Latin preface to Rhau's *Symphoniae iuncundae*. They include an *Encomium musicae* penned by Luther's colleague Johann Spangenberg in 1542,[70] Georg Fabricius's *Elogium musicae*, for which Joachim Heller composed a two-part musical setting in 1549, and the extended acrostic poem, *Encomium musicae*, by Johann Holtheuser, published with twelve other shorter poems in praise of music in 1551.[71] These poems, like Luther's, also echo the thoughts of medieval music theorists, such as one by Widkind Witkop, an acrostic on *"Musica laetificat cor hominiss"* (music gladdens the human heart), an almost exact quotation of Tinctoris's 13th proposition: *"Musica homines letificat."*[72]

The occasion for which Holtheuser's poem was written appears to have been some kind of music festival held in Wittenberg, appropriately on Cantate Sunday, 26 April 1551.[73] Music theorist Heinrich Faber lectured on music,[74] and although it is not identified, music must have been performed as well. This may have included Joachim Heller's two-part setting of Fabricius's *Elogium musicae* — or perhaps even Wolfgang Figulus's four-part setting of the same text[75] — since Fabricius's Latin poem appears at the beginning of Holtheuser's pamphlet containing the poetry written for the occasion; the first and last stanzas of Fabricius's poem are identical:

Diuina res est Musica	Music is a divine thing,
Mulcet Deum, mulcet viros,	delighting God, delighting men,
Quicunq. Musicam colit	whoever honors music
Hunc Deus amat, colunt viri.[76]	is loved by God, cherished by men.

Other music performed on this occasion most likely included pieces composed by the "immortals" who are praised at the end of Holtheuser's poem: Josquin, Senfl, Gombert, Lupus, Galliculus, Sixt Dietrich, Brettel, Stoltzer, Martin Agricola, Resinarius, and Reusch (who also contributed a Latin poem praising music in 1551).[77] Many of these are composers whose music is known to have been in the Wittenberg repertory, and many of them had connections with Luther.

What is particularly significant is that Holtheuser's long poem (402 lines) at various points closely reflects the general content of Luther's German "Frau Musica" and more especially his 1538 Latin preface. This connection can be clearly seen in Holtheuser's marginal headings throughout his poem. For example, *"De origine Musica"*[78] appears alongside the section that discusses the claims of Orpheus, Linus, Pythagoras, and Boethius, as inventors of music, who are then dismissed as the poet moves on to the next section that is headed *"Deus primus author Musices"* (God is the primary creator of music),[79] which reviews the biblical evidence and includes references to Jubal (Tubal), Moses and David. But the following marginal headings in Holtheuser's poem are virtually *verbatim* citations of Luther:

Holtheuser:	Luther:
Musica proxima Theologiae[80]	*Musica est . . . theologiae proxima*[81]
Musica gubernatrix affectuam[82]	*Musicam . . . gubernatrix affectuum humanorum*[83]
Musica expellit Sathanas[84]	*Musicam . . . expelli Satanam*[85]

Luther clearly established a close connection between theology and music that influenced both his contemporaries and those in the following generation who had connections with Wittenberg, an influence that continued in succeeding generations and indeed is still being exerted today. Some of the elements of this connection were a continuation of elements of medieval views of music, but the main thrust of Luther's understanding of music and theology substantially broke new ground.

A Proposed Treatise on Music

The doctrine of justification is central to Luther's theological thought and yet when one examines his tremendous literary output it is surprising to find that there is not one work devoted to a full-scale presentation of the doctrine.[86] From a comment he made in his open letter *On Translating* (1530), he did, however, plan to write one,[87] but, although there are a few notes and outlines for such a work, it was never written. Similarly, there is no fully worked-out treatise from his pen on the subject of music, only prefaces and letters, together with many scattered references throughout his voluminous writings. But, like the doctrine of justification, he did propose to write a treatise on music, though again, apart from a draft also dating from the same year (1530), it was another unfulfilled intention.[88]

The draft is partially in Greek, Περὶ τῆς μουσικῆς (Concerning Music), in essence a summary of the primary headings of the proposed study that reflects some of the medieval thinking Luther inherited, as well as his own distinctive perspectives, statements that were echoed many times in his various writings. In content it has many parallels with his letter to the composer Ludwig Senfl of October 1530, which suggests that this draft outline was written around the same time:

I love music.

Its censure by fanatics does not please me

For

1. [Music] is a gift of God and not of man
2. For it creates joyful hearts
3. For it drives away the devil
4. For it creates innocent delight, destroying wrath, unchastity, and other excesses.

I place music next to theology.

This is well known from the example of

David and all the prophets, who all

produced poetry and songs.

5. For [music] reigns in times of peace.

It will be difficult to keep this delightful skill after us.

The Dukes of Bavaria are to be praised in this, that they honor music.

Among our Saxon [Dukes] weapons and cannons are esteemed.[89]

The following is a commentary on the points raised in Luther's outline of a treatise on music.

Introduction

Luther's opening statement, "I love music,"[90] underscores his personal attachment and commitment to music, not just in theory but also in practice. For Luther is not here expressing an intellectual appreciation of the structures and forms of music but rather an experiential response to music as performed and heard. Many medieval treatises on music were primarily concerned with theory; Luther's proposed treatise would by contrast stress the fundamental practice of music.[91] In the same way that Luther discovered the doctrine of justification after an intensely personal struggle, by asking the biblical question, "What must I do to be saved?" and receiving the answer, "Believe on the Lord Jesus Christ" (see Acts 16:30-31), so Luther's theological understanding of music began with his personal involvement in and attachment to music. The doctrines of justification and music both can — and must — be objectively defined, but both are subjective in their effects. A purely intellectual appreciation of the doctrine — which Luther consistently dismissed as "historic faith" — is not enough; justifying faith is both practical and personal: "Oh, it is a living, busy, active, mighty thing, this faith. . . . Faith is a living, daring confidence in God's grace, so sure and so certain that the believer would stake his life on it a thousand times."[92] Similarly, an intellectual appreciation of music, its forms and structures as expressed in written notation on the page, is insufficient, for it cannot be experienced as music until its vibrations have excited the air and entered the outer ear. But even that is not enough, for the outward sound needs to be perceived within and move the inner heart:

> But to chant *(cantare)* means to praise with the mouth only, to jubilate *(iubilare)* is to do it in the heart, etc. [on Psalm 68:25][93]

> Wherever the word "song" *(canticum)* is used in psalm titles, it must always be understood that such a psalm is one of joy and dancing and is to be sung with a feeling of rejoicing. For a song and singing spring from the fullness of a rejoicing heart. But a spiritual song, or spiritual melody, is the very jubilation of the heart. [on Psalm 45][94]

> Some people confess with their lips only. They are the ones who say one thing in the heart and another with the mouth, like the sinner who has evil intentions and sings to God nevertheless. [on Psalm 9:1][95]

> Note that there is a difference between singing and saying, as there is between chanting or saying a psalm and only knowing and teaching with the understanding. But by adding the voice it becomes a song, and the voice is the feeling. Therefore, as the word is the understanding, so the [singing] voice is its feeling. [on Psalm 101:8][96]

Luther can even make the extravagant correlation that if faith is real it will involve music, and the believer must needs sing. He therefore employs the same kind of language he used to describe justifying faith in his Preface to the Epistle to the Romans (cited above) and applied it to the music of faith:

> For faith does not rest and declare a holiday; it bursts into action, speaks and preaches of this promise and grace of God, so that other people may also come up and partake of it. Yes, his great delight impels him [David] to compose beautiful and sweet psalms and to sing lovely and joyous songs, both to praise and to thank God in his happiness and to serve his fellowmen by stimulating and teaching them.[97]

Similarly, in his preface to the Bapst *Gesangbuch* of 1545 he wrote:

> For God has cheered our hearts and minds through his dear Son, whom he gave for us to redeem us from sin, death, and the devil. He who believes this earnestly cannot be quiet about it. But he must gladly and willingly sing and speak about it so that others also may come and hear it. And whoever does not want to sing and speak of it shows that he does not believe and that he does not belong under the new and joyful testament, but under the old, lazy, and tedious testament.[98]

Luther's love for music, therefore, is undergirded by theology, and his second premise in his draft outline of a treatise on music is the logical consequence of the first: "[Music's] censure by fanatics does not please me." Here a polarity of opposites is established: "I love music; fanatics hate it." The reason for Luther's displeasure is that for such "Schwärmerei" (enthusiasts) music is inherently biased towards evil, and must therefore be kept within strict limits. But nothing could be further from Luther's mind. If music is the creation and gift of God then it should be cherished rather than despised, and Luther could not bring himself to undervalue such a precious gift. He already had to deal with Karlstadt who had expounded a negative attitude towards music in Wittenberg with his *De cantu Gregoriano disputatio* (Disputation on Gregorian Chant) of 1521.[99] Thus when Johann Walter's set of part-books, known as the *Chorgesangbuch*, was published in 1524, Luther provided a preface in which he took aim against such negative views of music. He knew that music could be misused[100] and put to base ends, but would not concede that music itself was the problem — how could it be, if it is the gift from God?

> These songs were arranged in four [to five] parts to give the young — who should at any rate be trained in music and other fine arts — something to wean them from love ballads and carnal songs and to teach them

something of value in their place, thus combining the good with the pleasing, as is proper for youth. Nor am I of the opinion that the Gospel should destroy and blight all the arts, as some of the pseudo-religious claim.[101]

1. Music Is a Gift of God

Having stated his positive against the negative of the "pseudo-religious" enthusiasts Luther then enumerates a sequence of statements concerning music, several of which sound very similar to the aphorisms of Tinctoris, or the poetic expressions of Gerson. Luther begins, however, with a categorical statement that is not found in either of the earlier writers, a statement that conditions the meaning of those that follow: "1. [Music] is a gift of God and not of man." Here again is the repeated antiphon of Luther's thinking about music. Variant forms of the statement have been noted earlier in this chapter but here in this outline of the proposed treatise on music it takes on a special significance: its context underscores its content. Here it is not just a pithy saying that can be found elsewhere in Luther's literary output, it is the foundation stone on which his views of music are based. That music comes from God as a gift means that it has dimensions of meaning, power and effectiveness that far exceed any human art or science. Music is not an *inventio*, a work of humankind, but a *creatura*,[102] a work of God. Again there are parallels here with the doctrine of justification. In the same way as justification is God's gift of grace rather than the reward for human effort, so music is in essence God's gift of creation rather than a human achievement. Oskar Söhngen rightly points out that Luther's personification of music as "Frau Musica" in his vernacular poem is no mere allegory but rather the expression of the ontological reality that from the beginning of the world music has been an essential element within God's creation, and it — "she" — continues to inspire and influence human lives.[103] Thus, Luther wrote in the Preface to *Symphoniae iuncundae*:

> Next to the Word of God, music deserves the highest praise. She is a mistress and governess *(domina et gubernatrix)* of those human emotions . . . which as masters govern men or more often overwhelm them. No greater commendation than this can be found — at least not by us.[104]

The following headings in Luther's sketch are in a sense consequences of the first-numbered statement. This is demonstrated by the fact that when one attempts to find illustrative citations in Luther's writings, what are distinct in his draft outline are frequently found overlapping and complementing each other in his commentaries and other writings.

2. Music Creates Joyful Hearts

Luther's second point in the draft is: "[Music] creates joyful hearts" *(facit letos animos)*. Although this is a distant echo of Tinctoris's thirteenth aphorism *(Musica homines letificat),* Luther is not simply making an arbitrary list of attributes but rather creating a sequential and inter-related structure for a proposed treatise. Thus the primary reason why music creates joyful hearts is that it is the gift from God. Thus commenting on Psalm 4:1 in his first lectures on the Psalms, he wrote:

> It is the function of music to arouse the sad, sluggish, and dull spirit. Thus Elisha summoned a minstrel so that he might be stirred up to prophesy [2 Kings 3:15]. Hence מְנַצֵּחַ properly means stimulus, incitement, challenge, and, as it were, a spur of the spirit, a goad, and an exhortation. . . . For in all these the listless mind is sharpened and kindled, so that it may be alert and vigorous as it proceeds to the task. But when these are at the same time sung to artistic music, they kindle the mind more intensely and sharply. And in this manner David here composed this psalm לַמְנַצֵּחַ, that is, as something inciting, stirring, and inflaming, so that he might have something to arouse him to stir up the devotion and inclination of his heart, and in order that this might be done more sharply, he did it with musical instruments. Thus in ancient times the church used to read psalms before Mass as an incentive. To the present day some verses remain in the Introit. And to the present day the church has the invitatory psalm in Matins, namely, "O come, let us sing to the Lord" [Ps. 95:1], whereby the people invite each other to praise God. And the psalm is rightly called "invitatory," because the psalmist summoned not only himself but also others to praise God. This is what St. Ambrose did with a chant, by means of which he dispelled the sadness of the Milanese, so that they might bear the weariness of the time more lightly. But it can, not without sense, also be called "invitatory" for the reason that the Holy Spirit is invited in the same way. For when we are challenged, God is soon aroused also. And therefore we learn from these words that whoever wants to arouse himself to devotion should take up the Psalms.[105]

Similarly, almost twenty years later, he wrote on Psalm 118:16-18:

A good song is worth singing twice. It is customary for people, when they are really happy or joyful, to repeat a word two or three times. They cannot say it often enough, and whoever meets them must hear it. This is the case here, that the dear saints are so happy and joyful over the miracles God does for them when He delivers them from sin and death, that is, from every evil of body and soul, that out of sheer joy they sing their song over and over again.[106]

At the beginning of his poem on music "Frau Musica" says:

Of all the joys upon this earth
none has for men a greater worth
than what I give with my ringing
and with voices sweetly singing.

In his letter to Ludwig Senfl (1530) Luther states that "except for theology [music] alone produces what otherwise only theology can do, namely, a calm and joyful disposition."[107] But this joyful disposition is brought about by music that is more than just the human voice, individually or combined with others. Therefore in 1541 he could write in much the same way as he did in commenting on Psalm 4 in 1513-1516 (see above):

The stringed instruments of the . . . Psalms are to help in the singing of this new song; and Wolff Heinz[108] and all pious, Christian musicians should let their singing and playing to the praise of the Father of all grace sound forth with joy from their organs, symphonias,[109] virginals, regals, and whatever other beloved instruments there are (recently invented and given by God), of which neither David nor Solomon, neither Persia, Greece, nor Rome, knew anything.[110]

Observe Luther's parenthetical comment: the development of new and wonderful musical instruments is due to human skill, but the raw materials used to make them, together with music itself, are the prior gift of God in creation.

For Luther, therefore, musical instruments have a fundamental part to play in the praise of God. The many references to Luther's practice of singing at table should not be thought of as primarily an *a capella* performance practice. Johann Mathesius reports in his autobiography that in the early 1540s Luther's regular after-dinner "Kantorei" was accompanied by instruments:

It is an authentic "Musica" and Kantorei, in which one can sing and play to praise God with honorable people, and sing good Psalms, as David did with harps, a good Swiss hymn,[111] or a Josquin psalm, fine and gentle, together with the text, and also sung with instruments.[112]

The use of instruments in Wittenberg is confirmed by Martin Agricola, who wrote in 1545:

> I have been astonished to see, when boys come to Wittenberg and especially to the university, how they fare with their fellow students, who when they sit down at table or get up from it, joyfully engage in singing and playing instruments such as lutes, fiddles, and winds; or they pick up harps and other instruments.[113]

For Calvin instrumental music presented a theological problem, because it was so closely intertwined with the sacrificial cultus of the Temple, a cultus that was abrogated by the sacrifice of Christ on the cross. Commenting on Psalm 92:4 Calvin wrote:

> . . . the Levites who were appointed . . . singers . . . employ their instruments of music — not as if this were in itself necessary, only it was useful as an elementary aid to the people of God in these ancient times . . . now that Christ has appeared . . . it were only to bury the light of the Gospel, should we introduce the shadows of a departed dispensation.[114]

Luther has a different perspective: for him voices and instruments sounding together are a theological opportunity, the sound of joy of the redeemed as they glorify the God of grace. Commenting on Isaiah 5:11 Luther wrote: "Elisha says: [2 Kings 3:15] 'Bring me a minstrel, etc.' Amos 6:5 says: 'Like David [they] invent for themselves instruments of music.' Certainly if you make use of music as David did, you will not sin."[115] Similarly, in a letter to Prince Joachim of Anhalt, 16 June 1534, Luther wrote:

> So Elisha was awakened by his minstrel [2 Kings 3:15] and David himself declares in Psalm 57[:8] that his harp was his pride and joy: "Awake up, my glory; awake psaltery and harp." And all the saints made themselves joyful with psalms and stringed instruments.[116]

3. *Music Drives Away the Devil*

Luther's third numbered point in the draft is "[music] drives away the devil" *(Quia fugat diabolum)*, a sequence of words that is almost identical with Tinctoris's ninth aphorism *(Musica diabolum fugat)*. The concept was a general one that Luther inherited, but it was a matter of great personal concern to him since his letters, table talks, and other writings contain frequent references to the personal onslaughts of the devil. But for Luther music was more than a means of distraction, in the hope that temptation would be forgotten. From his point of view the corollary of music being the gift of God is that the devil, being opposed to God, must therefore abhor music. Thus this third heading is a logical consequence of the first, but it also follows naturally from the second, since the devil is antagonistic to pure joy. In his table talks are recorded a number of similar statements, such as: "Satan is a spirit of sadness; therefore he cannot bear joy, and that is why he stays very much away from music."[117] In his letter to composer Ludwig Senfl, 4 October 1530, he wrote:

> For we know that music, too, is odious and unbearable to the demons. Indeed I plainly judge, and do not hesitate to affirm, that except for theology there is no art that could be put on the same level with music, since except for theology [music] alone produces what otherwise only theology can do, namely, a calm and joyful disposition. Manifest proof [of this is the fact] that the devil, the creator of saddening cares and disquieting worries, takes flight at the sound of music almost as he takes flight at the word of theology.[118]

Here Luther makes the profound connection between "the sound of music" and the "word of theology": both repel the devil. Thus Luther's view that "music is next to theology" is not just a formula of words but an important fundamental working principle: music is next to theology because both accomplish similar results. Like theology, music "serves to cast out Satan, the instigator of all sins, as is shown in Saul, the king of Israel [I Sam. 16:23]."[119] Thus in Luther's poem in praise of music "Frau Musica" is heard to say:

> But God in me more pleasure finds
> than in all joys of earthly minds.
> Through my bright power the devil shirks
> his sinful, murderous, evil works.

4. *Music Creates Innocent Delight*

Luther's fourth heading in his outline for a treatise on music is the logical consequence of the third. If the devil is thwarted by music, then the evil he fosters must similarly be destroyed by means of music and good promoted instead: "[Music] creates innocent delight, destroying wrath, unchastity, and other excesses." So he can write in his treatise on the Last Words of David (1543): "For the evil spirit is ill at ease wherever God's Word is sung or preached in true faith. He is a spirit of gloom and cannot abide where he finds a spiritually happy heart, that is, where the heart rejoices in God and in His Word."[120] In the draft outline the fourth point is elaborated further. Luther adds: "I place music next to theology. This is well known from the example of David and all the prophets, who all produced poetry and songs." This parallels what Luther wrote in his letter to Senfl:

> Manifest proof [of this is the fact] that the devil, the creator of saddening cares and disquieting worries, takes flight at the sound of music almost as he takes flight at the word of theology. This is the reason why the prophets did not make use of any art except music; when setting forth their theology they did it not as geometry, not as arithmetic, not as astronomy, but as music, so that they held theology and music most tightly connected, and proclaimed truth through Psalms and songs.[121]

As passages already cited make clear, Luther makes frequent references to David banishing Saul's evil mood through music, Elisha's call for a musician to play so that he could prophesy, as well as general comments on the use of musical forms by various prophets. The following are other examples:

> The Holy Ghost himself honors her [music] as an instrument for his proper work when in his Holy Scriptures he asserts that through her his gifts were instilled in the prophets, namely, the inclination to all virtues, as can be seen in Elisha [2 Kings 3:15]. On the other hand, she serves to cast out Satan, the instigator of all sins, as is shown in Saul, the king of Israel [1 Sam. 16:23]. Thus it was not without reason that the fathers and prophets wanted nothing else to be associated as closely with the Word of God as music.[122]

> For by it [music] also the evil spirit of Saul was driven off [1 Samuel 16:23], and the prophetic spirit was given to Elisha [2 Kings 3:15].[123]

And as David initiated the writing of psalms and made this a vogue, many others were inspired by his example and became prophets. These followed in David's footsteps and also contributed beautiful psalms; for example, the Sons of Korah, Heman, Asaph, etc.[124]

That it is good and God pleasing to sing hymns is, I think, known to every Christian; for everyone is aware not only of the example of the prophets and kings in the Old Testament who praised God with song and sound, with poetry and psaltery, but also of the common and ancient custom of the Christian church to sing Psalms. St. Paul himself instituted this in 1 Corinthians 14[:15] and exhorted the Colossians [3:16] to sing spiritual songs and Psalms heartily unto the Lord so that God's Word and Christian teaching might be instilled and implanted in many ways.[125]

5. Music Reigns in Times of Peace

Luther's fifth heading is: "[Music] reigns in times of peace." To this he adds the observation: "It will be difficult to keep this delightful skill after us. The Dukes of Bavaria are to be praised in this, that they honor music. Among our Saxon [Dukes] weapons and cannons are praised." Here Luther registers the irony that the Catholic Bavarian Dukes, who opposed evangelical reforms, richly support music while the Lutheran Dukes of Saxony, patrons of Luther in other respects, had actually disbanded their musical foundations, refused to give financial support to the teaching of music in their university of Wittenberg,[126] and seemed more prepared for war rather than peace. He made much the same point in his letter to Senfl, who was, of course, composer to the Bavarian court:

> Even though my name is detested, so much that I am forced to fear that this letter I am sending may not be safely received and read by you, excellent Louis, yet the love for music, with which I see you adorned and gifted by God, has conquered this fear. This love also has given me hope that my letter will not bring danger to you. For who, even among the Turks, would censure him who loves art and praises the artist? Because they encourage and honor music so much, I, at least, nevertheless very much praise and respect above all others your Dukes of Bavaria, much as they are unfavorably inclined toward me.[127]

The previous statements in Luther's draft outline for a treatise on music are easily amplified by his comments in other writings, but on this last point[128] it is not exactly clear how he would have expounded it in the study had he completed it. The comparative reference to the Dukes of Bavaria and Saxony would suggest that his primary thought was of civil peace rather than theological peace, that music tempers the war-like spirit. But does this mean that this fifth proposition is merely a continuation of the fourth, that Luther was simply illustrating music's power over one of the most significant "other excesses" by stating in effect that "music creates peace and destroys war"? That is possible, except that Luther will often link civil peace and theological peace. For example, in 1541 his response to the threat of the advancing Ottoman Empire across Europe was to call the people to prayer in public worship that had a significant musical content.

> The people need to be challenged to earnest devotion through public prayer in the churches. It has been my practice, with permission of the pastors and the congregation, to chant alternately with the choir, as is customary, Psalm 79 after the sermon on Sunday, either at the morning or at the evening service. Then a choirboy with a good voice, from his place in the choir, sings on his own the antiphon or tract, "Lord, not according to our sins" [*Domine, non secundum*, Psalm 103:10]. After that, a second choirboy may chant the other tract, "Lord do not remember the iniquities of our forefathers" [*Domine ne memineris*, Psalm 79:8]. Following that the whole choir, kneeling, may sing, "Help us, O God" [*Adiuva nos, Deus*, Psalm 79:9]. . . . Thereupon, when desired, the congregation may sing, "Grant us peace" [*Verleih uns Frieden gnädiglich*] or the Lord's Prayer in German [*Vater unser im Himmelreich*].[129]

Luther had created a German version of the Latin antiphon *Da pacem domine in diebus nostris* (Grant us peace, Lord, in our time), *Verleih uns Frieden gnädiglich*, some years earlier, probably first appearing in the no-longer-extant 1529 edition of Klug's Wittenberg *Geistlicher lieder*.[130] Instead of the traditional melody Luther created a new one, closely related to *Nun komm der Heiden Heiland* and *Erhalt uns, Herr, bei deinem Wort* (see Example 13.2). *Erhalt uns, Herr, bei deinem Wort* was written around the same time as his Appeal for Prayer Against the Turks (1541), though probably after he had penned the sentences cited above, because instead of the Latin antiphons Luther originally suggested, these two hymns based on the same melodic material, *Erhalt uns, Herr, bei deinem Wort*[131] and *Verleih uns Frieden gnädiglich*, were soon sung together at the end of Sunday services.[132] But even before this both Luther's *Formula missae* (1523) and *Deutsche Messe* (1526) made significant use of chanted forms of prayer for peace with strong theological overtones. In their provisions for the Lord's Supper both liturgical orders indicate that the *Agnus Dei*, or its German version, with the final prayer, "*dona nobis pacem*/gib uns deinen Frieden" (grant us your peace), could be sung during the distribution of Communion,[133] and both orders include the (chanted) Aaronic blessing (Numbers 6), with its final words, ". . . and grant you peace."[134] In the *Formula missae* Luther directs that the distribution of Communion is to be introduced by "*Pax Domini*," and in his explanation of its meaning equates peace with forgiveness:

> "The peace of the Lord," etc., which is, so to speak, a public absolution of the sins of the communicants, the true voice of the Gospel announcing remission of sins, and therefore the one and most worthy preparation for the Lord's Table, if faith holds to these words as coming from the mouth of Christ himself.[135]

For Luther, the liturgical greeting "the peace of the Lord be always with you" carries within it the proclamation of the gospel, the declaration of forgiveness. Given this understanding it seems likely that in his exposition of the fifth point of his projected treatise on music he would have included some thoughts about music and peace, both theological as well as civil. Although we cannot be certain that he would have done so, it must be observed that there is a strong connection between Luther's words in the *Formula missae* about the *Pax Domini* being "the true voice of the Gospel announcing remission of sins," and his statements concerning the proclamatory function of music, such as "God has preached the Gospel through music."[136]

Theology and Music

Various aspects of Luther's theology of music are discussed in the chapters that follow, in which musical catechesis and liturgico-musical hermeneutics are explored. Here in the final section of this chapter the concern is with how Luther expressed theology in musical terms.

Medieval music theorists, such as Johannes de Muris, whose writings were widely used in German universities, including Erfurt,[137] drew a parallel between the doctrine of the Trinity and the essential nature of music. For example, de Muris wrote in his *Notitia artis musicae*:

> That all perfection lies in the ternary number follows from many likely reflections. In God, who is most perfect, there is one substance, yet three

persons; he is threefold, yet one, and one, yet threefold. Very great, therefore, is the correspondence of unity to trinity. . . . All music, especially
mensural music, is founded in perfection, combining in itself number
and sound. The number, moreover, which musicians consider perfect in
music is, as follows from what has been said, the ternary number. Music,
then, takes its origin from the ternary number. . . .[138]

By the time de Muris wrote this in the fourteenth century the threefold nature of music had been customarily expounded in musical treatises for many
centuries. Thus the twelfth century Hugo St. Victor, among others, divided
musica practica into the following three parts:

Primo, *voce humana* [human voice]
Secundo, *tibiarum sono* [sounding pipes]
Tertio, *fidium tinnitu* [ringing strings].[139]

Others, including later theorists whose works were published in Wittenberg,
such as Rhau (1531) and Martin Agricola (1561, though written earlier), classi-
fied *musica practica* as *plana* [plain = plainsong, monodic chant], *figurata*
[figural = polyphony], and *instrumentalis* [instrumental], and Finck, in another Wittenberg treatise (1556), divided *Musica* itself into the threefold
structure of *theoretica, practica,* and *poetica* [composition].[140] While such ternary expositions in theoretical treatises were not always explicitly linked to
the doctrine of the Trinity it was nevertheless commonly interpreted in this
way, as the de Muris citation above indicates. The connection between the nature of music and Trinitarian theology had long been undergirded by the use
of the "ternary number" (Greek τρίας; Latin *trias*) as a synonym for
Trinitatis.[141]

For Luther, the Trinitarian connections with music were explicit rather
than implicit. The *Tischreden* records his statements concerning the way in
which the Trinity of God is reflected in the created order, such as in arithmetic, geometry, astronomy,[142] grammar, and rhetoric.[143] But he was also careful to include the following statement: "In music [the Trinity is expressed] in
the three [notes] *re, mi, fa.*"[144] At first sight Luther's choice of the three notes
seems arbitrary. In the treatises of music theory, which were mostly designed
as instruction manuals for singing Gregorian chant, the musical scale was
designated as a sequence of six notes which could be sung at different pitches:
ut, re, mi, fa, sol, la (= hexachord = sequence of intervals: tone, tone, semitone, tone, tone).[145] The hexachord, which could be based on C, F, or G, was
divided into two groups of three notes, each note within the respective group

Example 3.1. Hexachords

being separated from its neighbor by a whole step: *inferior* (lower pitches) = *ut, re, mi; superior* (upper pitches) = *fa, sol, la* (see Example 3.1).[146] Thus Luther could have used either of these sequences of three notes — *ut, re, mi,* or *fa, sol, la,* to make his Trinitarian point, but to have done so would have meant ignoring a fundamental aspect of the basic hexachord. The interval between the two groups of three notes, between *mi* and *fa,* is a semitone. Thus to choose either *ut, re, mi,* or *fa, sol, la,* would be incomplete from a musical point of view and therefore invalid for a representation of the "completeness" of the Trinity. Thus Luther chose the three notes *re, mi, fa,* which embrace the two fundamental intervals of the musical scale — a whole tone between *re* and *mi,* and a semitone between *mi* and *fa* — the two intervals on which music depends. Thus *re, mi, fa* is as fundamental to music as the doctrine of the Trinity is fundamental to theology.[147]

With the beginnings of the shift from modal to major/minor tonality in the later sixteenth century,[148] Luther's melodic Trinitarian model was reinterpreted harmonically. Instead of a succession of adjacent notes (D, E, F = Luther's *re, mi, fa)* the Trinitarian harmonic triad (Latin, *trias)* became the model (C, E, G). Thus Joachim Burmeister's *"Epigramma de Musica Origine,"* in his *Hypomnematum musicae poeticae* ([Rostock: Reusner], 1599), begins:

> That from the one godhead of the triad who would deny you derived
>   your beginning, O divine music?
> You represent the mysteries of the divine triad;
>   like the nourishing triad you celebrate the uneven number.
> For we see the threefold clef open the musical piece.
>   We discern a concordant combination to be of threefold
>   pitch. . . .[149]

Luther's fundamental view of the musical dimensions of the Trinity is reflected in his hymns and liturgical chants, which are as much theological statements as they are musical forms. Many include references to the Trinity and some are not only Trinitarian in content but are also Trinitarian in form. The most obvious are hymns such as *Gott der Vater wohn uns bei, Wir glauben all an einen Gott, Erhalt uns, Herr, bei deinem Wort,* and, of course, his translation of the Latin hymn *O lux beata trinitas, Der du bist drei in Einigkeit,* or liturgical chants, such as his threefold *Kyrie* in the *Deutsche Messe* and his German *Agnus Dei, Christe du Lamm Gottes,* which of course follow earlier liturgical models. But Trinitarian theology undergirds many of his other hymns, especially *Nun freut euch,* which Oswald Bayer considers "the most telling and appropriate confession of the triune God that I know."[150]

As has been demonstrated in this and the preceding chapters, many of Luther's statements about music are to be found in the *Tischreden,* the Table-talk, a collection of verbatim reports of the Reformer's conversations at table and elsewhere, recorded by various students and colleagues, mostly during the last twenty years of his life. The title, *Table-talk,* witnesses to the most frequent occasions when Luther waxed eloquent on many and varied subjects, that is, "at table" before, during and after meals, particularly in the evening. It is also recorded in the table-talk and elsewhere that this was the usual location and time of day when those who had shared the meal joined with Luther to form an informal Kantorei to make music together. It is therefore understandable that there should be musical references in the transcribed accounts of these table-talks. Johann Aurifaber, a close colleague of Luther in Wittenberg from 1537, became an indefatigable collector of Luther's words, editing several volumes of his correspondence, as well as other volumes in both the Wittenberg and Jena editions of the Reformer's collected works, and bringing together a vast collection of the table-talks, which were published in 1566.[151] Aurifaber's *Tischreden* is a large folio volume of approaching 1,300 pages with the contents of Luther's thoughts structured according to basic Lutheran dogmatic theology under 82 *loci*,[152] such as "The Word of God or Holy Scripture," "Creation," "The Trinity," "Law and Gospel," and so forth. It is significant indeed to find that the 69th *locus* is "Von der Musica," and under this heading there are such striking statements concerning music as the following:

> I am not satisfied (says D.M.L.) with him who despises music, as all fanatics do; for music is an endowment and gift of God, not a human gift. It also drives away the devil and makes people cheerful; one forgets all anger, unchasteness, pride, and other vices. I place music next to theology and give it the highest praise. And we see how David and all saints put their pious thoughts into verse, rhyme, and song. . . .[153]

But Luther's statements about music are not confined to the *locus* on music in the *Tischreden* but are found scattered throughout the volume under various *loci,* therefore demonstrating that for Luther the closeness of music to theology was not just a pithy saying but was essential to his theological methodology. For him music provided a hermeneutic by which fundamental theology was to be expounded, such as when he was speaking about the Trinity (see above), or when dealing with the distinction between Law and Gospel (see below).

The distinction between Law and Gospel is a topic to which the Reformer returns again and again throughout his writings, and one that is of fundamental importance in both Luther's and Lutheran theology. From time to time he uses musical metaphors to explain the distinction, for example in one of the non-Aurifaber Table-talks:

> That *lex iram operatur* [the Law works wrath] is evidenced by the fact that Goerg Planck [organist in Zeitz] plays better when he plays for himself than when he plays for others; for what he does to please others sounds *ex lege* [from obedience to the Law] and where there is *lex* [Law] there is lack of joy; where there is *gratia* [Grace] there is joy.[154]

On the same page of Aurifaber's edition of the *Tischreden*, under the *locus* "Law and Gospel," there are two significant passages in which Luther makes reference to music. One is the much-quoted reference to the music of Josquin:

> What is Law does not make progress, but what is Gospel does [that is, the Law is static but the Gospel is dynamic, or, the Law is negative and the Gospel positive]. God has preached the Gospel through music, too, as may be seen in the songs of Josquin, all of whose compositions flow freely, gently, and cheerfully, are not forced or cramped by rules like the song of the finch.[155]

In the second passage on the same page in Aurifaber's *Tischreden*, Luther likens the gospel to music in performance and the Law to musical notation on the page:

> The Gospel is the same as the b *fa* [b♭] b *mi* [b♮] as it is performed, the other pitches [*Claves*, that is, written pitches] are the Law. And the same as the Law obeys the Gospel so must the written pitches submit to the b *fa* b *mi*. And in the same way that the Gospel is a lovely and gracious doctrine, so is the *mi* and *fa* the most beautiful in all voices [that is, discant, alto, tenor, bass]. But the other tone [the Law] is a poor, weak sinner, which allows both b *fa* and b *mi* — *mi* and *fa* — to be sung.[156]

Accidentals, indicating whether or not a note should be natural or flattened — common in modern scores — were not notated in sixteenth-century sources. Given their theoretical training in hexachordal solmization, late medieval and renaissance musicians were expected to know whether B♭ or B♮ was to be sounded, even though a simple B was notated on the page,[157] rationalizing those pitches through *musica recta,* for example the B♭ of the soft hexachord on F, or through *musica ficta,* for accidentals not covered by the hexachordal system. This was a cultivated skill on the part of the singers and instrumentalists. As Luther said on one occasion, "a musician may sing the whole song before another discerns and discovers whether *sol* or *fa* [that is, a whole-step or half-step] is to be sounded in a key."[158] Thus with inexperienced performers it was quite possible that one sang (or played) a half-step at the same time as another sang a whole-step, resulting in an unpleasant dissonance. There was therefore a distinction between the pitches in the written music and the sung pitches that were actually heard. This reveals that Luther had a sophisticated understanding of the nature of music: the "law" of music, as enshrined in written notation on the page, must be tempered by "grace" in performance by the singers and players as they make the music live.[159] Luther recognized that the difference between written notation and its actual performance is exactly analogous to the theological differentiation between Law and Gospel.

Here we return to the issue of Luther's musicianship that was discussed in the previous chapter. His understanding of music was more than that of a dilettante or semi-skilled dabbler. He had a good grounding in the practical aspects of music in school and university, and throughout his adult life continued to make music with his friends and colleagues, many of whom were accomplished musicians. Thus Erasmus Alber, friend and colleague of Luther from 1518, hymn writer and creator of hymn melodies,[160] wrote: "He was a good musician and also had a fine, clear, pure voice, both for singing and speaking."[161] Luther's physician, Matthäus Ratzeberger, reported that "in polyphonic settings he sang the Alto part,"[162] a fact confirmed by his handwritten verses of "Frau Musica" inscribed in the alto part book of Arnold von Bruck's *Hundert und ainundzweintzig newe lieder* (Nuremberg, 1534).[163] He did not sing the principal melody (usually) in the tenor part but sang the alto line in the middle of the polyphonic texture where he would be aware of the other voices surrounding his own. Hermann Finck, writing some years after Luther's death, probably accurately reflects vocal performance practice in Wittenberg during earlier decades. The concern was for balance among the voices, that within the texture of sound the inner voices — such as alto, Luther's preferred voice-part — should balance with the outer voices:

The Treble should be sung with a delicate and sonorous tone, the Bass, however, with a harder and heavier tone; the middle voices should move with uniformity and try to match themselves to the outer parts sweetly and harmoniously.

But Finck adds that in the case of imitative counterpoint, where the voices enter one at a time with the same motive, each voice-entry should be clearly heard:

> When there is a tasteful point of imitation at the beginning of a work, this is to be rendered with a more definite and distinct tone of voice than is employed elsewhere; and the following parts, if they start with the same point as the first, should perform it in the same way. This should be observed by all the parts whenever a new point [of imitation] occurs, so that the relationship between the voices and organization of all the points can be heard.[164]

Luther's experience of singing the alto part within sophisticated polyphonic music gave him a perspective and an understanding of how the different voices moved in counterpoint with each other that enabled him, for instance, to appreciate the skill of Josquin in his motet *Haec dicit Dominus,* where two of the voices sing a chant melody in strict canon [= Law] and the other voices in free counterpoint [= Gospel] (see Example 2.3):

> It beautifully comprehends the difference between Law and Gospel, death and life. Two voices make the plaintive lament *Circumdederunt me gemitus mortis etc,* against which four voices sing *Haec dicit Dominus, de manu mortis liberabo populum meum etc.* It is a very good and comforting composition.[165]

Luther's competence and experience in music were equal to his acumen and expertise in theology: together they created a distinctive and discriminating synthesis in which music has theological dimensions and theology musical meaning.

PART II

Musical Catechesis

CHAPTER 4

Erhalt uns, Herr, bei deinem Wort

A Children's Hymn, to Be Sung against the Two Arch-enemies
of Christ and His Holy Church, the Pope and the Turk[1]

[1.] Erhalt uns, Herr, bey deinem Wort
Und steur des Bapst und Türcken Mord,
Die Jhesum Christum, deinen Son
Wolten stürtzen von deinem Thron.

Preserve us, Lord, by thy dear Word,
from Turk and pope defend us, Lord,
who now would thrust out from his throne
our Savior, Jesus Christ, thy Son.

[2.] Beweis dein Macht, Herr Jhesu Christ,
Der du Herr aller Herren bist.
Beschirm dein arme Christenheit
Das sie dich lob in ewigkeit.

Lord Jesus Christ, show forth thy might;
for thou art Lord of Lords by right:
thine own poor Christendom defend,
that it may praise thee without end.

[3.] Gott heilger Geist, du Tröster werd,
Gib deim Volck einrley sinn auf Erd.
Sthe bey uns in der letzen Not.
Gleit uns ins Leben aus dem Todt.[2]

O Comforter, of priceless worth,
give thy people one mind on earth,
stand with us in our final strife
And lead us out of death to life.[3]

The singing of hymns creates "genuine faith [recht gläuben], Christian life,
patient suffering and a blessed death." This was a common Lutheran understanding, endorsed at the beginning of the eighteenth century by Johann
Christoph Olearius, one of the Lutheran church's pioneer hymnologists.[4] A
blessed death is the fulfilment of a Christian life, a Christian life is dependent
on a genuine faith, and such faith is formed by the Word of God. In essence
this is expressed in Luther's children's hymn, *Erhalt uns, Herr, bei deinem
Wort* (1542), written towards the end of his life.

It is because the classic Lutheran hymns were Scripture-based that they
functioned not only as worship songs, expressing the response of faith to be
sung within a liturgical context, but also as theological songs, declaring the

substance of the faith to be sung with catechetical intentions. In this early part of the twenty-first century, we hear much about hymns of "Christian experience," but almost nothing about the essential *catechesis* of hymnody. Yet the catechetical function of hymns has been fundamental to Lutheran theology and practice which, at least until the eighteenth century, ensured that every hymnal would have a substantial section of specific "Catechism Hymns,"[5] because through catechesis Christian experience is both created and interpreted.

All the early hymns produced by the Wittenberg circle of hymn writers in 1523-24 are essentially catechetical. Towards the end of 1523, when Luther was encouraging friends and colleagues to join him in the task of writing hymns, the Reformer saw these corporate songs as being fundamentally catechetical: "I intend to make vernacular psalms for the people, that is, spiritual songs so that the Word of God even by means of song may live among the people."[6] These early hymns were originally issued on individual broadsheets. In 1524 an enterprising printer in Nuremberg, Jobst Gutknecht, reprinted eight of them in a booklet as *Etlich Christlich lider Lobgesang/und Psalm* (Some Christian songs, canticles, and psalms), the so-called *Achtliederbuch* (Eight-Song-Book). The title indicated that these songs were "dem rainen wort Gottes gemess/auss der heyligen schrifft . . ." (according to the pure Word of God, from Holy Scripture), reflecting Luther's letter to Spalatin, cited above, in which he stated that the new German hymns should be the "Word of God in song." Of these eight hymns, three were psalm-hymns by Luther, including *Aus tiefer Not* (Psalm 130), which would later be sung as a catechism hymn. The five others have specific catechetical implications, revealed in their respective headings. Luther's *Nun freut euch* is described as a "Christian song . . . comprehending the inexpressible grace of God and right faith [rechten Glaubens]." The three hymns by Paul Speratus are each given with an appendix detailing the Scripture proofs, stanza by stanza: the first, *Es ist das Heil,* is described as "a song . . . of Law and Gospel"; the second, *In Gott gelaub ich,* as "a song . . . to confess the faith"; and the third, *Hilf Gott, wie ist der Menschen Not,* as "a song . . . to pray for a complete [spiritual] renewal." The anonymous *In Jesus Namen heben wir an* is headed "a Christian song of true faith [waren glauben] and right love for God and neighbor."[7] All five are explorations of the doctrine of justification and the distinction between Law and Gospel, which would later be directly addressed in the first two parts of Luther's catechisms: Commandments and Creed. These early Lutheran hymns were thus clearly and self-consciously the Word of God in song that would allow the people to learn and experience fundamental theology as they sang.

In his *Formula missae* (1523), written around the same time that the

Wittenberg circle began writing hymns, Luther recommended that the old folk-hymn *Gott sei gelobet und gebenedeiet,* suitably revised, should be sung during communion.[8] This implies that he had already begun thinking about his own revision of the hymn, which appeared in print the following year, 1524. This sacramental hymn also pointed forward to the fifth part of the catechism.

Late in the year 1525 Luther was preparing his vernacular *Deutsche Messe* (1526). In it he again indicates that *Gott sei gelobet und gebenedeiet* could be sung during communion, as could the hymn attributed to Jan Hus, *Jesus Christus unser Heiland,*[9] or the German Sanctus *Jesaja dem Propheten,*[10] and also that the hymn *Wir glauben all an einen Gott* should be sung as the Creed.[11] Thus hymns on the Creed and the Lord's Supper were being developed in Wittenberg even though a direct connection between hymnody and catechism had not yet been explicitly made. Luther, however, had already seen the need for a specific catechism. In the *Deutsche Messe* he wrote: "First, the German service needs a plain and simple, fair and square catechism."[12] Three years later Luther met this need in his Large and Small Catechisms of 1529.[13] In both catechisms the Lutheran hymn, the chorale, is given prominence. In the Small Catechism, in the section on morning and evening prayers in the home, Luther suggests that the morning devotion should conclude with the singing of a hymn, "possibly a hymn on the Ten Commandments," that is, a hymn on one of the principal parts of the catechism.[14] Towards the end of the preface to the Large Catechism Luther makes the following summary:

> Thus we have, in all, five parts covering the whole of Christian teaching, which we should constantly teach and require recitation word for word. For you should not assume that the young people will learn and retain this teaching from sermons alone. When these parts have been well learned, one may assign them also some psalms or hymns, based on these subjects, to supplement and confirm their knowledge. Thus young people will be led into the Scriptures and make progress every day.[15]

The same year that Luther issued his catechisms he also published a new collection of hymns for the congregations in Wittenberg. Instead of a simple anthology of hymns appearing in no particular order — the characteristic of Walter's *Chor-Gesangbuch* of 1524 — *Geistliche Lieder auffs new gebessert zu Wittemberg D. Mart. Luther* (Wittenberg, 1529) presented its hymns within a carefully constructed and orderly plan.[16] The first main part of the hymnal was devoted to Luther's hymns. Following ten hymns arranged according to the church year, from Advent to Trinity, eight further hymns are given:

Dies sind die heiligen zehn Gebot (Law)
Mensch, willst du leben seliglich (Law)
Mitten wir im Leben sind (Effect of Law/Repentance)
Wir glauben all an einen Gott (Creed)
Nun freut euch, lieben Christen gmein (Effect of Faith/Law and Gospel/
    Justification)
Jesus Christus, unser Heiland, der von uns den Gottszorn (Lord's Supper)
Gott sei gelobet und gebenedeiet (Lord's Supper)
Psalm 111 (prose)[17] (Lord's Supper)
Ein neues Lied wir heben an (Cross/Martyrdom)[18]

Although not so named, these hymns together form a section of catechism hymns, but "catechism" employed in a broader sense than later became
customary, meaning the teaching of the basic essentials of the Christian faith.
Thus in this 1529 section of catechism hymns Luther employed two approaches: one that dealt with the fundamentals of Law, Gospel, prayer, and
sacraments, the other with the effect of these fundamentals in life and experience, that is, faith with its components of repentance and forgiveness, and
love expressed towards one's neighbor and in the willingness to suffer perse-
cution and even martyrdom for one's faith. These two approaches, here combined in the 1529 hymnal, Luther clarified in later hymnals. But the 1529 hymnal marked a major hymnological development that was followed in later
hymnals, clearly establishing that in the reforming movement hymns were
not only meant to be liturgical, but also expressly catechetical.

A feature of the 1533 edition of the Wittenberg hymnal is the inclusion
of collects following some of the hymns.[19] The hymn before the catechism
hymns is *Gott der Vater wohn uns bei*, Luther's re-working of fifteenth-
century vernacular saint's-day hymns into an emphatic statement of Trinitarian theology. The following appears after this hymn, Luther's vernacular version of the Latin Collect for the Feast of the Trinity:

> Almighty eternal God, who hast taught us to know and confess in true
> faith that thou art one eternal God in three Persons of equal power and
> glory and to be worshiped as such: we beseech thee that thou wouldst at
> all times keep us firm in this faith in spite of whatever opposition we may
> incur; who livest and reignest, world without end. Amen.[20]

Gott der Vater wohn uns bei is the final item in the section of hymns on
the major festivals of the church year, assigned to Trinity Sunday, the feast day
that celebrates fundamental theology. Thus the collect not only accompanies

the Trinity hymn but also introduces the sequence of "catechism" hymns that are also creedal expositions of the primary tenets of Trinitarian faith. By this time catechesis had become more explicit and now revolved almost exclusively around the sections of Luther's 1529 catechisms. This is reflected in the 1543 edition of the Wittenberg hymnal in which a more coherent and complete collection of catechism hymns was created, with all five parts of the catechism being represented. They were preceded by a short preface that clearly identifies them as catechism hymns:

> Now follow spiritual songs in which the Catechism is covered, since we certainly must commend Christian doctrine in every way, by preaching, reading, singing, etc., so that young and unlearned people may be formed by it, and thus in this way it will always remain pure and passed on to our descendants. So may God grant us his grace and his blessing through Jesus Christ. Amen.[21]

[I.]   *Dies sind die heiligen zehn Gebot* [Commandments]
        Mensch, willst du leben seliglich [Commandments]
[II.]   *Wir glauben all an einen Gott* [Creed]
[III.] *Vater unser im Himmelreich* [Lord's Prayer]
[IV.]   *Christ unser Herr zum Jordan kam* [Baptism]
[V.]   Psalm 111 (prose) [Lord's Supper]
        Jesus Christus, unser Heiland, der von uns den Gottszorn
        [Lord's Supper]
        Jesaja dem Propheten [Lord's Supper][22]

In later Lutheran usage it was customary to divide the catechism into six main parts, the extra part being created out of the section on confession/repentance, the "Office of the Keys," that Luther included at the end of his treatment of Baptism. Although there were other catechism hymns that were added to the basic corpus,[23] six hymns by Luther became the primary catechism hymns:

[I.]   *Dies sind die heiligen zehn Gebot* [Commandments]
[II.]   *Wir glauben all an einen Gott* [Creed]
[III.] *Vater unser im Himmelreich* [Lord's Prayer]
[IV.]   *Christ unser Herr zum Jordan kam* [Baptism]
[V.]   *Aus tiefer Not schrei ich zu dir* [Confession]
[VI.]   *Jesus Christus, unser Heiland, der von uns den Gottszorn*
        [Lord's Supper]

These hymns are discussed in the following chapters; not all appear in modern Lutheran hymnals, with the LBW employing fewer than the three other Lutheran hymnals currently being used. Taking Luther's hymns as a whole, LBW, which included twenty of them, was an advance on one of its predecessors, the *Service Book and Hymnal* (1958), which had just seven, though not as many as the other LBW precursor, *The Lutheran Hymnal* (1941), which included twenty-eight.[24] But the fact is no earlier twentieth-century American Lutheran hymnal included all of Luther's catechism hymns.[25] In his review of Luther's hymns found in LBW, Lowell C. Green regarded the inclusion of only three of the six catechism hymns as a missed opportunity.[26] But it is significant that the three American Lutheran hymnals published after LBW (LWor, CW, and ELH) have included all six of these hymns, although none groups them together in sequence under the rubric "Catechism hymns."

In previous centuries Luther's six catechism hymns were the principal hymns that were regularly sung when the catechism was taught in church, school and home. The various sixteenth-century *Kirchenordnungen* (Church Orders) frequently speak of singing suitable hymns when the catechism was taught publicly in church. Thus the Church Order for Electoral Saxony (1580) directs that village sacristans should teach the children the catechism hymns of Luther,[27] and that during the special catechizing in Lent appropriate hymns should be sung.[28] In schools where the catechism was regularly taught throughout the week, the singing of catechism hymns was mandatory. For example, the Saxon Church Order directed that in schools "the children shall be taught with diligence the catechism and with it the spiritual hymns and psalms of Dr. Luther."[29] In the home many catechetical handbooks were available for use in which, following Luther's directives in the Small Catechism, the singing of hymns was encouraged in daily devotions. One of the most widely used was *Kurtze Fragen und Antwort über die Sechs Häupstücke deß heiligen Catechismi D. Martini Lutheri* [Short questions and answers on the six main parts of the holy catechism of Dr. Martin Luther] by Bartholomäus Rosinus, first published by Johan Berger in Regensburg in 1581, incorporated into later catechetical handbooks such as those issued in Weimar (1590) and Torgau (1594), and reprinted numerous times until at least the end of the first third of the eighteenth century. Rosinus arranged the six parts of the catechism over six days, morning and evening. In the morning one of the main parts of the Small Catechism was rehearsed, with Rosinus's questions and answers. In the evening a Psalm from "David's Catechism" was prayed, followed by the singing of a catechism hymn.[30] Similarly, when Andreas Reyher, rector of the Latin school in Gotha, drew up a teaching plan for the schools in ducal Gotha in 1642, he directed that the children be taught one of the chief parts of the Small Catechism each day, Monday through Saturday.[31] Since Eisenach came within the duchy of Gotha, reunited since 1680, it seems likely that the Latin school attended by Johann Sebastian Bach would have sung catechism hymns according to Reyher's directives on each school day, Monday through Saturday. The section of Katechismuslieder in the *Eisenachisches Gesangbuch* (1673), the first hymnal that the young Bach would have known, comprised no less than 93 hymns,[32] spanning almost 200 pages, but included all six of Luther's primary catechism hymns in their respective sections. Even though it contained many more hymns this Eisenach hymnal was structured the same as the Wittenberg hymnals of the sixteenth century: the first section was made up of hymns for the church year, and the second section included hymns on the Catechism.[33]

Luther's six catechism hymns were the principal catechetical hymns sung in church, school and home. They were frequently cited in catechism sermons, and their melodies were employed in choral and organ "catechism" music written by many different Lutheran composers, notably Johann Sebastian Bach. In the sixteenth and seventeenth centuries some composers created *quodlibets* of the melodies of the catechism hymns. A *quodlibet* is a single vocal work in which different melodies are intertwined. In a catechism *quodlibet* all the melodies of the six catechism hymns are set in counterpoint to each other, with each voice singing a different melody against the others.[34] Thus the theological unity of the teaching of the catechism was proclaimed in the ingenuity of the musical form.

There was, however, another hymn by Luther that had catechetical significance for later Lutheranism. In the 1543 edition of the Wittenberg hymnal the hymn, *Erhalt uns, Herr, bei deinem Wort,* was placed after the catechism hymns listed above.[35] In many respects the hymn is a summary of the theological roots of the catechism. It establishes the Word of God as the source of theology, "Preserve us, Lord, in thy dear Word," and its threefold stanzaic structure upholds the doctrine of the Trinity, the substance of the Creeds: the Father who preserves, the Son who defends, and the Spirit who unifies. But the first and third stanzas form a fairly close paraphrase of Luther's explanation of the third petition of the Lord's Prayer in the Small Catechism. In answer to the question, How is God's will done?, Luther responds:

Whenever God breaks and hinders every evil scheme and will — as are present in the will of the devil, the world, and our flesh — that would not allow us to hallow God's name . . . and whenever God strengthens and *keeps us steadfast in his Word* and in faith until the end of our lives. . . .[36]

The hymn's catechetical connections were made explicit when it was appended to the 1549 Leipzig edition of the Small Catechism and headed "A Children's Catechism Hymn."[37] *Erhalt uns, Herr, bei deinem Wort* almost certainly appeared in print in 1542 in a no-longer-extant broadsheet. It was very much a hymn for those particular times. Lutherans were in a precarious position in that the future was in jeopardy on three counts. First, there was the constant need for God's Word in the face of unbelief; hence the opening prayer: "Preserve us, Lord, in thy dear Word." Second, there was the external military threat of the Ottoman Empire that was steadily expanding northwestwards across Europe towards Vienna, an Islamic empire that threatened both Protestant and Roman Catholic alike; thus the reference to "Turk" in the second line. Third, there was the external ecclesiastical threat of Roman Catholicism that, through efforts of emperor Charles V, was pressurizing Lutherans to conform to the old faith; hence the reference to the "pope" at the beginning of the hymn.[38] Later hymnal editors re-wrote this stanza and eliminated the references to "Turk" and "pope." The context we now find ourselves in is very different from the one Luther found himself addressing towards the middle of the sixteenth century, and such revision is necessary if we are to sing Luther's hymn today. But we should not lose sight of the robustness of Luther's spirituality that enabled him to deal directly with contemporary issues in this hymn, rather than sidestep them with empty pious platitudes.

Erhalt uns, Herr, bei deinem Wort was a hymn that had wide usage, frequently being sung at the end of public worship, before the benediction.[39] But it also retained its strong catechetical connections: it was appended to editions of Luther's Small Catechism,[40] and was specified as the hymn to conclude the *Catechismusexamen.*[41]

Around the time of Luther's death Justus Jonas added two further stanzas to the hymn, and another was added in Straßburg in 1565.[42] Other stanzas were added from time to time that did not enter into general use.[43] A Latin version was created by Johannes Stigel, *Serva, Deus, verbum tuum* (1544), with two later expansions, one by Hermann Bonn and the other by Wolfgang Ammonius.[44] *Erhalt uns, Herr, bei deinem Wort* was also the inspiration for other hymns. Over the following generations there were numerous hymns that either quoted or alluded to the opening first line of Luther's original. Its status as a primary hymn for Lutherans tempted Catholics to parody it, such as the one that begins with a pun on "Wort/Wurst" (word/sausage): *Erhalt uns Herr bey deiner Wurst.*[45] As well as inspiring other hymns with the same or similar first line, the influence of Luther's hymn can be detected in the inner stanzas of other later hymns; for example, the second stanza of Nicolaus Selnecker's hymn based on Psalm 22, *Herr Jesu, hilf, dein Kirch erhalt* (1578):

Erhalt uns nur bey deinem Wort
und wehr des Teuffels trug und mord,
Gib deiner Kirchen gnad und huld,
fried, einigkeit, mut und gedult.[46]

Now keep us only by thy Word
and curb the devil's murd'rous fraud,
give thy churches grace and favor,
peace, oneness, courage and honor.

The most durable of hymns inspired by Luther's *Erhalt uns, Herr* was Ludwig Helmbold's *Herr Gott, erhalt uns für und für*,[47] a summary of the six parts of the catechism. It is in the same meter, was written to be sung to the same tune, and echoes Luther's vocabulary. It witnesses to the important Lutheran tradition of catechism hymns that begins with Luther, continues through several centuries, but which is hardly detectable in later Lutheran hymnals.[48]

For Teaching Children the Catechism[49]

1. Herr Gott, erhalt uns für und für
   die schlechte Catechismus lehr,
   Der jungen einfeltigen Welt
   durch deinen Luther für gestelt.

   Lord God, keep us for evermore
   in catechism doctrine pure —
   that through your Luther is made known
   for simple youth to make their own.

2. Das wir lernen die Zehn Gebot,
   beweinen unser Sünd und Not
   Und doch an dich und deinen Son
   gleuben, im Geist erleuchtet schon.

   The Ten Commandments here we learn,
   repent of sin, and so discern
   to live by faith in you alone,
   the Father, Son, and Spirit, one.

3. Dich unsern Vater ruffen an
   der allen helffen wil und kan,
   Das wir als Kinder nach der Tauff
   Christlich volbringen unsern lauff.

   Our Father, source of heavenly grace,
   we pray to you before your face,
   that we baptized, may come to be
   fulfilled in Christ eternally.

4. So jemand felt, nich liegen bleib
   sondern zur Beichte kom und gleub,
   Zur sterckung nehm des Sacrament:
   Amen, Gott geb ein seligs End![50]

   And when we fall, we seek relief
   and make confession, with belief,
   and take the Body and the Blood.
   Amen. God grant our end be good.[51]

CHAPTER 5

Dies sind die heiligen Zehn Gebot

The Ten Commandments, Long Version

[1.] Diß sind die heilgen zehen gebott,
die uns gab unser Herre Gott.
Durch Moses sinen diener trüw
hoch uff dem berg Sinai.
    Kyrieleison.

That man a godly life might live,
God did these Ten Commandments give
by his true servant Moses, high
upon mount Sinai.
    Kyrieleison.

[2.] Ich byn allain dein Gott, der herr,
keyn Götter solto haben meer.
Du solt mir gantz vertrauen dich,
von hertzen grund lieben mich.
    Kyrieleison.

I am thy God and Lord alone,
no other god beside me own;
put thy whole confidence in me,
and love me right heartily.
    Kyrieleison.

[3.] Du soltt nicht brauchen zu unehrn
den namen gottes, deines herrn;
du soltt nicht preysen recht noch gut
on was God selbst redt unnd thut.
    Kyrieleison.

By idle word and speech profane
take not my name, the Lord, in vain,
and praise but that as good and true
what God shall but say and do.
    Kyrieleison.

[4.] Do solt heilgen den sybend tag,
das du und dein hauß rugen mag;
do soltt von deim thun lassen ab,
das Gott seyn werck ynn dir hab.
    Kyrieleison.

Hallow the seventh day as blest,
that thou and all thy house may rest;
keep hand and heart from labor free,
that God may so work in thee.
    Kyrieleison.

[5.] Du solt ehrn und gehorsam seyn
den vatter und der mutter dein.
Und wo dein hant yhn deien kan,
so wirstu langes leben han.
    Kyrieleison.

Give to thy parents honor due,
be dutiful and loving too;
and help them when their strength decays,
so shalt thou have length of days.
    Kyrieleison.

[6.] Do solt nich todten zornigklich,
nicht hassen noch selbs rechen dich,
Gedult haben und sanfften mut
und auch dem feind thun das gut.
    Kyrieleison.

In sinful wrath thou shalt not kill
nor hate nor render ill for ill,
Be patient and of gentle mood,
and to thy foe do thou good.
    Kyrieleison.

[7.] Dein Ee soltu bewaren rein
das auch dein hertz keyn ander meyn,
Und halten keusch das leben dein
mit tzucht und messigkeit feyn.
    Kyrieleison.

Be faithful to thy marriage vows,
thy heart give only to thy spouse;
keep thy life pure, and lest thou sin,
use temp'rance and discipline.
    Kyrieleison.

[8.] Do solt nicht stelen gelt noch gut,
nicht wuchern ymands schweys und blut;
do solt auffthun dein mylde hand
den armen yn deynem land.
    Kyrieleison.

Steal not thy neighbor's goods or gold,
nor profit by his sweat and blood;
but open wide thy loving hand
to all the poor in the land.
    Kyrieleison.

[9.] Du soltt keyn falscher zeuge seyn,
nicht liegen auff den nehsten deyn.
Seyn unschult solt auch retten du
und seyne schand decken.
    Kyrieleison.

Bear not false witness, nor belie
thy neighbor by false calumny.
Defend his innocence from blame,
with charity hide his shame.
    Kyrieleison.

[10.] Do solt deins nehsten weib und haus
begeren nicht, noch etwas draus;
du solt yhm wundschen alles gut,
wie dir dein hertz selber thut.
    Kyrieleison.

Thy neighbor's wife desire thou not,
his house, nor aught that he hath got;
but wish that his such good may be
as thine heart wish for thee.
    Kyrieleison.

[11.] Die gepot all uns geben synd,
das du dein sundt, o menschen kynd,
erkennen solt und lernen wol,
wie man fur Gott leben soll.
    Kyrieleison.

God these Commandments gave, therein
to show thee, child of man, thy sin,
and make thee also well perceive
how man unto God should live.
    Kyrieleison.

[12.] Das helff uns der herr Jhesu Christ,
der unnser midler worden yst.
Es ist mit unserm thun verlorn,
verdienen doch eytel zorn.
    Kyrieleison.[1]

Help us, Lord Jesus Christ, for we
a Mediator have in thee;
our own work is a hopeless thing,
'tis wrath alone it can bring.
    Kyrieleison.[2]

Luther's Decalogue hymn, *Dies sind die heiligen Zehn Gebot*, was probably written during the early months of 1524 and almost certainly first circulated as a single broadsheet. The earliest extant source is the Loersfelt *Enchiridion* (Erfurt, 1524).[3] It is one of the hymns that grew out of that impressively creative and productive period during the fall, winter and spring of 1523-1524 in which Luther and his colleagues were putting the Word of God into song. Some of them, such as *Nun freut euch* and *Es ist das Heil* (by Paul Speratus), broadly summarized Scripture teaching, while others were versifications of specific passages of Scripture, such as Luther's metrical psalms, *Ach Gott vom Himmel sieh darein* (Psalm 12), *Aus tiefer Not* (Psalm 130), and this versification of Exodus 20.

The biblical background is reinforced by the first stanza. In his treatment of the German Sanctus, *Jesaja dem Propheten,* written some years later, Luther provided not simply a translation of the liturgical Sanctus but a versification of the broader Isaiah 6 passage.[4] Similarly here he presents the Ten Commandments in their biblical setting. The first stanza is a kind of prelude that establishes the context of the giving of the Law: the commandments are God's, the instrument of God's giving was Moses, and the place of reception was Sinai. Then Luther devotes one stanza to each of the first eight commandments, in the same order he would later follow in his catechisms (stanzas 2-9). Commandments nine and ten are expounded together in stanza 10. Stanza 11 answers stanza 1 by declaring why the commandments were given: that we should know and mark well that the Law reveals sin and makes clear that our lives fall short of God's purpose for them. But Luther could never state the demands of the Law without also expounding the grace of the Gospel. In the final stanza he therefore proclaims that only the Lord Jesus Christ, in contrast to any futile attempt at law-keeping, can assist us. So Moses and Christ, at the beginning and end of the hymn, stand in contradistinction: Moses the servant introduced the demands of the Law; Christ the Mediator fulfils the Law's demands. In hymnic form the theological distinction between Law and Gospel is therefore effectively expounded.

Luther was not the first to write a hymn on the Ten Commandments in the vernacular. Examples can be found in manuscripts dating from the thirteenth century, and some are perhaps as early as the twelfth century.[5] But Luther did not model his hymn on any of these. Instead he wrote his own hymn text, but, with a stroke of genius, fitted it to a tune of an old German folk hymn: *In Gottes namen faren wir,* originally sung by pilgrims on their way to visit the holy places in Jerusalem. The earliest form dates from the twelfth century, and the hymn exists, both textually and musically, in variant forms.[6] The folk hymn begins thus:

In gottes namen faren wir,	In God's name we are traveling,
siener gnaden begeren wir,	and for his grace we are praying,
nu helfe uns allen gottes kraft	that all may be aided by God's pow'r
verleihe uns allen große macht.	and all be strengthened to endure.
Kyrieleison.[7]	Kyrieleison.

Here is another example of Luther employing musical hermeneutics.[8] By choosing a known melody Luther was therefore able to use the association of the old text along with the meaning of his new text. The old text, the pilgrim song, was a prayer for God's grace and thus with every stanza of this new Decalogue hymn the singers were likely to connect the familiar prayer for grace to each of the commandments as expounded in Luther's new text. The fact that the melody was a pilgrim song would have also interpreted the concept of Christian life as a pilgrimage. Further, by adapting the old folk-hymn [*Leisen*] form, each stanza was concluded with the familiar liturgical prayer for mercy: the contracted form *Kyrieleison*. Thus by his choice of tune, Luther was underscoring the need for the mercy of the Gospel with every itemized declaration of the Law.

The only problem with the hymn may have been that it was perhaps too long for some children. Thus soon after writing his "long" Commandments hymn Luther wrote a "short" one:

The Ten Commandments, Short Version

[1.] Mensch, wiltu leben seliglich
und bey Gott bleyben ewiglich,
Soltu halten die zehn gebot,
die uns gebeut unser Gott.
          Kyrieleis.

Wilt thou, O man, live happily,
and dwell with God eternally,
thou Ten Commands should keep, for thus
God himself commanded us.
          Kyrieleis.

[2.] Deyn Gott alleyn und Herr byn ich;
keyn ander Gott soll yrren dich,
Trauen soll myr das hertze deyn;
meyn eygen reich solltu seyn.
          Kyrieleis.

I am thy Lord and God, take heed
no other god doth thee mislead.
Thy heart shall trust alone in me,
mine own kingdom thou shalt be.
          Kyrieleis.

[3.] Du sollt meyn namen ehren schon
und ynn der nott mich ruffen an.
Du sollt heylgen den Sabbath tag,
das ich ynn dyr wircken mag.
          Kyrieleis.

Honor my Name in word and deed,
and call on me in time of need.
Keep holy, too, the Sabbath day,
so in thee I work alway.
          Kyrieleis.

[4.] Dem vater und der mutter deyn
solltu nach myr gerhorsam seyn,
Niemand todten noch zornig seyn
und deyne ehe halten reyn.
          Kyrieleis.

To father and to mother be
obedient always, next to me.
Kill no one, even anger dread;
and keep pure thy marriage bed.
          Kyrieleis.

[5.] Du sollt eym andern stelen nicht
auff niemand falsches zeugen icht,
Deynes nehsten weyb nicht begern
und all seyns gutts gern empern.
          Kyrieleis.[9]

Steal not, nor do thy neighbor wrong
by bearing witness with false tongue;
thy neighbor's wife thou shalt not eye:
let his be his willingly.
          Kyrieleis.[10]

His starting point appears to have been the penultimate stanza of the "long" hymn. Here it is stated that the Commandments remind us that "man für Gott leben soll" [one should live before God]. At the beginning of his short hymn this became *Mensch willst du leben seliglich* [Man will you live blessedly].[11] The first hymnal to include the shorter hymn was Johann Walter's so-called *Chorgesangbuch* (Wittenberg, 1524), where it was set to a tune almost certainly composed by Walter.[12] The following year Loersfelt issued a supplement to his *Enchiridion,* under the title *Etliche Christliche Gesenge vnd Psalmen* (Erfurt, 1525), which included Luther's short Commandments hymn. The heading notes: ". . . zu syngen yn dem thon [to be sung to the tune:] In Gottis namen faren wir,"[13] that is, to the same tune as *Dies sind die heiligen Zehn Gebot.* This means that the "short" hymn was probably issued as a Wittenberg broadsheet, which would have been Loersfelt's source, and that the two Commandments hymns were closely associated in Luther's mind, in that both were originally intended to be sung to the same tune.

The "short" hymn has a remarkable structure: after the prologue of the first stanza the Commandments are grouped in an increasing mathematical sequence:

St. 2 = Commandment 1
St. 3 = Commandments 2, 3
St. 4 = Commandments 4, 5, 6
St. 5 = Commandments 7, 8, 9, 10

Luther had been preaching regularly on the Ten Commandments since 1516,[14] and these two hymns epitomize his teaching on the Law. But, as with the early church that began its liturgy with the *Missa catechumenorum,* Luther and his Wittenberg colleagues did not separate teaching from worship, but understood liturgy as *catechesis.*[15] The year after the two Ten Commandments hymns were published, March 1525, Bugenhagen made reference to both of them in his Wittenberg catechism sermons, and afterwards they were regularly sung during such catechism services, especially during Lent.[16] This is confirmed in the Wittenberg Church Order of 1533 which indicates that, in addition to the weekly teaching of the catechism, there was intensive catechization four times a year, one of them in Lent. During these two-week periods special catechism sermons were preached at vespers on Mondays, Tuesdays, Thursdays, and Fridays, according to the following liturgical order:

Psalm with antiphon
Scripture readings

Hymn: *Dies sind die heiligen Zehn Gebot*
Catechism sermon
Hymn: *Mensch willst du leben seliglich*
Magnifcat with Latin antiphon
Versicle
Collect
Benedicamus Domino[17]

Similarly, when the catechism was taught daily in the home, the fundamental theology was not to be relegated to a mere intellectual process of learning a series of theological propositions. The context for this *catechesis,* teaching and learning, was worship in which faith, prayer and hymnody were component parts. In his Short Preface to the Large Catechism Luther charges the head of every household to teach the catechism[18] and that this teaching should be accompanied by the singing of catechism hymns.[19] In the Small Catechism he indicates that a hymn should conclude domestic morning prayers, "possibly a hymn on the Ten Commandments."[20] In Bartholomäus Rosinus's popular *Kurtze Fragen und Antwort über die Sechs Häupstücke deß heiligen Catechismi D. Martini Lutheri* (Regensburg, 1581) Luther's suggestions were expanded into a daily sequence in which each of the main parts of the catechism was the focus for morning and evening prayers, one day at a time.

The first part of the holy catechism with its questions and answers the children at home can rehearse and practice after breakfast and after the *Gratias*[21] has been said. Following the evening meal, and after the *Gratias* has been said, the children at home can pray out of "David's Catechism" Psalm 90 . . . , and thereafter sing from the hymnbook of Luther the Ten Commandments: [either] the fine short form, Dr. Martin Luther's *Mensch willst du leben seliglich,* "Man, will you live blessedly" — and certainly without all your merits, *Kyrieleison;* [or] the Ten Commandments somewhat longer, *Dies sind die heiligen Zehn Gebot,* "These are the holy Ten Commandments" — that earn only wrath, *Kyrieleison.*[22]

Here the old adage of the church comes to mind, *lex orandi, lex credendi,* which might be slightly mistranslated as "the Law prayed is the Law believed." What Luther understood clearly was that without a true understanding of the theological function of the Law to expose sin, the doctrine of justification becomes confused and the essence of the Gospel is obscured. Therefore the Law is to be taught, prayed and sung in catechism, worship (public and private), and hymnody.

CHAPTER 6

Wir glauben all an einen Gott

The German Patrem

[1.] Wyr gleuben all an eynen Gott,
schepfer hymels und der erden,
der sich zum vater geben hat,
das wyr seynen kinder werden.
Er will uns allzeyt erneren
leyb und seel auch wol bewaren.
Allem unfal wil er waren;
Kleyn leyd soll uns widerfaren.
Er sorget fur uns, hutt und wacht
es steht alles ynn seyner macht.

[2.] Wyr gleuben auch an Jhesum Christ,
seynen son und unsern Herren,
Der ewig bey dem vater ist
gleicher Gott von macht und ehren.
Von Maria, der iungfrauen,
ist eyn warer mensch geboren
Durch den heyligen geyst y glauben
für uns, die wyr warn vorloren,
Am kreutz gestorben und vom tod
widder aufferfstanden durch Gott.

[3.] Wyr gleuben an den heylgen geyst,
Gott mit vater und dem sone
Der aller blöden tröster heyst
und mit gaben zieret schone.
Die gantz Christenheyt auff erden
hellt ynn eynem synn gar eben.
Hie all sund vergeben werden,
das fleysch soll auch widder leben.
Nach diesem elend ist bereyt
uns eyn leben ynn ewigkeit.[1]

We all believe in one true God,
who created earth and heaven,
the Father, who to us in love
hath the right of children given.
He both soul and body feedeth,
all we need he doth provide us;
he through snares and perils leadeth,
watching that no harm betide us.
He careth for us day and night,
all things are governed by his might.

We all believe in Jesus Christ,
his own Son, our Lord, possessing
an equal Godhead, throne, and might,
source of every grace and blessing.
Born of Mary, virgin mother,
by the power of the Spirit,
made true man, our elder brother,
that the lost might life inherit,
was crucified for sinful men
and raised by God to life again.

We all confess the Holy Ghost,
who sweet grace and comfort giveth
and with the Father and the Son
in eternal glory liveth;
who the Church, his own creation,
keeps in unity of spirit.
Here forgiveness and salvation
daily come through Jesus' merit.
All flesh shall rise, and we shall be
in bliss with God eternally.[2]

Luther's creedal hymn *Wir glauben* (1524) is in part a reworking of an older creedal hymn and in part a newly-written hymnic statement of faith. The older creedal hymn exists in variant forms in three manuscripts: one in the university library of Leipzig, dating from the end of the fourteenth or the beginning of the fifteenth century; another in the university library of Wroclaw (Breslau), dated 1417; and the third in the town library of Zwickau, dating from around 1500.[3] The original text appears to have been a Latin paraphrase of the three paragraphs of the two primary creeds, Apostolic and Nicene. It is found in the Wroclaw/Breslau manuscript, with its associated melody:

Credo in deum patrem	I believe in God, Father
omnipotentem.	Almighty.
Credo et in filium	I believe also in the Son
sanctum dominum	the holy Lord
patri natura uniformen.	of the same nature as the Father.
Credo et in spiritum	I believe also in the Spirit
peccatorumque paraclitum	the Comforter of sinners
utrique consubstancialem,	the same substance of both
	[Father and Son],
trinitatem individuam	undivided Trinity
ab utroque fluentem	proceeding from both
et in essentia unum.[4]	and in essence one.

The creedal hymn is primarily a theological statement of personal belief in the fundamental essence of the Trinitarian Godhead. But the Wroclaw/Breslau manuscript also gives a German text underneath the Latin that was clearly entered at a later date. The same German text, with some minor variants, is also found in the Leipzig and Zwickau manuscripts: The text as it appears in the Zwickau manuscript is given here, together with a literal translation:

Wir gelauben all an einen Gott,	We all believe in one God,
Schöpfer Himmels und der Erden,	Creator of heaven and earth,
uns zu Trost gegeben,	who has given us consolation;
alle Ding stehn seim Gebot.	all things stand by his command.
Von der Keusch[en] war er geboren,	Of a virgin was he born,
Maria der Zarten auserkoren,	Mary the tender was chosen,
uns zum Trost und aller Christenheit	to comfort us and all Christendom
vor uns er wollte leiden	he willed to suffer for us
das wir möchten vermeiden	that we should escape
schwere Pein des Tods der Ewigkeit.[5]	oppressive pain of eternal death.

This German version is obviously not a translation of the Latin text but a newly-written stanza that encompasses the first two paragraphs of the two primary creeds. What is significant is the change from first person singular (*Credo*, "I believe") to first person plural (*Wir gelauben*, "we believe"), implying corporate use.

There has been some discussion regarding which of the sources, Wroclaw/Breslau or Zwickau, Luther used. While it is uncertain whether the Zwickau document was written by Stephan Roth, as claimed by Wilhelm Lucke,[6] it is possible that Roth drew Luther's attention to the Zwickau version of the creedal hymn when he visited Wittenberg in 1523.[7] But whatever his source (or sources), Luther took over the first two lines of the older German text[8] and created what amounts to a new, three-stanza confession of faith. He ironed out the metrical irregularities of the earlier text, creating uniform lines of eight syllables, and the substance of each stanza is expressed in three logical units (4 + 4 + 2 lines).

There has also been some debate about Luther's original intentions with regard to this hymn. Towards the end of the nineteenth century Friedrich Spitta argued that Luther wrote *Wir glauben* in the first place as a Trinity hymn, rather than as a creedal hymn for liturgical use. The primary evidence for this suggestion is its proximity to another Trinitarian hymn, *Gott der Vater wohn uns bei* in Johann Walter's Wittenberg hymnal of 1524, the so-called *Chorgesangbuch*. Spitta was followed by Lucke, who discussed the two hymns together as "Trinitatislieder."[9] But the argument is overstated. Of course it is a Trinity hymn, but it is unlikely that Luther disconnected it from the liturgical use of the creeds, especially since the prototype on which Luther's hymn is partially based, as well as its subsequent appearance in other hymnals, confirms the explicit creedal connection. The Zwickau manuscript of around 1500 gives the vernacular creedal hymn in a two-part musical setting. The melody is in the Tenor with the German text, but the upper voice (Discant) has part of the liturgical credo, beginning with *Patrem omnipotentem*, the words traditionally sung by the choir after the priest has intoned *Credo in unum Deum*.[10] Although Walter's 1524 *Chorgesangbuch* carries no heading to the hymn, later hymnals include a creedal connection, usually by reference to the Latin *Patrem* (see Table 6.1).[11] Luther's hymn probably first circulated on a Wittenberg broadsheet, and these later headings thus reflect this original printing. Similarly, the use of *Wir glauben* as a vernacular liturgical creed in the *Form vnd ordnung eynes Christlichen Mess . . .* (Nuremberg, 1525), also reflects the original understanding of the hymn. Further confirmation of this is found in the *Deutsche Messe*, completed towards the end of the year 1525, in which Luther directs that the hymn should be sung in the location of the Nicene Creed in the traditional structure of the Mass: "After the Gospel the whole church sings the creed in German, *Wir glauben all an einen Gott*."[12] Thereafter in Lutheran church orders, liturgical books, and hymnals the liturgical use of the creedal hymn became virtually universal.

Table 6.1. Headings of *Wir glauben* in hymnals published in Saxony and Thuringia before 1546

Place of Publication	Year	Heading
Zwickau	1525	Das Patrem odder der Glawbe.
Erfurt	1525	. . . der glaub.
Leipzig	ca. 1530	Das Patrem zu deudsch. Martinus Luther.
Erfurt	1531	Das deutsche Patrem. Martinus Luther.
Wittenberg	1533	Das deutsche Patrem. Martinus Luther.
Wittenberg	1535	Das deutsche Patrem. Martinus Luther.
Wittenberg	1544	. . . Patrem. D. Mart. Luther.
Leipzig	1545	. . . patrem.

If Spitta and Lucke had investigated Johann Walter's *Chorgesangbuch* somewhat further they might have come to different conclusions regarding this hymn. Although there does not appear to have been a coherent plan for the arrangement of the hymns in Walter's hymnal, it is possible to detect groups of hymns within it that have a similar content. Towards the end of the collection, before the Latin pieces that conclude the work, there are five hymns in the following sequence:

Gott der Vater wohn uns bei (Luther)
Wir glauben all an einen Gott (Luther)
Es ist das Heil uns kommen her (Speratus)
Hilf Gott, wie ist der Menschen Not (Speratus)
In Gott gelaub ich, daß er hat (Speratus)

The content of these hymns deals in turn with the substance of prayer to the Trinity, the Creed, the doctrine of justification, the need for repentance, and a second, longer exposition of the Creed. When the three hymns of Speratus first appeared in 1524 each one was supplied with an appendix in which the scriptural proof-texts for every line of every stanza were given in full.[13] These hymns were literally the Word of God in song for the people to sing, the specific aim that Luther expressed in letters to his friends, written towards the end of 1523, encouraging them to join him in the task of writing hymns.[14]

These German hymns at the end of Walter's 1524 *Chorgesangbuch* are therefore catechetical in a broad sense in that they dealt with the essential theology of Trinitarian faith. Luther apparently first publicly advocated a three-fold division of the content of the Creed in 1520.[15] Later he explained his reasoning in the Large Catechism:

> The Creed used to be divided into twelve articles. Of course, if all the elements contained in Scripture and belonging to the Creed were gathered together, there would be many more articles. . . . But to make it most clear and simple for teaching to children, we shall briefly sum up the entire Creed in three main articles, according to the three persons of the Godhead, to whom everything that we believe is related. Thus the first article, concerning God the Father, explains creation; the second, concerning the Son, redemption; the third, concerning the Holy Spirit, being made holy. . . .[16]

What is particularly significant is that in this creedal hymn Luther anticipates his three brief paragraphs on the Creed in the Small Catechism he wrote some five years after the hymn. In many respects the expositions of each of the three articles of the Creed in the Small Catechism read like a commentary on each of the stanzas of the hymn, with an overlap of vocabulary and content. Here is another example of Luther's theological consistency especially when the teaching of children was concerned.

In *Kurtze Fragen und Antwort über die Sechs Häupstücke deß heiligen Catechismi D. Martini Lutheri* (Regensburg, 1581) Rosinus prescribes the following hymns by Luther to be sung in connection with the second part of the catechism: after the first article of the Creed, *Wir glauben all an einen Gott*;[17] after the second article, either *Gott der Vater wohn uns bei* — confirming the catechetical connection of this hymn that was included towards the end of Walter's *Chorgesangbuch* of 1524 (see above) — or *Gelobet seist du, Jesu Christ*; and after the third article, *Nun bitten wir den Heiligen Geist*.[18]

As the hymn is a summary of Christian faith it had quite wide usage, in addition to its regular use as the vernacular liturgical Creed and as a catechism hymn. For example, Luther included it in his *Christliche Gesang Lateinisch vnd Deudsch zum Begrebnis* [funeral hymns] (Wittenberg, 1542). But the catechetical connections remained strong, and Luther included *Wir glauben* within the specific catechism sections in Klug's *Geistliche Lieder* (Wittenberg, 1543) and Bapst's *Geystlicher Lieder* (Leipzig, 1545). By the eighteenth century some hymnals had begun to include the hymn under the rubric "Trinitarian hymns," but usually in close proximity to such Latin Trinitarian hymns of the liturgy as the *Kyrie* and *Gloria in excelsis Deo*. Official hymnals published in Hamburg throughout the eighteenth century gave it as a Trinitarian hymn, whereas those published in Leipzig over the same period included it within the section of catechism hymns.

Although the hymn is included in contemporary American Lutheran hymnals,[19] it does not seem to be sung often in the churches, except perhaps in Missouri Synod congregations. Three of the four hymnals include an outline of a "Chorale Service," based on Luther's *Deutsche Messe* of 1526, and all three specify Luther's "We all believe in one true God" as the creedal hymn.[20] But from what I can gather, this option is not frequently used, and, in congregations using the hymnals of the Missouri and Evangelical Lutheran Synods, one suspects that when the chorale service is used the creedal hymn by Thomas Clausnitzer — with the same first line[21] — is sung, rather than Luther's. The reason is almost certainly musical. The tune associated with Clausnitzer's text, first published in Darmstadt in 1699, is a "modern" tune in a regular meter, whereas Luther's sturdy tune in the Dorian mode, dating from the early fifteenth century, is perceived to be archaic, with an unusual metrical structure, and an elaborate melisma on the second syllable of the first line, on the word "all" in each stanza.[22]

Multiculturalism, rightly understood, has chronological as well as geographical dimensions, and our worship is enriched when we sing such hymns of faith that originate in earlier times and under different conditions than our own. The faith does not change but expression of it does. In our frenetic world we need to sing such expressions of theological praise that are more concerned with the timelessness of the substance of what we believe, instead of singing only in a currently fashionable style that quickly goes out-of-date. Further, our contemporary popular culture is not as monolithic and all-pervasive as some of our church leaders would have us believe.[23] Witness the widespread popularity of Gregorian chant recordings in recent years — as well as recordings of chant-related music, such as the compositions of the twelfth-century Hildegard von Bingen, on the one hand, and such twentieth-century compositions as those by Arvo Pärt and John Tavener, on the other. There is a certain irony in the fact that at a time when many within our churches are seeking to eliminate our specific traditions of church music, many more in the secular society outside the churches have embraced such music as the aural expression of a spirituality that contrasts strongly with the brash sounds of the propaganda music of our time.

We need the continuity of Luther's creedal hymn, with its different perspective on time and eternity, the hymn that teaches rather than simply exhorts, that confesses faith rather than simply defines it dogmatically, that is evangelical without confusing evangelism with worship, or vice versa.

CHAPTER 7

Vater unser im Himmelreich

The Our Father, briefly and well expounded,
and made into a song

[1.] Vater unser ym hymelreich,
der du uns alle heisest gleich
bruder sein und dich ruffen an
und wilt das beten von uns han.
Gib das nicht bett allein der mund.
Hilff das es geh von hertzen grund.

Our Father, thou in heaven above,
who biddest us to dwell in love,
as brethren of one family,
to cry in every need to thee,
teach us no thoughtless word to say,
but from our inmost heart to pray.

[2.] Geheiliget werd der Name dein.
Dein Wort bey uns hilff halten rein,
Das auch wir leben heiliglich
Nach deinem Namen wirdiglich.
Behüt uns, Herr, für falscher ler.
Das arm verfüret Volck beker.

Thy name be hallowed. Help us, Lord,
in purity to keep thy Word,
that to the glory of thy name
we walk before thee free from blame.
Let no false doctrine us pervert;
all poor, deluded souls convert.

[3.] Es kom dein Reich zu dieser zeit
Und dort hernach inn ewigkeit.
Der Heilig Geist uns wone bey
mit seinen gaben mancherley.
Des Satans zorn und gros gewalt
Zebrich, Für im dein Kirch erhalt.

Thy kingdom come. Thine let it be
in time and in eternity.
Let thy good Spirit e'er be nigh
our hearts with graces to supply.
Break Satan's power, defeat his rage;
preserve thy Church from age to age.

[4.] Dein will geschehe, Herr Gott, zu gliech
Auff Erden wie im Himelreich.
Gib uns gedult inn leidens zeit,
Gehorsam sein inn lieb und leid.
Wehr und steur allem fleisch und blut,
Das wider deinen willen thut.

Thy gracious will on earth be done
as 'tis in heaven before thy throne;
obedience in our weal and woe
and patience in all grief bestow.
Curb flesh and blood and every ill
that sets itself against thy will.

[5.] Gib uns heut unser teglich Brot
Und was man darff zur liebs nott.
Behüt uns, Herr, für unfried und streit,
Für seuchen and für theurer zeit.
Das wir inn gutem frieden stehn,
Der sorg und geitsens müssig gehn.

Give us this day our daily bread
and let us all be clothed and fed.
From war and strife be our defense,
from famine and from pestilence,
that we may live in godly peace,
free from all care and avarice.

[6.] All unser schuld vergib uns, Herr,
Das sie uns nicht betrüben mehr.
Wie wir auch unsern Schüldigern
Ir schuld und feil vergeben gern.
Zu deinen mach uns all bereit
Inn rechter lieb und einigkeit.

Forgive our sins, Lord, we implore,
remove from us their burden sore,
as we their trespasses forgive
who by offenses us do grieve.
Prepare and make us willingly
to dwell in love and unity.

[7.] Für uns, Herr, inn versuchung nicht,
Wenn uns der böse geist anficht.
Zur lincken und zur rechten Hand
Hilff uns thun starcken widerstand,
Im glauben fest und wolgerüst
Und durch des Heiligen Geistes trost.

Into temptation lead us not.
When evil foes against us plot
and vex our souls on every hand,
O, give us strength that we may stand
firm in the faith, a well-armed host,
through comfort of the Holy Ghost!

[8.] Von allem Ubel uns erlös.
Es sind die zeit und tage bös.
Erlös uns von dem ewigen Tod
Und tröst uns inn der letzten not.
Bescher uns auch ein seligs end,
Nim unser Seel inn deine hand.

From evil, Lord, deliver us;
the times and days are perilous.
Redeem us from eternal death,
and when we yield our dying breath,
console us, grant us calm release,
and take our souls to thee in peace.

[9.] Amen, das ist: Es werde war,
Sterck unsern glauben imerdar,
Auff das wir ia nich zweiveln dran,
Das wie hiemit gebeten han
Auff dein Wort inn dem Namen dein;
so sprechen wir das Amen fein.[1]

Amen, that is, So shall it be.
Confirm our faith and hope in thee
that we may doubt not, but believe
what here we ask we shall receive.
Thus in thy name and at thy word
we say: Amen. O, hear us, Lord![2]

Vater unser im Himmelreich is a rarity in that it is one of only two hymns[3] for which Luther's manuscript draft is still extant.[4] The undated autograph reveals a number of alterations and corrections. Most of the revisions have to do with establishing word order, or with clarifying meaning. But some of the changes are more substantial. Stanza 2, line 5, began with "Behut uns Herr fur" (Keep us, Lord, from), but Luther was in two minds how the line should end, since he wrote alternative endings, one above the other:

Behut uns Herr fur $<$ falscher lehr [false doctrine]
Eitler ehr [empty praise]

At a later stage "Eitler ehr" was crossed out. Stanza 5, line 3, was originally "Behut uns Herr fur krieg und streit" (Keep us, Lord, from war and strife);

129

"krieg" was later deleted and "blut" (blood) substituted, but this was also struck through and "unfri[e]d" (discord) was Luther's final choice. The following line (stanza 5, line 4) was originally written as "fur krankheit und fur theurer zeit" (from sickness and from time of famine), but "krankheit" was later changed to "seuchen" (pestilence). In the last two lines of the hymn (stanza 9, line 5 and 6) Luther originally wrote:

Auf dein wort ynn deinem Namen	On thy Word and in thy Name
So sprechen wir frolich Amen.	thus we say joyfully Amen.

However, he had second thoughts and did not want the Amen to be simply joyful, but emphatic and excellent. But in revising the text he had to modify the word order to arrange for a different rhyming scheme:

Auf dein wort ynn dem namen dein	On thy Word and in the Name of thine
So sprechen wir das Amen fein.	thus we say the Amen fine.

But it was stanza 6 that gave Luther the most problems, for in the manuscript there are no less than three versions of it. The first exhibits changes in word order, substitutions of various words, and all six lines are crossed out, and a neater version is written directly below it:

Vergib uns Herr all unser sund	Forgive us, Lord, all of our sins
Der on zal und mas viel sind;	that are numberless and very great;
Wolst Herr uns die nicht rechten zu	Lord, account them not unto us
Nach deim gericht nicht mit uns thu,	nor deal with us by thy judgment,
Verzeych uns alles gnediglich	but regard us all graciously
~~Als~~ Wie wir thun andern williglich.	as we to others do willingly.

But this revised stanza was abandoned and a new one was written, appended to the manuscript after stanza 9 but clearly marked as stanza 6. This, apart from one small detail, was the final version that appeared in the published version of the hymn.

Although the manuscript bears no date — and the paper carries no watermark that might have established the time of writing — it seems likely that it was written sometime during 1538 or 1539. In the middle of the eighteenth century a broadside of the hymn was known that has since been lost: *Das Vatter unser kurz ausgelegt, unnd inn Gesang weyse gebracht durch D. Mar. Luth. M.D.XXXIX.*[5] The same year the hymn was included in *Geistliche lieder, auffs new gebessert vnd gemehrt zu Wittenberg. D. Marti. Luther* (Leipzig:

Schumann, 1539).[6] Here it appeared in the same form as the final version of the manuscript with two modifications: a change of word order in stanza 6, line 3, and "Satan" replaced "Teuffel" (devil) in stanza 3, line 5. Luther was not the first to write a hymnic version of the Lord's Prayer in German. Medieval hymn versions in the vernacular were known, and there were several others that had circulated fairly widely during the previous decade and a half before Luther wrote his hymn. Ambrosius Moibanus wrote several Lord's Prayer hymns — probably during the later period of his time in Wittenberg, 1523-25 — the earliest being *Ach Vater unser, der du bist* (3 stanzas)[7] that first appeared in *Eyn gesang Buchleyn* (Zwickau, 1525). Another was *Vater unser, der du bist* (9 stanzas),[8] first published in *Enchiridion* (Erfurt, 1527), and later in hymnals with strong Wittenberg connection, such as *Enchiridion* (Zwickau, 1528), the second edition of Johann Walter's *Chorgesangbuch* (Wittenberg, 1528), and Bapst's *Geystliche Lieder* (Leipzig, 1545).

The circulation of such Lord's Prayer hymns probably explains why Luther delayed writing his own version. Like Moibanus's *Vater unser, der du bist*, Luther's Lord's Prayer hymn is in nine stanzas, but is more expansive than the earlier version of Moibanus in that it employs a larger stanzaic form: six lines of eight syllables compared with four lines of eight syllables (though Moibanus's syllabication is less than perfect). It also seems likely that Luther wanted a hymn that would follow closely the structure of his treatment of the Lord's Prayer in his Small Catechism. His nine stanzas therefore correspond exactly to the sections of his explanation of the prayer in the revised 1531 catechism, with one stanza each for the seven petitions, one for the address at the beginning, and one for the commitment of faith expressed in the Amen at the end.

In this hymn, therefore, we have the opposite of the hymns on the two main parts of the catechism: they were written before the catechism appeared; this hymn was written after it. The twelve stanzas of *Dies sind die heiligen zehn Gebot* anticipate the later answers to the twelve questions "What does this mean?" of Luther's treatment of the Ten Commandments in the Small Catechism, and the three stanzas of *Wir glauben all an einen Gott* anticipate the three answers to the questions "What does this mean?" of his treatment of the Creed in the catechism. But the Lord's Prayer hymn was written approaching ten years after the Small Catechism. Like the two earlier catechism hymns, the nine stanzas of *Vater unser im Himmelreich* are directly analogous to the answers to the ninefold questioning, "What does this mean?" in the exposition of the Lord's Prayer in the Small Catechism. Here is the demonstration of the close affinity between the main parts of Luther's Catechism and his corresponding hymns on the substance of these parts.

Example 7.1. Luther's Melodies for *Vater unser im Himmelreich*

A=DORIAN (1539). Zahn No. 2561. DKL Ee35.

B=IONIAN (undated Ms.). Zahn No. 2562.

*Altered from *b* to *a* in Luther's Ms.

Vater unser im Himmelreich therefore had a double usage. First, all of the stanzas could be sung liturgically either in place of the prose Prayer or immediately following it. Alternatively, when a specific question and answer was being examined, either in church or home, three stanzas could be sung: the first, addressed to God "our Father," then the respective stanza on the petition being taught, and finally the "Amen" stanza at the end.[9]

Over the decades following its publication Luther's hymn was translated into a number of other European languages, such as Dutch (1551), Danish (1553), and English (ca. 1555)[10] — a translation appended to the Sternhold and Hopkins psalter (the Old Version) that was still in print in the second half of the nineteenth century.

Luther wrote two tunes for his Lord's Prayer hymn. The first was included at the end of his manuscript draft of the hymn, but was later crossed out.[11] Until recently it had not been noticed that Luther altered the fifth note of the fourth line from B to A (Example 7.1B).[12] When it appeared in print in the Leipzig hymnal of 1539 it was set to another melody, the one that has subsequently and almost universally been associated with Luther's German hymn, as well as with its translations into other languages (Example 7.1A).[13] The first tune is in the Ionian mode, approximating to the modern major scale, and the second in the Dorian mode, closely related to the modern minor scale. The earlier Ionian tune, in the same mode as Luther's *Ein feste Burg*, is too robust and assertive for the prayerful nature of the text, whereas the Dorian tune is much more reflective and matches the petitionary mood of the text. It is therefore understandable that Luther preferred the Dorian tune, the one that subsequently has been indissolubly linked with his Lord's Prayer hymn.[14]

The tune also brought other hymn texts into being. One was *Gott Vater in dem Himmelreich*,[15] by Johannes Freder, first published in the Bapst

Geystliche Lieder (Wittenberg, 1545). It is headed "The German Litany brought into rhyme . . . ," and assigned to the tune *Vater unser im Himmelreich*. Luther's hymn from time to time echoes his German Litany, for example, stanza 5 has the following:

> From war and strife be our defense,
> from famine and from pestilence,
> that we may live in godly peace. . . .

This may have been Freder's inspiration to write his versification of the litany. However, the connections with Luther's hymn are obvious in Freder's first line, as well as in others, and in its use of the Lord's Prayer melody. By the use of this tune Freder therefore makes a link between the litany and the catechism. Similarly later hymnals include Luther's German Litany under the heading "Prayer" within the section of Catechism hymns.[16] Another is the creedal hymn, *Ich glaub an den Allmächtigen Gott*, by Sebald Heyden in Nuremberg in 1545, which was assigned the tune *Vater unser im Himmelreich*.[17] Here the musical hermeneutic is more direct: the second and third parts of the catechism are thus linked by the use of the tune. The twelve stanzas of the confessional hymn are thus interpreted as musical prayer by the use of the melody of Luther's Lord's Prayer hymn.

Luther's hymn and its associated melody have also inspired more recent hymns. The late Martin Franzmann, remarkable preacher and perceptive hymn writer, was concerned that Luther's hymn was rarely sung by American Lutheran congregations, largely because it is considered to be too long for contemporary use. Franzmann reasoned that if he wrote a shorter hymnic version of the Lord's Prayer, to be sung to Luther's tune, some congregations might be encouraged to look at, and even perhaps to sing, Luther's longer hymn. Therefore Franzmann wrote his three-stanza hymn, *O thou who hast of thy pure grace*, which first appeared in the *Worship Supplement* of 1969, and subsequently in two Lutheran hymnals.[18] Franzmann's text gave rise to another. Instead of Franzmann's hymn *Lutheran Worship* has another three-stanza paraphrase of the Lord's Prayer, by Henry L. Lettermann, and set to Luther's tune.[19] "The verbal correspondences are so striking, especially in the third stanza, that they suggest that Lettermann's version almost certainly began as a revision of Franzmann's text."[20]

These shortened forms of hymnic versions of the Lord's Prayer are symptomatic of our modern age, which is impatient with hymns longer than three or four stanzas and with services of worship that last longer than fifty-nine minutes. But worship and prayer require time if we are to become attuned to what we are doing and why. Luther and his generation have much to teach us about hymns that have more to do with faith, rather than simply evoking feeling, hymns that are sometimes expressions of prayer, instead of always being thought of as expressions of praise, hymns that make us take time in worship and prayer to consider who God is, what God has done for us, what God continues to do for us, and what our real needs — as opposed to our wants — are. The catechesis of prayer not only defines what prayer is but also expresses itself in prayer, which is what Luther's catechism hymn on the Lord's Prayer takes time to do.

CHAPTER 8

Christ unser Herr zum Jordan kam

A Spiritual Song of our Holy Baptism, which is a fine summary
of What is it? Who established it? What are its benefits?[1]

[1.] Christ unser Herr, zum Jordan kam
nach seines Vaters willen,
Von S. Johans die Tauffe nam,
sein werck und ampt zurfüllen.
Da wolt er stifften uns ein Bad,
Zu waschen uns von sünden,
Erseuffen auch dem Bittern Tod
Durch sein selbs Blut und Wunden.
Es galt ein newes Leben.

To Jordan came our Lord the Christ,
to do God's pleasure willing,
and there was by Saint John baptized,
all righteousness fulfilling.
There did he consecrate a bath
to wash away transgression,
and quench the bitterness of death
by his own blood and passion;
a new life he would give us.

[2.] So hört und mercket alle wol,
was Gott heisst selbs die Tauffe
Und was ein Christen gleuben sol,
Zu meiden Ketzer hauffen:
Gott spricht und wil, das wasser sey,
Doch nicht allein schlecht Wasser.
Sien heiligs wort ist auch dabey
Mit reichem Geist on massen.
Der ist alhie der Tauffer.

So hear you all and well perceive
what God has named Baptism,
and what a Christian should believe,
who error shuns and schism:
that we should water use, the Lord
makes known his pleasure,
not simple water, but with the Word
and Spirit without measure;
he is the true Baptizer.

[3.] Sölches hat er uns beweiset klar
Mit Bildern und mit Worten.
Des Vaters stim man offenbar
Daselbs am Jordan horte.
Er sprach: "Das ist mein lieber Son,
An dem ich hab gefallen.
Den wil ich Euch befohlen han,
Das jr in höret Alle
Und folget seinem Leren."

To show us this, he has his Word
with words and symbols given.
On Jordan's banks was plainly heard
the Father's voice from heaven.
He said, "This is my own dear Son,
in whom I'm well contented.
To you I send him, every one —
that you may hear I've sent him,
and follow what he teaches."

[4.] Auch Gottes Son hie selber steht
In seiner zarten Menscheit.
Der heilig Geist ernider fert
In Taubenbild verkleidet,
Das wir nicht sollen zweiveln dran,
Wenn wir getauffet werden,
All drey Person getauffet han,
Da mit bey uns auff Erden
Zu wohnen sich ergeben.

Also God's Son himself here stands
in all his manhood tender.
The Holy Ghost on him descends,
in dove's appearance hidden,
that not a doubt should ever rise
that, when we are baptized,
all three Persons do baptize;
and so, here recognized
will make their dwelling with us.

[5.] Sein Jünger heisst der Herre Christ:
"Geht hin, all welt zu leren,
Das sie verlorn in Sünden ist,
Sich sol zur Busse keren.
Wer gleubet und sich teuffen lesst,
Sol dadurch selig werden.
Ein neugeborner Mensch er heisst,
Der nicht mehr könne sterben,
Das Himmelreich sol erben."

Thus Jesus his disciples sent:
"Go, teach to every nation,
that lost in sin they must repent
and know the Lord's salvation.
He that believes and is baptized,
receives a mighty blessing,
a new-born man, no more he dies,
eternal life possessing,
a joyful heir of heaven."

[6.] Wer nicht glebt dieser grosser Gnad
der bleibt in seinen Sünden
und ist verdampt zum ewigen Tod
tief in der Hellen grunde.
Nichts hilfft sein eigen heiligkeit;
All sein Thun ist verloren,
Die Erbsünd machst zur nichtigkeit
darin er ist geboren,
Vermag jm selbst nichts helffen.

But in this grace who puts no faith,
remains in his trespasses,
and is condemned to endless death
deep down in hell's abysses.
His holiness avails him not
nor works of his own doing;
his inborn sin brings all to nought,
and brings about his ruin;
to help himself he's helpless.

[7.] Das Aug allein das Wasser siht,
Wie Menschen Wasser giessen.
Der Glaub im Geist die krafft versteht
Des Blutes Jhesu Christi.
Und ist für im ein rote Flut,
Von Christus Blut geferbet,
Die allen Schaden heilen thut,
Von Adam her geerbet
auch von uns selbst begangen.[2]

All that the mortal eye beholds
is water as man pours it.
Before the eye of faith unfolds
the power of Jesus' merit.
Faith sees the flooding fountain red,
stained with the blood of Jesus,
which from the sins inherited
from fallen Adam frees us,
and those we have committed.[3]

Christ unser Herr zum Jordan kam (1539) was the last of Luther's catechism hymns to be written, and may have been the last hymn he wrote.[4] It is found in three undated broadsides that suggest, from typographical evidence, they were issued in 1542-43: two in Regensburg and one in Leipzig.[5] In the no-longer extant *Enchiridion Geistliker Gesenge unde Leder* (Lübeck, 1556), it was included with other catechism hymns and given the specific date "Anno M.D.XLI."[6] The implication is that all these imprints were derived from an original 1541 Wittenberg broadside that has also not survived. The date of writing therefore is likely to have been sometime between 1540 and 1541. In Easter week, April 1540, Luther preached two sermons on the early verses of

Matthew 3 in which he expounded the significance of baptism.[7] These sermons provide the immediate theological context and background of the hymn,[8] which may well have been written around the same time.

The links between this baptismal hymn and the Small Catechism could not be stronger. The heading to the hymn includes three questions that parallel the first three questions of the exposition of baptism in the Small Catechism:[9]

Heading of the Hymn:	Small Catechism:
[1] Was sie sei?	Was ist die Taufe?
What is it [baptism]?	What is Baptism?
[2] Wer sie gestiftet habe?	Welch ist denn solch Wort Gottes?
Who established it?	What is this Word of God?
[3] Was sie nütze?	Was gibt oder nützet die Taufe?
What are its benefits?	What does Baptism give or bestow?

The three questions supply the framework for the chiastic structure of the hymn.

The first question is answered by stanzas 1, 4, and 7. The focal point of the total hymn is stanza 4, an exposition of the role of each of the Persons of the Trinity in baptism, which is also an echo of the baptismal formula: "I baptize you in the name of the Father and of the Son and of the Holy Spirit." The hymn is framed by the first and last stanzas (1 and 7). They declare that baptism is the sacrament of spiritual cleansing, the granting of new life and forgiveness, through Christ's willingness to receive baptism from John in the Jordan and in his bearing the sin of the world on the cross.

The second question is answered in stanzas 2 and 3. Who established baptism? God — Father, Son, and Holy Spirit — by water and the Word.

The third question is answered by stanzas 5 and 6. Here the benefits of baptism are stated both positively (stanza 5) and negatively (stanza 6): to be baptized in the faith is to receive forgiveness of sin, new birth, and eternal life; to be unbaptized is to be without grace, condemned in sin, and subject to eternal death.

In the outer two stanzas of the hymn (1 and 7), there are references to "Jordan," "the flood," and "Adam," that are strong echoes of Luther's "Flood Prayer" in his Order of Baptism (1526):

Almighty eternal God, who according to thy righteous judgment did condemn the unbelieving world through the flood . . . and who didst drown hardhearted Pharaoh with all his host in the Red Sea and didst lead thy people Israel through the same on dry ground, thereby prefiguring this bath of thy Baptism, and who through the Baptism of thy dear Child, our Lord Jesus Christ, hast consecrated and set apart the Jordan and all water as a salutary flood and full washing away of sins: We pray thee through the same groundless mercy that thou wilt graciously behold this N. and bless him with true faith in the spirit so that by means of this saving flood all that has been born in him from Adam and which he has added thereto may be drowned in him and engulfed, and that he may be sundered from the number of the unbelieving, preserved dry and secure in the holy ark of Christendom. . . .[10]

The new baptism hymn was not given a new melody but one that was composed, almost certainly by Johann Walter,[11] for Luther's hymnic version of Psalm 67, *Es wollt uns Gott genädig sein* (1524).[12] Later Luther supplied another tune of his own for this psalm-hymn.[13] There were, therefore, two tunes associated with *Es wollt uns Gott genädig sein*. One was Walter's found in the 1524 *Chorgesangbuch,* and also in the congregational hymnal, based on Walter's 1524 collection, issued in 1526. The other was Luther's melody associated with the same psalm that presumably appeared in the no longer extant Wittenberg hymnal issued by Joseph Klug in 1529, in the edition of 1533, and other later hymnals. In the second edition of Walter's *Chorgesangbuch* (1528) — another hymnal that has not survived but its contents can be reconstructed from later editions[14] — Walter's 1524 setting of the earlier melody was replaced by a new setting of Luther's melody now assigned to his psalm-hymn. Thus a decade or so later, when Luther came to write his baptism hymn, there was a redundant tune available for him to use. He wrote *Christ unser Herr zum Jordan kam* in the same meter as *Es wollt uns Gott genädig sein,* therefore rescuing Walter's fine tune that might otherwise have fallen into disuse. However, it seems likely that Luther was not simply being pragmatic in utilizing Walter's melody but seems to have made a theological connection between his earlier psalm-hymn and his newly-written baptism hymn. *Es wollt uns Gott genädig sein* (Psalm 67) is a general prayer for grace and blessing, and *Christ unser Herr zum Jordan kam* is an exposition of the specific grace and blessing of baptism. This theological association between the psalm-hymn and baptism hymn may well have been the reason why Luther was drawn to the redundant tune associated with the former and used it as the appropriate musical vehicle for the latter. If this was the reason for the choice of the tune for the baptism hymn — a text-tune association that has remained constant ever since — Luther's decision was conditioned more by musical hermeneutics than by simple musical ecology.

A four-part setting of Luther's baptism hymn, composed by Wolff

Heintz, was published in Georg Rhau's *Newe Deudsche Geistliche Gesenge* (Wittenberg, 1544). Luther had known Heintz since about 1523 and retained a high regard for the organist and composer, who remained a Catholic in the service of Cardinal Albrecht of Brandenburg, while maintaining a close interest in the reforming movement. Following the death of the strongest and most committed Catholic prince of Germany, Duke Georg of Albertine Saxony, in 1539, cities in the dukedom began to espouse Reformation faith and practice. It was a further two years before the Lutheran Reformation was introduced into Halle. Early in 1541 the Cardinal Archbishop left the city, Wolff Heintz openly declared himself a Lutheran and was appointed the organist of the Marktkirche, and Luther's colleague Justus Jonas inaugurated the Halle Reformation by preaching in the Marktkirche in April that year. Almost immediately Jonas began drawing up evangelical liturgical forms for Halle, under Luther's direction in Wittenberg, and working closely with Heintz who was responsible for introducing the Lutheran hymns and for providing appropriate music for the new liturgical forms.[15] It therefore seems highly likely that in 1541 Heintz composed his setting of Luther's recently-written baptism hymn, and that he gave or sent a copy to Luther. This appears to be confirmed by the handwritten dedication Luther wrote in a Bible he presented to Heintz in 1541. In this dedication Luther echoes the imagery of the Flood Prayer of his baptism rite, a reference that makes particular sense if Luther was sending a thank-offering to the composer for the four-part setting of his baptism hymn. Luther wrote the following in the presentation copy:

> Ps. 149[:1]. Sing to the Lord a new song, etc. A new miracle deserves a new song, thanksgiving, and preaching, that is, the new miracle that God through His dear Son has parted the real Red, Dead Sea and has redeemed us from the real Pharaoh, Satan. This is singing a new song, namely, the holy Gospel, and thanking God for it. God help us to do so.[16]

Since Luther's hymn expounds the evangelical understanding of the meaning of baptism, as the rite of spiritual cleansing by water and the Word, it is understandable that Heintz should want to compose a musical setting of this hymn at an early stage of his collaboration with Jonas, in which he was to create suitable music for the new evangelical liturgical forms, then being drawn up for use in Halle. What is clear is that Heintz and Walter were not the only ones to provide musical settings for Luther's baptism hymn. Many later Lutheran composers wrote such music, including Michael Praetorius and Johann Hermann Schein, who each wrote several vocal settings of the hymn in the seventeenth century, and Dietrich Buxtehude and Johann

Sebastian Bach who composed organ chorale preludes on its melody in the later seventeenth and eighteenth centuries. Particularly significant is Bach's chorale cantata *Christ unser Herr zum Jordan kam* (BWV 7), composed in 1724, which is a careful musical exposition of Luther's hymn. The reason why such music was almost continuously composed in later generations is that Luther's *Christ unser Herr zum Jordan kam* was, and remains, the primary baptism hymn of the Lutheran church. Similarly, preaching on the fourth main part of the catechism made specific reference to Luther's baptism hymn. For example, August Pfeiffer, superintendent in Lübeck, included a sermon on Luther's baptism hymn in *Cithera Lutheri, d[as]. i[st]. Christliche Predigten Über Die allgemeinen Katechismus-Lieder* (Lübeck, 1709), a collection of eight sermons on Luther's five catechism hymns. Similarly, Erdmann Neumeister, pastor in Hamburg, published, over the years, a series of volumes of catechism sermons, each volume covering one of the main sections of the catechism, in which catechism hymns were employed in the exposition of the questions and answers of the catechism. Neumeister's *Das Wasserbad im Worte, Oder: Die Lehre von der Heil. Tauffe, so in LII. Predigten; und zugleich . . . Unterschiedliche Lieder erkläret worden* [The Water-bath in the Word, or, the Doctrine of Holy Baptism, which in 52 sermons, together with . . . various hymns, is expounded] has expositions of five baptism hymns, *Christ unser Herr zum Jordan kam* being the first and most prominent.[17]

In the later nineteenth century the tendency was to displace Luther's objective baptism hymn by more subjective texts, written under the influence of Pietism, notably Johann Jakob Rambach's *Ich bin getauft auf deinen Namen,* that first appeared in the author's hymnal, *Erbauliches Handbüchlein für Kinder* (Giessen, 1734). The trend is illustrated in the Missouri Synod's *Lutheran Hymnal* of 1941, which includes Rambach's hymn, and at least two others in a similar vein,[18] but not Luther's baptism hymn. However, in the last thirty years or so, as part of the general movement for liturgical renewal, there has been a concern to recover the integrity of the baptismal rite and its theology, the recognition that its proper context is the worshiping community of faith, rather than an isolated cultural ceremony for one family. Thus all the four recent American Lutheran hymnals have included *Christ unser Herr zum Jordan kam,* and rightly so, since it is a summary of Luther's catechetical teaching on baptism. In the Large Catechism he wrote:

> Do you think it was a joke that the heavens opened when Christ was baptized, that the Holy Spirit descended visibly, and that the divine glory and majesty were manifested everywhere? I therefore admonish you again that these two, the Word and the water, must by no means be separated

from each other. . . . [W]hen the Word is with it according to God's ordinance, Baptism is a sacrament. . . . we must also learn why and for what purpose it has been instituted. . . . This is the simplest way to put it: the power, effect, benefit, fruit, and purpose of Baptism is that it saves. . . . Here again you see how Baptism is to be regarded as precious and important, for in it we obtain such an inexpressible treasure.[19]

CHAPTER 9

Aus tiefer Not schrei ich zu dir

Psalm 130. *De profundis clamavi*

Early Version

[1.] Us tieffer not schry ich zu dir;
Herr Gott, erhör min rüfen.
Din gnädig oren keer zu mir
unnd miner bitt sey offen.
    Dann so du wilt das sehen an,
    wie manches sünd ich hab gethan:
    wär kan, Herr, vor dir blyben?

[2.] Es steet bey deiner macht allain,
die sünden zu vergeben,
Das dich fürcht beyde, groß und klain,
auch in dem besten leben.
    Darumb auff got wil hoffen ich;
    Mein hertz auff jn sol lassen sich.
    Ich wils seins worts erharren.

Later Version

[1.] Aus tieffer not schrey ich zu dyr;
Herr Gott, erhor meyn ruffen.
Deyn gnedig oren ker zu myr
und meyner bitt sie offen.
    Denn so du wilt das sehen an,
    was sund und unrecht ist gethan:
    wer kan, Herr, fur dyr bleyben?

[2.] Bey dyr gillt nichts den gnad und gonst,
die sunden zu vergeben.
Es ist doch unser thun umb sonst,
Auch ynn dem besten leben.
    Fur dyr niemant sich rhumen kan;
    Des mus dich furchten yderman
    Und deyner ganden leben.

[3.] Darum auff Gott will hofen ich,
auff meyn verdienst nicht bauen.
Auff yhn mayn hertz sol lassen sich
und seyner guete trauen,
    Die myr zu sagt seyn werdes wort;
    das ist meyn trost und treuer hort.
    Des will ich allzeyt harren.

142

[3.] Und ob es wert biß in die nacht
und wider an den morgen,
Doch sol mein hertz an Gottes macht
verzweyfeln nit noch sorgen.
So thu Israel rechter art,
der auß dem geyst erzeüget wardt,
Und seines gots erharre.

[4.] Ob bey uns ist der sünden vil,
bey Got ist vil mer gnaden,
Sein handt zu helffen hat kain zill,
wie groß auch sey der schaden.
Er ist allein der gute hyrt,
Der Israel erlösen wirt
auß seinen sünden allen.

Early Version

[1.] From trouble deep I cry to thee,
Lord God, hear thou my crying;
thy gracious ear, O turn to me,
open it to my sighing.
For if thou mean'st to look upon
the many sins that I have done,
who, Lord, can stand beside thee?

[2.] Who stands by his own might alone,
to cover all his failing,
should fear his efforts to atone,
the good works he is doing.
Hope therefore in my God will I,
upon him shall my heart rely;
for his Word I am waiting.

[4.] Und ob es wert bis ynn die nacht
und widder an den morgen,
Doch sol meyn hertz an Gottes macht
verzweyfeln nicht noch sorgen.
So thu Israel rechter art,
der aus dem geyst erzeuget ward,
Und seynes Gotts erharre.

[5.] Ob bey uns ist der sunden viel,
bey Gott ist viel mehr gnaden,
Seyn hand zu helffen hat keyn ziel,
wie gros auch sey der schaden.
Er ist alleyn der gute hirt,
der Israel erlosen wirt
Auß seynen sunden allen.[1]

Later Version

[1.] From trouble deep I cry to thee,
Lord God, hear thou my crying;
thy gracious ear, O turn to me,
open it to my sighing.
For if thou mean'st to look upon
the many sins that I have done,
who, Lord, can stand beside thee?

[2.] With thee counts nothing but thy grace
forgiving all our failing.
The best life cannot win the race,
good works are unavailing.
Before thee none can perfect stand,
and so must tremble every man,
and live by thy grace only.

[3.] Hope therefore in my God will I,
on my deserts not founding;
upon him shall my heart rely,
and on his goodness grounding.
What his true Word doth promise me,
my comfort shall and refuge be;
that will I always wait for.

[3.] And though it last into the night,
and up until tomorrow,
yet shall my heart hope in God's might,
nor doubt or take to worry.
Thus Israel must keep his post,
for he's born by the Holy Ghost,
and for his God must tarry.

[4.] And though it last into the night,
and up until tomorrow,
yet shall my heart hope in God's might,
nor doubt or take to worry.
Thus Israel must keep his post,
for he's born by the Holy Ghost,
and for his God must tarry.

[4.] Although our sin be great, God's grace
is greater to relieve us;
his hand in helping nothing stays,
the hurt however grievous.
The Shepherd good alone is he
who will at last set Israel free
from each and every trespass.

[5.] Although our sin be great, God's grace
is greater to relieve us;
his hand in helping nothing stays,
the hurt however grievous.
The Shepherd good alone is he
who will at last set Israel free
from each and every trespass.[2]

The earliest version of *Aus tiefer Not schrei ich zu dir* was not only Luther's first catechism hymn but also one of the first hymns he wrote in 1523, after his protest song — about two Augustinian monks who were burnt for their "Lutheran" views — *Ein neues Lied wir heben an*.[3]

These early "songs" were written as general expressions of Christian faith and biblical doctrine, but Luther was quick to see the liturgical significance of using such strophic forms for congregational singing. In his *Formula missae pro Ecclesia Vuittembergensi* (Wittenberg, 1523) he wrote:

I also wish that we had as many songs as possible in the vernacular which the people could sing during Mass, immediately after the Gradual and also after the Sanctus and Agnus Dei. For who doubts that originally all the people sang these which now only the choir sings. . . . But poets are wanting among us, or not yet known, who could compose evangelical and spiritual songs, as St. Paul calls them, worthy to be used in the church of God. . . . I mention this to encourage any German poets to compose hymns of faith for us.[4]

Around the same time that Luther was working on the *Formula missae* he apparently wrote letters to various friends and colleagues, encouraging them to write such "songs" in the vernacular, of which only his letter to Georg Spalatin at the Saxon court survives:[5]

Following this example of the prophets and fathers of the church, I intend to make vernacular psalms for the people, that is, spiritual songs so that the Word of God even by means of song may live among the people. Everywhere we are looking for good poets. Now since you are skillful and eloquent in German, I would ask you to work with us in this and to turn a psalm into a hymn as in the enclosed sample of my work [presumably *Aus tiefer Not*, see later in the letter]. But I would like you to avoid newfangled, fancied words and to use expressions simple and common enough for the people to understand yet pure and fitting. The meaning should also be clear and as close as possible to the Psalm. Irrespective of the exact wording, one must freely render the sense by suitable words. I myself am not sufficiently gifted to do these things as I would. . . . Perhaps I may recommend you to the 6th Psalm, *Domine, ne in furore*, or the 143rd Psalm, *Domine, exaudi*, and to Johann Dolzig the 32nd, *Beati quorum*; for I have already translated the *De profundis* [Psalm 130], and the *Miserere mei* [Psalm 51] I have ordered from someone else.[6]

Although Spalatin never produced such a hymn for evangelical worship, others did, such as Lazarus Spengler, who wrote *Durch Adams Fall* (1524), and Erhart Hegenwalt — the "someone else" of Luther's letter to Spalatin (see above) — who wrote the version of Psalm 51, *Erbarm dich mein, O Herre Gott* (1524), another penitential psalm-hymn that was later closely associated with Luther's *Aus tiefer Not* (see further below). Luther's letter to Spalatin indicates that his German version of Psalm 130, *De profundis*, was written sometime around September-October 1523.

There has been some confusion over the original form of the hymn because two versions appeared almost simultaneously in print in 1524. One was a four-stanza version published in the *Achtliederbuch* that was prepared for the press in Nuremberg during the winter of 1523-24. The implication is that this hymn, like others in the small collection, was reprinted from a 1523 Wittenberg broadside, though unlike a number of the others it does not include the year it was written. This four-stanza form is also found in three other hymnals bearing the imprint 1524: the two Erfurt *Enchiridia* and the Straßburg *Teütsch Kirchenampt*. The other was a five-stanza version, first published in Walter's *Chorgesangbuch* (Wittenberg, 1524), which became the standard form of the text for later Lutheranism.[7]

In the American edition of *Luther's Works*, Ulrich Leupold (following Wilhelm Lucke, in the respective volume of the Weimar edition)[8] concludes that the five-stanza version is Luther's original hymn and that the four-stanza version is an unauthorized revision. The latter

is a conflation of the second and third stanzas [of the former]. . . . Jobst Gutknecht in Nürnberg, the printer of the *Achtliederbuch*, may have received this corrupted version from someone who had heard the hymn in Wittenberg, but did not know the exact words.[9]

But, as Markus Jenny has convincingly argued,[10] rather than an original five-stanza version that was later mutilated and issued in a shorter form by someone other than Luther, the two versions were both written by Luther and reveal two different approaches to the Psalm on which it is based.[11] The first to be written, in late 1523, was the four-stanza version that stays quite close to the content of Psalm 130; the second, revised form, probably written in early 1524, explored more fully the themes of grace as opposed to works, the Word rather than rewards, in the newly-written second and third stanzas. Thus the 1523 Psalm-hymn was transmuted into the 1524 faith-hymn. Martin Bucer, who had personal connections with Luther over the years, included both versions of *Aus tiefer Not* in his *Gesangbuch, darinn begriffen sind, die allerfünemisten vnd besten Psalmen, Geistliche Lieder vnd Chorgeseng* (Straßburg, 1541), and the shorter version is specifically described as the form "first issued" by Luther.[12]

The earlier, four-stanza form of Psalm 130 that Luther presumably sent to Spalatin toward the end of 1523 conforms exactly to the guidelines he included in his covering letter: first, it is the Word of God in song; second, it uses a basic German vocabulary; and third, it is closely based on Psalm 130. Each stanza approximates to two verses of the Psalm, but with some overlap of content: stanza 1 is based on verses 1-3; stanza 2, on verses 3-5, stanza 3, on verses 5-7; and stanza 4, on verses 7-8. Although it is closely based on the Psalm Luther nevertheless expands the content, making explicit what he saw as implicit in it: in stanza 2, forgiveness is in the declarative Word of God; in stanza 3, "Israel" is the creation of God's Spirit; and in stanza 4, the Good Shepherd is the one who mediates the grace of God.

The later, five-stanza form was created by expanding the second stanza into two separate stanzas (see Figure 9.1). Lines 2 and 4 of the early version were left unaltered in the same positions in stanza 2 of the later version. Similarly lines 5 and 6 of the early version were taken over to form lines 1 and 3 of stanza 3 of the later version — line 5 *verbatim* and line 6 in a different word-order. "Furcht" (fear) in line 3 of the original version becomes a keyword in lines 5-7 in stanza 2 of the later version, and "seins Worts erharren" (waiting for the Word) in line 7 becomes the keynote of the final three lines of stanza 3 of the later version. But there is more than simple semantics involved in Luther's revision.

In his first version stanza 2 says two things: that we cannot atone for our sins by our own efforts, and that instead we must wait for God's Word. In the later version these two concepts are given expanded treatment. The first part of the original stanza 2 is essentially a negative statement concerning the futility of good works if they are done in the hope of securing salvation. In contrast, the re-written stanza 2 of the later version first states the positive of God's grace, which throws the negative of self-justification by good works into high relief. Instead of beginning with the limitations of one's own power (Macht), as the early version does, stanza 2 of the revision begins with God's limitless grace in forgiveness. Similarly, the new lines at the end of the new

Figure 9.1. Luther's Expansion of the Earlier Version of *Aus tiefer Not*

Early Version	*Later Version*
2. Es steet bey deiner macht allain *die sünden zu vergeben,* das dich FÜRCHT beyde, groß und klain, *auch in dem besten leben.*	2. Bei dir gilt nichts denn Gnad und Gunst *die Sünde zu vergeben;* es ist doch unser Tun umsonst *auch in dem besten Leben.* Vor dir niemand sich rühmen kann, des muß dich FÜRCHTen jedermann, und deiner Gnade leben.
Darumb auff got wil hoffen ich; *mein herz auff jn sol lassen sich.* Ich wil SEINS WORTS erHARREN.	3. *Darum auff Gott will hoffen ich,* auff meyn verdienst nicht bauen; *Auff yhn meyn hertz sol lassen sich* und seyner guete trauen, Die myr zu sagt SEYN werdes WORT; das ist meyn trost und treuer hort, Des will ich allzeyt HARREN.

Italics indicate lines common to both versions; SMALL CAPITALS mark key words in the original version that also occur in the expanded revision.

stanza 2 expound the *sola gratia* principle. In a sense these lines are a pre-echo of the refrain that is reiterated again and again throughout Luther's treatment of the Ten Commandments in the Small Catechism: "We should fear and love God,"[13] that dialectic between servile and filial fear, one the product of the Law that condemns, the other the gift of grace in the Gospel that forgives.

This *sola gratia* principle is further expounded in the new stanza 3 of Luther's later version of Psalm 130: the hope of forgiveness is founded on God's goodness, rather than on our own deserving, forgiveness that is promised in God's Word, the *sola scriptura* principle. Thus in the later version of *Aus tiefer Not* Luther re-created his earlier metrical Psalm into a Gospel hymn. Instead of simply following the structure and content of the penitential Psalm Luther makes it into a Reformation hymn. It begins where Luther began in the first of the 95 Theses of 1517, with the meaning of repentance. It then deals with the tension and distinction between Law and Gospel, the essence of the doctrine of justification, by effectively expounding the meaning of the Reformation principles of *sola gratia*, *sola fide* and *sola scriptura*.

The early version of *Aus tiefer Not* in the *Achtliederbuch* (Nuremberg, 1524) was not assigned its own melody but would have been sung to the melody of Speratus's hymn *Es ist das Heil*.[14] Similarly, when the four stanzas appeared in the Erfurt *Enchiridia* the same year (1524), it was assigned another pre-existing tune: "Im Thon *Salvum me fac*," that is, *Ach Gott vom Himmel*.[15]

Example 9.1. Visual Hermeneutic of the Incipit of *Aus tiefer Not.*
Zahn No. 4437. DKL Ea6.

But when the later, five-stanza version was published for the first time in Walter's *Chorgesangbuch* (also 1524), it appeared with the striking Phrygian melody almost certainly composed by Luther, beginning as it does with a musical hermeneutic, in which "Aus tiefer Not," "Out of deepest need," is given sonic (and visual) expression in the fall and rise of a fifth (see Example 9.1).[16] While another sixteenth-century Strassburg tune, in variant forms, had some currency, and wider use from the nineteenth century,[17] the Phrygian melody was the tune universally associated with Luther's Psalm 130 in Lutheran Germany. Luther himself appears to have had a particular affection for it. When in Coburg Castle during the Diet of Augsburg in 1530, he suffered from severe headaches. On one occasion it is reported that many remedies were tried and eventually he fell asleep. On waking, with his head clear, it is reported: "He said: 'Now let us distress and annoy the devil by singing the Psalm *Aus tiefer Not* in four parts.'"[18] This must have been Johann Walter's four-part setting in the *Chorgesangbuch* of 1524 that had introduced the 5-stanza version of Luther's hymn version of Psalm 130.[19] (Luther would have sung from the Alto part book; see Fig. 9.2.)

Luther's concern for this hymn can be seen in the kind of appendix he added to his preface to the Bapst hymnal of 1545. The third paragraph, which includes a commendation of this beautifully produced hymnal (including a pun on "Bapst"/"Papst" — Printer's Name/Pope), is concluded by "Amen," which suggests that this is where he had originally intended to conclude his preface. But he then continues with comments on the faults of other printers and publishers of hymnals. First he draws attention to the hymn *Nun lasst uns den Leib begraben*, which had appeared in various hymnals with authorship wrongly ascribed to him. He then has an extended comment about stanza 2, line 6, of the later version of his hymn:

And in *De profundis* [*Aus tiefer Not*] the reading should be: "Everyone must fear thee." Whether by mistake or deliberately, in most books this is made to read "everyone must be afraid." For the expression "that thou mayest be feared" [Psalm 130:4] is a Hebrew idiom. Compare Matthew 15[:9], "In vain they fear me with the commandment of men," and Psalm 14[:4-5] and Psalm 53[:4-5], "They have not called upon God. They fear where there is nothing to fear," that is, they show great humility, and bow and scrape in their worship, which worship I do not want. So also here the meaning is this: Since forgiveness of sins cannot be found except with thee, they must cease from all their idolatry and willingly bow and bend before thee, humble themselves, hold thee alone in honor, take refuge in thee, and serve thee as those who live by thy grace and not by their own righteousness, etc.[20]

The hymn has had wide usage in the history of Lutheran worship. As Psalm 130 was one of the invariable psalms in the traditional *Officium pro defunctis,* Luther's *Aus tiefer Not* was sung as a burial hymn. In Wittenberg it was sung at the funeral of Duke Frederick the Wise in 1525 and a little more than two decades later was sung to mourn the passing of Luther himself in 1546.[21] Some hymnals included it in among funeral hymns, as did Luther's in his *Christliche Geseng Lateinische und Deudsch zum Begrebnis* (Wittenberg, 1542). The 1529/1533 Wittenberg congregational hymnal included it as a Psalm-hymn,[22] as did later editions and other hymnals, such as Lucas Osiander's influential cantional *Füfftzig Geistliche Lieder und Psalmen* (Nuremberg, 1586). According to the Rostock hymnal of 1525 it was sung before the sermon in north Germany.[23] Liturgical orders issued in Nuremberg in 1526 and Halle in 1543 direct that it was to be sung as a congregational Introit at the beginning of worship.[24] In the church order of Naumberg, 1537-38, it was designated the Gradual hymn, sung between the Epistle and Gospel, for the Twenty-second Sunday after Trinity,[25] and later hymnals assigned *Aus tiefer Not* as a *de tempore* Graduallied for other Sundays.[26]

Aus tiefer Not was also sung as a primary catechism hymn, since it expounded generally the doctrine of justification and specifically paralleled an important section of Luther's Small Catechism. In 1529, at the end of his treatment of baptism, the fourth main part of the catechism, he included "A Short Method of Confessing."[27] This was replaced in 1531 by "How Plain People Are to Be Taught to Confess,"[28] which thereafter was commonly regarded as the separate, fifth section of the catechism. Such confession was simultaneously a realization of the sacrament of baptism and a preparation for the sacrament of the altar. Luther explained that

Confession consists of two parts. One that we confess our sins. The other is that we receive the absolution, that is, forgiveness, from the confessor as

Figure 9.2. Alto Part Book of Walter's *Chorgesangbuch* (Worms, 1525) — Cover and Alto part of *Aus tiefer Not.*

from God himself and by no means doubt but firmly believe that our sins are thereby forgiven before God in heaven.[29]

Table 9.1. *Aus tiefer Not* as a *de tempore* Gradual hymn

Author/Editor	Short title	Place	Date	Sunday(s)
Spangenberg	*Cantiones . . . Kirchengesenge*	Magdeburg	1545	Septuagesima
Keuchenthal	*Kirchen-Gesenge*	Wittenberg	1573	Trinity 21
Selnecker	*Christliche Psalmen*	Leipzig	1587	Trinity 11
Schein	*Cantional*	Leipzig	1627	Trinity 11 & 21

Luther continues at some length to say that the Commandments must be allowed to condemn the sinner, and the confessor should pronounce God's promise of forgiveness and declare God's Word from Scripture. Since all this is paralleled in Luther's *Aus tiefer Not,* it was frequently sung in connection with this part of the catechism, along with a number of other penitential hymns. Thus in Bartholomäus Rosinus's popular *Kurtze Fragen und Antwort über die Sechs Häupstücke deß heiligen Catechismi D. Martini Lutheri* (1581):

This fifth main part of the holy catechism with its questions and answers the children at home can rehearse and practice after breakfast and after the *Gratias* has been said. Following the evening meal, and after the *Gratias* has been said, the children at the table can pray out of "David's Catechism" Psalm 51 . . . , and thereafter sing from the hymnal the hymn by Erhart Hegenwalt, *Erbarm dich mein, O Herre Gott* [Psalm 51]. . . . Or from Luther's hymnbook, *Aus tiefer Not schrei ich zu dir.*[30]

That Hegenwalt's penitential Psalm-hymn was given before Luther's reflects the wider general use of *Aus tiefer Not.* Thus some hymnals follow Rosinus in specifying Hegenwalt's version of Psalm 51 first, before *Aus tiefer Not,* as an appropriate hymn associated with this section of the catechism, as for example, in the *Eisenachishes Gesangbuch* (Eisenach, 1673), the hymnal that Johann Sebastian Bach knew in his youth.[31] But this was only following the long-standing tradition of linking these two hymns together, Luther's *Aus tiefer Not* and Hegenwalt's *Erbarm dich mein:* beginning with the Loersfelt *Enchiridion* (Erfurt, 1524), they were closely associated together, appearing in sequence one after the other as catechism hymns in many hymnals, and continuing into the eighteenth century when they often appeared together in a "Busse" or "Busse und Beichte" (Repentance and Confession) section which by then had become customary. One example is the confession and communion hymnal, published in Nuremberg in 1724;[32] another is the so-called *Schemelli-Gesangbuch* of 1736, for which Johann Sebastian Bach was the musical editor.[33] However, when Bach came to compose his *Clavierübung III*, published in 1739, a work that included two sets of chorale preludes on the six catechism hymns — one small-scale and the other large-scale, corresponding to Luther's "Small" and "Large" Catechisms — he used *Aus tiefer Not* for the fifth section of the catechism as being the primary Lutheran hymn on repentance and faith.[34]

It is this hymn, one of the first Lutheran hymns to have been written, that expounds the essence of Reformation faith and theology, that the response to the Law and the Gospel is not "do acts of penance" but "repent and believe." It is therefore a hymn that cannot be omitted from a Lutheran hymnal if it is to be authentically "Lutheran."

CHAPTER 10

Jesus Christus unser Heiland

The Hymn of St. John Huss improved

[1.] Jhesus Christus, unser Heiland,
der von uns den Gottes zorn wand,
durch das bitter leiden sein
halff er uns aus der helle pein.

Jesus Christ, our blessed Savior,
turned away God's wrath forever;
by his passion, death to quell,
he saved us from the pains of hell.

[2.] Das wir nymmer des vergessen,
gab er uns seyn leib zu essen
verborgen im brot so klayn,
und zu tryncken seyn blut im weyn.

Forget not his love undying,
he, his precious food supplying,
gives his body with the bread
and with the wine the blood he shed.

[3.] Wer sich wil zu dem tisch machen,
der hab wol acht auff seyn sachen.
Wer unwirdig hye zu geet,
für das leben den tod empfeht.

Who to this table now repaireth
should take heed how he prepareth;
for if he does not believe,
then death for life he shall receive.

[4.] Du solt Gott den vatter preysen,
das er dich so wol wolt speysen
unnd für deyne missethat
in den tod seyn son geben hat.

Praise the Father, God from heaven
who to us such food hath given
and for misdeeds we have done,
gave unto death his only Son.

[5.] Du solt glauben und nicht wancken,
das ayn speyse sey der krancken
den jr hertz von sünden schweer
und für angst ist betrübet seer.

Believe that, with faith unshaken,
this meal by the sick is taken,
sinners who are sore distress'd,
with hearts that long for peace and rest.

[6.] Solch groß gnad und barmhertzigkayt
sucht ain hertz in grosser arbayt;
ist dir wol, so bleyb davon,
das du nicht kriegest bösen lon.

To such grace and mercy turneth
everyone that truly mourneth;
Art thou well? avoid this board,
lest judgment is upon thee poured.

[7.] Er spricht selber: kompt jr armen
last mich uber euch erbarmen;
kayn artzt ist dem starcken not
seyn kunst wirdt an jm gar ain spot.

Christ says: "Come, all ye that labor,
and receive my grace and favor;
they who feel no want nor ill
need no physician's help nor skill.

[8.] Hetst du dir was kund erwerben,
was dürfft denn ich für dich sterben?
Diser tisch auch dir nicht gilt,
so du selber dyr helffen wildt.

Useless for thee is my passion
if thy works can earn salvation.
This table is not meet for thee
if thine own helper thou wilt be."

[9.] Glaubstu das von hertzen grunde
und bekennest mit dem munde,
So bist du recht wol geschickt,
und die speyse deyn seel erquickt.

Make this truth thy heart's profession,
make this truth thy mouth's confession;
come then as a welcome guest,
partake and let thy soul be blest.

[10.] Die frucht soll auch nicht außbleyben:
deynen nächsten solt du lieben,
Das er deyn genyssen kan,
wie deyn Got hat an dir gethan.[1]

Fruit of faith should thus be showing
that to neighbors thou art loving;
so shall they both know and see
what thy Lord God hath done in thee.[2]

The hymn *Jesus Christus, unser Heiland, der von uns Gotteszorn wandt* appeared in three hymnal collections issued in 1524: Walter's *Chorgesangbuch,* published in Wittenberg, and the two Erfurt *Enchiridia.* It also appeared as a broadside, issued without date or place of printing/publication, almost certainly a reprint of an earlier, no longer extant Wittenberg broadside.[3] All four sources carry the same heading: "Das Lied S. Johannes Hus gebessert"[4] (The hymn of Johannes Huss improved). The hymn in question is the Latin *Jesus Christus nostra salus,* written either in the late fourteenth or early fifteenth century and sung by the Bohemian Brethren, the followers of Huss. The attribution of Huss as the author probably arose because the first eight stanzas are an acrostic on the name I-O-H-A-N-N-E-S. Later scholarship assigned authorship to Johann von Jenstein,[5] but Luther accepted the common attribution to Huss. It seems likely that the original hymn comprised the eight acrostic stanzas, which were expanded by a further two, together with a refrain that was sung after every two stanzas. The earliest extant manuscript, dating from 1410, gives the hymn as follows:

1. Jesus Christus, nostra salus,
   quod reclamat omnis malus,
   nobis in sui memoriam
   dedit in panis hostiam.

   Jesus Christ, our blest Redeemer
   (truth denied by proud blasphemer),
   gave his flesh in wondrous fashion
   in remembrance of his passion.

2. O quam sanctus panis iste,
   tu solus es, Jesu Christe,
   panis cibus sacramentum,
   quo nunquam maius inventum.

   O how pure this Bread, and holy!
   it is Thou, Christ Jesus, wholly,
   sacramental bread of heaven
   here is found and to us given.

3. Hoc donum suavitatis
    caritasque deitatis,
    virtus et eukaristia,
    communionis gracia.

    'Tis a gift, the best, the sweetest,
    pledge of love divine, completest,
    Eucharist of mighty power,
    grace's channel, heavenly dower.

4. Ave deitatis forma,
    dei unitas norma,
    in te quisque delectatur,
    qui te fide speculatur.

    Hail, thou divinity's true form,
    God united in thee, the norm,
    whoever in thee delighteth
    then the truth by faith observeth.

5. Non es panis, sed es deus
    homo liberator reus,
    qui in cruce pependisti
    et in carne defecisti.

    'Tis not bread, 'tis thy Creator,
    incarnate, our Liberator,
    who on the cross suspended high,
    suffered, our flesh to purify.

6. Non augetur consecratus,
    nec consumptus fit mutatus,
    nec divisus in fractura,
    plenus deus in statura.

    God's not changed by consecration
    nor subject to alteration,
    nor divided in the fraction
    but fully God in this action.

7. Esca digna angelorum,
    pietatis lux sanctorum,
    lex moderna comprobavit,
    quod antiqua figuravit.

    Manna, angels satisfying,
    pious light to saints supplying,
    law now visible and revealed,
    what of old was hidden and veiled.

8. Salutare medicamen,
    peccatorum relevamen,
    pasce nos, a malis leva,
    duc post ubi est lux ewa.

    Medicine that brings salvation,
    and for sins grants absolution,
    relieves our ills, also feeds us,
    and to light eternal leads us.

9. Ath quam magna tu fecisti,
    dum te Christe impensisti,
    panis et vini specie
    apparentum in facie.

    O how magnificent the grace
    by which, O Christ, thou interlace
    thyself within the bread and wine,
    common things thus made divine.

10. Caro cibus, sanguis vinum,
    est mysterium divinum.
    Huic sit laus et gloria
    in seculorum secula.

    Flesh as food, and blood as wine,
    it is the mystery divine.
    Thus praise and glory let there be
    now and in all eternity.

℞: Eja jubilate,
    voces attolite
    nostro creatori,
    symphoniis
    ympnidiacis
    Christum zelate.[6]

    Eya, rejoice,
    thy voices raise
    to our Creator,
    sound together
    and sing hymns
    zealously to Christ.[7]

The hymn was translated into Czech during the fifteenth century, and was sung by the Bohemian Brethren to the same melody associated with the Latin text. However, this vernacular version comprised the ten stanzas without the refrain.[8] Similarly, the Latin form that circulated in Germany around the same time also did not include the refrain,[9] which perhaps explains why Luther modeled his eucharistic hymn on the ten stanzas without the repeated refrain.

When Luther's German is compared with the Latin it becomes clear that his "improvement" of the original was more in the nature of substantial rewriting rather than a revised translation. Indeed, apart from the first line of the first stanza, and detectable echoes found in other stanzas (notably stanzas 2 and 4), it is essentially a new hymn, but written in the same meter and same number of stanzas as the "Hussite" model.[10] While the original Latin hymn focuses on the Eucharist, Christ's presence within it, with an unambiguous stress on the important *utraquist* concern of the Hussite movement — reception of both consecrated bread and wine, *sub utraque specie* — the imagery remains within a late-medieval mindset. In contrast, Luther's hymn expresses a different and broader theological understanding of the Lord's Supper as the surety of God's grace in forgiveness: the Supper is grounded in the Passion of Christ (st. 1-2, 4, 6); it is to be received by faith (st. 3, 5); and Christ's invitation to participate is expressed in scriptural paraphrase, which simultaneously warns against justification by works (st. 7-8). What is necessary to come to the sacrament is faith by which God's forgiveness in Christ is received; what is necessary to depart from the sacrament is love, the overflowing love of Christ, the fruit of faith, that is extended to others (st. 9-10). These were the themes of Luther's preaching on the First Sunday in Lent, Palm Sunday, and Maundy Thursday, 1524,[11] and the parallels are not only in similar concepts but also in specific words and expressions. It therefore seems likely that Luther wrote this hymn during the early months of 1524.[12]

Luther had a high regard for Huss, whom he regarded as the author of the Latin hymn on which his was based, and a number of German hymns of the Bohemian Brethren were taken over in the early Lutheran hymnals, among them the Passion hymn *Christus, der uns selig macht* and the funeral hymn *Nun laßt uns den Leib begraben*, translated by Michael Weiße.[13] Huss was an icon for Luther who frequently referred to the Czech reformer as the forerunner of his work. Fundamental in Luther's understanding of the Lord's Supper was the Word of Scripture, which has to be taken in its straightforward meaning. As he was to declare unequivocally against Zwingli at Marburg in 1529, to qualify the meaning of a passage of Scripture as figurative rather than actual undermines its authority and validity. In dealing with the same issue the year before the Marburg colloquy he made particular reference to Huss in his *Confession Concerning Christ's Supper* (1528):

> You may be sure that it is pure imagination when anyone says that this word "is" means the same as "represents." . . . We Germans customarily

prefix "real" or "true" or "a second" or "new," and we say, "You are a real dog," "The monks are real Pharisees," "The nuns are real daughters of the Moabites," "Christ is the real Solomon." Again, "Luther is a second Huss," "Zwingli is a second Korah," "Oecolampadius is a new Abiram." . . . And it is precisely the same if I say, "Luther is Huss," "Luther is a second Huss," "Luther is a real Huss," "Luther is a new Huss." . . . It does not sound right or ring true if I say, "Luther signifies Huss"; rather, "He is a Huss." In such expressions we are speaking of an essence, what a person is and not what he represents. . . .[14]

Notwithstanding his respect for Huss, when he came to write this Lord's Supper hymn, as indicated above, Luther followed his own understanding of the Sacrament rather than the details of the hymn *Jesus Christus nostra salus,* which he thought Huss had written. The hymn *Jesus Christus unser Heiland* of 1524 therefore contains echoes in substance and content of his various treatises on the Sacrament of the Altar written in previous years, demonstrating an underlying consistency of his thinking.

The ten stanzas can be divided into two unequal sections: the first comprises stanzas 1 to 8, which deal with the foundation, essence, and use of the sacrament; the second is formed by stanzas 9 and 10, a summary of the consequences of the Lord's Supper for the individual believer. The first section can be further divided into four main themes. First, stanzas 1 and 8 present the work of the cross as the foundation of the meaning of the Supper, together with the corollary that anyone who substitutes his or her own efforts as the basis for communion with God has no place at this table. Thus in his *Confession Concerning Christ's Supper* (1528), Luther wrote: "The passion of Christ occurred but once on the cross. But whom would it benefit if it were not distributed, applied and put to use? And how could it be put to use and distributed except through Word and sacrament?"[15]

Second, stanzas 2 and 7 deal with the presence of Christ in the Supper and the "for you" aspect of reception, that Christ gives his body and blood in bread and wine. In the *Small Catechism* he wrote:

What is the Sacrament of the Altar? Answer: It is the true body and blood of our Lord Jesus Christ under the bread and wine, instituted by Christ himself for us Christians to eat and drink. . . . What is the benefit of such eating and drinking? Answer: The words "given for you" and "shed [for you] for the forgiveness of sins" show us that forgiveness of sin, life, and salvation are given to us in the Sacrament through these words, because where there is forgiveness of sin, there is also life and salvation.[16]

In the *Large Catechism* he expressed it thus:

> Now, what is the Sacrament of the Altar? Answer: It is the true body and blood of the Lord Christ, in and under the bread and wine, which we Christians are commanded by Christ's word to eat and drink. And just as we said of Baptism that it is not mere water, so we say here, too, that the Sacrament is bread and wine, but not mere bread and wine such as is served at the table. Rather, it is the bread and wine set within God's Word and bound to it.[17]

Significantly, Christ's invitation of Matthew 11:28, which is the basis for stanza 7, is connected with the Lord's Supper in his later writings, for example, in the *Large Catechism:*

> For in this Sacrament he offers us all the treasures he brought from heaven for us, to which he most graciously invites us in other places, as when he says in Matt. 11[:28], "Come to me, all you that are weary and are carrying heavy burdens, and I will give you rest."[18]

Third, faith leads to the response of praise and thanksgiving (stanzas 3 and 4), because it receives mercy, in contrast to "unfaith" that receives judgment (stanzas 5 and 6). In his Admonition Concerning the Sacrament of the Body and Blood of our Lord (1530), Luther wrote:

> This is the primary benefit and fruit which accrues to you from the use of the Sacrament that you are reminded of such favor and grace and that your faith and love are stimulated, renewed, and strengthened so that you might not reach the point of forgetting or despising your dear Savior and his bitter suffering and the great, manifold, eternal need and death out of which he rescued you . . . in contrast, unbelief is a dangerous, daily, incessant devil who wants to tear us away from our dear Savior and his suffering by both force and deceit. It requires toil and trouble daily to practice, stimulate, and exercise such faith so that we do not forget Christ's suffering and benefit.[19]

The problem of eating and drinking to one's judgment became a particularly difficult pastoral problem in Lutheranism with the rise of Pietism in the seventeenth century. In that setting, purity of life and true contrition became the marks of the worthy. In some instances, reception of the sacrament outside of confirmation and just before death was seen as an indicator of spiritual pride. In contrast, Luther's hymn indicates that unworthiness arose from the claim to be worthy (by one's works or merits). Luther's position here ("art thou well? Avoid this board!") is reflected in the later discussion in the *Formula of Concord, Solid Declaration,* VII: "True and worthy guests . . . are the Christians who are weak in faith, fragile and troubled, who are terrified in their hearts by the immensity and number of their sins and think that they are not worthy of this precious treasure and of the benefits of Christ because of their great impurity. . . ."[20]

Fourth, in stanzas 9 and 10 there is the summary statement that we are to partake in the Supper by faith and then to express the fruits of faith in love to others, as in Luther's well-known post-communion collect, "We give thanks to thee Almighty God, that thou hast refreshed us with this thy salutary gift; and we beseech thy mercy to strengthen us through the same in faith toward thee, and in fervent love among us all."[21] Thus, in the paragraph following the one cited above from the Admonition Concerning the Sacrament, Luther continues:

Where such faith is continually refreshed and renewed, there the heart is also at the same time refreshed anew in its love of the neighbor and is made strong and equipped to do all good works and to resist sin and all temptations of the devil. Since faith cannot be idle, it must demonstrate the fruits of love by doing good and avoiding evil. . . .[22]

In the same treatise Luther speaks about the sung portions of the Mass as underscoring the keynote of thanksgiving:

As a result of such an understanding I believe that many hymns were included and retained in the Mass which deal with thanking and praising [God] in a wonderful and excellent way, as for example, the Gloria in excelsis, the Alleluia, the Creed, the Preface, the Sanctus, the Benedictus, and the Agnus Dei. In these various parts you find nothing about a sacrifice but only praise and thanks. Therefore we have also kept them in our [evangelical] Mass . . . whatever is publicly sung by the choir or the multitude is essentially a good thing and a hymn of praise.[23]

Luther's argument in this paragraph was that it was the publicly sung items of the Mass that preserved the integrity of the unreformed rite, in contrast to the secret prayers of the priest that contained the unacceptable sacrificial language and content. He therefore mentioned only the Latin "hymns" of the traditional mass. But in another context he probably would also have listed German hymns among "whatever is publicly sung by the choir or multitude." These hymns effectively became part of the Lutheran ordinary, since they were commonly sung during the distribution of communion: in the *Formula missae* (1523) Luther designated his revised version of the old folk-hymn *Gott sei gelobet*,[24] and in the *Deutsche Messe* (1526) added *Jesus Christus unser Heiland* and the German Agnus Dei, *Christe, du Lamm Gottes*,[25] as distribution hymns. In the subsequent Lutheran church orders, especially those drawn up by Johannes Bugenhagen, these three were listed as the common communion hymns.[26] In time *Jesus Christus unser Heiland* became the primary communion hymn and also the leading hymn associated with the teaching of the main section of the catechism dealing with the sacrament of the altar.[27]

CHAPTER 11

Nun freut euch, lieben Christen gmein

A Fine Spiritual Song, How a Sinner Comes to Grace

[1.] Nun freut euch, lieben Christen gmeyn
und last uns frolich springen.
Das wyr getrost und all ynn eyn
Mit lust und liebe singen,
Was Gott an uns gewendet hat
Und seine susse wunder that.
Gar theur hat ers erworben.

Dear Christians, one and all, rejoice,
with exultation springing,
and, with united heart and voice
and holy rapture singing,
Proclaim the wonders God hath done,
how his right arm the victory won;
what price our ransom cost him.

[2.] Dem Teüffel ich gefangen lag,
Im todt was ich verloren.
Mein sünd mich quellet nacht und tag,
Darinn ich was geboren.
Ich fiel auch ymmer tieffer drein.
Es was kain guts am leben mein.
Die sünd hatt mich besessen.

Fast bound in Satan's chains I lay,
death brooded darkly o'er me,
sin was my torment night and day;
in sin my mother bore me.
But daily deeper still I fell;
my life became a living hell,
so firmly sin possessed me.

[3.] Mein gute werk die golten nicht;
Es was mit jn verdorben.
Der frey will hasset gots gericht;
Er was zum gut gestorben.
Die angst mich zu versweyfeln trayb,
Das nichts denn sterben bey mi blayb.
Zur hellen must ich sincken.

My own good works all came to naught,
no grace or merit gaining;
free will against God's judgment fought,
dead to all good remaining.
My fears increased till sheer despair
left only death to be my share;
the pangs of hell I suffered.

[4.] Da jamert gott in ewigkait
Mein ellend über massen.
Er dacht an sein Barmhertzigkeit,
Er wolt mir helffen lassen.
Er wandt zu mit das vatter hertz.
Es was bey jm fürwar kain schertz.
Es ließ seyn bestes kosten.

But God had seen my wretched state
before the world's foundation,
and mindful of his mercies great,
he planned for my salvation.
He turned to me the Father's heart;
he did not choose the easy part
but gave his dearest treasure.

[5.] Er sprach zu seynem lieben son:
"Die zeyt ist hye zurbarmen.
Far hyn, meyns herzten werde kron,
Und sey das hayl dem armen.
Und hilff jm auß der sünden nodt.
Erwürg vor jn den bittern todt,
Und laß jn mit dir leben."

[6.] Der son dem vatter ghorsam ward:
Er kam zu mir auff erden
Von ainer Junckfrau rayn und zart.
Er solt mein brüder werden.
Gar haymlich fürt er sein gewalt:
Dr gieng in meiner armen gstalt.
Den Teüffel wolt er fahen.

[7.] Er sprach zu mir: "Halt dich an mich,
Es soll dir yetzt gelingen.
Ich gib mich selber gantz für dich;
Da will ich für dich ringen.
Denn ich bin dein und du bist mein,
Und wa ich bleyb, da soltu seyn.
Uns soll der feynd nicht schayden.

[8.] Vergiessen wirt er mir mein blutt,
Darzu mein leben rauben.
Das leyd ich alles dir zu gutt;
Das halt mit festem glauben.
Den todt verschlingt das leben mein;
Mein unschuld tregt die sünde dein.
Da bistu sälig worden.

[9.] Gen hymel zu dem vatter mein
Far ich von disem leben.
Da will ich seyn der mayster dein.
Den gayst will ich dir geben.
Der dich jm trübnus trösten soll
Und lernen mich erkennen wol
Und in der warhayt laytten.

[10.] Was ich gethon hab und gelert,
Das soltu thun und leeren,
Damit das reych Gots werd gemert
Zu lob und seynen eeren.
Und hüt dich vor der menschen satz,
Davon verdürbt der Edle schatz.
Das laß ich dir zu letze."¹

God spoke to his beloved Son:
"It's time to have compassion.
Then go, bright jewel of my crown,
and bring to all salvation.
From sin and sorrow set them free,
slay bitter death for them that they
may live with you for ever."

This Son obeyed his Father's will,
was born of a virgin mother;
and God's good pleasure to fulfill,
he came to be my brother.
His royal power disguised he bore,
a servant's form, like mine, he wore
to lead the devil captive.

To me he said: "Stay close to me,
I am your rock and castle.
Your ransom I myself will be;
for you I strive and wrestle;
for I am yours, and you are mine
and where I am you may remain;
the foe shall not divide us.

Though he will shed my precious blood,
of life me thus bereaving,
all this I suffer for your good;
be steadfast and believing.
Life will from death the victory win;
my innocence shall bear your sin;
and you are blest for ever.

Now to My Father I depart,
from earth to heaven ascending,
and, heavenly wisdom to impart,
the Holy Spirit sending;
in trouble he will comfort you,
and teach you always to be true
and into truth shall guide you.

What I on earth have done and taught,
guide all your life and teaching;
so shall God's kingdom thus be wrought
and God's praise be unending.
But watch lest foes with base alloy
the heavenly treasure should destroy;
This final word I leave you."²

Nun freut euch, lieben Christen gmein was one of the earliest hymns Luther wrote. It probably originally circulated as a no longer extant Wittenberg broadside, since there was an Augsburg broadside issued in 1524 that must have been a reprint of a Wittenberg original.³ In the Nuremberg *Achtlieder-buch* (1524), the small booklet containing eight hymns reprinted from pre-existing broadsides, the year "1523" appears at the end of the text,[4] indicating that it was written toward the end of the year when Luther and his colleagues were authoring what was to become the basic corpus of Lutheran hymnody. There has been much discussion about the origins of the hymn, especially the suggestion that it was based on an earlier prototype, but the specific content marks it out as being very different from any suggested model and it is generally regarded as an original hymn, one of Luther's finest.[5]

Its immediate popularity is underscored by the different tunes assigned to it. In 1524 it was associated with no less than three different melodies: the Nuremberg *Achtliederbuch* gave the sturdy tune, an adaptation of an earlier model, that became the primary melody for the hymn;[6] the Erfurt *Enchiridia* assigned it to the melody *Es ist das Heil,* another hymn that expounds the doctrine of justification;[7] and Johann Walter composed another tune for his *Chorgesangbuch.*[8] The Wittenberg hymnal of 1529/33 included another melody, also an adaptation of an earlier tune, later associated with the text *Es ist gewißlich an der Zeit.*[9] Another indication of the hymn's popularity are the various hymns that either parodied or quoted some of its content, among them Nicolas von Amsdorf's *Nun freut euch, lieber bürger gmein* (ca. 1540) and Paul Gerhardt's *Nun freut euch hier und überall* (1656).

Luther's use of the first person singular implies an autobiographical reflection, in much the same way that Charles Wesley's "And Can It Be" contemplates what its author called his "experience of justification," except that Luther's hymn is more objective than Wesley's subjective verse, and focuses on the work of Christ as the ground of faith rather than on the emotions of believing.

As a confession of faith this hymn stands alongside Luther's great Reformation writings that deal with the doctrine of justification and the distinction between Law and Gospel. It is a hymnic expression of Pauline theology and is in a sense a commentary on the first eight chapters of Romans. Following the opening imperatives, stanza 1 picks up the theme of Romans 1:16-17; the next two stanzas (st. 2-3) summarize the content of Romans 1:18 through 3:20, and the whole of chapter 7; stanzas 4-6 focus on the primary substance of Romans 3:21 through to the end of chapter 6; and the remaining four stanzas (st. 7-10) crystalize Paul's teaching in Romans chapter 8. Also to be observed is the Trinitarian theology that undergirds the hymn, but in a way that is different from such Trinitarian hymns as *Wir glauben all an einen Gott* and *Gott der Vater wohn uns bei.*[10] Here Luther was following the substance of Paul's first eight chapters rather than the classic creedal formulations of the doctrine. Thus, after the exposition of the meaning of redemption, achieved by Christ's merits rather than our own works (st. 1-3), the following stanzas explicate the synergy of the Godhead in redemption, in contrast to any suggested synergy of the saved in their salvation: God the Father loved and planned redemption (st. 4-5), God the Son accomplished it (st. 6-8), and God the Holy Spirit applies it (st. 9-10).

That Luther should use the structure of Romans as the basis for a hymn on the Christian life is hardly surprising. On the one hand, Philipp Melanchthon had lately published his summary of Christian theology, the *Loci communes theologici* of 1521/22, which uses Romans for its outline of topics,[11] and Luther had praised this work: there is "no better book after the Holy Scripture."[12] On the other hand, Luther had himself lectured on Romans in 1515-1516, and more recently, influenced by Melanchthon's *Loci,* he had written the lengthy preface to Romans for his translation of the New Testament (1522). In this preface he wrote: "This epistle is really the chief part of the New Testament, and it is truly the purest gospel. It is worthy not only that every Christian should know it word for word, by heart, but also that he should occupy himself with it every day, as the daily bread of the soul. We can never read it or ponder over it too much; for the more we deal with it, the more precious it becomes and the better it tastes."[13]

The confessional nature of the hymn in epitomizing the essence of evangelical faith and life is reflected in the various headings given to the hymn during Luther's lifetime (see Table 11.1),[14] and also in the way it was regarded in later Lutheranism. For example, in the preface to his comprehensive hymnal, *Geistliche Singe-Kunst, und ordentliche verfassetes vollständiges Gesangbuch* (Leipzig, 1671-72), Johann Olearius wrote:

> Luther's beautiful hymn, *Nun freut euch lieben Christen gemein,* is an excellent and comforting summary of the totality of the evangelical [= Lutheran] foundation of faith, and within which is thus found the whole of Theology, Christology, and Anthropology, or, what we should know from the word of God about God, about Christ and our wretchedness and its solution in the kingdom of grace though the merit of Christ, as well as the certainty of the eternal joyful kingdom.[15]

In the Wittenberg hymnal of 1529/33 *Nun freut euch* appeared among the catechism hymns, immediately following *Wir glauben.* The first five hymns in the embryonic catechism section were:

> *Dies sind die heiligen zehn Gebot* [Law]
> *Mensch, willst du leben seliglich* [Law]
> *Mitten wir im Leben sind* [Effect of Law/Repentance]

Table 11.1. Headings of *Nun freut euch* published during Luther's lifetime

Place of Publication	Year	Heading
Nuremberg	1524	A Christian song of Doctor Martin Luther comprehending the inexpressible grace of God and right faith
Erfurt	1524	There follows a handsome evangelical song which one sings before the sermon
Leipzig	1530	A song of the total Christian life
Wittenberg	1533	A fine spiritual song, how a sinner comes to grace
Leipzig	1545	A song of thanks for the highest blessings God in Christ has rendered us

Wir glauben all an einen Gott [Creed/Gospel]
Nun freut euch, lieben Christen gmein [Effect of Faith/Law and Gospel/
Justification][16]

In the same way that *Mitten wir im Leben sind* was a response to the Law, as given in the two Ten Commandments hymns that preceded it, so *Nun freut euch* was a response to the Gospel as expounded in the creedal hymn *Wir glauben*. But this sequence may be as much liturgical as it is catechetical. In the *Deutsche Messe* of 1526 *Wir glauben* was sung after the Gospel and before the sermon.[17] The heading of *Nun freut euch* in the Erfurt *Enchiridia* of 1524 (repeated in later imprints) indicates that it was customarily sung before the sermon (see Table 11.1 above), that is, after the creedal hymn *Wir glauben,* which is exactly the sequence in the Wittenberg hymnal of 1529/33. The implication is that *Nun freut euch* was commonly sung as a pulpit hymn in Wittenberg.

This liturgical use appears confirmed by its position in the Bapst *Gesangbuch* of 1545. The first section of this hymnal is devoted to the hymns of Luther and generally follows the earlier Wittenberg hymnals but with some additions and changes in sequence. First are given his church year hymns, from Advent to Trinity (Nos. 1-13); these are followed by the catechism hymns, given in the same topical sequence of Luther's catechisms (Nos. 14-21); next are his Psalm-hymns (Nos. 22-28). These are followed by a series of liturgical hymns, though there is no heading to this effect:

[29]   The German Sanctus: *Jesaia dem Propheten*
[30]   *Erhalt uns, Herr, bei deinem Wort*
[31]   *Verleih uns Frieden gnädiglich*
[32/33] *Nun freut euch,* set to two different melodies

[34]   *Sie ist mir lieb die werte Magd*
[35]   *Mitten wir im leben sind*
[36]   German Te Deum, *Herr Gott dich loben wir*
[37]   German Litany
[38]   Latin Litany
[39]   *Ein neues Lied wir heben an*

Most of these items had obvious liturgical uses. No. 29, the German Sanctus, first appeared in the *Deutsche Messe* (1526), which directed that it should be sung during the distribution of communion;[18] the German Sanctus also concluded the Lord's Supper section of catechism hymns in the Wittenberg hymnal of 1543/44. Nos. 30 and 31 were customarily sung together, one after the other, at the end of the Lord's Supper following the benediction.[19] Nos. 36-38 are recognizable liturgical items, and No. 39, the last item in the catechism section of the 1529/33 Wittenberg hymnal, is in keeping with the penitential orientation of the two litanies, since it deals with the way of the cross and martyrdom. *Nun freut euch* (Nos. 32/33) is probably included here as a pulpit hymn sung before the sermon, which had been its use hitherto. The fact that two tunes are given might imply that it was the regular pulpit hymn and the alternative melodies gave the opportunity of variety if the hymn was sung frequently throughout the church year. If this is correct, then Nos. 34 and 35 may have been intended as alternative pulpit hymns: *Sie ist mir lieb die werte Magd* is headed "A Song of the Holy Christian Church, from the 12th chapter of Revelation,"[20] and therefore perhaps appropriate for the Trinity season; *Mitten wir im leben sind*, another hymn that was included within the catechism section of the Wittenberg hymnal of 1529/33, is suitable for penitential seasons (as well as for funerals), since it is partly based on the Lenten antiphon *Media vita.*

Catechism hymns, therefore, were as much integral components of the liturgy as they were teaching tools by which the substance of the Christian faith was taught. For example, *Wir glauben* effectively became the common confession of faith in the vernacular, sung by the whole liturgical assembly at worship, as well as being sung as a catechism hymn. This liturgical catechesis is underscored by the statement in Art. XXIV of the Augsburg Confession: in the evangelical Mass,

> The people are instructed more regularly and with greatest diligence concerning the holy Sacrament. . . . Moreover, no noticeable changes have been made in the public celebration of the Mass, except that in certain places German hymns are sung alongside Latin responses for the instruc-

tion and exercise of the people. For after all, all ceremonies should serve the purpose of teaching the people what they need to know about Christ.[21]

Similarly, as has been noted in earlier chapters in this section, most of the catechism hymns were also sung as Graduallieder, hymns assigned for specific days in the church calender and sung between the Epistle and Gospel. These pericopes were in themselves catechetical: from Advent through Pentecost the focus was on the life and work of Christ; throughout the Trinity (now Pentecost) season the concentration was on the life of Christians in Christ. The catechetical function of the church year is underlined by Luther's two series of sermons on the annual cycle of pericopes, one "Large" and the other "Small," corresponding to his two catechisms: the *Kirchenpostille* parallels the *Large Catechism,* in that both were intended for the pastors to use, and the *Hauspostille* is analogous to the *Small Catechism,* since both are manuals primarily intended for home use.

Catechism sermons, as they developed over the following generations, were not simply expositions of the main parts of Luther's *Small Catechism,* together with the morning and evening prayers, graces at table, and the table of duties. The catechesis also included other related matters, such as the doctrine of Scripture, and the primary teaching enshrined in the pericopes of the church year. For example, Philipp Jacob Spener, notwithstanding his suspect understanding of Lutheranism from his Pietist perspective, engaged in such catechetical preaching. He was superintendent and pastor in Frankfurt am Main between 1666 and 1686, during which time he placed great stress on teaching the catechism. Thus in the *exordia,* the introductory sections, of his Sunday morning sermons he included expositions of the relevant passages of the catechism that would be the subject of the *Kinderlehre* following Vespers on Sunday afternoons. In 1686 he was called to Dresden as the Oberhofprediger, the most influential ministerial office in Lutheran Germany, and three years later these *exordia* were published as *Kurtze Catechismus-Predigten, Darinnen Die fünff Haupt-Stück, aus dem Catechismo . . . einfältig erkläret werden* (Frankfurt am Main: Zunner, 1689).[22] After exactly one hundred sermons on the substance of the catechism there are a further fifteen sermons that expound the principal teaching of the biblical lections of the church year from Advent to Trinity.[23] Whatever the variants from the doctrinal substance and nuance of orthodox Lutheranism in these sermons, it is clear that Spener stands in the general Lutheran tradition in holding that catechesis is more than simply teaching the main parts of catechism.

Similarly, hymnodic catechesis is not confined to Luther's catechism hymns, or to other hymns on the main parts of the catechism. The hymns associated with the Sundays and festivals of the church year are especially catechetical. For example, Spener's first sermon on the church year, dealing with the Advent season, begins with a reference to Luther's Advent hymn *Nun komm der Heiden Heiland.*[24] But for Luther, and the immediate generations that followed him, all hymns, whether sung in home, school, or church, were catechetical.[25] Whether they were songs of praise and thanksgiving, or of repentance and faith, they had a double function. The people sang them to express their faith and theology but found as they sang them their hearts and minds were being formed by what they sang. This is why the *Formula of Concord,* when dealing with the doctrine of original sin (*Solid Declaration,* I), did not cite some erudite treatise on the subject but made reference to the hymn by Lazarus Spengler, *Durch Adams Fall,* as being an appropriate summary of the Lutheran understanding of the doctrine.[26]

Luther's hymns were more than sung propaganda. They had a specific catechetical function in undergirding the principal teachings of the faith. They were sung during the narrow catechesis of teaching the main parts of the catechism in church and home. But there was a broader catechetical function when these same catechism hymns were sung on particular Sundays of the church year when a vital link was made between the celebration of that Sunday and a specific part of the catechism. Similarly, when such hymns as *Wir glauben* and *Jesus Christus, unser Heiland, der von uns den Gotteszorn wandt,* were sung as the creed and during communion, an important connection was again being made between these liturgical actions and fundamental theology as expressed in the catechism.

For Luther and his Wittenberg colleagues the singing of hymns was therefore more profound than the way we tend to sing them today. We sing them for nostalgic reasons, to remind us of an earlier time in our lives. We sing them as shibboleths, identifiers — usually enshrined in a specific musical style — that marks out what kind of contemporary Christians we are. We sing them because we have always sung them, and we like the emotions they evoke, though we do not necessarily understand what it is we are singing. Or we sing them because they are new and up-to-date, and we would not want to be heard singing stuffy hymns, especially those old German ones. But such modern criteria for the singing of hymns appear very superficial when compared with how hymn-singing-as-we-know-it began in the sixteenth century.

Luther's hymns, as well as those written by his Wittenberg contemporaries, were grounded in Scripture and functioned not only as worship songs, expressing the response of faith to be sung within a liturgical context, but also as theological songs, declaring the substance of the faith. Today the emphasis is on "Christian experience," and very little is heard about the essential catechesis of hymnody. But the catechetical function of hymns has been fundamental in Lutheran theology and practice, at least, until the later eighteenth century. In contemporary Lutheran hymnals now in use this hymnic catechesis is either somewhat muted or obscured. But perhaps in the Lutheran hymnals of the twenty-first century that have yet to be edited there will be a return to Luther's understanding that through catechesis — and in this case, hymnodic catechesis — Christian experience is both created and interpreted.

PART III

Liturgico-Musical Hermeneutics & Pedagogy

CHAPTER 12

Musical Hermeneutics in Luther's Liturgical Reforms

In the substantial literature relating to his liturgical reforms, Luther has frequently been characterized as an inept, inconsistent, and conservative Reformer who was conditioned more by late medieval thought than by primitive Christianity.[1] The criticism centers on his wholesale rejection of the Canon of the mass, the Eucharistic Prayer. For example, in the *Formula missae* of 1523 he wrote:

> From here on [i.e., from the Offertory] almost everything smacks and savors of sacrifice. And the words of life and salvation [i.e., the Words of Institution] are imbedded in the midst of it all, just as the ark of the Lord once stood in the idol's temple next to Dagon. . . . Let us, therefore, repudiate everything that smacks of sacrifice, together with the entire Canon and retain only that which is pure and holy.[2]

Luther consistently worked out this agenda in both the *Formula missae* (1523) and the *Deutsche Messe* (1525/26): the *Verba Testamenti*, the Words of Institution, were given an isolated prominence with neither anamnesis nor epiclesis. The Preface was retained, but kept distinct from the *Verba* by an appropriate pause,[3] and the Sanctus was appointed to be sung during the distribution.[4] Hans-Christoph Schmidt-Lauber characterized these far-reaching alterations to the traditional structure and content of the Mass as a false development derived from Luther's theology of consecration, which had its roots in medieval thinking.[5] Frank C. Senn came to a similar conclusion: "The truncating of the Canon, therefore, is the most serious defect of Luther's eucharistic revision. . . . Whatever defects we may find in Luther's liturgical work, they were primarily medieval defects."[6] William D. Maxwell described Luther's treatment of the Canon as "negative, illogical, and subversive,"[7] and Gregory Dix dismissed the German Reformer as being unconcerned with liturgical origins, and content merely to solve contemporary problems of worship in Wittenberg.[8] All these scholars, among others, came to their conclusions with the wisdom of hindsight, but it is both unfair and unhistorical to do so without investigating Luther's own motives for his liturgical reforms.

Luther's Theological Approach to Liturgical Reform

If one approaches these reforms from the point of view of comparative liturgiology, then only one conclusion can by drawn: that Luther *was* inept, inconsistent, and conservative. However, in a valuable and timely study, Bryan Spinks has reinvestigated both Luther's liturgical reforms and later criticisms of them from the comparative liturgiology standpoint.[9] Although there are older studies that are negative in their assessment of Luther's liturgical reforms, Spinks demonstrates that much recent criticism owes its origin to Yngve Brilioth's *Eucharistic Faith and Practice: Evangelical and Catholic,* issued in English in 1930.[10] As Spinks makes clear, Brilioth came to his position from questionable premises.[11] Nevertheless, other scholars have accepted Brilioth's conclusions — that Luther's work was conservative, unclear, and lacking any constructive thought — without examining Brilioth's premises. Spinks writes: "It is clear — from phraseology, footnotes, and bibliography — that Brilioth has passed on certain conclusions about Luther's work. . . . Simply to repeat his [Brilioth's] views without reference to his criteria, and to present them as established conclusions of liturgical scholarship, is highly misleading."[12]

To understand Luther's liturgical reforms, it is necessary to evaluate them from the standpoint of his own liturgical thinking in particular and his reforming work in general. It is this theological context, neglected by many scholars, that Spinks reviews. His conclusions are quite different from the widely held Brilioth-inspired position, and reinforce another but more authentic understanding of Luther's liturgical reforms.[13]

Luther may not have been the systematic theologian that Calvin was, but that is not to suggest that his theological thinking was a disjointed collection of half-formed ideas and opinions. Certainly Luther wrote a great deal about many disparate things, but there is an impressive unity in the diversity of his theological thought. The touchstone of this unity is his understanding of the doctrine of justification by faith alone. For Luther, the heart of the Gospel is at the heart of every question of theology and every practical concern. As I have written elsewhere: "It was not that Luther was first upset by abuses in the church and as he began to tackle them discovered the gospel. No. At the beginning it was the personal problem expressed in the biblical question, 'What must I do to be saved?,' and not until Luther received the biblical answer, 'Believe on the Lord Jesus Christ,'[14] did he go on to tackle church problems."[15] As with other issues, Luther's starting point for liturgical reform was the doctrine of justification.[16] At the beginning of 1530, Luther wrote to pastors in Lübeck advising them on how they should reform the church life of the city:

> We . . . both beg and urge you most earnestly not to deal first with changes in the ritual, which changes are dangerous, but to deal with them later. You should deal first with the center of our teaching and fix in the people's minds what they must know about our justification: that is, that it is an extrinsic righteousness — indeed it is Christ's — given to us through faith which comes by grace to those who are first terrified by the Law and who, struck by the consciousness of their sins, ardently seek redemption. . . . Adequate reform of ungodly rites will come of itself, however, as soon as the fundamentals of our teaching, having been successfully communicated, have taken root in devout hearts. These devout people will at once recognize what a great abomination and blasphemy that papistic idol is, namely, the Mass and the other abuses of the sacrament, so that it is not necessary to fish in front of the net, that is, first to tear down the ritual before the righteousness of faith is understood.[17]

It was not innate conservatism but theological radicalism which lay behind Luther's approach to liturgical reform. This was neither understood by Luther's contemporaries, such as Carlstadt, whose iconoclastic attempts at liturgical reform in Wittenberg had to be reversed by Luther in 1522,[18] or by our near-contemporaries, such as William D. Maxwell, who thought that Luther's "Protestant thunder" had been neutralized by his retention of the Latin language and most of the ceremonial lights, incense, and vestments in the *Formula missae*.[19] Both failed to appreciate that for Luther the prior requirement for liturgical reform was the preaching and teaching of the doctrine of justification, and until that had been adequately done, few changes in ritual or ceremony should be made. However, such a situation should be tolerated only until the preaching of the Gospel has revealed the "abominations," which can then be removed completely.[20] It is clear that the "abominations" Luther refers to are those related to the Canon of the Mass which speak in the language of sacrifice.[21]

Here is revealed Luther's theological and antithetical understanding of the Mass. Whereas the Roman Church spoke of the Mass in terms of *sacrificium, opus bonum, meritum* — supremely expressed in the eucharistic Canon — Luther spoke in terms of *beneficium, testamentum, donum*,[22] which are clearly presented in the proclamation of the *Verba Testamenti* alone.[23] This difference was no mere semantic illusion but a theological reality. The action of the Mass in traditional thinking was of humans making an offering to God, but for Luther the movement was entirely in the other direction: God's gift is brought to us. In his Admonition Concerning the Sacrament (1530), Luther wrote:

> The art of doing this is set forth briefly and surely in these words: "Do this in remembrance of me." Learn to remember him . . . by preaching, praising, honoring, listening, and giving thanks for grace revealed in Christ. If you do that . . . you have given nothing to God, nor are you able to, but you have and receive each and everything from him, particularly eternal life and infinite righteousness of Christ. . . . For this is the true God who gives and does not receive, who helps and does not let himself be helped . . . in short, he does and gives everything, and he has the need of no one; he does all things freely out of pure grace without merit, for the unworthy and undeserving, yes, for the damned and the lost. This kind of remembrance, confession and glory he desires to have.[24]

For Luther, therefore, at any celebration of the Mass, the work of God in Christ must be given prominence in proclamation and action. The proclamation is given in the Lord's own Words of Institution, with their repeated "for you"; the action is in the distribution of bread and wine to the whole congregation, which is the response to the "for you" proclamation of the gospel. This "for you" aspect lies at the heart of Luther's understanding of the doctrine of justification, and therefore is also at the center of his thinking about the Lord's Supper:

> These words, OUR, US, FOR US, must be written in letters of gold. He who does not believe this is not a Christian.[25]

> Therefore read these words "me" and *"for me"* with great emphasis, and accustom yourself to accepting this *"me"* with a sure faith and applying it to yourself. . . . Christ did not love only Peter and Paul and give himself for them, but the same grace belongs and comes to us as to them; therefore we are included in this "me."[26]

It is for this reason that the *Verba Testamenti* were for Luther the essence of the Lord's Supper. In his Treatise on Good Works (1520), he wrote:

> It is necessary that we attend with our hearts also; and we do attend when we exercise faith in our heart. Here we must listen to the words of Christ when he institutes the Mass and says, "Take, eat; this is my body, which is given for you." In like manner he says over the cup, "Take it and all of you drink of it: this is a new everlasting testament in my blood, which is shed for you and for many for the remission of sins. Do this as oft as you do it, in remembrance of me."[27] In these words Christ has made a memorial or anniversary. . . . To it he has added a wonderful, rich, great testament in which are bequeathed and distributed not interest, money, or temporal possessions, but the forgiveness of sins, grace, and mercy unto eternal life. . . . He died with the intent that this testament become permanent and irrevocable.[28]

Here Luther is not conservatively hanging on to the remnant of a medieval understanding of consecration, but radically exposing the doctrine of justification as it is expressed in the Savior's own words. He would answer those who would charge him of not being primitive enough in his liturgical thinking by saying that the tradition of Jesus is more primitive than the tradition of the early Church:

> When Christ himself first instituted this sacrament and held the first Mass, there was no tonsure, no chasuble, no singing, no pageantry, but only thanksgiving to God and the use of the sacrament. According to this same simplicity the apostles and all Christians for a long time held Mass, until there arose the various forms and additions, by which the Romans held Mass one way, the Greeks another. And now it has finally come to this: the chief thing in the Mass has been forgotten [i.e., the *Verba Testamenti*], and nothing is remembered except the additions of men! . . . Now the nearer our Masses are to the first Mass of Christ, the better they undoubtedly are; and the further from Christ's Mass, the more dangerous.[29]

Thus anything that would undermine, obscure or nullify these *Verba* was to be removed, and in practice that meant the whole of the Canon, apart from the essential *Verba Testamenti*. Luther's understanding of these Words of Institution was that they were not words to be uttered in prayer to God, but rather words to be proclaimed[30] to the attending congregation.[31] They are therefore no longer to be kept inaudible by whispering priests, but spoken loud and clear so that all should hear,[32] and in the vernacular so that all should understand:

> In the first place, let us pay no heed to the irreligious religion which those foolish people have invented and persuaded the whole world to believe, namely, that the words of consecration have been kept secret and their use and knowledge entrusted to no one but the priests, and to them only after they have celebrated Mass. These words, after all, should fittingly have been common knowledge to all people, because faith, consolation and salvation of all people are contained in them.[33]

> The whole power of the Mass consists of the words of Christ, in which he testifies that forgiveness of sins is bestowed on all those who believe that his body is given and his blood poured out for them. This is why nothing is more important for those who go to hear Mass than to ponder these words diligently and in full faith. Unless they do this, all else they do is vain.[34]

In consequence Luther urged that the *Verba Testamenti* should be memorized by all church people and therefore included them in his *Small Catechism* of 1529:

> What is the Sacrament of the Altar? Answer: It is the true body and blood of our Lord Jesus Christ under the bread and wine instituted by Christ himself for us Christians to eat and to drink.
>
> Where is this written? Answer: The holy evangelists Matthew, Mark, and Luke, and St. Paul, write thus: "Our Lord Jesus Christ, on the night in which he was betrayed, took the bread, gave thanks, and broke it and gave it to his disciples and said, 'Take; eat; this is my body which is given for you. Do this in remembrance of me.'
>
> "In the same way also he took the cup after supper, gave thanks, and gave it to them and said, 'Take, and drink of it, all of you. This cup is the New Testament in my blood, which is shed for you for the forgiveness of sins. Do this, as often as you drink it, in remembrance of me.'"
>
> What is the benefit of such eating and drinking? Answer: The words "given for you" and "shed for you for the forgiveness of sins" show us that forgiveness of sin, life, and salvation are given to us in the sacrament through these words, because where there is forgiveness of sins, there is also life and salvation.[35]

The rejection of a Eucharistic Prayer in favor of the *Verba Testamenti* meant that there could be neither epiclesis nor anamnesis, as traditionally understood, in Luther's eucharistic forms, but they were not eliminated altogether; instead, they were theologically reinterpreted. In the *Deutsche Messe* Luther in effect brought forward the epiclesis so that it occurred earlier in the eucharistic order, as part of the ministry of the Word, rather than the ministry of the Sacrament. He called for the hymn *Nun bitten wir den Heiligen Geist* (Now let us pray to the Holy Spirit) to be sung as the Graduallied, that is, before the Gospel pericope was chanted.[36] This text in this context functioned as an epiclesis hymn,[37] an invocation of the Holy Spirit, that the worshipers should, through the action of the Spirit of God, believe and receive forgiveness offered in the Gospel. By suggesting the use of the hymn at this juncture Luther was being theologically consistent with his understanding of the sacrament as an offering — not an offering made *to* God but rather an offering *from* God who, in the proclamation of the Gospel, offers forgiveness and grace. For Luther, therefore, it was a Word-orientated, rather than an elements-orientated, epiclesis.[38]

Similarly, Luther gave a new interpretation to the concept of anamnesis. For example, in the Admonition Concerning the Sacrament (1530) he wrote:

> Christ completely separates the two matters, sacrament and remembrance [Gedenken], when he says: "Do this in remembrance of me." The sacrament is one matter, the remembrance is another matter. He says that we should use and practice the sacrament and, in addition, remember him, that is, teach, believe, and give thanks. The remembrance is indeed supposed to be a sacrifice of thanksgiving; but the sacrament itself should not be a sacrifice but a gift of God which he has given to us and which we should take and receive with thanks.[39]

The keynote of anamnesis for Luther was "eucharist," that is, the giving of thanks. He continued:

> I believe that many hymns were included and retained in the Mass which deal with thanking and praising [God] in a wonderful and excellent way, as for example, the Gloria in excelsis, the Alleluia, the Creed, the Preface, the Sanctus, the Benedictus, the Agnus Dei. In these various parts you will find nothing about a sacrifice but only praise and thanks. Therefore we have also kept them in our Mass [in Wittenberg]. Particularly the Agnus Dei, above all songs, serves well for the sacrament, for it clearly sings about and praises Christ for having borne our sins and in beautiful, brief words powerfully and sweetly teaches the remembrance of Christ.[40]

For Luther both epiclesis and anamnesis had musical dimensions, as did the proclamation of the Gospel, which is fundamental in his eucharistic theology and practice.

Verba: Not Whispered, nor Simply Spoken, but Sung

Between 1521 and 1525 Luther progressively came to terms with the practical implications of the *Verba Testamenti* as words of proclamation. In the unreformed Mass the only words heard by the congregation were *hoc est enim corpus meum* and *hic est enim calix sanguinis mei, novi et aeterni testamenti: mysterium fidei: qui pro vobis et pro multis effundetur in remissionen peccatorum* [This is my Body. . . . This is the cup of my Blood, the new and eternal testament, the mystery of faith, which is poured out for you and for many for the remission of sins]; the remainder of the *Verba Testamenti,* indeed, the remainder of the Canon, was inaudibly whispered by the celebrating priest. Luther's first concern is that the total *Verba Testamenti* should be heard in the vernacular. In his Sermon on the Worthy Reception of the Sacrament of 1521 he wrote: "The priest utters these words [i.e., the *Verba Testamenti*] softly during Mass — would to God that he would shout them loudly so that all could hear them clearly, and moreover, in the German language."[41] Two years later he had moved to a more radical position and expressed the view, in the *Formula missae,* that the *Verba Testamenti* should be *sung:* "I wish these words of Christ — with a brief pause after the Preface — to be recited in the same tone as the Lord's Prayer is chanted elsewhere in the Canon so that those who are present may be able to hear them."[42] Instead of inaudible recitation, Luther wants the *Verba Testamenti* to be heard by everyone in the attending congregation, so he calls for these words to be sung, and suggests that existing chant could be used. For these words Luther recommends a particular chant form of the Roman Latin Mass. He knows that the traditional chant provided a unitive musical hermeneutic in which the Canon of the Mass was effectively framed by the same music: the Sursum corda and Preface at the beginning and the Pater noster at the end, were sung by the celebrant to the same melodic formulae.[43] Thus Luther argues that the same chant could be used for the *Verba Testamenti* — implying that the truncated Preface, Verba Testamenti, and Lord's Prayer in the *Formula missae* would all be sung to the same basic chant form. Although there was no musical notation included in the *Formula missae,* what he had in mind is approximated in Thomas Müntzer's *Deutsch Euangelisch Messze* of 1524, where musical setting of the *Verba Testamenti* is clearly an adaptation of the traditional melodic formulae of the Sursum corda, Preface and Lord's Prayer.[44]

In 1525, partly in response to vernacular liturgies published for use in Strassburg, Nuremberg, and Allstedt, and partly in response to requests that he should create his own vernacular Mass, Luther began working on what was to become the *Deutsche Messe*. In contrast to the *Formula missae*, in which he was content simply to outline the musical aspects, Luther concluded that music was fundamental to the new liturgy and that it should therefore include musical notation. When the *Deutsche Messe* was published in 1526, 27 of its 49 pages were filled with musical notation, and the remaining 22 pages contain frequent references to the musical aspects of the liturgy. In spite of this, the musical content of the *Deutsche Messe* has often been disregarded as being incidental to Luther's liturgical reform. But it is the music that underscores the theological consistency and liturgical integrity of his approach to vernacular worship.[45]

There is a single manuscript leaf, probably written sometime during the second half of 1525, which reveals that Luther experimented with the musical content of what was to become the *Deutsche Messe*,[46] a draft he presumably shared with his musical colleagues. Johann Walter recorded the following recollection sometime around 1565-66:

> When he wished to establish the German Mass in Wittenberg about forty years ago, he wrote to the Elector of Saxony and Duke Johann, of praiseworthy memory, for his Electoral Grace to allow his old songmaster, the honorable Conrad Rupsch and myself to go to Wittenberg in order to discuss with us the *choral notes* [*Choral Noten* = chant notation] and nature of the eight tones [modes]. And finally, he appointed the eighth tone for the Epistle and the sixth tone for the Gospel, saying: "Christ is a friendly Lord, and his sayings are gentle, therefore, we want to take the *Sextum Tonum* for the Gospel; and because St. Paul is a serious apostle, we want to appoint the *Octavum Tonum* for the Epistle."[47]

Walter's recollection is basically confirmed by Luther's manuscript draft of the musical elements he was considering for the forthcoming *Deutsche Messe*, in which the Epistle is assigned to the Tone VIII and the Gospel to the Tone V.[48] In continuity with classical, medieval, and Renaissance humanist music theory, Luther associated particular attributes with each of the eight modes.[49] For example, Adam von Fulda, composer and music theorist in Duke Frederick the Wise's employ, who died in Wittenberg in 1505, recorded that Tone VIII (Hypomixolydian) was the *modus sapiens* (mode of wisdom) and the Tone V (Lydian) the *modus laetus* (mode of joy).[50] By assigning the Epistle and Gospel to these particular modes Luther was not only utilizing a known tradition, but also creating a new one. The biblical pericopes of the Roman Mass had been customarily chanted to simple forms, essentially a monotone with inflections at punctuation points.[51] But Luther wanted the chanting of the different biblical texts to be distinguished from each other, so took known modal characteristics and assigned them specific hermeneutical functions: the words of the apostles, especially St. Paul, were to be distinguished from the words of Christ by the use of the different modes. But Luther's musical hermeneutics went much further.

The draft includes brief musical examples of how the two lections were to be sung. Rather than selecting propers for a given Sunday or celebration Luther included two biblical fragments to illustrate the notation he was considering. The passages he chose are highly revealing and underscore his understanding of the nature of the Lord's Supper. The Epistle fragment notated in Tone VIII (transposed) comprised the opening words of Romans 5:1: "Therefore, since we are justified by faith, we have peace with God through &c." Here is another confirmation of Luther's understanding of the Lord's Supper as being grounded in the doctrine of justification, especially since the passage from Romans 5 was not included in the traditional pericopes of the church year.

Luther's choice of a Gospel example in the draft document is even more significant; indeed, it is not directly taken from one of the Gospels but is a German translation of the beginning of the *Verba Testamenti* (see Example 12.1).[52] Here is a clear demonstration of the theological consistency and liturgical integrity of Luther's reforms. Right from the very beginning Luther understood that the chanting of the Gospel pericope and the chanting of the *Verba Testamenti* would be connected since they both had the same theological function: the declaration of God's forgiveness and grace in Christ. Luther therefore signaled this theological unity by assigning the two parts of the liturgy to the same melodic form:

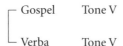

Further, as the Gospel pericope (usually) and the *Verba Testamenti* both contained the words of Christ, these words were to be emphasized by a different pitch. Thus in Luther's draft example the words of Christ are pitched a fourth below the words of the evangelist (D as opposed to G; see Example 12.1). The congregation would therefore be able to distinguish the words of the Savior in both the Gospel pericope and *Verba* by the lower pitch. This draft is an im-

Example 12.1. *Verba Testamenti* in Luther's Draft *Deutsche Messe*

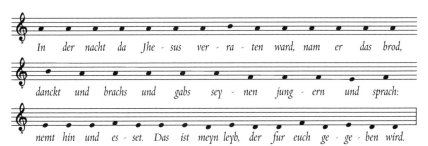

In der nacht da Jhe - sus ver - ra - ten ward, nam er das brod,

danckt und brachs und gabs sey - nen jung - ern und sprach:

nemt hin und es - set. Das ist meyn leyb, der fur euch ge - ge - ben wird.

portant witness to the evolution of Luther's thinking with regard to the hermeneutics of liturgical music. In the *Formula missae* — in contrast to the inaudibility of most of the traditional Canon of the Mass — he directs that the *Verba Testamenti* should be sung, and suggests they could both be sung to the same melodic formulae as the Preface and Lord's Prayer in the unreformed Mass. Here in the draft of the *Deutsche Messe* he goes further and makes a direct link between the Gospel of the day and the *Verba Testamenti* by assigning them both to the same chant form, a musical hermeneutic that Luther was to work out in greater detail in the published form of the *Deutsche Messe*.

The earliest reference to a vernacular Mass being celebrated in Wittenberg is at the end of the sermon that Luther preached in the Pfarrkirche on 29 October 1525:

> We have started our efforts to hold a German Mass. You know that the Mass is the foremost outward office which has been ordained for the comfort of the true Christians. Therefore, I ask you Christians that you will pray to God and implore him that he will be deigned to be pleased with it. You have often heard that one should not teach unless one is sure that what is taught is God's Word. Thus, one should not ordain or commence something unless one is certain that it pleases God. Neither should one only judge it by common sense, for if God does not see to it, nothing will come out of it. Also for this reason I have resisted to make an effort concerning the German Mass for so long, so that I did not become a cause for the gangs of spirits who put their foot in it thoughtlessly; they do not pay attention to whether God wants it so. But since so many people from all [German-speaking] countries now have asked me in writing and letters and the worldly power impels me, we could no longer make excuses or talk ourselves out of it, but must think and accept that it is God's will.

If there is something in it which is ours, it should perish and rot even if it should be considered, at the same time, fine and of great reputation. If it is from God, it must continue even if, at the same time, it seems foolish. Thus everything which God does must go on, even if it does not please anyone. Therefore, I ask you to beseech the Lord, that if this is a proper Mass it will be to his praise and glory.[53]

It is an open question whether the German Mass celebrated on 29 October 1525 was the same as the published form issued some months later. It may well have been an interim draft form, since Luther speaks of it in somewhat experimental terms. Whatever the form of this October Mass, a printed copy, presumably a proof-copy, of the *Deutsche Messe* was sent to Nikolaus Hausmann sometime in December 1525, it came into use in Wittenberg from the following Christmas Day, and copies of the imprint were generally available in early February 1526.[54]

In this printed form of Luther's vernacular liturgy the musical elements are more consistently worked out than in the earlier manuscript draft. Since the proclamation of the Gospel, the essence of the doctrine of justification, was central to Luther's understanding of the Lord's Supper, he gave careful attention to how the Gospel pericope was to be sung. The simple melodic formulae of the earlier draft gave way to a more complex, though clearly defined, system in which the narrative of the evangelist, the direct speech of various people, and the voice of Christ, were each given their own punctuation formulae and reciting tones: the evangelist was pitched on A; the speech of various people a third higher on C^1; and the voice of Christ a third below the evangelist (that is, a fifth below other direct speech) on F (see Example 12.2). The principle enunciated in the earlier draft, that the voice of Christ should be the lowest pitch, was thus made more emphatic in the final form of the *Deutsche Messe*. Again Luther is found modifying a known tradition in order to create a new one. The representation of the *dramatis personae* by different pitches had long been characteristic of the chanting of the passion narratives during Holy Week. In the *Deutsche Messe* Luther directed that this annual custom should become a weekly experience, a musical hermeneutic that taught the congregation to listen for the voice of Christ. By employing a system akin to the traditional passion tones Luther was therefore making emphatic his view that to participate in the Lord's Supper is to participate in the passion of Christ.[55]

The apparent contradiction between Walter, who stated that Luther set the Gospel in Tone VI, and Luther's specific reference to Tone V for the Gospel in the *Deutsche Messe,* is resolved in the fact that the two modes are almost

Example 12.2. Melodic Formulae for the Gospel in the
Deutsche Messe (1526)

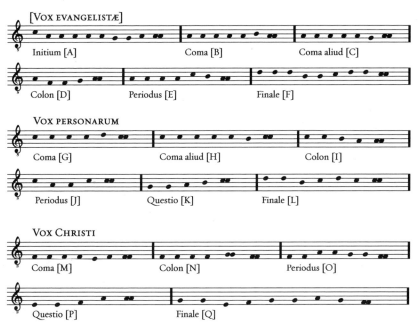

identical. The principal difference between them is that the former is centred on c^1 and the latter on f. Reference to Example 12.2 will confirm that Luther made use of both modes for the Gospel: the Lydian (Tone V) for the general content of the Gospel and the Hypolydian (Tone VI) — the "piously pleasant" mode[56] — specifically for the words of Christ.

As in his earlier draft, Luther assigned the same melodic forms to both Gospel and *Verba Testamenti*, because both share the same function of proclaiming the good news of grace to the worshiping congregation (see Example 12.3).[57] Thus in Luther's vernacular *Deutsche Messe* the two traditional parts of the liturgy, the ministry of the word and the ministry of the sacrament, both focus on the proclamation of forgiveness and grace in the Gospel pericope and the *Verba Testamenti*, and their unity of purpose is given audible form in the same music that was applied to both. Further, the Kyrie was set in the Dorian mode (Tone I) in a simple threefold form, and the German Agnus Dei, *Christe, du Lamm Gottes*,[58] similarly a threefold liturgical prayer for mercy, was also assigned to the same mode; indeed, the incipits of both the Kyrie and *Christe, du Lamm Gottes* are identical (see Example 13.1).[59] Thus

Example 12.3. *Verba Testamenti* in the *Deutsche Messe* (1526)

with the Gospel and *Verba Testamenti* sharing the same melodic forms, and
the Kyrie and German Agnus Dei being based on the same melodic material
— with the creedal hymn, the confession of faith in three stanzas, *Wir glauben
all an einen Gott*, set to its sturdy Dorian melody, in between — Luther created an impressive musical symmetry for his vernacular liturgy:[60]

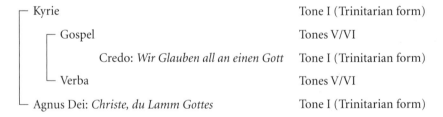

Kyrie	Tone I (Trinitarian form)
Gospel	Tones V/VI
Credo: *Wir Glauben all an einen Gott*	Tone I (Trinitarian form)
Verba	Tones V/VI
Agnus Dei: *Christe, du Lamm Gottes*	Tone I (Trinitarian form)

There are signs that Luther continued to develop the musical symmetry
of his vernacular liturgy after the publication of the *Deutsche Messe*. In the

1525 manuscript draft he had indicated that in place of the Introit the prose Psalm 34 should be sung in Tone I (Dorian), and in the *Deutsche Messe* the complete psalm is given, fully notated throughout. The psalm had longstanding eucharistic associations, especially verse 8: "O taste and see that the Lord is good." A few years later — probably in the no longer extant 1529 edition, but certainly in the 1533 edition, of the Wittenberg congregational hymnal — Luther included another vernacular prose psalm: Psalm 111 to be sung during communion.[61] In a similar way that Psalm 34, as the Introit, anticipated communion, Psalm 111 referred back to the *Verba Testamenti,* especially with verse 4: "He has instituted a memorial" (ein gedechtnis gestifftet) of his wonders." Thus with the addition of this psalm Luther extended the musical symmetry of his vernacular liturgy:

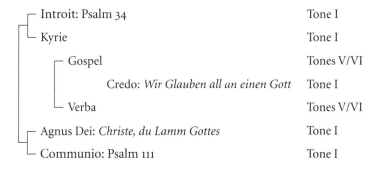

Introit: Psalm 34	Tone I
Kyrie	Tone I
Gospel	Tones V/VI
Credo: *Wir Glauben all an einen Gott*	Tone I
Verba	Tones V/VI
Agnus Dei: *Christe, du Lamm Gottes*	Tone I
Communio: Psalm 111	Tone I

This symmetrical structure, with its central double proclamation of the Gospel in pericope and *Verba Testamenti* either side of the confession of faith, was further enhanced by another pairing of vernacular versions of parts of the Ordinary. The *Deutsche Messe* was first sung during Advent 1525, which explains the omission of a German version of the Gloria in excelsis Deo. To supply the deficiency some areas adopted a prose version, while others sang Nikolaus Decius's hymnic version *Allein Gott in der Höh sei Ehr,* which ultimately came into almost universal use in Lutheran Germany. But in 1537 the manuscript *Formula Rituum* for Naumberg was completed, a church order drawn up by Nikolaus Medler in consultation with Luther, Jonas, and Melanchthon, that included a metrical version of the "Antiphona angelorum" that "Doctor Martin Luther has made" (Doctor Martin Luther gemacht hat): *All Ehr und Lob soll Gottes sein.*[62] This paralleled Luther's "German Sanctus," a metrical version of Isaiah 6:1-4, *Jesajah dem Propheten* included in the *Deutsche Messe* of 1526: both *All Ehr und Lob soll Gottes sein* and *Jesajah dem Propheten* are in similar rhymed couplets; both are set to modified forms of plainsong melodies, the former being based on the *Gloria tempore paschali,*[63] and the latter on the *Sanctus in Dominicis Adventus et Quadragesima*;[64] and both use similar cadential formulae.[65]

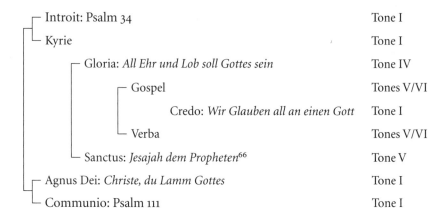

Introit: Psalm 34		Tone I
Kyrie		Tone I
Gloria: *All Ehr und Lob soll Gottes sein*		Tone IV
Gospel		Tones V/VI
Credo: *Wir Glauben all an einen Gott*		Tone I
Verba		Tones V/VI
Sanctus: *Jesajah dem Propheten*[66]		Tone V
Agnus Dei: *Christe, du Lamm Gottes*		Tone I
Communio: Psalm 111		Tone I

Theology and Practice of Later Lutheran Liturgy

The development of symmetrical, parallel musical elements in Luther's vernacular liturgy over the decade or so following the publication of the *Deutsche Messe*, reveals him to be a thoughtful liturgical reformer, rather than, as he has been characterized, an impetuous, cut-and-paste dabbler who did not really understand what he was doing. On the contrary, Luther knew exactly what he was doing, and there is an impressive theological and liturgical consistency in these developments, especially the musical components. But the key to these parallel musical elements is found in the connection between the Gospel pericope and the *Verba Testamenti*, the proclamation of grace that is emphasized by the common musical form.

The consequences of Luther's theological understanding of the essential proclamatory nature of the *Verba Testamenti* are that the liturgies of the church which took his name, and its eucharistic theology, were based primarily on biblical rather than liturgical sources. Of course, Luther and those who followed him did not overturn liturgical practices which in their view did not undermine this proclamation of the Gospel. But the reasons were in the first place theological, and only in the second place liturgical.

The classic Lutheran theologians followed Luther both in letter and spirit. Martin Chemnitz, in his *magnum opus, Examen Concilii Tridentini* (1565-73), wrote: "When Christ was about to die, he instituted the administration and use of the Lord's Supper in the form of a testament. Now it is a great crime to add anything even to a human testament when it has been ratified and confirmed. It is manifest, therefore, what the papalist Mass is, which adds to the testament of the Son of God something which is not contained in it, is not instituted, is not prescribed."[67] David Chytraeus, a colleague of Chemnitz, had a similar thrust in the *prolegomena* to his commentary on Leviticus (1569):

> The Mass, or Lord's Supper, is Christ's testament, that is, a promise of the remission of sins which was sealed by Christ's death; and it is at the same time the distribution and partaking of the body and blood. That it is not a sacrifice in which we offer Christ's body and blood to God is plainly demonstrated by the Words of Institution, where almost every letter contradicts the fundamental idea of such a sacrifice. Christ broke the bread and gave it to his disciples, saying: "Take . . ."; but to receive something from another is not to offer and sacrifice it to the one who is giving. . . . Then Christ says: "This is my body, which is given for you. This is my blood which is shed for you for the remission of sins." It is evident that these words are words of promise by which God offers and imparts his benefits to us. . . . Now a promise (by which God confers his benefits upon us) is utterly in conflict with a sacrifice (in which we ourselves offer something of our own to God). . . . From these *Verba* handed down by Christ we conclude most unmistakably that in the Mass, or Lord's Supper, Christ's body and blood are not offered to God either as a propitiatory sacrifice or as a eucharistic sacrifice but are given and presented by God through a minister and are only taken and received by us.[68]

But it was not only Lutheran theology but also Lutheran practice to center the Lord's Supper on the *Verba Testamenti*. Virtually all the sixteenth-century Lutheran liturgies replace the Canon by the Words of Institution.[69] There are but two exceptions among the many church orders of the period which have anything like a Eucharistic Prayer: the liturgy for Pfaltz-Neuberg (1543) and the Swedish order of 1576[70] — but both are atypical in Lutheran tradition.[71] Luther's understanding of the *Verba Testamenti*, as proclamation to the people of God, is also reflected in various Reformed liturgies, such as those of Zwingli and Bucer.[72]

It is only in fairly recent times that a Eucharistic Prayer has been introduced into Lutheran liturgies. One cannot help but observe that at the same time as there has been this growing interest in a Eucharistic Prayer within Lutheranism, there has been a corresponding decline in the understanding of the doctrine of justification as the central and controlling principle in theological matters. Similarly, the Lutheran tradition has long abandoned its earlier theological understanding of the nature and function of liturgical music. It is therefore not surprising to find that Luther is misunderstood and reinterpreted today. Thus, for example, the *Lutheran Book of Worship* gives in parallel columns the alternatives of a Eucharistic Prayer and the Words of Institution.[73] There is a theological inconsistency here, which has not gone unnoticed,[74] in that on the one hand there is a prayer addressed to God, in accordance with accepted liturgical tradition; and, on the other hand, there is a proclamation from God, which follows the theology and practice of Luther. It may well be a widely held contemporary view that the essence of the Lord's Supper is to be found in a Eucharistic Prayer, but to charge Luther with inconsistency simply because he took a different point of view is neither objective nor fair. Luther was totally consistent in applying the doctrine of justification as the controlling principle to liturgical as well as to all other theological and practical questions:[75] in the Lord's Supper is the offer of forgiveness and grace, and this proclamation of the Gospel is enshrined in the *Verba Testamenti,* which are not to be obscured by the addition of humanly-devised traditions, nor confused by making them into a God-directed prayer. Thus, as Spinks rightly concludes, "words such as 'conservative,' 'pruning-knife' or 'hatchet-job,' are completely inadequate, and even misleading. Far from being a conservative and unimaginative liturgiologist, Luther was in fact giving radical liturgical expression to justification by faith, and deserves to be regarded as a serious Reformation liturgist."[76] But the full extent of his astonishing creativity as the theological liturgiologist of the Reformation only becomes clear when his innovative approach to musical hermeneutics is taken into account.

CHAPTER 13

Liturgical Pedagogy in Luther's Musical Reforms

Luther was extremely sensitive to the continuity of Christian tradition, where it did not conflict with clear scriptural teaching. Thus, although he was quite severe in his elimination of the sacrificial language of the Offertory and in his destruction of the Canon of the Mass, apart from the *Verba testamenti*, he nevertheless retained the basic structure of the Latin rite, together with much of its content. With the continued use of the traditional liturgical texts, Luther also retained the song of the church, liturgical chant, and polyphonic choral music, though sometimes in modified forms, together with congregational hymnody. As discussed in the previous chapter, the Mass was theologically and liturgically reinterpreted as a gift rather than an offering, and the role of the people transformed from passive to active participation. Throughout these liturgical-musical reforms Luther and his colleagues pursued clear pedagogical goals. On the one hand, they sought to show that their reforms were in continuity with earlier traditions of the church, and on the other, to ensure that what appeared to the people as "new" was reinforced by creative pedagogy. This can be seen in four basic types of music that were created for the reformed, evangelical Mass: chant for the clergy, chant for the people, congregational hymnody, and choral settings of chorale melodies.

Chant for the Clergy

Although the previous chapter discussed Luther's liturgical chant at some length, it is necessary to review the primary details here in order to set them within the broader context of Luther's musical concerns for liturgical worship.

In continuity with the Catholic Church Luther preserved the practice of chanting the lections at Mass, the Epistle and Gospel, by the clergy. But instead of accepting the traditional reciting tones, Luther modified an existing tradition in the *Deutsche Messe* (1526), especially with regard to chanting the Gospel. During Holy Week it had been customary to sing the passion narratives, notably that of St. Matthew on Palm Sunday and St. John on Good Friday, in which the voice of the evangelist was pitched in the tenor range, the voices of various persons in the unfolding drama were pitched somewhat higher, but the voice of Jesus was always at the lowest pitched. What Luther did was to accept this principle of different pitches, heard only during Holy Week, and apply it to the weekly chanting of the Gospel of the day throughout the church year. The ears of those in Wittenberg who first heard the Gospel sung according to Luther's melodic formulae would have quickly registered that when they heard the lowest pitches they were hearing the words of Jesus. Luther's pedagogical purpose was that the people should learn to identify and listen closely to the words of Christ, and he employed a musical hermeneutic in order to achieve this end.

Luther did not stop there. The Canon of the Mass that he had excised from his liturgical forms had been largely unheard in the unreformed Mass, apart from a few fragments of the *Verba testamenti*. Luther wanted all of the *Verba testamenti* — and only these words — to be heard in the vernacular. But these words were to be sung rather than simply spoken. Part of the reason was that he understood these words as proclamation — proclamation from God rather than prayer to God, as was the Canon of the Mass. What is highly significant is that for the *Verba testamenti* Luther followed the same melodic formulae he had prescribed for the chanting of the Gospel of the day. The focal points of each part of the liturgy, Word and Sacrament, in Luther's vernacular liturgical form were both proclamatory in nature: the chanting of the Gospel of the day in the former and the chanting of the *Verba testamenti* — another proclamation of the Gospel — in the latter. These two similar functions were thus given a unity of purpose by the use of the same melodic formulae for both.

In the *Deutsche Messe* Luther indicated that the pastor was expected to chant more than the Epistle, Gospel, and *Verba Testament*. Leaving aside the question of the Introit (Psalm 34), which some suggest was sung by the pastor alone (see discussion below), Luther directs that the Collect of the day should be a monotone, chanted on F.[1] Although there is no specific direction, the implication is that the post-communion Collect was to be similarly intoned by the pastor, as well as the concluding Benediction from Numbers 6.

It is clear from the church orders drawn up by Luther's Wittenberg colleagues, as well as the correspondence of both Luther and Melanchthon, in the post–*Deutsche Messe* period, that in larger towns and cities the liturgy was an amalgam of Latin and German, with considerable variation of what was proportionally in each language depending on the nature of the celebration. Thus on ordinary Sundays there was a tendency for more German to be used; on festival days Latin predominated.[2] On such festivals, as the *Formula missae* directs,[3] the Sursum corda dialog between pastor and choir was sung, followed by the appropriate Preface.[4] Duke Henry's Church Order for Albertine Saxony, published in 1539, was drawn up by Luther's closest Wittenberg associates, including Justus Jonas, Georg Spalatin, and Caspar Creutziger, who must have done so in reference to Luther. The only music in the document is the notation for the *Verba Testamenti* taken from Luther's *Deutsche Messe*.[5] This is followed on the next page (the last of the document) by the post-Communion Collect and Benediction from the *Deutsche Messe*, and finally a directive concerning chants for the clergy:

> Melodies for singing the Epistles and Gospels in German should be created and transcribed by the clergy in larger towns, such as Dresden, Leipzig, Weissenfels, Seitz, etc.
> Prefaces for the Mass or Communion:
> Preface for Christmas
> Preface for Epiphany
> Preface for Easter
> Preface for Ascension
> Preface for Pentecost
> Preface for Trinity
> The pastors should take these Prefaces for Communion from Latin Missals, and all pastors should consult with the Superintendents so that they be appropriately and Christianly used.[6]

These prefaces continued to be sung in Latin to their traditional chant forms, since later editions of the Saxon Church Order include both the Latin texts and their respective chants fully notated.

In providing chant for the clergy Luther was motivated by clear pedagogical concerns. On the one hand, he could be radical, such as in his provision of melodic formulae for the *Verba Testamenti* (the same as he provided for the Gospel pericopes), the aim being to teach the attending congregation to listen for the words of Christ, always heard at the lower pitch. On the other hand, he could be conservative, not wishing the people to unlearn the profitable things they had experienced in the Mass, and he therefore retained traditional Latin Prefaces with their music, as well as other chant forms.

Chant for the People

One of the important theological principles of the Lutheran Reformation is the doctrine of the "common priesthood" of all Christians, which stood in contrast to the particular priesthood of Catholicism. For Luther and his colleagues it was necessary for all the people at worship to unite in corporate action. But, as Joseph Herl has effectively pointed out, the concept has been frequently misunderstood to mean something other than what Luther had in mind, especially with regard to worship.[7] The *Deutsche Messe* is often appealed to as an example of what Luther intended, a sung service of worship, completely in the vernacular for pastor and congregation, comprising mostly hymns, without the aid (or need) of a choir. While this would have been the case in those smaller towns and villages where there were no Latin schools, such a complete vernacular Mass was the exception rather than the rule. In larger towns and cities a macaronic liturgy became the norm, where Latin schools supplied choirs that had a role in worship, separate but closely connected to that of the congregation.

Herl also points out that when the *Deutsche Messe* was first introduced in Wittenberg in 1525-26 there is the strong possibility that congregational participation was somewhat limited. He provides significant evidence to show that it took some time for the Wittenberg congregations, and those elsewhere, to participate in the singing. It needs to be borne in mind, however, that the *Deutsche Messe* does not represent Luther's final word on the subject of evangelical worship; it met a pressing need for the use of the vernacular in liturgical worship at that time, but Luther and his colleagues continued to work on the content of liturgical worship, a fully integrated approach in which the provision of different genres of liturgical music, in Latin as well as German, choral as well as congregational, was fundamental.

Luther was certainly concerned to involve the whole congregation in worship through singing. In the *Formula missae* he wrote:

> I also wish that we had as many songs as possible in the vernacular which the people could sing during Mass, immediately after the Gradual and after the Sanctus and Agnus Dei. For who doubts that originally all the people sang these which now only the choir sings. . . .[8]

The Wittenberg congregations sang vernacular hymns, but did they sing any of the chants of the *Deutsche Messe*? Herl argues that the chanted Introit and Kyrie of the *Deutsche Messe* were sung by the choir rather than the congregation when vernacular service was first used in Wittenberg. Herl may well be right in these instances when the rite was introduced — if the question is: While both items are fully notated in the *Deutsche Messe*, would there have been enough printed copies available for the congregation to sing from? On the other hand, the argument could be countered by the fact that although the Introit, Psalm 34, with its notation, covers several pages, each verse is set to the same Tone I Psalmtone, and the members of the congregation were supplied with the text of the Psalm; they could have sung the simple repetitive Psalmtone tolerably well, especially if they were strongly led by a choir, which seems likely when the vernacular liturgy was first introduced.[9] Similarly, the threefold Kyrie is extremely simple and could have been quickly taught by rote before the service began. Herl's primary concern, however, is with how the *Deutsche Messe* was introduced and received, whereas the concern here is with Luther's ultimate intentions.

Hymnals published in the later 1520s and early 1530s that include versions of the *Deutsche Messe* imply that these items were intended to be sung congregationally (see Table 13.1). Two of these hymnals (Zwickau 1528 and Leipzig 1530) include a rubric similar to that of the *Deutsche Messe* for the Introit: "singet man ein geistlich lied oder ein Psalm" (Zwickau 1528 and Leipzig 1530), but without Psalm text or notation. Both hymnals, however, include vernacular prose Psalms within their versions of the Daily Office; thus any one of these could have been sung to a suitable Psalmtone as an Introit. Magdeburg 1536 also has a similar rubric and includes the text of Psalm 34, following the *Deutsche Messe*, but like the Psalms in the other hymnals it appears without notation. But again, it could have been sung to a Psalmtone without too much difficulty. Rostock 1531 only directs an "Introit Hymn," rather than a Psalm, which became the later widespread practice, but in this context underlines the congregational participation in the Introit. The Wittenberg Church Order (1533), however, envisages a variety of practice. The Introit could sometimes be sung in Latin — by implication by the choirboys — and sometimes in German, in which case it should be a German Psalm, rather than a translation of the traditional Latin Introit, the implication being that this German Psalm was to be sung by the congregation as a whole.[10]

The Kyrie in each of these hymnals also implies the congregational singing of the simple chant found in the *Deutsche Messe*. None give notation, but the simple melodic form is easily memorized. What is interesting is that while two hymnals give the transliterated Greek of the *Deutsche Messe*, "Kyrie eleison" (Zwickau 1528 and Leipzig 1530), the other two (Rostock 1531 and Magdeburg 1536) give a (Low) German translation, "Here vorbarme dy unser" (Herr erbarme dich unser). This is a strong indication that the Kyrie was meant to be sung by the whole congregation rather than by the boys of the choir alone, a principle underscored in the 1533 Wittenberg Church Order: "The schoolboys shall not sing in German except when the people sing along."[11]

The German Sanctus in the *Deutsche Messe* was intended for congregational singing,[12] and over the years various other chant forms were added to the Wittenberg hymnals. Luther's Te Deum, *Herr Gott, dich lobe wir* (ca. 1529), was intended to be sung antiphonally between choir and congregation, to a simplified version of the traditional chant. The Wittenberg Church Order (1533) directs at Vespers:

> After the hymn [at Vespers] let the choir intone the Te Deum laudamus, in Dr. Martin Luther's German translation, and let one of the choristers in the schoolboy's pew [pulpit?] in the middle of the church answer with the congregation at the half-verses. For a start he may also take a few boys into the pew to help him, until the congregation gets accustomed to singing along in this Te Deum.[13]

Luther's German Litany (1529) was similarly intended to be sung antiphonally by two "choirs," the first comprising boys and the second other boys leading the whole congregation. Again, the Wittenberg Church Order directs on Wednesdays: "Then, in the middle of the church, the boys sing the German Litany with the congregation."[14] At Vespers the German Magnificat, *Meine Seele erhebt den Herren* (1529/33), was sung by the congregation to the *Tonus peregrinus*, as, once again, the Wittenberg Church Order (1533) witnesses: "after the sermon shall the Deutsche Magnificat be sung, in the middle of the church, with the people."[15]

It is clear that Luther wanted the participation of the congregation not only in strophic vernacular hymns but also in vernacular chant forms. A feature of the published hymnals that are closely identified with Wittenberg is the inclusion of a good many of the Psalms in prose German translations that were clearly intended for corporate singing to the traditional Psalmtones. This is a measure of the influence of the *Deutsche Messe* in which Psalm 34 appears as the Introit, fully notated in Tone I (Dorian).[16] A few years later Luther included Psalm 111 in the congregational hymnal *Geistliche Lieder* (Wittenberg, 1529/33), to be sung during the distribution of communion, which he set to the same Tone I, though with different inflections and endings.[17] As argued in the previous chapter, this Communio (Psalm 111), sung towards the end of the evangelical Mass, echoes the Introit (Psalm 34) of the beginning of the *Deutsche Messe*. Luther signals their connection by using the same Psalmtone. It is another example of a musical

Table 13.1. Comparison of Deutsche Messen found in Gesangbücher 1528-1536

Zwickau 1528	Leipzig 1530	Rostock 1531	Magdeburg 1536
	Confession	Confession	
	Absolution	Absolution	
			Invocation
			Collect
Introit Psalm	Introit Psalm or Hymn	Introit Hymn	Introit Psalm
Kyrie	Kyrie	Kyrie (German)	Kyrie (German)
Gloria (prose)	*Allein Gott*	*Allein Gott*	*Allein Gott*
Collect	Collect	Collect	Collect
Epistle	Epistle	Epistle	Epistle
			Alleluia
Gradual Hymn	Gradual Hymn	Gradual Hymn	Gradual Hymn
		Alleluia	
Gospel	Gospel	Gospel	Gospel
Wir glauben	*Wir glauben*	*Wir glauben*	*Wir glauben*
Sermon	Sermon	Sermon	Sermon
Paraphrase of the Lord's Prayer	Lord's Prayer	Lord's Prayer	Lord's Prayer
Exhortation	Exhortation		
		Sursum corda	
		Preface [abbr.]	
Verba Testamenti	Verba Testamenti	Verba Testamenti	Verba Testamenti
German Sanctus	German Sanctus	German Sanctus	
Communion hymns	Communion hymns	Communion hymns	
			German Sanctus
		Collect	
		Pax Domini	
Agnus Dei:	Agnus Dei:	Agnus Dei:	Agnus Dei:
O Lamm Gottes	*Christe, du Lamm Gottes*	*O Lamm Gottes*	*O Lamm Gottes*
Collect	Collect	Collect	Collect
Blessing (Num. 6)	Blessing (Num. 6)	Blessing (Num. 6)	Blessing (Num. 6)

Zwickau 1528 = *Enchiridion geistliche gesenge* (Zwickau: Schönsperger, 1528).
Leipzig 1530 = *Enchiridion geistlicher gesenge* (Leipzig: Blum, 1530).
Rostock 1531 = *Geystlyke leder* (Rostock: Dietz, 1531).
Magdeburg 1536 = *Enchiridion Geistliker leder unde Psalmen* (Magdeburg: Lotter, 1536).

Example 13.1. Comparison of the Incipits of Luther's *Kyrie eleison* and *Christe, du Lamm Gottes*

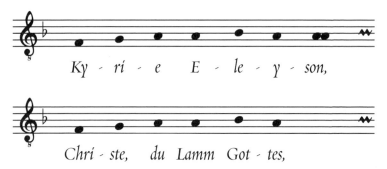

hermeneutic that, though somewhat more subtle than the melodic formulae that connect the Gospel and *Verba Testamenti,* nevertheless witnesses to the way Luther carefully prepared additional items for the congregation to sing.

Luther also used the same Tone I in a more striking manner in the *Deutsche Messe.* This concerns the brief threefold Kyrie that was included with notation and *Christe, du Lamm Gottes,* which was referred to in the text thus: ". . . the remainder of these [communion] hymns are sung, or the German Agnus Dei."[18] Although the text and melody of *Christe, du Lamm Gottes* first appeared in print in the Braunschweig church order, edited by Luther's colleague Johannes Bugenhagen and published in Wittenberg in 1528, this reference to it in the *Deutsche Messe* implies that it already existed when Luther was at work on the vernacular liturgical form, that is, towards the end of 1525.[19] Significantly, these two threefold liturgical prayers for mercy — "eleison" and "erbarm dich unser" — begin with exactly the same melodic form (see Example 13.1). The liturgical connection between these two sections of the Ordinary of the Mass is thus underscored in that both were created out of the same melodic Tone I material.[20] Again it is an example of musical hermeneutics and witnesses to Luther's pedagogical concerns. In singing the "German" Kyrie and the German Agnus Dei members of the singing congregation would quickly recognize that both melodic incipits are identical, thus making an aural link between the two liturgical prayers for mercy. Later Lutherans committed both melodies to memory, which allowed composers to explore the musical connection between the two. Thus if one only heard the opening melody, without a text, one could not be certain that what was being heard was the German Kyrie or the German Agnus Dei, but in a sense it would not matter because the prayer for mercy was the same in both cases; only as one heard more of the melodic form would the exact identity of the liturgical prayer become clear. It was an imaginative ambiguity that was effectively used by, for example, the composer Johann Sebastian Bach.[21]

Congregational Hymnody

For Luther worship was a corporate activity, an expression of the unity of the community of faith, a reality that was uniquely demonstrated in the song of the whole congregation. But because it was something of a novelty in the experience of the people of Wittenberg, Luther and his colleagues were concerned to find ways in order to encourage the corporate singing of the people. They took great care to create, and re-create, melodies that were singable and memorable.

One of the notable features of the Wittenberg hymnal of 1533 is the number of new tunes or revised tunes it introduced for hymn texts written by Luther and his colleagues that had been circulating in various hymnals during the previous decade (see Table 13.2).[22] When these new or revised melodies are compared with the earlier melodies there is a marked simplification in the rhythmic nature and melodic contours, consistent with a desire for forms that could be more readily sung by untrained congregations.[23] But this was not a new concern for Luther and his colleagues. Right from the very beginning, when the new vernacular hymnody was introduced into worship in Wittenberg, a primary concern was with the finding appropriate ways to encourage the congregation to sing.

For good pedagogical reasons, Luther wanted to establish the practice of congregational singing by building on what was already known to the people. Thus some of the "new" congregational hymns were re-workings of the old, para-liturgical German folk hymns, the *Leisen*. Others were newly composed but in a bar-form that was familiar because of its use by the Meistersänger, the composers of the *Hofweise* (court-song), and the ballad-singers who used the form for their narrative accounts of contemporary events. Another source was the hymns of the church, which the people had heard frequently, and therefore what was already in their ears could fairly readily be coaxed out of their mouths. One of these plainsong melodies was a medieval tune associated with the Ambrosian hymn *Veni redemptor gentium*. It originated in German-speaking areas and was widely dispersed and therefore a well-known melody.[24] This melody was reworked and reformed by Lu-

Table 13.2. New or Revised Melodies in the Wittenberg *Gesangbuch* of 1533 (DKL numbers)

Text	1533 Melodies	Earlier Melodies
Jesus Christus unser Heiland, der den Tod	Ee6	Ea9 (1524); Ec16 (1524)
Nun freut euch, lieben Christen	Ee7	B15 (1524); Ea2.a (1524); Ec6 (1524)
Jesus Christus unser Heiland, der von uns	Ee8	B14-T (1524)
Ach Gott vom Himmel, sieh darein	Ee9	Ea2.b (1524); Ea5 (1524); Ec3 (1524); Eb6 (1525); Ed1-4 (1526)
Wohl dem, der in Gottes Furcht steht	Ee10	B14-T, a (1525); Eb10 (1525); Ec12 (1524)
Wo Gott der Herr nicht bei uns hält	Ee11	Ea5 (1524); Ea18 (1525); Ec14, a (1525); Ee4 (1531)
Durch Adams Fall ist ganz verderbt	Ee12	Ec17 (1524); Ec8 (1524); Ec13, a (1526)
Hilf Gott, wie ist der Menschen Not so groß	Ee14	Ea3, a (1524/1528); Ec19 (1524)
In Gott gelaub' ich, daß er hat	Ee15	Ea3 (1524); Ec20 (1524)
O Gott Vater, du hast Gewalt	Ee16	Ee16A (pre-Reformation)
Ich ruf zu dir, Herr Jesu Christ	Ee17	B21 (1527)

ther (and later by Walter) to create a number of different congregational hymns (see Example 13.2).[25]

The first is *Nun komm der Heiden Heiland*. The text was a fairly literal translation that Luther made of the Ambrosian *Veni redemptor gentium*, and it is understandable that he should choose to adapt the melody associated with the Latin text for his vernacular translation. Although it seems quite likely that Luther's hymn with its melody appeared on a broadside published in Wittenberg during Advent 1523, the earliest extant appearance in print was in the "Schwartzen Horn" edition of the *Enchiridion Oder eyn Handbuchlein* (Erfurt, 1524) (**B** in Example 13.2).[26] The resulting tune, *Nun komm der Heiden Heiland*, is a skillful re-creation of the original melody by Luther. Most of the various adjustments and modifications made to the Latin melody were occasioned by the accented nature of the German text, in contrast to the fluidity of Latin. But making the fourth line identical with the first was a more radical change that allowed the plainsong-based melody to take on a character akin to religious folk melodies by giving it an ABCA structure.[27] The modifications to the basic melodic material may seem small, but, as Ulrich Leupold states, "they change the character of the melody completely and make a Lutheran chorale out of a medieval hymn."[28]

The second hymn melody to be derived from *Veni redemptor gentium* is *Verleih uns Frieden gnädiglich*, a prayer for peace (**C** in Example 13.2).[29] The

Example 13.2. Melodies Created from the *Veni redemptor gentium* Melody

changing political climate in Europe gave rise to the creation of this German hymn. The western advance across central Europe of the Ottoman Turks was a threat that not only had its political significance but also an important theological dimension, for both Catholics and Protestants alike.[30] It was seen as an Islamic onslaught on Christendom, a contemporary echo of the issues that had led to the Crusades of the early medieval era. Following the capture of Budapest and the Turkish control of the Hungarian crown, news of the advance of the Ottoman armies on Vienna in 1529 was greeted with dismay. In

Wittenberg Luther's response was to draw up a litany in both German and Latin. It appears that *Verleih uns Frieden gnädiglich*, textually a translation of the Latin antiphon *Da pacem Domine*, was completed around the same time he was working on the German litany, or shortly after. The German litany was issued in Wittenberg towards the end of 1529. It was reprinted the same year in Nuremberg with *Verleih uns Frieden gnädiglich* appearing on the final pages, which would otherwise have been blank,[31] implying that the hymn originally circulated as a Wittenberg broadside. What is significant is that Luther chose not to use the plainsong melody of the Latin antiphon *Da pacem Domine* but rather the Latin melody *Veni redemptor gentium* on which his earlier tune *Nun komm der Heiden Heiland* was based. The first four lines of the five-line melody are almost identical with the plainsong melody, the only changes being a few rhythmic adjustments. The fifth line is constructed from elements of the third and fourth lines of the plainsong tune.

The third hymn melody to be derived from *Veni redemptor gentium* is *Erhalt uns, Herr, bei deinem Wort*, another hymn that reflects current political pressures (**D** in Example 13.2).[32] The Turkish threat was intensified when Ferdinand of Austria was defeated at Budapest and most of Hungary became an Ottoman province in 1541. As with the German Litany of 1529, Luther's response was to underscore the need to pray. He published the treatise *Vermahnung zum Gebet wider dem Turken* [Admonition to Pray Against the Turks] (Wittenberg, 1541).[33] The Lutheran churches also faced the possibility of extinction should the Catholic princes of the Holy Roman Empire mount reactionary military actions against the areas ruled by Lutheran princes in the attempt to restore the unity of European Catholicism. There was also the danger of disaffection and division among the Lutheran churches. In response to such possible hazards Luther wrote what he called "Ein Kinderlied, zu singen wider die zween Ertzfeinde Christi und seiner heiligen Kirchen, den Bapst und Türcken" [A children's hymn to be sung against the two arch-enemies of Christ and his holy church, the pope and the Turks].[34] The text and its associated melody, both the work of Luther, first appeared in the congregational hymnal published by Joseph Klug in Wittenberg in 1543. The tune is again another reworking of the same melodic material. Instead of simply repeating the first line of *Veni redemptor gentium* unaltered, the three original repeated notes are replaced by the rise and fall of a minor third, thus emphasizing the second syllable. The second line eliminates the melisma on the seventh syllable, but retains the basic melodic shape. The third line owes little to the original tune, whereas the fourth line is essentially created out of the final phrase of line three. As indicated in Chapter 4, the two hymns *Erhalt uns, Herr, bei deinem Wort* and *Verleih uns Frieden gnädiglich* were closely associated together from their earliest appearance in print. Their use of the same melodic material reinforces the conclusion that they belong together. The three stanzas of *Erhalt uns, Herr, bei deinem Wort* are followed by *Verleih uns Frieden gnädiglich* in settings by Walter in the 1544 and 1551 editions of his *Gesangbüchlein,* and in two settings by Balthasar Resinarius in Georg Rhau's *Neue Deutsche Geistliche Gesenge* (Wittenberg, 1544).[35] The two hymns were employed in close proximity at the end of the vernacular liturgy. For example, Johann Spangenberg's *Kirchengesenge Deudsch, auff die Sontage und fürnemliche Feste, durchs gantze Jar* (Magdeburg, 1545) directs *Verleih uns Frieden gnädiglich* to be sung following the Benediction but before a final collect, and *Erhalt uns, Herr, bei deinem Wort* following this collect at the very end of the service.[36]

The fourth hymn melody to be derived from *Veni redemptor gentium* is *Gib unserm Fürsten und aller Obrigkeit,* an adaptation of *Erhalt uns, Herr, bei deinem Wort* rather than from the plainsong tune (E in Example 13.2).[37] The anonymous text first appeared in print in Walter's *Das Christlich Kinderlied D. Martini Lutheri Erhalt uns Herr . . .* (Wittenberg: Schwertel, 1566),[38] but is a slight revision of an earlier text, found in a Breslau manuscript dating from around 1560, that begins, *Gib unserm keyser und aller Obrigkeit.*[39] This collection of chorale motets was the last extensive work of the old composer who was then in his seventieth year. Walter had been a close colleague and staunch supporter of Luther. Following the Reformer's death in 1546 the young Lutheran churches were beset by a number of deeply divisive controversies. Many grew out of the imposition of the Leipzig Interim of 1548, a temporary agreement between Catholics and Protestants until such time as disputed doctrinal issues could be resolved by a general council of the church. The Philippists, the followers of Philipp Melanchthon, centered on the universities of Wittenberg and Leipzig, accepted the limitations on specific Lutheran theology and practice demanded by the Interim. The Philippists were energetically opposed by the Gnesio-Lutherans, centered on Magdeburg and the new University of Jena, founded in 1547 in opposition to Philippist Wittenberg University. In the bitter disputes that followed, Walter sided with the Gnesio-Lutherans. During the time he was Hofkapellmeister in Dresden, between 1548 and his retirement in 1554, he was careful to ensure that his own family, as well as the choirboys under his care, did not attend eucharistic worship presided over by clergy who had accepted the terms of the Leipzig Interim.[40] Although a measure of external security was afforded the Lutherans by the Peace of Augsburg of 1555, which adopted the principle of *cuius regio, eius religio* — that is, the religious affiliation of the rulers, Catholic or Protestant, determined the religious confession of the areas over which they ruled — internal insecurities continued to threaten the future of the Lutheran churches. A growing concern was the tendency for the Philippists to become Crypto-Calvinists and therefore depart from distinctive Lutheran theology.

This ferment was the immediate context in which Walter produced his penultimate published work, *Das Christlich Kinderlied D. Martini Lutheri Erhalt uns Herr.* The following year, 1567, he sent a copy to Duke Johann Wilhelm of Ernestine Saxony with a covering letter in which he said the following:

> . . . Gracious Lord and Prince, now indeed at this solemn time, in which all Christians must needs pray to God in the hour of need, I think often of the prophecy and warning of future punishment of the most worthy, holy and well-beloved prophet Dr. Martin Luther [that is, if the Lutherans were not kept by the Word of God they would be fragmented by sectarianism]; by God's grace I have newly set to music and committed to print the dearly-beloved hymn and prayer that he left behind, *Erhalt uns, Herr, bei deinem Wort,* together with other Christian prayers and hymns for the authorities and suchlike. . . .[41]

One of those hymns that includes prayer for political leaders is the following:

Gib unserm Fürsten und aller Obrigkeit	Give to our Prince and all [political] authorities
Fried und gut Regiment	peace and good government
daß wir unter ihnen	that we under them
ein geruhig und stilles Leben führen mögen	may lead a calm and quiet life
in aller Gottseligkeit und Ehrbarkeit.	in all blessedness and modesty.

The anonymous text almost certainly had a Gnesio-Lutheran origin. Walter was in complete sympathy with the movement that sought to preserve Luther's legacy. The single stanza is a kind of appendix to Luther's two hymns, *Erhalt uns, Herr, bei deinem Wort* and *Verleih uns Frieden gnädiglich,* and its content enshrines Luther's view of the Christian responsibility of rulers and governments. One of Luther's primary Reformation treatises of 1520 was the *Schrift an den christlichen Adel deutscher Nation* [Address to the Christian Nobility of the German Nation],[42] in which he stated that the future of the reforming movement would depend on secular power assuming a leadership role. In the 1560s, following the Peace of Augsburg, it was imperative that the local princes and governments remain faithful to Lutheran doctrine, otherwise their principalities and provinces could revert to Catholicism under the principle of *cuius regio, eius religio.*

As the single stanza is an appendix to the two earlier hymns of Luther, it is not surprising to find that it is also based on the same melodic material. The first line is made up of an abbreviated version of the first line and the almost unaltered second line of *Erhalt uns, Herr, bei deinem Wort;* the second line is similarly an abbreviated version of the third line of the earlier melody; the third line is mostly newly-composed but with echoes of the other melodies; the fourth line was developed from the third line of the earlier melody; and the fifth line is virtually the same as the final line of *Verleih uns Frieden gnädiglich* which links back to the third line of the original plainsong melody with a concluding cadential flourish.

In later Lutheranism *Gib unserm Fürsten* was frequently associated with the other two hymns, *Erhalt uns, Herr, bei deinem Wort* and *Verleih uns Frieden gnädiglich.* For example, in the later seventeenth century Johann Schelle included both *Verleih uns Frieden gnädiglich* and *Gib unserm Fürsten* in his chorale cantata *Nun danket alle Gott,*[43] Dietrich Buxtehude included all three in his chorale cantata *Erhalt uns, Herr, bei deinem Wort* (BuxWV 27),[44] and in 1725 Johann Sebastian Bach began his Sexagesima cantata with *Erhalt uns, Herr, bei deinem Wort* and ended it with *Verleih uns Frieden gnädiglich* (BWV 126).

It is part of Luther's (and Walter's) pedagogical creativity that all these different melodies were created from the same basic source: the similarity of their melodic form aided their assimilation by those who sang them, the music being an aid for memorizing the associated texts and their meaning.

Choral Settings of Chorale Melodies

When congregational singing was promoted in the worship of the Wittenberg churches, Luther and Walter adapted an earlier practice that was at the same time both pedagogical and liturgical. The older liturgical *alternatims praxis,* in which plainsong alternated with polyphony, was transmuted into an alternation between congregation and choir. The first stanza of a hymn would be sung in a strong, unaccompanied unison, with the choir supporting the congregation. The second stanza would then be sung by the choir, a cantus firmus chorale motet. The members of the congregation, following along with the text of the stanza being sung, would also have the basic chorale melody reinforced in their ears before they joined together to sing again, the third stanza in unaccompanied unison, and thereafter in alternation with the choir until all the stanzas had been sung. If the counterpoint of the chorale motet that the congregation heard sung for the intervening stanzas was constructed

Example 13.3. Voice Entries in Walter's 1524 Setting of *Nun komm der Heiden Heiland*

out of building-blocks of the chorale melody itself, then the essential character of that melody would enter quickly into the common memory of the congregation. This is exactly the compositional technique that Walter employed for many of his chorale motets. Modeled on Franco-Flemish cantus firmus compositions, such as those of Josquin, his effective settings are notable for their conciseness, and for the fact that instead of being based on plainsong melodies, they were composed on the melodies of the congregational hymns, with the cantus firmus usually in the Tenor. Further, he also used canonic devices and imitative voice-leading, all based on elements of the basic chorale melody, in the other voice-parts.

Almost any chorale motet by Walter could be chosen as an example but it is instructive to look at one of the earliest and one of the latest, *Nun komm der Heiden Heiland,* published in 1524, and the first of his settings of *Gib unserm Fürsten* published forty-two years later in 1566. There is a close connection between the two settings in that the melodies on which they are based were both created from the same plainsong melody, *Veni redemptor gentium.*

The 1524 setting of *Nun komm der Heiden Heiland* is in five voices with every initial voice-entry based on the incipit of the chorale melody (Example 13.3).[45] It has what amounts to a double cantus firmus as the Altus is in canon with the Tenor at the fifth. Three of the voice-parts (Discantus, Vagans, and Bass) clearly begin with the opening melodic phrase of the chorale melody.

206

Example 13.4. Voice Entries in Walter's 1566 Setting of *Gib unserm Fürsten* (note values halved)

The other two (Altus and Tenor) have a variant form of the melody (for example, the seventh note is F where one would expect A). But the piece as a whole, even though it uses this variant form of the melody, has the effect of reiterating the basic nature of the chorale melody, and thus became a teaching-aid to the congregation that was then beginning to learn such melodies.

The 1566 setting of *Gib unserm Fürsten,* also in five voices, is more closely based on the chorale melody than is the earlier example (Example 13.4).[46] Again there is a double *cantus firmus,* with the Discantus in canon at the octave with the Tenor. But the imitative counterpoint of the other voice-parts is more closely related to the chorale melody than those of the earlier setting of *Nun komm der Heiden Heiland.* But again, the way that the whole piece is constructed serves to underscore the fundamental chorale melody on which it is based.

Given Luther's intense interest in and practical experience of singing such vocal polyphony, together with his theological approach to music, especially within the liturgy,[47] there is the strong possibility that Luther had some significant influence on Walter's development of this compositional technique. After all, it was Luther who wrote the preface to the part books when they were first published in 1524. Walter was the composer but it may have been Luther who first saw the pedagogical implications of the concept on which these compositions were based.

The systematic use of thematic building-blocks to create a whole range of different forms of liturgical music is a remarkable achievement of the Lutheran Reformation in general and of the creative genius of both Martin Luther and Johann Walter in particular. It was a technique that was adopted and developed by many composers of succeeding generations. By using the same or similar melodic fragments to develop different aspects of liturgical music — chant for the clergy, chant for the congregation, congregational hymnody, and choral settings of chorale melodies — the development of the new Lutheranism was fostered:

First, the repetition of the same or similar melodic fragments was an extraordinarily effective technique for teaching, allowing the congregation to learn quickly what it should sing in worship. Congregational participation, one of the primary goals of the Reformation, required such a viable technique to promote it.

Second, the use of thematic, melodic building-blocks in the composition of liturgical music gave a strong unitive component to emerging Lutheran liturgy in which clergy, congregation, and choir shared similar melodic material.

Third, that these melodic fragments had their origin in the chant of the church and in the polyphonic styles that had been developing over the previous century or so demonstrated that the new Lutheran churches were in continuity with the practice of the church in the past.

Fourth, although the Lutheran Reformation was at heart a theological movement, it did not have a disdain for the affairs of this world. As the subject matter of these hymns that grew out of the *Veni redemptor gentium* melody indicates, when Lutherans sang their theology within a liturgical context, they did so fully aware of the political realities within which they had to live.

CHAPTER 14

Liturgical Chant in Church and School

By common consent the chorale is understood as the distinctive and — to some considerable extent — defining feature of Lutheran church music. The widely-accepted concept is of strong congregational singing with organ accompaniment. While it has almost universal currency, this understanding of the Lutheran chorale is nevertheless a fairly late development, a construct based largely on the practice of the later eighteenth and early nineteenth centuries, when the effects of the twin forces of Rationalism and Pietism had reduced Lutheran church music almost exclusively to congregational song. The chorale was, of course, a fundamental development of the Lutheran Reformation of the sixteenth century, but it was never the exclusive preserve of the congregation. As Joseph Herl has demonstrated, Lutheran congregational singing took quite some time to become established,[1] and while Michael Praetorius's substantial volumes of church music, published in the early seventeenth century, contain many hundreds of chorale settings, most of them are compositions for choirs rather than for congregations, ranging from simple two-part settings to massive polychoral concertos with anything up to twenty-one parts for voices and instruments.[2] Congregational participation in singing Lutheran chorales was certainly a primary goal of Luther's reformation of worship, but it was not meant to stand alone; it was to be augmented by a wide variety of vocal — choral as well as congregational — and instrumental music.

The sixteenth-century concept of the chorale was different from that of later times, being more akin to unison chant rather than harmonized melody. It tends to be forgotten that "chorale" (German: "choral") grew out of the common term for Gregorian chant. In the sixteenth century two forms of singing were distinguished by the terms "choraliter" and "figuraliter," meaning unison chant on the one hand and choral polyphony on the other. The early Lutheran hymns were to be sung "choraliter," that is, like Gregorian chant, in an unaccompanied unison. Thus the term "chorale" reflects its origin in the chant of the church, and many chorale melodies were in fact developed from specific chants, such as *Nun komm der Heiden Heiland* from *Veni redemptor gentium; Komm, Gott Schöpfer, heiliger Geist* from *Veni creator Spiritus; Christum wir sollen loben schon* from *A solis ortus cardine; Allein Gott in der Höh sei Ehr* adapted from the *Gloria paschale* melody, among many others. In sixteenth-century Lutheran Germany "choral" was an all-encompassing term that embraced both monodic chant *and* congregational song, designating unaccompanied melodic forms which might be sung by one or many voices.

An Early Chant Anthology

Traditional chant forms continued in use alongside the new church songs in evangelical worship, despite Carlstadt's early attempts to eliminate Gregorian chant from the Wittenberg churches.[3] For Luther there was no question that the traditional chant of the church would continue to be sung in the reformed liturgies, as is demonstrated by the many references to specific chant forms in his many writings,[4] and his adaptations and use of individual chant melodies.[5] Further, in the early 1530s Luther's primary musical collaborator, Johann Walter, was collecting and editing chants for the church year for use in evangelical worship. The information comes from Michael Praetorius — composer and major publisher of church music, whose father had taught alongside Walter in the Torgau Latin school — who reported at the beginning of the seventeenth century that he had access to an incomplete manuscript collection of chants that Walter had compiled:

Johann Walter . . . made somewhat of an attempt about eighty years ago [ca. early 1530s]. First of all, he separated the notes accurately, and then showed to which words they should be joined, and also corrected and removed the principal faults committed in Latin pronunciation, and the barbarisms which abounded in the old psalmody.[6] And that which seemed better left alone, considering carefully the quantity of the syllables, he believed that he should, of necessity, leave alone, lest the old and customary cadences, being disrupted, should sound quite new and strange, and offend the ears.[7]

During the early 1530s there was an intensification of the provision of various forms of liturgical music in Wittenberg and the surrounding area. In 1533 Luther and his colleagues (Jonas and Bugenhagen, among others) issued a revised edition of the Wittenberg hymnal and a new Wittenberg Church Order. Johann Walter must have been involved in this activity because around the same time he was assembling an anthology of liturgical chants, almost certainly with the involvement of Luther in the selection of individual items.

Walter, cantor in Torgau, was already at work in drawing together an extensive repertory of liturgical polyphonic music for his school choir to sing in liturgical worship throughout the church year. Praetorius supplies the additional information that Walter was also establishing a basic corpus of liturgical, monodic chant — with "purified" texts and notation, for doctrinal and musical reasons. The project however remained incomplete, was never published, and has not survived.[8] Some indication of its contents, however, can be gleaned from the manuscript cited by Praetorius in which Walter lists the primary chants for the festivals of the church year[9] that he may have already edited (see Table A4.1, col. 1, in Appendix 4). Walter also composed polyphonic settings on a good many of these melodies, the *cantus firmi* usually given in the Tenor voice (see Table A4.1, col. 3). Even though an unfinished work, Walter's collection of chants may have had some currency not only in Torgau and Wittenberg but also further afield. Martin Agricola, cantor in Magdeburg, observed in the early 1540s that schoolboys in Wittenberg and Magdeburg were competent singers of monodic chant as well as mensural music.[10] As no published anthologies of reformed liturgical chant were available at this time, such singing would have had to have been from manuscripts. Thus it seems likely that these schools in Wittenberg and Magdeburg used manuscript copies of Walter's anthology as it then existed.[11]

It is clear that in Wittenberg a complex pattern of traditional chant forms was used in the worship of the churches. In addition to the rubrics of the 1533 Wittenberg Church Order, which direct specific chants to be sung within liturgies on special days and celebrations, there is an important manuscript, dated 1543/44: "Ordenung der gesenge der Wittembergische Kirchen" (Order of Chants of the Wittenberg Churches).[12] This is a comprehensive listing of all the chants to be sung on every Sunday, festival or celebration in the church year according to their liturgical functions at the evangelical Mass, Matins and Vespers. Although most of the chants listed are Latin, a significant number of German hymns are included, confirming that the term "choral" covered both Latin monodic chant and strophic vernacular hymnody. The document lists by first line a complete repertory of chants required in Wittenberg for worship throughout the church year, and many of the chants for principal feasts are the same as those listed by Walter in the manuscript cited by Praetorius (see Table A4.1).

Erasmus Alber, who had been a student of Luther in Wittenberg, was another who advocated the continued use of such chant forms. He reported in a posthumous publication (written some time before 1553, the year of his death) that he used Latin chants throughout the church year, and, following the example of Luther's funeral Responsoria (see Chapter 15), had retained chant melodies but had replaced their theologically suspect texts with alternatives:

> In churches where there are schoolboys and educated citizens, it is excellent to sing Latin chants alongside German hymns. It is not now possible to create such beautiful melodies that these Latin chants have, such as: [for Christmas] *Verbum caro factum est, A solis ortus cardine, Puer natus est nobis, Illuminare Jerusalem;* [for Lent/Holy Week] *Laetere Jerusalem, Ossana filio David;* [for Easter] *Cum rex gloriae, Victimae paschali, Ad coenam agni providi;* [for Ascension] *Vita sanctorum, Festum nunc celebre,* &c. And the Latin text sounds much better under the same notes than the German. I have taken a good chant with a bad text and for the same notes have provided a good text, either Latin or German.[13]

Johann Spangenberg

Johann Spangenberg (1484-1550), another of Luther's ardent supporters, studied philosophy, theology, and music in Göttingen, Einbeck, and Gandersheim, before matriculating at the University of Erfurt in 1508, where Luther had studied some years earlier. In Erfurt he imbibed the spirit of Humanism, becoming an associate of Eobanus Hessius. On leaving Erfurt Spangenberg became Rector of the Latin school in Stolberg (1520-1524), and during the same period he completed a doctorate in theology and was ordained. Spangenberg now combined pastoral and preaching responsibilities with his teaching concerns. In 1524 he became the pastor of St. Blasiuskirche, Nordhausen, where he was to serve for the next twenty-two years. In 1546, on Luther's recommendation, Spangenberg became the pastor and superintendent in Eisleben, where he died in 1550.

One of Spangenberg's first significant projects was the founding of a Latin school in Nordhausen (1525) and creating its curriculum, which gave prominence to music. He authored a significant sequence of Latin textbooks on grammar, syntax, and etymology, as well as theological tracts, sermons,

Table 14.1. Representative Publications by Spangenberg 1533-1545

Prosodia. Wittenberg: Rhau, 1533

Syntaxis. Wittenberg: Rhau, 1535

Grammaticae Latinae Etymologia. Wittenberg: Rhau, 1535

Quaestiones musicae in usum scholae Northusionae. Nuremberg: Petreius, 1536

Computus ecclesiasticus in pueriles quaestiones redactus. Wittenberg: Rhau, 1539

Evangelia dominicalia in versiculos extemporaliter versa. Wittenberg: Rhau, 1539

Heubtartickel reiner Christlicher Lere : Frageweise gestellet. Wittenberg: Rhau, 1540

Ein geistlich Bad der Seelen. Erfurt: Sachse, 1540

Eine christliche Unterrichtung. Erfurdt: Sachse, 1540

Von den worten Christi, Matthej. XIII. Wittenberg: Rhau, 1541

Vom christlichen Ritter . . . Ein kurtzer unterricht aus der heiligen Schrifft. Wittemberg: Rhau, 1541

Trivii Erotemata. Hoc Est, Grammaticae. Dialecticae. Rhetoricae. Wittenberg: Rhau, 1542

Eine predigt . . . , Gestellet auff die wort S. Paulus Ephe. 5. Halle: Frischmut, 1543

Die Historia vom Leiden und sterben unsers Herrn Jhesu Christi. Magdeburg: Lotter, 1543

Ein new Trostbüchlin . . . zu einem seligen sterben. Wittenberg: Rhau, 1544

Der Apostel Geschichte. Kurtze auslegung, Fur die jungen Christen. Wittenberg: Rhau, 1545

Eine kurtze . . . Prediget vom hochwirdigen Sacrament des Abentmals . . . Magdeburg: Lotter, 1543

Funffzehen Leichprediget. Wittenberg: Rhau, 1545

and catechetical works, many of them published by Rhau in Wittenberg[14] (see Table 14.1), as well as being reprinted by other publishers in subsequent years. A significant number of Spangenberg's books had specific musical content, such as his *Prosodia in usam iuventutis Northusianae* (1533) that illustrated the principles of poetic meters with four-part musical settings. Rhau also re-published Spangenberg's *Quaestiones musicae in usum scholae Northusionae* (Nuremberg: Petreius, 1536), a basic, widely-used textbook of music theory and the principles of plainsong that by 1592 had been issued in twenty-five editions.

In addition to these publications Spangenberg also issued a significant series of anthologies of texts and melodies connected with the church year in German and/or Latin:

Alte und Neue Geistliche Lieder und Lobgesenge von der Geburt Christi/ unsers Herrn/Für die Junge Christen (Erfurt: Sachse, 1544) *Zwölff Christliche Lobgesenge und Leissen so man das Jar uber jnn der Gemeine Gottes singt auffs kürtzte ausgelegt* (Wittenberg: Rhau, 1545) *Cantiones ecclesiasticae/Kirchengesenge Deudsche* (Magdeburg: Lotter, 1545); *Hymni ecclesiastici*, 2 parts (Frankfurt: Egenolph, 1550).

Although others had published sermons on individual hymns, such as *Ein Kindelein so löbelich*, Spangenberg's *Zwölff Christliche Lobgesenge und Leissen* was the first of what was to become a distinctive Lutheran tradition of published collections of *Liedpredigten*, expository sermons on a number of different hymns.[15] But his most important publication was his anthology of chants: *Cantiones ecclesiasticae/Kirchengesenge Deudsche*.[16]

Spangenberg's *Cantiones ecclesiasticae/Kirchengesenge Deudsche*

Spangenberg in Nordhausen had been working along similar lines to Walter in Torgau, except that he completed his anthology of chants, whereas Walter's remained unfinished. Walter was cantor of the school and church in Torgau, and his projected anthology of chants was intended for the boys to sing from on the Sundays, festivals, and other celebrations of the church year. Spangenberg developed his collection of chants for the same purpose in Nordhausen. The large folio format of Spangenberg's printed volume, *Cantiones ecclesiasticae/Kirchengesenge Deudsche*, published in Magdeburg in 1545, would have been placed on a stand so that a number of boys could gather round to sing, as they had done in previous generations in connection with the unreformed Mass.

It therefore seems likely that since Walter's projected anthology of chants was still unfinished, Spangenberg was encouraged to publish his own anthology that he had prepared for use in Nordhausen. To judge from the 1543/44 "Ordenung der gesenge der Wittembergische Kirchen" (Order of Chants of the Wittenberg Churches) the specific chants in Spangenberg's collection are almost the same as those in use in Wittenberg. If, as seems likely, it was Luther who encouraged Walter to compile his anthology of liturgical chants, when it became clear that Walter would not be able to complete the work in the near future, there is the strong possibility that it was the Wittenberg Reformer who promoted the publication of Spangenberg's collection of chants. Support for this hypothesis comes from Spangenberg himself, who states that his anthology was not issued as a private undertaking but rather with the specific "direction and inspiration of our venerable patron Doctor Martin Luther."[17]

Given the connection with Luther, one might have expected the *Cantiones ecclesiasticae/Kirchengesenge Deudsche* to have been published in Wittenberg by Georg Rhau, the primary publisher of Lutheran music, who by this time had issued a significant number of titles authored by Spangenberg (see Table 14.1 above). In the end it was published in Magdeburg by Michael Lotter, another noted publisher of Lutheran literature, though not a particular specialist in music publishing. The reason for choosing the Magdeburg rather than the Wittenberg printer may well have been due to the fact that Rhau was already oversubscribed with projects at that time, since he published a wide range of literature for Luther, Melanchthon, Bugenhagen, among others, as well as music titles. Rhau was at work on a significant number of musical publications, some of them substantial works, between 1544 and 1545.[18] It therefore seems likely that Rhau's press was fully extended and that he was not in a position to take on another significant music publication.

Michael Lotter's printing and publishing career had begun in Wittenberg in 1523 when he started working with his father Melchior Lotter. In 1528 Michael took over the press and moved it to Magdeburg where he continued printing and publishing until his death in 1556.[19] Lotter therefore had strong connections with Wittenberg, and if Rhau found himself to be overcommitted it would have been an obvious solution to approach the Magdeburg printer about the printing and publishing of the *Cantiones ecclesiasticae/Kirchengesenge Deudsche*, especially since Lotter had recently published three non-musical titles by Spangenberg.[20] But it also seems highly likely that Martin Agricola, the Magdeburg cantor, was also involved in the choice of Lotter. Agricola held Georg Rhau in high regard and many of the eleven imprints of Agricola's musical publications that Rhau issued between 1528 and 1545 were dedicated to the Wittenberg publisher.[21] It therefore would have been natural for Rhau to have made contact with Agricola, when he realized that he would not be able to take on the Spangenberg project, especially as Lotter had apparently recently published Agricola's *Quaestiones vulgatiores in musicum* in 1543.

There were, however, other connections between Wittenberg and Magdeburg that could have influenced the publication of Spangenberg's chant anthology by Lotter. Two of Luther's closest colleagues had been active in Magdeburg. Between 1524 and 1542 Nikolaus von Amsdorf, one of Luther's earliest converts, was pastor of St. Ulrich's in the city, where he reformed liturgical worship according to Wittenberg principles and founded a Latin school. In 1529 Georg Major became the Rector of the Magdeburg Latin school[22] (where Agricola served as cantor) until he was called to Wittenberg to serve as pastor of the Castle Church in 1537. Both Amsdorf and Major had been associated with the Allerheiligenstift, the music foundation of the Castle Church, during their early years in Wittenberg, the former as a canon and the latter as a choirboy. The triumvirate of Amsdorf, Major, and Agricola — pastor, rector, and cantor — ensured that liturgical worship with its associated chants was promoted in Magdeburg.

The primary importance of Spangenberg's *Cantiones ecclesiasticae/ Kirchengesenge Deudsche,* is that it is the most extensive collection of Lutheran liturgical music to be issued during Luther's lifetime, the first in a significant sequence of chant anthologies issued for use in Lutheran worship (see further below). Its secondary importance is that it witnesses to the way in which Luther's liturgical provisions were put into practice. The *Cantiones ecclesiasticae/Kirchengesenge Deudsche* is a double volume in which the first part presents the necessary Latin chants for all the Sundays and celebrations of the church year, and the second part comprises German chants and hymns that are similarly presented according to structure of the Sundays and celebrations of the church year. The first part is in effect the outworking of the principles of Luther's *Formula missae* of 1523 and the second similarly follows the implications of Luther's *Deutsche Messe* of 1526.[23] In his preface to the second part, *Kirchengesenge Deudsche,* Spangenberg explains that "the Latin is for schoolboys and the learned; the German is for lay-people and the uneducated."[24] Thus the Latin forms were intended for churches in cities and towns where there were universities and/or Latin schools, and the German for churches in smaller towns and villages where only German was spoken.

In general, Spangenberg's *Cantiones ecclesiasticae* follows the structure of Luther's *Formula missae* (see Table 14.2). Luther's liturgy begins with the Introit but Spangenberg begins with Latin collects, which together approximate to the priest's *Confiteor* at the beginning of the Roman Mass. Instead of being the priest's private preparation, here it is a corporate invocation of the Holy Spirit in that the Antiphon was to be sung by the schoolboys who formed the choir. Other additions Spangenberg includes are an occasional Responsorium following the Gospel, and the Antiphon *Da pacem Domine* at the end of the liturgy, which would have been sung following the Benediction, in the same way that Luther's German version, *Verleih uns Frieden gnädiglich,* was sung after the Benediction in the German liturgy (see further below). Following the Epistle Spangenberg will occasionally give alternative "Sequentiae," sometimes as many as three: for example, Easter Day has *Haec dies quam fecit Dominus* (Responsorium), *Victime paschale laudes* (Se-

Table 14.2. Comparison of the Structures of Luther's and Spangenberg's
    Latin Masses

Luther 1523	Spangenberg 1545
	Veni sancte Spiritus
	Collects
Introit	Introit
Kyrie eleison	Kyrie eleison
Gloria in excelsis Deo	Gloria in excelsis Deo
Collect	Collect
Epistle	Epistle
Gradual	Gradual
Alleluia	Alleluia
Gospel	Gospel
	[Responsorium]
Nicene Creed	Nicene Creed
Sermon	
Dominus vobiscum &c	Dominus vobiscum &c
Sursum corda &c	Sursum corda &c
Preface (abbreviated)	Preface
	Sanctus & Benedictus
Verba Testamenti	Verba Testamenti
Sanctus & Benedictus	
Lord's Prayer	Lord's Prayer
Pax Domine	
Agnus Dei	Agnus Dei
Communion	
Collects	Collects
Benedicamus	
Benediction	
	Da Pacem Domine

quence), and *Salve feste dies* (Hymn). Spangenberg's omission of the Sermon,
Pax Domine, and Benediction is understandable since these were the responsibility of the pastor rather than the boys of the choir. Similarly the omission
of the Benedicamus is not surprising since in the *Formula missae* Luther indicates that it is optional.[25] The omission of Communion chants is similarly to

Table 14.3. Comparison of the Structures of Luther's and Spangenberg's
    Vernacular Masses

Deutsche Messe 1526	*Kirchengesenge Deudsch* 1545
Hymn or prose Psalm	Veni sancte Spiritus
	Deutsch: *Komm, Heiliger Geist, erfüll*
	(Luther 1524)
	Collects
Kyrie [x 3]	Kyrie [trope]
[Gloria]	*Allein Gott in der Höh sei Ehr* (Decius 1522)
Collect	Collect
Epistle	Epistle
Graduallied	Graduallied
	[Sequence]
Gospel	Gospel
Credal Hymn: *Wir glauben*	Credal Hymn: *Wir glauben* (Luther 1524)
Sermon	Sermon
	[Latin Responsorium]
	Preface
	Sanctus: *Jesaja dem Propheten* (Luther 1526)
Paraphrase of the Lord's Prayer	Paraphrase of the Lord's Prayer
Verba Testamenti [German]	Verba Testamenti [German]
Sanctus: *Jesaja, dem Propheten*	
Communion hymns	Communion hymns
Agnus Dei:	Agnus Dei
[*Christe, du Lamm Gottes*]	Deutsch: *O Lamm Gottes unschuldig*
	(Decius 1522)
Collect: *Wir danken dir*	Collect: *Wir danken dir*
Benediction [Num. 6]	Benediction [Num. 6]
	Da Pacem
	Deutsch: *Verleih uns Frieden gnädiglich*
	(Luther 1529)
	Collect
	Erhalt uns bei deinem Wort (Luther 1543)

be expected because by this time it had become customary to sing German
hymns during the distribution of Communion, as Luther had requested in
the *Formula missae*.[26] Spangenberg gives each Preface in full, which is the implication of Luther's *Formula missae*,[27] but immediately follows it with the

Sanctus and Benedictus, as in the traditional Mass: Luther had directed that these should be sung later in the liturgy, during the distribution of Communion.[28] For his Latin lectionary tones, both Epistle and Gospel, Spangenberg follows the melodic formulae found in Luther's *Deutsche Messe.*[29]

The second part of Spangenberg's anthology of chants, *Kirchengesenge Deudsche,* closely follows the structure of Luther's *Deutsche Messe* (see Table 14.3), but also incorporates a number of features of the first part, the *Cantiones ecclesiasticae.* Spangenberg also integrates a good many of Luther's liturgico-musical forms that had been published later than the *Deutsche Messe.*

In his *Deutsche Messe* Luther indicated that the vernacular Mass should begin either with a hymn or a prose Psalm, sung to an appropriate Gregorian Psalmtone. Luther's preference was for a sung Psalm, approximating to the practice of the early church of singing a complete Psalm as the Introit.[30] But in the twenty years or so since the publication of the *Deutsche Messe* the practice of singing a vernacular hymn in place of the Introit, often an invocation of the Holy Spirit as Spangenberg directs here, had already become widespread. Since Luther's *Komm, Heiliger Geist, erfüll* is a German version of the Pentecost Antiphon *Veni sancte Spiritus,* this hymn, with the following collects, exactly parallels the beginning of Spangenberg's Latin liturgy in his *Cantiones ecclesiasticae.*

Instead of Luther's simple threefold Kyrie in the *Deutsche Messe,* Spangenberg usually gives a German version of a troped Kyrie. Although Luther's *Deutsche Messe* omitted the *Gloria in excelsis Deo,* it is clear from later practice in Wittenberg and elsewhere that he had no intention of its permanent exclusion.[31] The omission from the *Deutsche Messe* was most likely due to the fact that it was drawn up at the end of 1525, that is, during Advent, a penitential season when the *Gloria* was not customarily sung. In the order for the First Sunday in Advent Spangenberg first gives the intonation, *Preis sei Gott in der Höhe,* after which the hymnic version by Decius is given: *Allein Gott in der Höh sei Ehr.* For Easter Day Spangenberg offers an alternative vernacular *Gloria* in rhymed couplets, almost certainly the work of Luther: *All Ehr und Lob soll Gottes sein.*[32] By this time Decius's version, *Allein Gott in der Höh sei Ehr,* had become almost universal throughout Lutheran Germany, but it was a rather free rendering of the traditional liturgical text. In contrast *All Ehr und Lob soll Gottes sein* follows the Latin text more closely and is similarly based on the same *Gloria Paschale* chant that Decius used. It therefore seems likely that Luther thought there was the need for a new text. *All Ehr und Lob soll Gottes sein* appears in the manuscript Kirchenordnung for Naumberg, drawn up in 1537/38 by Nicolaus Medler in close collaboration with his Wittenberg mentors, Martin Luther and Philipp Melanchthon. Here the Gloria was described as "Das deutzsch Et in terra wie als Martinus Luther gemacht hat."[33] This alternative *Gloria* appears in the Wittenberg hymnal issued by Klug in 1543/44 but without the associated melody: Spangenberg is therefore the first to publish both text and melody.[34] His decision to include it with the Propers for Easter Day was almost certainly based on the fact that the text is set to a version of the *Gloria Paschale* melody — the preceding Kyrie is specifically titled: "Kyrie Paschale Deudsch"[35] — thus especially appropriate for Easter season.

The collects would have been intoned, as Luther directs in the *Deutsche Messe*.[36] Both Epistle and Gospel are notated according to the melodic formulae found in Luther's *Deutsche Messe*. In between the two lections the Graduallied, the appropriate hymn for the Sunday or celebration, is sung. These hymns were taken primarily from the Wittenberg hymnals, beginning with *Nun komm der Heiden Heiland* on the first Sunday in Advent. Spangenberg frequently follows this with a German version of a Sequence and often supplies other alternatives. For example, for Easter Day *Christ lag in Todesbanden* is followed by "Das Victime Paschale Deudsch," that is, *Christ is erstanden,* and "Das salve festa dies Deudsch." Again there is confirmation that the concept "chorale" embraced both Latin chant and German hymn. The response to the Gospel is the singing of the German Credo, *Wir glauben all an einen Gott,* which is followed by the sermon. Then Spangenberg indicates that where there is a school that can provide a choir a Latin Responsorium can be sung in this otherwise German service. This is similar to the directive in his Latin liturgy, except there the occasional Responsorium is to be sung following the Gospel (see Table 14.3). The Preface follows, but without a vernacular equivalent of the Sursum corda, leading to the German Sanctus, that is, Luther's *Jesaja dem Propheten das geschah.* The paraphrase of the Lord's Prayer and Verba Testamenti, with notation, are taken from the *Deutsche Messe.* Similarly, the listing of the Communion hymns reflects Luther's directives in the *Deutsche Messe,* with the exception of the prose Psalm 111 (set to Tone I), which Luther had first included as a Communion Psalm in the Wittenberg hymnal issued by Klug, 1529/33. As in Luther's *Deutsche Messe,* the distribution of Communion is concluded by the singing of the German Agnus Dei, not *Christe, du Lamm Gottes,* however, but *O Lamm Gottes, unschuldig.* Here Spangenberg follows a number of contemporary hymnals, such as those published in Zwickau, Rostock, and Magdeburg, that similarly direct the use of *O Lamm Gottes, unschuldig* at this juncture of the vernacular Mass.[37] The form of the melody given in Spangenberg is the earliest printed source.

The post-Communion Collect, *Wir danken dir,* and Benediction (Numbers 6) are taken from the *Deutsche Messe,* and the service is concluded by the singing of two hymns by Luther (separated by another collect): *Verleih uns Frieden gnädiglich* and *Erhalt uns Herr bei deinem Wort*. Both the melodies of these hymns (together with that of *Nun komm der Heiden Heiland*) are based on the same material.[38] It seems likely that Luther himself connected the two hymns together since a year after *Erhalt uns Herr bei deinem Wort* appeared in print compositions were published by two composers who linked together their respective settings of these texts: Balthasar Resinarius in the composite set of part-books, *Newe Deudsche Geistliche Gesenge,* and Johann Walter in the third edition of his so-called *Chorgesangbuch* — *Wittembergisch deudsch Geistlich Gesangbüchlein* — both titles issued by Georg Rhau in Wittenberg in 1544. Thereafter numerous Lutheran composers, including Michael Praetorius, Schein, Buxtehude and Johann Sebastian Bach, created many different combined settings of these two hymns by Luther.

Impact and Significance

As stated earlier, Spangenberg's *Cantiones ecclesiasticae/Kirchengesenge Deudsche* was the most complete anthology of ecclesiastical chant to be published during Luther's lifetime. It therefore became the model for other such collections compiled by pastors and educators, with the active support of church leaders and theologians and strong connections with Wittenberg (see Table 14.4).

In 1530 Lucas Lossius (1508-1582) matriculated at Wittenberg University, where he was closely associated with both Luther and Melanchthon. On leaving Wittenberg, Lossius joined Superintendent Urban Regius, supporter and colleague of Luther, in introducing the Reformation into Lüneburg, becoming the conrector of the Latin school. It is here that Lossius edited his extensive anthology of chant for the use of schoolboys in the services of the church: *Psalmodia, hoc est, Cantica sacra veteris ecclesiae selecta,* first published in Nuremberg in 1553. It was revised and reprinted in Wittenberg 1561,[39] 1569, 1579, 1580, and 1595.[40] It thus became the most widespread anthology of chant in use in the sixteenth and seventeenth centuries. Unlike Spangenberg's anthology Lossius's is almost exclusively Latin, but does include chants for Vespers and Matins as well as the Hauptgottesdienst throughout the ecclesiastical year.

Johannes Keuchenthal (ca. 1522-1583) was the pastor of St. Andreasberg (Harz) where he compiled his *KirchenGesenge Lateinisch und Deudsch* (Wittenberg, 1573), with a preface by Christoph Pezel, professor in Wittenberg.[41] It is clear that Spangenberg was one of Keuchenthal's primary

Table 14.4. Published Collections of Chant for the Church Year

Location	Printer/Publisher	Editor	Year(s)
Magdeburg	Lotter	Spangenberg	1545
Nuremberg	Hayn	Lossius	1553
Wittenberg	Rhau	Lossius	1561
	Schwertel	Lossius	1569
	Seelfisch	Keuchenthal	1573
	Seelfisch	Lossius	1579, 1580, 1595
	Seelfisch	Ludecus	1589 (3 titles)
Copenhagen	Benedicht	Jesperssøn	1573
Leipzig	Beyer	Selnecker	1587
Hamburg	Wolff	Eler	1588

sources, except that for his anthology the Latin and German chants for the church year are integrated under each Sunday and celebration in his first section; the second section comprises a significant collection of vernacular chants and hymns.

Nikolaus Selnecker (1530-1592), professor and superintendent in Leipzig, was a leading theologian of second-generation Lutheranism. His *Christliche Psalmen, Lieder und Kirchengesenge, In welchen die Christlich Lehre zusam gefasset* (Leipzig, 1587)[42] is a comprehensive volume of German and Latin items which owes much to Spangenberg's anthology.

Franz Eler (d. 1590) was appointed the first Lutheran cantor of the Johanneum Latin school in Hamburg by Johannes Bugenhagen, Luther's Wittenberg colleague, sometime after 1529. His *Cantica sacra . . . in vsum ecclesiae jvventvtis scholasticae Hambvrgensis collecta* (Hamburg, 1588),[43] is structured similar to that of Keuchenthal, with a collection of German Kirchenlieder following the Latin chants.

Matthäus Ludecus (1527[?]-1606) was Stadtschreiber (city clerk) in Lüneberg in the early 1550s, where he would have been associated with Lossius. He later became canon (1562), then dean (1573), of Havelberg Cathedral.[44] Here he edited an extensive collection of chants for the Hauptgottesdienst throughout the church year, which follows the models of Spangenberg and Lossius: [I.] *Missale, hoc est Cantica, preces et lectiones sacrae quae ad Missae Officium . . . cantari usitate solent: prior pars de tempore . . .* [II.] *Missale . . . posterior pars de sanctis* (Wittenberg, 1589). He also edited chants for Sunday and weekday Matins and Vespers: *Vesperale et matutinale, hoc est*

Cantica, hymni et collectae sive precationes ecclesiasticae . . . ([Wittenberg, 1589]); this also had bound-in his *Psalterium Davidis . . . una cum antiphonis et psalmorum tropis . . . ad matutinas et vespertinas preces accomodatum* (Wittenberg, 1589).[45] The influence of Spangenberg's *Cantiones ecclesiasticae/Kirchengesenge Deudsche* was not restricted to German-speaking areas. In Denmark Niels Jesperssøn (1518-1587), bishop of Odense, created a chant collection that is very similar to Spangenberg's, except that his Danish chants and hymns are integrated with the appropriate Latin chants for each Sunday and celebration of the church year, rather than being separated into an independent section, as Spangenberg does with his German chants and hymns: *Gradual. En Almindelig Sangog* (Copenhagen, 1573).[46]

Many of the editors of these chant anthologies were educators (Spangenberg, Lossius, Eler) and/or pastors (Spangenberg, Keuchenthal, Selnecker, Ludecus). Some were directly supported by leading theologians, and one was one such theologian (Selnecker).

Philipp Melanchthon (1497-1560), Luther's closest colleague, had written frequently and positively on the role of music in church and school, beginning with *De artibus liberalibus* (Tübingen, 1517) — in which he articulated a new understanding of music as an art form akin to literary poetics — continuing with various prefaces to collections of music published in Wittenberg,[47] and two undated short treatises on music.[48] It is significant that he also contributed a preface to Lossius's *Psalmodia*, the collection of chants that had the widest circulation.

One of the authors of the Formula of Concord was David Chytraeus (1531-1600), a polymath who obtained his master's degree at the age of fifteen when he became a student and houseguest of Melanchthon in Wittenberg. Early in his career Chytraeus wrote a treatise, *De Musica,* in which he discussed basic music theory; it was later included as an appendix in his *Regulae studiorum: Seu, De ratione et ordine discendi, in praecipuis artibus, rectē instituendo* (Leipzig: Grosius, 1595). It is therefore understandable that he should write prefaces for two different collections of chant: the *Cantica sacra . . .* (Hamburg, 1588) of Franz Eler, who had studied with Chytraeus in Rostock; and the *Vesperale et matutinale, hoc est Cantica, hymni* (Wittenberg, 1589) of Matthäus Ludecus.

Another theologian involved with the final form of the Formula of Concord was Nikolaus Selnecker. At the age of twelve he was the organist of the Burgkapelle, Nürnberg, and subsequently studied theology in Wittenberg, becoming another guest in the Melanchthon household. He was also the author and composer of hymns and tunes, and was largely responsible for consolidating the music traditions of the Thomasschule in Leipzig, working with the cantor, Valentin Otto.[49]

These primary Lutheran theologians clearly did not restrict the role of music in worship to congregational hymnody. For them the "chorale" — the liturgical monody of the church — involved the continued use of chant forms, sung by the boys of the school choir throughout the church year, as well as the congregational singing of vernacular hymnody. They understood that worship was an ebb and flow of proclaiming and listening, that in corporate hymnody each member of the congregation proclaimed to the others the substance of their communal faith, and then, when the boys of the school choir sang the appropriate liturgical chants of the day or season, these congregants listened to the Word rather than proclaimed it. For Spangenberg it was important for the boys to understand the chants that they sang, and therefore, around the same time that he compiled his anthology of Latin and German chants, he also created another church year handbook: *Postilla Deudsch. Fur die jungen Christen, Knaben vnd Meidlein, jnn Fragstücke verfasset . . . durchs gantze Jar*, published by Georg Rhau in Wittenberg in 1544 (dedication dated 1542), with a preface written by Luther (dated 1543).[50] This was not an original work, but based primarily on the *Kirchenpostille* sermons of Luther, as well as the sermons of others such as Johannes Brenz (1499-1570) and Antonius Corvinus (1501-1553). Spangenberg turned these sermons on the Epistles and Gospels of the church year into a massive catechetical sequence of questions and answers. In many ways Spangenberg's *Cantiones ecclesiasticae/Kirchengesenge Deudsche* can be seen as the liturgico-musical counterpart of his homiletico-catechetical *Postilla*. The underlying principle appears to have been that if the congregation was to effectively hear the message of the chants sung to them by the boys of the choir then it imperative that these boys should understand what they sing. Lossius followed Spangenberg's example but instead of creating a separate homilectical/catechetical handbook he incorporated detailed expositions of the meanings of the texts of the chants and presented them in small type in the margins alongside the respective notation in his *Psalmodia*.

Liturgical chant — as understood by Luther and his colleagues as well as the second generation of Lutheran theologians and musicians — was more than just singing simple hymns: it was to be a rich experience in which theology was expressed in musical forms, undergirded by pedagogical and catechetical concerns, liturgically appropriate, and spiritually edifying.

PART IV

Liturgico-Musical Forms

CHAPTER 15

Sequences and Responsories

Jaroslav Pelikan has characterized Luther's Reformation in Wittenberg as an amalgam of "Catholic substance and Protestant principle," the continuity from the past integrated with the discontinuity of reform.[1] In an earlier essay I have explored the themes of continuity and discontinuity with regard to the music of worship in the Reformation era, in which Luther's liturgical provisions are discussed.[2] In this chapter our concern is with two specific liturgical-musical forms in which Luther combined Catholic principle with Protestant substance: the Sequence and the Responsory.[3]

The Liturgical Sequence

Although the exact origin of the Sequence is disputed, it appears that from the late eighth century it was sung by cantor and choir after the Alleluia at Mass on feastdays. It developed as an expansion of the Alleluia[4] and was therefore sung between the Epistle and Gospel, following the Gradual and Alleluia. The Sequence functioned as a musical hermeneutic, a homiletic exposition of the primary teaching of the day or celebration.[5] Early Sequences were prose texts but from the eleventh century they were written in meter and rhyme (somewhat irregularly), one of the earliest being *Victimae paschali laudes* for Easter Day.[6] From the first half of the twelfth century Sequences tended to be composed with a regular meter and rhyming scheme. Thus the Marian Sequence *Hodierne lux diei* comprises five six-line stanzas (each sung to its own repeated melody), with an *aabccb* rhyming scheme.[7] The Sequence for Pentecost, *Veni sancte Spiritus,* comprises 10 three-line stanzas, with a sim-

ple *aab* rhyming scheme — effectively a rhymed couplet followed by a third
line that always concludes with a word ending with "-um":

1. Veni, sancte Spiritus,
   et emitte caelitus
   lucis tuae radium.

   Come, thou Holy Spirit bright;
   come with thy celestial light;
   pour on us thy love divine.

2. Veni, pater pauperum,
   veni, dator munerum,
   veni, lumen cordium.

   Come, protector of the poor;
   come, thou source of blessings sure;
   come within our hearts to shine.

3. Consolator optime,
   dulcis hospes animae,
   dulci refrigerium.

   Thou, of comforters the best,
   thou, the soul's most welcome guest,
   of our peace thou art the sign.

4. In labore requies,
   in aestu temperies,
   In stetu solatium.

   In our labor, be our aid;
   in our summer, cooling shade.
   Every bitter tear refine.

5. O lux beatissima,
   reple cordis intima
   tuorum fidelium. . . .[8]

   Brighter than the noon-day sun,
   fill our lives which Christ has won;
   fill our hearts and make them thine. . . .[9]

By the beginning of the sixteenth century there was a proliferation of Sequences,
with one assigned to every saint's day, as well as every Sunday, every major feast,
and other celebrations of the church year. After the Council of Trent (1545-63)
Sequences, together with other liturgical tropes (expansions of the basic liturgical texts), were almost entirely eliminated, with only five remaining: *Victimae
paschali laudes* (Easter), *Veni sancte Spiritus* (Pentecost), *Lauda Sion* (Corpus
Christi), *Dies irae* (All Souls), and *Stabat mater* (feast of the Seven Sorrows of the
Blessed Virgin Mary). For Luther the traditional Latin Sequence provided both a
model and a form for different kinds of congregational song.

Luther's "Sequences"

Like the later Council of Trent, Luther was critical of most Sequences. In his
evangelical Latin Mass, the *Formula missae* published in Wittenberg in 1523,
he wrote:

> We allow no Sequences or Proses unless the bishop[10] wishes to use a short
> one for the Nativity of Christ, *Grates nunc omnes*. There are hardly any

which smack of the Spirit, save those of the Holy Spirit [at Pentecost]: *Sancti Spiritus* and *Veni sancti Spiritus*.[11]

Thus a few Latin Sequences continued to be sung in Wittenberg, principally those of the primary feasts of the church year. Later in the *Formula missae* Luther expressed his concern for congregational hymnody:

> I also wish that we had as many songs as possible in the vernacular which the people could sing during Mass, immediately after the Gradual [that is, in place of the traditional Latin Sequence] and also after the Sanctus and Agnus Dei. . . . The bishops [that is, parish pastors] may have these hymns sung either after these Latin chants, or use the Latin on one day and the vernacular on the next, until the time comes that the whole Mass is sung in the vernacular. But poets are wanting among us, or not yet known, who could compose evangelical and spiritual songs.[12]

Here it is clear that Luther wanted vernacular hymnody to effectively replace the Latin Sequence on most Sundays of the church year, but at this stage (1523), apart from a few vernacular folk-hymns, such as *Nun bitten wir den Heiligen Geist,* no such repertoire of hymns was available. Over the winter of 1523-24 Luther and his Wittenberg colleagues began writing vernacular hymns for congregational use. They were published in a number of collections in 1524, and in the *Deutsche Messe,* written towards the end of 1525, Luther again underscored the use of congregational songs as "Sequence" hymns — though the term that eventually came into use was "Graduallieder" (Gradual-hymns): "After the Epistle a German hymn, either *Nun bitten wir den Heiligen Geist* or any other, is sung with the whole choir."[13] The hymn as the congregational counterpart of the Sequence is underscored by the practice revealed during visitations in Wittenberg in 1528 and 1533:

> At Easter and until the Sunday after Ascension one shall sing after the Alleluia *Victimae paschali* together with *Christ lag in Todesbanden,* verse by verse, until both alike are completed; At Pentecost the sequence *Veni sancte Spiritus* with the hymn *Nun bitten wir den Heiligen Geist* [are sung], as arranged above.[14]

The verses of the respective Latin chant were sung in alternation with the stanzas of its vernacular partner, the former being sung by the choir, the latter by the congregation. But even here Luther was building on an earlier practice, since in some areas vernacular hymns had been sung in Germany during the

Mass on special feastdays, some in connection with the respective Sequence.[15] Luther, however, went much further than such occasional use and introduced seasonal "Sequence" hymns as a regular feature of his evangelical Mass. The first section of the Wittenberg congregational hymnal, issued in 1529, presents a church-year series of ten such hymns, translated, written or re-written by Martin Luther:[16]

Nun komm der Heiden Heiland	Advent
Christum wir sollen loben schon	Christmas
Gelobet seist du, Jesu Christ	Christmas
Mit Fried und Freud ich fahr dahin	Purification
Christ lag in Todesbanden	Easter
Jesus Christus, unser Heiland der den Tod	Easter
Komm, Gott Schöpfer, Heiliger Geist	Pentecost
Komm, Heiliger Geist, Herre Gott	Pentecost
Nun bitten wir den Heiligen Geist	Pentecost
Gott der Vater wohn uns bei	Trinity

Of these two are based on, or closely related to, specific Latin Sequences *(Christ lag in Todesbanden = Victimae paschali laudes; Komm, Heiliger Geist, Herre Gott = Veni sancte Spiritus);* three are reworkings of earlier *Liesen* (vernacular folk-hymns), a genre closely related to Latin Sequences *(Gelobet seist du, Jesu Christ, Nun bitten wir den Heiligen Geist,* and *Gott der Vater wohn uns bei),* to which should be added one more that, although no medieval model has been discovered, is clearly written in a *Leisen* style *(Jesus Christus, unser Heiland der den Tod);* and three are translations of Latin office hymns *(Nun komm der Heiden Heiland = Veni redemptor gentium* [Christmas], *Christum wir sollen loben schon = A solis ortus cardine* [Christmas], and *Komm, Gott Schöpfer, Heiliger Geist = Veni creator Spiritus* [Pentecost]). Only one can be said to be newly-written, *Mit Fried und Freud ich fahr dahin,* but even that is a versification of the Song of Simeon (Luke 2:29-32), the liturgical canticle known as the *Nunc dimittis.* The "new" "Sequence" hymns for the congregation to sing were therefore in every case effectively new forms of older liturgical material.

In addition to using the traditional Sequence as a model for hymns that were to be sung in the traditional position of the Sequence in the Mass, that is, in between the Epistle and Gospel, Luther also adapted the traditional form of the Latin Sequence to create new congregational versions of parts of the Ordinary of the Mass. The Ordinary comprised the unchanging elements of the Roman Mass that were customarily sung: Kyrie, Gloria, Credo, Sanctus, and Agnus Dei. In the *Deutsche Messe* of 1526 Luther introduced the concept of singing metrical, strophic forms of these parts of the Ordinary:

> After the Gospel the whole congregation sings the Creed in German, *Wir glauben all an einen Gott.* . . . Meanwhile [during the distribution of Communion], the German Sanctus or [Eucharistic hymns] . . . could be sung . . . or the German Agnus Dei.[17]

Neither the text of *Wir glauben all an einen Gott* nor the German Agnus Dei, *Christe, du Lamm Gottes,* was included in the *Deutsche Messe,* but the German Sanctus was given, complete with text and melody: *Jesaiah, dem Propheten, das geschah:*

Jesaiah, dem propheten, das geschach,	Isaiah 'twas the prophet who did see
das er ym geyst den herren sitzen sach	seated above the Lord in majesty
auff eynem hohen thron yun hellem glantz;	high on a lofty throne in splendor bright;
seines kleides saum den kor fullet gantz.	train of his robe filled the temple quite.
Es stunden zween seraph bey yhm daran.	Standing beside him were two seraphim;
Sechs flugel sach er eynen ydern han;	six wings, six wings he saw on each of them.
Mit zwen verbargen sie yhr antlitz klar,	With twain they hid in awe their faces clear;
mit zwen bedeckten sie die fusse gar,	with twain they hid their feet in rev'rent fear.
und mit den andern zwen sie flogen frey,	And with the other two they flew about;
gen ander ruffen sie mit grossem schrey:	one to the other loudly raised the shout:
"Heylig ist Gott der herre zebaoth.	Holy is God, the Lord of Sabaoth,
Heylig ist Gott der herre zebaoth.	Holy is God, the Lord of Sabaoth,
Heylig ist Gott der herre zebaoth.	Holy is God, the Lord of Sabaoth.
Sein ehr die gantze welt erfullet hat."	Behold his glory filleth all the earth.
Von dem schrei zittert schwel und balcken gar;	The angels' cry made beams and lintels shake;
das haus auch gantz vol rauchs und nebel war.[18]	the house also was filled with clouds of smoke.[19]

In the *Deutsche Messe,* from which Luther had eliminated the traditional Eucharistic Canon in favor of the *Verba testamenti* alone, there was also no place for a vernacular Sursum corda with a Preface leading to the Sanctus. Thus both the German Agnus Dei and the German Sanctus were to be sung as *musica sub communionem,* that is, during the distribution of Communion. The melodic form of Luther's chant for *Jesaiah, dem Propheten, das geschah* is an adaptation of the plainchant Sanctus for Sundays in Advent and Lent,[20] a reflection of the period when Luther was working on the *Deutsche Messe,* that is, during Advent 1525. Although it was called the "German Sanctus," and based on a traditional Sanctus chant melody, it is a versification of the broader biblical passage, Isaiah 6:1-4, rather than the narrower liturgical

Sanctus, Isaiah 6:3. In its form it is in a effect a vernacular Sequence. The traditional Sequence was an exposition of the primary teaching of the day or celebration, usually the Gospel on principal feasts. Here, following the form of a Latin Sequence, Luther gives the context of the origin of the Seraphic hymn rather than just the liturgical Sanctus. Further, it is written in rhymed couplets of ten syllables and thus in its form follows the traditional Sequence, even though it was to be sung during Communion rather than in between the Epistle and Gospel.

A further example of Luther's use of the Sequence form for another part of the Ordinary is the versification of the Gloria in excelsis Deo found in the manuscript liturgical provisions in the Church Order drawn up for use in Naumburg in 1537, and thereafter in a variety of hymnals. Some Luther scholars have been skeptical about its provenance, but recently the tendency has been to accept it as being the work of the Wittenberg Reformer. There are a number of features — such as the use of octosyllabic lines, the quotation from Luther's *Small Catechism* (see below), the general relationship between text and melody, and the similarity to *Jesaiah, dem Propheten, das geschah* — that suggest that Luther was its author.[21]

AL ehr und lob sol Gottes sein/	All glory, praise to God be giv'n,
ER ist und heist der höchst allein.	Who reigns supreme in highest heav'n.
SEin zorn auff erden hab ein end,	His wrath on earth comes to an end;
SEin fried und gnad sich zu uns wend.	His peace and grace to us extend.
DEn menschen das gefalle wohl,	Good will among humanity,
DAfür man hertzlich dancken sol.	Who thus should give thanks heartily.
ACh lieber Gott dich loben wir,	O dearest God, we honor thee
UNd preisen dich mit gantzen [be]gir.	And praise thee whole-heartedly.
AUch kniend wir anbeten dich.	Upon our knees we pray to thee,
DEin ehr wir rhümen stetiglich.	And honor thee continually.
WJr dancken dir zu aller zeit/	At all times we give thanks to thee
UMb dein grosse Herrligkeit.	For the greatness of thy glory.
HErr Gott im Himel König du bist,	Lord God, heav'n's King in majesty,
Ein Vater der allmechtig ist.	Who is the Father Almighty.
DU Gottes Son vom vater bist/	From the Father, made manifest,
EJnig geborn Herr Jesu Christ/	Only begotten Jesus Christ.
HErr Gott du zartes Gottes lamb	Lord God, tender Lamb, and holy,
EJn son aus Got des vaters stam.	Son of God the Father truly;
DEr du der welt sünd trägst allein.	Who alone the world's sin carries,
WOlst uns gnedig, barmhertzig sein.	Wills to us his grace and mercies.
DEr du der welt sünd tregst allein.	Who alone the world's sin carries
LAs dir unser bitt gefellig sein.	Be pleased to hear our prayers and cries.
DEr du gleich sitzst dem vater dein.	Thou, who thy Father's nature carries,
WOlst uns gnedig, barmhertzig sein.	Will to us his grace and mercies.

DU bist und bleibst Heilig allein.	Thou only art the Holy One,
UBer alles der Herr allein.	Over all things, the Lord alone.
DEr aller höchst allein du bist,	Thou the Highest, thou art solely,
DU lieber Heiland Jhesu Christ.	Dear Lord Jesus, Savior only,
SAmpt dem vater und heilgen geist.	With Father and Spirit truly
JN Göttlicher Maiestet gleich.	Divinity in majesty.
Amen/*das ist gewislich war*,[22]	Amen, most certain it is true,
DAs bekent aller Engel schar.	Confess'd by all the angels, too,
UNd alle welt so weit und breit.	And all the world, in unity,
VOn anfang bis in ewigkeit.[23]	Till now and in eternity.[24]

Like the German Sanctus the melody for this German Gloria is an adaptation of a traditional Ordinary chant, the *Gloria tempore paschali,* the Gloria for the Easter season.[25] Similarly, it is also written in rhymed couplets and thus is another example of Luther using the form of the Latin Sequence as a model for creating new liturgical music for the evangelical Mass.

The Liturgical Responsory

In general the Responsory was sung in "response" to the reading of Scripture, such as the Gradual in the Roman Mass. Some, such as those at Matins, could be quite lengthy and melismatic chants *(responsoria prolixa).* Others, such as those following the short lesson of the Little Hours of Prime, Terce, Sext, None, and Compline, were somewhat shorter and more syllabic *(responsoria brevia).*[26] At the Office of the Dead there were specific Responsories following each of the biblical lessons.[27] In the medieval church there were more funerary Responsories than were included in the Tridentine Office of the Dead. The form of a funerary Responsory comprises a "respond" followed by a verse (but without the Gloria Patri as with other Responsories), with the respond (or its concluding section) repeated after the verse:[28]

[Respond:] Rogamus te, Domine Deus noster, ut suscipias animas nostrorum defunctorum, quaesumus, pro quibus sanguinem tuum fudisti; recordare quia pulvis sumus, et homo sicut foenum et flos agri.	We implore thee, O Lord our God, to receive the soul of our departed, for whom thy blood was shed; remember that we are dust, and that man is as grass and a flower of the field.
[Versus:] Misericors et miserator et clemens Domine.	Merciful and pitying and forbearing art thou, O Lord.
[Respond:] Recordare quia pulvis sumus, et homo sicut foenum et flos agri.[29]	Remember that we are dust, and that man is as grass and a flower of the field.

233

The second part of the respond (repeated after the *Versus*) is closely based on Psalm 102 [Vulgate Psalm 103]:14-15 and the *Versus* is reminiscent of verse 8 of the same psalm. It is this Responsory form that Luther adapted for evangelical use during the last few years of his life.

Luther's Funeral Responsories

In 1542 the Wittenberg printer Joseph Klug published a small songbook: *Christliche Geseng Lateinsich und Deudsch zum Begrebnis. D. Martinus Luther* [Latin and German Christian Songs for Burials. Dr. Martin Luther]. It contained one Latin hymn, *Iam moesta quiesce querela*, by Prudentius, and six German hymns, all except one the work of Luther: *Aus tiefer Not* (Psalm 130), *Mitten wir im Leben sind, Wir glauben all an einen Gott, Mit Fried und Freud ich fahr dahin, Nun laßt uns den leib begraben* (by Michael Weiss),[30] and *Nun bitten wir den Heiligen Geist*. But these items are preceded by seven Latin biblical Responsories, complete with notated chants. Although reprinted in numerous Lutheran hymnals and anthologies of chant in the sixteenth and seventeenth centuries, they were neglected by later Luther scholarship: none were included in the various collected editions of Luther's works and the seven Responsories first appeared in a critical edition as late as 1984.[31] The Latin incipits are as follows:

I.	*Credo quod redemptor meus vivit*
II.	*Ecce quomodo moritur iustus*
III.	*Cum venisset Jesus*
IV.	*Ecce mysterium magnum dico vobis*
V.	*Stella enim differt a stella in claritate*
VI.	*Nolumus autem vos fratres*
VII.	*Si credimus quod Jesus Christus*

A further Responsory appears later in the volume[32] — together with three Antiphons: *Corpora Sanctorum, Media vita in morte sua* (that Luther translated as *Mitten wir im Leben sind*), and *In pace simil dormiam et requiescam* — a text that is similar to that of VII, but with an entirely different chant melody:

[VIII.] *Si enim credimus*

Of the associated melodies, four (and probably a fifth) are of Responsories of the medieval Office of the Dead:

III.   In tono *Rogamus te*
IV.   In tono *Absolve*
V.   In tono *Deus aeterne*
VI.   In tono *Ne tradas Domine*
[VIII.]   [In tono ??]

Two are texts that appear with their associated melodies:

I.   *Credo quod redemptor,* a variant form of the Responsory that
      follows the first lesson at Matins of the Office for the Dead.[33]
II.   *Ecce quomodo moritur,* a variant of the Responsory that
      follows the sixth lesson at Matins on Holy Saturday,[34] but
      used on Good Friday in the later medieval period.

One melody is based on a non-funerary Responsory:

VII.   In tono *Surge virgo* that employs the beginning of the
      medieval Responsory for the Ascension of Mary.

Luther's funerary Responsories therefore generally employ traditional
chant melodies with different texts; in every case the texts are entirely biblical:

Responsory	*Respond*	*Verse*
I.	Job 19:25	Psalm 146[145]:1-2
II.	Isaiah 57:1-2	Psalm 17[16]:15
III.	Matthew 9:23-24	Mark 5:41-42
IV.	1 Corinthians 15:51-52	1 Corinthians 15:54
V.	1 Corinthians 15:41-44	1 Corinthians 15:45
VI.	1 Thessalonians 4:13	1 Thessalonians 4:14
VII.	1 Thessalonians 4:14, 13	1 Corinthians 15:22
[VIII.]	1 Thessalonians 4:14	1 Corinthians 15:22

In contrast to the "doom and gloom" of many of the medieval funerary
Responsories, Luther's biblical Responsories were created from the primary
passages of the New Testament that stress resurrection. But in every case these
"new" Responsories used the traditional Responsory form, together with pre-
existing chant melodies. Luther's preservation of these earlier melodic forms
was a deliberate policy on his part. He explained his purpose in the preface to
the booklet:

We have collected the fine music and songs which under the papacy were used at vigils, masses for the dead, and burials. Some fine examples of these we have printed in this booklet and we, or whoever is more gifted than we, will select more of them in the future. But we have adapted other texts to the music so that they may adorn our article of resurrection, instead of purgatory with its torment and satisfaction which lets their dead neither sleep nor rest. The melodies and notes are precious. It would be a pity to let them perish. But the texts and words are non-Christian and absurd. They deserve to perish. . . . [The papists] also possess a lot of splendid songs and music, especially in the cathedral and parish churches. But these are used to adorn all sorts of impure and idolatrous texts. Therefore, we have unclothed these idolatrous, lifeless, and foolish texts, and divested them of their beautiful music. We have put this music on the living and holy word of God in order to sing, praise, and honor it. . . . We are concerned with changing the text, not the music.[35]

Thus, in a revised form, the Responsory had a continuing significance for Luther.

Continuity and Change

Luther's uses of both the Sequence and Responsory are examples of how his liturgical reform was a creative amalgam of existing practice with newly-espoused Reformation ideals. In some continuity was more prominent than change, such as Luther's acceptance of the traditional structure of the Mass in both his *Formula missae* (1523) and *Deutsche Messe* (1526), his conservative translations of the Latin collects,[36] and the retention of Latin in towns and cities that had Latin grammar schools and/or universities. On the other hand, in some of his other liturgical provisions change displaced continuity, such as his rejection of the Canon of the Mass, replacing it with the *Verba testamenti* alone,[37] and his creation of the so-called "Flood-Prayer" for the Order of Baptism (1523).[38] But much of his liturgical reforms are ingenious syntheses of continuity and change, of which his "Sequences" and Responsories are representative examples.

The Impact of Luther's "Sequences" and Responsories on Later Lutheranism

Although congregational hymnody was employed at various junctures within the Lutheran forms of worship of later generations, it remained customary for an appropriate hymn to be sung in between the Epistle and Gospel. Most of the time the hymn sung in this liturgical position effectively replaced the traditional Sequence. As more congregational hymnals were produced during the sixteenth century, the basic corpus of ten seasonal "Sequence" hymns of the 1529 Wittenberg hymnal was expanded so that there was at least one hymn for such use on every Sunday, feast and celebration of the church year, a "Sequence" hymn that was closely related to the particular Gospel lection. By the eighteenth century these "hymns of the day" had grown into a rich corpus which included many different hymns appropriate for the days and celebrations throughout the church year.[39] Although there were many options, in practice generally only one of the hymns for a given occasion — established by widespread usage — was sung as the specific "Sequence" hymn. Thus by the eighteenth century around 70-80 hymns became the primary ones sung as Lutheran "Sequences," chorales that were memorized by Lutheran congregations and sung on the respective Sundays and celebrations. The same chorales figure again and again over the next few centuries in the organ and vocal compositions of most of the composers of Lutheran Germany, notably in the music of Johann Sebastian Bach.

The Sequence principle — a homiletic commentary in musical form of the primary teaching of the day or celebration — not only influenced the development of an important aspect of the Lutheran congregational chorale, it also contributed to the evolution of two specifically Lutheran genres: the *Spruchmotette* and Cantata. The *Spruchmotette* ([biblical] verse motet), or *Evangelienmotette* (Gospel motet), was a choral setting of the primary verse(s) of the Gospel of the day that was customarily sung in between the reading/chanting of the Gospel and the sermon that was an exposition of the same passage. Many annual cycles of such motets were published between the middle of the sixteenth century and the end of the seventeenth century, by such composers as Raselius, Calvisius, Demantius, Vulpius, and Franck, among others, with settings that ranged from two to eight or more voices.[40] The Cantata form that evolved during the seventeenth century and reached its zenith in the cantatas of Bach, while in musical terms far from the chant forms of the traditional Sequence, was nevertheless an extension of the Sequence principle. Like the medieval Sequence, the Cantata was an exposition of the biblical lections (primarily the Gospel) of the day or celebration, but in a succession of different movements (choruses, arias, recitatives and chorales) with orchestral accompaniment. The musical form was more complex but the liturgical function was the same as the traditional Sequence.

The Latin Sequence was not entirely displaced but continued to be sung at major festivals in Lutheran worship when both a Latin Sequence and a vernacular hymn were sung in close proximity, such as *Grates nunc omnes* with *Gelobet seist du, Jesu Christ* at Christmas, *Victimae paschali laudes* with the old folk-hymn *Christ ist erstanden*, or Luther's reworking of its primary themes in *Christ lag in Todesbanden*, at Easter, and *Veni sancte Spiritus* with either *Komm, Heiliger Geist, erfüll die Herzen*, or *Komm, Heiliger Geist, Herre Gott* at Pentecost. In the sixteenth century the two forms were generally sung in an integrated pattern of alternation, each verse or stanza following its equivalent in the other language. In the sixteenth and seventeenth century the usual practice was for the congregation to sing the German hymn after the choir had sung the Latin Sequence. Latin Sequences thus survived well into the eighteenth century. For example, the *Neu Leipziger Gesangbuch* (Leipzig, 1682), edited by Gottfried Vopelius — still in use during Bach's time as the Thomaskantor in the city — includes seasonal Latin Sequences with notation, two of which are given with German translations so that either, or both, could be sung:

Advent:	*Mittit ad virginem (Als der gütige Gott)*
Christmas:	*Grates nunc omnes (Danksagen wir alle)*
Easter:	*Victimae paschali*
Pentecost:	*Veni sancte Spiritus*
Trinity:	*Benedicta semper sancta sit Trinitas*[41]

Luther's Sequence-like Gloria *All Ehr und Lob soll Gottes sein* did not enter in general use. It had been preceded by Nikolaus Decius' strophic form *Allein Gott in der Höh sei Ehr* (1522), with a melody also based on the same chant that Luther used, the *Gloria tempore paschali*. *Allein Gott in der Höh sei Ehr* quickly became the Gloria-hymn commonly sung by Lutheran congregations. *All Ehr und Lob soll Gottes sein* did appear in a number of mid-sixteenth century hymnals and was also adapted into a strophic form to be sung with the *Allein Gott in der Höh sei Ehr* melody in the Bapst *Gesangbuch* of 1545.[42] But it soon disappeared from mainstream hymnals, though it was resurrected in some nineteenth-century hymnals.[43] In contrast Luther's German Sanctus *Jesaiah, dem Propheten, das geschah*, in the Sequence form of rhymed couplets, has never been displaced from Lutheran hymnals.

Luther's Latin funerary Responsories had fairly widespread currency in hymnals and anthologies of chant published in the second half of the sixteenth century. But by the early seventeenth century the only Latin element from Luther's 1542 booklet generally found in hymnals was the Latin hymn by Prudentius, *Iam moesta quiesce querela*. This hymn is found in Johann Hermann Schein's *Cantional Oder Gesangbuch Augspurgischer Confession* (Leipzig, 1627) as well as in Vopelius' *Neu Leipzig Gesangbuch* (1682).[44] But the influence of one of the Responsories in Luther's 1542 collection was significant and widespread. While the second Responsory, *Ecce quomodo moritur iustus*, was not much used after the sixteenth century, its basic text, in a setting by Jacob Handl (Gallus) composed towards the end of the sixteenth century, was widely sung in Lutheran Germany during Holy Week. Handl's motet was included in Cantionals, such as Vopelius' *Neu Leipziger Gesangbuch* (1682).[45] For example, the motet was sung three times in Holy Week in the Leipzig churches during Bach's Kantorate, always after the singing of passion settings: on Palm Sunday it was heard after Johann Walter's *St. Matthew Passion*, sung as the Gospel of the day; on Good Friday morning it was similarly heard after Walter's *St. John Passion*, sung as the Gospel for that day; and on Good Friday afternoon it was sung again, at the close of a concerted setting of the passion, such as Bach's St. John or St. Matthew Passion.[46] Clearly the chant form *Ecce quomodo moritur iustus* found in Luther's funerary collection must have exerted some influence on the later use of the Handl motet on the same text.

Luther's funerary Responsories, however, were significantly influential in ensuring the continuity of chant forms being sung within the worship of the Lutheran churches. The Responsories themselves provided models to be followed by others, and in his preface to the 1542 collection Luther effectively set the agenda for the continued use of such chant forms:

> We have collected the fine music and songs which under the papacy were used at vigils, masses for the dead, and burials. Some fine examples of these we have printed in this booklet and we, or whoever is more gifted than we, will select more of them in the future. But we have adapted other texts to the music so that they may adorn our article of resurrection. . . . <But we do not hold that the notes need to be sung the same in all the churches. Let every church follow the music according to their own book and custom. For I do not like to hear the notes in a Responsory or other song changed from what I was accustomed to in my youth.> We are concerned with changing the text, not the music.[47]

The passage enclosed with angled brackets (< >) was quoted by Michael Praetorius in his appendix to the first volume of his *Syntagma musicum* (1614/

15).[48] In this appendix Praetorius quotes, from a manuscript source, Johann Walter's words about Luther's ability in adapting Latin chant forms to the German language. Though Walter's words about Luther have been often re-quoted, the context is frequently glossed over. Walter's broader purpose was to underscore the continued use of Gregorian chant forms, with both Latin and German texts, and as part of this he cites Luther's particular ability in adapting Latin chant forms for German texts. Praetorius' purpose in including Walter's words was to endorse the continued use of chant forms in Lutheran worship. Luther's policy expressed in his 1542 preface, and cited by Praetorius — "But we do not hold that the notes need to be sung the same in all the churches. Let every church follow the music according to their own book and custom" — was put into effect in the second half of the sixteenth century. Various anthologies of chant for the church year were published for Lutheran use that reflected the pre-Reformation usage of those areas: Nordhausen, edited by Johann Spangenberg (Magdeburg, 1545); Lüneberg, edited by Lucas Lossius (Nuremberg, 1553, and later editions); St. Andreasberg, edited by Johannes Keuchenthal (Wittenberg, 1573); Leipzig, edited by Nikolaus Selnecker (Leipzig, 1587); Hamburg, edited by Franz Eler (Hamburg, 1588); Havelberg, edited by Matthäus Ludecus (Wittenberg, 1589).[49] These publications, together with various hymnals that reprinted various items from them, ensured that pre-Reformation chant forms continued to be sung in Lutheran churches at least until the eighteenth century.[50] In those towns and cities where there were Latin schools Matins and Vespers continued to be sung in Latin by the pupils. Thus in Leipzig during Bach's time, though Luther's funerary Responsories were apparently no longer sung, seasonal Responsories were, since they were available in Vopelius' *Neu Leipziger Gesangbuch* (1682):

Rex noster adveniet	Advent
Verbum caro factum est	Christmas Day & Purification
Illuminare, illuminare Jerusalem	Epiphany
Discubuit Jesus	Maundy Thursday
Tenebrae factae sunt	Good Friday
Dum transisset Sabbathum	Easter Day
Ite in orbem universum	Ascension
Apparuerunt apostolis	Pentecost
Summae Trinitatis	Trinity
Inter natus mulierum	St. John the Baptist
Magnificat anima mea	Visitation
Te sanctum Dominum	St Michael
Fuerunt sine querela	Apostle Days[51]

These two pre-Reformation liturgical-musical forms, the Sequence and Responsory, which Luther adapted for use in Reformation worship are examples of the way he combined Catholic principle with Protestant substance, the marriage of *cantica sacra veteris ecclesiae* (sacred songs of the old church) with *sola scriptura* (Scripture alone). The Sequence supplied him with a model for expounding the primary message of the Gospel of the day in congregational hymnody, as well as providing a paradigm for the versification of two parts of the Ordinary that were scripturally based: the German Gloria and the German Sanctus. The Responsory presented him the opportunity to invest such melodies with consistent scriptural texts, and Luther's important models contributed significantly to the preservation of the older chant forms within Lutheran worship. Continuity and change lie at the root of Luther's liturgical reforms. As he wrote near the beginning of his *Formula missae:*

> We therefore first assert: It is not now or ever has been our intention to abolish the liturgical service of God completely, but rather to purify the one that is now in use from the wretched accretions which corrupt it and to point out pious [evangelical] use.[52]

CHAPTER 16

Biblical Canticles

Liturgical canticles are generally taken for granted or ignored,[1] yet they have been part of liturgical worship from the earliest times. For Luther such biblical canticles were not to be excised from the worship of the emerging Lutheran church, as is demonstrated by the contents of the hymnals, issued in Wittenberg and Leipzig, for which Luther exercised editorial oversight. There is, however, a surprising lack of literature devoted to discussions of the purpose and significance of these vernacular canticles. Their existence is noted in various places, such as in Hans Joachim Moser's *Die Evangelische Kirchenmusik in Deutschland*,[2] in Konrad Ameln's introductory material in the facsimiles of the 1533 Klug and the 1545 Bapst hymnals,[3] or in other literature cited here in the notes. Since they appear in these hymnals set to a variety of psalm tones, one might have expected to find some discussion of them in Otto Brodde's otherwise exhaustive study of the continued use of chant forms in the Lutheran church.[4] But there is none, and neither is there an entry in the older *Enzylopädie* of Kümmerle.[5] In much the same way that Luther's Latin funeral Responsories were ignored for centuries, until Markus Jenny produced a modern edition,[6] so these canticles, though not entirely neglected, have nevertheless remained essentially under-researched.[7] Part of the reason for this neglect is that the four-part, faburden settings of the psalm tones to which these canticles are set in the 1533 Klug *Gesangbuch* are regarded as the work of Johann Walter rather than Luther. That may be so (see the discussion below) but since Luther was the primary editor of the Wittenberg hymnals published by Joseph Klug, he was presumably responsible for the choice of these biblical canticles.

Luther's Latin funeral Responsories were included in a separate publication in 1542.[8] In contrast, the biblical canticles were never issued separately but originally formed the concluding section of the no longer extant 1529 *Geistliche Lieder,* edited by Luther and issued by Klug in Wittenberg. They continued to appear in the later editions of the Wittenberg hymnal issued by Klug in 1533, 1535, 1543/44, and 1545, as well as in the first part of the Bapst *Geystliche Lieder* (Leipzig, 1545), where they were included before the final section of the funeral hymns and Responsories that had been published separately in 1542. The general scholarly consensus is that the editorial process of the first part of the Bapst *Gesangbuch* was overseen by Luther, in contrast to the second part, which was probably compiled by someone else. These vernacular biblical canticles were therefore issued in hymnals that were closely connected to Luther. Further, the canticles are prose texts taken from various editions of Luther's Bible and thus constitute another link with the Reformer. The logical conclusion to be drawn is that Luther himself was responsible for selecting and editing the texts of these canticles, and may well have also assigned to them their particular musical chant forms.

Biblical Canticles in the Latin Liturgy[9]

Luther would have been familiar with the Latin biblical canticles that were sung in the daily office, particularly at Lauds. He would have regularly sung them while a boy at the Latin schools he attended in Mansfield, Magdeburg, and Eisenach,[10] and as a monk of the Erfurt Augustinian ("Black") cloister between 1505 and 1508. The Old Testament canticles sung at Lauds were as follows:

Sunday & Feasts	*Benedicite omnia opera*	Daniel 3:57-88
Monday	*Confitebor tibi, Domine*	Isaiah 12:1-6
Tuesday	*Ego dixi*	Isaiah 38:10-20
Wednesday	*Exultavit cor meum*	1 Samuel 2:1-10
Thursday	*Cantemus Domino*	Exodus 15:1-19
Friday	*Domine audivi*	Habakkuk 3:2-19
Saturday	*Audite caeli*	Deuteronomy 32:1-43

Three biblical canticles were also customarily sung at the third nocturn of Matins on Sundays and feasts. For example, for the third nocturn of Matins on Christmas Day the canticles were *Populus qui ambulabat* (Isaiah 9:2-7), *Laetare Jerusalem* (Isaiah 66:10-16), and *Urbs fortitudinis* (Isaiah 26:1-12). There were also a few occasions when Old Testament canticles were sung in the Mass. For example, on Holy Saturday, three of the twelve lessons of the

Mass were followed by canticles (whose texts began where the preceding lesson ended, thus creating a unity between lection and canticle): the fourth lesson was followed by *Cantemus Domino* (Exodus 15:1-19); after the eighth lesson the canticle *Vinea facta est* (Isaiah 5:1-9) was sung; and after the eleventh lesson, the canticle *Attende [Audite] caelum* (Deuteronomy 32:1-43). Other biblical canticles were assigned to specific occasions in various liturgical sources, but there was variety both in the choice of biblical passages and the celebration or observance on which they were sung.[11] In addition to these Old Testament canticles there were the New Testament canticles associated with particular hours of the daily Office: at Lauds the Benedictus (Luke 1:68-79) was sung; at Vespers the Magnificat (Luke 1:46-55); and at Compline the Nunc dimittis (Luke 2:29-31).

Luther's familiarity with these Latin canticles surfaces from time to time in his writings. In The Judgment of Martin Luther on Monastic Vows (1521) he writes (emphasis added):

> . . . the true worship of God established in the first three commandments lies dead [in monasticism]. . . . In place of . . . true worship they have substituted another which is most becoming to them. It is a great pomp of ceremonies distinguished by vestments and postures, by *canticles* and lections. In the whole lot there is nothing about faith, the divine name, or about the work of God. Everything about it is utterly and completely human. A trace of this kind of worship can be detected in the institution of Paul in 1 Corinthians 14[:1-19] where he teaches that three things should take place in the assembly of the church. First, speaking with tongues or singing psalms; second, prophesying or interpretation; third, prayer. In the first place, that means that something used to be recited from the Scriptures or the psalms. Then the prophets would interpret and teach. Third, they prayed together. That was a divine and most Christian institution ordained for teaching and exhortation. The first one is emulated today by the readings at Matins, by the Epistles, by the Gospels, and by the *selected canticles;* the second by the homilies; the third by responses, antiphons, graduals, and all the rest of the things generally read or sung. But none of it is done properly! All these things are done not with the intention of teaching or instructing, but simply with the desire of performing so many works. They are quite satisfied just to have read them, sung them, or bellowed them.[12]

Similarly, in the preface to his German commentary on Habakkuk (1526), after criticizing his predecessors for not attempting to learn Hebrew in order to expound the Old Testament, Luther writes:

And yet it would have been meet and right, also useful and necessary, to expound Habakkuk clearly, because the last chapter, his prayer, was used daily; it was both sung and read in all the churches, but probably according to the proverbial saying "the way the nuns read the Psalter" [that is, without understanding].[13]

It is clear that Luther was not condemning the canticles themselves but rather their misuse and the failure to understand their function in worship, a point that he made again in the short preface to the biblical canticles of the 1529 *Gesangbuch* (see further below). In order to promote an evangelical understanding of such songs, he expounded their content from time to time, such as his commentaries on the Canticle of Mary, the Magnificat (1521), and the Canticle of Habakkuk (1525/26).[14]

Psalms and Canticles in Wittenberg

The Latin canticles were sung to modified forms of the basic psalm tones. Thus the three canticles at Mass on Holy Saturday were all set in Tone VIII. It needs to be borne in mind that before strophic vernacular hymnody was introduced into the worship of Wittenberg Luther directed that psalmody should continue to be sung to the traditional psalm tones. This is the implication of his pamphlet Concerning the Order of Public Worship (1523), which reflects the simplified services that were begun in Wittenberg in March that year, replacing the daily Latin Mass:

> We should assemble daily at four or five in the morning and have [God's Word] read, either by pupils or priests, or whoever it may be, in the same manner as the lesson is still read at Matins; this should be done by one or two, or by one individual or choir after responding to the other, as may seem most suitable.
>
> Thereupon the preacher, or whoever has been appointed, shall come forward and interpret a part of the same lesson, so that all others may understand and learn it, and be admonished. . . . If this is not done, the congregation is not benefitted by the lesson, as has been the case in cloisters and in convents, where they only bawled against the walls.
>
> The lesson should be taken from the Old Testament. . . .
>
> Now when the lesson and its interpretation have lasted half an hour or so, the congregation shall unite in giving thanks to God, in praising him, and in praying for the fruits of the Word, etc. For this, the Psalms

should be used and some good Responsories and Antiphons. In brief, let everything be completed in one hour or whatever time seems desirable; for one must not overload souls or weary them, as was the case until now in monasteries and convents, where they burdened themselves like mules.

In like manner, come together at five or six in the evening . . . [and] have reading, interpreting, praising, singing, and praying just as in the morning, also for an hour. For all that matters is that the Word of God be given free reign to uplift and quicken souls so that they do not become weary. . . .

. . . to select the chants and Psalms for the daily morning and evening service shall be the duty of the pastor and preacher. For every morning he shall appoint a fitting responsory or antiphon with a collect, likewise for the evening; this is to be read and chanted publicly after the lesson and exposition.[15]

Although the document was in German the simplified daily offices were conducted in Latin — they had to be, because, apart from translations included with Luther's exposition of seven penitential psalms (1517),[16] and one or two others,[17] at that time there were no other German psalms available for such daily services. Thus the Latin texts of the psalms were sung to the traditional psalm tones. Although these daily Offices to some degree represented an interim measure — since Wittenberg eventually reverted to the traditional forms of Matins and Vespers — the principle was established that the singing of the prose text of Scripture was to be continued in evangelical worship. Thus in the *Deutsche Messe* (1526), in place of the traditional Introit, Luther directed that a complete psalm was to be sung in the vernacular (the example he gave was Psalm 34 set to Tone I),[18] and the 1529/33 Klug *Gesangbuch* included the prose German text of Psalm 111 (Tone I), "to be sung during the distribution of the Sacrament."[19]

Around 1529 there was a marked increase in the provision of vernacular chant forms for use in the Wittenberg churches. This formed part of the intensification of instruction and edification that was put in place after the results of the 1528 visitation had revealed that there was still much misunderstanding about evangelical faith and practice. Luther's response was to issue his two catechisms, the expanded edition of his *Betbüchlein* (which included sermons on parts of the catechism),[20] and to provide additional liturgical forms, mostly in the vernacular, that were incorporated into the 1529 hymnal (which included a section of catechism hymns).[21]

On 13 February 1529, Luther reported to Nikolaus Hausmann that the Litany, in both German and Latin, was being sung in Wittenberg and that he was thinking of publishing the two versions with their chant melodies.[22] The German Litany was issued in Wittenberg in a no longer extant imprint, with at least three Nuremberg reprints before the end of the year (1529), as well as being incorporated into the 1529 *Gesangbuch* in a slightly modified form.[23] It is likely that the Latin Litany was also issued as a separate imprint, though there is no supporting evidence. The Latin Litany was apparently not included in the first appearance of the 1529 Klug *Gesangbuch,* but was integrated into the second imprint issued later the same year[24] (on the two 1529 imprints, see further below). Around the same time that the German and Latin forms of the Litany came into use, that is, the end of 1528 or the beginning of 1529, Luther also created his vernacular version of the Te Deum, in rhymed couplets, with music based on the traditional chant: *Herr Gott, dich loben wir.*[25] It was almost certainly issued in a separate Wittenberg imprint in 1529, since two extant imprints were issued the same year, one in Zwickau and the other in Nuremberg.[26] Like the two versions of the Litany, the German Te Deum was also incorporated into the 1529 Klug *Gesangbuch,* though not within the section of biblical canticles (the custom in Latin sources).[27]

Biblical Canticles in the 1529 *Gesangbuch*

The *Geistliche Lieder* published by Joseph Klug in Wittenberg in 1529 is no longer extant. There is a reference to a known copy in a 1693 Leipzig dissertation,[28] and towards the end of the eighteenth century, a description appeared in the fifth volume of the *Journal von und für Deutschland* (1788).[29] At least one copy was known in the mid-nineteenth century, since in volume 56 (published in 1854) of the first Erlangen edition of Luther's works it is described thus:

> Geistliche Leider auffs new gebessert zu Wittemberg D. Mar. Luther. M.D.XXJX. Am Ende: Gedruckt zu Wittemberg durch Joseph Klug. 1529. 160 Blätter 12°, die letzte Seite leer. Mit Tit. Einfassung und vielen Holzschnitten [160 leaves 12°, the last page blank. With titlepage border and many woodcuts].[30]

A single copy of the 1533 edition was discovered in the Lutherhalle, Wittenberg, in 1932, which was eventually issued in facsimile in 1954.[31] There are some leaves missing from the end of the volume, since the last page (fol. 180^v) has just the beginning of the index (A-D), which would have covered a few more pages, plus a colophon and final woodcut that each would have filled a page. This means that the 1533 edition probably comprised 24 gatherings (each gathering = 8 leaves) = 192 leaves = 384 pages, which contrasts with the 1854 Erlangen report that the *Gesangbuch* comprised 160 leaves, that is, 20 gatherings = 320 pages. This might suggest that the biblical canticles, which conclude the 1533 edition, were not part of the 1529 edition. But this cannot be the case because two hymnals published in 1531, both closely dependent on the 1529 Klug *Gesangbuch* (one High German and the other Low German), include most of the biblical canticles: *Geistliche lieder aufs new gebessert zu Wittemberg D. Mar. Luth. M.D.XXXj* (Erfurt: Rauscher, 1531), and *Geystlyke leder vppt nye gebetert tho Wittēberch dorch D. Martin Luther* (Rostock: Dietz, 1531). The biblical canticles therefore must have been included in the 1529 *Gesangbuch,* and the discrepancy between the two different bibliographical descriptions requires an alternative explanation.

In a letter Georg Rörer wrote to Stephan Roth at the end of 1529 there is a reference to two books of German songs,[32] implying that there were two editions of the Klug *Gesangbuch* issued that year. In another letter written to Roth around the same time Rörer reported on the expanded content of what must have been the second 1529 imprint:

> I have diligently emended this booklet and added summaries of the songs/hymns *(canticorum)* whereby these canticles *(cantica)* can also be understood by the simple [uneducated]; the booklet grows by the addition of the Latin litany and the German psalm "Da Israel aus Ägypten zog" [Psalm 114/115] with its melody."[33]

According to the two bibliographical descriptions of the 1529 *Gesangbuch* there is a difference between them amounting to over sixty pages. It appears therefore that the first imprint did not include the Latin litany (21 pages) nor Psalm 114/115, the last item in the later imprint (7 pages), that is, the two items that Rörer states were added to the later imprint. If the earlier imprint had included the biblical canticles with simple monodic chant, rather than the two-page spreads required for the four-part settings of the later imprint, it would have been some twenty or more pages shorter. Further, when the four-part settings of the canticles were added to the later imprint, in one or two cases, in order to create a two-page spread for the four individual parts of the setting of the chant, the otherwise preceding blank recto page was filled with a repeated woodcut. For example, the woodcut of the Crucifixion appears before Canticle v (fol. 152^r) and Canticle xv (fol. 175^r). Thus the earlier imprint may not have included these woodcut repetitions. Thus most of the 60+ pages can be accounted for by the probability of two different 1529 imprints. Utilizing this information, together with a comparison with *Geystlyke*

Table 16.1. Biblical Canticles in the Two 1529 *Gesangbuch* Imprints
(Compared with Rostock 1531)

		1531	1529^I	1529^{II}
[i]	Exodus 15:1-18	+	+	+
[ii]	Deuteronomy 32:1-13	+	+	+
[iii]	Judges 5:2-31	+	+	+
[iv]	1 Samuel 2:1-10	+	+	+
[v]	Isaiah 12:1-6	+	+	+
[vi]	Isaiah 26:1-21	+	+	+
[vii]	Isaiah 38:10-20	+	+	+
[viii]	Isaiah 61:10-11	–	?	+
[ix]	Isaiah 63:7-19; 64:1-12	+	+	+
[x]	Jonah 2:3-10	+	+	+
[xi]	Habakkuk 3:1-19	+	+	+
[xii]	Psalm 117	–	?	+
[xiii]	Luke 1:46-55	+	+	+
[xiv]	Luke 1:68-79	+	+	+
[xv]	Luke 2:29-31	+	+	+
[xvi]	Luke 2:14	+	+	+
[xvii]	Psalm 114–115	–	–	+

leder (Rostock, 1531),[34] which appears to have been closely based on the first 1529 imprint, it is possible to identify the content of the final section of biblical canticles in the two imprints of the 1529 Gesangbuch (see Table 16.1).

The Texts of the German Biblical Canticles

Luther was not the first to prepare biblical canticles for evangelical worship. Thomas Müntzer included five canticles and the Te Deum in his *Deutzsch kirchen ampt* ([Eilenburg: Widemar, 1523/24]):

Lauds: *Mein hertz ist frölich im Herten* (1 Samuel 2:1-10)[35]
Herre, ich wil dich bekennen (Isaiah 12:1-6)[36]
Ich hab gesaget: in mittel meynes lebens (Isaiah 38:10-20)[37]
Gesegnet sey Got der Herr von Ißrael (Luke 1:68-79)[38]
Vespers: *Meyne sele erhebet den Herren* (Luke 1:46-55)[39]
Matins: *O Got, wir loben dich* (Te Deum)[40]

The Zwickau hymnal of 1525 began with three canticles, Benedictus, Magnificat, and Nunc dimittis, *Gesegnet sey Gott der herr von Israel, Meyn Seel erhebt den herren,* and *Herr, nun lassestu deynen diener ym fride faren,* respectively.[41] A version of Psalms 114 and 115, *In aussgang Israel von Egypten,* appeared under the title "Psalmus Jn exitu Jsrael verdeutscht," in *Etliche Christliche Gesenge vnd Psalmen/wilche vor bey dem Enchiridion nicht gewest synd* ([Erfurt], 1525), almost certainly the work of Johannes Loersfelt.[42] Luther was undoubtedly aware of these examples but his concern was more comprehensive than these earlier sources with canticles in the vernacular.

That it was Georg Rörer who reported to Roth about his collaboration on Luther's 1529 *Gesangbuch* is particularly significant with regard to the biblical canticles. Rörer was a close colleague of Luther — to some extent his amanuensis — and his primary proofreader, especially in connection with revisions of Bible translations. A year or two later he would be the primary reviser of *New deudsch Psalter* (Wittenberg: Lufft, 1528, a revision of the Psalter first issued in 1524), published as *Der Deudsch Psalter* (Wittenberg: Lufft, 1531; effectively the third edition).[43] Although others were involved with Luther in this second revision process with regard to the Psalter, such as Melanchthon, Creuciger, and Jonas, the principal collaborator was Rörer. The rhythmic nature and singability of the Psalm texts received special attention in the 1531 Psalter, and Luther was particularly pleased with the result.[44]

Most of the texts of the biblical canticles in 1529[I] were presumably taken from those parts of the German Bible that had been published prior to this year: Canticles xiii-xvi from *Newen Testaments Deutzsch* (1522); Canticles i and ii from the first part of the *Alten Testament deutsch* [the Pentateuch] ([1523]); Canticles iii-iv from the *Andern teyls des Alten Testaments* [Joshua-Esther] (1524); Canticle x from the commentary and translation of Jonah (1526); Canticle xi from the commentary and translation of Habakkuk (1526); Canticles v-ix from *Der Prophet Jesaia Deudsch* (1528); Canticles xii and xvii from the first revision of the Psalter (1528). However, since Canticles viii and xii were not included in *Geystlyke leder* (Rostock, 1531; see Table 16.1), it may mean that they were not in 1529[I] and therefore represent some of the additions that Rörer mentioned in the letter to Roth referred to above. In the 1533 edition there are four canticles (nos. x-xii, xvii) that have a text that postdates 1529 (see Table 16.2 below).[45] These modifications might have been made for the 1533 edition, but could well have been among the "diligently emended corrections" that Rörer informed Roth that he had introduced into 1529[II], therefore anticipating the subsequent published revisions of the German Bible, especially the versions of Psalms 114, 115, and 117 that appeared in the 1531 Psalter.

The section of canticles was reprinted in the 1535 edition of the

Table 16.2. Biblical Canticles in the 1533 Klug *Gesangbuch*

	First Line	Biblical Reference	Folio	Year	WA DB
[i]	*Ich wil dem Herrn singen*	Exodus 15:1-18	134^v-137^r	1523	8:244, 248
[ii]	*Mercket auff, jr himel*	Deuteronomy 32:1-13	138^v-144^r	1523	8:662, 664
[iii]	*Lobet den Herrn/ an denen die freywillig*	Judges 5:2-31	144^v-148^v	1524	9^1:98, 100, 102
[iv]	*Mein hertz ist frölich jnn dem Herren*	1 Samuel 2:1-10	151^v-152^v	1524	9^1:188
[v]	*Ich danke dir, Herr*	Isaiah 12:1-6	152^v-153^v	1528	11^1:54, 56
[vi]	*Wir haben eine starcke Stad*	Isaiah 26:1-21	154^v-156^v	1528	11^1:82, 84, 86
[vii]	*Ich sprach, nu mus ich zur helle*	Isaiah 38:10-20	157^r-158^v	1528	11^1:116, 118
[viii]	*Ich frewe mich jnn dem HERREN*	Isaiah 61:10-11	159^r	1528	11^1:174
[ix]	*Ich wil der güete des HERRN gedencken*	Isaiah 63:7-19; 64:1-12	160^r-163^r	1528	11^1:178, 180
[x]	*Ich rieff zu dem Herrn jnn meiner angst*	Jonah 2:3-10	163^v-165^r	1532	11^2:264
[xi]	*HERR, ich hab dein gerücht gehöret*	Habakkuk 3:1-19	165^v-168^r	1532	11^2:306, 308
[xii]	*Lobet den Herren alle Heiden*	Psalm 117	168^v-169^v	1531	10^1:491
[xiii]	*Meine seel erhebt den Herren*	Luke 1:46-55	171^v-172^v	1527	6:212, 214
[xiv]	*Gelobet sey der Herr der Gott Israel*	Luke 1:68-79	173^r-174^v	1527	6:214
[xv]	*HERR/nu lessestu deinen diener*	Luke 2:29-31	175^v-176^v	1526	6:218
[xvi]	*Preis sey Gott jnn der höhe*	Luke 2:14	176^v	1527	6:216
[xvii]	*In exitu Israel de Aegypto/ Du Israel aus Egypten zoch*	Psalm 114–115	[177^v]-180^r	1531	10^1:485, 487

Gesangbuch, but in the 1543 edition some of the texts were revised. For example, the beginning of Canticle i was changed from "Ich will dem Herrn singen, denn er hat herrlich gehandelt" (1533) to "Ich will dem Herrn singen, denn er hat eine herrliche Tat getan" (1543). Similarly the beginning of Canticle iii was changed from "Lobet den Herrn/an denen die freywillig waren im Volk" (1533) to "Lobet den Herrn, daß Israel wieder frei is worden" (1543).[46] In the 1545 Bapst *Gesangbuch* which, though published in Leipzig rather than Wittenberg, was effectively the continuation of the series of hymnals begun by Klug, the canticles were further revised. In general they reflect the text of the 1545 *Deutsche Bibel* (see Table 16.3). However, some of the texts are not quite the same as the 1545 Bible. Examples include: Canticle vii where the 1545 *Gesangbuch* renders Isaiah 38:10 as "Nu mus ich zur Helle pforten faren, ehe ich michs versahe, Und gedacht noch lenger zu leben," the 1545 Bible has "Nur

Table 16.3. Biblical Canticles in the 1545 Bapst *Gesangbuch*

	First Line	Biblical Reference	No.	Year	WA DB
[i]	*Ich wil dem HERRN singen*	Exodus 15:1-18	lxiiii	1545	8:245, 247
[ii]	*Mercket auff, ir himel*	Deuteronomy 32:1-13	lxv	1545	8:663, 665
[iii]	*Lobet den HERRN das Israel*	Judges 5:2-31	lxvi	1545	9^1:99, 101, 103
[iv]	*Mein hertz ist frölich in dem HERREN*	1 Samuel 2:1-10	lxvii	1545	9^1:189
[v]	*Ich danke dir, HERR*	Isaiah 12:1-6	lxviii	1545	11^1:55, 57
[vi]	*Wir haben eine feste Stad*	Isaiah 26:1-21	lxix	1545	11^1:83, 85, 87
[vii]	*Ich sprach, Nu mus ich zur helle*	Isaiah 38:10-20	lxx	1545	11^1:117, 119
[viii]	*Ich frewe mich im HERREN*	Isaiah 61:10-11	lxxi	1545	11^1:175
[ix]	*Ich wil der güte des HERRN gedencken*	Isaiah 63:7-19; 64:1-12	lxxii	1545	11^1:179, 181
[x]	*Ich rieff zu dem HERRN in meiner angst*	Jonah 2:3-10	lxxiii	1545	11^2:265
[xi]	*HERR ich habe dein gerücht gehöret*	Habakkuk 3:1-19	lxxiiii	1545	11^2:307, 309
[xii]	[Psalm 117; omitted]				
[xiii]	*Meine seel erhebt den HERREN*	Luke 1:46-55	lxxv	1545	6:213, 215
[xiv]	*Gelobet sey der HERR, der Gott Israel*	Luke 1:68-79	lxxvi	1545	6:215
[xv]	*HERR, nu lessestu deinen diener*	Luke 2:29-31	lxxvii	1545	6:219
[xvi]	*Preis sey Gott jnn der höhe*	Luke 2:14	lxxviii	1545	6:217
[xvii]	*In exitu Israel de Aegypto/ Du Israel aus Egypten zoch*	Psalm 114–115	lxxix	1545	10^1:485, 487

mus ich zur Helle pforten faren, da mein zeit aus war, Da ich gedacht noch lenger zu leben"; Canticle viii of the 1545 *Gesangbuch* renders Isaiah 61:10 as "wie an Breutgam in seinem schmuck, wie ein Priester pranget . . . ," whereas the 1545 Bible has "wie an Breutgam mit priestlichem Schmuck, gezieret . . ."; Canticle xv in the 1545 *Gesangbuch* begins "Preis sey Gott in der höhe," whereas in the 1545 Bible it begins "Ehre sey Gott in der höhe." Where the text of the 1545 *Gesangbuch* differs from the 1545 Bible it is usually found to be the same as the 1543 Klug text. This suggests that the Bapst *Gesangbuch* was sent to the printer before the revision of the 1545 Bible had been completed.

One of the "canticles" was omitted from the 1545 Bapst *Gesangbuch*: Canticle xii, Psalm 117. Including this Psalm among the canticles in the 1529 *Gesangbuch* was something of a novelty, in that there does not appear to be an earlier source that included the Psalm among biblical canticles. No doubt its content was the primary factor for its inclusion. Luther seems to have had a preoccupation with the Psalm during the period around 1529-1530. In the summer of 1530, while at Coburg Castle, he wrote a commentary on Psalm 117, which was later revised, expanded, and published by Georg Rhau around the middle of October that year.[47] Of significance is the dedication to Hans von Sternberg, who had chaired the visitation commission of the churches in Franconia in 1528-29. This is perhaps further confirmation that the 1529 *Gesangbuch* formed part of the response to the results of that visitation. It is not clear exactly why this psalm was omitted from the 1545 *Gesangbuch*.

Viewing the texts of these canticles as they appeared in the sequence of hymnals published between 1529 and 1545, it is clear that there was a concern that these biblical songs should parallel the work on the revision of the vernacular Bible. The principle seems to have been that when Scripture was sung in evangelical worship these texts should be clear and unambiguous. The singing of Scripture within the context of worship in which other Scripture was read and preached upon was fundamental for Luther. Thus he wrote at the end of his exposition of the third commandment of the Decalogue in the *Large Catechism* of 1529:

> Therefore you must constantly keep God's Word in your heart, on your lips, and in your ears. For where the heart stands idle and the Word is not heard, the devil breaks in and does his damage before we realize it. On the other hand, when we seriously ponder the Word, hear it, and put it to use, such is its power that it never departs without fruit. It always awakens new understanding, pleasure, and devotion, and it constantly creates clean hearts and minds. For this Word is not idle or dead, but effective and living.[48]

The Chants of the German Biblical Canticles

When the biblical canticles were sung in German they were sung to the same basic tones that had been used for centuries with Latin canticles, a modification of traditional psalm tones (Tones I-VIII and *tonus peregrinus*). Thomas Müntzer assigned 1 Samuel 2:1-10 to Tone IV, Isaiah 12:1-6 to Tone VI, and Isaiah 38:10-20 to Tone II;[49] the Benedictus was given four settings: Tones I, IV, VII and VIII;[50] and the Magnificat was set to Tone I.[51] In the Zwickau hymnal of 1525 the Benedictus and Magnificat were both given Tone VI chants (the Nunc dimittis appears without notation).[52]

As stated earlier, it seems almost certain that in the 1529 Klug *Gesangbuch* the canticles were set to simple monodic chants, rather than the

Table 16.4. Psalm Tones Assigned to the 1529/1533 Biblical Canticles

	Canticle	Tone	HEK 1/1 No.
[i]	*Ich wil dem Herrn singen*	Tone I	464
[ii]	*Mercket auff, jr himel*	Tone II	466
[iii]	*Lobet den Herrn/an denen die freywillig*	Tone III	468
[iv]	*Mein herz ist frölich jnn dem Herren*	Tone IV	469b
[v]	*Ich danke dir, Herr*	Tone V	472
[vi]	*Wir haben eine starcke Stad*	*	
[vii]	*Ich sprach, Nu mus ich zur helle*	*	
[viii]	*Ich frewe mich jnn dem HERREN*	*	
[ix]	*Ich wil der güete des HERRN gedencken*	*	
[x]	*Ich rieff zu dem Herrn jnn meiner angst*	Tone VI	481
[xi]	*HERR, ich hab dein gerücht gehöret*	Tone VII	483
[xii]	*Lobet den Herren alle Heiden*	Tone III†	457c
[xiii]	*Meine seel erhebt den Herren.* Magnificat	Tonus peregrinus	499d
[xiv]	*Gelobet sey der Herr der Gott Israel.* Benedictus	Tone VII†	488d
[xv]	*HERR/nu lessestu deinen diener.* Nunc Dimittis	Tone VIII	501a
[xvi]	*Preis sey Gott jnn der höhe*	*	
[xvii]	*In exitu Israel de Aegypto/Du Israel aus Egypten zoch*	Tonus peregrinus	–

*= no notation

faburdened four-part settings of the 1533 edition (see further the discussion below). Even in the 1533 *Gesangbuch* two canticles were not assigned faburdened four-part settings but given as simple monodic chants: Canticle xii (Psalm 117) and Canticle xiv (Benedictus).[53] There is no reason to believe that the 1529 canticles would have been set to different tones than those of the 1533 *Gesangbuch*. Not all the 1533 canticles appear with notation but those that do reveal a logical sequence of tones: the first seven psalm tones appear in their numerical order; then after the hiatus of the two monophonic chants and the *tonus peregrinus* assigned to the German Magnificat (Canticles xii-xiv), the next canticle (Canticle xv) completes the sequence by being set in the eighth Tone (see Table 16.4). Since Luther was the primary editor of the Wittenberg hymnal it seems most likely that he was responsible for the allocation of the psalm tones. The aim seems to have been to ensure that the long-standing tradition of using all the psalm tones for singing biblical canticles, as well as the Psalms, was continued within evangelical liturgical worship.

Luther thus most likely chose the psalm tones for the canticles, but did he also produce the simplified forms of these melodies? There is a strong possibility that he did. If the draft and final form of the use of a psalm tone in Luther's *Deutsche Messe* are compared with examples of tones found in both the

Example 16.1. Comparison of Luther's Two Versions of Tone I for the Introit Psalm

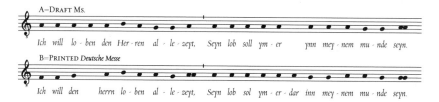

Example 16.2. Comparison of Tone VI in "Wittenberg" Hymnals

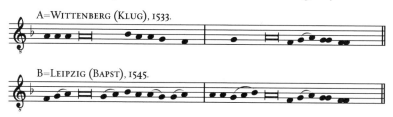

1533 and 1545 hymnals, then a clear pattern emerges. In Luther's 1525 manuscript draft of the chants for the *Deutsche Messe*, Tone I for the Introit Psalm is given in a simplified form (Example 16.1A),[54] whereas in the published *Deutsche Messe* (1526) it is closer to the standard form of Tone I, complete with intonation (Example 16.1B).[55] Since it is known that the composer Johann Walter collaborated with Luther with regard to the music of the *Deutsche Messe*, a reasonable explanation would seem to be that the draft version in Luther's hand represents his own work and the published version reflects Walter's editorial assistance. Similarly, the tones in the 1533 *Gesangbuch* conform to the simple type found in Luther's 1525 *Deutsche Messe* draft manuscript, and those in the 1545 *Gesangbuch* are more like the form exhibited in the published *Deutsche Messe* of 1526 (Example 16.2A & B).[56] Therefore it may well be that in the same way the music of the *Deutsche Messe* was the result of a collaboration between Luther and Walter, so the tones for the biblical canticles were similarly the product of the two men, Luther providing the forms for the 1529 *Gesangbuch* and Walter those for the 1545 *Gesangbuch*.

In the 1533 *Gesangbuch* ten psalm tones are faburdened (Tones I-VIII and two settings of the *tonus peregrinus*), with each of the four parts being printed independently: discant and tenor on the left-hand page and alto and bass on the right (see Fig. 16.1). There is the possibility that Luther was re-

Figure 16.1. Farburdened Psalm tone (Wittenberg *Gesangbuch*, 1533).

sponsible for these settings. He certainly had the ability to create such simple harmonizations that follow established formulae, as is demonstrated by his four-part setting of the canticle version of Tone VIII for the antiphon, *Non moriar sed vivam D. Martin Lutheri IIII vocum aus seinem schönen Confitemini* (Psalm 118:17), published in Wittenberg in 1545.[57]

The 1533 setting of Tone I (Canticle i) is known in two later published sources. In 1540 it was included in *Vesperarum precum officia*, published by Georg Rhau in Wittenberg, where it was assigned to Psalm 110 (109 Latin), *Dixit Dominus Domino meis*, and ascribed to "J. Vualther."[58] In 1922 a printed broadside of Psalm 64, *Höre Gott meine stim*, which contained no reference to the place of publication, name of the printer/publisher, nor year of issue, was discovered in Zerbst. However, an examination of the paper, watermark, and typography revealed that it was printed by Joseph Klug in Wittenberg in 1546.[59] The complete text of Psalm 64 is given, together with the four-part setting of Tone I found in the 1533 *Gesangbuch*, with authorship given as "D. Mart. Luther."[60] Thus each source appears to ascribe the setting of Tone I to two different composers. However, Rhau's *Vesperarum precum officia* includes not just one faburden psalm tone by Johann Walter but eight, one on each of the tones (see Table 16.5).[61] Three (settings of Tones I, IV, and VI) are virtually identical to those found in the 1533 *Gesangbuch*, and the remaining five are only slightly different from their equivalents found in the Wittenberg hymnal. Therefore the editors of the *Handbuch der deutschen evangelischen Kirchenmusik*, as well as the editors of *Johann Walter Sämtlicher Werke*, conclude that all eight faburden settings in the 1533 *Gesangbuch* were most likely the work of Walter rather than Luther, that is, the settings for Canticles i-v, x, xi and xv.[62] "D. Mart. Luther" on the 1546 broadside must therefore refer to his authorship of the text of Psalm 64, which is taken from his German Bible, rather than to the four-part musical setting.

There are two other faburden settings in the 1533 *Gesangbuch*, both of the *tonus peregrinus*: Canticle xiii (Magnificat), with the chant in the Discant voice, and Canticle xvii (Psalm 114-115) with the chant melody in the Tenor. The editors of *Johann Walter Sämtliche Werke* do not include them as settings by Walter, probably because there are no such settings of the *tonus peregrinus* in Rhau's *Vesperarum precum officia*. However, it would seem highly likely that these two settings were also the work of the same composer of the eight psalm tone settings in the small volume, that is, almost certainly Johann Walter.

The *Vesperarum precum officia* includes other faburdened psalm tones in addition to the eight by Walter: four each by Thomas Stolzer and Adam Rener, and three anonymous.[64] Together they form settings for the Psalms sung at Vespers on the respective days of the week. Such faburden psalmody in Latin was widespread in late medieval practice,[65] and there were such settings in the part-books compiled between 1510 and 1520 for use in the Wittenberg court chapel (All Saints), which also served as the university church.[66]

A significant sequence of faburden settings, mostly published by Rhau, was issued in printed sources in the post-1528 visitation period. Rhau had studied in Wittenberg before being appointed tutor at the University of Leipzig and Cantor of the Thomaskirche in the city in 1518. He composed the no longer extant twelve-voice Mass, *Missa de Sancto Spiritu*, sung before the 1519 Leipzig Disputation in which Eck confronted Luther. Before Rhau left Wittenberg he had published a textbook of basic music theory: *Enchiridion utriusque musicae practicae* (Wittenberg: Rhau-Grunenberg, 1517). Second and third editions were issued in Leipzig by Valentin Schumann in 1518 and 1520. Returning to Wittenberg by 1523 Rhau became one of Luther's primary printers, producing a wide variety of literature,[67] including an important sequence of music editions for church and school. The musical *Enchiridion* was reprinted and issued in re-edited editions by Rhau and his successors in Wittenberg in 1530, 1531, 1532, 1535, 1536, 1538, 1546, 1551, and 1553,[68] thus becoming a widely used textbook in Lutheran schools. The 1520 edition in-

Table 16.5. Faburdened Psalm Tones in Rhau's *Vesperarum precum officia* (1540)
by Johann Walter

		Voice	RMD	WGA
Tone I	D	*Dixit Dominus* (Psalm 109/110)[63]	4:465-46	4:63-64
Tone II	D	*Beatis omnes qui timent* (Psalm 127/128)	4:123-124	4:65-66
Tone III	T	*Laudate nomen Domini* (Psalm 134/135)	4:138-141	4:66-67
Tone IV	D	*Confitebor tibi* (Psalm 110/111)	4:49-51	4:67
Tone V	D	*Confitebor tibi* (Psalm 137/138)	4:151-152	4:68-69
Tone VI	D	*Benedictus Dominus* (Psalm 143/144)	4:1-5	4:70-71
Tone VII	T	*Laudate pueri Dominum* (Psalm 112/113)	4:55-57	4:72
Tone VIII	T	*Exaltabo te Deus* (Psalm 144/145)	4:7-11	4:72-73

cluded simplified chant forms of all eight psalm tones;[69] the 1531 edition gave the eight psalm tones in faburden settings,[70] including those of Tone V and VIII that were to appear later in the 1533 *Gesangbuch*[71] — anonymous in both sources but ascribed to Walter in the 1540 *Vesperarum*. In the 1530 dedication in the *Enchiridion* Rhau mentioned that he had also published a similar book, written by Martin Agricola, "an erudite musician and a singular friend of ours."[72] This is almost certainly a reference to Agricola's *Ein kurtz deutsche Musica* that Rhau had published in 1528. The title page of Agricola's textbook included the following information: "Mit 63 schonen lieblichen Exempeln yn vier stymmen verfasset. Gebessert mit 8. Magnificat, nach ordenung der 8 Thon" [presented with 63 beautiful and lovely examples in four voices, improved by eight Magnificats, according to the order of the eight tones]. Rhau reprinted Agricola's book with a new title: *Musica Choralis Deudsch* (Wittenberg: Rhau, 1533). Agricola included a section of faburdened settings, which, like those of Walter in the 1533 *Gesangbuch*, and those of Rhau's *Enchiridion*, were of the basic eight psalm tones.[73] Then in 1540 Rhau published his comprehensive anthology of music for vespers, *Vesperarum precum officia*, which included nineteen faburden settings, including those of Walter on the eight psalm tones. All these sources were associated with Latin Psalms, with the exception of the 1533 *Gesangbuch*, which assigned them to the vernacular biblical canticles.

What might appear as a somewhat haphazard pattern of publication of such faburdened settings can in fact be seen as part of an ongoing coherent strategy for the consolidation of evangelical faith and practice, especially in the period between the two visitations of 1528 and 1533. As referred to above, the publication of the 1529 *Gesangbuch* was part of the response to the findings of the 1528 visitation. It was clear that the people needed to be more aware of Scripture and have a better grasp of basic theology. Thus, addressing the former issue, biblical canticles were provided in the 1529 *Gesangbuch*, and to meet the latter need Luther published his two catechisms in the same year, 1529.

This was a continuation of the policies Luther had advocated in his *Deutsche Messe* (1526):

> First, the German service needs a plain and simple, fair and square cate-chism. Catechism means the instruction in which the heathen who want to be Christians are taught and guided in what they should believe, know, do, and leave undone, according to the Christian faith. . . .
>
> This is what we do to train the schoolboys in the Bible. Every day of the week they chant a few Psalms in Latin before the lesson, as has been customary at Matins hitherto. . . . After the Psalms, two or three boys in turn read a chapter from the Latin New Testament, depending on the length. Another boy then reads the same chapter in German to familiarize them with it and for the benefit of any layman who might be present and listening. Thereupon they proceed with an antiphon to the German les-son mentioned above. After the lesson the whole congregation sings a German hymn, the Lord's Prayer is said silently, and the pastor or chap-lain reads a collect and closes with the *Benedicamus Domino* as usual.
>
> Likewise at Vespers they sing a few of the Vesper Psalms in Latin with an antiphon, as heretofore, followed by a hymn if one is available. Again two or three boys in turn then read a chapter from the Latin Old Testa-ment or half a one, depending on length. Another boy reads the same chapter in German. The Magnificat follows in Latin with an antiphon or hymn, the Lord's Prayer said silently, and the collects with the Bene-dicamus. This is the daily service throughout the week in cities where there are schools.[74]

The parish schools were at the center of teaching evangelical faith and prac-tice: first, the younger generation were grounded in scriptural faith, and sec-ond, the older generations were instructed in turn by the younger generation. The schools supplied the musical leadership in the liturgy of the churches in the form of choirs.[75] What these choirs sang *to* their respective congregation, together with what they sang *with* that congregation, informed the faith and understanding of the whole worshiping assembly.[76] The post-1529 visitation strategy (which is reflected in the 1533 visitation) had a particular concentra-tion on the daily Office: at Matins Latin predominated and was attended mostly by the schoolboys; at Vespers, when, apparently, the laity were more in evidence, German texts were added. Thus the 1529 *Gesangbuch* included biblical canticles in German. The Wittenberg *Kirchenordnung* of 1533 makes it clear that when the service was in Latin it was to be sung by the school choir alone, but when German texts were used they were to be sung by the whole congregation:

> The schoolmaster [that is, the teacher of music, later known as the Kantor] should not just sing one thing with the children but many Antiphons, Responsories, [Latin] hymns and other songs, that are purely taken from holy Scripture. He should lead and sing with them. . . . When German is used the scholars should not sing on their own but should sing with the people.[77]

The Visitation Articles of 1533 follow closely the order and sequence of the 1533 Wittenberg *Kirchenordnung,* though usually in an abbreviated form, and similarly stress the significance of Vespers:

> Vespers is held as follows: first the schoolmaster and the scholars sing a Psalm; then a boy first reads a piece from the Old Testament, then another [reads the same] in German, then a [Latin] hymn is sung, then follows the Magnificat, and lastly the collect. . . .[78]

Apart from the reference to the biblical readings, the 1533 Visitation Articles do not distinguish what was to be sung in Latin and/or German. The 1533 Wittenberg Church Order is more specific in giving such detail, which can be correlated with the canticles in the 1533 *Gesangbuch:*

> On the evening of celebration before a special festival . . . after the sermon [the choir] will sing with the people the German Magnificat [Canticle xiii]. . . .
>
> Before everything in the Mass first shall be sung the German Benedictus of Zachariah with a short Antiphon [Canticle xiv], then an Introit, sometimes Latin, sometimes German, in which case it should be a German Psalm [sung to a psalm tone, as in the *Deutsche Messe*]. . . .
>
> At Vespers . . . after the sermon the whole congregation sings the German Magnificat to the *tonus peregrinus* [Canticle xiii] with this Antiphon: *Christum, unsern heilandt.* . . . Immediately thereafter the German Nunc dimittis is sung, as follows: *Herre nu lestu deinen diener fride faren.* . . . *Amen* [Canticle xv].[79]

The vernacular biblical canticles were thus primarily intended to be used in the daily Office, especially at Vespers, sung by both the school choir and congregation together. In the first imprint of the 1529 *Gesangbuch*, as argued above, only the melodies of the chant forms for the canticles were given. It is likely that in the second 1529 imprint they were given in the faburdened, four-part settings. In Rörer's letter cited above, he states that the second edition of 1529 was expanded by the addition of the Latin Litany and Psalm 114/115.[80] The first 1529 imprint was clearly congregational in content but it seems that Luther and his colleagues saw that, with some additions, it might also be used by the Wittenberg schoolboys. Thus the second 1529 imprint included the Latin Litany and Psalm 114/115, which, though in German, had the first verse in Latin interlined with each of the four parts of the faburden setting: *In exitu Israel de Aegypto*.[81] Such Latin items would only have been sung by the school choir and not by the congregation. It would therefore seem most likely that the faburdened settings were first added to the second 1529 imprint rather than that of 1533, that is, at the same time that the other "choir" items were added. The school choir would have sung the simple four-part settings, accompanying the congregation that sang just the chant melodies in unison. There was an incentive to include these faburdened settings in the Wittenberg *Gesangbuch* because, apart from the handbooks of basic music theory of Rhau and Agricola, such settings were not readily accessible for liturgical use. Therefore the eight faburdened psalm tones in the *Gesangbuch* could also be used by the school choir for singing Latin psalms at Vespers (and at Matins). The faburden settings continued to appear in later imprints of the Wittenberg *Gesangbuch* but were dropped from the 1545 Bapst *Gesangbuch*, which gave the canticles only with the monophonic tones. Part of the reason for the reversion to the unison chant forms must have been that after the publication of Rhau's *Vesperarum* in 1540, such faburdened chants were readily accessible for choral use. Thus there was no longer the necessity of continuing to include them in the *Gesangbuch*. But there may have been another reason as well. As Joseph Herl has documented, getting the congregations to sing in Wittenberg proved to be somewhat problematic.[82] The faburdened chant settings of the biblical canticles may not have been sung too well in the Wittenberg churches, especially since the chant melody that the congregation was required to sing was sometimes sung in the Tenor voice of the supporting choir and at other times in the Discant (soprano) (see Table 16.5, col. 2), which may have been confusing. Thus when the new edition of the *Gesangbuch* was being prepared (1544/45) the decision was taken to eliminate the four-part settings of the biblical canticles, presumably so that the congregation could be supported more effectively by the unison choir.

The psalm tones for the biblical canticles in the Bapst *Gesangbuch* of 1545 are different in a number of respects from those of the previous Wittenberg Klug editions: first, they are monophonic; second, the psalm tones are more developed than the earlier simple forms; third, canticles that appeared without notation in the earlier hymnals are assigned their own chant; and fourth, while some canticles are assigned to the same tone as in the earlier hymnals, there is quite a different pattern of psalm tones (see Table 16.6, and compare with Table 16.4).

There was a longstanding tradition that accorded each psalm tone a specific emotional content and the capacity to convey a particular meaning.[83] Hermann Finck explained each of these meanings at the end of the fourth chapter of his *Practica Musica*, published by Rhau's successors in Wittenberg in 1556.[84]

Finck states that Tone I (Dorian) "has the liveliest melody of all, arouses the somnolent, refreshes the sad and disturbed . . . the foremost musicians today use this tone the most."[85] In the *Deutsche Messe* Luther used Tone I for the Introit Psalm, Kyrie, and his German Agnus Dei, *Christe du Lamm Gottes*, which is referred to in the *Deutsche Messe* but did not appear in print until 1528.[86] Luther also set the thanksgiving Communion Psalm (Psalm 111) to Tone I in the 1529/33 *Gesangbuch*. In the Bapst *Gesangbuch* Canticle v (Isaiah 12), a song of thanksgiving, is set to Tone I.

Tone II (Hypodorian) "is diametrically opposed to the former [Tone I] . . . produces tears, makes morose . . . pitiable, heavy, serious, most subdued of all."[87] In the Bapst *Gesangbuch* Canticle iv, Hannah's song of praise (1 Samuel 2), is assigned to Tone II, presumably because of Hannah's humility in dedicating Samuel, the son she had prayed for, to the exclusive service of God.

Tone III (Phrygian) ". . . moves to choler and biliousness . . . loud words, hideous battles, and bold deeds suit it" (Finck).[88] The Bapst *Gesangbuch* assigns no less than three canticles to Tone III: Canticle iii (Judges 5), also assigned to Tone III in the 1533 *Gesangbuch*, is a battle song; Canticle x (Jonah 2) is an anguished prayer; and Canticle xi[89] (Habakkuk 3) is another anxious prayer.

Tone IV (Hypophrygian) "represents the parasite [dependent], who caters to the passions of his master . . . to whom he brings gifts and sings words of praise."[90] The Bapst *Gesangbuch* assigns Tone IV to Canticle vii (Isaiah 38), Hezekiah's song of dependence upon God who had delivered him from sickness.

Tone V (Lydian) ". . . corresponds with cheerfulness, friendliness, the gentler affects, since it pleases most of all . . . joyful, modest, the delight of the sorrowful, the restoring of the desperate, the solace of the afflicted. . . ."[91] For Luther Tone V was closely associated with the proclamation of the Gospel and the reception of the grace of forgiveness. In the *Deutsche Messe* he di-

Table 16.6. Psalm Tones Assigned to the 1545 Biblical Canticles

Canticle		Tone	HEK 1/1 No.
[i]	*Ich wil dem HERRN singen*	Tone V	465
[ii]	*Mercket auff, ir himel*	Tone VI	467
[iii]	*Lobet den HERRN das Israel*	Tone III*	468
[iv]	*Mein herz ist frölich jnn dem HERREN*	Tone II	470
[v]	*Ich danke dir, HERR*	Tone I	473
[vi]	*Wir haben eine feste stad*	Tone VIII†	475
[vii]	*Ich sprach, nu mus ich zur helle*	Tone IV†	477
[viii]	*Ich frewe mich im HERREN*	Tone VI†	478
[ix]	*Ich wil der güte des HERRN gedencken*	Tone VIII†	480
[x]	*Ich rieff zu dem HERRN In meiner angst*	Tone III	482
[xi]	*HERR, ich hab dein gerücht gehöret*	"Im vorgehenden thon"	
[xii]	[omitted]		
[xiii]	*Meine seel erhebt den HERREN.* Magnificat	Tonus peregrinus*	499e
[xiv]	*Gelobet sey der HERR, der Gott Israel.* Benedictus	Tone VII*	488e
[xv]	*HERR, nu lessestu deinen diener.* Nunc Dimittis	Tone VIII*	501a
[xvi]	*Preis sey Gott in der höhe*	–	48
[xvii]	*In exitu Israel de Egypto/Du Israel aus Egypten zoch*	Tonus peregrinus	–

*= same as 1533
†= no notation in 1533

rected that the Gospel lection and the *Verba Testamenti* in the evangelical Mass were both to be intoned in Tone V.[92] Thus it is not surprising to find that in the Bapst *Gesangbuch,* Canticle i (Exodus 15), Moses' song of redemption, is assigned to Tone V.

Tone VI (Hypolydian) is "contrary to the former [Tone V] . . . not infrequent in prayers [i.e., pious]."[93] In the *Deutsche Messe* Luther assigned the *Vox Christi* [Voice of Christ] within the chanted Gospel lection and *Verba Testamenti* to Tone VI.[94] The Bapst *Gesangbuch* gives two canticles in Tone VI: Canticle ii (Deuteronomy 32), the song of Moses, and Canticle viii (Isaiah 61), a song of praise, and both celebrate the acts of God, past and future, on behalf of his people.

Tone VII (Mixolydian) "shows itself with a stentorian voice and great shouts."[95] As in the 1533 *Gesangbuch,* in the Bapst *Gesangbuch* Canticle xiv (Luke 1, Benedictus), the proclamation of God's "blessedness," is to be sung to Tone VII.

Tone VIII (Hypomixolydian) "is not unlike an honest matron, who tries to soften and calm the wrath of her husband with agreeable discourse . . . studiously avoids offence . . . pacific."[96] In the *Deutsche Messe* Luther directed that the Epistle in the evangelical Mass was to be chanted in Tone VIII. The Bapst *Gesangbuch* assigns three canticles to Tone VIII: Canticle vi (Isaiah 26), a song of victory, Canticle ix (Isaiah 63/64), a song in praise of God's mercy, and Canticle xv (Luke 2, Nunc dimittis), a song of salvation (also assigned to Tone VIII in the 1533 *Gesangbuch*).

In the 1529/33 *Gesangbuch* the primary concern was to ensure that all the eight tones were given substantially in their numerical sequence, but in the Bapst *Gesangbuch* of 1545 more attention was given to matching the musical hermeneutic of the tones, that they should accord with the substance of the canticles.

The Hermeutical Function of the Biblical Canticles

The choice of the specific tone for each canticle was important because both text and tone undergirded the basic hermeneutic that Luther wanted the people who sang them to understand. They were scriptural models that enabled them to interpret their own lives. This is the substance of the introductory preface that Luther wrote for this section of biblical canticles that first appeared in the 1529 *Gesangbuch*, reprinted in the subsequent Klug editions, and then taken over in the Bapst *Gesangbuch* of 1545:

> In this booklet we have also taken — as good examples — the sacred songs of Holy Scripture, which the dear patriarchs and prophets made and sang. Thus we are not now as new masters contemplating this work but are following the example of all the saints before us. So each Christian will affirm, without great pains, how they — as we do likewise — praise only the grace of God and not the works of humankind. One may despise these hymns and us, but cannot condemn them along with us.
>
> But above all, we have desired to sing these songs or psalms with sobriety and devotion, with heart and mind, and not as in religious foundations and monasteries, where still today, with great abuse and idolatry, one bleats and roars without knowledge, understanding and trouble, instead of singing with devotion and profit, and thus God is angered rather than pleased.[97]

This is not an isolated preface, since each section of the 1529 *Gesangbuch* was introduced by such prefatory words. Although none of these prefaces are signed there is no reason to believe they were written by anyone other than Luther. There are many distinctive features that indicate that he was the primary editor of the hymnal and thus the author of these prefaces.[98] There are also expanded headings or summaries of each of the biblical canticles, but these were almost certainly written by Georg Rörer, under Luther's direction. In Rörer's letter to Roth cited above, he stated that "I have . . . added summaries of the songs/hymns *(canticorum)* whereby these canticles *(cantica)* can also be understood by the simple [uneducated]."[99] The hymns have straightforward headings in the Wittenberg *Gesangbuch* and the only summaries as such are those found in the section of biblical canticles. Even though they were probably written by Rörer, these summaries echo Luther's thought and vocabulary, such as the use of "Anfechtung" (temptation/struggle), and amplify not only the sentiments that Luther expressed in his introductory preface to this final section of the hymnal but also in his other writings.

Canticle i, Moses' song of faith and redemption, is introduced by Rörer's summary: "Moses and the children of Israel sang the following song to the Lord, when he rescued them from the hand of the Egyptians, as written in Exodus, chapter 15."[100] The substance of the song is reinforced by the woodcut illustrating the crossing of the Red Sea on the page immediately preceding. For the 1545 Bapst *Gesangbuch* a completely new series of woodcuts, much more carefully and artistically executed, were made. The subject matter remained basically the same but to each one was added a scriptural quotation, which functioned somewhat like an antiphon, that is, interpreting both the visible image as well as the following biblical canticle. Thus to the woodcut before Canticle i the Bapst *Gesangbuch* adds Hebrews 11:29: "By faith they passed through the Red Sea as on dry land, which the Egyptians attempted and drowned."[101] This Red Sea image of redemption was one that Luther referred to again and again in his writings, especially when dealing with baptism. Above all it is a primary image of his "Flood Prayer" that first appeared in his *Order of Baptism* of 1523:

Almighty eternal God, who according to thy righteous judgment didst condemn the unbelieving world through the flood and in thy great mercy didst preserve believing Noah and his family, and who didst drown hardhearted Pharaoh with all his host in the Red Sea and didst lead thy people Israel through the same on dry ground, thereby prefiguring this bath of thy baptism, and who through the baptism of thy dear Child, our Lord Jesus Christ, hast consecrated and set apart the Jordan and all water as a salutary flood and a rich and full washing away of sins: We pray through the same thy groundless mercy that thou wilt graciously behold this N. and bless him with true faith in the spirit so that by means of this saving flood all that has been born in him from Adam and which he himself has added thereto may be drowned in him and engulfed, and that he may be sundered from the number of the unbelieving, preserved dry and secure in the holy ark of Christendom, serve thy name at all times fervent in spirit and joyful in hope, so that with all believers he may be made worthy to attain eternal life according to thy promise; through Jesus Christ our Lord. Amen.[102]

Thus to sing Canticle i was to sing of redemption and be reminded of one's own baptism.

Rörer's summary of Canticle ii reads: "Moses spoke all the words of the following song in the ears of the whole congregation of Israel, as written in Deuteronomy, chapter 32."[103] The preceding woodcut, which has no counterpart in the 1545 *Gesangbuch*, depicts Moses receiving the Law. The woodcut was first used in the hymnal with Luther's Ten Commandments hymn, *Dies sind die heilgen Zehn gebot*. This later use of the woodcut in the hymnal is consonant with Luther's commentary on Deuteronomy 32 (1525):

The song of Moses is full of denunciation and reproof respecting the many great benefits shown by God to an ungrateful and evil people. He clearly affirms that when they have left God and turned to strange gods, the aforementioned curses will break over them. . . . Here one can see as in a mirror the power and nature of the Law, that it works wrath and holds under the curse.[104]

The phrase "gantzen gemeine" [the whole congregtion] in Rörer's summary echoes Luther's "Nach . . . singt die gantzen kirche" [then the whole church sings] in the *Deutsche Messe*,[105] and elsewhere. Although here the reference is to "hearing," the biblical canticle would have to be sung for it to be heard, and the activity of the whole worshiping community was not only an important principle for Luther but for most of the Reformers of the sixteenth century.[106]

Rörer's summaries for the next two canticles (iii and iv), essentially setting the biblical context of each, were taken over into the 1545 *Gesangbuch* without alteration:

[iii] Deborah and Barak sang to the Lord this song, as follows, when he delivered Sisera, the field-marshall, and Jabin, the Canaanite king, into their hands, together with their chariots and great army, as written in the book of Judges, chapter 5.[107]

[iv] Hannah, Elkanah's wife, who was barren, prayed to the Lord as follows, that he should hear and give to her Samuel, her son, which he delivered to her after her supplication, as is written in 1 Samuel, chapter 2.[108]

In the 1533 *Gesangbuch* (but not in 1545) there is the interesting visual hermeneutic of the woodcut that precedes Canticle iv: it depicts the Presentation of the Christ-Child in the temple.[109] Thus Hannah's "presentation" of Samuel in the place of worship prefigures the Presentation of Christ, thus giving Canticle iv a Christological hermeneutic.

Canticle v was introduced thus by Rörer: "There follows a song of praise in which you can see what is the authentic service of God [warhafftig Gottes dienst] and correct priestly ministry of the New Testament, Isaiah chapter 12."[110] A Christological hermeneutic is applied to "the authentic service of God [i.e., worship]" by the use of the woodcut of the Crucifixion that had appeared earlier in the hymnal with Luther's German Sanctus, *Jesaia dem Propheten*.[111] There is no equivalent woodcut in the 1545 *Gesangbuch* but the earlier summary was replaced by a new one (by Luther?): "There follows a song of praise, by the prophet Isaiah, in which he enumerates what should be preached, and how God is to be served by the people of the New Testament, namely, that God be thanked, praised, his name preached and confessed."[112] In his exposition of Isaiah 12, in his lectures on Isaiah (1527-1530), Luther not only gave the song a Christological interpretation but linked it specifically to the Lord's Supper:

> Here the prophet depicts the true and lawful worship and sacrifice of the New Testament and sets up, as it were, a certain hidden antithesis over against the Old Testament and its sacrifices, which were many and varied. But in the New Testament there was a single sacrifice of praise and thanksgiving. Thus the Lord's Supper is called Eucharist, that we may gather around it and give thanks to God. . . . The prophet foresaw this future preaching and confession of the Gospel, which did not take place in the Old Testament. In the voice of the Gospel God is glorified and preached in Christ. . . . Nor shall anything else be heard in the church but the voice of praise and proclamation of God's blessings which we have received. This song is in conflict with all human wisdom and righteousness, which are our works and in which we seek our own glory rather than give thanks to God. Hence, to be pleasing to God is simply to acknowledge that we are the recipients of His blessings, not the donors.[113]

Canticle vi is similar to Canticle v in that the earlier summary was replaced in the 1545 *Gesangbuch*. Rörer's summary: "There follows another song of praise in which high praise is accorded to the heavenly Jerusalem, that is, holy Christendom, together with Christ their King, &c. Isaiah chapter 26."[114] The 1545 summary (Luther's?): "There follows another song of praise, by the prophet Isaiah, in the 26th chapter, concerning Christ and his Christendom, what they should be as a people, namely, a righteous and peaceable people, that are dependent on their King, and mindful of his Word, by whom they are assisted and saved from all temptation [anfechtung], spiritual and temporal, &c."[115] The Christological hermeneutic is provided by both summaries, which parallel Luther's interpretation of the passage in his lectures on Isaiah (1527-1530):

> We have a firm and powerful city. This is the praise and preaching of the church, against which the gates of hell shall not prevail (Matt. 16:18), because the city is strong in government and priesthood. . . . This is not a city that is accessible to the few but one that is open to all who enter and is full of people. Thus all should have access to the church. . . . The righteous, by faith indeed, these are the inhabitants of this city. Thus there will be sung in that city what the city is, what kind of people it has, who is its governor, etc. . . . What we have, namely, Christ and His grace, is not an ordinary good. No one has more than the other, and therefore there cannot be discord, but peace, because in the Lord we are all equal in the likeness of hope and confidence. . . .[116]

Rörer's brief summary of Canticle vii was taken over unaltered into the 1545 *Gesangbuch*: "This is the writing of Hezekiah, King of Judah, who was sick and who was healed from this sickness. Isaiah 38."[117] Luther's commentary is more expansive, but consistent with the general tenor of his introductory preface to these biblical canticles:

> v. 17. *Behold, in peace.* The church's double peace is the severest kind of persecution. There is no plague worse for the church than a peace in which the Word of the Spirit and its diligent use are lacking. For the purpose of obtaining the true peace, however, we need nothing but the Word. . . . We labor and worry and exert ourselves in one kind of toil, care, and vexation, so that we may fall into something worse, because we rely on our care instead of relying on God. . . . Hence this verse is like a maxim. The fact that this most godly king in seeking peace apart from God found bitterness is something that will come to us all. . . .

> v. 20. *The Lord will save me.* . . . Here he comes to a close, as if to say: "Let us sing this song which I have composed. Only save us. Thou hast given

us health; help us to remain in it." So today we ought to sing: "Lord, preserve us in the truth that we have come to know."[118]

The summary for Canticle viii that appeared in the Klug hymnals was taken into the Bapst *Gesangbuch* unaltered: "Another song in which the prophet Isaiah, on behalf of the whole of Christendom, praises and thanks God for his truthful Word, who shows inexpressible goodness to the faithful and creates [for them] great things. And celebrates like the Magnificat. Isaiah 61."[119] Here is an echo of Luther's commentary on Isaiah 61 in his 1527-1530 lectures, including the reference to the Magnificat:

> This is a song which the prophet sings as representative of the church. This was Isaiah's feeling: As long as something is present, we pay no attention to it, but when it is gone, we long for it, because all these tasks, like baptizing and preaching, are considered worthless. Yet it is these very things that the prophet rejoices over. It is almost the same emotion as that expressed in the Magnificat, because the prophet sees God as not approving the ungodly and as rejecting the righteous hypocrites. He sees God approving His own people and promoting His church. Then there arises supreme glory and rejoicing of the spirit.[120]

Canticle ix, yet another from Isaiah, is given a somewhat longer summary:

> Another song in which the prophet instructs the faithful, by his example, how one should endure against temptations [anfechtungen] and distresses, namely, that they should remember the previous benefits which God has accomplished from the beginning, by Word and deed, to comfort and redeem. Besides, one should not forget to pray to God that one should live aright &c. Isaiah 64.[121]

Again, there are parallels with the respective passage in Luther's lectures on Isaiah:

> Now follows another chapter which contains a song that runs up to chapter 65. . . . Now the prophet sings a song and gathers the praises into a poem. In all of Scripture, however, it is customary for all the saints and prophets to console themselves in times of trial by recalling past benefits.[122]

Rörer's summary of Canticle x was slightly modified in the Bapst *Gesangbuch*. Rörer: "Jonah prays to the Lord his God in the body of the fish and says, as follows. Jonah chapter 2."[123] Bapst 1545: "Jonah prays to the Lord his God in the body of the fish and says, as it stands written in Jonah chapter 2."[124] In this case the two versions of the summary simply describe in the briefest terms the context of the song but without reference to the content, in contrast to Luther's commentary on the passage (1529):

> It was not as you might think, that the prophet versified this song while he was in distress. Rather, when he was finally released, he put into an orderly arrangement the things he had been thinking about in adversity and temptation. It is a fine song and one that shows that he did not put trust in his works.[125]

Rörer's words introducing Canticles xi and xii are brief. Canticle xi: "This is the prayer of the prophet Habakkuk for the innocent,"[126] to which the 1545 Gesangbuch simply added the reference, "As it is written in Habakkuk chapter 4 [= 3]."[127] Canticle xi (not included in the 1545 Bapst *Gesangbuch*): "Psalm 117 to be sung to God in thanksgiving for the Gospel and the kingdom of Christ."[128]

By contrast, the summary appearing before Canticle xiii is the longest:

> Mary's song of praise, the Magnificat.
>
> First, she sings with a joyful heart of the grace and blessing which the merciful God had shown to her, praising and thanking him for it.
>
> Second, she sings of the blessing and great and wonderful work which God continually does for all the people in the whole world, namely, that he has mercy on the fearful and desolate, raises the lowly and enriches the poor, deposes the great from their seat so they lose their power and might, and makes the rich into beggars.
>
> Third, she sings of the proper and all-highest work, that God has visited and redeemed Israel through his only Son Jesus Christ.[129]

The 1545 *Gesangbuch* repeated the summary, with some minor revisions but the meaning remained the same, and added the following to the accompanying woodcut of Elizabeth meeting Mary: "It came to pass as Elizabeth heard the greeting of Mary, the child in her body leaped. And Elizabeth was full of the Holy Spirit" (Luke 1:41).[130] This woodcut therefore established the biblical context for the Magnificat, whereas the Klug woodcut gave a more general reference to the Incarnation by depicting the Annunciation. The addition of

Luke 1:41, with its reference to the influence of the Holy Spirit, echoes Luther's preface to his commentary on the Magnificat (1521):

In order properly to understand this sacred hymn of praise, we need to bear in mind that the Blessed Virgin Mary is speaking on the basis of her own experience, in which she was enlightened and instructed by the Holy Spirit. No one can correctly understand God or His Word unless he has received such understanding immediately from the Holy Spirit. But no one can receive it from the Holy Spirit without experiencing, proving, and feeling it. In such experience the Holy Spirit instructs us as in His own school, outside of which nothing is learned but empty words and prattle. When the holy virgin experienced what great things God was working in her despite her insignificance, lowliness, poverty, and inferiority, the Holy Spirit taught her this deep insight and wisdom, that God is the kind of Lord who does nothing but exalt those of low degree and put down the mighty from their thrones, in short, break what is whole and make whole what is broken.[131]

With the summary for Canticle xiv, the Benedictus, there is similar addition in the 1545 *Gesangbuch* that again underscores the work of the Holy Spirit. Rörer: "The song of praise of Zechariah, father of John the Baptist, from which to learn, following his example, to be grateful to God for his holy esteemed Gospel, &c."[132] The 1545 *Gesangbuch adds*, "which is a word of grace and life."[133] There was no accompanying woodcut in the Klug *Gesangbuch* but there was in the Bapst *Gesangbuch,* a depiction of Zechariah with his son, together with the text of Luke 1:67: "And his father Zechariah was full of the Holy Spirit, prophesied and said."[134] In his preaching on the Benedictus Luther took the opportunity to stress the distinction between Law and Gospel, between works and faith, echoing his words in the preface to these biblical canticles. Thus in a sermon preached on John the Baptist Day in 1532 he said (specifically on Luke 1:77):

Such preaching [in the Benedictus] brought comfort and taught people correctly how they are to be saved. The Jews had the Law, that part of doctrine which is preached so that we learn what we are to do and not to do. Indeed, this knowledge is wonderful and great, but it bodes evil for us because we are unable to follow it. . . . On the other hand, John was now to come and give God's people another knowledge, which was not a recognition of sin, wrath and death, but a knowledge of salvation, that is, a preaching whereby people might learn how they might be rescued from death and sin.[135]

Canticle xv, the Nunc dimittis, is briefly introduced by Rörer: "There follows the song of praise of ancient Simeon, Luke chapter 2."[136] In the Bapst *Gesangbuch* Simeon was described (by Luther?) as "the dear, holy patriarch."[137] In the earlier Klug hymnals the canticle was accompanied by the woodcut of the Crucifixion, emphasizing the salvific content of the Nunc dimittis. In the Bapst *Gesangbuch* the new woodcut displays Simeon with the Christ-Child in his arms, and is headed by Luke 2:34: "Behold, this one is set for the fall and rising of many in Israel, and a sign that will be spoken against."[138] In his preaching Luther stressed the Christocentric nature of the canticle, such as in his 1537 Purification sermon:

. . . let us remember that with these words everything except Christ is to be excluded from contributing to righteousness and salvation before God. . . . This is the song that Simeon has sung to us today. Now, filled with joy he wants to depart in peace; for he has seen so much that there is nothing that now frightens him. Since he has seen the Savior and the Light which God has prepared, he no longer beholds either sin or death and is prepared and willing to die. . . . This was a song not just in the mouth, on his tongue, on paper, but in his heart! May our dear God and Father, for the sake of Jesus Christ, his Son, grant us his grace through his Holy Spirit that we may join to sing along with beloved Simeon and also depart in peace. Amen.[139]

Canticle xvi — which comprised just the song of the angels at the Nativity rather than the complete liturgical *Gloria in excelsis Deo* in the vernacular — was given the briefest introduction by Rörer, "The angelic song of praise. Luke 2[:14],"[140] which was only very slightly modified in the Bapst *Gesangbuch*.[141] For Luther the angelic song epitomized the nature and content of worship. In a sermon, preached in the Stadtkirche, Wittenberg, in December 1533, he said:

The dear angels have in effect drawn together a whole service of worship with their hymn of praise: they give God his glory, earth peace, and goodwill to mankind, so that good things come to pass no matter what. Indeed, a short but rightly excellent angelic, heavenly little song! It is not a song that has to do with outward liturgical forms prescribed for the sake of the child Jesus, as when the temple was built and Levitical offerings instituted, but only that God in heaven might have his glory, earth peace, and mankind goodwill. . . . The song of the angels . . . resounds only where this Child is received. There is nothing written here about things pertaining to hell or concerning death. For that would be another song, with other singers.[142]

The last canticle mirrors the first and together they frame the whole section of biblical canticles. Canticle xviii was given no introduction in the second imprint of the 1529 *Gesangbuch,* and in the 1545 *Gesangbuch* was simply headed "Der CXIIII. Psalm/In exitu Israel de Egypto."[143] In the 1533 Gesangbuch, and almost certainly in the second 1529 imprint, the canticle was preceded by a repetition of the Crossing of the Red Sea woodcut that had appeared with Canticle i, the song of Moses after the Exodus. Similarly, the same pattern occurs in the 1545 Gesangbuch, and its woodcut of the same event is associated with Canticle i and Canticle xvii, both of which deal in different ways with thanksgiving for redemption from Egypt, seen as a typological anticipation of redemption in Christ, the new Exodus. Thus Luther in his *Dictata super psalterium* (1513-1516) wrote on Psalm 114:

. . . this exodus is spiritual and takes place with the feet of the soul, namely, with the intellect and the feeling. One to whom the spirit begins to be known and loved is truly going forth from Egypt, and that all the more, the more clearly he understands and the more ardently he loves. Thus he goes out and enters the promised land, that is, the church. He goes out when he hates and begins not to know the world and turns his back to it and his face toward heavenly things.[144]

The biblical canticles as a whole formed an important part of the sung component of evangelical worship. They were included in all the editions of the hymnals that Luther personally supervised between 1529 and 1545. The evidence shows that during these years textual refinements were made, bringing them into line with the progress being made on the translation of the German Bible, and that there were also changes made to the musical forms of these canticles, relating to whether they should be sung in unison or in parts, and which tone was most appropriate for each canticle. Further, careful attention was given to the visual hermeneutic of the accompanying woodcuts. A great deal of care and attention was given to these biblical canticles so that they could contribute a distinctive element to evangelical worship, by encouraging the faith and commitment of those who sang them.

The Later Tradition

Although the singing of these vernacular canticles survived into the seventeenth century, by the eighteenth century the only one that was usually included in the hymnals and regularly sung was the German Magnificat, *Meine Seele erhebt den Herren,* with its *tonus peregrinus* chant. But for the rest, they mostly disappeared from later hymnals. One interesting exception is the so-called *Londoner Gesangbuch* (1753) of the Moravians. This massive hymnal began with a section of "Bibel-Gesang," comprising 110 biblical canticles, including eleven of the seventeen found in Luther's hymnals.[145]

In the later nineteenth and early twentieth century, as part of the movement for liturgical renewal, biblical canticles were included from time to time in German and American hymnals. But what is included in hymnals is not always sung. It is the Lutheran chorale tradition that has largely eclipsed the Lutheran canticle tradition. What is true in the practice of the churches is also mirrored in Luther studies. Many generations of Luther scholars have laid great stress on the introduction into evangelical worship of congregational, vernacular, strophic hymnody. This, of course, is part of the unique Lutheran heritage and should never be understated, but the consequence has been to largely ignore the biblical canticles that appeared in Luther's hymnals. In writing about Luther's hymnody most have quoted his famous letter, written to Georg Spalatin towards the end of 1523, in which Luther explained his intentions:

> [Our] plan is to follow the example of the prophets and the ancient fathers of the church, and to compose psalms for the people [in the] vernacular, that is, spiritual songs, so that the Word of God may be among the people also in the form of music.[146]

What is now clear is that, while his focus was on strophic hymnody in 1523, a few years later Luther came to see that the principle of "the Word of God . . . among the people . . . in the form of music" must also include the singing of the unaltered, prose words of Scripture, that is, biblical canticles.

PART V

Implications & Consequences

CHAPTER 17

Luther's Theology of Music in Later Lutheranism

Later Lutheranism, following its mentor Martin Luther, characterized music as the *viva voce evangelii*, the living voice of the gospel, the understanding that music is closely connected to the preaching and teaching ministry of the church. Previous chapters of this book have been concerned with Luther and his colleagues in the sixteenth century; this chapter, and the next, explore some of the later strands of the theory and practice of music that developed within the Lutheran church in subsequent generations. In the discussion that follows, many of the examples center on the life and works of the composer Johann Sebastian Bach. This is because, on the one hand, Bach represents the high point of the Lutheran tradition of church music, and, on the other hand, the tradition significantly declined in the decades immediately following Bach's death (1750); indeed, the signs of that decline were already apparent during Bach's lifetime. In the sixteenth and seventeenth centuries, however, two far-reaching implications of Luther's theological understanding of music were clearly enunciated: pedagogics in church and school, and homiletics from pulpit and music gallery.

Music and Theology in Church and School

As has been referred to numerous times throughout this study, the close connection between music and theology in Luther's thought had practical implications for education in the emerging Lutheran church: if music is this important, then it should be part of the basic curriculum in parish schools. In the *Tischreden* the following is found:

Music I have always loved. He who knows music has a good nature. Necessity demands that music be kept in the schools. A schoolmaster must know how to sing; otherwise I do not look at him. And before a youth is ordained into the ministry, he should practice music in school.[1]

This is a truly remarkable statement: a teacher must be able to sing, and seminarians must have practical experience of music in the school system before they can be ordained. It was a maxim that had practical consequences for Lutheran churches and schools for at least the next two centuries. It became customary for pastors and teachers to study music as well as theology, and for church musicians to study theology along with music.[2] Luther and his colleagues modified the choral tradition of the medieval school system and insisted that the teaching of music in these reformed institutions should have a primary importance, since through them the music of the church was both promoted and undergirded.[3] One such institution was the St. Thomas School in Leipzig which detailed the content and extent of the teaching and practice of music in its published regulations of 1634, 1723, and 1733.[4]

Many Lutheran teachers were also church musicians, such as the Krebs family, father and three sons, who all studied with Johann Sebastian Bach. The father, Johann Tobias Krebs, the elder, studied organ with Bach in Weimar between 1714 and 1717 before becoming church organist and school rector (headmaster) in Büttstädt. All of his three sons were successively taught by Bach in Leipzig: the eldest son, Johann Ludwig — one of the most gifted of all Bach's students — went on to study philosophy at Leipzig University before becoming organist in Zwickau in 1737, then organist in Altenburg from 1756; the youngest son, Johann Carl, succeeded his father as rector of the school in Büttstädt, where his father was also town organist, and became assistant organist when his father's eyesight began to fail; the middle son, Johann Tobias, the younger, also one of Bach's organ students, studied theology at Leipzig university before becoming conrector first in Chemnitz (1746), then in Grimma (1751), where he became rector of the school in 1763.[5] This middle son was not only an organist and educator, like his father and brothers, but also a theologian, publishing books of criticism and interpretation of the language and content of the New Testament, with special reference to the writings of Josephus and early Judeo-Christian connections.[6]

This close association between music and theology, initiated by Luther, manifested itself in Lutheran tradition by pastors and theologians who were also competent musicians. Numerous examples could be given; the following are representative. Nikolaus Selnecker (1530-1592), professor of theology and pastor of the Thomaskirche, Leipzig, one of the primary authors of the *For-*

mula of Concord (1577), was first a church organist (at the age of 14) before ordination, and was the composer of many hymns, both melodies as well as
texts.[7] Lucas Osiander (1534-1604), church historian, biblical commentator,
and court preacher in Stuttgart, also produced four-part settings of the basic
corpus of Lutheran chorales, *Fünfftzig Geistliche Lieder vnd Psalmen* (Fifty
Spiritual Songs and Psalms), published in Nuremberg in 1586, which created
the simple note-against-note, so-called "cantional," style that came into almost universal use thereafter. Nikolaus Stenger (1609-1680), who was first
cantor, later preacher, and ultimately professor of theology in Erfurt, produced a music textbook, edited the Erfurt hymnal, and published collections
of his sermons.[8] The noted hymn-writer, Johann Christoph Olearius (1611-
1684), senior court preacher and superintendent in Weissenfels, in addition to
published theological works in Latin and German, including an extensive Bible commentary,[9] also wrote a modest treatise on singing.[10] "The Father of
American Lutheranism," Henry Melchior Muhlenberg (1711-1787), was an accomplished organist as well as a pastor (ordained in Leipzig in 1739), who not
only taught Luther's small catechism to children in Pennsylvania in the early
1740s, but also taught them how to sing.[11]

On the other hand, Lutheran cantors were not only church musicians;
they were also teachers in the schools attached to the churches they served.
Further, their teaching responsibilities were not confined to music matters
alone. In most Latin schools the cantor and the other teachers were expected
to know in detail the content of the basic theological textbook used in such
schools: Leonard Hutter's *Compendium Locorum Theologicorum Ex Scripturis
sacris, & libro Concordiae . . . Facultate Theologica Lipsiensis & Wittebergensi
approbatum* (Compendium of Theological Loci Drawn from Sacred Scripture and the Book of Concord . . . Approved by the Theological Faculties of
Leipzig and Wittenberg), originally published in Wittenberg in 1610.[12]
Hutter's compendium was an epitome of, and an introduction to, Lutheran
confessional theology (with a particular stress on the Augsburg Confession,
its Apology, and the Catechisms), and although it was usually taught by the
school rector and conrector, the cantor was expected to be familiar with its
catechetical questions and answers, because he was required to teach the substance of Luther's small catechism as part of his duties. For example, in the
regulations of the Thomasschule in Leipzig published in 1634 it was specifically stated that the cantor's responsibilities included the teaching of Luther's
small catechism on Saturday mornings,[13] a duty that was still a requirement
when J. S. Bach became the Thomascantor in Leipzig in 1723. Further, it was
also the responsibility of the cantor to provide music for the regular Sunday
Vespers services at which it was customary to include the *Catechismus-*

Examen, expositions of one or other parts of the small catechism.[14] Generations of Lutheran composers thus provided catechism-music that accompanied this confessional teaching: among the earliest was *Catechesis numeris musicis inclusa* (Nuremberg, 1559), a collection of mostly freely-composed three-part vocal settings of the main parts of the catechism in Latin, composed by Mattheus Le Maistre, Saxon electoral Kapellmeister in Dresden;[15] and among the most profound are organ chorale preludes on Luther's catechism hymns[16] found in Bach's *Clavierübung III* of 1739, for which Bach composed two settings of each chorale melody, one long and one short, corresponding to Luther's two catechisms.[17] But there are many other examples of such catechism music, perhaps the most intriguing being the catechism *quodlibet*, that is, a single vocal work in which five or six melodies of catechism hymns are heard in counterpoint to each other, the ingenuity of the musical form demonstrating the theological unity of the teaching of the catechism.[18] Here the musical form was used to express a theological reality that could not be as effectively expressed by words alone.

The fact that Lutheran school teachers and cantors were intimately involved with fundamental theology in their day-to-day work meant that before they were confirmed in appointments they had to undergo a *viva voce* theological examination, and also, like the clergy, had to give written assent to doctrine as defined and expounded in the *Book of Concord,* the anthology of Lutheran confessional writings. Thus when the city council had finally decided that Johann Sebastian Bach should be their next cantor in Leipzig, he was first examined by Johann Schmid, professor of theology in the university, on or before 8 May 1723, on which date the professor reported to the Leipzig Consistory that the cantor-elect "Mr. Jo. Sebastian Bach replies to the questions propounded by me in such wise that I consider that the said person may be admitted to the post of cantor in the St. Thomas School."[19] This examination covered basic biblical and theological knowledge, quite detailed and widely compassed, and certainly was no formality. Almost exactly a year before, Conrad Küffner, the cantor-elect of Zwickau, went through a similar examination process.[20] There was nothing wrong with his musical abilities, indeed, his audition, the direction of concerted music on Cantate (Fourth Sunday after Easter, 3 May 1722), was accorded "great applause."[21] But the Leipzig Consistory could not confirm Küffner as the new cantor in Zwickau because Dr. Schmid — the same professor who examined Bach a year later — reported that the candidate could not answer satisfactorily basic Biblical and elementary theological questions.[22] Küffner therefore would not be appointed cantor in Zwickau because, in addition to teaching and directing music in church, the position included the teaching of basic theology in the school, a task for which he was clearly ill equipped. There was plainly no such problem with Bach, but he did have to undergo a second examination a few days after the first. This time he was examined by Salomon Deyling, superintendent (senior pastor) and professor of theology in Leipzig, who had also countersigned Schmid's certificate of examination a few days earlier. In a letter to the Consistory, dated 13 May 1723, Deyling states that Bach had subscribed to the *Formula of Concord*,[23] and therefore to the theological position of the *Book of Concord* as a whole. The actual document that Bach signed on 13 May 1723 reveals that he subscribed to the *Formula of Concord* twice: once positively, endorsing Lutheran doctrines, and once negatively, denying non-Lutheran beliefs, which is how the *Formula of Concord* was written.[24] The suggestion that this confessional subscription was of minimal significance[25] runs counter to the climate of the time and, in fact, intensifies rather than diminishes Bach's connection with Lutheran Orthodoxy. For Orthodox Lutherans confessional subscription was almost an article of faith, in contrast to the Pietists, who were not only critical of the church's confessionalism but also argued against the necessity of such subscription.[26] Thus at the beginning of his cantorate, Bach was not simply required to be a skillful musician but an able church musician with a specific level of competence in Lutheran confessional theology. The primary reason for this, as stated above, was that as cantor he was responsible for teaching basic theology in the St. Thomas School as well as directing the music of the principal churches of the city.

That there was a confessional aspect to the role of music in worship is exemplified in the change in the title of later editions of an influential *Gesangbuch* published in Frankfurt am Main that appeared a few years after the publication of the *Book of Concord*. The first edition was issued with the title: *Kirchen Gesäng Aus dem Wittenbergischen und allen andern den besten Gesangbüchern . . . gesamlet* (Church Songs assembled from the Wittenberg and other best hymnals . . .) (Frankfurt: Wolff, 1569). But in later editions issued from 1584 the basic title was expanded to become *Kirchen Gesäng So bey der predigt deß Göttlichen Worts und außspendung der H. Sacrament in den Kirchen Augspurgischer Confession, gebraucht werden, Aus dem Wittenbergischen und andern den besten Gesangbüchern gesamlet* (Church Songs as used in the churches of the Augsburg Confession with the preaching of the divine Word and the distribution of the holy Sacrament, assembled from the Wittenberg and other best hymnals . . .).[27] The addition is significant and echoes Art. VII of the *Augsburg Confession:* "The church is the assembly of saints in which the gospel is taught purely and the sacraments are administered rightly."[28] Singing was therefore closely associated with these two primary marks of the church, and confessional theology was seen to have important musical implications.

Music and Theology in Homiletic Partnership

If theology and music are interconnected, if musicians share in the teaching of theology, and if clergy are expected to have some musical background, then it is inevitable that there should be some overlap in the ministerial vocation of both musicians and clergy. This vocational interconnection was worked out in a variety of ways in Lutheran tradition. For example, it was underscored by the insistence that musicians should make the same subscription to the Lutheran Confessions as the clergy were required to do (see above), and also in the way that music was accorded homiletic functions akin to preaching.

Luther frequently made the link between music and preaching; the following constitute a representative sampling. In his exposition of Psalm 98, in his first series of lectures on the Psalms given between 1512 and 1515, he made the following comment: "To make music with hammered trumpets is to preach [*predicare*] the mystery of the kingdom of heaven and exhort to spiritual good things. To make music with the voice of the bronze horn is to preach [*predicare*] and to reprove our sins and evil."[29] In his treatise on the *Last Words of David* (1543) he wrote:

> When David uses the word *sweet* he is not thinking only of the sweetness and charm of the Psalms from a grammatical and musical point of view, of artistic and euphonious words, of melodious song and notes, of beautiful text and beautiful tune; but he is referring much more to the theology they contain, to the spiritual meaning. . . . The Book of Psalms is a sweet and delightful song because it sings and proclaims [*predigt*] the Messiah even when a person does not sing the notes but merely recites and pronounces the words. And yet the music, or the notes, which are a wonderful creation and gift of God, help materially in this, especially when the people sing along and reverently participate.[30]

In the *Tischreden* there are a number of such instances, including: "God has preached [*praedicavit/geprediget*] the Gospel through music"; and "Music is God's greatest gift. It has often so stimulated me and stirred me that I felt the desire to preach [*predigen*]."[31] In his preface to Georg Rhau's *Symphoniae iucundae* of 1538 he wrote:

> It was not without reason that the fathers and prophets wanted nothing else to be associated as closely with the Word of God as music. Therefore we have many hymns and Psalms where message [*sermo*] and music [*vox*]

join to move the listener's soul. . . . The gift of language combined with the gift of music was only given to man to let him know that he should praise God by proclaiming through music [*sonora praedicatione*] and by providing sweet melodies with words.[32]

Perhaps Luther's most extensive reflection on the connection between music and preaching is found in his letter to the composer Ludwig Senfl (4 October 1530) — a letter that was widely circulated during the sixteenth century and frequently cited in later literature:

> . . . Indeed I plainly judge, and do not hesitate to affirm, that except for theology there is no art that could be put on the same level as music, since except for theology [music] alone produces what otherwise only theology can do, namely, a calm and joyful disposition. . . . This is the reason why the prophets did not make use of any art except music; when setting forth their theology they did it not as geometry, not as arithmetic, not as astronomy, but as music, so that they held theology and music most tightly connected, and proclaimed [*dicentes*] the truth through Psalms and songs.[33]

Luther's views were paraphrased and expanded by others, beginning with Johann Walter, Luther's composer-colleague and the first Lutheran cantor. In a poem published in 1538 Walter wrote:

> Music and theology are the gift of God.
> God has finely clothed music in the outer-garment of theology.
> He has combined both in peace that none should claim the honor
>   above the other.
> They are in friendship so closely connected that they are known as
>   sisters. . . .
> Music abides with God eternally; all other arts are excluded.
> In heaven after Judgment Day only it will continue. . . .
> In heaven you will not need the art of grammar, fine logic,
> geometry, astronomy, no medicine, jurisprudence,
> philosophy, rhetoric, [but] only beautiful music.
> There will all his [God's] singers use this art alone.[34]

A similar statement can be found in *Grundlage einer Ehrenpforte* (Hamburg, 1740), by Bach's contemporary Johann Mattheson (1681-1764), composer, promoter of opera, the foremost Baroque music critic and theorist, pioneer music journalist and lexicographer in Hamburg:

> Music is a noble art and a great embellishment for a noble spirit. All other arts and sciences will die with us. A lawyer cannot use his skill in heaven, for there will be no trials like in Speyer. Nobody in heaven will ask a doctor for a prescription or a purgative. But the things that theologians and musicians learned on earth they will also practice in heaven, that is, to praise God.[35]

These words, however, are not Mattheson's; they comprise a quote within a quote. Mattheson's *Grundlage einer Ehrenpforte* is a kind of biographical dictionary of notable musicians, and this quotation occurs within the section devoted to one Bernhard von Sanden. Sanden was not a musician but the Prussian Oberhofprediger (principal court preacher) who had delivered a sermon in Königsburg on the occasion of the installation of Johann George Neidhardt as Capellmeister, published as: *Daß Kirchen-Musik, wenn solche wohl und christlich eingerichtet, eine Gabe Gottes sey, zu Gottes Dienst und Ehren zu brauchen* (Königsburg: Zäncker, 1720).[36] Mattheson's entry on Sanden is a summary of this Königsburg sermon in which quite a number of Sanden's quoted sources are repeated *verbatim*, and it is clear that Mattheson endorsed the views that he found there. The above quotation, which is closely parallel to the statements of Luther and Walter, is attributed to Johann Balthasar Schupp (1610-1661), theologian and ultimately pastor of the Jacobikirche in Hamburg. Thus the quotation of a quotation by Mattheson underlines the continuity of the connections between theology and music in later Lutheranism.

Johann Mattheson was, like Bach, a devout Lutheran who believed that the foundation of his art was theological and that the primary function of music was within the worship of the church. For example, in *Der Musikalische Patriot* of 1728 he wrote:

> All the efforts of our composers, singers, and instrumentalists will be of not the least avail unless, without the slightest hypocrisy and with the true earnestness of David himself, they aim directly or indirectly at the honor and praise of God. They may sing or play in operas, they may explain and compose as much as they want — in the end all must be fixed, immutably, in the church.[37]

Almost twenty years later Mattheson expressed the same thought more emphatically: "Operas are the academies of music, as concerts are its grammar schools, but in the church is found its true calling, and in heaven its eternal place, yes, so to speak, its place and voice."[38]

Mattheson was an avid reader of the Bible, especially the Psalms,[39] as well as the writings of Martin Luther. For example, on the title page of his *Die neueste Untersuchung der Singspiele* (Hamburg, 1744) he quotes Luther — "The [musical] notes make the text live"[40] — and the short work has many references to Luther.[41] But Mattheson's encounter with Luther's writings had begun much earlier. For example, in 1717 he edited the third part of Friedrich Erhardt Niedt's *Musikalischer Handleitung* (Hamburg, 1717), which also included another work as an appendix to Niedt's treatise: *Deutliche Beweis-Gründe*, by "Veritophilus" (= "lover-of-truth"), who is identified by Mattheson in the preface as Christoph Raupach, organist in Stralsund.[42] In the same preface Mattheson cites the Latin of Luther's letter to Ludwig Senfl, 4 October 1530,[43] and in the text of the treatise Raupach makes reference to numerous passages in Luther's writings where the Reformer speaks of the connections between music and theology.[44]

Similarly, in *Der Musikalische Patriot* of 1728 Mattheson calls his contemporary musicians to listen to Luther on the connection between music and theology:

Ask your father Luther, you Lutheran! He will tell you what a lovely, divine gift you have in music! His pure teaching is this: "Music is a beautiful and excellent gift of God, and next to theology. I give to music, after theology, the next *locus* and the highest praise. . . ."[45]

On 31 October 1717, Mattheson performed his oratorio, *Der reformirende Johannes,* in Hamburg Cathedral, in which the significance of Luther's reforms was recounted, the Reformer being interpreted as another John the Baptist.[46] Given Mattheson's numerous references to Luther, it is therefore difficult to understand Joyce Irwin's statement, as part of her argument that Bach was a "non-theologian": "Bach is more likely to have been influenced by his eighteenth century contemporaries [i.e. Mattheson] than by a long-lost teaching of Luther."[47] On the contrary, Luther's teaching was not "long-lost" and could be found quoted and expounded in Mattheson's publications; thus if Mattheson influenced Bach then it would have been the opposite of what Irwin suggests.

In his own writings Mattheson frequently explored the connections between music and theology.[48] Although there have been recent discussions of various aspects of Mattheson's voluminous literary output,[49] there is as yet no substantial investigation of his many writings with the aim of presenting a coherent assessment of his understanding of the connections between theology and music.

Mattheson was not the only contemporary of Bach who was aware of the significance of Luther's understanding of music. Daniel Vetter (1657/8-1721), organist of the Nikolaikirche in Leipzig, issued a collection of organ chorales in two installments: *Musikalischer Kirch- und Hauß-Ergötzlicheit* (Leipzig, 1709 and 1713). In the preface to the second part, dated 24 April 1713, Vetter writes of the spiritual benefits of music, especially the practice of singing hymns after meals, and does so by reference to Luther. The ultimate source is Ratzeberger's manuscript account of Luther's life,[50] which Vetter cites from Veit Ludwig von Seckendorf, *Commentarius historicus et apologeticus de lutheranismo* . . . (Leipzig: Gleditsch, 1692).[51] Although it is possible that Bach knew of the passage in Seckendorf's history of the Reformation, since both Latin and German editions were published in Leipzig, it is almost certain that he had read the same material in Vetter's preface to the second part of his *Musikalischer Kirch- und Hauß-Ergötzlicheit*. In the very next paragraph to his references to Luther Vetter draws attention to the hymn by Caspar Neumann, *Liebster Gott, wenn werd ich Sterben?*,[52] and then explains that he had composed a four-part vocal setting of it, with organ accompaniment, for the funeral of a Breslau cantor in 1695; the setting concludes the second part of Vetter's collection.[53] Significantly, Bach used this setting by Vetter, slightly modified, for the final movement of his chorale cantata on Neumann's hymn: *Liebster Gott, wenn werd ich Sterben?* (BWV 8), composed in 1724,[54] which implies that he had probably read Vetter's preface referring to Luther.[55]

Mattheson, Vetter, and Bach, therefore, in common with their contemporaries, shared the common Lutheran perspective on the connections between theology and music that ultimately derive from Luther and that were reiterated again and again throughout the sixteenth to eighteenth centuries.

The close connection between music and theology, and the consequential overlap of the ministries of preacher and musician, was a primary theme explored by musicians and theologians who followed Luther. By the end of the sixteenth century it had become customary to refer to a passage in a writing by Justin Martyr that expressed the view that the Word of God is not only to be proclaimed by singing but also by instrumental music. Even though two important facts were unknown to these writers — that the source was "Pseudo-Justin" rather than Justin, and the citation was corrupted by a transcription error — the passage continued to be cited over the following centuries in Lutheran writings.[56] For example, the Justin connection is found in the commentary on the Psalms by the Wittenberg theologian Salomon Gesner (1559-1605): *Commentationes in Psalmos Davidis . . . sub finem harum commentationum adjectus est libellus ejusdem autoris quem ipse sub titulo*

Meditationis generalis Psalterij antea seorsim editit, first published in Wittenberg in 1605, with at least a further five editions issued by 1665. At the end of the commentary Gesner appended *Meditatio Psalteri,*[57] a discussion of various topics relating to the Psalms. It is in this appendix that Gesner makes reference to Justin.[58] Similar references to the Justin citation can be found in numerous later writings in which the concept was often expanded or elaborated. An important example is the passage in Michael Praetorius's preface to his *Polyhymnia Caduceatrix et Panegyrica* (Wolfenbüttel, 1619); it includes the quotation from Justin, but with an effective word-play on *cantio* (song) and *concio* (sermon):

> Consequently, for the completeness and certainty of church authority, and also for the completeness of worship, it is not only appropriate to have a CONCIO, a good sermon, but also in addition the necessary CANTIO, good music and song. Thus correct and true is the meaning of Justin: ῥῆμα γὰρ ἔστιν Θεοῦ τὸ ἐνθυμούμενον καὶ ᾀδόμενον, καὶ ἀναχρουόμενον. *Verbum Dei est, sive mente cogitetir, sive canatur, sive pulsu edatur.* "It is and remains God's Word in the thinking of the mind, the singing of the voice, and also in the beating and playing upon instruments."[59]

Here Michael Praetorius asserts an unequivocal connection between *cantor* (musician) and *concionator* (preacher): both are bearers of the Word of God. Similarly the Limburger *Kirchenordnung* of 1666[60] contains the following paraphrase of the Justin passage:

> God's Word is accordingly, as expressed in the fine words of the old teacher Justin, conveyed in three different ways: 1) in teaching and preaching, 2) in prayer and song, 3) in music for organ, strings or [other] instruments.[61]

Johann Mattheson also makes reference to the Justin source and in doing so, as Söhngen suggests, places "preacher and cantor on the same level."[62] Much of the second volume of Mattheson's music journal, *Critica Musica,* issued in 1725, is taken up with the text of a treatise on how to write good melodies, *Die melodische Vorhof,* by Heinrich Bokemeyer, cantor in Wolfenbüttel, which appears with Mattheson's annotations that counter almost everything that Bokemeyer states. In section XVI Bokemeyer takes issue with composers who become "fledgling versifiers," using self-made texts for their church music.[63] Mattheson objects to this criticism, broadens the issue, and responds:

. . . a right-minded cantor, by the function of his holy vocation [Amt],[64] proclaims in the same way as a preacher in the pulpit: for both promote God's Word. *Verbum Dei est, sive mente cogitetir, sive canatur, sive pulsu edatur* [the Word of God is uttered by the thinking of the mind, by singing, and by playing (lit. = striking)], as expressed in the words written by Justin Martyr. *Vid. Gesneri Medit. super Psalter. cap. 27.*[65]

Mattheson's source was almost certainly the treatise by Raupach ("Veritophilus"), *Deutliche Beweis-Gründe* that he had appended to the third part of Niedt's *Musikalischer Handleitung* in 1717:

> *Justinus Martyr . . .* aus dem Griechischen übersetzet: "*Verbum Dei est, sive mente cogitetir, sive canatur, sive pulsu edatur.*" Das ist: Gottes Wort ist und bleibt Gottes Wort/es werde entweder im Gemühte gedacht/oder gesungen und ausgesprochen/oder auf *musicali*schen *Instrumen*ten geschlagen/angedeutet und zu verstehen gegeben. *Vide. Meditat. D. Salomonis Gesneri super Psalterium cap. 27.*[66]

Mattheson simply abbreviated Raupach's text but without omitting anything of substance.

Later in life Mattheson again quoted the words of "Justin":

> [Sanden] on p. 12 of his fine singular address [the 1720 Königsburg sermon], quotes thus from Justin Martyr, *Quaest. 107. ad Orthod.*: *Verbum Dei est, sive mente cogitetir, sive canatur, sive pulsu edatur.* It is and remains God's Word, whether it be carried in the thoughts of the heart, or by singing, or by playing. It is thus not secondary but primary. This may each Christian certainly believe: that God's Word can be no secondary matter.[67]

Irwin draws the following conclusion: "Even if the power of music to preach the Word was sometimes implicit in Lutheran thought prior to the eighteenth century, my research leads me to conclude that Johann Mattheson was not the end of a line which placed the preacher and cantor on the same level but was the first to make such a claim explicit."[68] But Mattheson is by no means the first to make explicit this connection between the similar functions of cantor and preacher: as he was ready to admit, many earlier writers, including Luther,[69] had made explicit statements concerning the commonality of function on the part of both preacher and cantor.[70] This commonality was the natural outgrowth of Luther's insistence on the indissoluble connection between theology and music.

The connection between composing sermons and composing music was also underscored by the commonality of terminology applied to both activities by Lutheran theologians and music theorists. The classical categories of rhetoric had long been applied to homiletics.[71] But, following the Reformation with its insistence on the primacy of the Word, such rhetorical categories were increasingly employed by music theorists to define and explain specific compositional techniques.[72] If therefore both homiletics and music were structured and analyzed according to similar rhetorical concepts it was inevitable that theologians and musicians would draw attention to the analogous functions of preaching and performing, of preachers and musicians.

Bach as Musical Theologian and Theological Musician

Johann Sebastian Bach was as much a musical theologian as a theological musician. Although there has been some resistance in musicological circles to the suggestion that there are distinctive theological dimensions to Bach's music, as the previous paragraphs demonstrate, the connection between theology and music has a long history in Lutheran tradition.

There are certainly difficulties in speaking about music in theological terms that are not restricted to musicians and musicologists, who tend to regard theology as an extra-musical dimension that has little or nothing to do with the essence of music itself. Pastors and theologians have their own difficulties, such as their propensity to regard music as an optional extra to worship that, while it might have certain propagandistic possibilities, lacks theological substance. But neither point of view represents the essential nature of pre-nineteenth-century Lutheran theology and practice, before they were diluted by the twin forces of Pietism and the Enlightenment.

In one sense, of course, Bach was not a "professional" theologian — he was neither a pastor nor a theology professor — but in another sense he was very much a professional "theologian," since as a cantor it was his duty to teach the basic theology of the catechism and to be intimately involved in providing music to be heard within specific liturgical and homiletic contexts which presupposed distinctive theological contents.[73] It is in his music that Bach demonstrates his theological acumen, as can be seen in the following representative examples.

The *Symbolum Nicenum* of what was to become known as the *B minor Mass* (BWV 232[II]) is as much a significant theological statement as it is a profound musical one, symmetrically arranged around the center-point of the *Crucifixus*, literally the theological *crux* of Christian, Trinitarian theology.

The Kyrie movement (BWV 233a) composed in Weimar and later incorporated into the *Missa* in F (BWV 233) is another striking musical statement of Trinitarian theology. In the five-part texture the three-voice fugal *Kyrie* is framed by the German Agnus Dei, *Christe, du Lamm Gottes,* in the upper soprano part, and by the Kyrie from the end of Luther's German litany (1529) in the bass. The Trinity is formally symbolized in the three-sectioned, three-voiced fugal counterpoint (SAT). The fugal theme of *Christe eleison* is an almost exact inversion of the theme of *Kyrie I,* and *Kyrie II* combines both themes *(Kyrie I* and *Christe)* in a double fugue. Again, this is as much a theological statement as a musical one. The three-fold structure of the liturgical *Kyrie* has traditionally been interpreted as an expression of Trinitarian faith, and, according to the Nicene Creed, the Son is "begotten from the Father" and the Holy Spirit proceeds "from the Father and the Son." Here Bach contrives to expound this Trinitarian theology in the thematic material and musical form of this remarkable movement.

Bach does something similar at the end of the *Magnificat* (BWV 243), in the nineteen measures at the beginning of the *Gloria,* before the music of the opening "Magnificat" returns for the remainder of the text of the *Gloria patri.* Trinitarian theology is expressed in three sections, one for each Person, in which the voice entries are in triplets and parallel thirds. Further, the voice entries for "Gloria patri" progress from the lowest to the highest, with a pedal-point in the middle of the three measures of the bass part. "Gloria filio" has staggered voice entries, beginning with soprano I, which is now assigned the vocal pedal-point in the middle of these three measures, that is, the inversion of what appears in the bass part of the "Gloria patri." Then for the "Gloria et Spiritui Sancto" the voices enter in a simple descending order, in five steps from soprano I to bass. Here again Bach gives musical form to Trinitarian theology: the Son is the image of the Father, and the Holy Spirit proceeds from the Father and the Son.

In the six cantatas that together form the *Christmas Oratorio* (BWV 248) there are various allusions to the purpose for which Christ was born: he was born to die; hence the first and last chorale of the total work employ the melody *Herzlich tut mich verlangen,* otherwise known as the Passion Chorale. Again, in the final recitative of the *Christmas Oratorio* the four voices in turn (SATB) sing the same basic melodic form that Bach used for the words "Der Held aus Juda" that erupt toward the end of the aria *Es ist Vollbracht* in the St. John Passion — a fanfare signaling the triumph of the cross. Thus in the *Christmas Oratorio* Bach uses musical means to link together the doctrines of Incarnation and Atonement.

In a number of Bach's other vocal works the theological distinction between Law and Gospel is expressed in musical form. In the *St. John Passion* (BWV 245) Law is depicted in the strict counterpoint of *Wir haben ein Gestz,* and the grace of the Gospel is expressed in the much freer imitative counterpoint of *Ich folge dir gleichfals.* Similarly, in the cantata *Gottes Zeit* (BWV 106) the demand of Law, expressed fugally by "Es ist ein alte Bund," is contrasted by the freedom of the Gospel, "Ja, komm Herr Jesu" in which the soprano freely floats away, unencumbered by the *basso continuo.* But there are many other examples of the way in which Bach expresses theological concepts with specific musical forms.[74]

Notwithstanding Irwin's proposition, Bach cannot simply be dismissed as a mere musician without theological competence. Two contemporary professors of theology in Leipzig witness to the contrary. But in addition to their judgment of his theological knowledge is the existence of his personal theological library. Bach owned a significant collection of theological books. He had many volumes of sermons, Bible commentaries, studies of the Council of Trent, the Augsburg Confession, the Lord's Supper, and baptism, as well as devotional writings.[75] He owned two different collected editions of Luther's works, an additional volume of his Psalm commentaries, two editions of the *Hauspostille,* and a copy of the *Tischreden,*[76] in which could be found many of Luther's statements concerning the connections between theology and music, views that clearly influenced Bach's approach to composition.[77] An example is the fifth movement of Cantata 9, *Es ist das Heil und kommen her,* a study in contrast, a duet for Soprano and Alto, that breathes a light and airy spirit and yet it is written in very strict counterpoint. In fact, it is an extraordinary combination of overlapping canons for the upper instruments (flute and oboe d'amore) and the two solo voices, Soprano and Alto. The text speaks of Christ fulfilling the Law, and Bach's music illustrates this by his legalistic canons, which can be clearly seen in the score, but what is heard is pure Gospel! It is a superlative example of Bach being at his musical and theological best, implying that he had carefully read the passage in Luther's *Tischreden,* under the *locus* "Law and Gospel," in which Luther declares that musical notation written on the page is Law but the sound of the same music in performance is Gospel.[78] Bach was indeed a lay theologian of some sophistication, someone who could be called a Doctor of Holy Scripture, according to Luther's judgment that anyone who could truly distinguish between Law and Gospel should be granted the title.[79]

The *Deutsche Messe* from Luther to Bach

Luther's *Deutsche Messe* is one of the most important liturgical documents of the Reformation era. It was not the first German vernacular liturgical order. German Masses had appeared in such places as Nürnberg, Straßburg, Augsburg, and Alstedt, before Luther's work on his *Deutsche Messe* was completed at the end of 1525. But most of these vernacular liturgies were substantially *verbatim* translations of the Roman Mass, with various truncations of the Canon of the Mass. Luther similarly accepted the liturgical continuity of the basic form and structure of the Mass, but at the same time he also created a discontinuity by his innovations. As discussed above in Chapter 12 above, he gave the traditional form a radically new theological interpretation. He reversed the accepted action of Mass: instead of prayer and intercession directed from the church to God, he saw it as the proclamation of the Gospel from God to the worshiping community, gathered at the altar. The proclamation of the Gospel was the unifying principle of Luther's *Deutsche Messe:* the chanting of the Epistle and Gospel was thus given a prominence; the sermon on the Gospel of the day became an integral part of the Abendmahl, in contrast to its infrequent appearance in the medieval Roman Mass; and the *Verba testamenti* were not only to be fully heard but were also sung to the same tones as the Gospel of the day, again in contrast to the medieval Roman Mass in which the Canon was mostly unheard by the attending worshipers. The role of each member of the congregation was no longer to be one of mute spectator but rather one of active participant. The whole church, rather than the choir alone, was to sing hymnic versions of the Ordinary of the Mass, as well as the newly introduced hymns at appropriate places throughout the liturgical order. Above all the *Deutsche Messe* was essentially a musical service of worship, a combination of chant and hymnody, with the sermon and the paraphrase of the Lord's Prayer being the only spoken elements of the liturgical form. But Luther's *Deutsche Messe* was and continues to be frequently misunderstood. First, it has been assumed that Luther intended his *Deutsche Messe* to be the definitive Lutheran liturgy to be followed to the letter by all evangelicals who were associated with the reforms of Wittenberg. This assumption both misunderstands Luther's theology in general and his specific directions in the *Deutsche Messe* in particular. To make his liturgical order prescriptive for the churches of the German Reformation would be an inappropriate legalistic imposition, destroying Christian liberty. Worship should be undergirded by the forgiveness and grace of the Gospel rather than being imposed as an expression of legalistic uniformity. For Luther there was always the danger of turning the Gospel back into Law. Therefore his *Deutsche Messe* was issued as an expression of Gospel worship by which no one was to be bound. Luther's preface to the *Deutsche Messe* begins with these words:

> In the first place, I would kindly and for God's sake request all those who see this order of service or desire to follow it: Do not make it a rigid law to bind or entangle anyone's conscience, but use it in Christian liberty as long, when, where, and how you find it to be practical and useful.[1]

Luther was more concerned that the Gospel principles enunciated in his *Deutsche Messe,* rather than a slavish adherence to its content and detail, should be expressed in evangelical worship. Thus in the numerous church orders of sixteenth-century Lutheran Germany, which continued in use virtually unaltered into the eighteenth century, while many features of the *Deutsche Messe* were retained, nevertheless the liturgical forms in each of these territorial church orders differed in specific content and detail. An example is the Saxon *Kirchen-Agenda* of 1539/40, still in use during Bach's lifetime.

Second, it has been assumed that with the publication of the *Deutsche Messe* in 1526, the earlier Latin *Formula missæ* of 1523 was thereby superseded and thereafter only the vernacular form was to be used in Lutheran worship. But Luther specifically rejects this assumption in the preface to the *Deutsche Messe:*

> [The Latin Mass] we published earlier under the title *Formula missæ.* It is not now my intention to abrogate or to change this service. It shall not be affected in the form which we have followed so far; but we shall continue to use it when and where we are pleased or prompted to do so. For in no

wise would I want to discontinue the service in the Latin language, because the young are my chief concern. . . . I do not at all agree with those who cling to one language and despise all others. . . . These two orders of service must be used publicly, in the churches, for all the people. . . .[2]

Therefore in the later Lutheran church orders, particularly those for use in larger towns and cities, both Latin and German liturgical forms existed side-by-side. Thus the Hauptgottesdienst in Leipzig during Bach's time included both Latin and German texts.

Third, it has been assumed that the musical elements of the *Deutsche Messe* are not fundamentally integral to its liturgical form and can therefore be ignored. But even before the *Deutsche Messe* was completed Luther was critical of attempts to produce vernacular liturgical forms — it is almost certain that he had Thomas Müntzer's *Deutsch Euangelisch Messze* (1524) in mind. His primary criticism was that these vernacular forms failed to understand the essential musical nature of liturgical worship. In his treatise *Wider die himmlischen Propheten* (1525) Luther wrote:

> I would gladly have a German Mass today. I am also occupied with it. But I would very much like it to have a true German character. For to translate the Latin text and retain the Latin tone or notes has my sanction, though it does not sound polished or well done. Both the text and notes, accent, melody, and manner of rendering ought to grow out of the true mother tongue and its inflection, otherwise all of it becomes an imitation, in the manner of the apes.[3]

Nevertheless, later scholars have not always appreciated Luther's standpoint on the issue and have been dismissive of the musical elements of the *Deutsche Messe*. Thus in Germany the editions prepared by Hans Lietzmann, Joachim Beckmann, and Wolfgang Herbst contain none of the musical notation that Luther carefully prepared for the *Deutsche Messe,* with the assistance of the composers Conrad Rupsch and Johann Walter.[4] Similarly, in America English versions of the *Deutsche Messe* edited by Paul Zeller Strodach and Bard Thompson also omit the musical notation.[5] But the *Deutsche Messe* cannot be fully understood without its music, which makes up a high proportion of its content. Approximately eighty percent of the 39 pages of the original edition of the *Deutsche Messe* include musical notation. For Luther worship should be a musical experience, a combination of chant and hymnody, choral and instrumental. It is from Luther's conviction that "music is a beautiful and magnificent gift of God, and next to theology,"[6] and therefore a fundamental component of liturgy and worship, that the distinctive Lutheran musical tradition developed under the leadership of its Kantors of church and school, beginning with Luther's colleague Johann Walter and culminating in Johann Sebastian Bach.

It is one of those curious facts of history that both Martin Luther and Johann Sebastian Bach should have attended the same school, and in their early years experienced church music in the same church building. Between 1498 and 1501 Martin Luther was a pupil of the Latin school in Eisenach, sang in the choir of the Georgenkirche, and experienced a wide range of music through the influence of the patrician families Schalbe and Cotta. Between 1693 and 1695 Johann Sebastian Bach was also a pupil of the Latin school in Eisenach, and sang in the Georgenkirche, the church of his baptism, where his uncle Johann Christoph was the organist, Andreas Christian Dedekind the Kantor, and where his father, Johann Ambrosius, played as the leading town musician.

When Luther came to reform the liturgy, music was a fundamental component to those reforms, and his agenda for liturgical and musical reform was rooted in the schools. Instead of abolishing Latin schools, such as the Latin school in Eisenach he attended as a boy, Luther (with his colleagues) reconstituted them and gave them a key role in the reforming movement. Music was retained as an essential element of the curriculum in these schools, but it was to be taught and learned not to support the unreformed Mass but to proclaim the Gospel within the evangelical Mass. The children in the schools were to be taught the new music first, so that the school choirs could then lead their congregations in the new hymnody by singing the melodies in unison with the congregation, and also by singing polyphonic settings of these melodies in alternation with the congregational unison. The part-books of Johann Walter's *Chorgesangbuch* of 1524 (and later editions) were specifically compiled to meet these educational and liturgical needs. As Luther wrote in the preface to the *Chorgesangbuch*:

> And these songs were arranged in four [to five] parts to give the young — who should at any rate be trained in music and other fine arts. . . . Nor am I of the opinion that the gospel should destroy and blight all the arts, as some of the pseudo-religious claim. But I would like to see all the arts, especially music, used in the service of him who gave and made them.[7]

As has been observed a number of times throughout this book, music was to be taught in the school not only as part of the liberal arts curriculum but also to enable the school choir(s) to lead the music of the local church. Theory and practice of music in the classroom was augmented by daily experience of worship in the parish church, as well as on Sundays and the major festivals of the church year. This close connection between musical pedagogy and practical theology can be seen in various comments found in Luther's writings. In particular, according to Luther, the training of both preachers and teachers should include the theory, practice and experience of music. Thus the oft-quoted *Tischreden* of Luther:

> A schoolmaster must be able to sing, otherwise I will not consider him. Also young men should not be ordained into the ministry, unless they have experienced and practiced music in school.[8]

The parish church and the parish school, their ministers and teachers, worked together for the worship life of the community. The school choir was the pedagogical tool whereby the congregation learned to sing the new melodies, so that both choir and congregation could proclaim to each other the essence of the Gospel. Thus when Luther came to draw up the *Deutsche Messe* in 1525, he enlarged on this basic concept he had referred to in the preface to Walter's *Chorgesangbuch* and described the daily worship that was necessary in the schools, if they were to effectively lead the worship of the congregations Sunday by Sunday:

> This is what we do to train the schoolboys in the Bible. Every day of the week they chant a few Psalms in Latin before the lesson, as has been customary at Matins hitherto. For as we stated above, we want to keep the youth well versed in the Latin Bible. After the Psalms, two or three boys in turn read a chapter from the Latin New Testament, depending on the length. Another boy then reads the same chapter in German to familiarize them with it and for the benefit of any layman who might be present and listening. Thereupon they proceed with an antiphon to the German lesson mentioned above. After the lesson the whole congregation sings a German hymn, the Lord's Prayer is said silently, and the pastor or chaplain reads the collect and closes with the *Benedicamus Domino* as usual.
>
> Likewise at Vespers they sing a few of the Vesper Psalms in Latin with an antiphon, as heretofore, followed by a hymn if one is available. Again two or three boys in turn then read a chapter from the Latin Old Testament or half a one, depending on length. Another boy reads the same chapter in German. The Magnificat follows in Latin with an antiphon or hymn, the Lord's Prayer said silently, and the collects with the Benedicamus. This is the daily service throughout the week in cities where there are schools.[9]

This kind of daily and weekly worship was Johann Sebastian Bach's experience when he was a pupil at schools in Eisenach, Ohrdruf, and especially in Lüneberg, where he sang in the Matins choir of St. Michael's school. Bach's education was to a large extent therefore conditioned by patterns of worship that Luther outlined in his *Deutsche Messe*, worship that had a high musical content. Later in life, as the Thomaskantor in Leipzig, his primary responsibility in the Thomasschule was to teach and lead music within the context of daily and weekly worship. The weekly pattern of worship of the Leipzig churches was particularly full, as is outlined in Günther Stiller's *Johann Sebastian Bach und das Leipziger gottesdienstlichen Leben seiner Zeit,*[10] and the Sunday and festival services were enriched with concerted choral music. Chapter 5 of the *Schule-Ordnung* (1723) is headed "Vom Amt des Cantoris, so viel die Music betrifft," and contains thirteen numbered paragraphs listing the Kantor's responsibilities in leading the music of the churches of Leipzig.[11]

Here Bach is again to be seen as the inheritor of a school-system, designed to serve the musical needs of the worship of the Lutheran church, that was initiated by Luther in the *Deutsche Messe*. What he had learned and experienced as a schoolboy, beginning in Eisenach, Bach was called upon to teach and lead in Leipzig. Further, the music Bach composed for Lutheran worship can be seen as the consequence, as well as the culmination, of the principles articulated in Luther's *Deutsche Messe*.[12]

The heart of Reformation theology was Christology, the *solus Christus* aspect of the Christian Gospel that was summarized by three further Latin formulæ: *sola scriptura, sola fidei,* and *sola gratia.* Together they encapsulate the Protestant understanding of the Christian faith, that is: a Christian's standing before God depends not on the authority of the church but on the authority of Scripture that centers on the person and work of Christ; salvation is offered and received as a gift by faith and not as a reward for a worthy life; and this salvation is from beginning to end the work of God's grace in Christ. A fourth dimension was added with the doctrine of universal priesthood of all believers that was directly antithetical to the particular priesthood of Catholicism. These four theological concepts were translated into the practical concerns of teaching the laity at large the essence of biblical theology and the substance of Christian faith, which were to be expressed in forms of worship and in congregational song. These four dimensions of Reformation theology were epitomized in four different types of publications that came from the pen of Luther: Bible, Catechism, Hymnal, and Liturgical Order.

These four manifestations of theological principle, which can be found in the *Deutsche Messe,* need to be examined further.

Bible

The *sola scriptura* principle gave rise to the need for vernacular translations of the Bible. Luther began by making a translation of the New Testament into German, which he published in 1522, and his complete German Bible was first issued in 1534 and subsequently revised a number of times. The Bible contained the Word of God which the people needed to read for themselves and to hear being read in public worship. Thus in the *Deutsche Messe* Luther gave careful consideration to how the Word of God, in the Epistle and Gospel, was to be appropriately chanted with clarity and precision. All the melodic formulæ for chanting the Epistle and Gospel were carefully explained, and in addition to the fully notated Epistle and Gospel included in the main text of the *Deutsche Messe*, two further examples were given in a kind of appendix. By a stroke of genius Luther took the concept of the traditional Passion tones, heard only during Holy Week — in which the voices of Jesus, the Evangelist, and the crowd are indicated by different pitches — and applied them to the Gospels which would be sung this way every Sunday and festival of the church year. This dramatic musical interpretation of the words of the Gospel of the day had significant consequences for the development of Passion music within the Lutheran tradition. The two great passions of Bach, St. Matthew and St. John, grow out of the tradition of the sung Gospel, which Luther articulated in his *Deutsche Messe*. The complete biblical narrative of the Passion in these two Gospel accounts is given musical form by Bach; sometimes, especially in the St. John Passion, it is given in a highly dramatic musical form. But the seeds of this kind of dramatic musical interpretation of the Gospel narrative are to be found in Luther's *Deutsche Messe*. Although Bach's biblical recitative is much more expressive than Luther's melodic formulæ in the *Deutsche Messe*, there are nevertheless significant points of contact. One example is that Luther directed that the asking of a question should be indicated by a rise in pitch. Bach frequently does the same. Thus Judas's question "Bin ichs, Rabbi?" in the St. Matthew Passion ends with a rising fifth (BWV 244:11, mm. 13-14), and Jesus's question "Wen suchet ihr?" in the St. John Passion is first a rising fifth (BWV 245:2^a, mm. 16-17) and then a rising fourth (BWV 245:2^d, mm. 29-30). Another example is the *vox Christi* (the voice of Christ) in Luther's melodic formulæ for the chanting of the Gospel of the day in the *Deutsche Messe*, which is, as in the traditional Passion tones, notated in the bass range. Thus in many of Bach's cantatas the solo bass is frequently the *vox Christi*, especially where there is dialogue between the soul (soprano) and Christ (bass), in such cantatas as the early *Ich hatte viel Bekümmernis* (BWV 21/8) and *Wachet auf* (BWV 140/3 & 6), written approaching twenty years later.

Luther's concern for the Gospel to be sung Sunday by Sunday also encouraged the ultimate development of the church cantata which in Bach's hands reached its most developed form. The cantata became the musical counterpart of the sermon, the sermon which was itself an exposition of the Gospel of the day. In a similar way that Bach's passions include meditations — both textual and musical — on the Passion narrative, the cantata (usually) is a textual and musical exposition of some aspect of the Gospel for the day, the major difference being that the cantata is a more concise form based on the leading ideas of the Gospel, whereas the Passion includes *verbatim* the biblical text. The function of each is also different. Bach's Passions, heard at Good Friday Vespers, took the place of the biblical lection and therefore it was necessary to include the complete biblical narrative. Bach's cantatas, in the eucharistic Hauptgottesdienst, were essentially musical commentaries on the Sunday and festival Gospels and therefore were heard in addition to, rather than in place of, the biblical lection. There was therefore no need to include the whole biblical text. Cantatas were therefore musical homilies that expounded the Gospel of the day in much the same way as the sermons that were preached at those services in which these cantatas were heard. But this close homiletic relationship with the Gospel of the day indicates that the musical form of the cantata is an extension of Luther's concept of the Gospel as a musical form.

Catechism

The *sola fidei* principle led to the formulation of catechisms in which the basic tenets of Reformation faith were expounded. In the *Deutsche Messe* Luther had registered the need for a basic catechism that should be taught within the context of worship.

> First, the German service needs a plain and simple, fair and square catechism. . . . This instruction or catechization I cannot put better or more plainly than has been done from the beginning of Christendom and retained until now, i.e., in these three parts, the Ten Commandments, the Creed, and the Our Father. These three plainly and briefly contain exactly everything that a Christian needs to know.[13]

There follows the question and answer form he would later expand into five main articles, with the addition of sections on the two sacraments, baptism and Lord's Supper. In 1529 Luther published his *Großer Katechismus* for pastors and *Kleine Katechismus* for laypeople, especially children. The Wittenberg hymnals included hymns on the mach sections of the catechism, though it took a little time before they were gathered together under the rubric "Katechismuslieder":[14]

Ten Commandments	*Dies sind der heilgen zehn Gebot* (1524)
Creed	*Wir Glauben all an einen Gott* (1524)
Lord's Prayer	*Vater unser im Himmelreich* (1539)
Baptism	*Christ unser Herr zum Jordan kam* (1541/43)
Confession	*Aus tiefer Not schrei ich zu dir* (1523/24)
Lord's Supper	*Jesus Christus unser Heiland, der von uns* (1524)

On Sunday afternoons and other specified days the catechism was expounded within the context of the Vespergottesdienst, sometimes called *Katechismusexamen*, derived from the fact that it was customary to teach the substance of Luther's catechisms at Sunday vespers, as well as on some weekdays. The melodies associated with these Katechismuslieder formed the basis for numerous congregational, choral, and organ settings by many Lutheran composers, including Bach, who as the Leipzig Thomaskantor was required to teach the substance of the Catechism in the Thomasschule each week.[15] The second part of Bach's *Clavierübung III* is made up of two complete cycles of organ chorale preludes on these Catechism hymns: one of settings for manuals alone and the other for manuals and pedal, corresponding to Luther's "Kleine" and "Großer" Catechisms:

	Kleine	Großer
Dies sind der heilgen zehn Gebot	BWV 679	BWV 678
Wir Glauben all an einen Gott	BWV 681	BWV 680
Vater unser im Himmelreich	BWV 683	BWV 682
Christ unser Herr zum Jordan kam	BWV 685	BWV 684
Aus tiefer Not schrei ich zu dir	BWV 687	BWV 686
Jesus Christus unser Heiland, der von uns	BWV 689	BWV 688

Hymnal

The doctrine of universal priesthood led to the necessity for the members of the worshiping congregation to express their faith with unanimity, a need that was fulfilled by introduction of the new evangelical hymns which were collected into hymnals. One of the principal differences, apart from language, between the *Formula missæ* of 1523 and the *Deutsche Messe* of 1526 is the expanded role of congregational singing in the vernacular liturgy. In the *Deutsche Messe* Luther employed congregational hymns in three different ways. First, hymns could be substituted for the Propers or Ordinary in any celebration of the evangelical Mass. At the beginning of the Deutsche Messe, in place of the traditional introit, Luther's preference is for the whole congregation to sing a complete prose psalm to a plainsong psalm tone. The example he gives is Psalm 34 to be sung "in primo Tono." But the Introit-psalm could be replaced by a hymn; indeed, that option is stated first. Luther wrote: "To begin the service we sing a hymn or a German Psalm."[16] This principle of substituting hymns for items of sung liturgical prose was also applied to the Ordinary. Instead of the prose *Credo* the congregation is to confess its faith by singing the vernacular hymn *Wir Glauben all an einen Gott*. Similarly, Luther included in the *Deutsche Messe* his vernacular version of the Sanctus in rhymed couplets, *Jesaja dem Propheten das geschah*, and also referred to the singing of the German Agnus Dei. In the course of time the principle was expanded and hymns for all five parts of the Ordinary came into almost universal use throughout Lutheran Germany:

Kyrie	*Kyrie, Gott Vater in ewigkeit*
Gloria	*Allein Gott in der Höh sei Ehr*
Credo	*Wir glauben all an einen Gott*
Sanctus	*Jesaja dem Propheten das geschah*
Agnus Dei	*Christe, du Lamm Gottes,* or *O Lamm Gottes, unschuldig*

The Gloria hymn, *Allein Gott in der Höh sei Ehr*, was used almost every Sunday, which accounts for the large number of extant chorale preludes on the melody written by numerous Lutheran composers, including Bach (for example, BWV 675-677, 711, 715, 717, 771). Bach also included extensive organ settings of the Kyrie and Gloria melodies in the first part of his *Clavierübung III*;[17] composed various chorale preludes and at least one vocal setting of *Wir glauben* (for example, BWV 437, 740, 765, 1098, as well as BWV 680-681 in *Clavierübung III*); and included both German versions of the Agnus Dei in his choral music, for example, *Christe, du Lamm Gottes* in the final movement of Cantata 23, and *O Lamm Gottes, unschuldig* in the opening chorus of the St. Matthew Passion. With the passage of time the German Sanctus, *Jesaja dem Propheten*, was not as frequently sung as the others, and Bach, apparently, did not compose a setting of it. But these vernacular hymns did not displace the Latin prose originals on which they were based. As has been emphasized throughout this book, Luther had no wish to abolish the use of Latin with the publication of the *Deutsche Messe*. Thus in towns and cities where there were Latin schools or universities, such as Eisenach and Leipzig, German and Latin liturgical texts either alternated Sunday by Sunday, or were sung sequentially within a single Hauptgottesdienst. Even though it became customary for the congregation to sing *Allein Gott in der Höh sei Ehr* at almost every Hauptgottesdienst, it could be preceded by the Latin *Gloria in excelsis Deo,* sung by the Kantorei, in either monodic chant or a concerted setting, as in Bach's four *Missæ* (BWV 233-236), and especially in the 1733 *Missa* (BWV 232) that eventually was expanded to become the monumental B-minor Mass. On the other hand, at the Vespergottesdienst, the Magnificat was either sung congregationally in its vernacular form, *Meine Seele erhebt den Herren,* to the *Tonus peregrinus* (see BWV 733: *Fuga sopra Magnificat*), or sung chorally to a Latin psalm tone, or in a concerted setting, such as Bach's great *Magnificat* (BWV 243).

Second, hymns were to be sung in response to the Epistle and in preparation for the Gospel. Luther wrote: "After the Epistle a German hymn . . . is sung with the whole choir."[18] Thus the concept of the Gradual as the song of the choir was expanded to embrace the whole church, congregation and choir together. In Wittenberg this Graduallied became the primary hymn at the evangelical Mass. At the time that Luther wrote the *Deutsche Messe* the corpus of hymns was relatively small. Thus he named the epiclesis hymn *Nun bitten wir den Heiligen Geist* as a general Graduallied. But already there were seasonal hymns that were being sung as Graduallieder, such as *Nun komm der Heiden Heiland* on the Sundays in Advent and *Christ lag in Todesbanden* during the Easter season. Over the years the basic corpus of Graduallieder expanded to include appropriate hymns for all the Sundays and festivals of the church year. The primary examples of these Graduallieder, many of them written by Luther, figure prominently in Bach's compositions for the church. A major part of the *Orgelbüchlein* (BWV 599-644) is primarily a collection of chorale preludes on the principal Graduallieder of the church year. Similarly, many of the chorale cantatas of his second Jahrgang in Leipzig (1724-25) are based on such Graduallieder, and many of his other cantatas make use of the respective Graduallied of the day or celebration, either as the concluding chorale or incorporated in some way into one of the other movements.

Third, hymns were to be sung during the distribution of communion. Luther wrote: "Meanwhile the German Sanctus or the hymn *Gott sei gelobet,* or the hymn of John Huss, *Jesus Christus unser Heiland,* could be sung . . . or the German Agnus Dei [= *Christe, du Lamm Gottes*]."[19] The establishment of congregational song at the time of the distribution encouraged the growth of a rich tradition of communion hymns in the Lutheran church. By the time of

Bach it had been expanded to include special vocal music as well as hymns, that is, *musica sub communione.* This could include a part of a cantata, or even a complete cantata, such as *Du wahrer Gott und Davids Sohn* (BWV 23), *Schmücke dich, o Liebe Seele* (BWV 180), *Barmherziges Herze* (BWV 185), and *Mein Herze schwimmt im Blut* (BWV 199), which Bach is known to have used for this purpose in Leipzig. But this *musica sub communione* did not supplant the singing of communion hymns during the distribution. As Bach recorded on the cover of the Advent Cantata *Nun komm der Heiden Heiland* (BWV 61), in an outline of the Leipzig Hauptgottesdienst, probably penned in November 1723: during Communion "Preluding on [and performance of] the music [= second part of the Cantata, or another cantata]. After which alternate preluding and the singing of chorales until communion is ended."[20] It is also possible that Bach's three chorale partitas (BWV 766-768), with their various alternate settings of their respective chorale melodies, were intended to be played during the distribution of communion. But this later *musica sub communione,* comprising vocal music and hymnody with organ chorale preludes, developed from the directions found in both Luther's *Formula missæ* and *Deutsche Messe.*

Liturgical Order

The *sola gratia* principle led to a reevaluation of the theological presuppositions undergirding worship in general and the Mass in particular. For Luther it was therefore necessary to reform existing orders of worship, especially the Mass, so that they were consistent with evangelical theology. The *sola gratia* principle meant that the Eucharist was to be seen in terms of *beneficium, testamentum,* and *donum,* rather than *sacrificium, opus bonum,* and *meritum,* the terms employed in Catholic theology of the Mass.[21] Notwithstanding this theological shift, what is significant about Luther's *Deutsche Messe* is its adherence to traditional liturgical form. Even though it has its radical components and is an essentially simple order, it preserves the historic liturgical form and retains much of the traditional content that was consistent with evangelical theology. Unlike some Reformed orders of the sixteenth century, which often appear to be loosely-connected amalgams of prayer, preaching, and singing, Luther did not reject the traditional, sequential liturgical paradigm: Introit-psalm (or hymn), Collect, Epistle, Graduallied, Gospel, Creed, sermon, Preface/prayer, Verba, distribution, thanksgiving collect, and Benediction. Nor did Luther overlook the chant associated with traditional liturgical forms. In the *Deutsche Messe* he either took them over with little alteration, as in his use of the "primo Tono" for the Introit-psalm, or adapted and/or simplified them, as in the Kyrie and the Epistle- and Gospel-tones.

Luther's respect for liturgical form and content meant that later regional church orders in Germany maintained a continuity with the liturgical traditions of Western Christendom, a continuity that was unbroken until the late eighteenth century when it was effectively dismantled by the combined influences of the Enlightenment and Pietism. While this process had begun during Bach's lifetime, traditions of liturgical worship remained strong in Leipzig. Thus much of Bach's music was written to be heard within a liturgical framework and context that owed much to Luther's *Deutsche Messe*. Many of Bach's choral compositions were not conceived as freestanding, independent works but rather as dependent musical creations that were intended to be heard at a particular juncture of the liturgical sequence. These pieces were meant to be heard with chant, prayers, readings, sermon, hymns, and so forth, appropriate to the day or celebration. Echoes of this liturgical context can be found woven into the fabric of some of Bach's compositions, such as: the opening four-measure statement, and the fugal theme that follows it, at the beginning of the first Kyrie of the 1733 *Missa*, are based on the melodic contour of Luther's Tone 1 Kyrie of the *Deutsche Messe;* the opening measures of movement 1 of the *Symbolum Nicenum* of the B-minor Mass (BWV 232[II]) cite the plainsong intonation *"Credo in unum Deum,"* and in movement 8 the chant for the words *"Confiteor unum baptisma in remissionem peccatorum"* is incorporated into the musical texture; and the German Agnus Dei, alluded to by Luther in the *Deutsche Messe,* is employed in the counterpoint — sometimes obviously and sometimes disguised — in the concerted Kyrie (BWV 233a), two movements of *Du wahrer Gott und David's Sohn* (BWV 23), and the opening movement of *Herr Jesu Christ, wahr' Mensch und Gott* (BWV 127).[22]

In the *Deutsche Messe* Luther established the principles of worship for Lutheran churches. Lutheran worship was a musical form of worship, to be promoted and undergirded by the choirs and the teaching of music in the schools. The church music of Johann Sebastian Bach is in many respects the product and culmination of Luther's principles. This music was also rooted in the teaching and practice of music in the schools. Much of Bach's music was written for the choirs of the Thomasschule in Leipzig, and his own early career was strongly influenced by his participation in the school choirs of his youth, that sang in the worship of the churches to which they were attached. For Bach, as well as for Luther, this early experience of musical worship was in Eisenach.

APPENDIX 1

Luther's Hymns and Liturgical Chants in Critical Editions and Hymnals

	WA 35	AWA 4	LW 53	LH	LBW	LWor	CW	ELH
Ach Gott, vom Himmel sieh darein	+	+	+	260	–	–	205	440
All Ehr und Lob soll Gottes sein	–	–	+	238	–	210	262	36
Aus tiefer Not schrei ich zu dir	+	+	+	329	295	230	305	452
Christ ist erstanden	–	+	–	187	136	124	144	344
Christ lag in Todesbanden	+	+	+	195	134	123	161	343
Christ, unser Herr, zum Jordan kam	+	+	+	–	79	223	88	247
Christe, du Lamm Gottes	–	+	+	147	103	–	–	[+]
Christum wir sollen loben schon	+	+	+	104	–	–	39	267
Der du bist drei in Einigkeit	+	+	+	–	–	–	–	–
Dies sind die heilgen zehn Gebot	+	+	+	287	–	331	285	490
Ein feste Burg ist unser Gott	+	+	+	262	228/9	297/8	200/1	250/1
Ein neues Lied wir heben an	+	+	+	259*	–	–	–	556*
Erhalt uns, Herr, bei deinem Wort	+	+	+	261	230	334	203	589
Es spricht der Unweisen Mund	+	+	+	–	–	–	–	–
Es wollt uns Gott genädig sein	+	+	+	500	335	288	574	591
Gelobet seist du, Jesu Christ	+	+	+	80	48	35	33	136
Gott der Vater wohn uns bei	+	+	+	247	308	170	192	18
Gott sei gelobet und gebenedeiet	+	+	+	313	215	238	317	327
Herr Gott, dich loben wir	+	+	+	–	–	–	–	45
Jesaja, dem Propheten, das geschah	+	+	+	249	528	214	267	40
Jesus Christus unser Heiland, der den Tod	+	+	+	–	–	–	–	–
Jesus Christus unser Heiland, der von uns	+	+	+	–	–	236/7	313	316/7
Komm, Gott Schöpfer, Heiliger Geist	+	+	+	–	–	–	177	10
Komm, heiliger Geist, Herre Gott	+	+	+	224	163	154	176	2

	WA 35	AWA 4	LW 53	LH	LBW	LWor	CW	ELH
Kyrie eleison	–	+	+	–	–	–	–	–
Litanie	–	+	+	–	–	–	–	–
Mensch, willst du leben seliglich	+	+	+	–	–	–	–	–
Mit Fried und Freud ich fahr dahin	+	+	+	137	–	185	269	48
Mitten wir im Leben sind	+	+	+	590	350	265	534	52
Nun bitten wir den Heiligen Geist	+	+	+	231	317	155	190	33
Nun freut euch, lieben Christen	+	+	+	387	299	353	377	378
Nun komm, der Heiden Heiland	+	+	+	95	28	13	2	90
Nun laßt uns den Leib begraben	–	+	–	596	–	–	–	–
Sie ist mir lieb, die werte Magd	+	+	+	–	–	–	–	–
Unser große Sünde und Schwere Missetat	–	+	–	–	–	–	–	–
Vater unser im Himmelreich	+	+	+	458	–	431	410	383
Verleih uns Frieden gnädiglich	+	+	+	–	471	219	522	584
Vom Himmel hoch, da komm ich her	+	+	+	85	51	37/8	38	123/4
Vom Himmel kam der Engel Schar	+	+	+	103	–	52	53	154
Wär Gott nicht mit uns diese Zeit	+	+	+	267	–	–	202	396
Was fürchst du, Feind Herodes, sehe	+	+	+	–	–	–	–	–
Wir glauben all an einen Gott	+	+	+	251	374	213	271	38
Wohl dem, der in Gottes Furcht steht	+	+	+	–	–	–	–	–

* = abbreviated
[ ] = in liturgical section

Jean Gerson's Poem "In Praise of Music"

Introduction

Jean Gerson (1363-1429), French theologian, educator, poet, and mystic, also wrote on music, notably *Tres tractatus de canticis* which comprises *De canticorum originali ratione* (ca. 1426), *De canticordo* (ca. 1423) and *De canticis* (between 1424 and 1426). His poem in praise of music is found in the second part of *De canticis*. The following translation, commissioned for this work, is by Leofranc Holford-Strevens, who also supplied the critical annotation ("LH-S" in the notes). The material enclosed thus << >> identifies the passages cited by Adam von Fulda in his treatise *De musica*, I, cap. 2 (1490), which amount to a high proportion of the poem but presented in fragmentary form which is often at variance with the sequence of lines in Gerson's original.[1]

Carmen de laude Musicae

<<New music that comes about through the impulse of divine love
cannot be adequately exalted by any praise;
it refreshes the spirit,[2] drives away cares, and soothes ennui,
and is a congenial companion to the travelers whom it bears along.[3]
Through the midst of snows and through [blazing] suns, in reliance on
　　song
I shall go, patient in hope, happy, eager, and cheerful,
for miserable cares flee at [the sound of] song through the empty air,
and every hostile plague that might lie in wait is dispelled.
On encountering the string-players[4] Saul is turned as it were

into another man, he plays the strings and becomes a new prophet.[5]
While the evil spirit torments him the shepherd David who sings to
    the cithara[6]
forces it to depart through song.[7] >>
At one time Elisha lacked the prophetic spirit;
as the string-player sang the spirit filled him.[8]
Pythagoras had been moved to compose on strings,
taking his composed melodies to the cithara.
Behold, the spirit breathing through the songs of the seers[9]
moves all creatures together to the praise of the Lord
that they shout for joy, play the strings, exult, that they give
    [= honor Him with] the cithara,
drums with strings, organs, harps, and choir.[10]
Bodies are organs consonant with spirits, the world is[11]
a single choir with which the mind loves to play.
With the harmony of the world the evil will, at discord with itself,
becomes concordant with the whole under God's direction.
Even remorseless death adorns the muse with short or long notes,
varying the vicissitudes of life;
merciful grace gives soft discant to the hoarse,
crime screeches about punishment in a deep tenor.
Alas, flee, flee I beg you from being in such a tenor;[12]
that you may be under a soft one, take on a soft heart.
Moreover, music is beneficial in healing bodies,
in that it rejoices, soothes, and relieves the spirit.
The heathens allot you both, [O] handsome Phoebus Apollo,
inventor of song and of medical assistance.
The music of the heart is inferred from the pulse of the veins:[13]
what is its temperament, its expression and beat.
By this touch the doctor conjectured the young man's love,
whose heart raged with grievous fire for [St] Agnes.[14]
We are not speaking now of the accursed spells[15] of magicians;
nor, unless he be a mystic, does even the poet please.
<<Amphion and Orpheus are said to have moved by song,
the one stones, the other the grim furies of hell. >>
If you take this metaphorically for teaching hard [strict] morality
and the good of changing [repentance?], they sing sound teaching.
Furthermore, every people's own music changes ways of behavior
or if they have already been altered inculcates them.
It is grave for this people,[16] wanton for another, soft or rustic;

one kind of music expands the heart and bears it along, another
constrains it.
There is the fourth, there is the fifth together with the octave:
a threefold grouping bound together by lawful pitches.
Again the Church undertakes to divide all singing into eight tones,
an ending, a reciting tone, and an intonation.[17]
Ignatius provided appropriate antiphons for the psalms
according as he had heard above on a mountain.[18]
I beg you, take care not to infect the impressionable minds
of children with disgraceful and foul songs.
The active power of song speeds into tender ears;
the slippery voice will sting your heart like nettles.
A woman stings by singing, and often does the same by seeing
    [i.e. being seen?];
she pours in both crime-poisons.
<<Why should we count the birds that are captured by human song,
though none despises its own song?
Fish and deer are soothed by songs, and music
has often been an antidote for various sick persons.
Believe [= If you believe] the Greeks, a dolphin bore Arion
through the midst of the waves while the lyre pleased it.
The shepherd's pipe soothes the beasts, herds, and flocks,
nor does the apparition of the wolf frighten them.
Then they graze the pastures free from care, and that rustic sound
diminishes the tiresomeness of feeding them for the herdsman.
Pan's rustic pipe contended with Apollo's cithara;
you judged, Midas, that Apollo lost.>>
Thus has everyone his own judgement, his own pleasure;
thus nature brings variety to its great melody.
<<The terrible trumpet sharpens the spirited breasts of horses
for war; the rider's wrath is roused.>>
When a woman weaves, or lulls the child in the cradle to sleep,[19]
in her want of education she sings stupid songs.
<<The heavenly host sings the celebratory songs of Jesus' birth
"Peace to man on earth, lofty glory to God."
The rustic cultivating the fields makes merry in shouting;[20]
the traveler sings and thereby lightens his journey.
Everyone eases his craft and its hard toil
with whatever kind of sound he can, even if it be somewhat harsh. >>
The devout voice placates God's wrath, and pleases the kindly citizens

[of heaven],
it sings together with the choirs of angels.
Father Augustine, you confess that you were moved
by the voices of the Church to drench your face with tears.[21]
Happy was he whose sins were uncovered, O Mary,
who so often receive voices from heaven in your ear.
We read that while the organs played[22] Cecilia sang to herself
only in her heart, a heart full of God.
You instructed us, Paul, to sing psalms to God in our hearts,[23]
for such action brings blessing in twofold way.
Here and now begins heaven, and dwells in exile
with the custom and manner of the blessed life;
death comes in time that looses the bonds of the flesh
and victoriously raises the singer of psalms aloft.

Carmen de laude Musicae[24]

<<Musica divini nova pulsu quae fit amoris
    Extolli nulla laude satis poterit;
Cor recreat, curas abigit, fastidia mulcet
    Fitque peregrinus quos vehit apta comes.
Per medias hyemes, per soles carmine fisus
    Ibo spe patiens, laetus alacris ovans
Nam fugiunt tristes cantu per mania curae,
    Omnis et insidians hostica pestis abest.
Vertitur occursu psallentium Saul velut alter
    Factus homo, psallit fitque propheta novus.
Exagitat nequam dum Spiritus hunc citharaedus
    Pastor per numeros cogit abire David.>>
Vatidicus deerat Elisaeo spiritus olim;
    Dum cecinit psaltes protinus implet eum.
Pythagoras motus fuerat componere chordis
    Adjectis citharae compositis numeris.
Spiritus ecce movet spirans per carmina vatum
    Ad Domini laudes cuncta creata simul
Ut jubilent, psallant, exultent ut citharam dent
    Tympana cum chordis, organa, nabla, chorum.
Corpora spiritibus sunt organa consona, mundus
    Et chorus unus quo ludere noys amat.
Carmine mundano sibi dissona prava voluntas

Concordans toti fit moderante Deo.
Ornat et ipsa notis brevibus longisve camaenam
   Improba vivendi mors variando vices;
Discantum mollem miserans dat gratia raucis.
   Stridet de poenis culpa tenore gravi.
Heu fuge te tali, fuge deprecor esse tenore;
   Ut sis sub molli, molle cor adde tibi.
Quid quod corporibus curandis musica prodest,
   Dum cor laetificat, lenit et alleviat.
Dant utrumque tibi gentiles, pulcher Apollo
   Carminis et medicae Phoebe repertor opis.
Colligitur pulsu venarum musica cordis,
   Quae sit temperies, quae phrasis atque thesis.
Hoc medicus tactu juvenis conjecit amorem
   Cujus in Agnete cor furit igne gravi.
Carmina non loquimur nunc execranda magorum;
   Nec nisi mysticus est, ipse poeta placet.
<<Amphion ac Orpheus cantu movisse feruntur
   Hic lapides, diras hic furias Erebi.>>
Moribus haec duris si transfers instituendis
   Mutandique bono, dogma salubre canunt.
Adde quod in populis mutat vel jam variatos
   Insinuat mores musica cuique sua.
Est gravis huic, petulans ill, mollis vel agrestis
   Unaque dilatans cor vehit, ista premit.
Est diatessaron, est diapente cum diapason
   Triplex legitimis copula nexa tonis.
Rursus in octo tonos, finem medium caput omnis
   Cantus partiri suscipit Ecclesia.
Antiphonas dedit ad psalmos Ignatius aptas
   Monte prout quodam desuper audierat.
Turpibus et foedis infantum quaeso cavete
   Flexibiles animos cantibus inficere.
Festinat in teneras energia carminis aures.
   Uret ut urticae cortibi lubrica vox.
Urit cantando, facit idem saepe videndo
   Femina flagitii fundit utrumque virus.
<<Quid numeremus aves humano quae capiuntur
   Cantu, nec cantum despicit ulla suum.
Pisces et cervi mulcentur cantibus, aegris

Antidotum variis musica crebro fuit.
Praebe fidem Graecis, delphinus Ariona vexit
    Fluctus per medios dum lyra mulcet eum.
Fistula pastoris pecudes armenta gregesque
    Solatur, nec eas terret imago lupi:
Pascua tunc secura metunt minuitque magistro
    Taedia pascendi rusticus iste sonus.
Fistula Pan Phoebi citharae certavit agrestis;
    Iudice te, Mida, victus Apollo fuit.>>
Iudicium sic cuique suum, sua cuique voluptas,
    Sic natura suum grande melos variat.
<<Buccina terribilis animosum pectus equorum
    Bellis exacuit, militis ira viget.>>
Femina dum texit dumve pueroque soporem
    Ducens in cunis cantat inepta rudis.
<<Coelica turba Jesu nati fascennia cantat
    Pax homini terris, gloria celsa Deo.
Rusticus arva colens in vociferando jocatur;
    Cantat et alleviat inde viator iter.
Artem quisque suam mulcet durumque laborem
    Qualicumque sono, sit licet asperior.>>
Vox devota Deum placat iratum, placet almis
    Civibus, ipsa choris concinit angelicis;
Vocibus Ecclesiae, pater Augustine, fateris
    Motum te lacrimis ora rigasse piis.
Felix cuius erant peccata retecta, o Maria,
    Quae totiens voces coelitus aure capis.
Organa dum cantant sibi soli corde canentem,
    Corde Deo pleno Ceciliam legimus.
Cordibus ut nostris psallamus, Paule, monebas,
    Actio nam talis jure beat duplici.
Inchoat hic et nunc coelum vitaeque beatae
    Moribus et ritu degit in exilio;
Mors venit interea quae carnis vincla resolvit,
    Cantantem in psalmis victor in alta vehit.

The Two Versions of Luther's *Encomion musices* (1538)

In Chapters 1 and 3 attention is drawn to the researches of Walter Blankenburg who conclusively argued that the German preface to Wolfgang Figulus's *Cantionem sacrum . . . primi tomi decas prima* (Nuremberg, 1575), rather than being another translation of Luther's preface to *Symphoniae iuncundae atque adea breves quattuor vocum*, published by Rhau in 1538, is in fact Luther's own vernacular draft that he translated into Latin for the 1538 Rhau publication.[1] While the Weimar edition gives the Latin text in parallel with Johann Walter's somewhat free 1564 translation, Blankenburg offers the Latin text alongside Luther's German draft as published by Figulus in 1575.[2] English translations of Luther's vernacular draft and his Latin version are given in parallel here, followed by the original texts as given by Blankenburg. The translation of the Latin text is that by Ulrich S. Leupold;[3] the translation of the German text is essentially my own but borrows from the Leupold translation where the two versions are in essence the same.

German Version

*To all lovers of the free Art of Music,
I Doctor Luther wish grace and peace
from God the Father and our Lord
Christ, etc.*

I would certainly have all Christians
value and treasure my beloved music, that God has given to humans,
yes, to love and retain it for it is
such an excellent treasure, though I
do not know how to speak about it
adequately.

There is nothing on earth that is
without its sound and its harmony,
yes even the air, which is invisible
and imperceptible, makes sound
when a stick is struck through it.

This noble art has its image in all
creatures. Ah, with what delightful

Latin Version

*Martin Luther to the
Devotees of Music
Greetings in Christ.*

I would certainly like to praise music with all my heart as the excellent
gift of God which it is and to commend it to everyone. But I am so
overwhelmed by the diversity and
magnitude of its virtue and benefits
that I can find neither beginning
nor end or method for my discourse. As much as I want to commend it, my praise is bound to be
wanting and inadequate. For who
can comprehend it all? And even if
you wanted to encompass all of it,
you would appear to have grasped
nothing at all. First then, looking at
music itself, you will find that from
the beginning of the world it has
been instilled and implanted in all
creatures, individually and collectively. For nothing is without sound
or harmony. Even the air, which of
itself is invisible and imperceptible
to all our senses, and which, since it
lacks both voice and speech, is the
least musical of all things, becomes
sonorous, audible, and comprehensible when it is set in motion. Wondrous mysteries are here suggested
by the Spirit, but this is not the
place to dwell on them.

music the Almighty Lord has blessed his song-master, the dear nightingale, together with his young scholars and many thousands of birds in the air, that each kind has its own mode and melody, its delightful sweet voice and fantastic coloratura, that no one on earth can comprehend.

This dear David saw with great wonder and spirit, for so he says in Psalm 104[:12]:

"By them the birds of the heaven sit and sing under their branches."

And above all this he [God] has graced humans yet more with this art [= music], so that there is no comparison when a person sings. Heathen philosophers have labored to explain how the human tongue can wonderfully express the thoughts of the heart, both in speaking and singing, but without success.

Music is still more wonderful in living things, especially birds, so that David, the most musical of all the kings and minstrel of God, in deepest wonder and spiritual exultation praised the astounding art and ease of the song of birds when he said in Psalm 103 [= 104:12], "By them the birds of the heaven have their habitation; they sing among the branches."

And yet, compared to the human voice, all this hardly deserves the name of music, so abundant and incomprehensible is here the munificence and wisdom of our most gracious Creator. Philosophers have labored to explain the marvelous instrument of the human voice: how can the air projected by a light movement of the tongue and an even lighter movement of the throat produce such an infinite variety and articulation of the voice and of words? And how can the voice, at the direction of the will, sound forth so powerfully and vehemently that it can not only be heard by everyone over a wide area, but also be understood? Philoso-

Truly they have come no further than establishing the "abc" of music, namely, that of all known creatures only humans can use it to express the joy of their hearts in laughter and their afflictions in weeping.

In short, noble music is next to God's Word, the highest treasure on earth: it governs all thought, perception, heart and mind.

Whether you wish to make a sad person joyful, an insolent uncouth person civilized, a fearful person courageous, an assertive person meek, and so forth,

phers for all their labor cannot find the explanation; and baffled they end in perplexity; for none of them has yet been able to define or demonstrate the original components of the human voice, its sibilation and (as it were) its alphabet, e.g., in the case of laughter — to say nothing of weeping. They marvel, but they do not understand. But such speculations on the infinite wisdom of God, shown in this single part of his creation, we shall leave to better men with more time on their hands. We have hardly touched on them.

Here it must suffice to discuss the benefit of this great art. But even that transcends the greatest eloquence of the most eloquent, because of the infinite variety of its forms and benefits. We can mention only one point (which experience confirms), namely, that next to the Word of God, music deserves the highest praise. She is a mistress and governess of those human emotions — to pass over the animals — which as masters govern men or more often overwhelm them. No greater commendation than this can be found — at least not by us. For whether you wish to comfort the sad, to terrify the happy, to encourage the despairing, to humble the proud, to calm the passionate, or to appease those full of hate — and who could number all these masters of the human heart, namely, the emotions, incli-

what could be better than to use this lofty, beloved, and noble art? The Holy Ghost himself honors it and holds it in high regard, as he witnesses that the evil spirit left Saul when David played on the harp [1 Samuel 16:23]. Similarly, when the prophet wanted to prophesy a minstrel was brought to play the harp for him [2 Kings 3:15].

Thus it was not without reason that the dear fathers and prophets wanted music to always be in the church in the form of many songs and Psalms.

And it is this cherished gift alone given to humans that they thereby should remember and use it to laud and praise God.

nations, and affections that impel men to evil or good? — what more effective means than music could you find? The Holy Ghost himself honors her as an instrument for his proper work when in his Holy Scriptures he asserts that through her his gifts were instilled in the prophets, namely, the inclination to all virtues, as can be seen in Elisha [2 Kings 3:15]. On the other hand, she serves to cast out Satan, the instigator of all sins, as is shown in Saul, the king of Israel [1 Samuel 16:23].

Thus it was not without reason that the fathers and prophets wanted nothing else to be associated as closely with the Word of God as music. Therefore, we have so many hymns and Psalms where message and music join to move the listener's soul, while in other living beings and instruments music remains a language without words. After all, the gift of language combined with the gift of song was only given to man to let him know that he should praise God with both word and music, namely, by proclaiming [the Word of God] through and by providing sweet melodies with words. For even a comparison between different men will show how rich and manifold our glorious Creator proves himself in distributing the gifts of music, how much men differ from each other in voice and manner of speaking so that one amazingly excels the other. No two men can be found with exactly the same voice and manner of speaking, although they often seem to imitate each other, the one as it were being the ape of the other.

But when [musical] learning is added to all this and artistic music which corrects, develops, and refines the natural music, then at last it is possible to taste with wonder (yet not to comprehend) God's absolute and perfect wisdom in his wondrous work of music. Here it is most remarkable that one single voice continues to sing the tenor, while at the same time many other voices play around it, exulting and adorning it in exuberant strains and, as it were, leading it forth in a divine roundelay, so that those who are the least bit moved know nothing more amazing in this world. But any who remain unaffected are unmusical indeed and deserve to hear a certain filth poet or the music of the pigs.

But the subject is much too great for me briefly to describe all its benefits. And you, my young friend, let this noble, wholesome, and cheerful creation of God be commended to you. By it you may escape shameful desires and bad company. At the same time you may by this creation accustom yourself to recognize and praise the Creator. Take special care to shun perverted minds who prostitute this lovely gift of nature and of art with

Thus one sees in this art the great inexpressible, incomprehensible, and inexplicable wisdom of God, that a single voice proceeds according to its fine and simple manner, and the other [voices] play so marvelously in every way, beside it and around it, together in friendly consort,

with one heart and delightful harmony, so that whoever is only mildly moved and heeds not the inexpressible marvel of the Lord, should not be considered human, and should hear nothing else than the bray of the donkey and the grunt of a sow.

Therefore let us recognize the Creator in this costly creation and not misuse it to serve the devil, but therewith to laud and praise the

Lord God. But misuse, such as drunkenness, carousing, wantonness, and lewdness, the things that are attested yet within the devil's kingdom, which is hostile to God, nature and the every good thing that God has made. Herewith I commend you all to the Lord God.

Wittenberg 1538.

their erotic rantings; and be quite assured that none but the devil goads them on to defy their very nature which would and should praise God its Maker with this gift, so that these bastards purloin the gift of God and use it to worship the foe of God, the enemy of nature and of this lovely art. Farewell in the Lord.

German Text	Latin Text
Allen liebhabern der freien Kunst Musica/wünsch ich Doctor Martinus Luther, Genad und Fried von Gott dem Vater under unserm HERRN Christo/etc.	*Martinus Luther musicae studiosis. Salutem in Christo.*

Ich wolt warlich das alle Christen den theuren/werden hohen schatz/ die lieben Musicam meine ich/so Gott uns Menschen gegeben/ja lieb und werdt hielten/denn es ist ein solch/herlich Kleinot/das ich nicht weis wo ichs nemen soll/davon/ wie sichs gebüret zu reden./

Vellem certe ex animo laudatum, et omnibus commendatum esse donum illud divinum et excellentissimum Musicum. Sed ita obrour multitudine et magnitudine virtutis et bonitatis eius, ut neque initium neque finem, neque modum orationis invenire queam, et cogar in summa copia laudum, ieiunius et inops esse laudator. Quis enim omnia complectatur? Atque si velis omnia complecti, nihil complexus videare.

Ist doch nichts auff Erden/das nicht seinen klang hat/und seine zal/ja auch die Lufft/so doch unsichtbar und unbegreifflich ist/wenn man darein schlegt mit einem stabe/so klinget sie.

Primum, si rem ipsam spectes, invenies Musicam esse ab initio mundi inditam seu concreatam creaturis universis, singulis et omnibus. Nihil enim est sine sono, seu numero sonoro, ita, ut et aer ipse per sese invisibilis et inpalpabilis, omnibusque sensibus inperceptibilis, minimeque omnium musicus, sed plane mutus et nihil reputatus, tamen motus sit sonorus et audibilis, nunc etiam palpabilis, mirabilia in hoc significante spiritu mysteria, de quibus hic non est locus dicendi.

Das also diese edle Kunst in allen Creaturen ihr bildnus hat. Ach wie eine herrliche Musica ists/damit der Allmechtige HERR im Himel seinen Sangmeister/die liebe Nachtigal/ sampt jren jungen Schülern/und so

viel tausend mal vögel in der Lufft/
begnadet hat/do ein jedes geschlecht
seine eigene ahrt und Melodey/seine
herrliche süsse stim und
wünderliche Coleratur hat/die kein
Mensch auff Erden erlangen noch
begreiffen kan./

Der liebe David hat solches mit
größern verwundern im Geist
angeshehn/do er spricht im 104.
Psalm: An demselben sitzen die
Vogel des Himmels/und singen
unter jren zweigern.

Und uber das alles hat er die
Menschen mit dieser Kunst noch
höher begnadet/das nichts dargegen
zurechen ist/wenn eines Menschen
stimm erklingt.

Die Heydnische Philosophi haben
sich hefftig bemüht zuerforschen/
wie doch des Menschen Zunge also
wunderlich die gedancken ds
Hertzens/beide mit reden und
singen dargeben möge/aber sie
habens nicht können ergründen/

ja es ist noch keiner so weit
kommen/der da hette können

*Sed mirabilior est Musica in
animantibus, praesertim volucribus,
ut Musicissimus ille Rex, et divinus
psaltes David, cum ingenti stupore et
exultante spiritu, praedicit mirabilem
illam volucrum peritiam et
certitudinem canendi, dicens Psalmo
centesimo tertio. Super ea volucres
coeli habitant, de medio rammorum
dant voces.*

*Verum ad humanam vocem, omnia
sunt prope immusica, tanta est
optimi Creatoris in hac una re
supereffusa et incompraehensibilis
munificentia et sapientia. Sudarunt
Philosophi, ut intelligerent hoc mira-
bile artificium vocis humanae, quo
modo tam levi motu linguuae,
leviorique adhuc motu gutturis,
pulsus aer funderet illam infinitam
varietatem et articulationem vocis et
verborum, pro arbitrio animae
gubernantis, tam potenter et
vehementer, ut per tanta intervalla
locorum, circularitur ab omnibus,
distincte, non solum audiri, sed et
intelligi possit. Sed sudant tantum,
numque inveniunt et cum
admiratione desinunt in stuporem.
Quin nulli adhuc reperti sunt, qui
definire et statuere potuerint, quid sit
ille sibilus et alphabetum quoddam*

ausgründen das abc. Von der
Musica/Nemlich das unter allen
sichtbarn Creaturen/der Mensch
allein die freude seines hertzens also
darthun kan/wenn er lacht/und
dagegen/wenn er betrübet ist/das er
weinet.

In summa die edle Musica ist nach
Gottes wordt/der höchste Schatz
auff Erden. Sie regiret alle
Gedanken/sinn/hertz und muth.

Wilstu einen betrübten frölich
machen/einen frechen wilden
Menschen zeumen das er gelinde
werde/einem zaghafftigen einen
muth machen/einen hoffertigen
demütigen/und dergleichen/

    was kann besser dazu dienen/
denn diese hohe/theure/werde und
edle kunst. Der heilige Geist ehret
sie selbst/unnd helt sie hoch/do er
zeuget wie der böse Geist von Saul
gewichen sey/wenn David auff der
Harffen schluge. Item da der
Prophet Elisa weissagen solte/befahl
er man solte jm ein spielman her
bringen, der auff der Harffen

vocis humanae, seu materia prima,
nempe risus (de fletu nihil dicam)
mirantur, sed non complectuntur,
Verum haec speculabilia de infinita
sapientia Dei, in hac una creatura,
relinquamus melioribus et
otiosioribus, nos, vix gustum
attingimus.
    De usu tantae rei dicere hic
oportuit. Sed et ille ipse sua infinita
varietate et utilitate longe superat
eloquentissimorum eloquentissimam
eloquentiam. Hoc unum possumus
nunc afferre, quod experientia testis
est. Musicam esse unam, quae post
verbum Dei merito celebrari debeat,
domina et gubernatrix affectuum
humanorum (de bestiis nunc tacen-
dum est) quibus tamen ipsi homines,
ceu a suis dominis, gubernantur et
saepius rapiuntur. Hac laude Musicae
nulla maior potest (a nobis quidem)
concipi. Sive enim velis tristes erigere,
sive laetos terrere, desperantes
animare, superbos fragere, amantes
sedare, odientes mitigare, et qui
omnes illos numeres dominos cordis
humani, scilicet affectus et impetus
seu spiritus, impulsores omnium vel
virtutum vel vitiorum? Quid invenias
afficacius quam ipsam Musicam?
Honorat eam ipse Spiritus sanctus,
ceu sui proprii officii organum, dum
in scripturis suis sanctis testatur, dona
sua per eam Prophetis illabi, id est
omnium virtutum affectus, ut in
Eliseo videre est. Rursus per eandem
expelli Satanam, id est omnium
vitiorum impulsorem, ut in Saule rege
Israel monstratur.

schlüge. Daher auch nicht die
lieben Veter und Propheten/ohn
ursach gewolt haben/das bey der
Kirchen die Musica alzeit bleiben
solt/daher sind kommen so viel
geseng und Psalmen.

Und ist diese theure gabe allein den
Menschen geben/das er sich dobey
erinner er sey dazu geschaffen/das
er Gotte loben und preisen sol.

Auch sihet man in dieser Kunst/die
grosse unaussprechliche/
unbegreiffliche und unerforschliche
weisheit Gottes/das die eine stimme
jhrer art nach fein gerate und
einfeltig her gehet/und die andern
so wunderbarlichen auff allen
örtern/daneben und umbher
spielen/freundlich einander/
begenen/und sich gleich hertzen

*Unde non frustra, Patres et
Prophetae, verbo Dei nihil voluerunt
esse coniunctius quam Musicam.
Inde enim tot Cantica et Psalmi, in
quibus simul agunt et sermo et vox
in animos auditoris, dum in ceteris
animantibus et corporibus sola
musica sine sermone gesticulatur.
Denique homini soli prae ceteris,
sermo voci copulatus, donatus est, ut
sciret, se Deum laudere oportere
verbo et Musica, scilicet sonora
praedicatione et mixtus verbis suavi
melodiae. Iam si comparationem
feceris inter ipsos homines, videbis
quam multiplex et varius sit Creator
gloriosus in donis Musicae dispertitis,
quantum differat homo ab homine in
voce et verbo, ut alius alium
mirabiliter excellat, negant enim
posse duos homines inveniri similes
per omnia vocis et loquelae, etiam si
saepius imitari alii alios videantur,
velut alii aliorum simiae.
Ubi autem tandem accesserit
studium et Musica artificialis, quae
naturalem corrigat, excolat et
explicet. Hic tandem gustare cum
stupore licet (sed non compre-
hendere) absolutam et perfectam
sapientiam Dei in opere suo mirabili
Musicae, in quo genere hoc excellit,
quod una et eadem voce canitur suo
tenore pergente, pluribus interim
vocibus circum circa mirabiliter
ludentibus, exulantibus et
iuncundissimis gestibus laudem
ornantibus, et velut iuxta eam
divinam quandam choream
ducentibus, ut iis, qui saltem modico*

und lieblichen umbfangen/das/wer
jm ein wenig nach dencket/und es
nicht für ein unaussprechliches
wunderwerck des Herrn helt/der ist
nicht werdt/das er ein Mensch
heist/und solte nichts anders hören/
denn wie der Esel schreiet unnd wie
die Saw gruntzet.

         Darumb last uns in
diesem thewren geschöpff/den
Schöpfer erkennen und ihr nicht
misbrauchen/noch dem Teuffel
damit dienen/sondern Gott der
HERREN damit loben und preisen.
Die sie aber misbrauchen/zu
sauffen/schwelgen/leichtfertigkeit
und unzucht/die bezeugen damit
das sie noch ins Teuffelsreich sein
welcher ist ein feind Gottes, der
natur und alles des/so Gott gemacht
und gut heist: Hiemit wil ich euch
allen Gott dem HErrn bevolen
haben. Wittenberg 1538.

*afficiunter, nihil mirabilius hoc
saeculo exstare videatur. Qui vero
non afficiuntur, ne illi vere amusi et
digni sunt, qui aliquem
Merdipoetam interim audiant vel
porcorum Musicam. Sed res est
maior, quam ut in brevitate utilitates
eius describi queant. Tu iuvenis
optime commendatam hanc nobilem,
salutarem et laetam creaturam tibi
habeas, qua et tuis affectibus interim
medearis contra turpes libidines et
pravas societates. Deinde assuescas in
hac creatura Creatorem acnoscere et
laudare. Et depravatos animos, qui
hac pulcherrima et natura er arte
abutuntur, ceu impudici poetae ad
suos insanos amores, et summo studio caveto et*

*vitato, certusque Diabolus eos rapiat
contra naturam, ut quae in hoc dono
vult et debet Deum solum laudare
auctorem, isti adulterini filii, rapina
ex dono Dei facto, colunt eodem
hostem Dei et adversarium naturae
et artis huius iuncundissimae. Bene
in Domino vale.*

Johann Walter on Luther

Introduction

In various studies of Luther and music Johann Walter's later recollections of Luther's musical abilities are frequently quoted but usually only with passing reference to the context in which they are found. The primary source was a manuscript, no longer extant, accessible to Michael Praetorius at the beginning of the seventeenth century. Although the provenance of the manuscript is unknown the most likely line of transmission from Walter to Praetorius (who was born in 1571, the year after Walter's death) would have been through Praetorius's father, Michael Schultheiss, who had been a colleague of Walter at the Latin school in Torgau.

Praetorius published the words of Walter twice, first at the end of the preface to his *Leiturgodia Sionia Latina* (Wolfenbüttel, 1612)[1] and again as an appendix to his *Syntagma musicum* I (Wittenberg, 1615; preface dated Dresden, 24 June 1614). Walter's primary concern was not with Luther but with the continuing use of chant forms in the Lutheran church, and the references to Luther serve this end. Similarly, the two instances of Praetorius's citation of Walter's words occur in connection with discussions of liturgical chant, first as an introduction in the *Leiturgodia* and then as an afterthought in the *Syntagma*. Praetorius explains that while he had mentioned Walter at the end of his section on traditional chant *("Psalmodia veterum")* he had neglected to include Walter's words, a deficiency he was now rectifying.[2]

The citation of Walter is introduced by two full pages of Latin text, under the heading: *"De vitiis quibusdam Musicis, quae in antiquis cantionibus Choralibus occurunt, & eorundem per Waltherum correctione"* ("Of certain musical faults which occur in ancient chants, and their correction by Walter").³ Praetorius draws attention to the errors and misreadings that occurred over many centuries when chant manuscripts were copied and recopied, some through undue haste or inexperience on the part of the copyists, others because of the dilapidated state of the sources being copied.

> Although this sort of thing occurs so frequently that to cure all [these faults] and to clean out this Augean stable would be nearly impossible, and would require not [just] one Hercules; nevertheless, Johann Walter, who was then master of choral music to the Elector of Saxony, made somewhat of an attempt about eighty years ago [ca. early 1530s]. First of all, he separated the notes accurately, and then showed to which words they should be joined, and also corrected and removed the principal faults committed in Latin pronunciation, and the barbarisms which abounded in the old psalmody. And that which seemed better left alone, considering carefully the quantity of the syllables, he believed that he should, of necessity, leave alone, lest the old and customary cadences, being disrupted, should sound quite new and strange, and offend the ears.⁴

It is clear from these words that the manuscript accessible to Praetorius contained more than the German text of Walter he cites. That he is able to describe in some detail chants as revised and emended by Walter implies that the manuscript actually contained revised chant forms. Further, that Praetorius is able to specify that this work was done around the early 1530s presupposes that the document was dated. Praetorius therefore witnesses to the fact that around the time that there was an intensification of liturgical music in Wittenberg — which included the issuing of the Wittenberg Church Order⁵ and a new edition of the Wittenberg hymnal in 1533 — and when Walter was establishing the polyphonic musical traditions of Torgau as the first Lutheran Cantor, he (Walter) was also at work on establishing an appropriate corpus of liturgical monody for use throughout the church year. That the project remained incomplete and unpublished is hardly surprising considering the amount of work Walter was involved in, to say nothing of the various upheavals that disturbed the Lutheran church following Luther's death. After citing some words from Luther's 1542 preface to the funeral hymns in which he commends the continued use of traditional chant forms, Praetorius continues:

> It would have been highly desirable if those labors of Walter's had had greater success, and had seen the light in public. But that torch, which Walter was unable to carry un-extinguished to the desired goal, has been

taken up by Lucas Lossius. His psalm-melodies [i.e., chant melodies], no less correct and purified, appeared in public a little later, and were received with incredible acclaim. Indeed, that work was helpful, not only to those who devote themselves to sacred music in schools and churches, who were assisted by its many labors of transcription, but at the same time, to all the pious, who were concerned for and love divine worship.[6]

The reference to Lucas Lossius is to his *Psalmodia, hoc est, Cantica sacra veteris ecclesiae selecta,* first published in Nuremberg in 1553, revised and reprinted in Wittenberg 1561, 1569, 1579, 1580, and 1595.[7] Praetorius was writing from the perspective of the early seventeenth century and it is natural for him to refer to the anthology of chant that was widely used in the Lutheran churches of his day. But there was another, post-Walter, collection of chants with connections to Wittenberg: Johann Spangenberg's *Cantiones ecclesiasticae latinae/ Kirchengesenge Deutsch,* published in Magdeburg in 1545.[8] Spangenberg, pastor in Nordhausen since 1524, had been a fellow student with Luther in Erfurt and remained one of his closest associates. In many respects his work in Nordhausen paralleled Walter's in Torgau, except Spangenberg was a pastor with musical gifts and Walter was a musician with theological acumen, but in each place both were involved in establishing a close connection between church and school, where the school provided the singers to lead the worship of the church. Part of the effort involved the provision of monodic chant for the schoolboys to sing in church. Thus in the early 1530s, in addition to his other duties, Walter apparently began work on assembling an appropriate collection of chants for the major festivals of the church year, but for some reason he was prevented from completing the project.

As is discussed in Chapter 14, when it became clear that Walter would be unable to finish the work it seems likely that Spangenberg was encouraged to publish his own anthology that he had probably already created for the use of the church in Nordhausen. Since both Walter and Spangenberg were close associates of Luther there is a strong possibility that it was the Wittenberg Reformer who encouraged Walter in the first place to undertake the revision of the chants and to make an appropriate collection, and then, when Walter was unable to take the matter further, it was Luther again who encouraged the publication of Spangenberg's anthology. Luther's love of traditional chant melodies and his concern that they should continue to be sung in the churches are expressed in many comments scattered throughout his various writings, or found in accounts recorded by his colleagues and friends. For example, Matthäus Ratzeberger, Luther's physician, reported that Luther liked to sing Gregorian chant or chant-based compositions at table after meals. He would sing with his sons Martin and Paul the chants appropriate to the day or season in the church year *("responsoria de tempore")*, such as ". . . at Christmas *Verbum caro factus est* [Antiphon], *In principio erat verbum* [Responsory]; at Easter *Christus resurgens ex mortuis* [Alleluia], *Vita sanctorum* [Hymn], [and] *Victimae paschali laudes* [Sequence]. . . ."⁹ Thus Walter's manuscript and Spangenberg's anthology can be seen as responses to Luther's concerns.

As most of the published collections of chants were issued either very late in Luther's life or after his death, there has been the tendency to regard them as developments of the second generation of Lutherans. But Walter's no longer extant manuscript, witnessed to by Praetorius, establishes that the continued use of traditional chants in the Lutheran liturgy was no afterthought on the part of Luther's successors but grew out of the intense period of liturgical and educational reform emanating from Luther and his colleagues in Wittenberg in the early 1530s. The role of parish schools was a particular concern: Luther expounded the basic strategy, Melanchthon created the detailed curriculum, and Walter (in Torgau but with close connections to Wittenberg)¹⁰ worked on music for church and school, both monody and polyphony. It is significant that two students in Wittenberg during this period were involved in the provision of liturgical chant some years later. One was Nikolaus Medler, a student in Wittenberg in the early 1520s who returned to study for his doctorate between 1531 and 1535, during which time he was one of Luther's assistants as well as a close associate of Melanchthon. In 1536 Medler was called as Superintendent of Naumberg and almost immediately began work on a church order in collaboration with the leading reformers in Wittenberg; the manuscript church order is headed: *Formula Rituum in sacris observandorum a Medlero conscripta A° 1537 atque a Luthero, J. Jona et Melanchthone approbata.*¹¹ The second part of the manuscript (dated 1538) dealt with liturgical matters and included a number of chants, among them the earliest appearance of the rhymed version of the Gloria, *All Ehr und Lob soll Gottes sein,* almost certainly by Luther and based on the *Gloria paschali* chant.¹² The other student was Lucas Lossius, who studied with both Melanchthon and Luther in Wittenberg between 1530 and 1533. In 1533 he went to Lüneberg to teach in the gymnasium and work closely with the superintendent, Urban Regius, who, in reforming the churches and schools in the area from 1530, maintained personal contact with Luther in Wittenberg. Lossius also continued his connection with Wittenberg but, being an educator, was particularly close to the "Preceptor of Germany," Philipp Melanchthon, who wrote the preface to his *Psalmodia,* an extensive anthology of liturgical chant.

In Walter's German text, written some decades later (see below), he lists a significant number of incipits according to the major festivals of the church year. The way they are introduced seems to imply that these would have formed the basic corpus of his proposed anthology of chants. Just how many he had in fact edited by the time he penned these paragraphs cannot be known without access to the original (now lost) manuscript. More than half are found in polyphonic settings in the music manuscripts compiled under Walter's supervision for use in Torgau, most being his own compositions (see Table A4.1, col. 3),[13] which implies that at least these chants, the *cantus firmi* on which the compositions are based, had been edited by Walter by the time he came to write the German paragraphs cited by Praetorius. Spangenberg included only about a third of the chants listed by Walter, compared with Lossius who included all of the Latin chants in the list (cf. cols. 5 and 6 in Table A4.1). This is presumably to be explained by the fact that Lossius was in Wittenberg during the reforms of the early 1530s and therefore his chant anthology reflects more of the Wittenberg repertory (cf. Cols. 4 and 6 in Table A4.1), whereas Spangenberg, who had been the pastor of Nordhausen since 1524, worked somewhat more independently in the compilation of his collection of chants. That there should be differences in chant repertories is in accord with Luther's directives in both the *Formula missae* (1523) and *Deutsche Messe* (1526), that different areas must be free to establish their own liturgical forms. Thus Walter's collection of chants was prepared in Torgau in the early 1530s, reflecting Wittenberg usage; Medler's church order containing chants was drawn up for the church in Naumberg in 1537/38; Spangenberg's anthology was prepared for Nordhausen in the early 1540s (or possibly earlier) and published in Magdeburg; and Lossius's Psalmodia was developed for use in Lüneburg in the 1550s, first published in Nuremberg and then in Wittenberg. Later in the century Johannes Keuchenthal created another anthology of chant in St. Andreasberg, published in Wittenberg in 1573,[14] and Franz Eler compiled and published a similar work in Hamburg in 1588.[15] At the beginning of the next century Praetorius, working mostly in Wolfenbüttel, was particularly impressed by the chant forms he found in Lossius and linked them to work on chant revision that Walter was engaged in during the early 1530s:

> For my part, I liked that book [Lossius's *Psalmodia*] so much that I resolved, with God's grace and help, to set all of it in harmony. For, aside from the fact that, from my very youth, I was moved by an incredible and singular zeal for that sort of melody, I was persuaded by other reasons and arguments, but especially by those found in the above-mentioned manuscript of Johann Walter, a pious man and a cultivated musician, and I was more and more confirmed in that intention.[16]

Table A4.1: Concordances of Later Use of Chants Listed in the Walter Ms. Cited by Praetorius[17]

Walter Ms	Genre	Walter Sources	Witten-berg	Spangen-berg	Lossius	Prae-torius
CHRISTMAS						
Verbum caro factum est	Antiphon	+	–	–	+	–
Puer natus est nobis	Introit	+	+	+	+	–
Grates nunc omnes reddamus	Sequence	+	+	+	+	+
Natus ante secula Dei filius	Sequence	–	–	–	+	–
A solis ortus cardine	Hymn	–	+	–	+	+
Corde natus ex parentis	Hymn	–	+	–	+	+
Dies est laetitiae = Ein kindelein so löbelich	Graduallied	+	+	–	+	+
Illuminare, Hierusalem	Responsory	–	–	+	+	–
EASTER						
Christus resurgens	Alleluia	+	–	–	+	–
Victimae paschali laudes	Sequence	+	+	+	+	+
Salve festa dies	Hymn	+	+	+	+	–
Resurrexit Dominus	Invitatory	–	–	–	+	–
Ad coenam agni providi	Hymn	–	–	–	+	+
Pax vobis ego sum, alleluia	Antiphon	–	–	–	+	–
Christ ist Erstanden	Graduallied	+	+	+	–	+
ASCENSION						
Ascendo ad Patrem	Antiphon	+	+	–	+	–
Summi triumphum regis	Sequence	–	–	–	+	–
Ite in orbem universum	Responsory	+	+	–	+	–
Christ fuhr gen Himmel	Graduallied	–	–	–	–	+
PENTECOST						
Apparuerunt apostolis	Responsory	+	+	–	+	–
Veni sancte Spiritus, & emitte	Sequence	+	+	+	+	–
Sancte Spiritus adsit nobis gratia	Sequence	–	–	–	+	–
Veni creator Spiritus	Hymn	–	+	–	+	+
Nun bitten wir den heiligen Geist	Graduallied	+	+	–	–	+
TRINITY						
Summae Trinitati	Responsory	–	+	–	+	–
Benedicta semper sit Trinitas	Sequence	+	+	+	+	–
O lux beata Trinitas	Hymn	+	+	–	+	+

Praetorius's intention remained unfulfilled, although he did create poly-phonic settings of nearly half of the chants listed by Walter, some of them several times (see Table A4.1, col. 7).

Praetorius's Latin paragraphs do more than simply introduce Walter's words that include citations of Luther on music. Even before giving Walter's German text he reveals important information regarding Luther and Lutheran liturgical music: that the continuation of liturgical monodic chant was in large measure due to Walter, acting on Luther's clearly expressed views, rather than being the product of second generation Lutherans.

Having made his prefatory remarks Praetorius then gives the extended quotation of Walter's German text, which is unusual in this learned Latin treatise.[18] Walter's paragraphs do not date from the same period as the revised chants (early 1530s) but from a later time, since he refers to his collaboration with Luther on the *Deutsche Messe* in 1525 as occurring around forty years earlier. Thus they were penned sometime around 1565, that is, a few years before Walter's death in 1570. Whether these words were written on a separate sheet and tipped into the manuscript or whether they were entered directly into it is unknown. The structure and content suggest that Walter was preparing the manuscript anthology of chants for publication — even though it probably represented an incomplete corpus — and that these paragraphs were to form the preface. In commending his own work he comments on Luther's abilities as well as citing the Reformer, and in the process reveals unique information concerning the genesis of Luther's *Deutsche Messe*, especially its monodic chant.

The following is a complete translation by Michael David Fleming, with some minor modifications and additional annotation.[19]

[Preface][20]

The reasons why I have corrected the *choral* song [i.e. chant] (which is textually pure, but musically quite debased)[21] are these:

First, I was moved to do so by the beautiful, precious, clever, [and] artful Latin and German songs of our ancestors before our time, dear Christians and saints, who drew [these songs] out of the writings of the Prophets and Apostles, made them in honor of Christ, and sang them in their parishes in praise of God. In these songs, one feels and one sees clearly from their joyful melodies the great joy and ardor of their spirits over the godly, inexpressibly lofty work of the Incarnation of Christ, and of our redemption. I must name some of them, such as:

Verbum caro factum est
Puer natus est nobis
Grates nunc omnes reddamus Domino Deo
Natus ante secula Dei Filius
A solis ortus cardine
Corde natus ex parentis ante mundi exordium
Dies est laetitiae
Ein Kindelein so löbelich[22]
Illuminare Hierusalem

Likewise, of the joyful Resurrection of Christ:

Christus resurgens[23]
Victimae Paschali laudes
Salve festa dies
Resurrexit Dominus
Ad coenam Agni providi
Pax vobis ego sum, Hallelujah
Christ ist erstanden

Of the Ascension of Christ:

Ascendo ad patrem
Summi triumphum regis
Ite in orbem universum
Christ fuhr gen Himmel

Of the Holy Spirit:

Apparuerunt Apostolis
Veni sancte Spiritus, & emitte coelitus
Sancte Spiritus adsit nobis gratia
Veni creator Spiritus
Nun bitten wir den heiligen Geist

Of the Holy Trinity:

Summae Trinitati
Benedicta semper sit Trinitas
O adoranda Trinitas,
O veneranda Unitas, &c[24]
O lux beata Trinitas

And there are many more such songs all Christians must acknowledge in regard to these, that they contain a lofty [and] rich understanding of Holy Scripture, and when they are sung with devotion and attention, they powerfully stir human hearts to God and stimulate [them] to praise him.

And, although one finds people who consider only the old German Christian songs good, and praise [them], calling the aforementioned Latin songs Popish, that seems unimportant to me. For, if these Latin songs should be called Popish because they are sung by the Papists in their monasteries, so must the old German Christian songs be Popish, and be so named, because the Papists sing them in their churches, just as we do.[25]

2. Second, I have been enabled to do such work by commission and support from certain pious Christians, for God's glory and praise, and for the honor of the precious Gospel of Christ, and I did not wish to bury the talent received from God.

3. Third, I know and bear true witness that the holy man of God, *Luther,* the Prophet and Apostle to the German *nation,* had a great love for *music* in *plainsong* and *polyphony* [*Choral* und *Figural*]. Many precious hours have I sung with him, and have often seen how the dear man became so merry and joyful in spirit from singing, that he could hardly become tired and weary of singing and speaking so splendidly about *music.* For when he wished to establish the German Mass in Wittenberg about forty years ago, he wrote to the Elector of Saxony and Duke Johann, of praiseworthy memory, for his Electoral Grace to allow his old songmaster [Sangmeister], the honorable *Conrad* Rupsch and myself to go to Wittenberg in order to discuss with us the *choral notes* [*Choral Noten* = chant notation] and nature of the eight *tones.* And finally, he appointed the eighth tone [*Choral Noten octavi Toni*] for the Epistle, and the sixth tone for the Gospel, saying: "Christ is a friendly Lord, and his sayings are gentle, therefore, we want to take the *Sextum Tonum* for the Gospel; and because St. Paul is a serious apostle, we want to appoint the *Octavum Tonum* for the Epistle." He wrote himself the notes for the Epistles, Gospels, and the Words of Institution of the true Body and Blood of Christ; these he sang to me, wishing to hear my opinion of them. He kept me three weeks in Wittenberg to write in an orderly fashion the choral notes for certain Gospels and Epistles, until the first German Mass was sung in the town church [Pfarrkirche]. Then I had to listen to this first German Mass, and take a copy of it with me to Torgau, and hand it over to his Electoral Grace, on orders from the *Doctor* himself. Since he ordered *Vespers,* as it is [sung] in many places, to be arranged with short, pure choral songs [= chants] for the students and youths, likewise he ordered that the poor students who go [begging] for bread should sing Latin songs, *Antiphons* and *Responsoria* before the doors, as they

had opportunity. And it did not please him for the students to sing only German songs at the doors. Therefore, those who cast out all Latin Christian songs from the churches are not to be praised, and are incorrect if they believe it is not evangelical or properly Lutheran when they sing or hear Latin *chants* [*Choral* Gesang] in church. On the other hand, it is also wrong to sing for the common people nothing but Latin songs, by which the common folk are not improved. Thus, the German, holy, pure, old, and Lutheran songs and psalms [Lieder und Psalmen] are most useful for the general congregation [gemeinen hauffen], but the Latin is for the young to practice and for the learned.[26]

And let it be seen, heard, and understood, how the Holy Spirit himself collaborates, both with these *authors* of Latin [songs] and with Herr Luther, who until now has written most of the German *chants* [deutschen Choral Gesänge] and set them to music. Therefore, it may be observed in the German *Sanctus* (Jesaja dem Propheten das geschah, etc.) and in other places, how carefully he fitted all the notes so masterfully and so well to the text, according to the right *accent* and *concent*.[27] And I also had the occasion to ask his Reverence how, or from what source, had he been taught or instructed. Then the dear man laughed at my innocence and said: "The poet Virgil taught me this, who is also able to apply his poetry and vocabulary so artfully to the story he is writing. So should *music* arrange all its *notes* and songs in accord with the text."[28]

[JOHANN WALTER] [CA. 1565]

Des alten Johan Walthers

Die Ursachen/warumb ich den *Choral* Gesang (welcher im Text reine/in den Noten aber sehr verfelschet) corrigiret/seynd diese:

Dann 1. erstlich/haben mich darzu bewegt unserer Vorfahren/vor unserer zeit/lieben Christen und Heiligen/schöne/köstliche/Geistreiche künstliche lateinische unnd deutsche Gesänge/aus der Propheten und Aposteln Schrifften gezogen/welche sie Christo zu ehren gemachet/und in jrer Gemeine/Gott zu lobe/gesungen. In welchen Gesängen man spüret/unnd aus den frölichen Melodyen klärlich siehet/die grosse Frewde und Brunst jres Geistes/uber dem Göttlichem/unerforsschlichem hohem Werck der Menschwerdung Christi und unser Erlösung/Derer ich etliche erzehlen muß: Also da ist/das

Verbum caro factum est.
Puer natus est nobis.

Grates nunc omnes reddamus Domino Deo.
Natus ante secula Dei Filius.
A solis ortus cardine.
Corde natus ex parentis ante mundi exordium.
Dies est laetitiae.
Ein Kindelein so löbelich.
Illuminare Hierusalem.

Item/von der frölichen Aufferstehung Christi.

Christus resurgens.
Victimae Paschali laudes.
Salve festa dies.
Resurrexit Dominus.
Ad coenam Agni providi.
Pax vobis ego sum, Hallelujah.
Christ ist erstanden.

Von der Auffarth Christi.

Ascendo ad patrem.
Summi triumphum regis.
Ite in orbem universum.
Christ fuhr gen Himmel.

Vom heiligen Geist.

Apparuerunt Apostolis.
Veni sancte Spiritus, & emitte coelitus.
Sancte Spiritus adsit nobis gratia.
Veni creator Spiritus.
Nun bitten wir den heiligen Geist.

Von der hiligen Dreyfaltigkeit.

Summae Trinitati.
Benedicta semper sit Trinitas.
O adoranda Trinitas.
O veneranda Unitas, &c.
O lux beata Trinitas.

Und solcher dergleichen Gesänge seind vielmehr: von welchen herrlichen Gesängen alle Christen bekennen müssen/daß sie hohen reichen verstand der heiligen Schrifft in sich haben/Und wann sie mit andacht und auffmerckung gesungen werden/die Hertzen der Menschen kräfftiglich zu Gott erwecken/und zu seinem Lobe reitzen.

Und wiewol man Leute findet/welche allein die deutsche alte Christliche Lieder für gut achten und loben/die Lateinsiche erzehlete Gesänge aber Päpstisch heissen/Solches ficht mich wenig an. Denn/so gedachte lateinische Gesänge deßhalben Päpstisch sein solten/daß sie von den Papisten in jhren Stifften gesungen werden/so müsten die deutsche Christliche alte Lieder auch Papistisch sein und heissen/weil sie die Papisten eben so wol als wir in ihren Kirchen singing.

2. Zum andern/so habe ich/Gott zu lobe und preiß/unnd dem lieben Evangelio Christi zu ehren/zu solchem Wercke/auff bitte und anhaltung etlicher frommer Christen/mich vermögen lassen/und das empfangene Pfund/von Gott/nicht vergraben wollen.

3. Zum dritten/so weis und zeuge ich warhafftig/daß der heilige Mann Gottes *Lutherus,* welcher deutscher *Nation* Prophet und Apostel gewest/zu der *Musica* im *Choral* und *Figural* Gesange grosse lust hatte/mit welchem ich gar manche liebe Stunde gesungen/und offtmahls gesehen/wie der thewre Mann vom singen so lustig und frölich im Geist ward/daß er des singens schier nicht köndte müde und satt merden/und von der *Musica* so herrlich zu reden wuste. Denn da er vor viertzig Jahren die deutsche Messe zu Wittenberg anrichten wolte/hat er durch seine Schrifft an den Churfürsten zu Sachsen/ und Hertzog Johansen/hochlöblicher gedächtnuß/seiner Churfürstlichen Gnaden die zeit alten Sangmeister Ehrn *Conrad* Rupff/und Mich gen Wittemberg erfordern lassen/dazumahlen von den *Choral Noten* und Art der achrt *Ton* unterredung mit uns gehalten/und beschließlich hat er von jhm selbst die *Choral Noten octavi Toni* der Epistel zugeeignet/unnd *Sextum Tonum* dem Evangelio geordnet/unnd sprach also: Christus is ein freundlicher H E R R/und seine Rede sind lieblich/darumb wollen wir *Sextum Tonum* zum Evangelio nehmen/und weil S. Paulus ein ernster Apostel ist/wollen wir *Octavum Tonum* zur Epistel ordnen: Hat auch die *Noten* über die Episteln/Evangelia/und uber die Wort der Einsetzung des wahren Leibes unnd Bluts Christi selbst gemacht/mir vorgesungen/und mein bedencken darüber hören wollen. Er hat mich die zeit drey Wochen lang zu Wittemberg auffgehalten/die *Choral Noten* uber etliche Evangelia unnd Episteln ordentlich zu schreiben/biß die erste deutsche Meß in der Pfarkirchen gesungen ward/do muste ich zuhören/und solcher ersten deutschen Messe Abschrifft mit mir gen Torgaw nehmen/und hochgedachten Churfürsten

jhrer Churf. Gn. Aus befehl des Herrn *Doctoris* selbst uberantworten. Denn er auch die *Vesper,* so die zeit an vielen Orten gefallen/mit kurtzen reinen *Choral* Gesängen/für die Schuler und Jugend widerumb anzurichten/befohlen: Deßgleichen/daß die arme Schüler/so nach Brod lauffen/für den Thüren lateinische Gesänge/*Antiphonas* und *Responsoria,* nach gelegenheit der zeit/ singen solten: Und hatte keinen gefallen daran/daß die Schüler für den Thüren nichts denn deutsche Lieder sungen. Daher seind die jenien auch nicht zu lobe/thun auch nicht recht/die alle Lateinsiche Christliche Gesänge aus der Kirchen stossen/lassen sich düncken es sey nicht Evangelisch oder gut Lutherisch/wenn sie einen Lateinischen *Choral* Gesang in der Kirchen singen oder hören solten: Wiederumb ists auch unrecht/wo man nichts denn lateinisch Gesänge für der Gemeine singet/daraus das gemeine Volck nichts gebessert wird. Derowegen seind die deutsche Geistliche/reine/alte und Lutherische Lieder und Psalmen für den gemeinen hauffen an nützlichsten: die Lateinischen aber zur ubung der Jugend und für die Gelärten.

Und sihet/höret unnd greiffet man augenscheinlich/wie der heilige Geist/so wol in denen *Autoribus,* welche die lateinischen/als auch im Herrn Luthero/welcher jetzo die deutschen *Choral* Gesänge meistestheils gedichtet/ und zur Melodey bracht/selbst mit gewircket: Wie denn unter andern aus dem deutschen *Sanctus* (Jesaia dem Propheten das geschah/&c.) Zuersehen/ wie er alle *Noten* auff den Text nach dem rechtem *accent* und *concent* so meisterlich und wol gerichtet hat/Und ich auch die zeit seine Ehrwürden zu fragen verursachet ward/woraus oder woher sie doch diß Stücke oder Unterricht hetten: Darauff der thewre Mann meiner Einfalt lachte/unnd sprach: Der *Poët Virgilius* hat mir solches gelehret/der also seine *Carmine* und Wort auff die Geschichte/die er beschreibet/so künstlich *applicirn* kan: Also so auch die *Musica* alle jhre *Noten* und Gesänge auff den *Text* richten.

The Misreading of Pseudo-Justin
in Lutheran Writings on Music

As indicated in Chapter 17, one of the most frequently cited passages found in Lutheran writings on music from the sixteenth to the twentieth centuries is one that purports to be by "Justin," that is, Justin Martyr. The work in question is the Pseudo-Justinian Greek document, known in Latin as *Questiones et responsiones ad orthodoxos,* now generally accepted as a work by Theodoret of Cyrrus (Syria) in the fifth century. The passage in question in fact confirms the exact opposite of what the Lutheran writers were contending, though it does make a clear distinction between Law and Grace, which may have drawn them to the passage in the first place:

> Question 107. If songs were invented by unbelievers as a ruse, and introduced to those under the Law because of their simplemindedness, while those under Grace have adopted better practices . . . , why have they used these songs in the churches as did the children of the Law?

> Response. It is not singing as such which befits the childish, but singing with lifeless instruments, and with dancing and finger clappers; wherefore the use of such instruments and other things appropriate to those who are childish is dispensed with in the churches and singing alone has been left over. . . . Paul calls it [singing] a sword of the Spirit by which pious fighters for God are equipped against the invisible enemy. *For it is and remains God's Word, whether it is contemplated, sung or listened to,* a protection against demons.[1]

The words in italic are those supposedly given in Greek by Michael Praetorius in 1619, who does not cite a source: ῾Ρῆμα γὰρ ἔστιν Θεοῦ καὶ ἐνθυμούμενον καὶ ᾀδόμενον καὶ ἀκουόμενον.[2] But when Praetorius's text is examined it will be discovered that, apart from small variations, there is one substantial difference, the final participle is different from the original document: ῥῆμα γὰρ ἔστιν Θεοῦ τό ἐνθυμούμενον καὶ ᾀδόμενον, καὶ *ἀναχρουόμενον*. In the original it reads ἀ[να]κουόμενον (to listen) rather than ἀναχρουόμενον (to beat upon) as cited by Praetorius. The second term gives the impression of being a transcription error, since the two words are similar. It is possible that the error was created when this Pseudo-Justin passage was being transcribed by someone who knew the writings of St. Augustine, and subconsciously interpreted the Pseudo-Justin passage in terms of Augustine's statements concerning the threefold nature of music. The first is in Augustine's *In psalmum* (commenting on Psalm 150:5-6):

> . . . there are three kinds of sound, by voice, by breath, and striking: by voice, that is by the throat and wind pipe of a singing man without any sort of instrument; by breath, as with the tibia or anything of that kind [= blown instruments]; by striking, as with the cithara or anything of that sort [= plucked strings].[3]

Another similar passage is found in *De doctrina christiana* (lib. 2, cap. 17):

> All sound which furnishes the material of music is threefold in nature. For it is produced either by voice, as with those who sing with their throats and without an instrument, or by breath, as with trumpets and tibias, or by striking, as with citharas and tympana and whatsoever other instruments sound when beaten.[4]

For whatever reason, the idea of creating sound by striking something, rather than listening, was introduced into the Pseudo-Justin text. What is unclear is when the alteration first occurred, almost certainly sometime before 1600. What is clear is that from a common source, as yet unidentified, in which the alteration was made, the later Lutheran tradition was developed, with various writers simply accepting the attribution to "Justin," repeating the error, and even expanding upon it. Thus not only Praetorius and the authors of the *Limburgische Kirchenordnung* in the seventeenth century, among others, and Mattheson in the eighteenth century, but also Hans-Joachim Moser and Oskar Söhngen[5] in the twentieth century, were content to perpetuate the tradition without verifying the source. What is important is that, even though it was based on a corrupted source, there is this consistent strand within Lutheranism that has stressed the validity of instrumental music in proclaiming the Word of God.

Postscript

As explained in the Preface, many of these chapters are revisions of material originally prepared as conference papers, or as commissioned articles published in *Lutheran Quarterly* or other publications. These occasions and sources are given in detail below.

Chapters 1-3 were newly written for this book; Chapter 2 appeared in a slightly abbreviated form in *Lutheran Quarterly* 18 (2004): 125-183, and part of Chapter 3 in *Lutheran Quarterly* 20 (2006): 1-21, in anticipation of this volume.

Chapters 4-11 were originally written as a series of articles for *Lutheran Quarterly* under the general title "Luther's Catechism Hymns": *Lutheran Quarterly* 11 (1997): 397-421 and 12 (1998): 79-98, 160-180, 303-323. Abridgments of these articles appeared in *Luther Digest* 8 (2000) & 9 (2001).

Chapter 12 first appeared as "Verba Testamenti versus Canon: The Radical Nature of Luther's Liturgical Reform," in *Churchman* 97 (1983): 123-131; it was later substantially revised and expanded to become "Theological Consistency, Liturgical Integrity, and Musical Hermeneutic in Luther's Liturgical Reforms" in *Lutheran Quarterly* 9 (1995): 117-138.

Chapter 13 was originally given as a paper at the First International Conference of Frühe Neuzeit Interdisziplinär, Duke University, April 1995 (see *17th Century Music* 5/1 [Fall 1995]: 5); it was later revised and published as "Thematic Building Blocks: Liturgical, Pedagogical and Political Concerns in Early Lutheran Church Music," in *Cross Accent: Journal of the Association of Lutheran Church Musicians* 8/2 (Summer 2000): 24-36.

Chapter 14 originally appeared as "Johann Spangenberg and Luther's Legacy of Liturgical Chant" in *Lutheran Quarterly* 19 (2005): 23-42, an article that grew out of research undertaken for the introduction to a facsimile edition of Johann Spangenberg's *Cantiones ecclesiasticae/Kirchengesenge Deudsche* (Magdeburg: Lotter, 1545) to be published by Georg Olms Verlag, Hildesheim.

Chapter 15 originally appeared as "Sequences and Responsories: Continuity of Forms in Luther's Liturgical Provisions," in *Worship in Medieval and Early Modern Europe: Change and Continuity in Religious Practice*, ed. Karin Maag and John Witvliet (Notre Dame: University of Notre Dame Press, 2004), 300-328.

Chapter 16 originally appeared (without musical examples) under the title "The Biblical Canticles in Luther's Hymnals," in *Lord Jesus Christ, Will You Not Stay: Essays in Honor of Ronald Feuerhahn on the Occasion of His Sixty-Fifth Birthday*, ed. J. Bart Day et al. (St. Louis: Concordia Publishing House, 2002), 23-64.

Chapter 17 was first published as "Johann Sebastian Bach: Theological Musician and Musical Theologian" in *BACH, the Journal of the Riemenschneider Bach Institute* 31/1 (2000): 17-33; it was subsequently substantially revised and reissued as "Johann Sebastian Bach and the Lutheran Understanding of Music" in *Lutheran Quarterly* 16 (2002): 153-194.

Chapter 18 was first given as a paper at the conference *Von Luther zu Bach* in Eisenach, Germany, organized by the Internationale Arbeitsgemeinschaft für theologische Bachforschung and sponsored by the Ständigen Konferenz Mitteldeutsche Barockmusik in Sachsen, Sachsen-Anhalt und Thuringen e.V., and published with other conference papers as "The Deutsche Messe and the Music of Worship: Martin Luther and Johann Sebastian Bach," *Von Luther zu Bach. Bericht über die Tagung 22.-25. September 1996 in Eisenach*, ed. Renate Steiger (Sinzig: Studio, 1999), 115-127; a revised form appeared in *Lutheran Quarterly* 15 (2001): 317-335.

Notes

Notes to Chapter 1

1. See the discussion in Chapter 12 below.

2. *The Cambridge Companion to Martin Luther,* ed. Donald K. McKim (Cambridge: Cambridge University Press, 2003). The contributions to this volume are somewhat uneven in quality and some suffer from oversimplification, misleading summaries, and faulty or nonexistent citations; see Timothy J. Wengert, "Review Essay: The Cambridge Luther, an Unreliable Companion," *Lutheran Quarterly* 19 (2005): 79-84.

3. Helmar Junghans, ed., *Leben und Werk Martin Luthers von 1526 bis 1546: Festgabe zu seinem 500. Geburtstag* (Berlin: Evangelische Verlagsanstalt, 1983); Albrecht Beutel, ed., *Luther Handbuch* (Tübingen: Mohr Siebeck, 2005).

4. The literature referred to in the following paragraphs is representative rather than exhaustive; other contributions are discussed elsewhere in this book and listed in the Bibliography.

5. The first section of this two-part work was originally published as *Musica Christiana, oder Predigt uber die Wort Psalm 98 . . . darrinnen von dem Ursprung, Brauch und Erhaltung Christlicher Musica fürnemlich gehandelt wird* (Leipzig: Börners & Rehfeldt, 1615).

6. Cyriacus Spangenburg, *Cythera Lutheri* (Erfurt: Bauman, 1569-70); Johann Adolf Liebner, *Ueber D. Martin Luthers Dichtkunst und Lieder* (Wittenberg: Kühne, 1791); August Jakob Rambach, *Ueber D. Martin Luthers Verdienst um den Kirchengesang* (Hamburg: Bohn, 1813; repr. Hildesheim: Olms, 1972); Justin Heinrich Knecht, *Luthers Verdienste um Musik und Poesie* (Ulm: Wohler, 1817); Friedrich Adolf Beck, *Dr. Martin Luther's Gedanken über die Musik* (Berlin: Mittler, 1825), and August Gebauer, *D. Martin Luther und seine Zeitgenossen als Kirchenliederdichter: nebst Luthers Gedanken über die Musik und einigen poetischen Reliquien* (Leipzig: Klein, 1828).

7. Johannes Rautenstrauch, *Luther und die Pflege der Kirchen Musik in Sachsen* (Leipzig: Breitkopf & Härtel, 1907; repr. Hildesheim: Olms, 1970). Karl Anton, *Luther und die Musik,* 4th ed. (Berlin: Evangelische Verlagsanstalt, 1957). Hermann Abert, *Luther und die*

Musik (Wittenberg: Verlag der Luther-Gesellschaft, 1924); reprinted in Hermann Abert, *Gesammelte Schriften und Vorträge*, ed. Friedrich Blume (Halle: Niemeyer, 1929), 103-19. Hans Joachim Moser, "Die Wittenbergisch Nachtigal," L-J 7 (1925): 87-91. Friedrich Blume, *Die evangelische Kirchenmusik* (Potsdam: Academische Verlagsgesellschaft Athenaion, 1931; repr. New York: Musurgia, 1949), esp. 4-40. Christhard Mahrenholz, *Luther an die Kirchenmusik*, (Kassel: Bärenreiter, 1937); reprinted in *Musicologica et Liturgica: Gesammelte Aufsätze vom Christhard Mahrenholz zu seiner 60. Geburtstag*, ed. Karl Ferdinand Müller (Kassel: Bärenreiter, 1960), 136-153.

8. Griefswald and Hanover (1945); Eßlingen (1948); Görlitz and Schleuchtern (1947); Bayreuth, later in Erlangen (1948); Frankfurt am Main, Herford, Dresden and Düsseldorf (1949); and Eisenach (1950).

9. Karl Honemeyer, "Luther's Musikanschauung: Studien zur Fragen ihrer geschichtlichen Grundlagen" (diss., University of Münster, 1941). Christoph Wetzel, "Die theologische Bedeutung der Musik im Leben und Denken Martin Luthers" (diss., University of Münster, 1954); see also Christoph Wetzel, "Studie zur Musikanschauung Martin Luthers," *Musik und Kirche* 33 (1955): 238-245, 274-279. Walter Blankenburg, "Luther und die Musik," *Luther: Mitteilungen der Luther-Gesellschaft* 28 (1957): 14-27; reprinted in Walter Blankenburg, *Kirche und Musik: Gesammelte Aufsätze zur Geschichte der gottesdienstlichen Musik, zu seinem 75. Geburtstag*, ed. Erich Hübner and Renate Steiger (Göttingen: Vandenhoeck & Ruprecht, 1979), 17-30. Oskar Söhngen, "Theologische Grundlagen der Kirchenmusik," *Leiturgia: Handbuch des evangelischen Gottesdienstes*, ed. Karl Ferdinand Müller and Walter Blankenburg, Bd. 4: *Die Musik des evangelischen Gottesdienst* (Kassel: Stauda, 1961), 62-81; revised and reissued as *Theologie der Musik* (Kassel: Stauda, 1967), 80-112. Winfried Kurzschenkel, *Die theologische Bestimmung der Musik* (Trier: Paulinus, 1971), 151-197.

10. Ulrich S. Leupold, "Luther's Conception of Music in Worship," *The Lutheran Church Quarterly* 13 (1940): 66-69. Walter E. Buszin, "Luther on Music," *The Musical Quarterly* 32 (1946): 80-97; issued separately as *Luther on Music* (St. Paul: North Central, 1958), with the information, "The author is currently working on a more detailed discussion of the subject which will be published at some later time," an intent that remained unfulfilled. Paul Nettl, *Luther and Music*, trans. Frida Best and Ralph Wood (Philadelphia: Muhlenberg, 1948; repr. New York: Russel & Russel, 1967). Robert M. Stevenson, "Luther's Musical Achievement," *Lutheran Quarterly*, first series, 3 (1951): 255-262; reprinted in Robert M. Stevenson, *Patterns of Protestant Church Music* (Durham: Duke University Press, 1953), 3-12. Theodore Hoelty-Nickel, "Luther and Music," in *Luther and Culture* [Martin Luther Lectures 4] (Decorah, Ia.: Luther College Press, 1960), pp. 143-211.

11. For example, the chapter "Luther on Music: A Theological Basis for German Baroque Music," in Dietrich Bartel, *Musica Poetica: Musical-Rhetorical Figures in German Baroque Music* (Lincoln: University of Nebraska Press, 1997), 3-9, is almost exclusively based on citations found in Buszin's article.

12. Carl Schalk, *Luther on Music: Paradigms of Praise* (St. Louis: Concordia, 1988).

13. Daniel Reuning, "Luther and Music," *Concordia Theological Quarterly* 48 (1984): 17-21; Edward Foley, "Martin Luther: A Model Pastoral Musician," *Currents in Theology and Mission* 54 (1987): 405-418, reprint, Edward Foley, *Ritual Music: Studies in Liturgical Musicology* (Beltsville: Pastoral Press, 1995), 89-106; see also the discussion of music within a broader cul-

tural context by George W. Forrell, "Luther and Culture," L-J 52 (1985): 152-163, esp. 159-160.

Other non-American English-language studies include John Wesley Barker, "Sociological Influences upon the Emergence of Lutheran Music," *Miscellanea musicologica: Adelaide Studies in Musicology* 4 (1969): 157-198; B. L. Horne, "A Civitas of Sound: On Luther and Music," *Theology* 88 (1985): 21-28; Helga Robinson-Hammerstein, "The Lutheran Reformation and Its Music," in *The Transmission of Ideas in the Lutheran Reformation,* ed. Helga Robinson-Hammerstein (Dublin: Irish Academic Press, 1989), 141-171; Helen Pietsch, "On Luther's Understanding of Music," *Lutheran Theological Journal* 26 (1992): 160-168.

14. Robin A. Leaver, "Luther, Martin," New Grove 2, 15: 364-369.

15. See Honemeyer, *Luther's Musikanschauung.*

16. Notably Karl Honemeyer, *Thomas Müntzer und Martin Luther, ihr Ringen um die Musik des Gottesdienstes: Untersuchungen zum "Deutzsch Kirchenampt" 1523* (Berlin: Merseburger, 1974). See also Henning Frederichs, "Zur Wort-Ton-Beziehung in Thomas Müntzers Deutschen Messen und Kirchenämtern," in Walter Elliger, *Thomas Müntzer Leben und Werk,* 3rd ed. (Göttingen: Vandenhoeck & Ruprecht, 1976), 339-360.

17. Joyce L. Irwin, "The Theological and Social Dimensions of Thomas Müntzer's Liturgical Reform" (Ph.D. diss., Yale University, 1972).

18. Joyce Irwin, *Neither Voice nor Heart Alone: German Lutheran Theology of Music in the Age of the Baroque* (New York: Lang, 1993), 1-7.

19. Matthias Silesius Viertel, "Kirchenmusik zwischen Kerygma und Charisma: Anmerkungen zu einer protestantischen Theologie der Musik," JbLH 29 (1985): 111-123.

20. See, for example, Walter Blankenburg, "Zu Karl Honemeyers Thomas Müntzer-Buch," JbLH 19 (1975): 228-231, and Christoph Krummacher, *Musik als Praxis pietatis: Zum selbstverständnis evangelischer Kirchenmusik* (Göttingen: Vandenhoeck & Ruprecht, 1994), 11-40.

21. LW 51: 47; Sermon on Raising of Lazarus (1518); WA 1: 275: "Lasset faren werck, wie gros sie sind, Gebet, Gesange, geplerre, gekleppere. Denn es wird sicherlich keiner durch diese alle zu Gott komen."

22. LW 36: 52; Babylonian Captivity (1520); WA 6: 523: "*A Missa Christi fuit simplicissima sine ulla vestium, gestium, cantuum aliarumque ceremoniarum pompa.*"

23. LW 39: 262-263; Against the Spiritual Estate of the Pope (1522); WA 10^{II}: 120: "Widderumb thut er hyntzu, wie man durch platten, kappen, orden, fasten, bettle, milch, eyer, fleysch, butter essen, singen, orgeln, reuchern, leutten, feyeren, ablaß lößen und der gleychen gott diene und gute werck thue, davon got nichts weyß."

24. LW 52: 38; Christmas Postil on Luke 2 (1522); WA 10^{I}: 138: "Wyr . . . nit viel orgelln, glocken unnd plerren bedarff."

25. LW 52: 59; Christmas Postil on John 1 (1522); WA 10^{I}: 205: "Die . . . vornunfft . . . ist sie stockblind und hebt an und spricht: man soll fasten, beten, singen und die werck der gesetz thun, unnd narret alßo fortan mit den wercken biß das sie fzo tieff kompt, das sie meynett, man diene gott mit kirchen bawen, glocken leutten, reuchernn, plerren, singen, kappen tragen, platten haben, kertzle brennen und des untzehlichen narrnwercks, des itzt alle wellt vol unnd uber voll ist."

26. LW 52: 79 (slightly modified); Christmas Postil John 1 (1522); WA 10^{I}: 234: "St Paulus . . . Alsdenn sihet er ßo klerlich, wilch groß narren sehen alle, die mit wercken wollen frum werden, da geb er denn nit eyn heller umb aller Pfaffen, Munch, Bischoff, Bapst,

platten, kappen, reuchernn, leutten, kertzen brennen, singen, orgelln, beten mit allem yhrem euβerlichen weβen." See also the Epiphany Postil on Matthew 2 (1522): "They have tonsures, are anointed with oil, have white albs, celebrate mass, sing with a high voice and read with a low voice, play organs and pipes, ring and tinkle bells and cymbals, consecrate churches and chapels, burn incense and sprinkle water, wear the cross and carry banners, and clothe themselves in silk and velvet"; LW 52: 221 (slightly modified); WA 10[1]: 646: "Haben sie doch platten, sind mit öle gesalbt, haben auch weysse korröck, halten auch Messe, singen hoch und leβen nyder, orgelln und pfeyffen, leutten glockeln und klengelln schellen, weyhen kirchen und cappellen, reuchen weyrauch und sprengen wasser, tragen creutz und fanen, kleyden sich mit seyden und sammet."

27. LW 44: 324; The Judgment of Martin Luther on Monastic Vows (1521); WA 8: 621-622: "Si intret (ut Paulus ait) aliquis infidel is in medium horum mugientium, murmurantium, boantium, videns eos neque prophetare neque orare, sed tantum suo more sonare ceu fistulas illas organorum, quae sibi optimo consilio socia verunt, et simile iuxta simile suum posuerunt, nonne optimo iure dicet: Quid insanatis? Quid enim sunt nisi fistulae aut tibiae illae, quas Paulus dicit nullam vocam distinctionem dare, sed tantum in aera sonare?"

28. LW 42: 39; An Exposition of the Lord's Prayer for Simple Laymen (1519); WA 2: 97: "Dyse beten dis gebeet mit dem munde, aber mit dem hertzen widdersprechenn sie dem selben und feind gleych den pleyern orgel pfeiffen, die plerren und schreyen fast yn der kirchen unnd haben doch weder worth nach vorstandt, und villeichtn seind die orgelen der selben senger und beter figur und antzeyger."

29. The Travel Journal of Antonio de Beatis: Germany, Switzerland, the Low Countries, France and Italy, 1517-1518, trans. and ed. J. R. Hale and J. M. A. Lindon (London: Hakluyt Society, 1979), 62. The instrument in Speyer cathedral was described as "a fine organ with many stops," 74.

30. For example, in the 1525 liturgical provisions for the Castle Church of All Saints, Wittenberg, drawn up by Bugenhagen and Jonas in consultation with Luther, the use of the organ is specified; see Georg Rietschel, Die Aufgabe der Orgel im Gottesdienste bis in das 18. Jahrhundert (Leipzig: Dürr, 1893; repr. Buren: Knuf, 1979), 18. Wolfgang Musculus gave an eyewitness account of the worship of the Town Church, Wittenberg, on the Sunday after Ascension, 1536, in which the use of the organ is described; the account is cited in full in Rietschel, Orgel im Gottesdienste, 20. See also Herbert Gotsch, "The Organ in the Lutheran Service of the 16th Century," Church Music 67/1 (1967): 7-12; R. Schmidt-Rost, "Martin Luthers Gedanken über die Orgel im Gottesdeinst," Württembergische Blätter für Kirchenmusik 52 (1985): 40-45 (regrettably the sources of the Luther citations are not identified). Erasmus Alber, who had studied in Wittenberg with Luther, reported that Luther "loved the noble art of painters and organists" ("Die edle Kunst der Maler und Organisten . . . hatte lieb"); Erasmus Alber, Wider die verkehrte Lehre der Carlstader, und alle fürnemste Häupter der Sacramentirer: Rottengeister, Widerteuffer, Sacramentlsterer, Eheschender, Musica Verächter, Bildstürmer, und Verwüster aller guten Ordnung (1556) (Neubrandenburg, 1594), sig. Nn7[r].

31. See further in Chapter 2 below.

32. LW 44: 39; Treatise on Good Works (1520); WA 6: 217: "Nach dem glauben mugen wir nichts grossers thun, dan gottis lob, ehre, namen preiszen, predigen, singen, und allerley weisz erheben und groszmachen."

33. See the further discussion in Chapter 3 below.

34. LW 36: 254 (slightly modified); Receiving Both Kinds of the Sacrament (1522); WA 10[II]: 29: "Auffs erst, den alten brauch lasßen bleyben, das man mit geweyheten kleydern, mit gesang unnd allen gewönlichen cerimonien auff latinisch mesß halt, angesehen, das solchs eytell eußerlich ding ist, daran den gewissen keyn fär ligt, daneben mit der predigt die gewissen frey behallten, das der gemeyn man erlerne, das solchs geschehe nicht darumb, das es müsse geschehen odder ketzerey sey, wer anders thett, wie die tollen gesetz des Bapsts dringen."

35. As in other instances, the translators of LW misread "Patrem" as "Lord's Prayer" instead of the Nicene Creed, "Patrem . . ." being the continuation sung by the choir after the celebrant has intoned "Credo in unum Deum."

36. LW 38: 123; Concerning the Sacrament (1530); WA 30[II]: 614-615: "Und daher achtlich, das viel gesang inn der Messe, so fein und herrlich vom dancken und loben gemacht und bis her blieben ist, als das Gloria in excelsis Et in terra, Das Alleluia, Das Patrem, Die Prefation, Der Sanctus, Das Benedictus, das Agnus Dei, In welchen stücken findestu nichst vom opffer, Sondern eitel lob und danck, Darumb wir sie auch jnn unser Messen behalten, Und sonderlich dienet das Agnus uber allen gesengen aus der massen wol zum Sacrament. Denn es klerlich daher singet und lobet Christum, das er unser sunde getragen habe, und mit schonen kurtzen worten das Gedechtnis Christi gewaltiglich und lieblich treibt. Und summa, was bose jnn der Messe ist vom opffer und werck, das hat Gott wunderlich geschickt, das fast alles des priester heimlich lieset, und heisset die stillmesse, Was aber offentlich durch den Kor und unter dem hauffen gesungen wird, fast eitel gut ding und lobesang ist, als solt Gott mit der that sagen, Er wolle seiner Christen mit der stille Messe schonen, das ihr oren solch grewel nicht musten horen, und also die geistlichen mit ihrem eigen grewel sich plagen lassen." "Those who added the Kyrie eleison also did well. We read that under Basil the Great, the Kyrie eleison was in common use by all the people. . . . Later, when chanting began, the Psalms were changed into the *Introit;* the Angelic Hymn Gloria in Excelsis: et in terra pax, the Graduals, the Alleluias, the Nicene Creed, the Sanctus, the Agnus Dei, and the Communio were added. All of these are unobjectionable, especially the ones that are sung *de tempore* or on Sundays. For these days by themselves testify to ancient purity, the canon excepted"; LW 53: 20-21; *Formula missae* (1523); WA 12: 206-207: "*Diende qui Kyrieleison addiderunt, et ipsi placet. Nam sub Basilo magno legimus Kyrie Eleison fuisse in usu totius populi publico. . . . Post vero, ubi cantus cepit, mutati sunt psalmi in introitum, tum additus est hymnus ille angelicus 'Gloria in excelsis, Et in terra pax.' Item gradualia et alleluia et symbolum Nicenum, Sanctus, Agnus dei, Communio. Que omnia talia sunt, ut reprehendi non possint, presertim quae de tempore seu dominicis diebus cantantur. Qui dies soli adhuc priscam puritatem testantur, excepto Canone.*"

37. LW 54: 360; Table Talk (June 25, 1539), emphasis added; WA TR No. 4676: "Man mogte wol die gantz meße *cum suis cantilenis* behalten *modo canone omisso.*" Luther had given similar advice to the clergy in Lübeck when the Reformation was introduced into the area some years before, Letter 12 January 1530: "We . . . both beg and urge you most earnestly not to deal first with changes in the ritual, which [changes] are dangerous, but to deal with them later. You should deal first with the center of our teaching and fix in the people's minds what [they must know], about our justification . . . for they understand nothing but the external changes in the ritual, with which they are titillated for one hour, but as saturated peo-

ple they soon loathe all sound teachings. Adequate reform of ungodly rites will come of itself, however, as soon as the fundamentals of our teaching, having been successfully communicated, have taken root in devout hearts . . . so that it will not be necessary to fish in front of the net, that is, first to tear down the ritual before the righteousness of faith is understood"; LW 49: 263; WA BR 5: 221: "*. . . tamen pia sollicitudine rogamus et hortamur, ut mutationem rituum, quae pericolosa est, non primo, sed posteriore loco tractetis, primo loco autem caput doctrinae nostrae tractetis et plantetis . . . non enim capiunt nisi externam rituum mutationem, qua titillantur ad horam, mox fastidiunt saturi omnis sanae doctrinae. Satis autem per se ipsam sese urgebit mutatio impiorum rituum, ubi caput illud doctrinae bene traditum radices egerit in piis cordibus.*" Thus in Leipzig, Lübeck, as well as Wittenberg, monodic chant and polyphonic settings continued as an essential component of Lutheran worship.

38. LW 53: 38; *Formula missae* (1523); WA 12: 219: "*Hic vero . . . agendum est, ut iste cantus non sit tantum lingua loqui, vel potius tantum sicut sonus fistulae aut cytharae, sine sensu.*"

39. LW 53: 333; Preface to the Bapst *Gesangbuch* (1545); WA 35: 476: "Frölich und lustig mus hertz und mut sein, wo man singen sol. Darum hat Gott, solchen faulen und unwilligen Gottes dienst faren lassen."

40. See Notes 7 and 10 above.

41. See Note 10 above.

42. While Schalk (see Note 12 above) uses the American edition of *Luther's Works* wherever possible, he simply cites many of Buszin's translations without identifying their locations in the Weimar edition.

43. WA 50: 368-374; the two versions are also given in parallel in Walter Blankenburg, *Johann Walter, Leben und Werk*, ed. Friedhelm Brusniak (Tutzing: Schneider, 1991), 439-445.

44. Anton, *Luther und die Musik*, 53-58.

45. August Jakob Rambach, *Über D. Martin Luthers Verdienst um den Kirchengesang* (Hamburg: Bohn, 1813; repr. Hildesheim: Olms, 1972), 190, Anhang 90.

46. Karl Anton, *Luther und die Musik*, 53, gives the year as 1733; Kurt Aland, *Hilfsbuch zum Lutherstudium*, 4th ed. (Witten: Luther-Verlag, 1996), 608, gives the year as 1734.

47. Hugo Holstein, "Eine unbekannte Schrift Luthers über die Musik," *Die Grenzboten* 42 (1883): 79.

48. Karl Anton, *Luther und die Musik*, 53-58.

49. See the facsimile in *Georg Rhau: Musikdrucke aus den Jahren 1538 bis 1545 in praktischer Neuausgabe*, ed. Hans Albrecht and Joachim Stalmann (Kassel, 1955-), 10: viii.

50. Buszin, "Luther on Music," 81-82.

51. Buszin, "Luther on Music," 83.

52. Walter Blankenburg, "Überlieferung und Textgeschichte von Martin Luthers 'Encomion musices,'" L-J 39 (1972): 80-104, esp. 87; the German and Latin texts are given in parallel, 90-94. An English translation of Luther's original German version appears in this volume as Appendix 3.

53. See the discussion in Joseph Herl, *Worship Wars in Early Lutheranism: Choir, Congregation, and Three Centuries of Conflict* (New York: Oxford University Press, 2004), 21-22.

54. WA 35: 411-415; AWA 4: 217-220; LW 53: 214-216. Like *Aus tiefer Not*, written shortly after (see Chapter 9 below), *Ein neues Lied* exists in two forms; the two final stanzas of the later version are not the same as those of the earlier version. See the discussions of Paul F.

Casey, "'Start Spreading the News': Martin Luther's First Published Song," *In laudem Caroli: Renaissance and Reformation Studies for Charles G. Nauert* (Kirksville: Thomas Jefferson University Press, 1998), 75-94; and Martin Rössler, "'Ein neuer Lied wir heben an': Protestsong Martin Luthers," in *Reformation und Praktische Theologie: Festschrift für W. Jetter*, ed. Hans Martin Müller, Dietrich Rössler and Martin Brecht (Göttingen: Vandenhoeck & Ruprecht, 1983), 216-232.

55. Franz M. Böhme, *Altdeutsche Liederbuch: Volkslieder der Deutschen nach Wort und Weise aus dem 12. bis zum 17. Jahrhundert*, 3rd ed. (Leipzig: Breitkopf & Härtel, 1925), No. 389.

56. See Frances H. Ellis, *The Early Meisterlieder of Hans Sachs* (Bloomington: Indiana University Press, 1974).

57. See Philipp Wackernagel, *Das deutsche Kirchenlied von der ältesten Zeit bis zu Anfang des XVII. Jahrhunderts* (Leipzig: Teubner, 1864-1877; reprint, Hildesheim: Olms, 1964), 5:55-57, and Philipp Wackernagel, *Bibliographie zur Geschichte des deutschen Kirchenliedes im XVI. Jahrhundert* (Frankfurt: 1855; repr. Hildesheim: Olms, 1961), 165-166.

58. Zahn No. 8283. DKL Ee16. See Daniela Wissemann-Garbe, "Neue Weisen zu alten Lieder: Die Ersatzmelodien im Klugschen Gesangbuch von 1533," JbLH 37 (1998): 118-138, esp. 134-136.

59. Adam von Fulda was active in Wittenberg in the early years of the university; see further in Chapter 2 below.

60. This adaptation of the secular original to create a poetic dialogue form representing the individual worshiper, the "Sinner," and the person worshiped, "Christ," became an important devotional device in later Lutheran verse, especially in the work of baroque poets, which would culminate in the "Dialogus" cantatas of Johann Sebastian Bach (BWV 32, 49, 57, 58, 60 and 66).

61. The basic study is Kurt Hennig, *Die geistliche Kontrafaktur im Jahrhundert der Reformation: Ein Beitrag zur Geschichte des deutschen Volks- und Kirchenliedes im XVI. Jahrhundert* (Halle: Niemeyer, 1909; repr. Hildesheim: Olms, 1974). Hennig identifies 300 *contrafacta*, but not all are Lutheran; also included are examples by Roman Catholic, Reformed, Anabaptist, Bohemian Brethren, and Schwenkfelder authors. See also Wolfgang Suppan, *Deutsches Liedleben zwischen Renaissance and Barock: Die Schichtung des deutschen Liedgutes in der zweiten Hälfte des 16. Jahrhunderts* (Tutzing: Schneider, 1973).

62. Böhme, *Altdeutsche Liederbuch*, No. 271a; Zahn No. 344a; DKL Ee18. See also Chapter 2, notes 74 and 75. It is possible that Luther was influenced by Ludwig Senfl's six-voice setting of the melody with three stanzas of another secular song, which occurs in an undated Munich manuscript, later published in *Hundert und fünff guter newer Liedlein* (Nuremberg: Ott, 1544); see AWA 4, 110, and Böhme, *Altdeutsche Liederbuch*, No. 281. But it may well have been a widely-known melody and Luther would therefore have already been familiar with it.

63. Böhme, *Altdeutsche Liederbuch*, Nos. 271b; Zahn No. 344b; DKL Ee18A.

64. Walter Blankenburg, in Friedrich Blume, *Protestant Church Music: A History* (New York: Norton, 1974), 509-510.

65. Rebecca Wagner Oettinger, *Music as Propaganda in the German Reformation* (Aldershot: Ashgate, 2001), 207. The interrelationships between liturgical vernacular hymn and non-ecclesiastical religious folk song have been generally neglected; Dr. Oettinger's study is a notable exception.

66. LW 53: 316; WA 35: 474-475: "Und sind dazu auch ynn vier stymme bracht, nicht aus anderer ursach, denn das ich gerne wollte, die iugent, die doch sonst soll und mus ynn der Musica und andern rechten künsten erzogen werden, ettwas hette, damit sie der bul lieder und flyschlichen gesenge los werde und an derselben stat ettwas heylsames lernete, und also das guete mit lust, wie den iungen gepürt, eyngienge."

67. See Luther's letter to Georg Spalatin, late 1523: LW 49: 68; WA BR 8: 220.

68. Recent studies have tended to balance the two emphases; see, for example: Patrice Veit, *Das Kirchenlied in der Reformation Martin Luthers: Eine thematische und semantische Untersuchung* (Stuttgart: Steiner, 1986); Hubert Guicharrouse, *Les Musiques de Luther* (Geneva: Labor et Fides, 1995); Wichman von Meding, *Luthers Gesangbuch: Die gesungene Theologie eines christlichen Psalters* (Hamburg: Lova, 1998); Johannes Block, *Verstehen durch Musik: Das gesungene Wort in der Theologie: Ein hermeneutischer Beitrag zur Hymnologie am Beispiel Martin Luthers* (Tübingen: Francke, 2002).

69. Three other hymnals were issued in 1524, the Nuremberg *Achtliederbuch*, and the two editions of the Erfurt *Enchiridion*, were created from individual broadsides originally issued in Wittenberg. Walter's so-called *Chorgesangbuch* (though it is a set of part-books rather than a single-bound book), was therefore the first hymnal to be planned and published in Wittenberg.

Notes to Chapter 2

1. WA TR No. 6248 (uncertain date): "Musicam semper amavi"; WLS No. 3092; see also WA 30^{II}: 696: "μουσικὴν ἐράω" (I love music).

2. WA 38:338; see also WA TR No. 4640 (1539); Preface to Urban Regius, *Widerlegung der Münsterischen neuen Valentinianer und Donatisten Bekenntnis, an die Christen zu Osnabrück* (1535). Regius — superintendent of Lüneberg at the time, working with Lucas Lossius who would later produce one of the most important collections of chant for Lutheran use — must have had some musical abilities since he wrote a vernacular parody of the Latin hymn *Christe, qui lux es et dies,* issued with its associated melody (DKL B12), in a broadside published in Augsburg in 1523; see the facsimile in Friedrich Blume et al., *Protestant Church Music: A History* (New York: Norton, 1974), 11. The first stanza ran:

Christ der du bist des liecht vnd tag	Christ who is to us both Light and Day
Des yetz vns Wittenberg vermag	in Wittenberg now shows the way;
Glauben wir recht dem liechtes schein	we have right faith within these rays
So Martin Luther fieret ein.	and join with Martin Luther's praise.

3. WA TR No. 5050: "*Reliqui ebrii sunt laeti et suaves ut pater meus, cantant, iocantur, at tu totus in furorem converteris.*"

4. Martin Brecht, *Martin Luther* [1]: *His Road to Reformation, 1483-1521,* trans. James L. Schaaf (Minneapolis: Fortress, 1985), 12.

5. For the background, see Otto Scheel, "Luther und die Schule seiner Zeit," L-J 7 (1925): 141-175; and the overview in Ulrich Leupold, "Luther's Musical Education and Activities," *The Lutheran Church Quarterly* 12 (1939): 423-428. There is the interesting comment of Luther recorded in the *Tischreden* that indicates that he understood music as part of the *triv-*

ium: WA TR No. 5603 (1543): "S. Maria ist mehr celebrirt worden in Grammatica, Musica und Rhetorica, denn ihr Kind, Jesus" ("Mary is celebrated more than her child Jesus in grammar, music and rhetoric").

6. Scheel, "Luther und die Schule seiner Zeit," 148.

7. For the background, see Ernest F. Livingstone, "The Place of Music in German Education from the Beginnings through the 16th Century," *Journal of Research in Music Education* 15 (1967): 243-277.

8. Scheel, "Luther und die Schule seiner Zeit," 153-154; cf. Friedrich Gebhardt, "Die musikalischen Grundlagen zu Luthers Deutscher Messe," L-J 10 (1928): 69-70.

9. Brecht, *Martin Luther* [1], 16.

10. LW 16:76; Lectures on Isaiah (1527-1530) [On Isaiah 6]; WA 30^{II}: 53: "'Sanctus' in Missa cantus puerorum est."

11. LW 22:76; Sermons on John 1-2 (1537-38) [on John 1]; WA 46:713, 716: ". . . sie singen unserm Herrn Gott: *Gloria in excelsis Deo*, das singen jr auch, das jr zu den grossen gnaden komen seid, das jr Gottes Kinder und Erben und Miterben seines lieben Sons, des heiligen Geistes und aller güter teilhaftig worden seid . . . wir predigen Christum und rhümen jn al unsern Heiland, singen jm auch: *Gloria in excelsis Deo.*"

12. Luther probably had in mind the triple Alleluia of the Easter Vigil Mass, *Confitemini Domino, quoniam bonus* (Psalm 105[106]:1) (LU 759). The injunction *Confitemini,* to praise, occurs in various Psalms, such as Psalm 32[33]:2, "*Confitemini Domino in cithara in psalterio decem cordarum psallite illi*" (Praise the Lord with the harp and psaltery of ten strings), and three Psalms begin with the word: Psalms 105, 106, and 117 [106, 107 and 118]. Thus commenting on Psalm 118:2 Luther states: "Job, you see, knew very well how to sing this beautiful *Confitemini* and this particular verse; for he said [Job 1:21]: 'As God wills, so let it be; the name of the Lord be praised'"; LW 14:50. *Das Schöne Confitemini, an der Zahl der 118. Psalm* (1535); WA 31^{I}: 74.

13. LW 3:155; Lectures on Genesis (1535-1545) [on Genesis 17:18]; WA 42:659: "*Quad si caro nos impediret, et essemus veri Christiani, nihil possemus canere per omnem vitam, quam Magnificat, Confitemini: Gloria in excelsis Deo: Sanctus Sanctus, etc.*"

14. LW 22:102-103; Sermons on John 1–2 (1537-38) [on John 1:14]; WA 46:624-625: "Also ist auch dis wort: *Et verbum caro factum est,* in grossen ehren bleiben und teglich in allen Messen gesungen worden und fein mit langsamen und sonderlichen Noten denn die anderen wort, das, wenn man gesungen hat: *Ex Maria virgine, et homo factus est,* jederman die knie gebenget, und sein Hütlin abgezogen hat. Und were noch billich und recht, das man für dem wort: *Et homo factus est,* nieder kniet und mit langen Noten sünge (wie vorzeiten) und mit frölichem Hertzen hörete, das die Göttliche Maiestat sich so tieff herunter gelassen, das sie uns armen Nadensecken gleich ist worden, und wir Gott für feine unaussprechliche gnade und barmhertzigkeit danckten, das die Gottheit selbs ist fleisch worden. . . ." "When the pupils kneel and fold their hands as the schoolmaster beats time with his baton during the singing of 'And was made man,' the common people will imitate them"; LW 41:137; On the Councils and the Church (1539); WA 50:619: "Wenn sie [die schüler] niderknien und die hende falten, so der Schulmeister mit dem stecken klopfft unter dem gesang: *Et homo factus est,* so thuts der hauffe hinach." Apparently chant was still being sung with a basic tactus in seventeenth-century Germany. In Erasmus Sartorius, *Institutionum musicarum tractatio nova* (Hamburg, 1635), chant notation is given with vertical tactus marks, and in the introduction to his *Historia de Geburt*

Jesu Christi (Dresden, 1664), Heinrich Schütz directs that the evangelist's recitatives should not be sung like chant but in a natural speech rhythm "without any time-beating with the hand [ohne einege Tactgebung mit der Hand]"; see Heinrich Schütz, *Neue Asugabe sämtlicher Werke* (Kassel: Bärenreiter, 1955-), 1:4; Frederick K. Gable, "Rhythm in 17th-Century German Chant," *Proceedings of the Göteborg International Organ Academy, 1994* (Göteborg: University of Göteborg, 1995), 173-185; and Frederick K. Gable, "The *Institutionum musicarum* of Erasmus Sartorius and the Rhythm of Plainsong in Seventeenth-Century Germany," in *Music in Performance and Society: Essays in Honor of Roland Jackson*, ed. Malcolm S. Cole and John Koegel (Warren: Harmonie Park Press, 1997), 149-162.

15. LW 10:410; *Dictata super psalterium* (1513-1516) [on Psalm 72:6]; WA 3:468: "*Et pro utroque canitur in Sequentia 'Sancto rorante pneumate parituram divini floris amydalem signavit Gabriel.'*" The citation is from the Marian Sequence *Ave praeclara maris stella, in lucem gentium;* Lossius, fol. 208ᵛ-211ʳ, esp. 209ʳ.

16. These are the opening words of the second verse of the Pentecost sequence *Veni, Sancte Spiritus;* LU 880-881; Lossius, fol. 145ʳ-146ʳ. During Luther's schooldays it was customary for each day to begin with the singing of either the *Veni, Sancte Spiritus* or *Veni, Creator Spiritus;* Scheel, "Luther und die Schule seiner Zeit," 154.

17. LW 15:275; On the Last Words of David (1543); WA 54:69: ". . . die Kirche singet, auch von hieligen Geist: *Veni pater pauperum,* kum du Vater der Elenden. . . . Da her singet man in den artickel des Glaubens von dem Heiligen Geist also: 'Der durch die Propheten geredet hat' [*qui locutus est per prophetas*]."

18. LW 21:197; Sermons on the Sermon on the Mount (1532) [on Matthew 6:27]; WA 32:462: ". . . und singen feiner und lieblicher jrem herrn Laudes und metten des morgens frue ehe sie essen, und . . . machen ein schones langes Benedicite und lassen unsern Herrn Gott sorgen, auch wenn sie iungen haben die sie neeren sollen." The *Benedicite,* Canticle of the Three Children (Daniel 3:57-88, 56), was sung at Lauds of feasts; LU 222, 398-399. Luther created a German version of the canticle; see Chapter 16.

19. LW 29:151; Lectures on Hebrews (1517-1518) [on Hebrews 3:10]; WA 57ᴵᴵᴵ: 145: "*Id, quad usitatur in cantu Ecclesie: 'Quadraginta annis proximus fui,' sumptum est ex psalterio Romano, quod solum sic habet.*" Psalm 95, the *Venite,* is the Invitatory Psalm at Matins; see LU 370; Lossius, fol. 351ᵛ-353ᵛ.

20. LW 6:218; Lectures on Genesis (1535-1545) [on Genesis 34:30]; WA 44:162: "*Sed hoc est natura fidei: quando Sol lucet et coelum est serenum, acquiescimus consolationibus propositis, et canimus: Te deum laudamus etc. Benedicam Dominum omni tempore etc.*" Luther made frequent reference to the *Te Deum,* for instance: "For we should continually be happy, dance, spring, and sing the *Te Deum laudamus*"; LW 22:254-255; Sermons on John 1-4 (1537-1540) [on John 2:24]; WA 46:768: "Denn wir solten jmerdar uns frewen, tantzen, springen und singen das TE DEUM LAUDAMUS." The *Te Deum* was one of the Matins canticles that was also sung at times of thanksgiving; LU 1832-1837; Lossius, fol. 346ʳ-349ʳ. Luther also created a vernacular version in rhymed couplets, *Herr Gott, dich loben wir;* see Jenny AWA 4:107-109, 276-284; Lossius, fol. 348ᵛ-351ʳ.

21. LW 32, 57; Defense and Explanation of All Articles (1521); WA 7:390: "Die Kirche Singt auch ynn dem hymno *Verbum Supernum:* 'Er hat seinen jungern gebenn unter zweien gestalt sein fleisch und blut, auff das er den gantzen menschen speiset, wilcher von zweien naturn gemacht ist.' Ist die kirch ynn dießem gesang recht, Szo sollen yhe beide gestalt geben

werden allen Christen, Seyntemal nit allein die priester, szondern auch die leyen menschen sehn von zweyen naturen, wilchen dieße speiß gantz unnd gantzen menschen zu gesungen wirt." The reference is to the third stanza of the hymn *Verbum supernum prodiens* by Thomas Aquinas, sung at Lauds on Corpus Christi; LU 940-942.

22. WA TR No. 2557: *"Optimi hymni sunt: Rex Christe, factor omnium, et: Inventor rutili."* Both were Easter office hymns; the former continued in Lutheran use; see, for example, Lossius, fol. 94^{r-v}.

23. LW 53:328; Preface to the Burial Hymns; WA 35:480: "Denn ichs selbs auch nicht gerne höre, wo in einem Responsorio oder Gesang die Noten verruckt, anders gesungen werden bey uns, weder ich der in meiner Jugent gewonet bin."

24. LW 18:334; Lectures on the Minor Prophets (1524-1526) [on Zephaniah 1:15]; WA 13:490: *"Quia dies irae celebratus est hoc locus in omni templis, si quando naenias canebant sacrifices traxeruntque ad diem iudicii extremi."* In the Vulgate the verse forms the first line of the medieval Sequence *Dies irae;* LU 1810-1813.

25. LW 31:130; Explanation of the 95 Theses (1518); WA 1:558: *"Ad id facit auctoritas ecclesiae, quae canit 'Libera eas de ore leonis, ne absorbeat eas tartarus' . . . nec vana esse verba ecclesiae credo."* *"Libera eas de ore leonis"* = 4th line of the Tone II Offertory, *Domine Jesu Christe, Rex gloriae;* LU 1813; *"a porta inferi"* = the beginning of the 4th antiphon at Lauds (LU 1802), or *"vadam ad portas inferi"* = from the first verse (Isaiah 38:10) of the Canticle of Hezekiah (Isaiah 38:10-20); LU, 1802; Luther created a German form of the Canticle of Hezekiah; see Chapter 16.

26. LW 4:116; Lectures on Genesis (1535-1545) [on Genesis 22:11]; WA 43:218-219: *"Si enim legem audias, dicet: Media vita in morte sumus, iuxta veteram illam et piam cantionem in Ecclesia, sed est legalis tantam. Euangelium autem et fides invertunt hanc cantionem, et sic canunt: Media morte in vita sumus. . . ."* The reference is to the antiphon *Media vita in morte sumus,* sung at funerals as well as on other occasions. The Latin form continued in Lutheran use; see for example, Franz Eler, *Cantica sacra* (Hamburg: Wolff, 1588; facsimile, Hildesheim: Olms, 2002), cii, where it is assigned to Vespers on Judica Sunday [Lent 5]. Luther made many references to the *Media vita;* see for example WA TR Nos. 3139 (1532) and 6028 (uncertain date).

27. See WA TR No. 6418 (uncertain date).

28. The Latin hymn was attributed to Jan Hus; Luther commended the vernacular version as a communion hymn in the *Deutsche Messe* (1526); LW 53:82; WA 19:99. On this hymn, see Chapter 10.

29. See WA TR No. 4627 (1539): *"De compositione prosae: Veni, sancte Spiritus, et mitte coelitus etc., dixit: Das lied hatt der Heilige Geist selber von ihme gemacht et verbis et melodia . . .";* "On the composition of the sequence *Veni, sancte Spiritus* [for Pentecost], he [Luther] said: 'The hymn was written by the Holy Spirit himself, both words and melody.'"

30. On the background see Walther Lipphardt, "Die älteste Quelle des deutschen "Media vita," eine Salzburger Handschrift vom Jahre 1456," JbLH 11 (1966): 161-162; on *En mitten in des lebens zeyt* and *Chum heiligergeist, herre got,* see Walther Lipphardt, "Deutsche Antiphonenlieder des Spätmittelalters in eine Salzburger Handschrift," JbLH 27 (1983): 40-82, esp. 70-75, and 54-69.

31. Luther knew that it was a popular late medieval hymn, since he argued that it expressed the concept and practice of communion under both kinds; see WA 38:245-246; Of Se-

cret Masses and Priestly Consecration (1533). Earlier he commended it as an appropriate communion hymn, if suitably revised: "But poets are wanting among us, or not yet known, who could compose evangelical and spiritual songs, as Paul calls them [Colossians 3:16], worthy to be used in the church of God. In the meantime, one may sing after communion, *Gott sey gelobet und gebenedeyet* (Let God be blest and praised), omitting the line, 'Und das heylige sacramente, an unserm letzten ende, aus der gewyeten priesters hende' (And the holy sacrament, at our last end from the consecrated priest's hand), which was added by some devotee of St. Barbara, who, having neglected the sacrament all his life, hoped that he would on his deathbed be able to obtain eternal life through this work rather than through faith. For both the musical meter and structure prove this line to be an interpolation"; LW 53:36-37; *Formula missae* (1523); WA 12:218: "*Interim placet illam cantari post communionem:* 'Gott sey gelobet und gebenedeyet, der uns selber hatt gespeyset, etc.' *Omissa ist particula:* 'Und das heylige sacramente, an unserm letzten ende, aus des geweyeten priesters hende,' *quae adiecta est ab aliquo d. Barbarae culture, qui sacramentum tot vita parvi ducens in morte hoc opera bono speravit vitam sine fide ingredi. Nam et numeri et musicae ratio illam superfluam probant.*" Luther makes a similar endorsement of the communion hymn in the *Deutsche Messe* (1526); LW 53:82; WA 19:99.

32. There are frequent references to this hymn in Luther's writings. For example: "We are called 'believers in Christ,' and on the day of Pentecost we sing, "Now let us pray to the Holy Ghost above all for true faith"; LW 39:69; On the Papacy in Rome (1520); WA 6:296: "Darumb heysset auch unßer name 'christglewbegenn,' unnd am Pfingstag wir singenn 'Nu bittenn wir den heyligenn geist umb den rechten glawben aller meyst.'" See also LW 13:356; Exposition of Psalm 111 (1530) [on Psalm 111:1]; WA 31^I: 398. He also commended its use as a communion hymn in the *Formula missae* (1523) (LW 53:37; WA 12:218), and as a gradual hymn in the *Deutsche Messe* (1526) (LW 53:74; WA 19:90).

33. On this hymn, see Chapter 6.

34. "After a time one tires of singing all other hymns, but *Christ ist erstanden* one can sing all year"; WA TR No. 4795 (1541): "Aller lieder singet man sich mit der zeit müde, aber das 'Christ ist erstanden' must all jar erfur, wollte kein ende haben!" See also LW 13:356; Exposition of Psalm 111 (1530) [on Psalm 111:1]; WA 31^I: 398; Martin Rössler, *Die Liedpredigt: Geschichte einer Predigtgattung* (Göttingen: Vandenhoeck & Ruprecht, 1976), 21 and *passim*.

35. The original hymn was written by Michael Weisse (1531).

36. The vernacular folk song was widely known and Luther made numerous references to it; see, for example, WA TR No. 1961 (1531) and No. 4975 (1540):

O du armer Judas, was hast du getan	O poor Judas, what is it you have done,
daß du deinen Herren also verraten hast!	that you have betrayed the Lord?
Darum mußt du leiden in der Hölle Pein;	Therefore you must suffer the pains of hell
Lucifers Geselle mußt du ewig sein.	eternally with Lucifer's horde.
Kyrieleison.	Kyrieleison.

[Philipp Wackernagel, *Das deutsche Kirchenlied von der ältesten Zeit bis zu Anfang des XVII. Jahrhunderts* (Hildesheim: Olms, 1964), 2:468-469 (Nos. 616-618)]

The angry song was parodied in the sixteenth century by a number of different authors — including Luther himself — in order to score points against various enemies; see Rebecca Wagner Oettinger, *Music as Propaganda in the German Reformation* (Aldershot:

Ashgate, 2001), 214-221 [Nos. 3-5]. *Unser grosse sunde* first appeared anonymously in Georg Rhau's *Newe Deudsche Geistliche Gesenge* (Wittenberg, 1544), with polyphonic settings by Thomas Stoltzer and Ludwig Senfl. Markus Jenny, the editor of the new edition of Luther's hymns for the supplementary volumes of the Weimar edition (AWA 4:123-124), makes a convincing argument for ascribing authorship of the parody to Luther. It is quite a remarkable text, especially the first stanza, that is very different from the original *O du armer Judas,* and is in stark contrast to Luther's violent words against the Jews, though consistent with the thoughts expressed in his sermon on the Passion, "How to Contemplate Christ's Holy Sufferings" (1519), which went through an astonishing number of reprints, making it one of Luther's most popular writings (see WA 2:136-142; LW 42:3-14):

Unser grosse sunde und schwere misethat	All our heavy sin, all our misdeeds and our loss
Jhesum, den waen Gottes Son ans Creutz geschlagen hat.	have nailed our Lord Jesus, God's true Son, to the cross.
Drumb wir dich, armer Juda, darzu der Jüden schar,	Therefore you, O poor Judas, with all Jewish seed,
Nicht feintlich dürffen schelten;	must not take our blame;
die schult ist unswer zwar.	for the debt is ours indeed.
Kyrieleison.	Kyrieleison.
Gelobet seistu, Christe, der du am Creutze hingst	We praise you, O Christ, upon the cross suspended,
Und vor unser Sunde viel schmach und streich empfingst,	where, for our great sin, all stripes and scorn accepted,
itzt herschest mit deim Vater in dem Himmelreich;	who now reigns with the Father in heav'ns kingdom great;
mach uns alle selig auff diesem erdreich.	make us all as blessed in this earth's lower state.
Kyrieleison.	Kyrieleison.

AWA 4:313-314; see also WA TR No. 6897 (uncertain date).

37. See WA BR 1:610; LW 48:145.

38. WA BR 1:610; LW 48:145; see also WA TR No. 5347 (1540). On the background, see Friedrich Henning, "Martin Luther als Lateinschüler in Eisenach," *Luther: Zeitschrift der Luther-Gesellschaft* 67 (1996): 109-113.

39. LW 46:250; Sermon on Keeping Children in School (1530); WA 30^II: 576: "Man spricht und ist die warheit, der Pabst ist auch ein schuler gewest. Darumb verachte mir nicht die desellen, die fur der thür *panem propter Deum* sagen und den brot reigen singen. . . . Ich bin auch ein solcher parteken hengst gewest und hab das brot fur den heusern genommen sonderlich zu Eisenach ynn mein lieben stad, wie wol mich hernach mein lieber Vater mit aller lieb und trew, ynn der hohen schulen zu Erffort hielt. . . . Aber dennoch bin ich parteckenhengst gewest."

40. LW 7:335; Lectures on Genesis (1535-1545) [on Gen. 43:24], emphasis added; WA 44:548: *"Atqua idem nobis accidit, quod olim puero mihi et sodalibus meis, cum quibus stipem collegere solebam, unde nos et studia nostra sustentaremus. Cum enim eo tempora, quo in*

Ecclesia natalis Christi celebratur, in pagis ostiam decantaremus quatuor vocibus carmina usitata de puero Iesu nato in Bethlehem. . . ."

41. Johann Mathesius, *Dr. Martin Luthers Leben* [original title: *Historien, Von des Ehrwirdigen inn Gott seligen theuren Manns Gottes, D. Martin Luthers*... Nuremberg: Berg, 1576] (St. Louis: Concordia, 1883), 4. For the background and the identity of the matron, see Brecht, *Martin Luther*, 18-19. Mathesius was also something of a composer in that he created a number of melodies for some of the hymn texts he wrote; for example, see DKL A295-A297.

42. See Brecht, *Martin Luther*, 20.

43. See Herman Degering, "Aus Luthers Frühzeit: Briefe aus dem Eisenacher und Erfurter Lutherkreis," *Zentralblatt für Bibliothekwesen* 33 (1916): 69-95; Scheel, "Luther und die Schule seiner Zeit," 151. "Johannes Braun . . . whose love for poetry and music represented broader cultural interests than Luther had previously experienced"; Harold J. Grimm, *The Reformation Era 1500-1650*, 2nd ed. (New York: Macmillan, 1973), 77.

44. For the background of music in German universities, see Nan Cooke Carpenter, *Music in the Medieval and Renaissance Universities* (Norman: University of Oklahoma Press, 1958), 100-111, 224-271.

45. On the musical writings of de Muris, see Lawrence Gushee, et al., "Muris, Johannes de," New Grove 2, 17:410-412.

46. Gerhard Pietzsch, *Zur Pflege der Musik an den deutschen Universitäten bis zur Mitte des 16. Jahrhunderts* (Hildesheim: Olms, 1971), 113.

47. Pietzsch, *Musik an den deutschen Universitäten*, 115-120 & 192, offers only a partial listing of Erfurt faculty and students with musical connections. According to custom many of these students did not study exclusively in Erfurt but attended other universities as well. For the background, see Heinz Endermann, "Martin Luther in Erfurt: Student, Mönch und Wissenschaftler," *Luther: Zeitschrift der Luther-Gesellschaft* 72 (2001): 83-95.

48. See Pietzsch, *Musik an den deutschen Universitäten*, 120; Wilibald Gurlitt, "Johannes Walter und die Musik der Reformationszeit," L-J 15 (1933): 11; Victor H. Mattfeld, "Weinmann, Johann," New Grove 2, 27:243.

49. He probably also taught music in the university; see Carpenter, *Music in the Medieval and Renaissance Universities*, 265.

50. See Irmgard Höß, "Spalatin, Georg," OER 4:96-99.

51. LW 53:221; WA BR 8:220.

52. See Siegfried Fornaçon, "Jonas, Justus," MGG² *Personenteil* 7, cols. 1161-1162.

53. For a summary of Jonas's connection with Luther, see Hans-Günther Leder, "Luthers Beziehungen zu seinen Wittenberger Freunden," *Leben und Werk Martin Luthers von 1526 bis 1546: Festgabe zu seinem 500. Geburtstag*, ed. Helmar Junghans (Berlin: Evangelische Verlagsanstalt, 1983), 1:433-436; see also Hans-Christian Müller, "Jonas, Justus," New Grove 2, 13:186.

54. See Walter Serauky, *Musikgeschichte der Stadt Halle* (Hildesheim: Olms, 1971), 1:183-206.

55. Siegfried Fornaçon, "Wolfgang Dachstein, der erste evangelische Organist," *Der Kirchenmusiker* 7 (1956): 37-40.

56. Zahn No. 4438a; DKL Eb2.

57. See Victor Mattfeld, "Rhau [Rhaw], Georg," New Grove 2, 21:255-257.

58. Clement Miller and Clytus Gottwald, "Johann Spangenberg," New Grove 2, 24:155.

Johann Spangenberg also wrote a 20-line Latin *Encomium musicum* that his son, Cyriacus, used as a preface for his manuscript on music and mastersingers; see Cyriacus Spangenberg, *Von der Musica und den Meistersängern*, ed. Adelbert von Keller (Stuttgart: Hiersemann, 1861; repr. Hildesheim: Olms, 1966), 2.

59. See Chapter 14 below, and Daniel Zager, "Music for the Lutheran Liturgy: Johannes Spangenberg: *Cantiones ecclesiasticae/Kirchengesenge Deudsche* (1545)," *This Is the Feast: A Festschrift for Richard Hillert at 80* (St. Louis: Morning Star, 2004), 45-60.

60. The term first appeared in Nicolaus Listenius, *Rudimenta musicae in gratiam studiosae iuventutis . . . comportata* (Wittenberg: Rhau, 1533); for the background, see Heinz von Loesch, *Der Werkbegriff in der protestantischen Musiktheorie des 16. und 17. Jahrhunderts: Ein Mißverständnis* (Hildesheim: Olms, 2001).

61. For a summary of the curricula of schools and universities, see Livingstone, "Place of Music in German Education," 263-270. "Since the dividing line between the artistic faculty of the universities (the preliminary stage for the study of law, medicine and theology) on the one hand, and the schools that prepared for the university on the other, was not a sharp one, we find the *ars musica*, properly part of the *quadrivium*, not infrequently in the curriculum of the secondary schools"; Frederick W. Sternfeld, "Music in the Schools of the Reformation," *Musica disciplina* 2 (1948): 110.

62. See Sternfeld, "Music in the Schools of the Reformation," 106-108. Such simple homophonic settings are found in manuscripts and in later imprints, such as Petrus Tritonius, *Melopoiae, sive harmoniae tetracenticae* (Augsburg: Oglin, 1507), Nicolas Faber, *Melodiae Prudentianae et in Virgilium* (Leipzig: Faber, 1533), Martin Agricola, *Melodiae scholasticae* (Wittenberg: Rhaus Erben [heirs of Georg Rhau], 1557; apparently composed in Magdeburg around 1520), and Lucas Lossius, *Erotemata musicae practicae* (Nuremberg: Gerlach, 1563). Some of these simple settings are identified with such composers as Hofhaimer, Ducis, and Senfl; others are anonymous. More complex motets on these poetic texts were composed by such composers as Josquin, Willaert, among others; see Rudolf Wustmann, *Musikgeschichte Leipzigs I: Bis zur mitte de 17. Jahrhunderts* (Leipzig: Teubner, 1909), 46-48; W. Oliver Strunk, "Vergil and Music," *Musical Quarterly* 16 (1930): 482-497, esp. 488-490; Édith Weber, *Musique et théâtre dans les pays rhénans* ([Paris]: Klincksieck, 1974), 1:271-309.

63. Mathesius, *Martin Luthers Leben*, 246-247. The composition has not survived, though an anonymous four-part setting of the words appeared in two Rhau imprints in 1538 and 1542 that could be Luther's composition, especially since he contributed the preface to the 1538 imprint, *Symphoniae jucundae*; see WA 35:538-42. The last words of Dido were set by numerous composers, including Josquin, Mouton, Willaert, and Lassus, among others; see Strunk, "Vergil and Music," 485, and Helmuth Osthoff, "Vergils Aeneis in der Musik von Josquin des Prez bis Orlando di Lasso," *Archiv für Musikwissenschaft* 11 (1954): 85-102, esp. 88-94.

64. The full text in both German and English is given in Appendix 4 below.

65. WA TR No. 5603 (1543). Probably *Ein thurnier sich erheben hat*, found in *Bergkreyen. Etliche Schöne gesenge* ([Nuremberg?]: n.p., n.d.), No. 7, and in *Schöner auserlesener lieder* (Nuremberg: Hergotin, n.d.), No. 9. Both imprints are found in the Weimar exemplar containing 71 folksong pamphlets, issued in facsimile as *Das Weimarer*

Liederbuch: Schätzbare Sammlung alter Volkslieder (Leipzig: Edition Leipzig, 1976), [12-14] and [90-93] respectively.

66. WA TR No. 6707 (before 1542). *Eyn schön reygenlied*, published without place or year of publication; see Philipp Wackernagel, ed., *Das deutsche Kirchenlied von der ältesten Zeit bis zum Anfang des XVII. Jahrhunderts* (Leipzig: Teubner, 1864-1877; reprint, Hildesheim: Olms, 1964), 3:396-397 (No. 470).

67. WA TR No. 4628 (1539). Probably a variant of *Der scheffer von der newen stat*, dating from the end of the fifteenth century; see Franz M. Böhme, *Altdeutsche Liederbuch: Volkslieder der Deutschen nach Wort und Weise aus dem 12. bis zum 17. Jahrhundert*, 3rd ed. (Leipzig: Breitkopf & Härtel, 1925), 382 (No. 298). There was also a Christological parody; see Wackernagel, *Das deutsche Kirchenlied*, 3:396-397, and Walther Lipphardt, "Das wiedergefundene Gesangbuch-Autograph von Adam Reißner aus dem Jahre 1554," JbLH 10 (1965): 76-77.

68. WA TR No. 2619 (1532). *Es für ein Bawr in das holtz;* see Böhme, *Altdeutsche Liederbuch*, 587-589 (No. 472).

69. WA TR No. 4628 (1539).

70. Böhme, *Altdeutsche Liederbuch*, No. 568; DKL Ea1A.

71. Zahn No. 1951; DKL Ea1; see Chapter 5 below.

72. See Otto Brodde, "'Ein neues Lied wir heben an': Martin Luther als 'Phonascus,'" *Luther: Zeitschrift der Luther-Gesellschaft* 34 (1963): 74-75.

73. Zahn No. 4427; DKL B15; see Chapter 11 below.

74. Böhme, *Altdeutsche Liederbuch*, No. 271.

75. Zahn No. 344a; DKL Ee18; see also Chapter 1 above.

76. Zahn No. 346; DKL Ei1.

77. Crotus Rubeanus, *Intimation der hoch berüempten Uniuersitet Erdtfurt, in Martinum Luther. Durch Wolffgang Rusen verteütschet* (Augsburg: Schönsperger, 1521); see Brecht, *Martin Luther* [1], 448-449.

78. Julian Köstlin, *The Theology of Martin Luther*, trans. Charles E. Hay (Philadelphia: Lutheran Publication Society, 1897; repr. St. Louis: Concordia, 1986), 1:39; WA BR 1:541: *"Quod summa familiaritate Erffordiae bonis artibus simil operam dedimus aetate iuvenili."*

79. Köstlin, *The Theology of Martin Luther*, 1:39; WA BR 2:91: *"Eras in nostro quondam contubernio musicus et philosophus eruditus."*

80. Paul Tschackert, "Justus Jonas' Bericht aus dem Jahre 1538 über Martin Luthers Eintritt in das Kloster (1505). Aus dem handschriftlichen Zusatz zu einem Urdruck der Confessio Augustana," *Theologische Studien und Kritiken* 70 (1897): 579: *"Jonas hanc historiam et legendam mihi recitavit in domo Christophori Seszen, qui est questorerarius in Czerbst, sub prandiolo, anno 38, die Karoloj Cesaris & tercia die post Conversionis Paulj";* trans. Ernest G. Schwiebert in *Luther and His Times: The Reformation from a New Perspective* (St. Louis: Concordia, 1950), 137. Jonas was in Zerbst in 1538 compiling and introducing the new church order.

81. Tschackert, "Justus Jonas' Bericht aus dem Jahre 1538," 578-579 (emphasis added): "Es hat sich begeben zei und dreissigjharen . . . zu Erffurdt . . . verkauft er alle die bücher der juristerey heymlich, und lest zurichten eine herliche *collacion*, ein abendtessen in Porta Celi (dan so heisset zu Erffurdt die enie burs) lesset bitten etzliche gelerten zu ym, zuchtige tugensame jungfrauen und frauen und ist mit yn uber die masse frölich, schleth auf der

lauten (wilches er dan fast wol kan). Sindt so all frölich. Als sie ym aber noch verlaufener zeith freundtlich dancken, wusten nicht, was er ym sinne hatte, gehen sie frolich darvon. Er aber, Martinus Luther, ging so baldt yns augustinercloster zu Erfurdt yn der nacht. Dan das hat er also bestaldt, und wardt ein munch"; trans. Schwiebert, *Luther and His Times*, 137.

82. Luther's Wittenberg physician, 1538-1546.

83. Matthäus Ratzeberger, *Die handschriftliche Geschichte Ratzeberger's über Luther und seine Zeit*, ed. Christian Gotthold Neudecker (Jena: Mauke, 1850), 46; see also the comment of Cyriacus Spangenburg, reflecting on the time he was Luther's houseguest in the early 1540s: ". . . seeligen Doctore Lutherus . . . er ein gueter Musicus wehre . . ." (Spangenberg, *Von der Musica*, 15).

84. Wackernagel, *Das deutsche Kirchenlied*, 1:168 (No. 269). Bruno Stäblein suggests that the text was customarily sung to melody No. 606 in Germany [*Monumenta monodica medii aevi, I: Die mittelalterlichen Hymnen des Abendlandes*, ed. Bruno Stäblein, 2nd ed. (Kassel: Bärenreiter, 1995), 333, 673, 684]; however, the text is in 6-line stanzas of 8 syllables, whereas the melody is in 4 lines of 8 syllables. For the background, see Brecht, *Martin Luther* [1], 58-59. On Augustinian thinking with regard to music, see Beat A. Follmi, *Weiterwirken der Musikanschauung Augustins im 16. Jahrhundert* (Frankfurt: Lang, 1994).

85. Luther's knowledge of the late medieval Mass is discussed in detail in Gebhardt, "Die musikalischen Grundlagen zu Luthers Deutscher Messe," L-J 10:79-117. On the different parts of the Mass assigned to the clergy as opposed to the schoolboys, see, for example, the following: ". . . the psalm was to be sung under the leadership of the chief singers or Levites, much as in the cathedral churches the Epistle and Gospel are not read by the students but by the ministers"; LW 12:200; *Enarratio psalmi secundi D. M. Luthero dictata* (1532); WA 40[II]: 475: "*ut indecet Psalmum hunc fuisse tali ritu canendum, ut praecineretur a principalibus Cantoribus seu Levitis, Sicut in Ecclesiis cathedralibus leguntur Epistola et Euangelion non a scholasticis, sed ministris.*"

86. LU 826; Lossius, fol. 127[r-v].

87. See Luther's letter to Braun, dated April 22, 1507; WA BR 1:10-11; LW 48:3-5; see also Brecht, *Martin Luther* [1], 72.

88. See WA TR No. 4174 (1538); LW 54:325.

89. Ratzeberger, *Die handschriftliche Geschichte*, 59.

90. WA TR No. 5408 (1542); LW 54:420.

91. "The psalms and music have been designed to arouse devotion. But if they are handled with excessive noise, they quench the spirit rather than restore it"; LW 10:42; *Dictata super psaltarium* (1513-1516)[on Psalm 4:1]; WA 3:40: "*Psalmi enim et Musica ad exitandam devotionem reperta sunt, quae si nimis inordinato clamore ageantur, magis extinguunt spiritum quam recreent.*"

92. For the background, see Brecht, *Martin Luther* [1]: 98-105.

93. See *The Travel Journal of Antonio de Beatis: Germany, Switzerland, The Low Countries, France and Italy 1517-1518*, trans. & ed. J. R. Hale and J. M. A. Lindon (London: Hakluyt Society, 1979), 80: "Both women and men go to church frequently. . . . They do not talk business or make merry in church as in Italy; they simply pay attention and follow the Mass and the other divine services and say their prayers all kneeling."

94. The reference is to "*Patrem*" meaning *Patrem omnipotentem*, the continuation of

the Nicene Creed following the intonation *Credo in unum Deum.* The reference is therefore not to the Lord's Prayer, *Pater noster.*

95. Quotes added to convey Luther's irony in comparing the sexton's lute to an organ.

96. WA TR No. 3926: "*Recitavit quandam historiam sibi contigisse, cum esset Erfurdiae iuvenis monachus et exisset terminatum in villam quandam, et cum ad celebrandam missam se apparasset, tunc custodem incepisse canere in testudine: Kyrie eleyson, et Patrem. Ibi ego cogebar canere missam, qui vix a risu me continere potuit,* den ich solcher orgeln nicht gewonnet war; must mein Gloria in excelsis nach seinem Kyrie richten!"

97. The reminiscence might also suggest that chant was customarily accompanied at that time.

98. Josquin was intermittently connected with the cathedral of Milan between 1459 and 1476, and with the papal chapel in Rome between 1489 and 1502; see Allan A. Atlas, *Renaissance Music: Music in Western Europe, 1400-1600* (New York: Norton, 1998), 254-255.

99. "In the chief church [St. Jakob's] there is an organ which, while not particularly large, is most beautiful, with many stops which produce the purest tone representing trumpets, fifes, flutes, cornets, crumhorns, bagpipes, drums, and the choruses and spring songs of various birds . . . ; indeed, of all the many other organs we saw in the course of the whole journey, this was pronounced the most perfect," *The Travel Journal of Antonio De Beatis,* 62.

100. LW 54:271: "Afterward there was mention of large churches which are not suited to preaching. 'Cologne has a cathedral [Martin Luther said] that is so large that it has four rows of columns, each row consisting of twenty columns. These are extraordinary buildings, but they aren't suitable for listening to sermons. Good, modest churches with low arches are the best for preachers and for listeners, for the ultimate object of these buildings is not the bellowing and bawling of choristers but the Word of God and its proclamation. The cathedral of St. Peter in Rome and the cathedrals in Cologne and Ulm are very large but inappropriate'"; WA TR No. 3781 (1538) "*Postea fiebat mentio* von großen kirchen, *quae essent inconvenientes ad praedicationem. Nam colonia haberet tantum* da 4 riegen pfeilen stunden, auff jeder riege 20 pfeiler: Es feind ungewonlich beu, *nec sunt apta aedificia pro contionibus percipiendis.* Feine meßige kirchen nit nidrigen gewalben sind die besten *pro contionatoribus et pro auditoribus, non enim finalis causa est illorum templorum rugitus et boatus choriantium, sed verbum Dei illiusque praedicatio.* Sanct Peters münster zu Rom, *Coloniae et Ulm templa sunt amplissima inopportuna.*" Luther visited Cologne on behalf of his order in 1512; see Brecht, *Martin Luther* [1]: 105.

101. See David C. Steinmetz, "Staupitz, Johann von," OER 4:109-111.

102. WA 3 & 4; LW 10-11.

103. WA 5; the commentary on the first two Psalms is given in LW 14:279-349. For a complete translation, see *Martin Luther's Complete Commentary on the First Twenty-Two Psalms,* trans. Henry Cole (London: Simpkin and Marshall, 1826).

104. Mathesius, *Martin Luthers Leben,* 227: "Die gehen mich nicht an . . . sondern unsern Herren Christum; will er sich von der Rechten seines Vaters stoßen und seinen Kircheüberwältigen lassen, da sehe er zu."

105. For a summary of the leading members of the Hofkapelle and its repertory, see Gurlitt, "Johann Walter und die Musik der Reformationszeit," 16-25.

106. Georg Major became a choirboy of the Allerheiligenstift in 1511 at the age of nine. He later studied at Wittenberg university, translated Luther's Small Catechism into Latin,

served as a teacher in Magdeburg under Luther's colleague Nicholas von Amsdorf, and eventually became professor of theology in Wittenberg (1545); see Robert Kolb, "Major, George," OER 2:501-502.

107. See Kathryn Ann Pohlmann Duffy, "The Jena Choirbooks: The Music and Liturgy at the Castle Church in Wittenberg under Frederick the Wise, Elector of Saxony" (Ph.D. diss., University of Chicago, 1995), and Jürgen Heidrich, *Die deutschen Chorbücher aus der Hofkapelle Friedrichs des Weisen: Ein Beitrag zur mitteldeutschen geistlichen Musikpraxis um 1500* (Baden-Baden: Valentin Koerner, 1993).

108. See, for example, Ronald Lee Gould, "The Latin Lutheran Mass at Wittenberg 1523-1545: A Survey of the Early Reformation Mass and the Lutheran Theology of Music, as Evidenced in the Liturgical Writings of Martin Luther, the Relevant Kirchenordnungen, and the Georg Rhau Musikdrucke for the Hauptgottesdienst" (SMD diss., Union Theological Seminary, 1970); Victor H. Mattfeld, *Georg Rhaw's Publications for Vespers* (Brooklyn: Institute of Mediaeval Music, 1966); Bartlett Russell Butler, "Liturgical Music in Sixteenth-Century Nürnberg: A Socio-Musical Study" (Ph.D. diss., University of Illinois at Urbana-Champaign, 1971).

109. Johannes Cochlaeus, *Commentaria de actis et scriptis Martini Lutheri Saxonis* (Maintz: Behem, 1549), 31: "*In diuersorijs multa propinatio, leta compotatio, Musices quoq. gaudia: adeo, ut Lutherus ipse alicubi sonora testudine ludens, omnium in se oculos conuerteret, uelut Orpheus quidam, sed rasus adhuc et cucullatus, eoq. mirabilior*"; trans. (slightly modified), Elizabeth Vandiver, Ralph Klein, and Thomas D. Frazel in *Luther's Lives: Two Contemporary Accounts of Martin Luther* (Manchester: Manchester University Press, 2002), 84.

110. See Atlas, *Renaissance Music*, 72-73.

111. See Carpenter, *Music in the Medieval and Renaissance Universities*, 262.

112. See Carpenter, *Music in the Medieval and Renaissance Universities*, 260.

113. The manuscript was destroyed by fire in 1870 but had already been published in Martin Gerbert, *Scriptores ecclesiastici de musica sacra potissimum* (St. Blaise: Typis San Blasius, 1784; repr. Hildesheim: Olms, 1963), 3:329-381.

114. WA TR No. 76 (1531).

115. "*. . . ita ut interdum differentia plus congrua videatur vero tono, quem Gregorianistae Euouae vocant, id est, seculorum amen, propter psalmorum finem; nam finis dat tonum, sicut generale est proverbium: in fine videbitur, cuius toni*"; Gerbert, *Scriptores ecclesiastici de musica sacra potissimum*, 3:355.

116. The Latin saying survived at least into the later eighteenth century; for example, it is cited in *Der Hofmeister oder Vortheile der Privaterziehung* (1774), a comedy by Jakob Michael Reinhold Lenz.

117. Andreas Ornithoparchus, *Musicae activae micrologus* (Leipzig: Schumann, 1517; facsimile Hildesheim: Olms, 1977); trans. by John Dowland as *Micrologus, or Introduction* (London: Adams, 1609).

118. See Carpenter, *Music in the Medieval and Renaissance Universities*, 265. It was republished in Leipzig in 1519 and 1521, and in Cologne in 1533 and 1535; later writers incorporated some of its chapters into their own works of music theory.

119. His letters from the Wartburg were often signed "from the kingdom of the birds"; see, for example, his letter to Philipp Melanchthon, May 12, 1521; LW 48:217; WA BR 2:333. He used a similar imagery in letters sent from Coburg castle where he stayed while the Diet of

Augsburg was meeting in 1530; see Martin Brecht, *Martin Luther* [2]: *Shaping and Defining the Reformation 1521-1532*, trans. James L. Schaaf (Minneapolis: Fortress, 1990), 373.

120. See Hermann Barge, *Andreas Bodenstein von Karlstadt* (Leipzig: Brandsetter, 1905; repr. Nieukoop: de Graaf, 1968), 1:491-493. See also discussions in Charles Garside, *Zwingli and the Arts* (New Haven: Yale University Press, 1966), 28-33, and Gurlitt, "Johannes Walter und die Musik der Reformationszeit," 30-31.

121. Barge, *Karlstadt*, 492: "*11. Levitae hoc tempore vocum sonoritate probuntur, olim honestate vitae*"; Garside, *Zwingli*, 29. This is almost a direct quotation from a decretal of Gregory I; see Jacques-Paul Migne, ed., *Patrologiae cursus completus . . . Series latina* (Paris: Migne, 1844-1891), 77:1334.

122. Barge, *Karlstadt*, 493: "*37. Ecclesia, cuius Gregorius caput fuit, haec murmura instituit. 38. Sed non ecclesia, cuius caput ist Christus*"; Garside, *Zwingli*, 29.

123. Barge, *Karlstadt*, 492: "*17. In altum quippe ascendens Hylani vocat, descendens vero profundum tarantantura. 18. Sic cum illo et organa, tubas et tibias in theatra chorearum et ad principum aulas relegamus*"; Leslie Korrick, "Instrumental Music in the Early 16th-century Mass: New Evidence," *Early Music* 18 (1990): 360.

124. Barge, *Karlstadt*, 493: "*Si ergo cantum in ecclesia permanere volueris, hunc non nisi unisonum velis, Vt sit unus deus, unum baptisma, una fides, unus cantus*"; Garside, *Zwingli*, 31. From the context of these theses by "one chant" something other than traditional chant is meant: simple congregational song.

125. WA 10^{III}: 1-64; LW 51:70-100. For the background, see Brecht, *Martin Luther* [2], 59-66.

126. LW 45:369; To All the Councilmen of All the Cities in Germany That They Establish and Maintain Christian Schools (1524); WA 15:46.

127. The part books were reprinted in Worms in 1525; see the facsimile: *Das geistliche Gesangbüchlein: "Chorgesangbuch"* (Kassel: Bärenreiter, 1979).

128. LW 53:316; WA 35:474-475: "Und sind dazu auch ynn vier stymme bracht, nicht aus anderer ursach, denn das ich gerne wollte, die iugent, die doch sonst soll und mus ynn der Musica und andern rechten künsten erzogen werden, ettwas hette, damit sie der bul lieder und flyschlichen gesenge los werde und an derselben stat ettwas heylsames lernete, und also das guete mit lust, wie den iungen gepürt, eyngienge. Auch das ich nicht der meynung byn, das durchs Euangelion sollten alle künste zu boden geschlagen werden und vergehen, wie ettliche abergeystlicher fur geben, Sondern ich wollt alle künste, sonderlich die Musica gerne sehen ym dienst des, der sie geben und geschaffen hat."

129. WA BR 4:90: "Zu letzt, gnedigster herr, bitte ich fur mich, wie vor mals, das E.c.f.g. die Cantorey nicht wolt lassen zu zugehen, sonderlich weil die itzige personen drauff erwachsen, Und sonst auch die Kunst werd ist, von fursten und herren zu erhalten, und doch sonst wol nicht, denn so viel anders, wo villeicht nicht wol nott, gewand wird. Sie kundten zu Wittemberg wol sein. An Solche und der gleichen personen weren der Closter guter nützlich gewand, und geschehe gott gefallen dran." Translation based on Walter E. Buszin, "Luther on Music," *Musical Quarterly* 32 (1946): 86.

130. Philipp Melanchthon, *Opera quae supersunt omnia*, ed. Carolus Gottlieb Bretschneider (Halle: Schwetschke, 1834-1860), 1:799: "Johannes Walter, der Componist in der Cantorei . . . denn er das Gesang, so jetzund sehr gebraucht wird, gemacht. Es ist auch in diesem Läuften, da Kirchengesang geändert, solcher Leut von Nöten, die da helfen konnten,

daß nicht alt Gesang allein unterdrückt werden, sondern auch neue und besser wieder angericht werden. Solche Leute halten, acht ich gänzlich für ein gut und recht Werk, dem Gott Wohlgefallen an hat. Man hat bisher Singerei an viel Orten zu unnützem Pracht oder andern unziemlichen Sachen gehalten, warum wollte jetzund die edel Kunst Musica nicht handhaben um Gottes willen, so sie zu Gottes Dienst und Ehre recht gebraucht würd." Trans. Buszin, "Luther and Music," 86. The continued use of Walter's polyphonic settings is confirmed by the Tenor part book of the first edition of the *Chorgesangbuch* (1524), now in the library of the Lutherhalle, Wittenberg, shelfmark ss 2181. At the end of the volume are a significant number of extra leaves which contain numerous additional musical settings in manuscript, some of which are given dates that range between 1534 and 1538.

131. WA TR No. 2545b (1532): "*Nobiles putant, sie haben unserm gnedigen herrn jährlich 3000 fl. ersparet an der musica, et interim dilapidant 30000 fl. Konig und fursten mussn musicam erhalten. Monarcharum opera sunt, artes concervare et leges, privati, utcunque illas amant, tamen conservare illas non possunt. Dux Georgius, Comes Hassiae et Fridericus noster elector habuerunt musicam, iam habent caesar, Ferdinandus Bauari. Ideo legitur de David: Fecit cantares et cantrices.*"

132. See Carpenter, *Music in the Medieval and Renaissance Universities*, 262.

133. On March 22, 1534 the Visitation concluded that under Walter's leadership, "God Almighty has graciously blessed this city of Torgau above many others with an illustrious Kantorei and with glorious music." Gurlitt, "Johannes Walter und die Musik der Reformationszeit," 48; trans. Buszin, "Luther on Music," 93.

134. For an overview of Rhau's musical publications issued in Wittenberg between 1528 and 1548, see Mattfeld, *Georg Rhaw's Publications for Vespers*, 351-353.

135. See Carl Parrish, "A Renaissance Music Manual for Choirboys," in *Aspects of Medieval and Renaissance Music: A Birthday Offering to Gustave Reese*, ed. Jan LaRue (New York: Norton, 1966), 649-664.

136. The work was revised in 1537 and has been translated: Nicolaus Listenius, *Music (Musica)*, trans. Albert Seay (Colorado Springs: Colorado College Music Press, 1975); see also the facsimile of the 1549 Nuremberg imprint, *Musica Nicolai Listenii*, ed. Georg Schünemann (Berlin: Breslauer, 1927).

137. The preface was written by Bugenhagen; see Schünemann's introduction, *Musica Nicolai Listenii*, x. For the background of these Wittenberg publications of music theory, see Ralph Lorenz, "Pedagogical Implications of *music practica* in Sixteenth-century Wittenberg," PhD diss. (Indiana University, 1995).

138. Adolf Aber, "Das musikalische Studienheft des Wittenberger Studenten Georg Donat (um 1543)," *Sammelbände der Internationalen Musik-Gesellschaft* 15 (1913): 68-98; Carpenter, *Music in Medieval and Renaissance Universities*, 267.

139. See the discussion concerning Faber in Wittenberg in 1551 in Chapter 3 below.

140. Lorenz, "Pedagogical Implications," 286-289. Faber produced two other music treatises: *Ad musicam practicam introductio* (Nuremberg: Berg & Neuber, 1550), and *Musica poetica* (1548) which was never published.

141. Adrianus Petit Coclico, *Compendium musicis* (Nuremberg: Montan & Neuber, 1552; facsimile, Kassel: Bärenreiter, 1954); Adrianus Petit Coclico, *Musical Compendium*, trans. Albert Seay (Colorado Springs: Colorado College Music Press, 1973).

142. Lorenz, "Pedagogical Implications," 282-286.

143. Lorenz, "Pedagogical Implications," 281-282.

144. Lorenz, "Pedagogical Implications," 293-294.

145. See Werner Merten, "Die Psalmodia des Lucas Lossius," JbLH 19 (1975): 1-18; 20 (1976): 63-90; 21 (1977): 39-67.

146. Facsimile: *Bibliotheca musica bononiensis,* II/53 (Bologna: Forni, 1980).

147. Lorenz, "Pedagogical Implications," 295.

148. WA TR No. 6248 (uncertain date): "Man muß *musicam necessario* in der schulen behaltten. Ein schulmeister muß singen können, sonst sehe ich ihn nicht an. *Et adolescens, antequam ad ministerum ordinetur, exerceat se, in schola.*" WLS No. 3092.

149. LW 41:176; On the Councils and the Church (1539); WA 50:651: "Uber das, wo Schulmeister Gottfürchtig ist, und die knaben Gottes wort rechten glauben leret verstehen, singen und uben, und zu Christlicher zucht helt, Da sind die Schulen, wie droben gesagt, eitel junge, ewige Concilia, die wol mehr nutz schaffen, weder viel andere grosse Concilia."

150. For discussions of the role of schools in the establishment and development of Lutheran church music in Saxony in the sixteenth century, see: Johannes Rautenstrauch, *Luther and die Pflege der kirchlichen Musik in Sachsen* (Leipzig: Breitkopf & Härtel, 1907; reprint, Hildesheim: Olms, 1970), 60-234; Sternfeld, "Music in the Schools of the Reformation," 99-122; Livingstone, "The Place of Music in German Education," 243-277; Kyle C. Sessions, "Hymns and School Music in the Reformation," *Illinois State University Journal* 31 (1968): 21-31; Joe Eugene Tarry, "Music in the Educational Philosophy of Martin Luther," *Journal of Research in Education* 21 (1973): 355-365; the first chapter of John Butt, *Music Education and the Art of Performance in the German Baroque* (Cambridge: Cambridge University Press, 1994), 1-12; and Joachim Kramer, "Change and Continuity in the Reformation Period: Church Music in North German Towns, 1500-1600," *Music and Musicians in Renaissance Cities and Towns,* ed. Fiona Kisby (Cambridge: Cambridge University Press, 2001), 118-130.

151. At root the issue was one of finance. While the teaching of music remained a private concern, the students had to pay the teacher individually for his services. But if there was a professor of music matriculated students would be able to attend his lectures without further fees. While private teaching of music remained the practice it meant that poorer students were effectively excluded from music studies.

152. Carpenter, *Music in Medieval and Renaissance Universities,* 267, n. 165.

153. Carpenter, *Music in Medieval and Renaissance Universities,* 268.

154. WA BR 9:340: "Wir haben bis her großen Mangel [in Wittenberg] gehabt an einem Musico, Aber weil nichts furhanden gewest, haben wir E.k.f.g. nicht mugen mit viel supplicieren bemuhen. Nu aber das einkommen Licentiat Blanckens verledigt, dunkt michs wol gut, das davon ein stattlicher Musicus wurde gehalten. Denn zu der Zeit hatten wir noch vorrhat aus dem Bapstum (wie andere personen auch), die singen kundten. Nu wir aber selbs eigene erzihen sollen, wills mangeln." Trans. Buszin, "Luther on Music," 93.

155. "His magistris licet nobis omne nephas, licet probis, omnis obstrepere.

Cum Iubilo.

Conculare iura, legis: infamare licet Reges, Papamq. Cum Caesare.

Cum Iubilo. . . .

Septa claustri dißipamus, sacra uasa compilamus, sumptus unde suppetat.

Cum Iubilo.

I Cuculla, uale Cappa, uale Prior, Custus, Abba, cum obedientia. Cum Iubilo. . . .
Io Io Io Io Gaudeamus cum iubilo Dulces Lutheriaci. Cum Iubilo."

Cochlaeus, *Commentaria*, 118; trans., Vandiver, Klein, Frazel, *Luther's Lives*, 166.

156. *"Quod & Quatuor uocum concentu decorauit"*; Cochlaeus, *Commentaria*, 118; trans., Vandiver, Klein, Frazel, *Luther's Lives*, 166. In 1789 a substantial collection of books and manuscripts from the library of Johann August Ponickau was received by the Wittenberg university library, doubling its holdings; among them was a manuscript of Emser's poem with musical notation; see Johann Christian August Grohmann, *Annalen der Universität zu Wittenberg* (Meissen: Erbstein, 1801-1802), 1:193-194. Emser had earlier written a vernacular text and its associated melody, issued as a broadside in 1524; DKL B16.

157. LW 45:369; To All the Councilmen of All the Cities in Germany That They Establish and Maintain Christian Schools (1524); WA 15:46: "Ich rede fur mich: Wenn ich kinder hette und vermöchts, Sie müsten mir nicht alleyne die sprachen und historien hören, sondern auch singen und die musica mit der gantzen mathematica lernen."

158. See Johannes Luther, "Die Nachkommenschaft Martin Luthers des Reformators," L-J 7 (1925): 126-127.

159. WA TR No. 6707 (before 1542).

160. Ratzeberger, *Die handschriftliche Geschichte*, 59.

161. LW 50:231; WA BR 10:134: *"Sicut inter te et me convenit, Mi Marce, mitto ad te filium meum Johannem, ut adhibeas eum exercendis pueris in Grammatica et Musica. . . . Si videro successum in isto filio, mox, me vivo, etiam alios duos filios habebis. . . . Vale in Domino et Johannem Waltherum iubeas sauum esse oratione mea, et ut filium sibi commendatum habeat in Musica. Ego enim parturio quidem Theologos sed Grammaticos et Musicos parere etiam cupio."* See also WA TR Nr. 1096 (1530): "Grammar and music are the preservers of the sense"; *"Grammatica [et] musica [sunt] conservatores rerum."*

162. Ratzeberger, *Die handschriftliche Geschichte*, 58: "D. Luther Im Anfang seines kampfes wieder die Bebstische mißbraucht . . . und auch sonsten *privatim* von Sathana viel große anfechtunge ausstehen muste, begab sichs oftermal, wen er In seinem schreibstublin seines studirens und schreibens wartete, Das Ihn derselbe uff mancherley weise und wege *turbite*, Einsmals kam *M. Lucas Edemberger* (Hertzog Johann Ernst Zu Sachsen *praeceptor*) mit etzlichen feinen gessellen, allen guten *Musicis,* und Georgen Rhauen, Ihne zu besuchen, So wirdt Ihme angezeigt das sich Luther In sein stublin verschlossen habe, und dasselbe uber die Zeit zugehalten, habe auch etzlicher Zeit nichts sonderlichs gessen, noch getruncken, und niemand zu Ihme lassen wollen, Da gedencket *M. Lucas* Es musse gewiß nicht recht umb Ihn stehen, klopfet an, beckommet aber keine antwort, so schauet er Zu einem lochlin durch die thur hinein und siehet, Das Luther an der Erden auf seinem Angesichte ligt In einer Onmacht mit Ausgestrecken armen, Da offenet er die thur mit gewalt, ruttelet Ihn auf und fuhret Ihn Ins unter Losament, lesset Ihn ein wenig essen zurichten und fehet darauf an mit seinen gesellen zu musiciren. Da solches geschieht kombt D. Luther allgemach wieder Zu sich selbst und vorgieng Ihm sein schwermutt und Traurikeit, also das er auch anfehet mit Ihnen zu singen, hieruber wirdt er so frolich und bittet gedachten *M. Lucam* und seine gesellen ufs vleissigste, Sie wolten Ihn Ja oft besuchen, Insonderheit wan sie lust zu *musiciren* hetten und sich nichts Irren noch abweisen lassen, Er hatte auch gleich zu schaffen, was er wolle, Dan er befandt, sobald er Musicam höretе, das sich seine *tentationes* und schwermut enderten." One

must treat such anecdotal incidents recorded by Ratzeberger and others, appearing in the *Tischreden* and other sources, with some caution with regard to their veracity. However, taken together, such sources present a consistent view of Luther's love for music and of his continuous involvement in music-making in his home.

163. Article III/4: Concerning the Gospel: "God is extravagantly rich in his grace . . . through the mutual conversation and consolation of brothers and sisters [*per mutuum colloquium et consolationem fratrum*]"; BC-W/K 319. In footnote 128 the editors of BC-W/K raise the possibility that this reflects the monastic practice of mutual confession, since Luther speaks of "the power of the keys and also through the mutual conversation and consolation of brothers and sisters." But given the frequency of Luther's admonitions to sing with others when melancholy and when temptations arise, it would seem more likely that he was thinking of such mutual encouragement in addition to the office of the keys.

164. Is this second-hand reportage, or is Luther speaking personally? He is known to have played the flute and this sounds like a reminiscence of his relationship with Katie, who frequently dealt firmly with her husband.

165. WA BR 7:104-105: "Aber, lieber Mattia, folget hierin nicht Euren Gedanken, sondern höret, was Euch ander Leute sagen. . . . So höret nu, was wir in Gottes Namen zu Euch sagen. . . . Darumb, wenn Ihr traurig seid, und will uberhand nehmen, so sprecht: Auf! Ich muß unserm Herrn Christo ein Lied schlagen auf dem Regal (es sei *Te Deum laudamus* oder *Benedictus*, etc.); denn die Schrift lehret mich, er höre gern fröhlichen Gesang und Saitenspiel. Und greift frisch in die *Claves* und singet drein, bis die Gedanken vergehen, wie David und Elisäus taten. . . . Und wie jener Ehemann tät, wenn seine Ehefrau anfang zu nagen und beißen, nahm er die Pfeifen unter dem Gürtel herfür und pfiff getrost, da wird sie zuletzt so müde, daß sie ihn zufrieden ließe, also greift Ihrauch ins Regal, oder nehmet gute Gesellen und singet dafur, bis Ihr lernet ihn spotten." Trans. *Luther: Letters of Spiritual Counsel*, trans. and ed. Theodore G. Tappert (Philadelphia: Westminster, 1955), 96-97.

166. Mathesius, *Martin Luthers Leben*, 227: "Über und nach Tische sang auch der Doktor bisweilen, wie er auch ein Lautenist war. Ich hab mit ihm gesungen." Mathesius, deacon (1541) then pastor (from 1545) in Joachimsthal, wrote a number of hymns and probably composed or arranged their associated melodies; at least one of them was a probable collaboration with Luther: *Nun trieben wir den Bapst hinaus*, issued as a broadside (Wittenberg, 1545), in a four-part setting; DKL B50.

167. Mathesius, *Martin Luthers Leben*, 246: "Wenn nun Doktor Luther sich müde und hellig gearbeitet, war er am Tische fröhlich. Ließ bisweilen eine Kantorei anrichten."

168. See Appendix 4 below.

169. Mathesius, *Martin Luthers Leben*, 58 & 246 respectively.

170. The young Johann Zink sang soprano; when he died Luther wrote to his father, 22 April 1532: "We were all very fond of the boy; he was especially dear to me — so that I made use of him many an evening for singing in my house"; LW 50:51; WA. BR 6:301: "Denn er uns allen fast ein lieber Bube ist, und sonderlicher mich, daß ich viel Abend sein gebraucht habe zu singen in meinem Hause."

171. WA TR No. 5408 (1542); LW 54:420.

172. WA BR 7:154: "Wir singen, so gut wir hie können, über Tische, und geben's darnach weiter. Machen wir etliche Säue darunter, so ist's freilich Eure Schuld nicht, sondern unsere Kunst, die noch sehr gering ist, wenn wir's schon zwei- dreimalübersingen. . . . Und

wenn es schon all Componisten gut machen, so ist unser Ernst wohl noch weit drüber, und können's böse genung singen." Trans. Blume, *Protestant Church Music*, 6-7.

173. Ratzeberger, *Die handschriftliche Geschichte*, 59: "Vormercket er aber bisweilen an einem Neuen gesang, das er falsch abnotiert wahr, so setzet er denselben als bald wieder ab uf die Lineen und rectificirt."

174. LW 13:173; Commentary on Psalm 101 (1534) [on Psalm 101:2]; WA 51:221: ". . . solch lied ja nicht höher singe, Er wird sonst gewislich heisch werden und eine saw machen, ehe er funff noten erreicht."

175. The extent of Luther's collection of music is unknown and must have been dispersed after his death, but it would have included various editions of Walter's *Chorgesangbuch*, and many of the musical publications issued by Georg Rhau. It is reported that while he was at Coburg in 1530 he joined with his fellows in singing Aus tiefer Not "in four parts" ("mit vier Stimmen"); Johannes Manlius, *Locorum communium . . . Schöne ordentliche Gattierung allerley alten und newen Exempel, Gleichniß, Sprüche, Rathschläge . . .* [translated from the Latin (originally published by Oporinus in Basle in 1563) by Johann Huldrich Ragor] (Frankfurt am Main: Feyerabend & Hüter, 1574), fol. 7^r, which must have been Johann Walter's four-part setting, suggesting that Luther owned at least the first edition (1524) of these part-books. He also must have owned other published part books, such as those that included polyphonic settings of his chorales that were probably presented to him by their composers when they were published. Thus he most likely owned Arnold von Bruck's *Hundert und ainundzweintig newe lieder* (Nuremburg: Formschneider, 1534), which included Bruck's four-part settings of three of his chorales *(Komm Heiliger Geist, Herre Gott, Gott der Vater wohn uns bei,* and *Mitten wir im Leben sind).* Veit Dietrich is reported to have owned a set of these part-books and into one of them — the Alto part-book — Luther inscribed his German poem in praise of music (see WA 35:383; WA 48:293, and the discussion in Chapter 3 below). It is also probable that he would have owned musical manuscripts of works by various composers, some of whose music he highly regarded, such as Josquin, and others with whom he had personal contact, such as Senfl. See further the discussion below concerning specific publications that were used for singing at his table.

176. Ratzeberger, *Die handschriftliche Geschichte*, 59: "Auch hatte sonsten *Lutherus* den brauch, sobalde er die abendtmalzeit mit seinen Dischgesellen gehalten hatte, brachte er aus sienem schreibstublein seine *partes* und hielte mit denen, so zur *Musica* lust hatten, eine *Musicam,* Insonderheit gefiel Ihm wol, wo eine gute *compositio* der alten Meister uff dei *Responsoria* oder *hymnos de tempora anni* mit einfiel, und sonderlichen hatte er zu dem *Cantu Gregoriano* und dem *Choral* gute lust. . . . Insonderheit sang er gerne mit, wo ettwa ein *hymnos* oder *responsorium de tempora* von den *Musicis componirt* war uf den *Cantum Gregorianum* wie gemeldet, und musten Ihm sein Junger sohn *Martinus* und *Paulus* die *responsoria de tempore* nach essens fur Dische auch singen, als zu Weinachten *Verbum caro factus est, In principio erat verbum.* Zu Ostern *Christus resurgens ex mortuis, Vita sanctorum, Victimae paschali laudes,* Da er allzeit selbst solche *responsoria* mit seinen sohnen, und *in cantu figurali* den alt mit sang."

177. "Es war ein guter Musicus/hatte auch ein fein helle reine Stimme/beyde zu sing und zu reden"; Erasmus Alber, *Wider die verkehrte Lehre der Carlstader, und alle fürnemste Häupter der Sacramentirer: Rottengeister, Widerteuffer, Sacramentlsterer, Eheschender, Musica Verächter, Bildstürmer, und Verwüster aller guten Ordnung* (1556) (Neubrandenburg: [s.n.],

1594), sig. Nn7ʳ. In the middle of the eighteenth century it was reported that Alber was the author of an unpublished manuscript, *Buch von der heiligen, himmlischen und holdseligen Musica* (Book of holy, heavenly and most charming music); see Christian Gottleib Jöcher, *Allgemeines Gelehrten-Lexicon* (Leipzig: Gledisch, 1750-1751), 1, col. 211. The manuscript has not survived but most likely would have contained other references to Luther and music.

178. LW 53:324; the Latin is given in Appendix 3 below. Compare the earlier German draft of the Latin text: "Thus one sees in this art the great inexpressible, incomprehensible, and inexplicable wisdom of God, that a single voice proceeds according to its fine and simple manner, and the other [voices] play so marvelously in every way, beside it and around it, together in friendly consort, with one heart and delightful harmony, so that whoever is only mildly moved and heeds not the inexpressible marvel of the Lord, should not be considered human, and should hear nothing else than the bray of the donkey and the grunt of a sow"; the German is also found in Appendix 3 below.

179. See Charles Anders, "Luther and the Composers of His Time," *The Musical Heritage of the Church* 7 (1970): 41-50.

180. See Appendix 4 below.

181. WA BR 7:105-106.

182. See Kurt Gudewill, "Forster, Georg," New Grove 2, 9:105.

183. Markus Jenny, "Ein brief von Sixt Dietrich über Luther und die Kirchengemeinde in Wittenberg," JbLH 5 (1960): 134: "D. M. Luther hat sonderlich grosse lieblin zu der music, mit dem ich vil vnd oft gesungen."

184. Ratzeberger, *Die handschriftliche Geschichte*, 58.

185. WA TR No. 4897 (1540).

186. WA TR No. 5391 (1542).

187. WA 48:85-86; WLS No. 3100.

188. WA 48:35-36. Carl Philipp Emmanuel Bach, Johann Sebastian's son, owned a woodcut of Paminger, who is described as "Lutheri Amicus" (Luther's friend), which may have come from J. S. Bach's collection; see *Verzeichniß des musikalischen Nachlasses de verstorbenen Capellmeisters Carl Philipp Emanuel Bach* (Hamburg: 1790; facsimile, Buren: Knuf, 1991), 115.

189. WA TR No. 3516 (1537): "*Egregas cantilenas post coenam cecinerunt. Quas cum admiraretur Doctor Martinus, dixit cum singultu:* Ach, wie feine musici sindt in 10 jharen gestorben! Iosquin, Petrus Loroe, Finck *et multi alii excellentes.*" Josquin died in 1521; la Rue in 1518; and Heinrich Finck im 1527. Thus Luther's "10 years" is an approximation and has more to do with receiving news of their deaths rather than their actual decease.

190. See Carl Gerhardt, *Die Torgauer Walter Handschriften: Eine Studie zur Quellenkunde der Musikgeschichte der deutschen Reformationszeit* (Kassel: Bärenreiter, 1949), 116-120.

191. On Senfl generally, see Martin Bente, *Neue Wege der Quellenkritik und die Biographie Ludwig Senfls: Ein Beitrag zur Musikgeschichte der Reformationszeitalters* (Wiesbaden: Breitkopf & Härtel, 1968).

192. See WA 35:535.

193. For the background, see Brecht, *Luther* [1]: 251, 260, 445, 452-453, 456, 465 and 468.

194. For the background, see Stephanie P. Schlagel, "The *Liber selectarum cantionum* and the 'German Josquin Renaissance,'" *The Journal of Musicology* 19 (2002): 564-615.

195. See Helmut Kind, *Die Lutherdrucke des 16. Jahrhunderts und die Lutherschriften der Niedersächsischen Staats- und Universitätsbibliothek Göttingen* (Göttingen: Vandenhoeck & Ruprecht, 1967), Nos. 110, 279, 688, 882, 925, 937 and 1202.

196. For the complete Latin text with English translation, see Schlagel, "The *Liber selectarum cantionum*, 613-615.

197. Schlagel characterizes the work as "the humanist luxury book" that "was likely planned as a presentation volume"; Schlagel, "The *Liber selectarum cantionum*," 568 and 571.

198. The Hofkapelle was disbanded on Maximilian's death in 1519.

199. WA TR No. 1258: "Josquin des alles composition frolich, willig, milde heraus fleust, ist nitt zwungen und gnedigt *per* [*regulas*] *sicut* des fincken gesang." "According to old German usage, 'milde' means 'liberal,' 'generous,' 'abundant'; we render it . . . 'overflowing'"; Walter Wiora, "The Structure of the Wide-Spanned Melodic Lines in Earlier and Later Works of Josquin," *Josquin des Prez: Proceedings of the International Conference Held at the Juilliard School at Lincoln Center in New York City, June 1971*, ed. Edward E. Lowinsky (London: Oxford University Press, 1976), 312, n. 7. There are a number of ambiguities regarding this oft-quoted statement. Some regard "regulas" as an addition by Aurifaber, editor of Luther's *Tischreden*, though it seems to be necessary given the context in which Luther is distinguishing between Law (rules) and Gospel. Theodore Tappert's translation (LW 54:129, following Buszin, "Luther on Music," 91) makes Luther say that Josquin's compositions "are like the song of the finch." But Luther actually stated the opposite: Josquin's compositions are free in contrast to the song of the finch that always obeys the rules. Luther therefore seems to be drawing attention to repetitious birdsong — beautiful but made up of unaltered repeated phrases. At the same time the reference to "fincken gesang" is probably also to be taken as a pun on the name of the composer Heinrich Finck; see, for example, the discussions of Oskar Söhngen, *Theologie der Musik* (Kassel: Stauda, 1967), 93, note 219; Walter Wiora, *Historische und systematische Musikwissenschaft: Ausgewählte Aufsätze* (Tutzing: Schneider, 1972), 229-239; Martin Stähelin, "Luther über Josquin," *Festschrift für Martin Ruhnke zum 65. Geburtstag*, ed. Mitarbeitern des Instituts für Musikwissenschaft der Universität Erlangen-Nürnberg (Stuttgart: Hänssler, 1986), 326-338; and Eyolf Østrem, "Luther, Josquin and *des fincken gesang*," *The Arts and the Cultural Heritage of Martin Luther*, ed. Eyolf Østrem, Jens Fleisher and Nils Holger Petersen (Copenhagen: Museum Tusculanum Press, 2003), 51-79.

200. For the background, see Brecht, *Martin Luther* [2], 384-410.

201. Antiphon at Matins on Holy Saturday, i.e., a pre-Resurrection antiphon.

202. LW 49:427-29; WA BR 5:639: "*Quamvis nomen meum sit invisum, adeo ut vereri cogar, ne satis tuto recipiantur a te et legantur, optime Ludovice, quas mitto literas, vicit tamen hanc formidinem amor musicae, qua te video ornatum et donatum a Deo meo. Qui amor spem quoque fecit, fore ut nihil periculi sint tibi allaturae meae. . . . Ego sane ipsos tuos Duces Bavariae, ut maxime mihi parum propitii sint, vehementer tamen laudo et colo prae caeteris, quod musicam ita fovent et honorant. . . . Ad te redeo et oro, si quod habes exemplar istius cantici: 'In pace in id ipsum,' mihi transcribi et mitte cures. Tenor enim iste a iuventute me delectavit, et nunc multo magis, postquam et verba intelligo. Non enim vidi eam antiphonam vocibus pluribus compositam. Nolo autem te gravare componendi labore, sed praesumo te habere aliunde compositam. Spero sane, finem vitae meae instare, et mundus me odit nec ferre potest, ego rursus mundum mihi fastidio et detestor; tollat itaque animam meam pastor optimus et fidelis. Idcirco hanc antiphonam iam coepi cantillare et compositam cupio audire. Quod si non*

habes aut non nosti, mitto hic suis notis pictam, quam vel post mortem meam, si voles, componere potes."

203. Thought to be no longer extant, the motet has recently been identified in the *Schalreuter Codex* in the Ratsschulbibliothek, Zwickau; see Ole Kongsted, "Ludwig Senfl's 'Luther-Motetter': En forskningsberetning," *Fund og Forskning* 39 (2000): 7-41.

204. Rediscovered in the early twentieth century; see Josef Müller-Blattau, "Die musikalischen Schätze der Staats- und Universitätsbibliothek zu Königsburg in Preußen," *Zeitschrift für Musikwissenschaft* 6 (1923/24): 215-239. The information regarding the Senfl motets was reported by Mathesius; see Mathesius, *Martin Luthers Leben*, 143.

205. It was reported as still being visible twenty years later; see WA 35:536.

206. In discussing Senfl's motet Rebecca Wagner Oettinger inexplicably makes no reference to the personal significance of the text for Luther; see Rebecca Wagner Oettinger, "Ludwig Senfl and the Judas Trope: Composition and Religious Tolerance at the Bavarian Court," *Early Music History* 20 (2001): 214-215.

207. See Brecht, *Martin Luther* [2], 376.

208. Cited by Schlagel, "The *Liber selectarum cantionum*," 590: "IOSQUINVM celeberrimum huius artis Heroem facile agnoscent omnes, habet enim vere diuinum et inimitabile quiddam Neque [sic] hanc laudem grata & candida posteritas ei inuidebit"; Brecht, *Martin Luther* [2], 376, n. 61.

209. WA TR No. 4316 (1538): "*Estque egregia muteta legem et euangelium, mortem et vitam comprehendens. Duae voces querulae lamentatur: Circumdederunt me gemitus mortis etc, diende quatuor voces uberschreien dise; Haec dicit Dominus, de manu mortis liberabo populum meum etc.* Es ist sehr wol und trostlich componirt."

210. "*Nimphes, nappés* is articulated with considerable transparency, and strikes the listener most immediately by way of its opulent harmonic sonority. To do so, it must stress the vertical dimension of its texture, which it manages to accomplish — despite the presence of strict canon — by its reliance on relatively undifferentiated rhythmic values. A manner of 'homorhythm by default' results that enables harmony to gain prominence over the other parameters of musical style"; Lawrence F. Bernstein, "Chansons for Five and Six Voices," *The Josquin Companion*, ed. Richard Sherr (Oxford: Oxford University Press, 2000), 408. The use of the chant melody within the structure of the motet produces a striking cross-relation that occurs twice (from $E_\natural$ to $E_\flat$), a sudden darkening of the harmony; see Patrick Macey, "An Expressive Detail in Josquin's *Nimphes, nappés*," *Early Music* 31 (2003): 400-411.

211. See Martin Just, "Josquins Chanson 'Niphen, napées' als Bearbeitung des Invitatoriums 'Circumdederunt me' und als Grundlage für Kontrafaktur, Zitat und Nachahmung," *Die Musikforschung* 43 (1990): 305-335; John Milsom, "*Circumdederunt*: 'A Favourite cantus firmus of Josquin's'?," *Soundings* 9 (1982): 2-10; Marcus van Crevel, *Adrianus Petit Coclico: Leben und Beziehungen eines nach Deutschland emigrierten Josquinschülers* (The Hague: Nijhoff, 1940), 102-134.

212. WA TR No. 4316: "26 December canebant: Haec dicit Dominus, sex vocum, a Conrado Rupff compositium, qui cupiit in agone mortis hoc sibi decantari."

213. Mathesius, *Martin Luthers Leben*, 227-228: "Zwischen dem Gesang brachte er gute Reden mit ein. 'Josquin,' sagt er, 'ist der Noten Meister: die haben's müssen machen, wie er wollte; die andern Sangmeister müssen's machen, wie es Noten haben wollen. Freilich hat der Komponist auch seinen guten Geist gehabt, wie Bezaleel, sonderlich da er das *Haec dicit*

Dominus und das *Circumdederunt me gemitus mortis*, werklich und lieblich ineinander richtete.'" In a Tenor part book of Ott's anthology, with a Wittenberg provenance, now in Jena university library, there is a manuscript addition confirming Josquin, rather than Rupsch, as the composer of *Haec dicit dominus:* "Joskin nymphes Napees"; see Wolfram Steude, *Untersuchungen zur mitteldeutschen Musiküberlieferung und Musikpflege im 16. Jahrhundert* (Leipzig: Peters, 1978), 86.

214. WA TR No. 4316: "*Diende canabant: Sancta Trinitas, etiam sex vocum, sed duae erant adulterinae. Ubi dixit: Es hats ainer wollen besser machen et simplicitatem depravavit. Nam quatuor illae voces mirae sunt suavitatis et simplicitatis. Nam simplicia in omnibus artibus sunt iuncundiora*. . . . Darumb sol man einem iedem sein composition laßen un sol ym seine stim nit verderben."

215. See Othmar Wessely and Walter Kreyzig, "Bruck, Arnold von," New Grove 2, 4:457; Howard Mayer Brown and T. Herman Keahey, "Févin, Antoine de," New Grove 2, 8:753.

216. See Patrick Macey, "Josquin and Musical Rhetoric: *Miserere mei, Deus* and Other Motets," in *The Josquin Companion,* ed. Richard Sherr (Oxford: Oxford University Press, 2000), 485-530; and Willem Elders, "Symbolism in the Sacred Music of Josquin," in the same volume, 531-568.

217. "The three canonic voices are equally spaced apart at the interval of a fifth, the arithmetical rigidity producing a canon at the ninth, an unlikely canonic interval that can nevertheless be read in this context as another Trinitarian reference (9 = 3 × 3)"; Schlagel, "The *Liber selectarum cantionum,*" 577-578. On la Rue's extensive use of canon, see Honey Meconi, *Pierre de la Rue and the Musical Life at the Hapsburg-Burgundian Court* (New York: Oxford University Press, 2003), 101-104.

218. See Chapter 3 below.

219. See Diana Pulton and Tim Crawford, "Lute, § 8 (ii). Repertory: Germany, Bohemia and Austria." New Grove 2, 15:353-355; Arthur J. Ness and C. A. Kolczynski, "Sources of Lute Music, § 3: Central European Sources to *c.* 1650," New Grove 2, 24:44-48, esp. 45.

220. See WA 35:538-42.

221. From May 10 Luther was incapacitated by exhaustion for several days; see his letter to Melanchthon, dated May 12, 1530; WA BR 5:316.

222. Luther used the term *"in cloaca,"* "in the toilet," but almost certainly did not mean it to be taken literally. "In cloaca" was a term known to medieval monks who used it to convey the state of being under attack from the devil, the *cloaca* being the most vulnerable and degrading place for a human to be and therefore the natural habitat for the devil; see Heiko A. Oberman, *Luther: Man between God and the Devil,* trans. Eileen Walliser-Schwarzbart (New Haven: Yale University Press, 1989), 155.

223. WA BR 5:320-321: "*Verum mitto hic ad vos materiam exercitii vestri cantionem quandam. Cum enim qautriduo neque legere scribere mihi liceret, forte in cloaca inveni chartam, in qua vetus haec cantilena tribus vocibus erat composita, quam ego expurgavi, correxi et emendavi, adiecta voce quarta, et textum subito finxi, hoc scilicet consilio, quod vellem nostrum Capellanum M. Georgiam fallere, ut eam cantionem a vobis ad me missam tanquam noam Augustae pro Caesaris adventu Ferdinandi in cantaria editam acciperet. Spes est autem, eum falli posse, si vos aliquantulum mihi eam laudabitis, praesertim quod audieritus simplicitatem in ea multis probari, porro textum reliquum vos esse missuros. Si mihi placere senseritud, tum ego haec omnia illi mittam, et, si res successerit, ut istum Bavarium criticum et*

Momum musicae, qua non parum sibi placet." Translation partially based on Buszin, "Luther and Music," 96.

224. See WA 35:542-544.

225. See the discussion in Chapter 16 below.

226. WA 35:535-538; LW 53:337-341.

227. WA TR 968 (uncertain date): "Da man etliche feine, liebliche Moteten des Senfels sang, verwunderte sich D.M.L. und lobt sie sehr, und sprach: 'ein solche Motete vermöcht ich nicht zu machen, wenn ich mich auch zureißen sollte, wie er denn auch wiederum nicht einen Psalm predigen konnte als ich.'"

228. For the background, see Konrad Ameln, *The Roots of German Hymnody of the Reformation Era* (St. Louis: Concordia, 1964).

229. Zahn No. 4437; DKL Ea6.

230. Heinrich Glarean, *Dodecachoron* (Basle, 1547); See Atlas, *Renaissance Music,* 555-556.

231. *Monumenta monodica medii aevi,* ed. Stäblein, I: 217 [No. 503].

232. Zahn No. 1174; DKL Ea10.

233. Zahn No. 1945; DKL D1A.

234. Zahn No. 350; DKL Ee21. See also the discussion of these three melodies in Chapter 13 below.

235. See Walter Blankenburg, "Geschichte der Melodien des Evangelischen Kirchengesangbuchs: Ein Abriß," *Handbuch zum Evangelischen Kirchengesangbuch,* ed. Christhard Mahrenholz and Oskar Söhngen (Berlin: Evangelische Verlagsanstalt, 1954-1990), 2/2:59-63; see also Edward Foley, *Ritual Music: Studies in Liturgical Musicology* (Beltsville: The Pastoral Press, 1995), 95-96.

236. A skillful and substantial re-creation of part of the Sanctus chant for Sundays in Advent and Lent; see LU 61.

237. This was the melody that appeared in a Luther holograph of his Lord's Prayer hymn that was later crossed out; for a facsimile, see the insert in AWA 4; see also Example 7.1.

238. See Ursula Aaburg, "Zu den Lutherliedern im jonischen Oktavraum," JbLH 5 (1960): 125-131.

239. Wilhem Bäumker, *Das katholische deutsche Kirchenlied in seinen Singweisen von den frühesten Zeiten* (Freiburg: Herder, 1883-1911; repr. Hildesheim: Olms, 1962), 1:29-30.

240. Ameln, *Roots of German Hymnody,* 20. See also the detailed critique by Johannes Linke, "Die Melodie: 'Ein feste Burg ist unser Gott' und die Bäumker'sche Analyse," *Blätter für Hymnologie* [2] (1884): 82-88, 101-105.

241. See Appendix 4. See also the similar comment of David Chytraeus in his preface to Eler's *Cantica sacra* (Hamburg: Wolff, 1588; reprint, Hildesheim: Olms, 2002), sig. (:) 4ᵛ. Bäumker's citation of Chytraeus is abbreviated more than the single ellipsis suggests; see Bäumker, *Das katholische deutsche Kirchenlied,* 1:21.

242. WA TR No. 968 (uncertain date): "Die Noten machen den Text lebendig."

243. See the facsimile, Thomas Müntzer, *Deutsche Evangelische Messe 1524,* ed. Siegfried Bräuer (Berlin: Evangelische Verlagsanstalt, 1988).

244. LW 40:141; Against the Heavenly Prophets (1525); WA 18:123: "Ich wolt heute gerne eyne deutsche Messe haben, Ich gehe auch damit umbe, Aber ich wolt ja gerne, das sie eyne rechte deutsche art hette, Denn das man den lateinischen text verdolmetscht und lateinischen

don odder noten behellt, las ich geschehen, Aber es laut nicht ertig noch rechtschaffen. Es mus beyde text und notten, accent, weyse und geperde aus rechter mutter sprach und stymme komen, sonst ists alles eyn nachomen, wie die affen thun." For Müntzer's German version of *Veni redemptor gentium,* see Example 13.2 below.

245. "Das Lutherus, unter allen Meistersängern, steder der Apostel zeit her, der beste und kunstreichste gewesen. . . . Es fleusset und fellet ihme doch alles auffs lieblichste und artlichste, voller Geists und Lere. . . . Die Meinung klar und verstendlich, Die Melodien und Thon, lieblich und hertzlich, Und in Summa, alles herrlich und köstlich, das es safft und krafft hat, hertzet und tröstet, Und ist fürwar, seins gleichen nicht, viel weniger seins Meisters zu finden"; Philipp Wackernagel, *Bibliographie zur Geschichte des deutschen Kirchenliedes im XVI. Jahrhundert* (Frankfurt: 1855; repr. Hildesheim: Olms, 1961), 654; cited from the 1581 Erfurt edition. The work was originally published in four sections between 1569 and 1570, each with its own preface. For the 1581 edition Cyriacus Spangenberg edited these prefaces into one document. For a description of the content of *Cithera Lutheri* and its publication history that extended into the mid-nineteenth century, see Martin Rössler, *Bibliographie der Liedpredigt* (Nieuwkoop: de Graaf, 1976), 24-26. See also C. Spangenberg, *Von der Musica,* 137-138, and Wolfhart Spangenberg (Johann's grandson; Cyriacus' son) in his manuscript "Von der Musica": Wolfhart Spangenberg, *Sämtliche Werke,* ed. Andor Tarnai and András Vizkelety (Berlin: de Gruyter, 1971-), 1:91-94.

246. See, for example, Hans Albrecht's introduction (dated fall 1957) to his edition of *Symphoniae jucundae* (1538), in Georg Rhau, *Musikdrucke aus den Jahren 1538 bis 1545* (Kassel: Bärenreiter, 1955-), 3: xi-xiv, esp. xii.

247. See, for example, Clytus Gottwald, "Von der babylonischen Gefangenschaft der Musik: Josquin und Luthers Encomion," *Ursprung der Biblia deutsch von Martin Luther: Ausstellung in der Württembergische Landesbibliothek Stuttgart, 21. September bis 19. November 1983,* ed. Stefan Strohm and Eberhard Zwink (Stuttgart: Württembergische Landesbibliothek & Quell-Verlag, 1983), 101-08.

248. Paul Henry Lang, *Music in Western Civilization* (New York: Norton, 1941), 207. This is the citation that Buszin used to conclude his study: Buszin, "Luther on Music," 97.

249. WA TR No. 4192 (17 December 1538): "*Cantores quidam aderant canantes egregias mutetas. Quas cum Lutherus miraretur, dixit:* So unser Her Gott in diesem leben in das scheißhauß solche edle gaben gegeben hat, was wirdt in ihenem ewigen leben geschehen, *ubi omni erunt perfectissima et iucundissima?*" See also WA TR No. 968.

250. Johannes Bugenhagen, *Eine Christliche Predigt/uber der Leich und begrebnis/des Ehrwirdigen D. Martini Luthers . . .* (Wittenberg: Rhau, 1546), sig. Civ^r: "Und volgend hat er drey mal gesagt. Inn deine hende beuehl ich meinen Geist/Du hast mich erlöset/du trewer Gott."

251. *The Last Days of Luther,* trans. and ed. Martin Ebon (New York: Doubleday, 1970), 68-69.

252. LU 269-271.

253. *The Last Days of Luther,* 90-91.

Notes to Chapter 3

1. WA TR No. 968: "Die Musik ist . . . nahe der Theologie"; WA TR No. 3815: "*Musica est . . . theologiae proxima*" (see WLS No. 3090); WA TR No. 7034: "Ich gebe nach der Theologia der Musica den nähesten *Locum* und höchste Ehre" ("I place music next to theology and give it the highest praise"; WLS No. 3091); WA 50:370, Preface to Rhau's *Symphoniae iucundae* (1538): "*Experientia testis est, Musicam esse unam, quae post verbum Dei merito celebrat . . .*" ("experience confirms that next to the Word of God, music deserves the highest praise"; LW 53:323).

2. LW 49:427-28; WA BR 5:639: "*Et plane iudico nec pudet asserere, post theologiam esse nullam artem, quae musicae possit aequari, cum ipsa sola post theologiam id praestet, quod alioqui sola theologia praestat, scilicet quietem at animum laetum. . . . Hinc factum est, ut prophetae nulla sic arte sint usi ut musica, dum suam theologiam non in geometriam, non in arithmeticam, non in astronomiam, sed in musicam digesserunt, ut theologiam at musicam haberent coniunctissimas, veritatem psalmis et canticis dicentes.*" See also WA 50:371, Preface to Rhau's *Symphoniae iucundae* (1538): "*Unde non frustra Patres et Prophetae verbo Dei nihil voluerunt esse coniunctius quam Musicam*" ("the fathers and prophets wanted nothing else to be associated as closely with the Word of God as music"; LW 53:323).

3. Herbert M. Schueller, *The Idea of Music: An Introduction to Musical Aesthetics in Antiquity and the Middle Ages* (Kalamazoo: Medieval Institute Publications, 1988), 321.

4. On the *quadrivium* in education, see Chapter 2 above.

5. Piero Weiss and Richard Taruskin, eds., *Music in the Western World: A History in Documents* (New York: Schirmer, 1984), 39; Martin Gerbert, ed., *Scriptores ecclesiastici de musica sacra potissimum* (St. Blaise: Typis San-Blasianis, 1784; repr. Hildesheim: Olms, 1963), 1:193: "*Hae enim quatuor disciplinae non sunt humanae inventionis artes, sed divinorum operum aliquantae investigationes, et in creatura mundi intelligenda mirabilissimis rationibus ingenuas mentes ducunt, ita ut sint inexcusabiles, qui per haec cognoscentes Deum, et sempiternam eius Divinitatem, non sicut Deum glorificaverunt, et gratias egerunt.*"

6. See note 2 above.

7. Such authors were also influenced by Augustine; see Christopher Page, "Reading and Reminiscence: Tinctoris on the Beauty of Music," *Journal of the American Musicological Society* 49 (1996): 1-31, esp. 12-13. Luther was clearly aware of such treatises, for example: "About the praise and power of music . . . [has] been sufficiently treated by others"; for the citation, see note 22 below.

8. See Chapter 2 above.

9. The title of the extended treatise by Tinctoris of which only brief fragments are known; some were published in Naples between 1481 and 1483, and others are found in a manuscript of ca. 1490; see *Johannes Tinctoris (1445-1511) und sein unbekannter Traktat "De inventione et usu musicae,"* ed. Karl Weinmann (Regensburg: Pustet, 1917), and Ronald Woodley, "The Printing and Scope of Tinctoris's Fragmentary Treatise *De inventione et vsv mvsice,*" *Early Music History* 5 (1985): 239-268.

10. For the background, see James McKinnon, "Jubal vel Pythagoras, quis sit inventor musicae?" *Musical Quarterly* 64 (1978): 1-28.

11. McKinnon, "Jubal vel Pythagoras," 2.

12. See McKinnon, "Jubal vel Pythagoras," 2-6.

13. Cambridge University Library, CUL Gg. 5.35, fol. 432^r-443^v.

14. *The Cambridge Songs (Carmina cantabrigiensia)*, ed. & trans. Jan M. Ziolkowski (New York: Garland, 1994), 54-57:

> *Vite dator, omnifactor,*
> *deus, nature formator,*
> *mundi globum sub potenti*
> *claudens uolubilem palmo,*
> *in factura sua splendet*
> *magnificus per euum.*
> *Ipse multos ueritatem*
> *ueteres necdum sequentes*
> *uestigando per sophie*
> *deuia iusserat ire*
> *improbabilis, errore*
> *parare nobis uiam.*
> *Inter quos subtilis*
> *per acumen mentis*
> *claruit Pitagoras*
> *. . .*
> *Ergo uir hic prudens*
> *die quadam ferri*
> *fabricam pret[er]iens*
> *pondere non equo*
> *sonoque diuerso*
> *pullsare [ferrarios]*
> *malleolos senserat*
> *sicque tonorum quamlibet*
> *informem uim latere*
> *noscens, forma addita*
> *artem pulchram*
> *primus edidit.*

15. For example, see Luther's comment on Genesis 2:21; LW 1:126; WA 42:94-95.

16. LW 1:317; WA 42:233: "*Est eadem origo, significat enim adductum, productum.*"

17. LW 1:317; WA 42:233-234: "*Continent autem haec duo nomina votum de familia augenda. Nam posteritas Cain hoc spectavit, ut numero superaret. Ac sine dubio eam benedictionem opposuit verae Ecclesiae, tanquam evidens Argumentum, quod non abiecti essent quoque populus Dei.*" Luther's interpretation of the true church as the descendants of Abel and the false church as the descendants of Cain was influential on later Lutheran theology. For example, in Nicolaus Hunnius's critique of the Reformed Synod of Dort [Nicolaus Hunnius, *Diaskepsis theologica de fundamentali dissensu doctrinae Evangelicae-Lutheranae, et Calvinianae, seu reformatea* (Wittenberg: Helwig, 1626)] Calvinists are characterized as the "Cainitic fraternity"; see Nicolaus Hunnius, *Diaskepsis Theologica: A Theological Examination of the Fundamental Difference Between Evangelical Lutheran Doctrine and Calvinist or Reformed Teaching*, trans. Richard J. Dinda and Elmer Hohle (Malone, Texas: Repristination,

2001), 4. One of the points of contention between Lutherans and Calvinists was the question of choral and instrumental music in worship, Lutherans arguing for their use and Calvinists arguing against; for example, August Pfeiffer, *Anti-Calvinismus, Das ist/Kurtzer/deutlicher/ aufrichtiger und beschneider Bericht und Unterricht Von der Reformierten Religion* (Lübeck: Böckmann, 1699); see August Pfeiffer, *Anti-Calvinism*, trans. Edward Pfeiffer (Columbus: Joint Synod of Ohio, 1881), 404-405.

18. LW 1:317-318; WA 42:234: "*. . . qui ideo fingunt, posteritatem Cain ad alias artes exercendas coactam, quod terra ipsis maledicta esset: Parasse itaque victum alia ratione, alios factos pastores, alios fabros aerarios, alios Musicae dedisse operam, Ut ab Adae posteris frumentum et alia terra nata ad victum necessaria compararent. Sed si ita fame pressi esst Cainitae, cytharae et aliorum organorum musicorum in ista inopia obliti essent. Nam musicae non est locus apud famelicos et sitibundos. Quod autem Musicam invenerunt, quod aliis artibus excogitandis dederunt operam, argumento est abundasse eos omnibus, quae ad victum requiruntur. Ideo autem versos ad hanc curam nec contentos rudi victu fuisse sicut Adae posteros, quod volebant dominari, quod singularem laudem et gloriam captabant tanquam homines ingeniosi. Credo tamen, fuisse inter eos aliquot, qui transierunt ad verum Ecclesiam, et religionem Adae secuti sunt.*"

19. LW 1:138; WA 42:104: "*Si itaque Adam in innocentia perstitisset, nati liberi etiam essent facti coniuges. . . . Nonnunquam venissent ad patrem Adam, cecinissent hymnum, praedicassent Deum, postea rediisent ad sua.*"

20. See note 18 above.

21. Hermann Finck begins his discussion of "*De Musicae inventoribus*" with the statement: "*Inter caeteras praeclaras artes quae uere DEI dona sunt, non infimum locum tenet Musica . . .*" (Among all the other excellent arts that are indeed gifts of God, music is by no means the least . . .); Hermann Finck, *Practica Musica* (Wittenberg: [Haeredum] Rhau, 1556), Aj[r].

22. Some have argued that since it is only in the 1530s that music is given particular emphasis in Luther's writings, it was therefore a subject of peripheral concern to him. But, as the previous chapter has demonstrated, music had a lifelong interest for Luther. The intensity of musical references in the 1530s should rather be taken as evidence of the culmination of Luther's thinking about music over the years, and his readiness to express his own views, contrasting to his earlier practice of summarizing the conclusions of others. See, for example, his comment on the superscription of Psalm 4 in his *Operationes in psalmos* (1518-1521): "About the praise and power of music, which have been sufficiently treated by others, I am silent except for the remark that here it appears that of old the use of music was sacred and was adapted to divine matters"; WLS No. 3094; WA 5:98: "*De laude et virtute musicae sileo, quae ab aliis abunde tractantur, nisi quod hic apparet: Usum musicae fuisse olim sacrum et divinis rebus accommodatum.*"

23. LW 16:62. Lectures on Isaiah (on Isaiah 5:11) (1528); WA 31[II]: 43: "*Musica donum dei est.*"

24. LW 53:321-323; Preface to Rhau's *Symphoniae* (1538); WA 50:368, 372: "*Vellem certe ex animo laudatum . . . esse donum illud diuinum et excellentissimum Musicum. . . . Denique homini soli prae caeteris sermo voci copulatus donatus est, vt sciret, se Deum laudere oportere verbo et Musica, scilicet sonora praedicatione et mixtis verbis suaui melodiae.*"

25. WLS No. 3090; WA TR No. 3815 (1538): *"Musica est insigne donum Dei et theologiae proxima."*

26. WLS No. 3102; WA TR No. 4441 (1539): *"Musica optimum Dei donum";* "Musica ist eine schöne, liebliche Gabe Gottes."

27. WLS No. 3091; WA TR No. 7034 (uncertain year): "Musica ist ein Gabe und Geschencke Gottes, nicht ein Menschen-Geschenk."

28. LW 15:274. 2 Samuel 23:1. On the Last Words of David (1543); WA 54:33-34: "Musica, oder noten . . . ein wunderliche Creatur und gabe Gottes."

29. See, for example, Luther's comment on Psalm 8:1 (1537): "In David's time music was not as artistic as it is nowadays. An instrument like the lyre with ten strings was just about the highest and most glorious and most artistic they had, while ordinary instruments had three or four strings. Now music has grown enormously, and we have many instruments that are more artistic; but in David's time there were only lyres, harps, violins, pipes, cymbals, and so forth." LW 12:98; WA 45:206: "Zu Davids zeiten ist die Musica nicht so Künstreich gewesen. Die andern gemeinen Instrumenten haben drey oder vier Seiten gehabt. Jtzt aber ist die Musica uber die mas gestiegen, Wir haben mancherley und viel Kunstreicher Instrumenta, da zu Davids zeiten nur Psalter, Harffen, Geigen, Pfeiffen, Cymbeln, etc. gewesen sind."

30. Around 1480 Tinctoris incorporated the document into *De inventione et usu musice,* his extended philosophical and theological exposition of the origins and development of music; see note 9 above.

31. Edmond de Coussemaker, ed., *Scriptorum de musica medii aevi nova series a Gerbertina altera* (Paris: Durand, 1864-76; reprint ed., Hildesheim: Olms, 1963), 4:195-200: *"Effectus primus est iste: Musica Deum delectat . . . Sequitur secundus effectus: Musica laudes Dei decorat . . . Tertius effectus est: Musica gaudia beatorum amplificat . . . Quartus effectus est: Musica ecclesiam militantem triumphanti assimilat . . . Quintus effectus est: Musica ad susceptionem benedictionis domini preparat . . . Sextus effectus est: Musica animos ad pietatem excitat. . . . Septimus effectus est: Musica tristitiam depellit. . . . Octavus effectus est: Musica duriciam cordis resolvit. . . . Nonus effectus est: Musica diabolum fugat. . . . Decimus effectus est: Musica extasim causam. . . . Undecimus effectus est: Musica terrenam mentem elevat. . . . Duodecimus effectus est: Musica voluntatem malam revocat. . . . Tertiusdecimus effectus est: Musica homines letificat . . . Quartus decimus effectus est: Musica egrotos sanat. . . . Quintus decimus effectus est: Musica labores temperat . . . Sextus decimus effectus: Musica animos ad praelia incitat. . . . Septimus decimus effectus: Musica amorem allicit. . . . Octavus decimus effectus: Musica jocunditatem convivii augmentat. . . . Nonus decimus effectus est: Musica peritos in ea glorificat. . . . Vicesimus effectus musice: Musica animas beatificat."* Tinctorus later expanded these 20 propositions to 27 in his *De inventione et vsv mvsice;* see Woodley, "The Printing and Scope of Tinctoris's Fragmentary Treatise," 263-266.

32. See Walter Dress, "Gerson und Luther," *Zeitschrift für Kirchengeschichte* 52 (1933): 122-161; see also Steven E. Ozment, *Homo Spiritualis: A Comparative Study of the Anthropology of Johannes Tauler, Jean Gerson and Martin Luther (1509-16) in the Context of Their Theological Thought* (Leiden: Brill, 1969).

33. See, for example, WA TR Nos. 312, 1288, 1346 and 5532; LW 54:42, 132, 141 and 443 respectively.

34. See Joyce L. Irwin, "The Mystical Music of Jean Gerson," *Early Music History* 1 (1981): 187-201.

35. See Appendix 2, where Gerson's poem is given in English (translated by Leofranc Holford-Strevens) and Latin, in which the lines cited by Adam von Fulda are indicated.

36. For Adam von Fulda in Wittenberg, see Chapter 2.

37. See Appendix 2 below.

38. Johannes Walter, *Lob und Preis der löblichen Kunst Musica 1538*, facsimile, introduced by Wilibald Gurlitt (Kassel: Bärenreiter, 1938). There was also another imprint which includes a prose foreword by Walter, presumably issued either in 1538 or soon after; see Walter Blankenburg, *Johann Walter, Leben und Werk*, ed. Friedhelm Brusniak (Tutzing: Schneider, 1991), 67-68 and 426-428 (facsimile of preface).

39. LW 53:319.

40. See Markus Jenny, *Luther, Zwingli, Calvin in ihren Liedern* (Zurich: Theologischer Verlag, 1983), 159. The complete publishing history of Wittenberg hymnals, is imperfectly known, for example, the 1529 Klug hymnal is no longer extant, and only the last signature of a word-only edition issued by Hans Lufft in 1538 survives; see WA 35:400-407.

41. See WA 48:293-297. Dietrich was born in Nuremberg and became the pastor of St. Sebald's in the city in 1535.

42. See WA 35:383. The part-books included four-part settings of three of Luther's chorales — *Komm Heiliger Geist, Herre Gott, Gott der Vater wohn uns bei*, and *Mitten wir im Leben sind* — composed by Bruck.

43. The photographic reproductions appear as an unnumbered and unpaginated appendix in WA 48.

44. Specific details are given in the following notes.

45. In the Ms. the heading is simply "Musica."

46. In the Ms. Luther first wrote "Und," which is struck through and replaced by "Auch" in the margin.

47. In the Ms. "Guts" is crossed out and replaced by "viel" above the line.

48. In the Ms. Luther first wrote: "Durchs harffen er den geist empfand," which is struck through and then "Da er den geist durchs harffen fand" was written underneath.

49. "Der" is omitted in Luther's Ms., thus leaving the line one syllable short.

50. In the Ms. Luther originally wrote "Guts gesengs das da lautet wol," at different times he then deleted "Guts" and replaced it with "Viel" in the margin, then deleted "s" at the end of "gesengs" and crossed out "das." But his revision was left incomplete since he did not add the required "gut" to the line.

51. When Luther wrote this line in the Ms. he omitted "ein" which he then had to insert in its place above the line.

52. WA 35:483-484.

53. Some of the lines of this translation are taken from that found in LW 53:319-320 (by Paul Nettl, revised by Ulrich S. Leupold), but it is essentially a new translation of my own; the primary concern has been accuracy of meaning rather than a rendering of polished poetry.

54. Cited by James McKinnon, *Music in Early Christian Literature* (New York: Cambridge University Press, 1987), 23 (No. 33) and 166 (No. 386) respectively.

55. See Chapter 2, note 119. Luther often makes reference to birds and their singing; see,

for example, his extended comment on Matthew 6:26-27 (Commentary on the Sermon on the Mount, 1532): "Behold the birds of the air . . ."; LW 21:196-198; WA 32:461-463.

56. Hans Sachs, *Die Wittenbergisch Nachtigall die mann yetzt höret uberal* [Nuremberg, 1523], with several contemporary reprints; Adelbert Keller and Edmund Goetze, *Hans Sachs* (Tübingen: Literarischen Verein, 1870-1908; repr. Hildesheim: Olms, 1964), 6:368-386. For an English translation of the complete poem, see Hans Sachs, *The Wittenberg Nightingale*, trans. C. W. Schaeffer (Allentown: Brobst & Diehl, 1883); for a discussion of the content, see Kyle C. Sessions, "Luther in Music and Verse," in *Pietas et Societas: New Trends in Reformation Social History: Essays in Memory of Harold J. Grimm*, ed. Kyle C. Sessions and Phillip N. Bebb (Kirksville: Sixteenth Century Journal, 1985), 123-139, esp. 127-129.

57. "Vorrede auff alle güte Gesangbücher. Fraw Musica," *Geistliche Lieder zu Wittemberg* (Wittenberg: Klug, 1543; the colophon gives the year as 1544), fol. 191^{r-v}.

58. "Fraw Musica," *Newe Deudsche Geistliche Gesenge [Tenor]* (Wittenberg: Rhau, 1544; facsimile, Kassel: Bärenreiter, 1969), fol. Aiij $^{r-v}$.

59. See the discussion in Chapter 1 above.

60. See Appendix 3 below, where the two versions are given in parallel in German and Latin as well as in English translation.

61. Luther is probably alluding to John 3:8: "The wind blows where it chooses, and you hear the sound of it, but you do not know where it comes from or where it goes. So it is with everyone who is born of the Spirit" (NRSV).

62. Poems in praise of music were not new in the sixteenth century; see Karl Honemeyer, *Luther's Musikanschauung: Studien zur Fragen ihrer geschichtlichen Grundlagen* (Ph.D. diss., University of Münster, 1941), 41-43. But Luther's distinctive emphases reappear in the poetry of those with close connections with Wittenberg, as is discussed in the following paragraphs.

63. See Wilibald Gurlitt, "Johannes Walter und die Musik der Reformationszeit," L-J 15 (1933): 95-98.

64. Both poems are given in *Johann Walter Sämtliche Werke*, ed. Otto Schröder et al. (Kassel: Bärenreiter, 1953-1973), 6:153-161; for a facsimile of the 1538 poem, see note 38 above. There are connections between some of the lines of Walter's 1538 poem and some in Voigt's poem, which have similar expressions and rhymes, but opinions differ concerning which was dependent on the other; see Blankenburg, *Johann Walter*, ed. Brusniak, 356-361. All of the 56 stanzas of Walter's 1564 poem are acrostics on either "musica" or its retrograde "acisum," and thus may have been influenced by the Latin poems written for the Wittenberg celebration of music, published in 1551; see note 71 below.

65. Agricola, *Musica instrumentalis deudsch* (1529), fol. xxx^r.

66. Agricola, *Musica instrumentalis deudsch* (1545), sigs. Aij^r, Av^r, Avij^v & Lvj^r.

67. Agricola, *Musica instrumentalis deudsch* (1545), sigs. Av^r, Avij^v, Bij^r & Lv^v.

68. *Newe Deudsche Geistliche Gesenge [Tenor]* (Wittenberg: Rhau, 1544; facsimile, Kassel: Bärenreiter, 1969), sig. Aiij^r; Agricola, *Musica instrumentalis deudsch* (1545), sig. Aj^v; it also appears, under the heading "Musica," as the frontispiece of Herman Finck's *Practica musica* (Wittenberg: Haeredum Rhau, 1556), §iv^v.

69. See Gurlitt, "Johannes Walter," 94-95, 108-109; Max Joseph Husung, "Die neuen Musen des Zeichners und Formschneiders Jakob Lucius von 1579," *Gutenberg-Jahrbuch* (1941): 163-173.

70. The poem was included at the beginning of Cyriacus Spangenberg's 1598 manuscript; see Cyriacus Spangenberg, *Von der Music und den Meistersängern*, ed. Adelbert von Keller (Stuttgart: Literarischen Verein, 1861; reprint, Hildesheim: Olms, 1966), 2.

71. Johann Holtheuser, *Encomium musicae, artis antiquiae: et divinae carmine elegiaco scriptum* (Erfurt: Dolgen, 1551), fol. Cij^v-Diij^r, under the heading: *"Epigrammata in laudem Musicae a varijs scripta Wittebergae. Anno 1551."* One poem is in Greek; the remainder is in Latin. All thirteen people associated with this 1551 publication were Wittenberg alumni, and five attended the university when Luther was still alive. The principal participants were four students who had matriculated in the previous two years, 1549-1550 (Johann Holtheuser, Heinrich Nortmeri [Nortmeyer?], Johann Fabri, and Michael Hofmann), and six who had matriculated a few years earlier, between 1543 and 1546 (Abraham Udalric [Ulrich?], Leonhard Venator, Paul Dölsch, Widkind Witkop, Andreae Stroph and his brother Johannis). Of the three remaining, two matriculated a month apart, Heinrich Faber (May 1542) and Johann Reusch (April 1542); and Georgius Fabricius, who matriculated in March 1536. There are further interconnections between these three: Reusch had studied music with Faber in Naumberg before matriculating in Wittenberg; in 1551 Reusch was rector of the Stadtschule, Meissen, and Fabricius the rector of the Landschule of St. Afra, in the same city; see the respective entries in the first volume of *Album academiae Vitebergensis 1502-1602*, ed. Karl Eduard Förstemann, Otto Hartwig, and Karl Gerhard (Leipzig & Halle, 1841-1905; reprint Tübingen: Niemeyer, 1976), and the entries on Faber, Fabricius, and Reusch in New Grove 2. Holtheuser later authored a small treatise on music: *Ein kleine deutsche Musica, für die Schulerlein auff dem Lande, daz sie die Psalmen und andere geistliche Lieder auß ihrem Gesangbuch künstlich können lernen singen* (Nuremberg: Knorr, 1586); see John Butt, *Music Education and the Art of Performance in the German Baroque* (Cambridge: Cambridge University Press, 1994), 8 and 95.

Many of the poems in Holtheuser's 1551 publication are acrostics on "Musica" and the respective names of the authors. Here they appear to follow the example of Martin Agricola, who included an acrostic on "Musica" in the first edition of *Musica instrumentalis deudsch* (1529, fol. xxx^r), and another, with an acrostic on his name, in the revised edition (1545, fol. Av^v). Similarly, these 1551 acrostic poems may have influenced Johann Walter's 1564 poem; see note 64 above.

72. Holtheuser, *Encomium musicae*, fol. Ciij^r; for Tinctoris, see note 30 above. Other examples include the poem by "Griselius, a scholar of Wittenberg" [possibly Leonhard Gresselius of Breslau, who matriculated in May 1554; see Förstemann et al., *Album academiae Vitebergensis 1502-1602*, 1:292] in Coclico's *Compendium Musices*, which speaks of music as the *"Dei donum tam grande, piumque"* [the great and pious gift of God]; Adrian Coclico, *Compendium Musices* (Nuremberg: Montani & Neuber, 1552; facsimile, Kassel: Bärenreiter, 1954), sig. A3^r; Adrian Petit Coclico, *Musical Compendium*, trans. Albert Seay (Colorado Springs: Colorado College Music Press, 1973), 2. Griselius's poem begins:

Mvsica diuinas laudes celebrare reperta est,
Vtque suis numeris seruiat ipsa Deo.
Non est scurriles inuentum munus ad usus,
Qui dedit hanc, fructu commodiore dedit.
Carmine, uoce, sono, Deus est laudandus et hymnis,

Huic famulas praebet Musica prompta manus.
Illa suis numeris longe super aethera tollit
Quos uirtus claros conspicuosque facit. . . .

Music has been invented to celebrate divine praises,
So that through its numbers it may serve God.
Its gift has not been made for vile uses;
He who gave this gave it for more pleasant fruit.
In song, in voice, in sound and in hymns God must be praised.
For this Music supplies her handmaiden with a ready hand.
She raises by its numbers far above the heavens
Those whom virtue makes noble and famous. . . .

Lucas Lossius begins and ends his treatise on music theory with poems *"In laudem Musices."* The first includes a line that is almost identical with the opening line of Griselius's poem, issued eleven years earlier by the same Nuremberg publishers: *"Musica diuinas laudes cantare reperta est"* — *"cantare"* replacing *"celebrare"* [Music has been invented to sing divine praises]; Lucas Lossius, *Erotemata Musicae practicae* (Nuremberg: Montani & Neuber, 1563; facsimile, Bologna: Forni, 1980), A1ᵛ.

73. Holtheuser, *Encomium musicae,* fol. Aiijʳ and Ciiᵛ. It is possible that such musical celebrations had begun a decade or more earlier. For example, Luther and his colleagues may have taken part in a Musikfest in Torgau on either 5 or 6 April 1538, the Friday and Saturday before Judica (Lent 5). Luther was in Torgau on his way back to Wittenberg, where, in Wolff Reißenbusch's house, he heard the Kantorei sing, almost certainly under the direction of Johann Walter; see WA TR Nos. 3803 and 3815. The likelihood is that the Kantorei sang some of the pieces from *Selectae Harmoniae Quatuor Vocum De Passione Domine* — particularly appropriate a week or so before Holy Week — and *Symphoniae iuncundae atque adea breves quattuor vocum,* which were then being prepared for publication (July 1538); see WA 48:294. In which case it is possible that Luther's "Frau Musica" and Walter's *Lob und Preis der löblichen Kunst Musica,* published together by Rhau that year, were also recited on this occasion.

74. The title page of Holtheuser's pamphlet states that the poem was *"recitatum in celeberrima Academia wittebergensi, in praelectione musicae Henrici Fabri"* [recited at a celebration at Wittenberg University, after a lecture on music by Heinrich Faber].

75. Although Figulus's composition was not published until two years later, 1553, since there were two headmasters at the 1551 Wittenberg musical celebration who came from Meissen, where Figulus had recently become Cantor, it is possible that the then unpublished work might have been performed at this Wittenberg celebration.

76. Holtheuser, *Encomium musicae,* fol. Aiᵛ.

77. *"Musica immortales fecit";* Holtheuser, *Encomium musicae,* fol. Ciiʳ. These names occur in the margin; a few more appear within the text of the poem. Many of these composers are represented in Rhau's 1544 anthology, *Neue Deudsch Geistliche Gesenge.* Compare the expanded list in Herman Finck, *Practica musica,* sig. Aijʳ⁻ᵛ.

78. Holtheuser, *Encomium musicae,* fol. Aivᵛ.

79. Holtheuser, *Encomium musicae,* fol. Aivᵛ.

80. Holtheuser, *Encomium musicae,* fol. Biᵛ.

81. WA TR No. 3815 (1538).

82. Holtheuser, *Encomium musicae*, fol. Bii^v.

83. WA 50:371. Preface to Rhau's *Symphoniae* (1538); see Appendix 3.

84. Holtheuser, *Encomium musicae*, fol. Bii^v.

85. WA 50:371. Preface to Rhau's *Symphoniae* (1538); see Appendix 3 below. This also echoes Tinctoris's ninth proposition, *"Musica diabolum fugat"* (see note 31 above).

86. See Robin A. Leaver, *Luther on Justification* (St. Louis: Concordia, 1975), 9.

87. "If God gives me grace, I shall have more to say about it in the tract 'On Justification,'" LW 35:198; WA 30^{II}: 643: "Weiter wil ich (so Gott gnade gibt) davon reden ym buchlin de iustificatione." See WA 30^{II}: 657-676.

88. It is interesting to note that the evidence for Luther's intention to write a treatise on justification and another on music dates from year 1530. It therefore seems likely that both these ideas germinated during the six months he was in Coburg Castle, during the Diet of Augsburg. Being removed from his day-to-day pressures in Wittenberg gave him the opportunity to think and write (see Martin Brecht, *Martin Luther* [1]: *His Road to Reformation, 1483-1521*, trans. James L. Schaaf [Minneapolis: Fortress, 1985], 379-384). In his correspondence between Coburg and Augsburg there was much preoccupation with the doctrine of justification — Luther was concerned that Melanchthon would concede too much. But he also wrote letters to Senfl and Johann Agricola in which music was the primary topic, including references to chant melodies that were important to him, as was the song of the birds; see Chapter 2 above.

89. WA 30^{II}: 696:

Περὶ τῆς μουσικῆς

μουσικῆς ἐράω

Eciam damnantes non placent Schwermerii

Quia

1. *Dei donum non hominum est*
2. *Quia facit letos animos*
3. *Quia fugat diabolum*
4. *Quia innocens gaudium facit*

$$\textit{Interim pereunt} \;\; \Big\langle \; \begin{array}{l} \textit{irae} \\ \textit{libidines} \\ \textit{Superbia} \end{array}$$

Proximum locum do Musicae post Theologiam. Hoc patet ex examplo David et omnium prophetarum, qui omnia sua metris at cantibus mandaverunt.

5. *Quia pacis tempore regnat.*

Durate ergo et erit melius arti huic post nos, Quia pacis sunt. Duces Bavariae laudo in hoc, quia Musicam colunt. Apud nos Saxones arma et Bombardae praedicantur.

For a German version, see WA TR No. 7034 (= WA 30^{II}: 695), translated in Buszin, "Luther and Music," 88.

90. See also WA TR No. 6248 (uncertain date): "*Musicam semper amavi*"; "Music I have always loved," WLS No. 3092.

91. See the discussion in Chapter 2 dealing with the similar shift in emphasis in the teaching of music among the teachers and alumni of Wittenberg University.

92. LW 35:370, Preface to Romans, 1522, WA DB 7: "O es ist eyn lebendig, schefftig, thettig, mechtig ding umb den glawben. . . . Glawb ist eyn lebendige erwegene zuuersicht auff Gottes gnade, so gewis, das er tausent mal druber sturbe."

93. LW 10:344; *Dictata super Psalterium* (1513-1516); WA 3:405: "*Cantare autem est ore tantum laudare, iubilare corde &c.*"

94. LW 10:208; WA 3:253: "*Ubicunque 'Canticum' in titulis habetur, semper debet intelligi, talem psalmum esse gaudii et tripudii et cum affectu exultandi cantandum. Nam Canticum et cantus ex abundantia gaudentis cordis oritur. Est autem Canticum spirituale seu melodia spiritualis ipse iubilus cordis.*"

95. LW 10:92; WA 3:89: "*Aliqui confitentur in labiis tantum. Hii sunt, qui aliud in corde, aliud in ore loquuntur, ut qui peccator est in proposito malo, psallens nihilominus deo.*"

96. LW 11:294; WA 4:139: "*Nota, quod cantare et dicere differunt, quod psallere vel psalmum dicere et tantummodo intellectu agnoscere et docere. Sed vocem addendo fit cantus, que vox est affectus. Sicut ergo verbum est intellectus, sic vox ipsius affectus.*"

97. LW 15:273. Treatise on the Last Words of David (1543). WA 54:33: "Denn der glaub ruget und feiret nicht, Er feret heraus, redet und prediget von solcher verheissung und gnade Gottes, das ander Leute auch dazu komen, und der telhafftig werden, Ja fur grosser freude fehet er an, tichtet schöne susse Psalmen, singet liebliche lustige Lieder, damit zu gleich Gotte frölich zu loben und zu dancken, Und auch die menschen nützlich zu reitzen und zu lernen."

98. LW 53:333. WA 35:477: "Denn Gott hat unser hertz und mut frölich gemacht, durch seinen lieben Son, welchen er für uns gegeben hat zur erlösung von sunden, tod und Teuffel. Wer solchs mit ernst gleubet, der kans nicht lassen, er mus frölich und mit lust davon singen und sagen, das es andere auch hören und herzu komen. Wer aber nicht davon singen und sagen wil, das ist ein zeichen, das ers nicht gleubet und nicht ins new fröliche Testament, Sondern unter das alte, faule, unlustige Testament gehöret."

99. See Chapter 2 above.

100. See the discussion in Chapter 1 above.

101. LW 53:316. WA 35:474-475: "Und sind dazu auch ynn vier stymme bracht, nicht aus anderer ursach, denn das ich gerne wollte, die iugent, die doch sonst soll und mus ynn der Musica und andern rechten künsten ersogen werden, ettwas hette, damit sie der bul lieder und fleyschlichen gesenge los werde und an derselben stat ettwas heylsames lernete, und also das guete mit lust, wie den iungen gepürt, eyngienge. Auch das ich nicht der meynung byn, das durchs Evangelion sollten alle künste zu boden geschlagen werden und vergehen, wie etliche abergeystlichen fur geben."

102. Preface to *Symphoniae iuncundae* 1538, WA 50:373; see Appendix 3 below.

103. Oskar Söhngen, *Theologie der Musik* (Kassel: Stauda, 1967), 84-85.

104. WA 50:371; see Appendix 3 below. Hermann Finck, who matriculated at Wittenberg University in 1545, reported some ten years after Luther's death: "*Inter caeteras praeclaras artes quae uere DEI dona sunt, non infimum locum tenet Musica. . . . Et reuerendus pater dominus Martinus Lutherus piae memoriae saepe dicere solitus est, multa semina bonarum virtutum inesse animis ijs, qui Musica afficerentur*" (Among all the other excellent

arts that are indeed gifts of God, music is by no means the least . . . the reverend father Herr Martin Luther, of pious memory, often used to say that many seeds of the finest virtues are sown in souls affected by music); Finck, *Practica Musica*, Aj^{r-v}.

105. LW 10:43. *Dictata super psalterium* (1513-1516); WA 3:40: *"Habet enim natura Musicae, excitare tristem, pilgrum et stupidum animum. Sic Helizeus vocavit psalten, ut excitaretur ad prophetiam. Quare Mnazeah est proprie incitabulum, invitatorium, provocatorium ac velut calcar spiritus, stimulus et hortatorium. . . . Quia in his omnibus acuitur et accenditur animus ignavus, ut vigil et strenuus eat ad opus. Quod si ista simul cantentur in Musica artificiali, vehementius et acrius accendunt animum. Et hoc modo hic David fecit hunc psalmum la mnazeah, i.e. pro invitatorio, excitatorio et inflammatorio, ut scilicet haberet, quo seipsum excitaret ad devotionem et affectionem cordis, et ut acrius hoc fieret, fecit in musicalibus. Sic olim Ecclesia solebat psalmos ante missam legere, scilicet pro incitatorio, cuius adhuc versus restant de introitu. Et adhuc in matutinis habet invitatorium psalmum, scilicet 'venite exaltemus,' quo sese mutuo invitant ad laudem dei. Et recte vocatur psalmus sic invitatorium, quia non solum se, sed etiam alios invitavit ad laudem Dei. Sicut Sanctus Ambrosius fecit cum cantu, quo Mediolanensium tristitiam depulit, ut levius ferrent tedium temporis. Sed et non vane potest invitatorium dici eo quod isto modo etiam spiritus sanctus invitetur. Quia cum nos sumus provocati, mox etiam deus excitatur. Ex istis igitur discimus, quod qui vult seipsum ad devotionem excitare, apprehendat psalmos."*

106. LW 14:83, *Das schöne Confitemini, an der Zahl der 118. Psalm* (1530); WA 30^{1}: "Denn ein gut liedlin mag man wol zwey mal singen, So ists auch aller menschen weise, wenn sie von hertzen frolich odder lustig sind, das sie ein wort, zwey, drey mal wider holen und konnen nicht gnug das selbige sagen, Was yhn begegenet, mus es horen. Also laut es hie auch, das die lieben heiligen so hertzlich fro und lustig sind uber den grossen wunder werckenm so Gott an yhn thut, das er sie von sunden und tod (das ist von allem ubel, beide leibs und seelen) erloset, das sie für freüden yhr lied ymer widder forne anfahen." "We often sing a good song over again from the beginning, especially one we have sung with pleasure and joy" (on Psalm 118:29); LW 14:105; WA 30^{1}: "So pflegt man die guten lieder, wenn sie aus sind, widder forn an zu heben, sonderlich wo sie mit lust und liebe gesungen sind."

107. LW 49:428; WA BR 5:639: *". . . quae musicae possit aequari, cum ipsa sola post theologiam id praestet, quod alioqui sola theologia praestat, scilicet quietem et animum laetum."*

108. Organist in Halle, see Chapter 2 above.

109. In medieval literature "symphonia" was used to designate a number of different instruments, usually those that produced more than one sound simultaneously, such as the bagpipe and hurdy-gurdy. Praetorius employs "symphonia" for all string keyboard instruments, which, given the context, seems to be Luther's meaning here; see Michael Praetorius, *Syntagma musicum II; De Organographia* (Wolfenbüttel: Holwein, 1619; facsimile, Kassel: Bärenreiter, 1958), 62.

110. WLS No. 3100 (slightly altered). Dedication in a Bible presented to Wolff Heinz, 1541. WA 48:85-86: "Solch new Lied sollen auch des folgenden psalms Seitenspiel helffen singen. Und Wolff Heinz auch beide mit seiner Orgeln, Symphonien, Virginal, Regal, und was der lieden Musica mehr ist, Davon (als seer newer kunst und Gottes gaben) weder David noch Salomon, noch Persia, Grecia noch Roma ichts gewust, sein singen und spielen mit freuden gehen lassen, zu lob den Vater all gnaden."

111. A composition by Senfl is meant.

112. *Hrn. M. Joh. Mathesii . . . Lebens-Beschreibung/so da Seine Geburth/Aufferziehung/ Studia, Beförderung/Tugenden/Ehestand/Priesterlich-Exemplarisches Ende/und was sonst zu seinem Lebens-Wandel gehöret,* ed. Johann Balthasar Mathesius (Dresden: Zimmermann, 1705), 32-33; cited by Wolfram Steude, *Untersuchungen zur mitteldeutschen Musiküberlieferung und Musikpflege im 16. Jahrhundert* (Leipzig: Peters, 1978), 90: ". . . eine ehrliche Musica und Cantorey, darinnen man von ehrlichen Leuten singet und klinget, Gott preiset, gute Psalmen singet, wie David in die Harffen, einen guten Schweitzersichen Choral oder Josquinschen Psalm, fein leise und gelinde, sammt den Text, auch in die Instrumenta singet."

113. *The "Musica instrumentalis deudsche" of Martin Agricola: A Treatise on Musical Instruments, 1529 and 1545,* trans. & ed. William E. Hettrick (Cambridge: Cambridge University Press, 1994), 71; Agricola, *Musica instrumentalis deudsch* (1545), sig. Biij^r:

Ich habe wunder vernomen
Wenn sie gen Wittemberg kommen
Und sonst zur Universitet
Wie es jhn bey der Burse geht/
Welche/wenn sie zu Tische gan
Odder widder dar von auffstan/
Sich üben frölich im singen
Auch auff Instrumenten klingen
Als Lauten/Geigen/und Pfeiffen
Odder die Harffen angreiffen
Und ander Instrumenta zwar. . . .

114. John Calvin, *Commentary on Psalms,* trans. James Anderson (Edinburgh: Calvin Translation Society, 1845-1849; repr. Grand Rapids: Eerdmans, 1949), 3:494-495; Johannes Calvin, *In librum psalmorum commentarius,* ed. August Tholuck (Berlin: Eichler, 1836), 2:153: "*Levitas, quibus iniunctum erat canendi munus, proprie compellat, ut musica etiam instrumenta adhibeant: non quia per se hoc necessarium foret, sed quia utile erat rudimentum veteri populo . . . quia quum exhibito Christo. . . . Evangelii lucem suffocant qui adhuc Ecclesiam involvunt veteribus umbris.*" For further representative examples, see Calvin's comments on Psalm 71:22, Psalm 81:3, Psalm 149:1; *Commentary on the Psalms* 3:98, 3:312, 5:312 respectively = *In librum psalmorum* 1:529-530, 2:76 & 522.

115. LW 16:62; Lectures on Isaiah (1528); WA 31^{II}: 43: "*Helizeus: 'adduc,' inquit, 'mihi psalten' etc. Amos 6. Sicut David putaverunt se etc. Certe si usus fueris musica ut David, non peccabis.*"

116. *Luther: Letters of Spiritual Counsel,* trans. & ed. Theodore G. Tappert (Philadelphia: Westminster, 1965), 94; WA BR 7:78: ". . . wie Elisäus sich ließ durch seinen Psalter erwecken, 2 Kön. 3, und David im Psalter selbs sagt Ps. 57, seine Harfe sei seine Ehre und Freude: *Exurge, gloria mea, exurge, Psalterium et Cithera,* und aller Heiligen machen sich fröhlich mit Psalmen und Saitenspielen."

117. WLS 3:983, n. 8; WA TR No. 194 (1532): "*Satan est Spiritus tristitiae. Ideo non potest ferre laetitiam, ideo longissime abest musica.*" See also WA TR Nos. 968, 2387 and 2545.

118. LW 49:427-428; WA BR 5:639: "*Scimus enim musicen daemonibus etiam invisam et intolerabilem esse. Et plane iudico, nec pudet asserere, post theologiam esse nullam artem, quae musicae possit aequari, cum ipsa sola post theologiam id praestet, quod alioqui sola theologia*

praestat, scilicet quietem et animum laetum, manifesto argumento, quod diabolus, curarum tristium et turbarum inquietarum autor, ad vocem musicae paene similiter fugit ad verbum theologiae." Luther is here speaking from personal experience; see, for example, Ratzeberger's account of Luther being revived by music after a period of spiritual exhaustion, and Luther's letter to Matthias Weller; Chapter 2, notes 162 and 165.

119. Preface to *Symphoniae iuncundae* 1538; see Appendix 3. "So you too must turn to your regal or gather some good companions about you and sing with them until you learn how to defy the devil." Letter to Matthias Weller (7 October 1534). *Luther: Letters of Spiritual Counsel,* trans. and ed. Theodore G. Tappert (Philadelphia: Westminster, 1955), 97. WA BR 7:106: "also greift Ihr auch ins Regal, oder nehmet gute Gesellen und singet dafur, bis Ihr lernet ihn spotten."

120. LW 15:274; WA 54:34: "Denn dem bösen geist ist nicht wol dabey, wo man Gottes wort im rechten glauben singet oder predigt. Er ist ein geist der traurigkeit, und kan nicht bleiben, wo ein hertz Geistlich (das ist, in Gott und seinem wort)."

121. LW 49:428; WA BR 5:639: "*Manifesto argumento, quod diabolus, curarum tristium et turbarum inquietarum autor, ad vocem musicae paene similiter fugit ad verbum theologiae. Hinc factum est, ut prophetae nulla sic arte sint usi ut musica, dum suam theologiam non in geometriam, non in arithmeticam, non in astronomiam, sed in musicam digesserunt, ut theologiam et musicam haberent coniunctissimas, veritatem psalmis et canticis dicentes.*"

122. Preface to *Symphoniae iuncundae* (1538), see Appendix 3.

123. WLS No. 3094. *Operationes in psalmos* (1518-1521). WA 5:98 — on the superscription of Psalm 4.

124. LW 15:273. Treatise on the Last Words of David (1543). WA 54:33: "Und da solch tichten den Psalmen David anfieng, und in schwanck bracht, wurden dadurch viel andere erleucht und zu Propheten erweckt, die auch da zu hlffen, und schöne Psalmen machten, als die kinder Korah, Heman, Assaph etc."

125. LW 53:315-316. Preface to Walter's *Chorgesangbuch* (1524). WA 35:474: "Das geystliche lieder singen gut und Gott angeneme sey, acht ich, sey keynem Christen verborgen, die wehl yderman nicht alleyn das Exempel der propheten und könige ym allten testament (die mit singen und klingen, mit tichten und allerley seytten spiel Gott gelobt haben) sondern auch solcher brauch, sonderlich mit psalmen gemeyner Christenheyt von anfang kund ist. Ja auch S. Paulus solchs 1. Cor. 14 eynfetzt und zu den Collossern gepeut, von hertzen dem Herrn singen geystliche lieder und Psalmen, Auff das da durch Gottes wort und Christliche leere auff allerley weyse getrieben und geübt werden."

126. See Chapter 2. On the Saxon fiscal policy that denied financial support to music foundations and the large amounts spent on other concerns, see WA TR Nos. 968, 2545a and 2545b.

127. LW 49:427; WA BR 5:639: "*Quamvis nomen meum sit invisum, adeo ut vereri cogar, ne satis tuto recipiantur a te et legantur, optime Ludovice, quas mitto literas, vicit tamen hanc formidinem amor musicae, qua te video ornatum et donatum a Deo meo. Qui amor spem quoque fecit, fore ut nihil periculi sint tibi allaturae literae meae; quis enim vel in Turca vituperet, si amet artem et laudet artificem? Ego sane ipsos tuos Duces Bavariae, ut maxime mihi parum propitii sint, vehementer tamen laudo et colo prae caeteris, quod musicam ita fovent et honorant.*"

128. Since the document is fragmentary it is an open question whether this was the last point in his intended treatise, or whether he intended further sections.

129. LW 43:231, slightly altered. Appeal for Prayer Against the Turks (1541). WA 51:606-607: "Damit aber das Volck zur andacht und ernst gereitztet würde durch offentliche Gebet in der Kirchen, Leisse ich mir gefallen, wo es den Pfarherrn und Kirchen auch gefeile, das man am Feiertage nach der Predigt (Es sey morgends oder abends) den Lxxviiij psalm sunge ein Chor umb einander, wie gewonet. Darnach tret ein wol gestimpter knabe fur den pült ynn yhrem Chor, und sunge allein die Antiphon oder tract, Domine Non secundum. Nach dem selben ein ander knabe, den andern tract, Domine ne Meminaris Und darauff der ganze Chor knyend, Adjüüa nos Deus. . . . Darauff (wo man wil) mag der Leye singen, Verleyhe uns frieden oder das deutsche Vater Unser etc."

130. In the 1533 edition of the Wittenberg hymnal following *Verleih uns Frieden* is a prayer for peace and good government, Luther's translation of the collect from the *Missa pro pace; Geistliche lieder* (Wittenberg: Klug, 1533; facsimile, Kassel: Bärenreiter, 1954), fol. 51^r-52^r; see WA 35:233; LW 53:138.

131. On *Erhalt uns, Herr, bei deinem Wort*, see Chapter 4.

132. See, for example, Johannes Spangenberg, *Kirchengesenge Deudsche* (Magdeburg: Lotter, 1545), fol. 26^r-27^r, the sequence being, Benediction, *Verleih uns Frieden*, Collect, *Erhalt uns, Herr*. Later practice was to sing the two hymns one after the other, *Erhalt uns, Herr*, then *Verleih uns Frieden*, following the Benediction. Singing a prayer for peace at this juncture may have been suggested by the earlier practice of singing the *Nunc dimittis . . . in pace* at the end of the Roman Mass. Luther had created his vernacular version of the *Nunc dimittis* in 1524: *Mit Fried und Freud ich fahr dahin;* see further in Chapter 14.

133. LW 53:29 and 82; WA 12:213 and WA 19:99.

134. LW 53:30 and 84; WA 12:213 and WA 19:102.

135. LW 53:28-29; WA 12:213: "*Pax domini etce., quae est publica quaedam absolutio a peccatis communicantium, Vox plane Evangelica, annuncians remissionem peccatorum, unica illa et dignissima ad mensam domini preparatio, si fide apprehendatur, non secus atque ex ore Christi prolata.*"

136. LW 54:129. WA TR 1258 (1531): "So hat Gott das Evangelium auch durch die Musik gepredigt."

137. See Chapter 2.

138. *Source Readings in Music History,* ed. Oliver Strunk, rev. Leo Treitler (New York: Norton, 1998), 262-264; *Johannes de Musis: Notitia artis musicae, et Compendium musicae, Petrus de Sancto Dionysio: Tractatus de musica,* ed. Hans Ulrich Michels ([Rome]: American Institute of Musicology, 1972), 67, 71: "*Quod autem in ternario quiescat omnis perfectio, patet ex multis veresimilibus coniecturis. In Deo enim, qui perfectissimus est, unitas est in substantia, trinitas in personis; est igitur trinus unus et unus trinus. Maxima ergo convenientia est unitatis ad trinitatem. . . . Tota musica, maxime mensurabilis, in perfectione fundatur, numerum et sonum pariter in se comprehendens. Numerus autem, qui in musica perfectus a musicis reputatur, ternarius appellatur, ut patet in praedictis. Musica igitur a numero ternario sumit ortum. . . .*" For an alternative translation, see Piero Weiss and Richard Taruskin, *Music in the Western World: A History in Documents* (New York: Schirmer, 1984), 68-69.

139. See Gerhard Pietzsch, *Die Klassifikation der Musik von Boetius bis Vgolino von Orvieto* (Halle: Niemeyer, 1929), 76.

140. See Heinz Funck, *Martin Agricola: Ein früprotestantischer Schulmusiker* (Wolfenbüttel: Kallmeyer, 1933), 90-91.

141. See the discussion in Benito V. Rivera, *German Music Theory in the Early 17th Century: The Treatises of Johannes Lippius* (Ann Arbor: University of Michigan Research Press, 1980), 120-126.

142. Note that these three, with music, form the subjects of the traditional *Quadrivium*.

143. On another occasion he expounded the Trinity in terms of *grammatica, dialectica,* and *rhetorica;* see WA TR No. 1143 (1530).

144. "In musica re me fa, tres"; WA TR No. 815 (1530).

145. The six notes of a hexachord are named after the initial syllables of the first six lines of the hymn *Ut queant laxis,* LU 1504; Lossius, fol. 216^{v}-217^{r}.

146. See, for example, Nicolaus Listenius, *Musica* (Nuremberg: Petri, 1549; facsimile, Berlin: Breslauer, 1927), sig a 6^{r}; Nicolaus Listenius, *Music,* trans. Albert Seay (Colorado Springs: Colorado College Music Press, 1975), 7.

147. It is possible that this particular connection between music and the doctrine of the Trinity had been expressed before Luther but I have not been able to locate an earlier example.

148. See, for example, Benito V. Rivera, "The 'Isagoge' (1581) of Johannes Avianius: An Early Formulation of Triadic Theory," *Journal of Music Theory* 22 (1978): 43-64. Avianius's treatise exercised a particular influence on the writings of Burmeister (see the following note).

149. Joachim Burmeister, *Musical Poetics,* trans. & ed. Benito V. Rivera (New Haven: Yale University Press, 1993), 213; the Latin is given on the previous page (212):

Abs uno triados, quis te duxisse negaret,
Numine, principium, musica dia, tuum?
Dum repraesentas triados mysteria diae:
Dum numero gaudes impare ut alma trias.
Nam trinam clavem cantum reserare videmus.
Syzigiam trini cernimus esse son. . . .

150. Oswald Bayer, *Living by Faith: Justification and Sanctification,* trans. Geoffrey W. Bromiley (Grand Rapids: Eerdmans, 2003), 53; see the whole section (pp. 52-57), and Oswald Bayer, "Poetological Doctrine of the Trinity," *Lutheran Quarterly* 5 (2001): 43-58. On *Nun freuet euch,* see Chapter 11.

151. [Johann Aurifaber], *Tischreden Oder Colloqvia Doct. Mart: Luthers/So er in vielen Jaren/gegen gelarten Leuten/auch frembden Gesten/vnd seinen Tischgesellen gefüret/Nach den Heubstücken unserer Christlichen Lere/zusammen getragen* (Eisleben: Gaubisch, 1566; facsimile reprint, Berlin: Nationales Druckhaus, 1967). While Aurifaber included a great many Table-talks, he did not include them all. The six volumes of the Weimar edition therefore include additional material collected and/or published by others.

152. In the preface Aurifaber states that his aim was to create a *Loci communes* — the term chosen by Melanchthon for his 1521 dogmatic theology — from the disparate writings of Luther he and others had assembled; fol. iiij^{r}. Of course, the structure of the *Tischreden*

was created by Aurifaber rather than Luther, but it needs to be borne in mind that it was in this form that later generations of Lutherans received these views of the Reformer.

153. Trans. based on WLS No. 3091; Aurifaber, *Tischreden,* 578^{r-v}: "Wer die Musicam verachtet (sprach D.M.L.) Wie denn alle Schwermer thun/mit denen bin ich nicht zu frieden. Denn die Musica ist ein Gabe vnd Geschencke Gottes/nicht ein Menschen Geschenck/So vertreibt sie auch den Teufel/vnd machet Leut fröliche/Man vergisset dabey alles zorns/ vnteuscheit/hoffart/vnd anderer Laster. Ich gebe nach der Theologia/der Musica den neheseten Locum vnd höchste Ehre. Vnd man sehet/wie David vnd alle Heiligen jre Gottselige gedancken in Verss/Reim/vnd Gesang gebracht haben"; WA TR No. 7034; cf. WA TR Nos. 968 and 3815.

154. Paul Nettl, *Luther and Music,* trans. Frida Best and Ralph Wood (Philadelphia: Muhlenberg, 1948), 18-19. WA TR No. 5391: "Daß *lex iram operatur,* sieht manan dem wohl, daß Görg Planck alles besser schlägt, was er von sich selber schlägt, denn was er anderen zu Gefallen schlagen muß und das klingt *ex lege.* . . . Wo *lex* ist, da ist Unlust, wo *gratia* ist, das ist Lust."

155. Trans. based on LW 54:129-130. Aurifaber, *Tischreden,* 172^v: "WAS Gesetz ist/das gehet nicht von stat/noch freiwillig von der hand/sondern sperret vnd wehret sich/man thuts vngern vnd mit vnlust/was aber Euangelium ist/das gehet von stat mit lust vnd allem willen. Also hat Gott das Euangelium geprediget auch durch die Musicam wie man ins Josquini gesang sihet/das all Composositio fein frölich/willig/milde vnd lieblich heraus fleusst vnd gehet/ist nicht gezwungen noch genötig/vnd die Regeln stracks vnd schnurgleich gebunden/ wie des Fincken gesang." WA TR No. 1258 gives a slightly abbreviated macaronic text: "*Lex et euangelium.* Was *lex* ist, gett nicht von stad; was *euangelium* ist, das gett von stadt/ *Sic Deus praedicavit euangelium etiam per musicam, ut videtur in Iosquin* das all compososition frölich, willig, milde heraus fleusst, ist nitt zwungen vnd gnedigt *per regulas, sicut* des Fincken gesang." See the discussion of "*Ficken gesang,*" Chapter 2, note 199 above.

156. Aurifaber, *Tischreden,* 172^v: "DAS Euangelium ist gleich wie das Bfa bmi in der Musica/als die von jm regiert wird/die andern Claues sinds Gesetz. Vnd gliech wie das Gesetz dem Euangelio gehorchet/also sind die ander Claues dem Bfa bmi gehorsam. Und gleich wie das Evangelium iene liebliche, holdselige Lehre ist, also ist das Mi and Fa unter allen Stimmen die lieblichste. Aber der ander Tonus ist ein armer schwacher Sünder, der läßt im Bfa bmi, Mi und Fa, singen"; WA TR No. 816; see also No. 2996. In the first of his two sermons published as *Music-Büchlein Oder Nützlicher Bericht Von dem Uhrsprunge/Gebrauche und Erhaltung Christlicher Music* (Lüneburg: Stern, 1631), 65, Christoph Frick cites this saying from the *Tischreden,* which is then used to create the prayer that concludes the sermon: "O Allmächtiger Gott/und bitten dich/lasse diese Kirche und Gemein in Gnaden dir befohlen seyn/erhalte darein für allen dingen die Cantorey/deines heilgen Geistes/daß alle unnütze Menschenlieder verworffen/und das reine Lied deines Worts/und Evangelii durch D. Lutherum wieder angestimmet/allezeit klar und unverfälscht darein klingen möge. Regiere uns/auch also/daß wir nicht den b. *mol* des heiligen des Evangelii/als des Lambs Liede/unser Gesissen trösten/sondern auch aus dem b. *dur* des Gesetzes/als Moses Liede/unser Leben bessern/auch beydes hie in deinen Hause/in der Gemeine/und wenn wir in unserem Beruffe seyn/aus Christlicher Andacht/und wahrem Glauben dich preisen und ansingen mögen . . ."; Frick, *Music-Büchlein,* 130-131 (O Almighty God, we pray to you, let this church and congregation be ordered by your grace, and keep therein the Kantorei in all things by your Holy

Spirit, that all empty human songs be cast aside, that the pure song of your Word and Gospel by Dr. Luther may be voiced again, which always sounds clear and genuine. Guide us, therefore, that our consciences be comforted not only by the b. *mol* [literally: B soft = B♭] of the holy Gospel, such as the Song of the Lamb, but also by the b. *dur* [literally: B hard = B♮] of the Law, as in Moses' Song [see Revelation 15:3], and our lives reformed, both here in your church [Hause] and congregation, and also in the practice of our particular calling, that with Christian devotion and true faith we may sing your praise).

157. Both the F and G hexachords have a notated B, but in the F hexachord it is *fa* = B♭ whereas in the G hexachord it is B♮; see Example 3.1 — the accidentals above the stave conform to modern convention; sixteenth-century performers were expected to know whether the written note B was to be performed as B♭ or B♮. (See Example 3.1 on page 99.)

158. LW 15:269. Last Words of David (1543); WA 54:30: "Also ein Musicus hat ein lied ausgesungen, ehe der ander sucht und findet, obs ein Sol oder Fa im clave sey."

159. Cf. his statement: "The [musical] notes make the text live"; WA TR No. 968 (uncertain date): "Die Noten machen den Text lebendig."

160. See, for example, Walther Englehardt and Konrad Ameln, "Eine Kirchenlied-Melodie von Erasmus Alber und seine Vorlage," JbLH 18 (1973/74): 196-197. Alber's text and melody, *Gott hat des Evangelium*, was originally published as a separate publication with a four-part setting composed by Luther's colleague Johann Walter: *Von der Zeichen des Jüngsten Tags: Ein schön Lied* (Wittenberg: Rhau, 1548).

161. "Es war ein guter Musicus/hatte auch ein fein helle reine Stimme/beyde zu sing und zu reden"; Erasmus Alber, *Wider die verkehrte Lehre der Carlstader, und alle fürnemste Häupter der Sacramentirer: Rottengeister, Widerteuffer, Sacramentlsterer, Eheschender, Musica Verächter, Bildstürmer, und Verwüster aller guten Ordnung* (1556) (Neubrandenburg, 1594), sig. Nn7ʳ.

162. Matthäus Ratzeberger, *Die handschriftliche Geschichte Ratzeberger's über Luther und seine Zeit*, ed. Christian Gotthold Neudecker (Jena: Mauke, 1850), 59: "*in cantu figurali den alt mit sang*."

163. See note 42 above.

164. F. E. Kirby, "Herman Finck on Methods of Performance," *Music & Letters* 42 (1961): 213: Herman Finck, *Practica Musica*, sig. Ssiijʳ⁻ᵛ: "*Discantus tenera ac sonora voce, Bassus vero asperiori & crassiori canatur, Mediae aequabili voce suas modulationes efficiant, & extremis vocibus sauviter & concinne se applicare studeant. . . . Meminisse & illud proderit, si in initio cantus, elegans fuga occurrerit, hanc voce clariore & explanata magis proferendam quam alioqui usu receptum est, & sequentes voces, si ab eadem fuga quam prior cecinit ordiantur, simili modo enuntiandas esse: Hoc in omnibus vocibus, cum novae fugae occurrunt, observandium est, ut possit audiri cohaeruntia & omnium fugarum systema.*"

165. WA TR No. 4316 (1538): "*Estque egregia muteta legem et euangelium, mortem et vitam comprehendens. Duae voces querulae lamentatur: Circumdederunt me gemitus mortis etc, deinde quatuor voces* uberschreien dise; *Haec dicit Dominus, de manu mortis librerabo populum meum etc.* Es ist sehr wol und trostlich componirt"; see also Chapter 2, note 212.

Notes to Chapter 4

1. "Ein Kinderlied, Zu singen wider die zween Ertzfeinde Christi und seiner heiligen Kirchen, den Bapst und Türcken, etc."

2. WA 35:467-468; AWA 4:304-305.

3. Translation based on Robert Wisdom (1561), incorporated into *The Whole Book of Psalms* of Sternhold and Hopkins of 1562 and many later reprints.

4. Johann Christoph Olearius, *Kurtzer Entwurff einer nützlichen Lieder-bibliotheck* (Jena and Arnstadt, 1702), cited by Martin Rößler, "Die Frühzeit hymnologischer Forschung," JbLH 19 (1975): 135.

5. Once the tradition of catechism hymns had been established in Wittenberg (see further below), later German Lutheran hymnals included a section of such hymns following the church year section. For example, in Leipzig the choir books of Johann Herman Schein, *Cantional, Oder Gesangbuch Augspurgischer Confession* (1627), and Gottfried Vopelius, *Neu Leipzer Gesangbuch* (1682), as well as the various editions of the congregational *Leipziger Gesangbuch*, issued between 1729 and 1734 (this edition was reprinted frequently until late in the eighteenth century), follow this pattern. In some hymnals catechism hymns formed the first main section, such as in the sequence of hymnals published for German congregations in Stockholm, Sweden, between 1683 and 1757; the *Deutsches Stockholmisches Gesangbuch* of 1743 began with a section of sixty catechism hymns. Similarly, nearer our own time, Wilhelm Stapel's edition and study of Luther's hymns and poetry, *Luthers Lieder und Gedichte: Mit Einleitung und Erläuterungen* (Stuttgart: Evangelisches Verlagswerk, 1950), begins with Luther's Katechismuslieder.

6. Letter to Georg Spalatin, LW 53:221; WA BR 3:220.

7. *Das Achtliederbuch Nürnberg 1523/24*, facsimile ed. Konrad Ameln (Kassel: Bärenreiter, 1957). Later editions and anthologies, including Wackernagel (see the citation in note 23 below), give the texts of the hymns of Speratus, but not his Scripture proofs.

8. LW 53:36; WA 12:218.

9. See Chapter 10 below.

10. See Chapter 15 below.

11. LW 53:81-82, 78; WA 19:99, 95; see Chapter 6 below.

12. LW 53:64; WA 19:75-76: "Ist auffs erste ym deudschen Gottis dienst eyn grober, schlechter, eynfeltiger guter Catechismus von nöten."

13. For the background, see Timothy J. Wengert, "Wittenberg's Earliest Catechism," *Lutheran Quarterly* 7 (1993): 247-260.

14. BC-W/K 363; BSLK 521.

15. BC-W/K 386; BSLK 558-559: "Also hätte man überall fünf Stück der ganzen christlichen Lehre, die man immerdar trieben soll und von Wort zu Wort fodern und verhören. Denn verlasse Dich nicht drauf, daß das junge Volk alleine aus der Predigt lerne und behalte. Wenn man nu solche Stücke wohl weiß, so kann man darnach auch etliche Psalmen oder Gesänge, so darauf gemacht sind, furlegen zur Zugabe und Stärke desselbigen und also die Jugend in die Schrift bringen und täglich weiter fahren."

16. The 1529 edition is no longer extant. For a reconstruction of its contents, see Robin A. Leaver, *"Goostly Psalmes and Spirituall Songes": English and Dutch Metrical Psalms from Coverdale to Utenhove 1535-1566* (Oxford: Clarendon, 1991), 281-85. The situation is fur-

ther complicated by the probability that there were two imprints of this Wittenberg hymnal in 1529; see the discussion in Chapter 16 below.

17. LW 53:181-83.

18. See AWA 4:329. At this stage the section was not introduced by a separate preface, as suggested in Leaver, *Goostly Psalmes*, 283. The short preface was added to a later edition of Klug's Wittenberg hymnal; see further below.

19. It is possible that the collects were first introduced in the 1529 hymnal.

20. LW 53:136; AWA 4:328: "Almechtiger, ewiger Gott, der du uns geleret hast, in rechtem glauben zu wissen und bekennen, das du jnn drey personen, gleicher macht und ehren, ein einiger ewiger Gott und dafur anzubeten bist, wir bitten dich, du wollest uns bei solchem glauben allzeit feste erhalten wider alles, das da gegen uns mag anfechten, der du lebest und regierest von ewigkeit. Amen." Note that the phrase "allzeit feste erhalten" anticipates *Erhalt uns, Herr*.

21. "Nu folgen Geistliche Gesenge, darin der Catechismus kurtz egfasset ist, Denn wir ja gern wolten, das die Christliche Lere auff allerley weise mit predigen, lesen, singen etc. vleissig getrieben, Und jmer dem Jungen und einfeltigen Volck eingebildet, Und also fur und fur rein erhalten und auff unser nachkomen gebracht würde, Dazu verley Gott Gnade und Segen, Durch Jhesu Christum, Amen."

22. *Geistliche Lieder Zu Wittemberg* (Wittenberg: Klug, 1543/44), fols. 30^v-65^r; see also WA 35:555-556. One of the features of this hymnal (as well as the Bapst *Gesangbuch* of 1545) is that each section of the catechism is illustrated with appropriate woodcuts; see Rosa Micus, "Zum Katechismusbild in der Wittenberg-Leipzig Gesangbuchfamilie," JbLH 35 (1994/95): 210-215. On the development of catechism hymns in these hymnals see: Christhard Mahrenholz, "Auswahl und Einordnung der Katechismuslieder in den Wittenberger Gesangbüchern seit 1529," in *Gestalt und Glaube: Festschrift für Vicepräsident Professor D. Dr. Oskar Söhngen zum 60. Geburtstag am 5. Dezember 1960* (Witten: Luther-Verlag, 1960), 123-132; and Wichman von Meding, "Luthers Katechismuslieder," *Kerygma und Dogma* 40 (1994): 250-271. The earliest English versions of Luther's catechism hymns, given in the sequence of the five main parts of the catechism, were by the Scots Wedderburn brothers, John and Robert, in the first edition of their hymnal, known as the *Gude and Godlie Ballads*, published around 1544-45; see Leaver, *Goostly Psalmes*, 85.

23. These were mostly individual hymns written by various authors on one or another part of the catechism. An exception was Nikolaus Selnecker, one of the architects of the Formula of Concord (and a church organist in his teens), whose sequence of six catechism hymns was first published in *Drey Predigten: Die Erster Von der Heiligen Tauffe. Die Ander Von der Heiligen Absolution. Die Dritte Von dem Heiligen Abendmal des Herrn . . . Durch D. Martinum Chemnicium, D. Nicolaum Selneccerum, M. Christophorum Vischer dem Eltern. Den 22.23.24 April 1572* (Heinrichstadt: Horn, 1572); Philipp Wackernagel, *Das deutsche Kirchenlied von der ältersten Zeit bis zum Anfang des XVII Jahrhunderts*, 5 vols. (Hildesheim: Olms, 1964), 5:252-257 (Nos. 359-364); see further Inge Mager, "Nikolaus Selneckers Katechismusbereimung," JbLH 34 (1992/93): 57-67.

24. See Lowell C. Green, "The Chorales of Martin Luther: How Have They Fared in the *Lutheran Book of Worship?*" *Church Music* 79 (1979): 63.

25. Strictly speaking, even LH included only four of Luther's catechism hymns, though

it also included a translation of the Latin original on which Luther's Lord's Supper hymn was based: *Jesus Christus nostra salus* (No. 311).

26. "Regarding the Catechism hymns, it is thankworthy that LBW has included those on the Catechism's second, fourth, and fifth chief parts. But the omission of Luther's texts *Dies sind die Heiligen zehn Gebot, Vater unser im Himmelreich,* and *Jesus Christus unser Heiland* will be regretted by many." Green, "Chorales of Martin Luther," 61.

27. See Emil Sehling, *Die evangelischen Kirchenordnungen des 16. Jahrhunderts* (Leipzig: Riesland, 1902-1913; repr. Tübingen: Mohr, 1955), 1:452. The 1580 Church Order is here repeating the instructions given in the Saxon *Generalartikel* of 1557; Sehling, *Die evangelischen Kirchenordnungen,* 1:326; see also Johann Michael Reu, *Dr. Martin Luther's Small Catechism: A History of Its Origin, Its Distribution and Its Use* (Chicago: Wartburg, 1929), 159.

28. Sehling, *Die evangelischen Kirchenordnungen,* 1:424; Reu, *Small Catechism,* 165.

29. Sehling, *Die evangelischen Kirchenordnungen,* 1:395: ". . . den catechismum die kinder mit fleis in der schulen lere, und mit ihnen d. Luthers geistliche geseng und psalmen treibe"; see also Reu, *Small Catechism,* 168.

30. See Johann Michael Reu, *Quellen zur Geschichte des kirchlichen Unterrichts in der evangelischen Kirche Deutschland zwischen 1530 und 1600,* 4 vols. in 9 (Gütersloh: Bertelsmann, 1904-1935), I/1:743-755; Reu, *Small Catechism,* 63.

31. [Andreas Reyher], *Special- vnd sonderbahrer Bericht/Wie nechst Göttlicher verleyhung/die Knaben vnd Mägdlein auff den Dorffschafften/vnd in den Städten die vnter dem vntersten Haffen der Schule Jugend begriffene Kinder im Fürstenthumb Gotha* (Gotha: Schmieden, 1642); see Martin Petzoldt, *Bach und die Bibel: Ausstellung der Leipziger Bibelgesellschaft* (Leipzig: Bibelgesellschaft, 1997), 18-20.

32. About half of this number were hymns on repentance and Communion.

33. *Neues vollständiges Eisenachisches Gesangbuch* (Eisenach: Rörer, 1673), 284-456. A copy of this hymnal is in the Herzog August Bibliothek, Wolfenbüttel, Signatur TL 450, and available in digital format: http://diglib.hab.de.

34. See Michael Praetorius, *Syntagma Musicum: Tomus tertius* (Wolfenbüttel: Holwein, 1619), 258; see also C. L. Hilgenfeldt, *Johann Sebastian Bachs Leben, Wirken und Werke* (Leipzig: Hofmeister, 1850; repr. Hilversum: Knuf, 1965), tab. 1, at the end of the volume.

35. *Geistliche Lieder* (Wittenberg: Klug, 1543/44), fols. 65^r-66^r.

36. BC-W/K 357 (italics added); BSLK, 513: "Wenn Gott allen bösen Rat und Willen bricht und hindert, so uns den Namen Gottes nicht heiligen . . . als da ist der Teufel, der Welt und unsers Fleischs Wille, sondern stärket und *behält uns feste in seinem Wort* und Glauben bis an unser Ende."

37. WA 30^I: 684.

38. During the later struggle with Calvinism, the so-called "Second Reformation" (see Bodo Nischan, *Prince, People, and Confession: The Second Reformation in Brandenburg* [Philadelphia: University of Pennsylvania Press, 1994]), an anonymous hymn was published, probably in Dresden around 1590, which, in a staggering 79 stanzas, added Calvinists to the threat of Turk and pope by indicating that it was to be sung to the melody of Luther's hymn, and by parodying its opening stanza: "Erhalt uns, Herr, bei deinem Wort, | und steur des Calvinisten Mord . . ."; Wackernagel, *Das deutsche Kirchenlied,* 5:171 (No. 246). Another from the same period, a single stanza, began: "Erhalt uns Herr bei reinem Lehr, | Dem Pabst und Calvinisten Wehr . . ."; Kaspar Stolzhagen, *Kinderspiegel/Oder Hauszucht/vnd*

Tischbüchlein (Eisleben, 1591), cited (in facsimile) by Siegried Fornaçon, "Kaspar Stolz-hagen," JbLH 2 (1956): 75.

39. See further in Chapter 14.

40. For example, the Bapst imprints, Leipzig, 1545; WA 30^I: 684.

41. See, for example, Reu, *Quellen*, I/2:329; Reu, *Small Catechism*, 30.

42. See Wackernagel, *Das deutsche Kirchenlied*, 3:27 (No. 46).

43. See Johann Christoph Olearius, *Evangelischer Lieder-Schatz* (Jena: Bielke, 1707), 4:94-95.

44. Wackernagel, *Das deutsche Kirchenlied*, 1:284, 281, and 336 (Nos. 484, 480, and 600 respectively).

45. Olearius, *Evangelischer Lieder-Schatz*, 4:95.

46. Wackernagel, *Das deutsche Kirchenlied*, 4:286 (No. 392).

47. It first appeared in Helmbold's *Dreyssig geistliche lieder auff die Fest durchs Jahr* (Mühlhausen, 1594); thereafter it appeared frequently among the "Catechism Hymns" of various hymnals, sometimes the first, as in the *Eisenachisches Gesangbuch* (Rörer, 1673), 285-287. There were other such hymns that summarized the catechism, including another by Helmbold (Wackernagel, *Das deutsche Kirchenlied*, 4:668-669 [No. 964]), and one by Thomas Hartman, archdeacon in Eisleben (Wackernagel, *Das deutsche Kirchenlied*, 5:310 [No. 310]), but they did not rival the currency of *Herr Gott, erhalt uns für and für.*

48. Although some of Luther's catechism hymns were included under various headings, and there were such sections as "Baptism" and "Communion" in later hymnals, a specific section of "Catechism" hymns had become a rarity by the nineteenth century.

49. "Bey der Kinder Lehr des Catechismi."

50. Wackernagel, *Das deutsche Kirchenlied*, 4:677 (No. 980).

51. My translation. A somewhat free translation by Matthias Loy (1880) is in ELH, No. 551.

Notes to Chapter 5

1. WA 35:426-428; AWA 4:149-153.

2. Translation based on Richard Massie, *Martin Luther's Spiritual Songs* (London: Hatchard, 1854), 55-58; for an alternative translation, see LW 53:278-279.

3. On the complex relationship between the Loersfelt *Enchiridion* and the Maler *Enchiridion*, both published in Erfurt in 1524, see Konrad Ameln, "Introduction," *Das Erfurter Enchiridion Gedrukt in der Permentergassen zum Ferbefaß 1524 und der Ergänzungs druck . . . 1525*, facsimile ed. (Kassel: Bärenreiter, 1983), 13-22.

4. The German Sanctus is discussed further in Chapter 15 below.

5. See WA 35:135-136.

6. See Feranz M. Böhme, *Altdeutsches Liederbuch: Volkslieder der Deutschen nach Wort und Weise aus dem 12. bis 17. Jahrhundert*, 3rd ed. (Leipzig: Breitkopf & Härtel, 1925), 677-680 (No. 568$^{I=III}$).

7. Böhme, *Altdeutsches Liederbuch*, No. 568^{III}.

8. See Chapter 12 below.

9. WA 35:428-429; AWA 4:226-227.

10. Translation based on Massie, *Martin Luther's Spiritual Songs*, 53-54, with lines taken from the alternative translation, LW 53:281.

11. Not included in modern hymnals, which suggests that the "long" hymn had the wider currency.

12. Zahn 1956; DKL Ec9.

13. *Etliche Christliche Gesenge,* fol. [Avii^v]; see facsimile, *Das Erfurter Enchiridion,* ed. Ameln, [no pagination].

14. For example, the sermons on the Commandments of 1516 (WA 1:398-521); the *Short Exposition of the Ten Commandments,* 1518 (WA 1:250-256), which was reissued in a revised form in 1520 together with expositions of the Creed and Lord's Prayer (WA 7:205-214); and the *Sermon on Good Works,* 1520 (WA 6:202-276 = LW 44:15-114).

15. For an exploration of the general concept, see Klaus Meyer zu Uptrup, "Liturgie und Katechese," JbLH 26 (1982): 1-19.

16. Johannes Bugenhagen, *Katechismuspredigten gehalten 1525 und 1532,* ed. Georg Buchwald (Leipzig: Heinsius, 1909), 12, 29 and 42.

17. Emil Sehling, *Die evangelischen Kirchenordnungen des 16. Jahrhunderts* (Leipzig: Riesland, 1902-1913; repr. Tübingen: Mohr, 1955), 1:700-701. Two-week periods of special catechization became customary in Lutheran practice. For example, August Pfeiffer, superintendent in Lübeck, preached eight catechism sermons over two weeks in 1698. They were based on the five primary catechism hymns of Luther (omitting *Aus tiefer Not*), later published as *Cithara Lutheri, das ist, Christliche Predigten Über die allgemeinen Katechismuslieder* (Lübeck: Böckmann, 1709); see Martin Rößler, *Bibliographie der deutschen Liedpredigt* (Nieuwkoop: De Graaf, 1976), 137.

18. At the time he wrote the Short Preface, "catechism" for Luther meant the Ten Commandments, the Apostles' Creed and the Lord's Prayer, not his explanations in the Small Catechism.

19. BC-W/K 383-384 and 386; BSLK 554 and 559.

20. BC-W/K 363; BSLK 521.

21. That is, the Thanksgiving after Eating appended to the Small Catechism; see BC-W/K 364; BSLK 523.

22. Johann Michael Reu, *Quellen zur Geschichte des kirchlichen Unterrichts in der evangelischen Kirche Deutschland zwischen 1530 und 1600,* 4 vols. in 9 (Gütersloh: Bertelsmann, 1904-1935; reprint Hildesheim: Olms, 1976), I/1:745-746: "Diß Erste Stück des heiligen Catechismi mit seinen fragen und antwort können die Kindlein nach der Früemahlzeit und gesprochenen Gratias daheim repetieren und uben. — Nach der Abendmalzeit und gesprochenen Gratias können die Kindlein daheim auß Davids Catechismo beten den 90. Psalm. . . . Und darauff singen auß dem Gesangbüchlein Lutheri: Die zehen Gebot fein kurtz. D. Martini Lutheri: Mensch, wiltu leben seligklich — unnd all seins guts gern entpern, Kyrieleison. Die zehen Gebot D. Martini Luther, etwas lenger: Diß sind die heiligen Zehen Gebot — verdienen doch eiteln zorn, Kyrieleison."

Notes to Chapter 6

1. WA 35:451-452; AWA, 4:238-241.

2. Composite translation LH 251; for an alternative translation, see LW 53:272-273.

3. Philipp Wackernagel, *Das deutsche Kirchenlied von der ältersten Zeit bis zum Anfang des XVII Jahrhunderts*, 5 vols. (Hildesheim: Olms, 1964), 2:509-510 (Nos. 664-665a-b); see also WA 35:172-173; AWA 4:89-95.

4. WA 35:172; AWA 4:91-95.

5. Wackernagel, *Das deutsche Kirchenlied*, 509-510 (No. 665b); WA 35:173; AWA 4:91-95.

6. WA 35:177.

7. WA 35:177. In any case, Roth was from Zwickau and was also involved in Wittenberg's catechesis; see Timothy J. Wengert, "Wittenberg's Earliest Catechism," *Lutheran Quarterly* 7 (1993): 247-260.

8. Some have detected the influence of the older creedal hymn in Luther's subsequent stanzas but it is difficult to determine whether this was so or whether Luther was directly drawing on his knowledge of the historic creeds themselves.

9. WA 35:172-180.

10. See AWA 4:90.

11. Information based on *AWA* 4:239-240, and the facsimile of *Etliche Christliche Gesenge vnd Psalmen* (Erfurt, 1525), ed. Konrad Ameln (Kassel: Bärenreiter, 1983), sig. Aii^r. Ulrich Leupold confuses the Zwickau hymnal of 1525 with the Erfurt hymnal of the same year; see LW 53:271.

12. See LW 53:78. "Nach dem Euangelio singt die gantze kirche den glauben zu deutsche, *Wir glauben all an einen Gott*"; WA 19:95.

13. See *Das Achtliederbuch Nürnberg 1523/24*, facsimile ed. Konrad Ameln (Kassel: Bärenreiter, 1957).

14. See Luther's letter to Georg Spalatin: LW 53:221; WA BR 3:220.

15. *Eine kurze Form des Glaubens* (1520); WA 7:214.

16. BC-W/K 431-432; BSLK 646-647: "Aufs erste hat man bisher den Glauben geteilet in zwelf Artikel, wie wohl, wenn man alle Stück, so in der Schrift stehen und zum Glauben gehören, einzelen fassen sollte, gar viel mehr Artikel sind. . . . Aber daß man's aufs leichteste und einfältigste fassen künnde, wie es für die Kinder zu lehren ist, wöllen wir den ganzen Glauben kürzlich fassen in drei Häuptartikel nach den dreien Personen der Gottheit, dahin alles, was wir gläuben, gerichtet ist, also daß der erste Artikel von Gott dem Vater verkläre die Schepfung, der ander von dem Sohn die Erlösung, der dritte von dem heiligen Geist die Heiligung. . . ."

17. This particular identification of *Wir glauben* with the first article of the Creed is underscored by Bach's larger chorale prelude on the melody (BWV 680) in his *Clavierübung III* (1739), a work that includes settings on all the melodies of Luther's catechism hymns. An ostinato in the pedal, developed from the opening phrase of the melody, is repeated six times, an allusion to the six days of creation; see Robin A. Leaver, "Bach's 'Clavierübung III': Some Historical and Theological Considerations," *The Organ Yearbook* 6 (1975): 17-32.

18. Johann Michael Reu, *Quellen zur Geschichte des kirchlichen Unterrichts in der evangelischen Kirche Deutschland zwischen 1530 und 1600*, 4 vols. in 9 (Gütersloh: Bertelsmann, 1904-1935; repr. Hildesheim: Olms, 1976), I/1:747-748.

19. In three hymnals *Wir glauben* is included in a section of liturgical hymns, variously titled: "Liturgical Hymns" (LWor); "Hymns of the Liturgy" (CW); "Worship and Praise" (ELH). LBW includes it in the more general section "Community in Christ."

20. LBW 120; LWor 197-198; ELH 107.

21. "We all believe in one true God," translated by Catherine Winkworth; LWor No. 212; ELH No. 37.

22. In the original German, the melisma is on the word "glauben" (believe), but in the English translation, on the word "all." The tune was widely used not only in the worship of European Lutheranism but also that of English-speaking Calvinists. It was adapted into a metrical psalm tune, first appearing in print in the second edition of the Anglo-Genevan psalter of 1558. Over the next century or so this psalm-tune version found its place in other psalters and tune books. For example, it is the tune for Psalms 1 and 67 in Henry Ainsworth's psalter, published in Amsterdam in 1612, that the Pilgrim Fathers brought to America in 1620; see Robin A. Leaver, *Goostly Psalmes and Spirituall Songes: English and Dutch Metrical Psalms from Coverdale to Utenhove, 1535-1566* (Oxford: Clarendon, 1991), 129-131.

23. See, for example, Barbara J. Resch, "Adolescents' Attitudes Toward the Appropriateness of Religious Music" (DME diss., Indiana University, 1996).

Notes to Chapter 7

1. WA 35:463-465; AWA 4:295-298.

2. LH 458, slightly altered; for an alternative translation, see LW 53:296-98.

3. The other is *Vom Himmel kam der Engel schar* (1543); the document is given in facsimile in WA 35:636-637, and separately in a pocket in the back cover of AWA 4.

4. The manuscript is in the Staatsbibliothek, Berlin; see WA 35:465-467, AWA 4:346-348, and Jenny's detailed discussion, AWA 4:349-351.

5. DKL 1539[05]; see Johann Bartholomäus Riederer, *Abhandlung von Einführung des teutschen Gesangs in die evangelischlutherische Kirche überhaupts und in die nürnbergische besonders: wobey auch von den ältesten Gesangbüchern und Liedern so bis zum Tode Lutheri herausgegeben und verfertigt worden gehandelt wird* (Nürnberg: Endter, 1759; facsimile, Leipzig: Zentralantiquariat, 1975), 162-163.

6. DKL 1539[04].

7. Philipp Wackernagel, *Das deutsche Kirchenlied von der ältersten Zeit bis zum Anfang des XVII Jahrhunderts*, 5 vols. (Hildesheim: Olms, 1964), 3:544 (No. 592).

8. Wackernagel, *Das deutsche Kirchenlied*, 3:545 (No. 594). Another, anonymous, 9-stanza Lord's Prayer hymn, *O Vater unser, der du bist*, issued in Zwickau in an undated publication, was probably written after Luther's; see Wackernagel, *Das deutsche Kirchenlied*, 3:180-181 (No. 207). The texts of Moibanus' Lord's Prayer hymns are also given in WA 35:271-272.

9. See further Wichmann von Meding, "Luthers Lied vom Vaterunser: Waffe aus Weise und Wort," *Zeitschrift für Theologie und Kirche* 93 (1996): 500-537.

10. The Dutch version, *Vader onser in Hemelryck*, was translated by Jan Utenhove and published in his *Eenige Psalmen* (London, 1551); the Danish, *Fader vor vdi Hiemmerig*, first appeared in *En Ny Psalmebog* (Copenhagen, 1553); and the English transation by Richard Cox, *Our Father which in heaven art*, first appeared in *Psalmes of Dauid in Metre* ([Wesel], [ca. 1555]).

11. WA 35:527, mel. a) = AWA 4:295, mel. A = Zahn No. 2562. DKL — .

12. See Markus Jenny, "Eine Korrektur Luthers an einer von seiner eigenen Melodien," JbLH 33 (1990/91): 204-205.

13. *WA* 35:527, mel. b) = AWA 4:295, mel. B = Zahn No. 2561. The tune in English use took on the nature of Psalm tune as it was also assigned to Psalm 112, thus acquiring the name Old 112th. Luther's Lord's Prayer hymn was assigned two other tunes in Georg Rhau's *Newe Deudsche Geistliche Gesenge* (Wittenberg, 1544, Nos. 46 and 51 = Zahn No. 2563 and 2564), but neither rivaled the 1539 tune (Zahn 2561). The hymn with this melody was published by Krießstein in Augsburg ca. 1540 (DKL 1540[05]), with the suggestion — a common practice of the time — that it could be sung to two alternative tunes already in the Augsburg repertory, but neither displaced Luther's sturdy Dorian melody.

14. On this melody and its later use by various composers, see Gerhard Schuhmacher, "Aspekte der Choralbearbeitung in der Geschichte des Liedes 'Vater unser im Himmelriech,'" *Sagittarius* 4 (1973): 110-136.

15. Wackernagel, *Das deutsche Kirchenlied*, 3:209-210 (No. 231); see also the variants, 3:206-208, 210-212 (Nos. 230, 232).

16. For example, *Neues vollständiges Eisenachisches Gesangbuch* (Eisenach: Rörer, 1673), 309-312.

17. Wackernagel, *Das deutsche Kirchenlied*, 3:557 (No. 605).

18. *Worship Supplement: Authorized by the Commission on Worship of the Lutheran Church–Missouri Synod and Synod of Evangelical Lutheran Churches* (St. Louis: Concordia, 1969), 767. LBW 442, and CW 407, revised as *O Lord, you have in your pure grace*.

19. LWor 430.

20. Robin A. Leaver, *Come to the Feast: The Original and Translated Hymns of Martin H. Franzmann* (St. Louis: Morning Star, 1994), 103.

Notes to Chapter 8

1. "Ein Geistlich Lied Von unser heiligen Taufe, darin fein kurtz gefasset, Was sie sey? Wer sie gestifftet habe? Wer sie nütze? etc."

2. WA 35:468-470; AWA 4:299-301.

3. Translation based on Richard Massie, *Martin Luther's Spiritual Songs* (London: Hatchard, 1854), 69-72; for an alternative translation, see LW 53:300-301.

4. It is possible that Luther wrote one more hymn. In 1544 the Wittenberg printer and publisher Georg Rhau issued a set of part-books under the title *Newe Deudsche Geistliche Gesenge*. It included two settings of the melody of the old vernacular passion Leise, *O du armer Judas*, one by Thomas Stölzer and the other by Ludwig Senfl. But neither setting used the traditional text. Instead there are two stanzas, beginning *Unser große Sünde and schwere Missetat*, that appear for the first time. Markus Jenny has argued that they were most likely written by Luther; see AWA 4:123-124; see also Chapter 2, note 36.

5. See AWA 4:117. There was also a Nuremberg imprint of ca. 1542, no longer extant, that included Luther's five primary catechism hymns: *Gar schöner vnd Christlicher Lieder fünffe, yetz new zusamen gebacht, vnd auffs trewlichest Corrigiert. 1. Die Zehen gebot Gottes.... 2. Die Zwolff stücke des Christlichen Glaubens.... 3. Die Sieben bitt im Vater unser.... 4. Die Christliche Tauffe....5. Das Abendtmal des Herren Jhesu Christi* (Five beautiful and Christian

hymns, now newly brought together, and faithfully corrected. 1. The Ten Commandments. . . . 2. The twelve articles of the Christian faith. . . . 3. The seven petitions of the Lord's Prayer. . . . 4. Christian Baptism. . . . 5. The Lord's Supper. . . .); see WA 35:380.

6. Philipp Wackernagel, *Bibliographie zur Geschichte des deutschen Kirchenlieds im XVI. Jahrhunderts* (Frankfurt: Wolf, 1855, repr. Hildesheim: Olms, 1961), 279; WA 35:281.

7. WA 49:111-124, and 124-135. The sermons were preached on Thursday and Friday, April 1 and 2, 1540.

8. Friedrich Spitta argued that Luther's *Christ unser Herr zum Jordan kam* was originally conceived as an Epiphany hymn, a reworking of the early Latin hymn *Inluxit orbi iam dies;* see the summary of Spitta's argument in WA 35:282-285. But Luther's hymn, while being appropriate for the Epiphany season, is more closely connected to his Baptism sermons of early April 1540 than to the earlier Latin hymn; Spitta's hypothesis has not been widely accepted.

9. BSLK 515.

10. LW 53:107-108; WA 19:539-540: "Almechtiger Ewiger Gott, der du hast durch die sindflut nach deinem gestrengen gericht die unglewbige welt derdampt und den glewbigen. . . . Und den verstockten Pharao mit allen seinen ym roten meer erseufft, und dein volck Israel trocken durch hyn gefurt, da mit dis bad deiner heiligen tauffe zukunfftig bezeichnet, und durch die tauffe deines lieben kindes, unsers herren Jhesu Christi den Jordan und alle wasser zur seligen sindflut und reichlicher abwasschung der sunden geheiliget und eingesetzt: Wir bitten durch die selbe deine grundlose barmhertzicheit, du woltest disen N. gnediglich ansehen und mit rechtem glawben ym geyst beseligen, das durch dise heysame sindflut an yhm ersauffe und untergehe alles, was yhm von Adam angeporn ist, und er selb dazu gethan hat; Und er aus der ungleubigen zal gesundert, yn der heiligen Arca der Christenheit trocken und sicher behalte. . . ."

11. Earlier scholars raised the possibility that it was an adaptation of a folksong melody; see S. Kümmerle, *Encyklopedie der evangelischen Kirchenmusik* (Gütersloh: Bertelsmann, 1888-1895; repr. Hildesheim: Olms, 1974), 1:277. But no model on which it might have been based has been located, which led Walter Blankenburg to conclude that the melody was composed by Johann Walter; see Walter Blankenburg, *Johann Walter: Leben und Werk*, ed. Friedhelm Brusniak (Tutzing: Schneider, 1991), 167.

12. Zahn No. 7246. DKL Ec4.

13. Zahn No. 7247. DKL B17; see Konrad Ameln, "'Es wolt vns Gott genedig sein': Ein 'Straßburger' melodie aus Wittenberg," JbLH 32 (1989): 146-157.

14. See Blankenburg, *Johann Walter,* 128-131, 137-145.

15. Walter Serauky, *Musikgeschichte der Stadt Halle 1: Von den Anfängen bis zum Beginn des 17. Jahrhunderts* (Halle: Weisenhaus, 1935; repr. Hildesheim: Olms, 1971), 192-193.

16. Translation based on WLS, No. 3100; WA 48:85: "Ps. 149. Singet dem Herrn ein newes Lied etc. Auff ein new Wunderwerck Gottes, das er durch seinen lieben Son das rechte rote todes Meer zurissen und uns von dem rechten Pharao, Satan, erloset hat, Das heisst ein neues Lied, nemlich das heilige Evangelium, singen und Gott dafur dancken, das helffe uns Gott." At the bottom of the title page Luther inscribed: "Wolffgango Hinrico Organiste Excellen[tissimo] Amico Optimo Mart. Lüther d. 1541"; WA 48:255. The Bible must have been sent to Heintz before November 10, 1541, the date of a letter Luther wrote to Jonas in Halle in

which he remarks that Heintz has not yet responded to his gift with its inscription: *"Nihil respondet Wolff Heintz de Biblia, quam ei donatum apud me habea"*; WA BR 9:548.

17. On the volumes by Pfeiffer and Neumeister, see Martin Rössler, *Bibliographie der deutschen Liedpredigt* (Nieuwkoop: De Graaf, 1976), 137 and 172 respectively. The composer Bach had a number of volumes by Pfeiffer, as well as the particular volume by Neumeister, in his personal library; see Robin A. Leaver, *Bachs theologische Bibliothek: Eine kritische Bibliographie* [Beiträge zur theologischen Bachforschung 1] (Stuttgart: Hänssler, 1983), Nos. 14-18, 37-39 (Pfeiffer); Nos. 46-47 (Neumeister).

18. Of the six baptism hymns in this hymnal: two were written in the nineteenth century, Albert Knaap (1841), and Samuel Gilman (1823); three in the eighteenth century, Benjamin Schmolck (1704), Rambach (1734), and the Reformed Philip Doddridge (1755); and one in the seventeenth century, Thomas Kingo (1689); see William Gustave Polack, *The Handbook to the Lutheran Hymnal*, 3rd ed. (St. Louis: Concordia, 1958), 214-217.

19. BC-W/K 459: BSLK 695-69: "Denn meinsest Du, daß ein Scherz war, da sich Christus täufen ließ, der Himmel sich auftäte, der heilige Geist sichtiglich erabfuhr, und war eitel göttliche Herrligkeit und Majestät. Derhalben vermahne ich abermal, daß man beileib die zwei, Wort und Wasser, nicht voneinander scheiden und trennen lasse . . . aber wenn es dabei ist, wie es Gott geordnet hat, so ist's ein Sakrament . . . müssen wir auch lernen, warümb und wozu sie eingesetzt sei. . . . Darümb fasse es aufs allereinfältigst also, daß dies der Taufe Kraft, Werk, Nutz, Frucht und Ende ist, daß sie selig mache. . . . Da siehest Du abermal, wie teuer und wert die Taufe zu halten sei, weil wir solchen unausprechlichen Schatz darinne erlangen."

Notes to Chapter 9

1. WA 35:419-422; AWA 4:188-193.

2. Composite translations; for an alternative translation, see LW 53:223-224.

3. WA 35:411-415, 487-488; AWA 4:217-220; LW 53:214-218. Like *Aus tiefer Not, Ein neues Lied* exists in earlier and later versions; see Chapter 1 above.

4. LW 53:36; WA 12:218: "*Cantica velim etiam nobis esse vernacula quam plurima, quae populus sub missa cantaret, vel iuxta gradualia, item iuxta Sancus et Agnus die. Qui enim dubitat, eas olim fuisse voces totius populi, quae nunc solus Chorus cantat vel respondet Episcopo benedicenti? . . . Sed poetae nobis desunt, aut nondum cogniti sunt, qui pias et spirituales cantilenas (ut Paulus vocat) nobis concinnent, quae dignae sint in Ecclesia dei frequentari. . . . Haec dico, ut, siqui sunt poetae germanici, extimulentur et nobis poemata pietatis cudant.*"

5. Luther's *Formula missae* was published in December 1523; his letter to Spalatin is undated but is generally thought to have been written in September/October 1523.

6. Translation based on LW 53:221; WA BR 3:220: "*Consilium est, exemplo prophetarum & priscorum patrum Ecclesię psalmos vernaculos condere pro vulgo, id est spirituales cantilenas, quo verbum dei vel cantu inter populus maneat. Quęrimus itaque vundique poetas. Cum vero tibi sit data & copia elegantia linguę germanicę, ac multo vsu exculta, ora, vt nobiscum in hac re labores, & tentes aliquorum psalmorum in cantilenam transferre, sicut hic habes meum exemplum. Velim autem nouas & aulicas voculas omitti, quo pro captu vulgi quam simplicissima vulgatissimaque, tamen munda simul & apta verba canerentur, deinde sententia perspicua &*"

psalmis quam proxima redderetur. Libere itaque hic agendum & accepto sensu, verbis relictis, per alia verba comoda vertendum. Ego non habeo tantum gratię, vt tale quid possem, quale vellum. . . . Aut si placet assignaro Tibi psalmum primum: 'domine, ne in furore,' vel septimum: 'Beati, quorum' assigno, nam 'Deprofundis' a me versus est, & 'Miserere mei' iam prędestinatus fieri." For an alternative translation see LW 49:68-70.

7. Two different doxological stanzas, by anonymous authors, were added to the five-stanza form: one is found in Rostock hymnals issued in 1525 and 1526, and the other in hymnals published in Augsburg in 1533 and 1539, and Straßburg in 1541; see *WA* 35:420-421.

8. WA 35:97-109.

9. LW 53:222.

10. Jenny reiterates earlier scholarship that regarded the longer version as the later expansion of the shorter version; see, for example, Philipp Wackernagel, *Das deutsche Kirchenlied von der ältersten Zeit bis zum Anfang des XVII Jahrhunderts*, 5 vols. (1864-1877; repr. Hildesheim: Olms, 1964), 3:7-8 (Nos. 5 & 6); A. F. W. Fischer, *Kirchenlieder-Lexicon*, 2 vols. (1878-79; repr. Hildesheim: Olms, 1967), 1:59.

11. See, Markus Jenny, *Geschichte des deutschschweizerischen evangelischen Gesangbuchs im 16. Jahrhunderts* (Basel, 1962), 196-197; Markus Jenny, "Vom Psalmlied zum Glaubenslied: vom Glaubenslied zum Psalmlied," *Musik und Kirche* 49 (1979): 267-278; AWA 4:68-70.

12. ". . . wie er zum ersten ist ausgegangen D.M.L. [= Doctor Martin Luther]"; see AWA 4:69. The 4-stanza hymn continued in Straßburg use as Luther's "first version" of the Psalm; see the heading in the 1648 Straßburg *Gesangbuch* cited in Fischer, *Kirchenlieder-Lexicon*, 1:59.

13. BC-W/K 351-354; BSLK 507-509.

14. Zahn 4430. DKL Ea2.

15. Zahn 4431. DKL Ea5.

16. Zahn 4337. DKL Ea6.

17. Zahn 4438. DKL Eb2.

18. ". . . sagte er: Nun wollen wir dem Teuffel zu leid unnd verdrieß dem Psalmen/Aus tieffer noht schrey ich zu dir/mit vier Stimmen singen." Johannes Manlius, *Locorum communium . . . Schöne ordentliche Gattierung allerley alten und newen Exempel, Gleichniß, Sprüche, Rathschläge . . .* [translated from the Latin by Johann Huldrich Ragor] (Frankfurt am Main: Feyerabend & Hüter, 1574), fol. 7ʳ.

19. See Johann Walter, *Sämtliche Werke*, ed. Otto Scroeder, et al. (Kassel: Bärenreiter, 1953-1973), 1:20-21.

20. LW 53:334, slightly altered; WA 35:477: "Und ym De profundis, sols also stehn, Des mus dich fürchten jederman. Ist versehen oder ist ubermeistert, das fast in Büchern stehet, Des mus sich fürchten jederman. *Vt timearis.* Denn es ist Ebraisch geredt, wie Mat. xv. Vergeblich fürchten sie mich mit menschen lere. Und Psal. xiiij. und Psal. liij. Sie ruffen den Herrn nicht an, Da fürchten sie, da nicht fürchten ist. Das ist, sie können viel demut bucken und tucken in jrem Gottes dienst, da ich keinen Gottes dienst wil haben. Also ist hie auch die meinung, Weil sonst nirgend vergebung der sunden zu finden ist, denn bey dir, So müssen sie wol alle abgötterey faren lassen und thuns gern, das sie sich fur dir bucken, tucken, zum creutz kriechen und allein dich in ehren halten, und zu dir zuflucht haben, und dir deinen, als die deiner gnaden leben, und nicht jrer eige gerechtigkeit etc."

21. See WA 35:107-108; and Chapter 2 above.

22. See Robin A. Leaver, *Goostly Psalmes and Spirituall Songes: English and Dutch Metrical Psalms from Coverdale to Utenhove, 1535-1566* (Oxford: Clarendon, 1991), 283.

23. "De profundis/to syngen vor der predekyge"; Joachim Slüter, *Ein gar schönes und sehr nützliches Gesangbuch 1525*, facsimile, ed. Gerhard Bosinski (Leipzig: Zentralantiquariat der DDR, 1986), 31 & 118.

24. See Leaver, *Goostly Psalmes*, 19; Emil Sehling, ed., *Die evangelischen Kirchenordnungen des 16. Jahrhunderts*, 15 vols. (Leipzig: Reisland, 1902-1913), 2:436.

25. Sehling, *Die evangelischen Kirchenordnungen*, 2:77.

26. Information extracted from Rochus, Freiherrn von Liliencron, *Liturgischmusikalische Geschichte der evangelischen Gottesdienste von 1523 bis 1700* (Schleswig: Bergas, 1893; repr. Hildesheim: Olms, 1970), 61-77, which also includes information on other hymnals published in Augsburg, Darmstadt, Frankfurt, etc., between 1601 and 1694; see also Detlef Gojowy, "Kirchenlieder im Umkreis von J. S. Bach," *JbLH* 22 (1978): 79-123, which covers a broader range of sources from a generally later period.

27. WA 30^I: 343-435.

28. BC-W/K 360-362; BSLK 517-519.

29. BC-W/K 360; BSLK 517: "Die Beicht begreift zwei Stück in sich. Eins, daß man die Sunde bekenne, das ander, daß man die Absolutio oder Vergebung vom Beichtiger empfahe als von Gott selbs und ja nicht dran zweifel, sondern feste gläube, die Sunde seien dadurch vergeben für Gott im Himmel."

30. Johann Michael Reu, *Quellen zur Geschichte des kirchlichen Unterrichts in der evangelischen Kirche Deutschland zwischen 1530 und 1600*, 4 vols. in 9 (Gütersloh: Bertelsmann, 1904-1935; repr. Hildesheim: Olms, 1976), I/1:751. "Diß fünffte Heubstuck des heiligen Catechismi mit seinen fragen unnd antwort können die Kindlein nach der Früemalzeit und gespröchenem Gratias daheim repetieren und eben. Nach der Abendmahlzeit desselben tags unnd gespröchenem Gratias können die Kindlein daheim fürm Tisch auß Davids Catechismo beten den 51. Psalm. . . . Und drauff singen auß dem Gesangbüchlein des gesang Erhard Hegenwald: Erbarm dich mein, O Herre Gott. . . . Oder auß dem Gesangbüchlein Lutheri: Aus tieffer noth schrey ich zu dir. . . ."

31. *Neues vollständiges Eisenachisches Gesangbuch* (Eisenach: Rörer, 1673), 329-332.

32. *Geistreiche alt und neue Gesänge, Welche bey der Beicht und Communion . . .* (Nuremberg and Leipzig: Stein, 1724), 6-8.

33. *Musicalisches Gesangbuch . . .*, ed. George Christian Schemelli (Leipzig: Breitkopf, 1736; facsimile repr. Hildesheim: Olms, 1975), 43-44.

34. See Robin A. Leaver, "Bach's 'Clavierübung III': Some Historical and Theological Considerations," *The Organ Yearbook* 6 (1975): 17-32.

Notes to Chapter 10

1. WA 35:435-437; AWA 4:168-170.

2. Composite translation; for an alternative translation, see LW 53:249-251.

3. See Philipp Wackernagel, *Bibliographie zur Geschichte des deutschen Kirchenlieder im XVI. Jahrhundert* (Frankfurt am Main: Heyden & Zimmer, 1855; repr. Hildesheim: Olms,

1961), 57 (No. 155). Although issued anonymously the imprint can be identified as being printed by Steiner in Augsburg; DKL 1524[02].

4. The heading does not appear with the hymn in Walter's *Chorgesangbuch* but is included with the first line in the index found at the end of the tenor part-book; see Johann Walter, *Das geistliche Gesangbüchlein "Chorgesangbuch,"* facsimile of the second printing (Worms, 1525), ed. Walter Blankenburg (Kassel: Bärenreiter, 1979), *Tenor. Geystliche Gsngbüchlin [sic]*, sig. Hvi[r].

5. See *Analecta hymnica medii aevi*, ed. Guido Maria Dreves and Clemens Blume, 55 vols. (Leipzig: Reisland, 1886-1922), 1:31-32.

6. Zdeněk Nejedlý, *Dějiny Husitského Zpěvu*, 6 vols. (Prague: československé akademie věd, 1954-1956), 3:408-412.

7. The first stanza and a few phrases in some of the other stanzas are taken from George Woodward's incomplete translation in his *Songs of Syon* (London: Schott, 1908), No. 141; the remainder is my own translation.

8. Nejedlý, *Dějiny Husitského Zpěvu*, 3:412.

9. For the text of a fifteenth-century Munich manuscript, see Philipp Wackernagel, *Das deutsche Kirchenlied von der ältersten Zeit bis zum Anfang des XVII Jahrhunderts*, 5 vols. (Leipzig: Teubner, 1864-1877; repr. Hildesheim: Olms, 1964), 3:218 (No. 367); WA 35:142-143.

10. The editors of LH are therefore misleading when they state that hymn No. 311, "Jesus Christ, our blessed Savior," is an unknown translation of the hymn by "Huss," *Jesus Christus nostra salus*, whereas it is actually a translation of eight stanzas (1-5, 7-9) of Luther's *Jesus Christus, unser Heiland*. However, the editors were simply following some German hymnals in which the hymn was ascribed to Huss without reference to Luther; for example, *Musicalisches Gesang-Buch*, ed. George Christian Schemelli [and Johann Sebastian Bach] (Leipzig: Breitkopf, 1736; repr. Hildesheim: Olms, 1975), No. 144.

11. WA 15:444-453, 481-509.

12. See WA 35:145-146.

13. Luther lightly revised the seven stanzas of Weiße's translation, and added an eighth stanza in 1540; see Konrad Ameln, "Luthers Anteil an dem Liede 'Nun laßt uns dem Leib begraben,'" JbLH 3 (1957), 108-112; AWA 4:120-122. In his preface to the Bapst hymnal of 1545 he wrote concerning this hymn: "the burial hymn *Nun laßt uns den Leib begraben* bears my name; but it is not mine, and hereafter it should not be credited to me. Not that I condemn it; for it pleases me very much, and a good poet wrote it, one named Johannes [= Michael] Weiss (only that on the sacrament he has come close to the enthusiasts). But I will not palm off anyone's work as my own"; LW 53:333-334, WA 35:477: ". . . das lied, so man zum grabe sunget, Nu last uns den leib begraben, füret meinen namen, aber es ist nicht mein und sol mein name hinfurt davon gethan sein, Nicht das ichs verwerffe, denn es gesellet mir sehr wol, und hat ein guter Poet gemacht, gennant Johannes Weis, on as er ein wenig geschwermet hat am sacrament, Sondern ich wil niemand sein erbeit mor zu eigen." Thereafter it became the most widely-used of Lutheran burial hymns (see further in Chapter 15). Only one contemporary American Lutheran hymnal (ELH) offers an English translation of the hymn.

14. LW 37:171, 173; WA 26:271, 273-274: ". . . solt yhr wissen, Das ein lauter geticht ist, wer do sagt, das dis wörtlin 'Ist' so viel heisse als 'deutet.' . . . Wir deudschen pflegen bey solchen verneweten worten 'recht' odder 'ander' oder 'new' zusetzen und sagen: Du bist ein rechter hund, Die münch sind rechte Phariseer, Die nonnen sind rechte Moabiter töchter, Christus

ist ein rechter Salomon. Item: Luther ist ein ander Hus, Zwingel ist ein ander Chore, Ecolampad ist ein newer Abiram. . . . Und gleich so viel ist, viel wenn ich sage: Luther ist Hus, Luther ist ein ander Hus, Luther ist ein rechter Hus, Luther ist ein newer Hus. . . . Denn es klapt noch klinget nicht, Wenn ich sage: Luther bedeut Hus, sondern: Er ist ein Hus. Vom wesen redet man ynn solchen sprüchen, was einer sey und nicht, was er bedeute. . . ."

15. LW 37:193; WA 26:296-297: "Denn Christus leiden ist wol nür ein mal am creutz geschehen, Aber wem were das nütz, wo er nicht ausgeteilet und ynn brauch bracht wurde? Wie sols aber ynn brauch komen und aus geteilet werden on durchs wort und sacrament?"

16. BC-W/K 362; BSLK 519-520: "Was ist das Sakrament des Altars? Antwort. Es ist der wahre Leib und Blut unsers Herrn Jesu Christ, unter dem Brod und Wein uns Christen zu essen und zu trinken von Christo selbs eingesetzt. . . . Was nützet den solch Essen und Trnken? Antwort. Das zeigen und diese Wort: "fur Euch gegeben" und "vergossen zur Vergebung der Sunden," nämlich, daß uns im Sakrament Vergebung der Sunde, Leben und Seligkeit durch solche Wort gegeben wird; denn wo Vergebung der Sunde ist, da ist auch Leben und Seligkeit."

17. BC-W/K 467; BSLK 709: "Was ist nu das Sakrament des Altars? Antwort: Es ist der wahre Leib und Blut des Herrn Christi, in und unter dem Brot und Wein durch Christus' Wort uns Christen befohlen zu essen und zu trinken. Und wie von der Taufe gesadt, daß nicht schlecht Wasser ist, so sagen wir hie auch, das Sakrament ist Brot und Wein, aber nicht schlecht Brot noch Wein, so man sonst zu Tisch trägt, sondern Brot und Wein, in Gottes Wort gefasset und daran gebunden."

18. BC-W/K 473-474; BSLK 721: "Denn da beut er uns an alle den Schatz, so er uns von Himmel bracht hat, dazu uns auch sonst locket aufs allerfreundlichste, als da er spricht Matthäi 11.: 'Kommpt her zu mir alle, die Ihr mühselig und beladen seid, ich will Euch erquicken.'"

19. LW 38:125-126; WA 30^II: 616-617: "So ist nu das der erste nutz und frucht, so dir kompt aus dem brauch des Sacrament das du solcher wolthat und gnade damit erinnert wirst, und dein glaube und liebe gereitzt, ernewert und gesterckt wird, auff das du nicht komest jnn ein vergessen odder verachtung deines lieben heilands und seines bittern leidens und deiner grossen, manchfeltigen, ewigen not und tod, daraus er dir gehofften hat. . . . Und dagegen der unglaube ein ferlicher, teglicher, unableslicher teuffel ist, der uns von unserm lieben heilande und seinem leiden, beide mit gewalt und list, reissen wil, Es ist muhe und erbeit, wo man teglich solchen glauben treibt, reitzt und ubet, das wir Christus leiden und wohlthat nicht vergessen."

20. BC-W/K 605; BSLK 996: "Denn die schwachgläubigen, blöden, betrübten Christen, die vonwegen der Größe und Menge ihrer Sünden von Herzen erschrocken sein und gedenken, daß sie in dieser ihrer großen Unreinigkeit dieses edlen Schatzes und Guttaten Christi nicht wert sein. . . ."

21. LW 53:84; WA 19:102: "Wyr dancken dir, almechiger herr gott, das du uns durch dise heylsame gabe hast erquicket und bitten deyne barmhertzigkeit, das du uns solchs gedeyen lassest zu starckem glauben gegen dir und zu binstiger liebe unter uns allen."

22. LW 38:126; WA 30^II: 617: "Wo solcher glaube jmer also erfrisschet und ernewert wird, da wird auch mit zu das hertz jmer von newem erfrisschet zur liebe des nehesten und zu allen guten wercken starck und gerust, der sunden und aller anfechtung des teuffels

403

widder zu stehen, Sintemal der glaube nicht kan mussig sein, Er mus frucht der liebe uben mit gut thun und böses meiden."

23. LW 38:123 (the mistranslation of "Das Patrem" as "Lord's Prayer," instead of "the Creed," has been corrected); WA 30[II]: 614-615: "Und daher acht ich, das viel gesang jnn der Messe, so fein und herrlich vom dancken und loben gemacht und bis her bleiben ist, als das Gloria in excelsis Et in terra, Das Alleluia, Das Patrem, Die Praefation, Das Sanctus, Das Benedictus, das Agnus Dei, In welchen stücken findestu nichts vom opfer, Sondern eitel lob und danck, Darumb wir sie auch jnn unser Messen. . . . Was aber offentlich durch den Kor und unter dem hauffen gesungen wird, fast eitel gut ding und lobesang ist. . . ."

24. LW 53:36; WA 12:218. All four contemporary American Lutheran hymnals include revisions of the composite translation, "O Lord, we praise you," that appeared earlier in LH. The opening couplet was the work of Martin Franzmann; see Robin A. Leaver, *Come to the Feast: The Original and Translated Hymns of Martin H. Franzmann* (St. Louis: Morning Star, 1994), 116-117.

25. LW 53:81-82; WA 19:99. Only LBW and ELH include English versions of *Christe, du Lamm Gottes*.

26. See Helmut Schwier, "Lehren, Züristen und Gedenken: Bugenhagens Abendmahlsvermahnung in ihren theologischen und liturgischen Dimensionen," JbLH 36 (1996/97): 35; see also Johannes H. Bergsma, *Die Reform der Messliturgie durch Johannes Bugenhagen* (Hildesheim: Bernward, 1966), *passim*.

27. Examples of collections of hymn-sermons include: Cyriacus Spangenberg, *Cythera Lutheri* (Erfurt, 1570), Simon Pauli, *Erklarung der Deutschen Geistliche Lieder . . . Martino Luthero* (Magdeburg, 1588), August Pfeiffer, *Cithera Lutheri* (Lübeck, 1709), and Erdmann Neumeister, *Tisch des Herrn* (Hamburg, 1722); see Martin Rößler, *Bibliographie der deutschen Liedpredigt* (Nieuwkoop: de Graaf, 1976), 25, 31, 137, and 158-159.

Notes to Chapter 11

1. WA 35:422-425; AWA 4:154-157.

2. Composite translation based on Richard Massie, *Martin Luther's Spiritual Songs* (London: Hatchard, 1854), 47-50; for an alternative translation, see LW 53:219-220.

3. DKL, 1524[10].

4. *Das Achtliederbuch Nürnberg 1523/24*, facsimile ed. Konrad Ameln (Kassel: Bärenreiter, 1957) [= DKL 1524[13]], sig. [Aii][v].

5. The basic literature includes: Paul Alpers, "'Nun freut euch, lieben Christen gmein' im Liederbuch der Anna von Köln [ca. 1500]," JbLH 5 (1960): 132-133; Hans Joachim Moser, "Nun freut euch, lieben Christen gmein," in *Gestalt und Glaube: Festschrift für Vicepräsident Professor D. Dr. Oskar Söhngen zum 60. Geburtstag am 5. Dezember 1960* (Witten: Luther-Verlag, 1960), 137-144; Ludwig Wolff, "Zu Luthers Lied: 'Nun freut euch, lieben Christen gmein,'" JbLH 7 (1962): 99-102; Alfred Jung, "'Nun freut euch, lieben Christen gmein': Eine theologische Untersuchung des Lutherliedes," JbLH 19 (1975): 200-209; see also Markus Jenny in AWA 4:58.

6. AWA 4, melody 2A. Zahn 4427. DKL No. B15. This is the associated tune in all four of the contemporary Lutheran hymnals.

7. AWA 4, melody 2B. Zahn No. 4430 DKL Ea2. In the Loersfelt Erfurt *Enchiridion* of 1524 the heading to *Nun freut euch* notes that the melody to which it is set, *Es ist das Heil*, was previously associated with an earlier Easter hymn beginning *Frewt euch yhr frawen und die man;* AWA 4:154. Later variant forms of another Easter hymn, beginning *Frew dich, du werde Christenheit,* was assigned this tune in Catholic hymnals; see Franz M. Böhme, *Altdeutsches Liederbuch: Volkslieder der Deutschen nach Wort und Weise aus dem 12. bis zum 17. Jahrhundert,* 3rd ed. (Leipzig: Breitkopf & Härtel, 1925), 668-671; and Wilhelm Bäumker, *Das Katholische deutsche Kirchenlied in seinen Singweisen,* 4 vols. (Hildesheim: Olms, 1962), 1:544-551.

8. AWA 4, melody 2C. Zahn No. 4428. DKL Ec6.

9. AWA 4, melody 2D. Zahn No. 4429a. DKL Ee7. LBW No. 321; LWor No. 462; CW No. 208; ELH No. 538.

10. See further Oswald Bayer, *Living by Faith: Justification and Sanctification,* trans. Geoffrey W. Bromiley (Grand Rapids: Eermans, 2003), 52-57; Oswald Bayer, "Poetical Doctrine of the Trinity," *Lutheran Quarterly* 5 (2001): 43-58.

11. See Heinz Scheible, "Melanchthon, Philipp," OER 3:41-45, esp. 42.

12. WLS No. 4370; WA TR 5511 (Winter 1542-43): *"Non est melior liber post scripturam sanctam."*

13. LW 35:365; WA DB 7:3: "Diese Epistel ist das rechte Heubstück des newen Testaments, und das allerlauterste Evangelium, welche wol wirdig und werd ist, das sie ein Christen mensch nicht allein von wort zu wort auswendig wisse, sondern teglich damit umbgehe, als mit teglichem brot der Seelen, Denn sie niemer kan zu viel und zu wol gelesen oder betrachtet werden, und je mehr sie gehandelt wird, je köstlicher sie wird, und das schmecket."

14. Information extracted from AWA 4, 155, 158.

15. ". . . des Hn. Lutheri schöner Gesang/Nun freut euch lieben Christen gemein/ist ein vortrefflicher tröstlicher Auszug des gantzen Evangelischen Glaubens-Grundes/also daß darinne die gantze *Theologia, Christologia,* und *Anthropologia* enthalten/oder/was wir von Gott/von Christo und unserm Elende und desselben Abwendung im Reich der Gnaden/durch Christi Verdienst/wie auch von der Versicherung des ewigen Freuden Reichs aus Gottes Wort zu mercken haben"; cited Johann Christoph Olearius, *Evangelischer Lieder-Schatz* (Jena: Bielcke, 1707), 2:63-64.

16. See AWA 4:329; Robin A. Leaver, *"Goostly psalmes and Spirituall Songes": English and Dutch Metrical Psalms from Coverdale to Utenhove 1535-1566* (Oxford: Clarendon, 1991), 283.

17. WA 19:95; LW 53:78.

18. WA 19:99-102; LW 53:81-83.

19. See Chapter 14.

20. WA 35:462; AWA 4:292: "Ein lied von der Heiligen Christlichen Kirchen, aus dem xij. capitel Apocalypsis"; see LW 53:293-294.

21. BC-W/K 68; BSLK 91-92: "So werden auch die Leute mit hochstem Fleisch zum oftern mal unterricht vom heiligen Sakrament. . . . So ist auch in den offentlichen Ceremonien der Messe keine merklich Anderung geschehen, dann daß an etlichen Orten teutsch Gesänge, das Volk damit zu lernen und du uben, neben lateinischem Gesang gesungen werden, sintermal alle Ceremonien furnemlich darzu dienen sollen, daß das Volk daran lerne, was ihm zu wissen von Christo not ist."

22. On the background, see Johann Michael Reu, *Dr. Martin Luther's Small Catechism: A History of Its Origin, Its Distribution and Its Use* (Chicago: Wartburg, 1929), 192-195.

23. Philipp Jacob Spener, *Kurtze Catechismus-Predigten, Darinnen Die fünff Haupt-Stück, aus dem Catechismo . . . einfältig erkläret werden* (Berlin: Rüdiger, 1727), 671-768.

24. Spener, *Kurtze Catechismus-Predigten,* 671.

25. See further, Robin A. Leaver, "The Chorale: Transcending Time and Culture," *Concordia Theological Quarterly* 56 (1992): 123-144, esp. 131-135.

26. BC-W/K 531; BSLK 844. The debate leading up to the *Formula* had centered on the meaning of this hymn, and the hymn continued to be cited as enshrining the Lutheran position on original sin; see, for example, Johann Benedict Carpzov, *Isagoge in libros ecclesiarum Lutheranarum symbolicos* (Dresden: Zimmermann & Gerlach, 1725), 1165.

Notes to Chapter 12

1. For a review of the general literature, see Frieder Schulz, "Der Gottesdienst bei Luther," *Leben und Werk Martin Luthers von 1526 bis 1546: Festgabe zu seinem 500. Geburtstag,* ed. Helmar Junghans (Berlin: Evangelische Verlagsanstalt, 1983), 297-302, and 811-825. Other recent literature, in addition to the following notes, includes: Frieder Schulz, "Luthers liturgische Reformen: Kontinuität und Innovation," *Archiv für Liturgiewissenschaft* 25 (1983): 249-275; Rudolf Padberg, "Luther und der Canon missae," *Catholica* 37 (1983): 288-305; Hans-Christoph Schmidt-Lauber, "Das Gottesdienstverständnis Martin Luthers im ökumenischen Kontext," *Theologische Literaturzeitung* 114 (1989): 321-338; Reinard Meßner, *Die Meßreform Martin Luthers und die Eucharistie der Alten Kirche: Ein Beitrag zu einer systematischen Liturgiewissenschaft* (Innsbruck: Tyrolia, 1989); A. P. Nirmal, "Faith's Provocations — Luther's Liturgical Reforms," *Gurukul Journal of Theological Studies* 3 (1992): 1-17; Helmar Junghans, "Luther on the Reform of Worship," *Lutheran Quarterly* 13 (1999): 315-333.

2. LW 53:26; WA 12:21: *"Et ab hinc omnia fere sonant ac olent oblationem. In quorum medio verba illa vitae et salutis sic posita sunt, ceu olim arca, domini in templo idolorum iuxta Dagon. . . . Proinde omnibus illis repudiatis, quae oblationem sonant, cum universo Canone, retineamus, quae pura et sancta sunt."*

3. WA 12:212; LW 52:28.

4. WA 12:212-213 and WA 19:97-99; LW 53:28 and 81-82.

5. Hans-Christoph Schmidt-Lauber, *Die Eucharistie als Entfaltung der Verba Testamenti* (Kassel: Stauda, 1957).

6. Frank C. Senn, "Martin Luther's Revision of the Eucharistic Canon in the *Formula Missae* of 1523," *Concordia Theological Monthly* 44 (1973): 118. "It would seem, therefore, that the Lutherans discarded what was most primitive in the eucharistic tradition, namely, the act of thanksgiving, and retained what was secondary," 109.

7. William D. Maxwell, *An Outline of Christian Worship: Its Development and Forms* (London, 1936; repr. London: Faith, 1960), 77. Maxwell adds: "By an indefensible innovation he attaches the Words of Institution to the Preface." But Luther did not so much "attach" as "detach" the *Verba* from the Preface; see note 4 above.

8. Gregory Dix, *The Shape of the Liturgy* (London: Dacre, 1945), 629-631.

9. Bryan Spinks, *Luther's Liturgical Criteria and His Reform of the Canon of the Mass* (Bramcote: Grove, 1982).

10. Yngve T. Brilioth, *Nattvarden i evangeliskt gudstjänstliv* (Stockholm: Svenska Kyrkans Diakonistyrelses Bokförlag, 1926); *Eucharistic Faith and Practice: Evangelical and Catholic,* trans. A. G. Hebert (New York: Macmillan, 1930; abbreviated and revised edition London: SPCK, 1965).

11. Spinks, *Luther's Liturgical Criteria,* 11-14.

12. Spinks, *Luther's Liturgical Criteria,* 14.

13. In addition to Spinks, *Luther's Liturgical Criteria,* see also: Vilmos Vajta, *Die Theologie des Gottesdienst bei Luther,* 2nd ed. (Göttingen: Vandenhoeck & Ruprecht, 1954), and its (unfortunately abridged) English translation, by Ulrich S. Leupold, *Luther on Worship: An Introduction* (Philadelphia: Fortress, 1958); Adolf Allwohn, *Gottesdienst und Rechtfertigungsglaube: Luthers Grundlegung evangelischer Liturgik bis zum Jahre 1523* (Göttingen: Vandenhoeck & Ruprecht, 1926); Theodor Knolle, "Luthers Deutsche Messe und die Rechtfertigungslehre," L-J 10 (1928): 170-203; Louis Novak, "The Liturgical Contributions of Martin Luther," *The Iliff Review* 32 (1975): 43-50; and the summary, largely based on Vajta, in Gerhard Hahn, *Evangelium als literarische Anweisung: Zu Luthers Stellung in der Geschichte des deutschen kirchlichen Liedes* (Munich: Artemis, 1981), 49-60.

14. See Acts 16:30-31.

15. Robin A. Leaver, *Luther on Justification* (St. Louis: Concordia, 1975), 13.

16. "Here is the first and chief article: That Jesus Christ, our God and Lord, 'was handed over to death for our trespasses and was raised for our justification' (Romans 4[:25]). . . . Nothing in this article can be conceded or given up. . . . On this article stands all that we teach and practice against the pope, the devil, and the world. Therefore we must be quite certain and have no doubt about it. Otherwise everything is lost, and the pope and the devil and whatever opposes us will gain the victory and be proved right. . . . That the Mass under the papacy has to be the greatest and most terrible abomination, as it directly and violently opposes this chief article. . . . As the canon of the Mass and all the handbooks say, the Mass is and can be nothing but a human work (even a work of rotten scoundrels), performed in order that individuals might reconcile themselves and others to God, acquire the forgiveness of sins and merit grace. . . . Thus the Mass should and must be condemned and repudiated, because it is directly contrary to the chief article [i.e., of justification], which says that it is not an evil or devout servant of the Mass with his work, but rather the Lamb of God and the Son of God, who takes away our sin"; Schmalcald Articles 1537, BC-W/K 301-302; BSLK 415-418: "Hie ist der erste und Häuptartikel: Daß Jesus Christus, unser Gott und Herr, sei 'umb unser Sunde willen gestorben und umb unser Gerechtigkeit willen auferstanden, Ro. 4. . . . Von diesem Artikel kann man nichts weichen oder nachgeben. . . . Und auf deiser Artikel stehet alles, das wir wider den Bapst, Teufel und Welt lehren und leben. Darum mussen wir des gar gewiß sein und nicht zweifeln. Sonst ist's alles vorlorn, und behält Bapst und Teufel und alles wider uns den Sieg und Recht. . . . Daß die Messe im Bapsttum muß der großeste und schrecklichste Greuel sein, als die stracks und gewaltiglich wider diesen Häuptartikel . . . nu aber die Messe nichts anders ist noch sein kann (wie der Kanon und aller Bucher sagen) denn ein Werk der Menschen (auch boser Buben), damit einer sich selbst und andere mit sich gegen Gottversuhnen, Vergebung der Sunden und Gnade erwerben . . . so soll und muß man sie verdammen und fallen lassen verwerfen; denn das ist stracks wider den

Hauptartikel, daß nicht der da nicht sagt, daß nicht ein Messeknecht mit seinem Werk, sondern das Lamb Gottes und Sohn Gottes unsere Sünde trägt."

17. LW 49:263. WA BR 5:221: *". . . tamen pia sollicitudine rogamus et hortamur, ut mutationem rituum, quae pericolosa est, non primo, sed posteriore loco tractetis, primo loco autem caput doctrinae nostrae tractetis et plantetis, quod est de iustificatione nostri . . . non enim capiunt nisi externam rituum mutationem, qua titillantur ad horam, mox fastidiunt saturi omnis sanae doctrinae. Satis autem per se ipsam sese urgebit mutatio impiorum rituum, ubi caput illud doctrinae bene traditum radices egerit in piis cordibus. Hi enim intelligent statim, quam sit grandis abominatio et sacrilega blasphemia idolum illud papisticum, Missa scilicet et alii abusus sacramenti, uti non sit necesse ante hamum piscari, hoc est, istud primo convellere, antequam iustitia fidei intelligatur."*

18. Luther returned from Wartburg to bring order out of the chaos created by Carlstadt's iconoclastic reforms; he preached eight pastoral sermons in the course of a week. In one he said: "The Mass is an evil thing, and God is displeased with it, because it is performed as if it were a sacrifice and work of merit. Therefore it must be abolished . . . and only the ordinary evangelical Mass be retained. . . . It should be preached and taught with tongue and pen that to hold Mass in such a manner is sinful, and yet no one should be dragged away from it by the hair; for it should be left to God, and his Word should be allowed to work alone, without our work and interference. Why? Because it is not in my power or hand to fashion the hearts of men. . . . I can get no further than their ears; their hearts I cannot reach. And since I cannot pour faith into their hearts, I cannot, nor should I force anyone to have faith. That is God's work alone, who causes faith to live in the heart. . . . We should preach the Word, but the results must be left solely to God's good pleasure"; LW 51:75-76; WA 10^{III}: 14-15: "Also die Meß ist ein böß ding und gott ist jr feynd, in dem also sie geschehe, als were sie ein opffer und verdienstlick werck, der halb müssen sie abgehan werden . . . und alle die gemeyne Evangelische Messe gehalten . . . predigen sol mans, schreiben und verkündigen sol mans, das die Messe auff solche weise gehalten die Messe in der weyse gehalten sonderlich ist: doch sol mann niemants mit dem haer darvon ziehen oder reyssen, dann gotte sol mans herjnn geben und sein wort alleyne würcken lassen, nit unser zuthun und werck. Warumb? dann jch hab nit in meiner gewalt oder handt jr hertzen (der menschen). . . . Ich kan nit weytter kommen dann zu den orn, jns hertz kan ich nit kommen: dieweyl ich dann den glauben jns hertz nit giessen kann, so kann noch sol ich niemants darzu zwingen noch dringen, wenn got thut das alleyne und macht, das er vor jm hertzen lebt. . . . Das wort soll wir predigen, aber die volge sol got alleyn in seim gefallen sein."

19. Maxwell, *Outline of Christian Worship*, 77.

20. *Formula Missae* (1523), WA 12:28; LW 53:22. This was not only theory but also Luther's practice; he had preached the gospel for years in Wittenberg before introducing this evangelical liturgy.

21. Luther had been consistently speaking against the sacrifice of the Mass in such writings as A Treatise of the New Testament, that is, the Holy Mass (1520), WA 6:353-378, LW 35:79-111; The Babylonian Captivity of the Church (1520), WA 8:482-563, LW 36:11-26; and The Misuse of the Mass (1521), WA 6:497-573, LW 35:162-198.

22. Although it is clear that the Lord's Supper as *"donum Dei"* is fundamental in Luther's theology, in this context it needs to be observed that he also spoke of music using the

same term, music is a *"donum Dei"*; see Chapter 3, especially the discussion of the similarity of language when Luther speaks about justification, on the one hand, and music on the other.

23. On *beneficium* and *sacrificium*, see Vajta, *Luther on Worship*, 27-63.

24. LW 38:107; WA 30^{II}:603: "Das ist aber die Kunst, kurtz, kurtz und gewis dargegeben: **Das thut meinem gedechtnis,** Lerne sein gedencken.... Predigen, preisen, loben zuhoren und dancken fur die gnade jnn Christo erzeigt. Thustu das ... das du Gott nichts gegeben habest, noch mugest, Sondern alles und alles von jhm habest und nemest, sonderlich das ewige leben und unendliche gerechtigkeit jnn Christo.... Denn das heisst ein rechter Gott, der da gibt und nicht nimpt, der da hilfft und nicht jhm helffen lesst.... Summa, der alles thut und gibt, und er niemands darff, und thut solchs alles umbsonst, aus lauter gnaden on verdienst, den unwirdigen und unverdieneten, ja den verdampten und verlornen, Solch gedechtnis, bekentnis und ehre wil er haben."

25. LW 17:221. Lectures on Isaiah (1527-30); WA 31^{II}:432: *"Aureis literis haec verba sunt scribenda NOSTRUM, NOS, NOBIS. Qui haec non credit, non est Christianus."*

26. LW 26:179. Lectures on Galatians (1535); WA 40^{I}:299: *"Lege igitur cum magna Emphasi has voces: 'ME,' 'PRO ME,' et assuefacias te, ut illud, 'ME' possis certa fide concipere et applicare tibi.... Item, quod Christus non tantum dilexerit Petrum et Paulum et seipsum pro eis tradiderit, sed quod illa gratia aeque ad nos pertineat et veniat ac ad illos, Ideo etiam comprehendimur in isto 'ME.'"* See also Theses Concerning Faith and Law (1535), WA 39^{I}:45-46; LW 34:10. For this "for you" aspect in Lutheran worship, see Peter Brunner, *Worship in the Name of Jesus,* translated by Martin H. Bertram (St. Louis: Concordia, 1968), 91, 165 and *passim.*

27. Cf. Matthew 26:26-28; Luke 22:17-19; 1 Corinthians 11:23-24.

28. LW 44:55-56; WA 6:230: "In der meß ist nodt, das wir auch mit dem hertzen uben. Hie mussenn wir die wort Christi ertzelen, da er die meß einsetzt und spricht 'Nemet hyn und esset, das ist mein leichnam, der fur euch gebenn wirt,' desselben gleichenn ubir den kilch 'Nemet hyn und trincket alle drausz, das ist ein newes ewiges testament in meinem blut, das fur euch und fur viel vorgossen wirt zu vorgebung der sund, das solt yhr thun, als offt yhrs thut, tzu meinem gedechtnis.' In diesem worten hat Christus yhm ein begencknisz odder jartag gemacht ... die zu dissem begencknisz kommen, sollen haben dasselb testament, und ist drauff gestorben, damit solch testament bestendig und unwidderrufflich worden ist."

29. LW 35:81. A Treatise on the New Testament, that is, the Holy Mass (1520), WA 6:354-355: "Dan do Christus sebst und am ersten diß sacrament einsetzt unnd die ersten meß hielt und übet, da war keyn platten, kein casell, kein singen, kein prangen, ßondern allein dancksagung gottis und des sacraments prauch. Der selben einfeltickeit nach hielten die Apostel und alle Christen meß ein lang tzeyt, biß das sich erhuben die mancherley weysen und zusetze, das anders die Romischen, anders die Kriechen meß hielten, und nu endlich dahyn kummen, das das häubtstück an der meß unbekannt worden ist, und nit mehr den die zu setze der menschen yn der andacht seyn.... Ihe neher nu unßere meße der ersten meß Christi sein, yhe besser sie on zweyffell sein, und yhe weytter davon, yhe ferlicher."

30. Luther's understanding of the *Verba Testamenti* as proclamation from God rather than prayer to God, is underscored in his preference, expressed in the *Deutsche Messe,* for the so-called westward position, with the celebrant facing the people when declaring these words, in contrast to his direction that the celebrant should face the altar when praying on

behalf of the gathered congregation. However, Luther never put the westward-facing celebration into practice; see WA 19:80 and 90; LW 53:69 and 74.

31. The recitation of these words is not focused on the elements of bread and wine so much as on the people who are to receive them. "The words of the Supper: 'He said, "Take, eat; do this,"' etc., are directed not to the elements but to those who are about to commune"; Martin Chemnitz, *Examination of the Council of Trent, Part II,* translated by Fred Kramer (St. Louis: Concordia, 1978), 311; Martin Chemnitz, *Examen Concilii Tridentini* [1578], ed. Eduard Preuss (Berlin: Schlawitz, 1861), 333: "*Verba illa coena, Dixit: Accipite, comedite, hoc facite etc. diriguntur non elementa, sed ad communicaturos.*" Compare the similar statement of the Reformed Peter Martyr: "the words of the Supper pertain rather to men than either to bread or to wine"; cited in Joseph C. McLelland, *The Visible Words of God: An Exposition of the Sacramental Theology of Peter Martyr Vermigli AD 1500-1562* (Edinburgh: Oliver and Boyd, 1957), 30.

32. See The Abomination of the Secret Mass (1525), WA 18:22-36; LW 36:311-28.

33. LW 36:164. The Misuse of the Mass (1521), WA 8:508: "Zum ersten, Fragen wyr nichts noch der ungeystlichen geystlickeyt, wilche die nerrischen leutt erfunden und der gantzen wellt eyngebildet haben, das man die wortt der benedeyung hatt heymlich gehallten und neimandt den priestern, und nicht eher, sie haben denn Messe gehallten, wollen handelln, reden und wissen lassen, wilche doch alle menschenn solten billich bekandt unnd offenbar gewest seyn, die weyl glawb, trost und selickeyt aller menschen."

34. LW 36:43. The Babylonian Captivity of the Church (1520), WA 6:517: ". . . *totam virtutem Missae consistere in verbis Christi, quibus testatur remissionem peccatorum donari omnibus, qui credunt corpus eius tradi et sanguinem eius fundi pro se. Atque ob hanc rem nulla re magis opus esse audituris Missam quam ut ipsa verba sedulo et plena fide meditentur. quod nisi fecerint, frustra omnia alia fecerint.*"

35. BC-W/K 362; BSLK 519-520: "Was ist das Sakrament des Altars? Antwort. Es ist der wahre Leib und Blut unsers Herrn Jesu Christi, unter dem Brot und Wein uns Christen zu essen und zu trinken von Christo selbst eingesetzt. Wo stehet das geschrieben? Antwort. So schreiben die heiligen Evangelisten Matthäus, Markus, Lukas, und S. Paulus: 'Unser HERR Jesus Christus in der Nacht, da er verraten ward, nahm er das Brot, dankt' und brach's und gab's seinen Jungern und sprach: Nehmet hin, esset, das ist mein Leib, der fur Euch gegeben wird. Solchs tut zu meinem Gedächtnis.

Desselbengleichen nahm er auch den Kelch nach dem Abendmahl, danket und gab ihn den und sprach: Nehmet hin und trinket alle daraus. Dieser Kelch ist das neue Testament in meinem Blut, das fur Euch vergossen wird zur Vergebung der Sunden. Solchs tut, so oft Ihr trinket, zu meinem Gedächtnis." In the *Large Catechism* (1529) Luther states that what the second sacrament is, what its benefits are, and who should receive it, "is established from the words Christ used to institute it. So everyone who wishes to be a Christian and go to the sacrament should know them. For we do not intend to admit to the sacrament and administer it to those who do not know what they seek or why they come. The words are these . . ."; BC-W/K 467; BSLK 708: "Und solchs alles aus den Worten gegründet, dadurch es von Christo eingesetzt ist, welche auch ein iglicher wissen soll, der ein Christ will sein und zum Sakrament gehen. Denn wir sind's nicht gesinnet, dazuzulassen und zu reichen denen, die nicht wissen, was sie da suchen oder warümb sie kommen. Die Wort aber sind diese. . . ."

36. WA 19:90; LW 53:74. In the *Formula missae* it was simply listed as a suitable eucharistic hymn; see WA 12:218; LW 53:37.

37. The use of hymns to supply what is otherwise missing from a liturgical form is a topic infrequently discussed; an exception is Alan Dunstan, *The Use of Hymns: A Practical Exploration of the Place of Hymnody within the Liturgy* (London: Mayhew, 1990). One example he cites is the former custom, in the chapel Pusey House, Oxford, an Anglo-Catholic foundation, "to sing *Wherefore, O Father . . .* directly after the 1662 [Book of Common Prayer] consecration prayer in order to supply what were considered to be the deficiencies of that prayer," 16. The hymn in question was:

> Wherefore, O Father, we thy humble servants
> Here bring before thee Christ thy well-beloved,
> All-perfect Offering, Sacrifice immortal,
> Spotless Oblation

(*The English Hymnal* [London: Oxford University Press, 1906], No. 335). Anglo-Catholics worshiping in the chapel of Pusey House were concerned to add the language of oblation and sacrifice to the Prayer Book Eucharistic rite that had been specifically excluded by Anglican liturgical reformers.

38. There is a parallel in Calvin's *La Forme des prières et chants ecclésiastiques* (Geneva, 1542). The important prayer before the sermon, though the verbal form was left to the discretion of the preacher, was essentially an epiclesis prayer, an invocation of the Holy Spirit that the Word may be effectively preached: "The Minister commences . . . to pray for the grace of His Holy Spirit, that his Word may be faithfully expounded to the honor of his name and the edification of the Church . . ."; Bard Thompson, *Liturgies of the Western Church* (1961) (Philadelphia: Fortress, 1980), 198-199. ". . . puis le Ministre commence de rechef à prier, pour demander à Dieu la grace de son sainct Esprit: afin, que sa parolle soit fidelement exposee à l'honneur de son Nom, & à l'edification de l'Eglise . . ."; [Jean Calvin], *La Forme des Prieres et Chantz ecclesiastiques* ([Geneva]: [s.n.], 1542; facsimile, Basel: Bärenreiter, 1959), sig. i6^{v}-i7^{r}. Thus the epiclesis is effectively transferred from a Eucharistic Prayer to the prayer before the sermon — from the ministry of the Sacrament to the ministry of the Word.

39. LW 38:122; WA 30^{II}:614: "Denn Christus scheidet hie die zwey stuck weit von einander, Sacrament und Gedechtnis, da er spricht: 'Solchs thut zu meinem gedechtnis.' Ein ander ding ist das Sacrament, und ein ander ding ist das Gedechtnis, Das Sacrament sollen wir uben und thun (spricht er) und daneben sein gedencken, das ist: leren, gleuben und dancken, Das gedechtnis sol wol ein danckopffer sein, aber das Sacrament selbs ist nicht eine opffer, sondern ein gabe Gottes sein, uns geschenckt, welchs wir zu danck an nemen und mit danck empfahen sollen." Note again the similarity of language when Luther speaks of the Sacrament and music as both being the gift of God.

40. LW 38:123; WA 30^{II}: 614-625: "Und daher acht ich, das viel gesang jnn der Messe, so fein und herrlich vom dancken und loben gemacht und bis her bleiben ist, als das Gloria in excelsis Et in terra, Das Alleluia, Das Patrem, Die Prefation, Das Sanctus, Das Benedictus, das Agnus Dei, In welchen stücken findestu nichts vom opffer, Sondern eitel lob und danck, Darumb wir sie auch jnn unser Messen behalten, Und sonderlich dienet das Agnus uber allen gesengen aus der massen wol zum Sacrament, Denn es klerlich daher singet und lobet

Christum, das er unser sunde getragen haben, und mit schonen kurtzen worten das Gedechtnis Christi gewaltiglich und lieblich treibt."

41. LW 42:173; WA 7:694: "Diße wort ob sie wol der priester heymlich spricht (unnd wolt gott, er sprecht sie auffs allerlaut, das sie yderman klerlich höret auch yn deutscher sprach)."

42. LW 53:28; WA 12:212: "*Haec verba Christi velim, modica post praefationem interposita pausa, in eo tono vocis recitari, quo canitur alias oratio dominica in Canone, ut a circumstantibus possit audiri.*"

43. For the two items within the context of the medieval mass of Easter Day, see Richard Hoppin, ed., *Anthology of Medieval Music* (New York: Norton, 1978), Nos. 16 and 18.

44. See Thomas Müntzer, *Schriften und Briefe: Kritische Gesamtausgabe*, ed. Günther Franz (Gütersloh: Mohn, 1968), 174-179.

45. Literature on the musical aspects of the *Deutsche Messe* includes: Johannes Wolf, "Luther und die musikalische Liturgie des evangelischen Hauptgottesdienst," *Sammelbände der internationalen Musikgesellschaft* 3 (1901/02): 647-670; Friedrich Gebhardt, "Die Musikalischen Grundlagen zu Luthers Deutscher Messe," L-J, 10 (1928): 128-169; Christhard Mahrenholz, "Zur musikalischen Gestaltung von Luthers Gottesdienstreform," *Musik und Kirche* 5 (1933): 281-296, reprinted in Christhard Mahrenholz, *Musicologica et liturgia: Gesammelte Aufsätze*, ed. Karl Ferdinand Müller (Kassel: Bärenreiter, 1960), 154-168; Theodore Hoety-Nickel, "Luther's Deutsche Messe," *Luther and Culture* [Martin Luther Lectures 4] (Decorah: Luther College Press, 1960), 183-211. On Johann Walter's collaboration with Luther on the musical aspects of the *Deutsche Messe*, see Walter Blankenburg, *Johann Walter, Leben und Werk*, ed. Friedhelm Brusniak (Tutzing: Schneider, 1991), 310-391.

46. WA 19:70-71, and also the facsimile at the end of the volume; LW 53:55-57.

47. Cited in Michael Praetorius, *Syntagma musicum* 1: *Musicae artis analecta* (Wittenberg: Richter, 1614/15, facsimile ed. Wilibald Gurlitt, Kassel: Bärenreiter, 1959), 451-452; see Appendix 4 for the full text in Latin and German, together with an English translation.

48. The apparent discrepancy between Walter's recollection of the sixth mode for the Gospel with Luther's prescription of the fifth mode is discussed below.

49. See Harold S. Powers and Frans Wiering, "Modal Theories and Polyphonic Music," New Grove 2, 16:798.

50. Martin Gerbert, *Scriptores ecclesiastici de musica sacra potissimum* (St. Blasien, 1784; reprinted Hildesheim: Olms, 1963), 3:356: "*sed postremus [octavi] sapientum*"; "*Quintum da laetis.*"

51. See, for example, Andreas Ornithoparchus, *Musicae activae micrologus libris* (Leipzig: Schumann, 1517), sig. Ki^r-Kii^r, where both "*de accentus epistolarum*" and "*de accentus Evangeliorum*" are directed to be intoned on the same basic pitch, with the simplest of inflections.

52. Luther also added an example of how to notate a question within a Gospel pericope. The text he chose was Matthew 26:1-2: "Jesus said to his disciples: You know that in two days it will be Passover [Oster]?" The choice is interesting in that there is a parallel between the disciples in the Gospel narrative, who were preparing for the Passover that would become the institution of the Lord's Supper, and Luther, who was preparing for a German vernacular form of this Abendmahl.

53. Translation in Nils Holger Peterson, "Lutheran Tradition and the Medieval Mass," *The Arts and the Cultural Heritage of Martin Luther*, ed. Eyolf Østrem, Jens Fleischer and Nils Holger Peterson (Copenhagen: Museum Tusculanum Press, 2003), 41-42; WA 17[1]:449: "Wyr haben angefangen zuversuchen eyn deutsche Messe anzurichten. Ihr wist, das die Messe ist das furnemest eusserlich ampt, das do verordnet ist zu trost den rechten Christen, Darumb bitt ich euch Christen, yhr wolt Gott bitten und anruffen, das er yhm das las wolgefallen, Ihr habt offt gehort, das man nicht leren solle, man wis denn, das es Gott wort sey, also soll man nicht ordnen und anheben, man wis denn, das es Got gefalle, man soll auch nicht mit der vernunfft dareyn fallen, denn so es nicht selber ansehet, so wird nichts daraus, Darumb hab ich mich auch so lang gewert mit der deutsche Messe, das ich nicht ursach gebe den rotten geystern, die hyneyn plumpen unbesunnen, achten nicht ob es Gott haben wolle. Nu aber so mich so viel bitten aus allen landen mit geschrifft und brieffen, und mich der weltlich gewalt darzu dringet, kunden wyr uns nicht wol entschuldigen und ausreden, sonder mussen darfur achten und halten, es sey der wil Gottis, wa nu da etwas gehet, das unser ist, das soll untergehen und stincken, wenn es gleich eyn schon und gros ansehen hat, Ist es aber aus Gott, so mus es fort gehen, ob es sich gleich nerrisch let ansehen, Also alle ding, die Gott thut, wnes gleich nymant gefelt, mus es fort, Darumb bitt euch, das yhr den Herren bitet, wenn es eyn rechtschaffne Mess sey, das sie yhm zu lob und ehren fort gehe."

54. See WA 19:50-51.

55. For example, in his Admonition Concerning the Sacrament (1530), Luther wrote: "Now because everyone wants to be reverent and devout, in order to honor Christ's sufferings and to worship God, one person undertakes this, another that, one person goes to Rome, another becomes a monk, a third person fasts. Who can enumerate all the forms of divine worship which we have up till now instituted and observed on the basis of the devil's inspiration and our own devotion? Because of them we have obscured and forgotten this lofty, beautiful worship, namely, his remembrance and the glory of the passion of Christ, which worship God himself established and to which he bore witness that he was indeed well pleased with it. He has established it in such a way that it can never be exhausted or observed enough, for who remembers God sufficiently? Who can praise him too much? Who can thank him too much? Who can honor Christ's passion too much?"; LW 38:105-106; WA 30[II]: 601-602: "Weil nu ein iglicher geneigt und andechtig sein wil, Christus leiden zu ehren und Gott einen dienst zu thun, und einer dis, der ander das fur nimpt: Einer eufft gen Rom, der ander wird ein Munch, Der dritte fastet. Und wer kan alle die Gottes dienst erzelen, die wir das aus teufels eingeben und eigener andacht bis her gestifftet und gehalten haben, damit wir diesen hohen, schonen Gottes dienst, nemlich sein gedechtnis und die ehre des leidens Christi, verfinstert und vergessen haben, welchen Gott selbs gestifft und bezeugt hat, das er jhm hertzlich wol gefalle? Und hat jhn also gestifft, das er nimer mehr kan aufgedienet noch gnug gehalten werden, Denn wer kan Gottes gnugsam gedencken? Wer kan jhn zu viel loben? Wer kan ihm zu seer dancken? Wer kan Christus leiden zu viel ehren?"

56. Adam von Fulda, in Gerbert, *Scriptores ecclesiastici de musica sacra potissimum*, 3:356: "*sextum pietate probatis.*"

57. The letters above the staves indicate the various melodic formulae as given in Example 12.2. Unlike the *Vox evangelistae* and the *Vox personarum*, the *Vox Christi* is not given an alternate comma, although the *Verba Testamenti* includes an alternative form (M^2 in Example 12.3).

58. The earliest appearance of *Christe, du Lamm Gottes* was in the 1528 Brunswick church order, but its earlier existence is implied both by Luther's manuscript draft (WA 19:71; LW 53:57), and by his reference to "the German Agnus Dei" in the *Deutsche Messe* (WA 19:99; LW 53:82). Most scholars accept 1525 as the year of its creation; see, for example, Markus Jenny in AWA 4:99.

59. This melodic connection was exploited by later composers, notably Johann Sebastian Bach; see, for example, Robin A. Leaver, "Bach and the German *Agnus Dei*," *A Bach Tribute: Essays in Honor of William H. Scheide*, ed. Paul Brainard and Ray Robinson (Kassel: Bärenreiter, 1993), 163-171. See also Chapter 13 below.

60. Examples of Luther's use of parallel and symmetrical relationships can be detected in his hymns. For example: the four stanzas of *Ein feste Burg* comprise two parallel groups, stanzas 1-2 and 3-4, and the "Christ" stanzas (1 and 3) are set in contrast to the "devil" stanzas (2 and 4); the 7 stanzas of *Christ lag in Todesbanden* are symmetrically centered on stanza 4: "ein Tod den andern fraß" (one death the other ate).

61. See AWA 4:315-317.

62. Scholarly opinion is divided on the question of Luther's authorship; see the discussions of Jenny (AWA 4:132-134), who argues against the possibility, and Konrad Ameln ("'All Ehr und Lob soll Gottes sein': Ein deutsches Gloria — von Martin Luther?" JbLH 31 [1987/88]: 38-52), who argues for its authenticity on the basis of the attribution in the earliest source, and the strong internal evidence of the relationship between text and melody; Ulrich S. Leupold (LW 53:184) also accepts the rhymed version as authentic.

63. LU 16-18. Decius's *Allein Gott in der Höh sei Ehr* is based on the same plainsong melody.

64. LU 61.

65. These two vernacular items, being based on pre-existing chants, keep their modal identity, Tone IV (which Adam von Fulda characterized as "soothing"; Gerbert, *Scriptores ecclesiastici de musica sacra potissimum*, 3:356: "*quartus dicitur fieri blandus*") for the German Gloria and Tone V ("joyful") for the German Sanctus. On Luther's metrical versions of the Gloria and Sanctus, see further in Chapter 15 below.

66. In both the *Formula missae* and *Deutsche Messe* the Sanctus was moved from its traditional position following the Preface, and was to be sung during the distribution of communion.

67. Chemnitz, *Examination of the Council of Trent, Part II*, 494; Chemnitz, *Examen Concilii Tridentini*, 403: "*Administrationem et usum coenae Dominicae, Christus moriturus testamenti forma instituit. Magnum autem scelus est, vel hominis testamento, quando ratum et confirmatum est, aliquid superordinare. Manifestum igitur est, quid sit Pontificia Missa, quae Testamento Filii Dei aliquid superordinat, quod in illo non continentur, non institutur, non praescribitur.*" See also Martin Chemnitz, *Fundamenta sanae doctrinae, de vera et substantiali praesentia, exhibitione & sumptione corporis & sanguis Domini in coena . . .* (1570) (Jena: Richtzenhain, 1590); English translation, *The Lord's Supper*, trans. J. A. O. Preus (St. Louis: Concordia, 1979).

68. David Chytraeus, *In Leviticum, seu tertium librum Mosis* (Wittenberg, 1569); English version of the *Prolegomena: Chytraeus on Sacrifice: A Reformation Treatise in Biblical Theology*, translated by John Warwick Montgomery (St. Louis: Concordia, 1962), 122-123, for

the passage cited here. Before these words the reader is directed to "those richer treatises of Luther: *On the Abrogation of Private Mass* and *The Babylonian Captivity*."

69. See Leonhard Fendt, *Der lutherische Gottesdienst des 16. Jahrhunderts* (Munich: Reinhardt, 1923).

70. See Luther D. Reed, *The Lutheran Liturgy*, 2nd ed. (Philadelphia: Fortress Press, 1959), 753-754. The Pfaltz-Neuberg church order was largely the work of Andreas Osiander and may well have exerted some influence on Cranmer and the 1549 Prayer Book; see John Dowden, *Further Studies in the Prayer Book* (London: Methuen, 1908), 66-70. However, it should be noted that it is not a Reformed Canon as such but rather an independent epiclesis to be prayed before the *Verba Testamenti;* see Aemilius L. Richter, *Die evangelischen Kirchenordnungen des sechsehnten Jahrhunderts* (Weimar: Verlag des Landes-Industriecomptoirs, 1846; repr. Nieuwkoop: De Graaf, 1967), 2:28.

71. It is significant that Brilioth's critique of Luther was made from a Swedish perspective; so also Frank C. Senn (note 6 above); and Senn's "Liturgia Svecanae Ecclesiae: An Attempt at Eucharistic Restoration during the Swedish Reformation," *Studia Liturgica* 14 (1980/81): 20-36.

72. See Thompson, *Liturgies of the Western Church*, 154, 177. The influence of Luther is also to be found in the early development of the English Prayer Book. The 1549 Eucharistic Prayer, a reduced and reformed version of the Sarum Canon, was in three parts, with the *Verba Testamenti* imbedded within the middle section. The outer sections were placed elsewhere in the 1552 Prayer Book, leaving the Words of Institution almost on their own. An interim position is discovered in Marbeck's *Booke of Common praier noted* (1550), which introduced an "Amen" after the first section, and a suitable space before the third section, which served to isolate the Words of Institution. Marbeck also followed Luther, and the German church orders derived from Luther, by indicating that the Reformed Canon should be sung, albeit in a monotone rather than in a melodic form such as Luther prescribed; see Robin A. Leaver, *Marbeck's Book of Common praier noted* (Appleford: Marcham Manor, 1982), 70-71. Luther, of course, would not have been entirely happy with the 1552 Prayer Book, which set the *Verba Testamenti* within the context of prayer to God, rather than being presented as God's proclamation of forgiveness and grace in Christ to his believing people.

73. LBW, 69-70.

74. See, for example, Paul Rorem, "Luther's Objection to a Eucharistic Prayer," *The Cresset* 38 (1978): 12-16.

75. For a summary of how Luther understood the doctrine of the church from the standpoint of the doctrine of justification, see Paul D. L. Avis, *The Church in the Theology of the Reformers* (London: Marshall Morgan and Scott, 1981), 1-25.

76. Spinks, *Luther's Liturgical Criteria*, 37.

Notes to Chapter 13

1. LW 53:72; WA 19:86.

2. For the background, see Joseph Herl, *Worship Wars in Early Lutheranism: Choir, Congregation, and Three Centuries of Conflict* (New York: Oxford University Press, 2004), 3-22.

3. LW 53:27; WA 12:212.

4. See the Wittenberg Church Order (1533), Emil Sehling, *Die evangelischen Kirchenordnungen des 16. Jahrhunderts* (Leipzig: Riesland, 1902-1913; reprint, Tübingen: Mohr, 1955), 1:704.

5. *Kirchen-ordnunge zum anfang/fur die Pfarher in Hertzog Heinrichs zu Sachsen v.g.h. Fürstenthumb* (Wittenberg: Lufft, 1539), sig. Fii^v-Fiii^v. Musical notation is not given by Sehling, *Die evangelischen Kirchenordnungen.*

6. *Kirchen-ordnunge* (1539), sig. Fiv^r: "Melodie der Evangelien und Episteln deudsch zu singen/mögen die Pfarher bey den Kirchen des grossen Stedte suchen/und abschrieben/Als Dresden/Leiptzick, Weissenfels/Saitz, etc.

> Prefation in der Messe/oder Communion/
> Prefatio in Natali Domini/
> Prefatio in Epiphania Domini.
> Prefatio in Festo Paschali.
> Prefatio in Festo Ascensionis Domini/
> Prefatio in Festo Pentecostes/
> Prefatio de S. Trinitate/

Item Prefationem communem/mögen die Pfarher aus den Lateinischen Missaln/und sollen die Pfarrer alles mit rat der Superattendenten ordentlich und Christlich halten." Sehling, *Die evangelischen Kirchenordnungen,* 281.

7. Herl, *Worship Wars in Early Lutheranism,* 17-21.

8. LW 53:36; WA 12:218: "*Cantica velim etiam nobis esse vernacula quam plurima, quae populus sub missa cantaret, vel iuxta gradualia, item iuxta Sanctus et Agnus dei. Quis enim dubitat, eas olim fuisse voces totius populi, quae nunc solus Chorus cantat. . . .*"

9. See note 13 below.

10. Sehling, *Die evangelischen Kirchenordnungen,* 1:704: ". . . darnach einen introitum, zu zeiten lateinisch, zu eiten deutsch, welches soll sein ein deutscher psalm." See also the following note.

11. Sehling, *Die evangelischen Kirchenordnungen,* 1:703: "Deutsch sollen die schüler nicht singen, on allein, wenn das volk mitsinget." The Church Order also makes it clear that the Kyrie was not invariable. "Then [after the Introit] a threefold Kyrie, or at times, especially at festivals, a ninefold [Kyrie] as customary." Sehling, *Die evangelischen Kirchenordnungen,* 1:704: "Darnach das recte kyrie dreimal, oder zu zeiten, besondern uf die feste, ein anders neunmal, wie gewonlich." This implication is that the threefold Kyrie from the *Deutsche Messe* was generally sung by the whole congregation, but at the major festivals the "customary" Kyries, that is, troped in Latin, would be sung by the choirboys.

12. This chant is discussed in Chapter 15 below.

13. LW 53:173 (modified); Sehling, *Die evangelischen Kirchenordnungen,* 1:705: ". . . nach dem hymno soll man im chor anheben das teutsch te deum laudamus, wie as doctor Martinus verdeutscht hat, und ein schulgesell soll in dem schulerstul mitten in der kirchen mit dem volck auf alle halbe vers, wie es gemacht ist, antworten. Er mag auch zum ersten etliche knaben in den stul zu hulf nehmen, bis das volck sich gewent, solch te deum mitzusingen."

14. Sehling, *Die evangelischen Kirchenordnungen*, 1:701: "Darnach singen die schuler mitten in der kirchen mit der gemein die deudschen Letanien."

15. Sehling, *Die evangelischen Kirchenordnungen*, 1:703: ". . . nach der predigt soll man mitten in der kirchen mit dem volck singen das Deutsch Magnificat." The Wittenberg Church Order also speaks of the singing of the Benedictus in German at the beginning of the evangelical Mass, which, according to its rubric of the choirboys never singing alone in German, implies congregational participation; Sehling, *Die evangelischen Kirchenordnungen*, 1:704.

16. WA 19:81-86; LW 53:70-71.

17. AWA 4, 315-19; LW 53:182-183.

18. LW 53:82; WA 19:99: ". . . und singe, was ubrig ist von obgenanten liedern oder das deudsch Agnus dei."

19. AWA 4:99.

20. See Chapter 12 above.

21. On Bach's use of the connections between Luther's German Kyrie and Agnus Dei, see Robin A. Leaver, "Bach and the German *Agnus Dei*," in *A Bach Tribute: Essays in Honor of William H. Scheide*, ed. Paul Brainard and Ray Robinson (Kassel: Bärenreiter, 1993), 163-71, and Robin A. Leaver, "*Agnus dei* Compositions of J. S. Bach: Some Liturgical and Theological Perspectives," in *Das Blut Jesu und die Lehre von der Versöhnung im Werk Johann Sebastian Bach*, ed. Albert A. Clement (Amsterdam: Koninklijke Nederlandse Akadamie van Wetenschappen, 1995), 233-249.

22. See Daniela Wissemann-Garbe, "Neue Weisen zu alten Lieder: Die Ersatzmelodien im Klugschen Gesangbuch von 1533," JbLH 37 (1998): 118-138.

23. See the comparative melodic incipits in Wissemann-Garbe, "Neue Weisen zu alten Lieder," 122-123.

24. See Bruno Stäblein, *Hymnen I: Die mittelalterlichen Hymnenmelodien des Abendlands*, [*Monumenta monodic medii aevi*, 1] (Kassel: Bärenreiter, 1956), 503; Wilhelm Bäumker, *Das katholische deutsche Kirchenlied in seine singweisen von den frühesten Zeiten bis gegen ende des Siebzehnten Jahrhunderts* (Hildesheim: Olms, 1962), 1:1.

25. Literature on the chorale melodies created from *Veni redemptor gentium* include: Salmon Kümmerle, *Encyklopädie der evangelischen Kirchenmusik* (Gütersloh: Bertelsmann, 1888-95), 3:768; Konrad Ameln, "Lateinischer Hymnus und deutsche Kirchenlied," *Musik und Kirche* 6 (1934): 138-48; Walter Blankenburg, "Geschichte der melodien des Evangelischen Kirchengesangbuch: Ein Abriß," *Handbuch zum evangelische Kirchengesangbuch*, ed. Christhard Mahrenholz, Oskar Söhngen, and Otto Schlißke, 2/2 (Berlin: Evangelische Verlagsanstalt, 1957), 55-56; Konrad Ameln, *Roots of German Hymnody of the Reformation Era* (St. Louis: Concordia, 1964); *Johann Walter sämtliche Werke 6: Das Christlich Kinderlied D. Martini Lutheri Erhalt uns Herr . . .* , ed. Joachim Stalmann (Kassel: Bärenreiter, 1970), 185; see also the discussion in Chapter 2 above.

26. Zahn No. 1174. DKL Ea10.

27. Some of the variant forms of the plainsong melody had already begun to move in this direction; see *The Hymnal 1982 Companion*, ed. Raymond Glover (New York: Church Hymnal Corporation, 1990-95), 3:102.

28. LW 53:235.

29. Zahn 1945a. DKL D1A.

30. On the background, see Cemal Kafadar, "The Ottomans and Europe," in *Handbook of European History 1400-1600: Late Middle Ages, Renaissance and Reformation*, ed. Thomas Brady, Jr., Heiko Oberman, and James D. Tracy (Leiden: Brill, 1994-95), 1:589-635, esp. 609-13; see also Gregory J. Miller, "Luther on the Turks and Islam," *Lutheran Quarterly* 14 (2000): 79-97, and the literature cited there.

31. The two extant copies of this 1529 Nuremberg imprint only came to light in recent decades, one in the library of Basle University, Switzerland, and the other in the Pitts Theology Library, Emory University, Atlanta, Georgia.

32. Zahn 350. DKL Ee21.

33. WA 51:585-625; LW 43:213-241.

34. The hymn is discussed further in Chapter 4 above.

35. Walter also included the Latin *Da pacem Domine* in the sequence; see *Johann Walter sämtliche Werke* 1: *Geistliches Gesangbüchlein, Wittenberg 1551, I: Deutsche Gesänge*, ed. Otto Schröder (Kassel: Bärenreiter, 1953), 112-17; *Georg Rhau Musikdrucke aus den Jahren 1538-1545 in practischer Neuausgabe* 11: *Neue deutsche geistliche Gesänge für die gemeinen Schulen*, ed. Joachim Stalmann (Kassel: Bärenreiter, 1994), 296-304.

36. See the discussion in Chapter 14 below.

37. Zahn No. 1945b. DKL D1Aα.

38. This led to the assumption that Walter was the author of the text; see Walter Blankenburg, "Wer schuf den Gesang 'Gib unserm Fürsten und aller Obrigkeit'?" JbLH 25 (1981): 102-103.

39. Breslauer Handschrift Sign. *Bohn 352*, fol. 60; see Konrad Ameln, "Nochmals zu 'Gib unserm Fürsten und aller Obrigkeit,'" JbLH 25 (1981): 103-104.

40. See Karl Brinkel, "Zu Johann Walters Stellung als Hofkapellmeister in Dresden," JbLH 5 (1960): 135-43.

41. *Johann Walter sämtliche Werke* 6: xviii (English) and ix (German): ". . . dem Gnediger her und fürst, itzt gar eine fherliche Zzeit, dorinnen allen Christen des gebet zcu Got hoch von nöten, und ich gar oftmals an die weißagung und warnung der zcukunftigen straffe, des Ehrwirdigen gotseligen teweren propheten Doctor Mar. Lutheri gedencke, So habe ich sein liebes hinderlassen liedt und gebet "Erhalt uns Her bey deinem Wort" sambt andern Christlichen gebet gesungen, fur die oberkeit und dergleichen aus gotes gnade, itzt auf new, in figural gesetz, und in Druck geben. . . ."

42. WA 6:404-469; LW 44:115-217.

43. Johann Schelle, *Six Chorale Cantatas*, ed. Mary S. Morris, Recent Researches in the Music of the Baroque Era 60-61 (Madison, Wis.: A-R Editions, 1988), 109-52.

44. *Dietrich Buxtehudes Werke* 8: *Neun Kantaten*, ed. Dietrich Kilian (Leipzig: Peters, 1958), 47-53.

45. *Johann Walter sämtliche Werke* 1:52.

46. *Johann Walter sämtliche Werke* 6:21.

47. See the discussions in Chapters 2 and 3 above.

1. Joseph Herl, *Worship Wars in Early Lutheranism: Choir, Congregation, and Three Centuries of Conflict* (Oxford: Oxford University Press, 2004).

2. See the summaries of the contents of Praetorius's publications in George J. Buelow, *A History of Baroque Music* (Bloomington: Indiana University Press, 2004), 207-209; and Carl Schalk, *Music in Early Lutheranism: Shaping the Tradition (1524-1672)* (St. Louis: Concordia, 2001), 110-112.

3. See Chapter 2 above.

4. See Chapter 2 above.

5. See Chapter 13 above and Chapters 15 and 16 below.

6. A comprehensive term for all kinds of chant forms.

7. See Appendix 4 below which includes the complete section from Praetorius's *Syntagma musicum I*.

8. Walter's surviving Torgau manuscripts are of polyphonic motets and other liturgical music. Many of these compositions employ chant *cantus firmi,* confirming Walter's continued use of monodic chant in Torgau; see Carl Gerhardt, *Die Torgauer Walter Handschriften: Eine Studie zur Quellenkunde der Musikgeschichte der deutschen Reformationszeit* (Kassel: Bärenreiter, 1949).

9. Praetorius, *Syntagma musicum tomus primum,* 449-450.

10. "... dieweil ich bey euch [Rhau] zu Wittemberg auch jnn unser löblichen schul/viel feiner junger knaben und gesellen spüre/die sich (welchs mir hertzlich wol gefelt) jnn den andern Musicus activis/als Plan und Mensurata ..."; Martin Agricola, *Musica Instrumentalis Deudsch* (Wittenberg: Rhau, 1545), fol. ii^v.

11. The other alternative would have been for these school choirs to have used pre-existing, unreformed chant sources, with handwritten corrections and emendations. The preference would have been to use new, "clean" versions, unencumbered by alterations, if they were available.

12. The document, originally in the Staatsarchiv, Zerbst (GAR V 209b), now in the Staatsarchiv, Göttingen; see Adolf Boës, "Die reformatorischen Gottesdienste in der Wittenberger Pfarrkirche von 1523 und die 'Ordenung der gesenge der Wittembergischen Kirchen' von 1543/44," JbLH 4 (1958/59): 1-40 — the document is also given in facsimile, between pp. 32-33, with a transcription as a supplement folded-in at the end of JbLH 4.

13. Erasmus Alber, *Wider die verkehrte Lehre der Carlstader, und alle fürnemste Häupter der Sacramentirer: Rottengeister, Widerteuffer, Sacramentlsterer, Eheschender, Musica Verächter, Bildstürmer, und Verwüster aller guten Ordnung* (1556) (Mecklenburg, 1594), sig. T 7^v: "In den Kirchen/da Schüler und gelehrte Bürger sind/ists fein das man Lateinische Gesenge neben den Teutschen Liedern singt. Denn schöner Melodey kan man nicht machen/ denn die Lateinische Gesenge haben/als *Verbum caro factum est. A solis ortus cardine. Puer natus est nobis. Illuminare Jerusalem. Laetere Jerusalem. Ossana filio David. Cum rex gloriae. Victimae paschali. Ad coenam agni providi. Vita sanctorum. Festum nunc celebre,* &c. Und der Lateinische Text klingt viel besser unter denselben Noten/wo gute Noten bösen Text haben/ da gebe ich den selben Noten ein guten Text/Lateinischer oder Teutsch."

14. See Josef Benzing, *Die Buchdrucker des 16. und 17. Jahrhunderts in deutschen Sprachgebiet* (Wiesbaden: Harrassowitz, 1963), 468.

15. See Martin Rössler, *Bibliographie der deutschen Liedpredigt* (Nieuwkoop: de Graaf, 1976); Martin Rössler, *Die Liedpredigt: Geschichte e. Predigtgattung* (Göttingen: Vandenhoeck & Ruprecht, 1976).

16. A facsimile of Spangenberg's double chant anthology, with an introduction by Robin A. Leaver, is forthcoming from Olms, Hildesheim.

17. "*Nec id quidem priuato consilio, Sed potius iussu et instinctu Venerabilis patris nostri D. Martini Lutheri*"; *Cantiones ecclesiasticae*, fol. ii^v.

18. In 1544 Rhau produced: Balthasar Resinarius, *Responsorium numero octoginta;* Johann Walter, *Cantio Septem vocum;* Johann Walter, *Wittembergisch deudsch Geistlich Gesangbüchlein; Newe deudsche geistliche Gesenge; Postremum Vespertini Officii Opus;* and *Etliche Psalmen.* In 1545: Sixtus Dietrich, *Novum Opus Musicum Tres Tomus Sacrorum Hymnorum; Bicinia Gallica, Latina, Germanica Tomus Primus . . . Tomus Secundus; Officiorum De Nativitate circumcisione;* as well as Spangenberg's *Zwölff Christliche Lobgesenge vnd Leissen.*

19. See Benzing, *Die Buchdrucker des 16. und 17. Jahrhunderts,* 466-467 & 292.

20. *Eine kurtze schöne christliche Prediget vom hochwirdigen Sacrament des Abentmals . . .* (1543); *Des ehelichen Ordens Spiegel und Regel inn zehen Capittel geteilt* (1544/1545); *Postilla dudesch van den vornemsten Festen dorch dat gantze Jar, vor de iungen Christen . . .* [first published in Wittenberg; see note 50 below] (1545).

21. Conversely, Rhau had a high regard for Agricola, whom he regarded as "musicus sane eruditus, et amicus noster singularis" (truly an erudite musician and our singular friend); *Enchiridion utriusque musicae practicae* (Wittenberg: Rhau, 1538), sig. Aiij^r. The dedicatory epistle of Spangenberg's *Quaestiones musicae* is addressed to Rhau, and he and Martin Agricola are described as "skilled musicians" (*Musici peritissimi*); Spangenberg, *Quaestiones musicae in usum scholae Northusianae* (Nuremberg: Iohannes Petreius, 1536), sig. Aij^r; see also Heinz Funck, *Martin Agricola: Ein frühprotestantischer Schulmusiker* (Wolfenbüttel: Kallmeyer, 1933), 63.

22. Early in 1537 Luther called it the "crown of all schools" ("die Kron aller Schulen") and gave the credit for this to its Rector Georg Major; see WA TR No. 3544.

23. See Daniel Zager, "Music for the Lutheran Liturgy: Johannes Spangenberg's *Cantiones ecclesiasticae/Kirchengesenge Deudsche* (1545)," *This Is the Feast: A Festschrift for Richard Hillert at 80* (St. Louis: Morning Star, 2004), 45-60.

24. "Das lateinisch vmb der schüler vnnd gelerten/Das deutsch vmb der leyen vnnd vngelerten willen"; *Kirchengesenge Deudsche,* fol. [Aii^r].

25. "In place of the *Ite missa* let the Benedicamus domino be said . . . or the Benedicamus may be borrowed from Vespers," LW 53:30; WA 12:213: "*Loco 'Ita Missa' dicatur: 'Benedicamus domino' . . . Vel ex vespertinis 'Benedicamus' mutuentur.*"

26. See LW 53:36-37; WA 12:218.

27. See LW 53:27; WA 12:212.

28. See LW 53:28; WA 12:212-213.

29. See LW 53:72-78; WA 19:87-94.

30. In the *Formula missae* he wrote: "we prefer the Psalms from which they were taken as of old"; LW 53:22; WA 12:208-209 (cf. 206): "*. . . probamus at servamus, quamquam psalmos mallemus, undi sumpti sund, ut olim. . . .*" In the *Deutsche Messe* he included Psalm 34 fully notated in Tone I; LW 53:70-71; WA 19:81-86.

31. In later hymnals that incorporated the *Deutsche Messe*, a vernacular version of the *Gloria in excelsis Deo* was included, usually Decius' *Allein Gott in der Höhe sei Ehr*, though one included a prose version: see for example, *Enchiridion geistliche gesenge* (Zwickau, 1528); *Enchiridion geistlicher gesenge* (Leipzig, 1530); *Geystlyke leder* (Rostock, 1531); and *Enchiridion Geistliker leder unde Psalmen* (Magdeburg, 1536); see Table 13.1.

32. LW 53:187-188; on the background, see Konrad Ameln, "'All Ehr und Lob soll Gottes sein': Ein deutsches Gloria — von Martin Luther?" JbLH 31 (1987/88): 39-52.

33. Cited in WA 35:629.

34. In the so-called "Bapstischen Gesangbuch" (Leipzig, 1545) — another publication closely associated with Luther — *All Ehr und Lob soll Gottes sein* is given with the *Allein Gott* melody, confirming that this alternative version was intended to replace that of Decius. In the event the Decius version proved to be already popular and was never effectively displaced.

35. *Kirchengesenge Deudsche*, fol. lxxxviii^r. Later in this second part Spangenberg also includes a prose German version of the *Gloria* (fol. clxxxiii^r — clxxxv^r), later reprinted in Nikolaus Selnecker's *Christliche Psalmen, Lieder und Kirchengesenge* (Leipzig: Beyer, 1587); see Ludwig Schoeberlein and Friedrich Samuel Riegel, eds., *Schatz des liturgischen Chor- und Gemeindegesangs: nebst den Altarweisen in der deutschen evangelischen Kirche* (Göttingen: Vandenhoeck & Ruprecht, 1865-1872), 1:154-157.

36. "Thereupon the priest reads a collect in monotone on F-fa-ut," LW 53:72; WA 19:86: "Darnach lieset der priester eyne Collecten ynns F faut ynn vnisono."

37. See note 30 above.

38. See the discussion in Chapter 13 above.

39. Lucas Lossius, *Psalmodia, hoc est, Cantica sacra veteris ecclesiae selecta* (Wittenberg: Rhau, 1561; facsimile, Stuttgart: Cornetto, 1996).

40. See Werner Merten, "Die Psalmodia des Lucas Lossius," JbLH 19 (1975): 1-18; 20 (1976): 63-90; 21 (1977): 39-67.

41. See Konrad Ameln, "Johannes Keuchenthal," JbLH 3 (1958): 121-124.

42. On the title page of *Christliche Psalmen, Lieder, und Kirchengesenge* Selnecker includes couplets that state that while David's harp sounds in heaven, on earth the singing is led by Luther, whose "Tenor" — that is, his hymn melodies that were customarily set in the Tenor voice — sings of God's Word, while we sing somewhat imperfectly, which God, however, will not hold against us:

Des Davids Harpff in Himmel klingt,
Wol dem, der mit nur frölich singt.
Lutherus singt uns allen vor,
Nach Gottes Wort führt den Tenor.
Wir singen nachnund zwitern mit,
Gott will solch stimm verachten nit . . .

Philipp Wackernagel, *Bibliographie zur Geschichte des deutschen Kirchenliedes im XVI. Jahrhundert* (Frankfurt: 1855; repr. Hildesheim: Olms, 1961), 414.

43. Franz Eler, *Cantica sacra* (Hamburg: Wolff, 1588; facsimile Hildesheim: Olms, 2003).

44. See Siegfried Fornaçon, "Matthäus Lüdtke (Ludecus)," JbLH 12 (1967): 167-170.

45. See Oskar Johannes Mehl, "Das 'Vesperale et Matutinale' des Matthaeus Ludecus (1589)," *Theologische Literaturzeitung* 80 (1955), cols. 265-270.

46. Niels Jesperssøn, *Gradual. En Almindelig Sangog* (Copenhagen: Benedicht, 1573; facsimile [ed. Erik Abrahamsen, Erik Dal and Henrik Glahn] Copenhagen: Den Fog, 1986). King Christian III of Denmark, who reigned from 1534 to 1559, ensured that the Danish church would follow the theology and practice of Wittenberg. He conducted extensive correspondence with Luther; he engaged Bugenhagen to draw up the Danish Kirchenordnung in 1537; and appointed clergy to important ecclesiastical positions only if they had studied theology in Wittenberg, which was termed "Den hellige Stad," the holy city. For the background, see Martin Schwaz Lausten, "Luther and the Reformation in Denmark," L-J 71 (2004): 115-130, esp. 124-130.

47. Rhau's *Selectae harmoniae* (Wittenberg, 1538) and *Officia de Nativitate* (Wittenberg, 1545); and Johann Reusch's *Zehen deudsch Psalm Davids* (Wittenberg, 1552).

48. *Epistola complectens commendationem musicae* and *Elogium de musica;* see *Corpus Reformatorum: Melanchthon,* 10:94-97.

49. Selnecker also published an oration on Luther's life and work, *Historia Oratio. Vom Leben und Wandel des Ehrwirdigen Herrn/und theuren Mannes Gottes/D. Martini Lutheri* (Leipzig: Rhambaw, 1576; facsimile, Fürth: Flacius-Verlag, 1992), a translation by Paul Heusler of the original Latin published the previous year. Given Selnecker's musical sensibilities, one would have expected more than Selnecker's two brief references to Luther and music — one of *Ein feste Burg* and the other of Luther's letter to Senfl from Coburg; see Selnecker, *Historia Oratio,* fol. 69^r^-70^r^.

50. WA 53:216-218. It also appeared in Latin: *Postilla Latina, Pro Christiana Iuuentute, per Quaestiones explicata* (Frankfurt am Main and Marburg: Egenolff, 1545). The German *Postilla* was reprinted continuously into the nineteenth century.

Notes to Chapter 15

1. Jaroslav Pelikan, *Obedient Rebels: Catholic Substance and Protestant Principle in Luther's Reformation* (New York: Harper, 1964); see also Jaroslav Pelikan, *Spirit versus Structure: Luther and the Institutions of the Church* (New York: Harper, 1968).

2. Robin A. Leaver, "Christian Liturgical Music in the Wake of the Protestant Reformation," in *Sacred Sound and Social Change: Liturgical Music in Jewish and Christian Experience,* ed. Lawrence A. Hoffman and Janet R. Walton (Notre Dame: University of Notre Dame Press, 1992), 124-144.

3. As the discussions in earlier chapters make clear, there are other instances of Luther's adaptations and use of traditional liturgical-musical forms, but these are chosen because they have not generally received the attention they deserve.

4. For the background, see David Hiley, *Western Plainchant: A Handbook* (Oxford: Clarendon, 1993), 172-195.

5. For the background, see William T. Flynn, *Medieval Music as Medieval Exegesis* (Lanham: Scarecrow, 1999).

6. LU, 780; Lossius, fol. 104^v^-105^v^.

7. See Hiley, *Western Plainchant,* 192 (Ex. II.22.11).

8. LU, 880-81; Lossius, fol. 145^r-146^r.

9. Translation by Charles P. Price, *The Hymnal 1982 Companion*, ed. Raymond F. Glover (New York: Church Hymnal Corporation, 1990-94), 3:226.

10. Luther means the senior pastor rather than diocesan bishop.

11. LW 53:24-25; WA 12:210-211: *"Sequentias et prosas nullas admittimus, nisi Episcopo placuerit illa brevis in Nativitate Christi 'Grates nunc omnes.' Neque ferme sunt, quae spiritum redolant, nisi illae de spiritu sancto: 'Sancti Spiritus' et 'Veni, Sancte spiritus.'"*

12. LW 53:36; WA 12:218: *"Cantica velim etiam nobis esse vernacula quam plurima, quae populus sub missa cantaret, vel iuxta gradualia, item iuxta Sanctus et Agnus Dei. . . . Possent vero ista cantica sic per Episcopum ordinari, ut vel simul post latinas cantiones, vel per vices dierum nunc latine, nunc vernacula cantarentur, donec tota Missa vernacula fieret. Sed poetae nobis desunt, aut nondum cogniti sunt. . . ."*

13. LW 53:74; WA 19:90: "Auff die Epistel singet man eyn deudsch lied: 'Nu bitten wyr den heyligen geyst, odder sonst eyns, und das mit dem gantzen Chor."

14. Cited in Adolf Boës, "Die Reformatorischen Gottesdienst in der Wittenberger Pfarrkirche von 1523 an und die 'Ordenung der gesenge der Wittenbergischen Kirchen'" von 1543/44," JbLH 4 (1958/59): 7: "Auf Ostern und bis auf Ascensionis domini soll man nach dem *alleluia* singen *victimae paschali*, und darunder *Christ lag in todes banden*, vers umb vers, so kombts bedes gleich aus."

15. See the examples cited by Anthony Ruff, "A Millennium of Congregational Song," *Pastoral Music* 21 (Feb-Mar, 1997): 11-15.

16. See Robin A. Leaver, *Goostly Psalmes and Spirituall Songes: English and Dutch Metrical Psalms from Coverdale to Utenhove 1535-1566* (Oxford: Clarendon, 1991), 282-83.

17. LW 53:78, 81-82; WA 19:95, 99: "Nach dem Evangelio singt die gantze kirche den glauben zu deudsch/Wir gleuben all an eynen gott. . . . Und die weyl singe das deudsche sanctus odder das lied[er] . . . oder das deutsch Agnus dei."

18. AWA 4:243-244; WA 35:455.

19. LW 53:82-83.

20. LU, 61.

21. See the discussion in Chapter 14 above.

22. The words in italics are cited from Luther's *Small Catechism*, where they appear at the end of each of the answers that expound the meaning of the three paragraphs of the Creed; see BSLK 510-12; BC-W/K 355-56. This would suggest that *All Ehr und Lob soll Gottes sein* was written after 1529, when the *Small Catechism* was first published. These last four lines may well have formed the prototype for the final stanza of Luther's Lord's Prayer hymn, *Vater unser im Himmelreich*, which first appeared in 1539; see Chapter 7.

23. Konrad Ameln, "'All Ehr und Lob soll Gottes sein': Ein deutsches Gloria — von Martin Luther?" JbLH 31 (1987/88): 45-46.

24. My own translation, an approximation of the octosyllabic couplets of the original; for an alternative translation, see LW 53:187-88.

25. LU, 16-18.

26. See Hiley, *Western Plainchant*, 69-76, 85-88.

27. See LU, 1772-1806.

28. The medieval performance practice was: respond (solo), respond repeated (choir), verse (solo), respond, or a truncated version of the respond (choir).

29. Cited in Markus Jenny, "Sieben biblische Begräbnisgesänge: Ein unerkanntes unediertes Werk Martin Luthers," in *Lutherana zum 500. Geburtstag Martin Luthers von den Mitarbeitern der Weimarer Ausgabe*, ed. Gerhard Hammer and Karl-Heinz zur Mühen (Cologne: Böhlau, 1984), 458.

30. Luther added a stanza; see Jenny, "Sieben biblische Begräbnisgesänge," 120-22.

31. Jenny, "Sieben biblische Begräbnisgesänge," 455-74.

32. Noted, but not included in Jenny, "Sieben biblische Begräbnisgesänge."

33. LU, 1785-86.

34. LU, 728.

35. LW 53:327-28; WA 35:479-480: "Zu dem haben wir auch, zum guten Exempel, die schönen Musica oder Gesenge, so im Bapstum. In Vigilien, Seelmessen und Begrebnis gebraucht sind, genomen, der etliche in dis Büchlin drücken lassen, und vollen mit der zeit derselben mehr nemen, Oder wer es besser vermag denn wir, Doch andere Text drunter gesetzt, damit unsern Artikel der Aufferstehung zu schmücken, Nicht das Fegfewr mit seiner Pein und gnugthuung, dafur jre Verstorbene nicht schlaffen noch rugen können. Der Gesang und die Noten sind köstlich, Schade were es, das sie solten untergehen, Aber unchristlich und ungereimpt sind die Text oder wort, die solten untergehen. . . . Also haben sie auch warlich viel teffliche schöne Musica oder Gesang, sonderlich in den Stifften und Pfarrhen, Aber viel unfletiger abgöttischer Text da mit geziert. Darumb wir solche abgöttische todte und tolle Text entkleidet, und jnen die schöne Musica abgestreifft, und dem lebendigen heiligen Gottes wort angezogen, dasselb damit zu singen, zu loben und zu ehren. . . . Es ist umb verenderung des Textes und nicht der Noten zuthun."

36. See LW 53:131-46.

37. See Chapter 12 above.

38. LW 53:107-108; WA 19:539-540.

39. See Rochus Freiherr von Liliencron, *Liturgisch-musikalische Geschichte der evangelischen Gottesdienste von 1523 bis 1700* (Schleswig: Bergas, 1893; repr. Hildesheim: Olms, 1970), 61-77; Detlef Gojowy, "Kirchenlieder im Umkreis von J. S. Bach," JbLH 22 (1978): 79-123.

40. In the twentieth century some composers returned to composing such liturgical motets, such as those by Ernst Pepping found in his *Spandauer Chorbuch* (1934-38).

41. See Jürgen Grimm, *Das Neu Leipziger Gesangbuch des Gottfried Vopelius (Leipzig 1682): Untersuchung zur Klärung seiner geschichtlichen Stellung* (Berlin: Merseburger, 1969), 54, 60, 63 and 66.

42. *Das Babstsche Gesangbuch von 1545*, facsimile, ed. Konrad Ameln (Kassel: Bärenreiter, 1966), No. LXI.

43. For example, it appeared as No. 142 in the Missouri Synod's *Kirchen-Gesangbuch für Evangelisch-Lutherische Gemeinden ungeänderter Augsburgischer Confession* (St. Louis: Concordia, 1847).

44. See Walter Reckziegel, *Das Cantional von Johann Herman Schein: Seine geschichtlichen Grundlagen* (Berlin: Merseburger, 1963), 216; Grimm, *Das Neu Leipziger Gesangbuch*, 90.

45. Grimm, *Das Neu Leipziger Gesangbuch*, 59.

46. See Charles Sanford Terry, *Joh. Seb. Bach Cantata Texts Sacred and Secular, With a Reconstruction of the Leipzig Liturgy of His Period* [1929] (London: Holland, 1964), 201, 207,

209. Both Walter Passions were to be found in Vopelius; see Grimm, *Das Neu Leipziger Gesangbuch*, 59.

47. LW 53:327-28; WA 35:479-480: "Zu dem haben wir auch, zum guten Exempel, die schönen Musica oder Gesenge, so im Bapstum. In Vigilien, Seelmessen und Begrebnis gebraucht sind, genomen, der etliche in dis Büchlin drücken lassen, und vollen mit der zeit derselben mehr nemen, Oder wer es besser vermag denn wir, Doch andere Text drunter gesetzt, damit unsern Artikel der Aufferstehung zu schmücken. . . . <Doch ist nicht dis unser meinung, das diese Noten so eben müsten in allen Kirchen gesungen werden. Ein igliche Kirche halte jre Noten nach jrem Buch und Brauch. Denn ich selbs auch nicht gerne höre, wo in einem Responsorio oder Gesang die Noten verruckt, anders gesungen werden bey uns, weder ich der in meiner Jugent gewonet bin.> Es ist umb verenderung des Textes und nicht der Noten zuthun."

48. Michael Praetorius, *Syntagma musicum I: Musicae artis Analecta. Wittenberg 1614/ 15*, facsimile, ed. Wilibald Gurlitt (Kassel: Bärenreiter, 1959), 447-453, here 448; see Appendix 4 below.

49. See the discussion in Chapter 14 above.

50. The chants began to be recovered for Lutheran use in the later nineteenth and early twentieth centuries. For a study of these German forms of traditional chant, see Otto Brodde, "Evangelische Choralkunde: Der gregorianische Choral im evangelischen Gottesdienst," *Leiturgia: Handbuch des evangelischen Gottesdienstes*, 4: *Die Musik des evangelischen Gottesdienstes*, ed. Karl Ferdinand Müller and Walter Blankenburg (Kassel: Stauda, 1961), 343-557.

51. Grimm, *Das Neu Leipziger Gesangbuch*, 50-68.

52. LW 53:20; WA 12: "*Imprimis itque profitemur, non esse nec fuisse unquam in animo nostro, omnem cultum dei prorsus abolere, sed eum, qui is usu est, pessimis additamentis vitiatum, repurgare et usum pium monstrare.*"

Notes to Chapter 16

1. "Canticles are songs that we don't notice"; Ronald Feuerhahn, "Healing in the Canticles of the Old and New Testaments," *Christ's Gifts for Healing the Soul: Toward a Lutheran Identity in the New Millennium* [The Good Shepherd Institute of Pastoral Theology and Sacred Music for the Church: Journal for the First Annual Conference, November 5-7, 2000], ed. Daniel Zager (Fort Wayne: Concordia Theological Seminary Press, 2001), 25.

2. Hans Joachim Moser, *Die Evangelische Kirchenmusik in Deutschland* (Berlin: Merseberger, 1954), 53.

3. *Das Klug'sche gesangbuch 1533 nach dem einzigen erhaltenen Exemplar der Lutherhalle zu Wittenberg*, ed. Konrad Ameln (Kassel: Bärenreiter, 1954); *Das Babstsche gesangbuch von 1545. Faksimiledruck*, ed. Konrad Ameln (Kassel: Bärenreiter, 1966).

4. Otto Brodde, "Evangelische Choralkunde: Der gregorianische Choral in evangelischen Gottesdienst," in *Leiturgia: Handbuch des evangelischen Gottesdiensts*, ed. Karl Ferdinand Müller & Walter Blankenburg, IV: *Die Musik des evangelischen Gottesdienst* (Kassel: Stauda, 1961), 343-557.

5. Salomon Kümmerle, *Encyklopädie der evangelischen Kirchenmusik* (Gütersloh: Bertelsmann, 1888-1895).

6. Markus Jenny, "Sieben biblische Begräbnisgesänge: Ein unerkanntes unediertes Werk Martin Luthers," in *Lutherana zum 500. Geburtstag Martin Luthers von den Mitarbeitern der Weimarer Ausgabe*, ed. Gerhard Hammer and Karl-Heinz zur Mühen [Archiv zur Weimarer Ausgabe der Werke Martin Luthers Bd. 5] (Cologne: Böhlau, 1984), 455-474; see also Chapter 15 above.

7. As with the Latin Responsoria, the recent scholar who has contributed most on Luther's canticles is again Markus Jenny, as the following notes demonstrate.

8. Martin Luther, *Christliche Geseng Lateinische vnd Deudsch/zum Begrebnis* (Wittenberg: Klug, 1542).

9. For the background, see: Fernand Cabrol, "Cantiques," *Dictionnaire d'archéologie chrétienne et la liturgie*, ed. Fernand Cabrol & Henri Leclerq (Paris: Letouzey et Ané, 1907-1953), 2/2: cols. 1975-1999; Markus Jenny, "Cantica," *Theologische Realenzyklopädie*, ed. Gerhard Krause & Gerhard Müller (Berlin: Gruyter, 1977-), 7:624-628; Milos Velimirović, Ruth Steiner, Keith Falconer, Nicholas Temperley, "Canticle," New Grove 2, 5:49-52.

10. In his preface to the Burial Hymns of 1542 Luther makes reference to the chants he had sung in his early years: "For I myself do not like to hear the notes in a responsory or other song changed from what I was accustomed to in my youth"; LW 53:328; WA 35:480: "Denn ich selbs auch nicht gerne höre, wo in einem Responsorio oder gesang die Noten verruckt, anders gesungen werden bey uns, weder ich der in meiner Jugent gewonet bin."

11. See Cabrol, "Cantiques," cols. 1985-6; Jenny, "Cantica," pull-out table opposite p. 624.

12. LW 44:323; WA 8:621: "*Ita iacet quidem verus ille cultus dei, tribus praeceptis primis institutus, et viae Zion lugent, eo quod non sit qui veniat ad solennitatem: in cuius locum illi alium subtituerunt sese plane dignissimum, qui est pompa illa cerimoniarum in veste, gestu, cantu, lectionibus, in quibus omnibus nihil fidei neque nominis neque operis est divini, sed omnia sunt humanissima. Atque ex instituto Pauli I. Corin. xiiii. videtur usus huius vestigium esse reliquum, ubi docet tria fieri in conventu Ecclesiae, linguis loqui seu psallere, prophetari seu interpretari et orare. Scilicet primo recitabatur aliquid e scriptura vel psalmis. Diende prophetae interpretabuntur et docebant. Tertio in communi orabur. Divina et Christianissima institutio, sed ad docendum et exhortandum, hoc est, ad fidem alendam ordinata. Primum aemulantur hodie lectionibus matutinalibus, Epistolis, Evangeliis et singularibus cantibus, Alterum Omiliis, Tertium Responsoriis, Antiphonis, Gradualibus, et quaecunque communiter leguntur vel cantantur, sed infoeliciter omnia. Non enim docendi aut exhortandi, sed operandi tantum studio omnia fiunt. Sic enim legisse, sic cantasse, sic boasse illis satis est. Hoc opus quaeritur et vocatur cultus dei.*"

13. LW 19:152; WA 19:349: "So doch wol billich und recht, auch nütz und not gewest were, das diser Habacuc klerlich ausgelegt were, weyl das letzte Capitel, sein gebet, so teglich ym brauch gewesen, beyde gesungen und gelesen ist ynn allen kirchen, doch fast nach dem sprichwort 'wie die Nonnen den Psalter lesen.'"

14. Magnificat: LW 21:295-358, WA 7:538-604. Habakkuk: LW 19:133-148, WA 13:439-448 (Latin 1525); LW 19:227-237, WA 19:424-435 (German 1526).

15. LW 53:12-14; WA 12:35-37: "das man teglich des morgens eyne stunde frue umb vier odder funffe tzu samen keme und daselbs lesen lieffe, es sey schuler odder priester, odder wer

sey, gleych wie man itzt noch die Lection ynn der metten ließet. Das sollen thun eyner odder tzween, odder eyner umb den andern, odder eyn Chor umb den andern, wie das am besten gefellet.

Darnach soll der prediger odder welchem es befolhen wirt, er fur tretten und die selb lection aus legen, das die andern alle verstehen, lernen und ermanet werden. . . . Und wo dis nicht geschicht, so ist die gemeyne der lection nicht verbessert, wie bis her ynn klostern und ztifften geschehen, da sie nur die wende haben angeblehet.

Diß Lection soll aber seyn aus dem alten Testament. . . .

Wenn nu die Lection und auslegung eyn halb stund odder lenger geweret hatt, soll man drauff yn gemeyn got dancken, loben und bitten umb frucht des worts etc. Dazu soll man brauchen der psalmen und ettlicher gutten Responoria, Antiphon, kurtz also, das es alles ynn eyner stund ausgerichtet werde, odder wie lange sie wollen, denn nan mus die seelen nicht uberschutten, das sie nicht mude und uberdrussig werden, wie bis her ynn klostern und stifften sie sich mit esels erbeyt beladen haben.

Desselben gleychen an dem abent umb sechs odder funffe widder also tzu samen . . . und gleych also lesen, auslegen, loben, singen und beten, wie am morgen, auch eyn stund lang. Denn es ist alles zuthun umb gottis wort, das dasselb ym schwang gehe und die seelen ymer auffrichte und erquicke, das sie nicht lassz werden.

. . . Aber das gesenge und psalmen teglich des morgens und abents zu stellen soll des pfarrers und predigers ampt seyn, das sie auff eyn iglichen morgen eyn psalmen, eyn Resposorion odder Antiphen mit eyner Collecten ordenen. Des abents auch also, nach der Lection und auslegung offentlich zu lesen und zusingen."

16. The translations were included with his expositions of these psalms: WA 1:158-220.

17. Psalm 109 (1518), WA 1:690-710; and Psalm 68 (1521), WA 8:4-35.

18. LW 53:69-71; WA 19:80-86.

19. LW 53:182-183; AWA 4:124-126, 315-319. The same hymnal also included Psalm 117, "to be sung to thank God for the Gospel and the kingdom of Christ," to Tone VIII, included within the section of biblical canticles; see further below.

20. Martin Luther, *Ein Betbüchlein mit Kalender und Passional, Wittenberg 1529*, facsimile, ed. Frieder Schulz (Kassel: Stauda, 1982). The biblical woodcuts were also used in the Klug *Gesangbuch* of 1529 and later editions.

21. See Christhard Mahrenholz, "Auswahl und Einordnung der Katechismuslieder in den Wittenberger Gesangbüchern seit 1529," *Gestalt und Glaube: Festschrift für . . . Oskar Söhngen* (Witten: Luther-Verlag, 1960), 123-132; see also Chapters 4-11 above.

22. LW 53:153; WA BR 5:38.

23. Jenny, AWA 4, 102. Latin Litany: LW 53:155-162; AWA 4:264-273. German Litany: LW 53:163-170; AWA 4:250-255 (separate imprint), 256-263 *(Gesangbuch)*.

24. Jenny, AWA 4:104.

25. LW 53:174-175; AWA 4:276-284.

26. Jenny, AWA 4:108.

27. Other liturgical provisions of 1529 included the *Short Order of Confession* (LW 53:116-117; WA 30[I]: 343-345), *Order of Marriage* (LW 53:110-115; WA 30[III]: 74-80), and various vernacular collects that appeared in the 1529 hymnal.

28. Jenny, AWA 4:37.

29. See Philipp Wackernagel, *Bibliographie zur Geschichte des deutschen Kirchenliedes*

im XVI. Jahrhundert (Frankfurt: Heyder & Zimmer, 1855; repr. Hildesheim: Olms, 1961), 108-109.

30. *Dr. Martin Luther's sämtliche Werke* (Erlangen: Heyder, 1826-1857), 56:368-369; cited Jenny, AWA 4:39. By using the information in this source, together with comparison with later hymnals that were virtual reprints, with minor modifications, of the 1529 Klug *Gesangbuch*, it is possible to reconstruct its contents, though on some points of detail some ambiguity remains; see Konrad Ameln, "Das Klugsche Gesangbuch, Wittenburg 1529: Versuche einer Rekonstruktion," JbLH 16 (1971): 159-62; Gerhard Bosinski, "Joachim Slüter und Luthers Gesangbuch von 1529," *Theologische Literaturzeitung* 108 (1983): 705-22; Konrad Ameln, "Eine neue Ausgabe der geistlichen Lieder und Kirchengesänge Luthers," JbLH 30 (1986): 113-14; Jenny's discussion in AWA 4:36-41; and "A Reconstruction of the Contents of the Wittenberg Congregational Gesangbuch (1529)," in Robin A. Leaver, *Goostly Psalmes and Spirituall Songes: English and Dutch Metrical Psalms from Coverdale to Utenhove 1535-1566* (Oxford: Clarendon, 1991), 281-285. On the 1529 Gesangbuch generally, see Markus Jenny, "Luthers Gesangbuch," *Leben und Werk Martin Luthers von 1526 bis 1546: Festgabe zu seinem 500. Geburtstag*, ed. Helmar Junghans (Berlin: Evangelische Verlagsanstalt, 1983), 1:301-321 & 2:825-832.

31. See note 3 above.

32. ". . . *duos libellos canticorum germanicorum*"; WA 35:620, note 1.

33. "*Illum libellum emendavi diligenter et adieci summas canticorum, quo etiam possint intelligi ista cantica a simplicioribus, accrevit libellus insuper litania latina et psalmo Germanico Da Israel aus Ägypten zog cum sua melodia*"; WA 35:619.

34. See Gerhard Bosinski, *Das Schrifttum des Rostocker Reformators Joachim Slüter* (Berlin: Evangelischen Verlagsanstalt, 1971), 184-185.

35. Thomas Müntzer, *Schriften und Briefe: Kritische Gesamtausgabe,* ed. Paul Kirn & Günther Franz (Gütersloh: Mohn, 1968), 44.

36. Müntzer, *Schriften,* 63.

37. Müntzer, *Schriften,* 87.

38. Müntzer, *Schriften,* 91-92.

39. Müntzer, *Schriften,* 99.

40. Müntzer, *Schriften,* 111-114.

41. *Das älteste Zwickauer Gesangbuch von 1525,* facsimile, ed. Otto Clemen (Zwickau: Hermann, 1935), fol. Ai^v-Aiii^v.

42. See Konrad Ameln, "Psalmus Jn exitu Jsrael verdeutscht," JbLH 28 (1984): 65-67, and *Das Erfurter Enchiridion Gedruckt in der Permentergassen zum Ferbefaß 1524 und der Ergänzungsdruck Etliche Christliche Gesenge vnd Psalmen,* facsimile, ed. Konrad Ameln (Kassel: Bärenreiter, 1983).

43. Nevertheless the 1531 revision of the Psalter was essentially Luther's as is evident from the manuscript notes — which grew out of his regular meditation on the Psalms — he entered into his personal copy of the 1528 Psalter; see WA DB 3: liii, lxii; and 4:510-577. See also Otto Reichert, "Der Deudsche Psalter D. Luthers zu Wittenberg 1531-1931," L-J 13 (1931): 29-68.

44. Heimo Reinitzer, *Biblia deutsch: Luthers Bibelübersetzung und ihre Tradition* [exhibition catalog] (Wolfenbüttel: Herzog August Bibliothek, 1983), 158; Willem Jan Kooiman, *Luther and the Bible,* trans. John Schmidt (Philadelphia: Muhlenberg, 1961), 148-151.

45. The fourth column records the year that the respective Bible translation appeared in print.

46. See *Handbuch der deutschen evangelischen Kirchenmusik nach den Quellen,* ed. Konrad Ameln, Christhard Mahrenholz, Wilhelm Thomas & Carl Gerhardt (Göttingen: Vandenhoeck & Ruprecht, 1932-) [= HEK], 1/1: Nos. 464 & 468.

47. LW 14:1-39; WA 31^I: 223-257. See the summary of Luther's "prophetic-Christological" exegesis of the Psalm: Heinrich Bornkamm, *Luther and the Old Testament,* trans. Eric W. and Ruth C. Gritsch, ed. Victor I. Gruhn (Philadelphia: Fortress, 1969), 98-101.

48. BC-W/K, 400; BSLK, 586: "Darümb muß Du immerdar Gottes Wort im Herzen, Mund und fur den Ohren haben. Wo aber das Herz müßig stehet und das Wort nicht klinget, so bricht er ein und hat dn Schaden getan, ehe man's gewahr wird. Wiederümb hat es die Kraft, wo man's mit Enst betrachtet, höret und handlet, daß es nimmer ohn frucht abgehet, sondern allezeit neuen Verstand, Lust und Andacht erwecket, rein Herz und Gedanken machet. Denn es sind nicht faule noch tote, sondern schäftige, lebendige Wort."

49. HEK 1/1 Nos. 469, 471 & 476.

50. HEK 1/1 Nos. 484, 485, 487 & 489

51. HEK 1/1 No. 490.

52. HEK 1/1 Nos. 486a & 496a.

53. These are also the only canticles that have an assigned antiphon (with notation).

54. WA 19:70. The notation is on a three-line stave and has no clef. When chants were faburdened the intonations were customarily omitted, which raises the possibility that Luther's first thoughts for the Introit psalm in the *Deutsche Messe* were that it should be sung in four parts rather than in its monophonic form.

55. WA 19:81-86; LW 53:69-71.

56. HEK 1/1, No. 481 (1533), & No. 467 (1545). Not all of the tones in the 1545 *Gesangbuch* include intonations. For example, Tone I in 1545 (HEK 1/1, No. 473) is almost identical with Tone I in 1533 (HEK 1/1, No. 464).

57. LW 53:339-341; WA 35:537. The faburden technique was explained and demonstrated in a succession of treatises of music theory. Early in the sixteenth century Johannes Cochlaeus explained and demonstrated the process; Johann Cochlaeus, *Tetrachordis Musices* (Nuremberg: Stuchsen, 1512; reprint, Hildesheim: Olms, 1971), sig. Fi^r-Fii^r; see Cristle Collins Judd, *Reading Renaissance Music Theory: Hearing with the Eyes* (Cambridge: Cambridge University Press, 2000), 86-90. For a later description of the compositional process, see Michael Praetorius, *Syntagma Musicum,* tom. 3 (Wolfenbüttel: Holwein for Praetorius, 1619; facimile ed. Wilibald Gurlitt, Kassel: Bärenreiter, 1954), 9-11.

58. Georg Rhau, *Musikdrucke aus den Jahren 1538 bis 1545 in praktischer neuausgabe,* ed. Hans Albrecht (Kassel: Bärenreiter, 1955-) [= RMD], 4:45-46.

59. See WA 35:542-544. The Psalm is headed: "Complaint and Prayer to God, Against the Old (the Old Beaten) Religion and Its Patron" [Klage vnd bitte zu Gott/wider Die alten (der alten schlagen) Religion vnd ihre Schutz herrn. Psalm Lxiiii.]; WA 35:543. This is reminiscent of the title of a work that Luther wrote the previous year, in response to the pope's call to the emperor to engage in a religious war against the Protestants: Against the Roman Papacy, an Institution of the Devil (1545); LW 41:257-376; WA 54:206-299. Alternatively, it might be a reference to the Council of Trent that began to meet in 1545.

60. WA 35:544.

61. Voice = the voice in which the tone occurs: D = Discant. T = Tenor. RMD (see note 58 above). WGA = *Johann Walter Sämtlicher Werke*, ed. Otto Schroeder (Kassel: Bärenreiter, 1953-70). See also the facsimile of the index pages of *Vesperarum precum officia*, that classify some of the contents according to the eight tones; WGA 4:xxviii.

62. HEK 1/2:546-547; WGA 4:xi-xii, xix-xx; see also the discussion in Walter Blankenburg, *Johann Walter Leben und Werk*, ed. Friedhelm Brusniak (Tutzing: Schneider, 1991), 296-301.

63. Facsimile in HEK 1/2:547.

64. See WGA 4:xxviii, and Victor H. Mattfeld, *Georg Rhaw's Publications for Vespers* (New York: Institute of Mediaeval Music, 1966), 171-172. Stolzer always placed the chant in the Discant voice, following Italian custom; Rener always in the Tenor voice, following German custom; in five of Walter's settings the chant is in the Discant and three in the Tenor (see Table 16.5).

65. For the background, see Günther Schmidt, "Über den Fauxbourdon," JbLH 4 (1958/59): 146-151; Brian Trowell, "Fauxbourdon," New Grove 2, 8:614-620.

66. See Blankenburg, *Johann Walter*, 298-299.

67. Rhau's imprints of Luther's writings include: exposition of the Benedictus (1525), the Large Catechism (1529), exposition of Psalm 117 (1530), the exposition of the Song of Moses (Deuteronomy 32) (1532), etc.

68. Mattfeld, *Georg Rhaw's Publications for Vespers*, 141.

69. Mattfeld, *Georg Rhaw's Publications for Vespers*, 354-355.

70. Werner Braun in WGA 4:xii, xix.

71. Rhau, *Enchiridion* (1538), fol. Fiv^v-Fviij^r.

72. *"Neq vero spes hec me omnino fefellit, Scripsit enim Martinus Agricola musicus sane eruditus & amicus noster singularis, hac de re, elegantissimos libellos, qui si sic in latino sermone, ut sunt germanice scripti, exarent, nihil ultra in hac artea quo piam merito desyderari posset"*; Rhau, *Enchiridion* (1538), fol. Aiii^r.

73. Martin Agricola, *Musica Choralis Deudsch* (Wittenberg: Rhau, 1533; facsimile, Hildesheim: Olms, 1985), fol. Diiij^r-Fiij^v.

74. LW 53:64, 69; WA 19:76, 80: "Ist auffs erste ym deudschen Gottis dienst eyn grober, schlechter, eynfeltiger guter Catechismus von nöten. Catechismus aber heyst eyne unterricht/ damit man die heyden/so Christen werden wollen/leret und weyset/was sie gleuben/thun/ lassen und wissen sollen ym Christenthum/daher man Catechumenos genennet hat/de leer iungen/die zu solcher unterricht angenomen waren/und des glaubë lernten/ehe denn man sie teuffet. . . . Fur die knaben und schuler ynn der biblia zu uben gehets also zu. Die wochen uber teglich/fur der lection/singen sie ettliche psalmen lateinisch/wie bis her zur metten gewonet/denn/wie gesagt ist. . . . Nach den psalmen lesen die knaben eyner umb den andern zween odder drey eyn Capitel lateinisch aus dem newen testament/darnachs lang ist/ Darauff liset eyn ander knabe dasselbige capitel zu deudsch sie zu uben/und ob yemands von leyen da were und zo höret. Darnach gehen sie mit eyner antiphen zur deudschen lection/ davon droben gesagt ist. Nach der lection singet der gantze hauffe eyn deudsch lied/darauf spricht man heymlich eyn von vater unser/Darnach der pfarherr odder Caplan eyne Collecten/und beschliessen mit dem benedicamus domino/wie gewonet ist.

Dasselbigen gleychen uyr vesper/singe sie etliche der vesper psalmen/wie sie bis her gesungen sind/auch latinsch mit eyner antiphen/darauff eynen hymnos/so e fur handen ist/

Darnach lesen sie abermal eyner umb den andern zween odder drey latinsch aus dem alten testament/eyn gantzes odder halbes Capitel/darnachs lang ist/Darnach lieset eyn knabe dasselbige Capitel zu deudsch/Darauff das magnificat zu latein/mit eyner antiphen/odder lied/Darnach eyn vater unser heymlich/und die Collecten mit dem Benedicamus. Das ist der Gottis dienst teglich durch die wochen ynn stedten da man schulen hat."

75. For this leadership the scholars were required to understand the rudiments of music, which formed an important part of the school curriculum. Thus the title page of the 1538 edition of Rhau's *Enchiridion* includes: "pro pueris in Schola VITEBERGENSI congestum" (compiled for the boys of Wittenberg school). According to Hans Albrecht (in the unpaginated "Nachwort" to the facsimile of the 1538 edition), these words were added to the 1536 edition; they were certainly absent from the 1530 edition, see WA 19:54; see also Chapter 14 above.

76. On the background regarding the liturgical function of these Lutheran schoolchoirs in the sixteenth and seventeenth centuries, see Robin A. Leaver, "Lutheran Church Music," New Grove 2, 15:369-381; Uwe Förster, "Lateinschule und Gymnasium zwischen Reformation und Neuhumanismus," *Struktur, Funktion und Bedeutung des deutschen protestantischen Kantorats im 16. bis 18. Jahrhundert*, ed. Wolf Hobohm, Carsten Lange, & Brit Riepsch (Oschersleben: Ziethen, 1997), 11-20.

77. "Der Schulmeister soll mit den kindern nicht stets einerley singen, sonder mancherley Antiphon, Responsoria, Hymnos und andere gesenge, so rein aus der heiligen schrifft genommen sein. Er soll sie auch leiten und mit jnen singen. . . . Deutsch sollen die schuler nicht singen, on allein, wenn das volck mit singet"; Aemilius Ludwig Richter, ed., *Die evangelischen Kirchenordnungen des sechzehnten Jahrhunderts* (Weimar: Landes-Industriecomtoir, 1846; repr. Nieuwkoop: de Graaf, 1967), 1:222; Emil Sehling, ed., *Die evangelischen Kirchenordnungen des XVI. Jahrhunderts* (Leipzig: Reisland, 1902-1913), 1/1:703.

78. "Die Vesper heldt man also, Erstlich singt der schulmeister mit den schulern ein psalm, Darnach liset ein knab ein stucklen aus dem alden Testament, Erstlich lateinisch, Der annder deutsch, darnach singt man eyn Hymnus, Folgend das Magnificat, Letzlich die Collect . . . ; Richter, *Kirchenordnungen*, 1:229. Sehling, *Kirchenordnungen*, 1/1:192.

79. "Wens ein feierabent ist vor einem sonderlichen feste . . . der predigt soll man mitten in der kirchen mit dem volck singen das Deutsch Magnificat. . . .

Vor allem in der Messen soll man erstlich singen das Deutsch Benedictus Sachariae mit seiner kurzen Antiphon, darnach einem Introitum, zu Zeiten Lateinisch, zu Zeiten Deutsch, welches soll sein ein deutscher Psalm. . . .

Zur Vesper Zeit. . . . Nach der predigt singt die gantze gemeine das deutzsch Magnificat sub *tono peregrino* mit dieser Antiphon: *Christum, unsern heilandt, ewigen Gottes und Mariä Son, preisen wir in ewickeit, Amen.* Bald darauf das deutzsche nunc dimmittis, also wie volget: Herre nu lestu deinen diener fride faren. . . . Amen"; Richter, *Kirchenordnungen*, 1:223; Sehling, *Kirchenordnungen*, 1/1:703-705.

80. See note 33 above.

81. *Geistliche lieder* (Wittenberg, 1533), fol. 177^v-178^r [misprinted as fol. 182^v-183^r].

82. Joseph Herl, *Worship Wars in Early Lutheranism: Choir, Congregation, and Three Centuries of Conflict* (Oxford: Oxford University Press, 2004).

83. Harold S. Powers and Frans Wiering, "Mode, III. Modal Theories and Polyphonic Music, 1-3," New Grove 2, 16:796-807, esp. 798-799.

84. *Practica mvsica Hermanni Finckii, exempla variorvm signorvm, proportionvm et canonvm, ivdicivm de tonis, ac quædam de arte svaviter et artificiose cantandi continens* (Wittenberg: Rhau [hæredum], 1556; facsimile, Bologna: Forni, 1969), fol. Rriij^v-Rriv^v; partial translation, Powers and Wiering, "Mode III," 799.

85. *"Proprietas primi Toni. Dorius . . . alacriorem ex omnibus melodiam habet, somnolentos excitat, tristesque & perturbatos recreat . . . Musicorum præstantissimi hodie hoc tono plurimum utuntur."*

86. See Chapter 12 above.

87. *". . . cum priori ex diametro pugnat: Nam lachrymas ciet, mœrorem creat . . . sic tonus hic flebilis, grauis, serius, omnibus alijs est submissior. . . ."*

88. *". . . propterea quod choleram atque bilem moueat . . . uerba sonora, horrida prælia, & arduæ res gestæ huic congruunt."*

89. No notation is given for Canticle xi but has the following note: "Im vorgehenden thon" (in the previous tone), that is, the tone of Canticle x, Tone III.

90. *". . . parasitum representat, qui affectibus heri sui seruit . . . cuius beneficijs fruitur, illius elogia decantur."*

91. *"Hic hilaritati, comitati, mitioribusque affectibus competit, quibus cum maxime delectetur . . . hilaris, modestus, gaudium mœstorum, desperantium recreatio, afflictorum solatium. . . ."*

92. See Chapter 12 above.

93. *". . . priori contrarius, in precationibus non est infrequens. . . ."*

94. See Chapter 12 above.

95. *". . . uoce Stentorea & magnis clamoribus se ostentat."*

96. *". . . non dissimilis est naturæ ac moribus honestæ matronæ, quæ mariti iram & commotionem oratione fauorabili lenire & sedare conatur . . . offensiones studiose (ut par est) uitat . . . Placabilis. . . ."*

97. Leaver, *Goostly Psalmes*, 284; AWA 4:333: "Wir haben auch zu gutem Exempel, jnn das büchlein gesetzt die heiligen lieder aus der heiligen schrifft, so die lieben Patriarchen und Propheten vorzeiten gemacht und gesungen haben. Auff das wir nicht als newe Meister, allein angesehen werden, jnn diesem werck, sondern für uns, aller Heiligen Exempel anzeigen können. Darumb ein jglicher Christ wol sehen wird, wie die selbigen, gleich wie wir thun, auch allein Gottes gnade, und nicht menschen werck preisen, welche man doch nicht so thar verdammen als uns, ob man sie gleich wol veracht als uns.

Aller meist aber darumb, das wir solche Lieder odder Psalmen gerne wolten, mit ernst und andacht, mit hertz und verstand, gesungen haben, nicht wie man sie jnn den Stifften und Klöstern, mit grossem missebrauch und Abgötterey, noch heutiges tages plöcket und heulet, noch zu verstehen willen oder vleis hat, schweige denn, mit andacht und mit frucht, singen solt. Darumb auch Gott mehr damit erzörnet denn versünet."

98. See, for example, Jenny, "Luthers Gesangbuch," 306-307.

99. See note 33 above.

100. "Mose und die kinder Israel haben dis nachfolgende Lied dem Herren gesungen, da er jn halff von der Egyptern hand. Wie im Andern buch Mose geschrieben steht. Am xv. Capitel"; *Geistliche lieder* (Wittenberg, 1533), fol. 133^v; AWA 4:333.

101. *Geystlycher Lieder* (Leipzig, 1545), fol. S[iv]^r.

102. LW 53:143. "Almechtiger Ewiger Gott, der du hast durch die sindflutt"; WA 12:43-44. The German text is given in Chapter 8, note 10.

103. "Moses hat geredt alle wort dieses nachfolgenden Lieds, für den ohren der gantzen gemeine Israel. Wie geschrieben stehet im Fünfften buch Mosi, jm xxxij. Capitel"; *Geistliche lieder* (Wittenberg, 1533), fol. 137^v; AWA 4:334.

104. LW 9:290; WA 14:732: "*Canticum Mose plenum est increpatione et exproratione super beneficiis tot et tantis populo ingrato et malo exhibitis a Deo. Et plane asserit futurum, ut deserto Deo ad alienos Deos conversi maledictiones praedictas incurrant . . . ut videre hic liceat velut in speculo vim et naturam legis, ut iram operatur et sub maledicto teneat.*"

105. WA 19:95; LW 53:78.

106. See Robin A. Leaver, "'Then the Whole Congregation Sings': The Sung Word in Reformation Worship," *The Drew Gateway* 60 (1990): 55-73.

107. "Dibora und Barack, sungen dem Herrn dis Lied, wie folget, da er jhnen Sissera den Feldheubtman Jabin, der Dananiter König, jnn jhre hende gab, mit seinen wagen und grossem heer. Wie jm Buch der Richter, am v. Capitel geschrieben hat"; *Geistliche lieder* (Wittenberg, 1533), fol. 144^r; AWA 4:334.

108. "Hanna, Elkana eheweib, die unfuchtbare, hat gebetet zum HERRN wie folget, Da er sie erhörete, und gab jr Samuel jren son, den sie dem HERREN bracht, nacht dem sie jn entwennet hatte. Wie jm Ersten buch Samuelis, jm Andern Capitel, geschrieben stehet"; *Geistliche lieder* (Wittenberg, 1533), fol. 148^v; AWA 4:335.

109. *Geistliche lieder* (Wittenberg, 1533), fol. 17^v.

110. "Folget ein lobgesang, darinne du sehen kannst, welches der warhafftig Gottes dienst und das rechte Priester ampt des Newen Testament sey, Jesaie am xij Capitel"; *Geistliche lieder* (Wittenberg, 1533), fol. 151^v; AWA 4:335.

111. *Geistliche lieder* (Wittenberg, 1533), fol. 50^r.

112. "Folget ein Lobgesang/des Propheten Jesaia/darinnin er anzeiget/welches die predigt/und der Gottes dienst sein wird/des volcks im newen Testament/nemlich/Gott dancken/loben/seinen namen predigen und bekennen"; *Geystlycher Lieder* (Leipzig, 1545), fol. T[viii]^r.

113. LW 16:128; WA 31^{II}:91: "*Propheta describit hic verum et legittimum cultum sacrificiumque novi testamenti et ponit quasi quandam occultam antithesin contra Vetus testamentum et sua sacrificia, quae multa erant ac varia. At in novo testamento unicum erat sacrificium laudis et graciarum accionis. Ita dicta est Cena domini εὐχαριστία, quod ad eam conveniamus et gracias agamus deo. . . . Hanc praeviderat propheta futuram praedicacionem et confessionem Evangelii, quae non fiebat in Vetere testamento. In voce Evangelii glorificatur et praedicatur deus in Christo. . . . Neque enim aliud audietur in ecclesia quam vox laudis et praedicationis beneficiorum dei, quae accepimus, et hoc canticum pugnat cum omni sapiencia et iustica hominum, quae sunt nostra opera, in quibus magis spectamus nostram gloriam, quam ut agamus gracias deo. Ideo gratum esse deo est simpliciter confiteri se acceptorum esse beneficiorum, non datorem.*"

114. "Folget ein Ander Lobgesang, darinne hoch gepreiset wird das himelisch Jerusalem, das ist, die heilige Christenheit, sampt Christo jrem König, &c. Jesaie xxvj. Capitel"; *Geistliche lieder* (Wittenberg, 1533), fol. 154^r; AWA 4:335.

115. "Folget ein ander Lobgesang/des Propheten Jesaia/am xxvj. Capitel/von Christo und seiner Christenheit/was sie für ein volck sey/Nemlich/ein gerecht/und friedsam volck/

und lust hat an seinem wort/Dem er auch beystehet und aus allerley anfechtung/Geistlich und leiblich errettet &c"; *Geystlycher Lieder* (Leipzig, 1545), fol. V[i]ʳ.

116. LW 16:200-201; WA 31ᴵᴵ: 141: "Wyr haben eyne feste, mechtige stadt. *Commendacio et praeconium ecclesiae, contra quam non praevalebunt inferorum portae, qui urbs potens regno et sacerdocio.* . . . *Non est civitas, quae exposita sit paucis, sed omnibus intrantibus pateat et sit populosa, ita in ecclesiam esse debet omnius aditus.* . . . *Iusti, siquidem per fidem, ii sunt huius civitatis incolae. Ita cantabitur in ista civitate, quae civitas, qualis populus, quis rector, etc.* . . . *Non commune bonum, Christum scilitet et eius graciam, habemus, nullus altero plus habet, ergo non potest esse discordia, sed pax, quia in domino omnes sumus equales in similitudine spei et fiduciae.* . . ."

117. "Dis ist die schrifft Hiskia des Königes Juda da er kranck gewesen, und von der krankheit gesund worden war. Jesaie. xxxviij." *Geistliche lieder* (Wittenberg, 1533), fol. 157ʳ; AWA 4:336.

118. LW 16:342-344; WA 31ᴵᴵ: 255-257: "*Ecce in pace etc. Pax ecclesiae duplex est summa persequucio. Nulla maior pestis ecclesiae quam pax, quae deficit verbum spiritus et eius exercicium. Ad acquirendam autem veram pacem nihil indigemus quam verbo* . . . *ex uno labore, sollicitudine, molestia laboramus, angustiamur, nitimur, ut in peiora cadamus, quia nostra cura freti, non deo.* . . . *Hic ergo versus est quasi γνομί. Quod hic piisimus rex quaerens pacem extra deum invenit amaritudinem, hoc omnibus nobise veniet.* . . . *Domine, me salvum fac.* . . . *Concludit hic q. d. hoc carmen, quod ego composui, hoc canemus. Modo salvos nos fac, tu donasti nobis sanitatem, hilff,* das wyr dar bey bleyben. *Ita hodie cantare debemus: Domine, serva nos apud veritatem cognitam.*"

119. "Ein Ander Lied, darinne der Prophet Jesaia, jnn der person der gantzen Christenheit, Gott lobet und danket, für sein tewres wort, das den glaubigen unaussprechliche güter bringet, und grossen nutz schaffet. Und fehet an wie das Magnificat. Jesaia lxj." *Geistliche lieder* (Wittenberg, 1533), fol. 158ᵛ; AWA 4:336.

120. LW 17:341; WA 31ᴵᴵ:525: "*Canticum, quad canit propheta in persona Ecclesiae. Ita autem fuit adfectus Esaias:* Wen eyn ding verhanden ist ßo achtet mans nicht, *deinde desideratur in absencia, qui monia opera illa, baptizare, praedicare, arbitrantur vilia, et tamen de illis exultat propheta. Idem fere adfectus ut in 'magnificat,' quia videt deum non approbantem impios et reiicientem iustos hypocritas. Videt suos approbare, Ecclesiam propagare. Tunc summa oritur gloria et gaudium spiritus.*"

121. "Ein Ander liede, darinne der Prophet die gleubigen, seinem Exempel nach, unterweiset, wie sie sicj jnn anfechtungen und trübsaln halten sollen, nemlich, das sie gedencken an die vergangen wolthaten, welche Got von anbegin, beide durch wort und werck, den gleubigen erzeuget hat, sie zu trösten und zu erlösen. Daneben, wie man on unterlas mit gebet zu Gott anhalten solle, das er solches fort an thun wolle &c. Jesaie. lxiiij." *Geistliche lieder* (Wittenberg, 1533), fol. 159ᵛ; AWA 4:337.

122. LW 17:355; WA 31ᴵᴵ: 535: "*Nunc sequitur aliud Capitulum, in quo est Canticum usque ad 65. Caput.* . . . *Nunc propheta cantat canticum, redigit laudes in carmen. Mos autem est in tota scriptura omnium sanctorum et prophetarum ses in tentacionibus consolari in praeteritis beneficiis.*"

123. "Jona bettet zu dem HERRN seinem Gott, jm leibe des fisches und sprach, wie folget. Jona am ij. Capitel"; *Geistliche lieder* (Wittenberg, 1533), fol. 163ʳ; AWA 4:337.

124. "Und Jona bettet zu dem HERRN seinem Gott/jm leibe des fisches und sprach. Wie geschrieben stehet/Jane am andern Capitel"; *Geystlycher Lieder* (Leipzig, 1545), fol. X[i]ᵛ.

125. LW 19:16; WA 13:249: *"Non est, quod putes prophetam hoc suum carmen sic digessisse, dum in angustii esset, sed quod liberatus tandem redegerit in ordinem ea, quae in adversitate et tentatione cogitavit. Est autem elegans carmen et evidens contra fiduciam operum.*

126. "Das ist das gebet, des Propheten Habacuc, für die unschuldigen"; *Geistliche lieder* (Wittenberg, 1533), fol. 165ʳ; AWA 4:337.

127. ". . . Wie geschrieben stehet/Habacuc am vierden Capitel"; *Geystlycher Lieder* (Leipzig, 1545), fol. X[iii]ʳ. For Luther's commentary on Habakkuk, see the citation in note 14 above.

128. "Der cxvij. Psalm zu singen Gott zu dancken für das Euangelion und Reich Gottes"; *Geistliche lieder* (Wittenberg, 1533), fol. 168ᵛ; AWA 4:338. For Luther's commentary on Psalm 117 (1530), see the citation in note 47 above.

129. Translation based on LW 53:176; *Geistliche lieder* (Wittenberg, 1533), fol. 170ʳ; AWA 4:338: "Der Lobesang Marie, das Magnificat.

Auffs erste, singet sie mit frölichem hertzen, von der gnade und wolthat, die jr der barmhertzig Gott jn jrer eigen person erzeiget hat, lobet und dancket jm dafur.

Zum andern, singet sie von der wolthat und von dem grossen wunderwerck, das Gott an unterlas ubet durch und durch, an allen menschen jnn der gantzen welt, Nemlich, das er barmhertig sey uber die furchtsamen und elenden, die nidrigen erhebe, Und die armen reich mache, Störtze vom stuel die grossen hansen, die sich auff jr gewalt, und macht verlassen, Und mache aus Reichen Betler.

Zum dritten singet sie von dem sonderlichen und aller höchstem werck, das Gott Israel heimgesucht, und erlöset hat, durch seinen einigen Son Jesum Christum."

130. *Geystlycher Lieder* (Leipzig, 1545), fol. X[vi]ʳ.

131. LW 21:299; WA 7:546: "Dieszem heiligen lobegesang ordentlich zuvorstgehen ist zu merckenn, das die hochgelobte junckfraw Maria ausz eygner erfarung redet, darynnen sie durch den heyligen geist ist erleucht unnd geleret worden. Denn es mag niemant got noch gottes wort recht vorstehen, er habs on mittel von dem heyligen geyst. Niemant kansz aber von dem heiligenn geist habenn, erfaresz, vorsuchs und empfinds denn, unnd yn der selben erfarung leret sie der heylig geyst alsz ynn seiner eygenen schule, auszer wilcher wirt nichts geleret, denn nur schein wort unnd geschwetz. Alszo die heylig Junckfraw, da sie ynn yhr selb erfaren, das got ynn yhr szo grosz dingk wircket, szo sie doch gering, unanfehlich, arm und voracht geweszenn, leret sie der heylig geyst diesze reiche kunst und weiszheyt, das got eyn solcher herr sey, der nit andersz zu schaffen habe, denn nur erhohen, was nydrig it, nydern, was da hoch ist, und kurtzlich, brechen, was do ist gemacht, und machen was zu brochen ist."

132. "Der lobsang Zacharie, Johannis des Teuffers vaters, daraus lerne, seinem Exampel nach, Gott danckbar sein, für sein heiliges werdes Euangelion, &c."; *Geistliche lieder* (Wittenberg, 1533), fol. 173ʳ; AWA 4:338.

133. ". . . das ein wort der gnaden und des lebens ist, &c."; *Geystlycher Lieder* (Leipzig, 1545), fol. X[vii]ʳ.

134. *Geystlycher Lieder* (Leipzig, 1545), fol. X[vi]ᵛ.

135. *Sermons of Martin Luther: The House Postils*, ed. Eugene F. A. Klug (Grand Rapids: Baker, 1996), 3:318. Two different transcriptions of Luther's *Hauspostille* were published, one

by Dietrich and the other by Rörer. Klug's translation is of Rörer's text, whereas WA 52 is based on Dietrich's text. The citations here are therefore made from the appropriate volume of the St. Louis Edition: *Dr. Martin Luthers sämmtliche Schriften*, ed. Johann Georg Walch, et al. (St. Louis: Concordia, 1880-1910), 13b, col. 2707: "Das heißt tröstlich predigen und die Leute recht lehren, wie sie sollen selg werden. Es hatten die Juden das Gesetz, welches ist eine solche Lehre und Predigt, daraus man weiß, was man thun und lassen soll. Solches ist wohl auch eine herrliche, große Erkenntniß, aber sie geräth uns sehr übel, weil wir ihr nicht folgen konnen. . . . Dagegen soll nun Johannes kommen, und einer andere Erkenntniß dem Volk Gottes geben, die da sei nicht eine Erkenntniß der Sünde, des Zorns, des Todes; sondern eine Erkenntniß des Heils, das ist, eine solche Predigt, daraus man lernt, wie man selig und vom Tode und Sünde möge errettet werden."

136. "Folget Simeonis des Altuaters lobesang, Luce am andern Capitel"; *Geistliche lieder* (Wittenberg, 1533), fol. 174ᵛ; AWA 4:338.

137. ". . . des lieben heiligen Ertzvaters Lobgesang"; *Geystlycher Lieder* (Leipzig, 1545), fol. Y[i]ʳ.

138. *Geystlycher Lieder* (Leipzig, 1545), fol. Y[i]ᵛ.

139. Luther, *The House Postils*, 3:282-283; St. Louis Edition, 13b, cols. 2666-2667: "Aber laßt uns auf diesmal das merken, daß mit diesem Worten alles ausgeschlossen wird, als unmöglich zur Gerechtigkeit und Seligkeit vor Gott, was nicht Christus ist. . . . Das ist das Liedlein, welches uns Simeon heute gesungen hat; darauf will er nun fröhlich hin fahren im Frieden; denn er hat so viel gesehen, daß er sich nichts schrecken läßt. Weil er den Heiland und das Licht, von Gott bereitet, gesehen hat, so sieht er weder Sünde noch Tod mehr, und ist bereit und willg zu sterben. . . . Solchen Gesang hat er nicht allein gehabt im Munde, auf der Zunge, auf dem Papier, sondern im Herzen. Unser lieber Gott und Vater verleihe uns um Jesu Christi, seinnes Sohnes, willen, durch seinen Heiligen Geist seine Gnade, daß wirs dem lieben Simeon nachsingen und auch im Frieden fahren mögen."

140. "Der Engel lobsang. Luce ij." *Geistliche lieder* (Wittenberg, 1533), fol. 176ᵛ; AWA 4:339.

141. "Der Engel lobgesang/Luce am andern Capitel"; *Geystlycher Lieder* (Leipzig, 1545), fol. Y[ii]ᵛ.

142. Luther, *The House Postils*, 1:129, 131; St. Louis Edition, 13b, cols. 1475, 1477: "So haben nun die lieben Engel den ganzen Gottesdienst in diesen Lobgesang gefaßt: sie geben Gott die Ehre, der Erde, Friede, den Menschen ein Wohlgefallen, daß sie guter Dinge feien, wenns nicht geht, wie es gehen soll. Laß das ein kurz, und doch recht fein engelisch und himmlisch Liedlein fein. Sie singen nicht von äußerlichen Ceremonien, als sei es dem Kindlein Jesu darum zu thun, wie der Tempel zu Jerusalem gebaut und die levitischen Opfer verrichtet werden; sondern darum sei es ihm zu thun, daß Gott im Himmel seine Ehre habe, Friede auf Erden sei und den Menschen ein Wohlgefallen. . . . Es singen aber . . . die lieben Engel allein, wie es zugeht bei denen, die dies Kindlein annehmen. Wie es aber in er Hölle zugeht, davon ist hier nicht geschrieben. Denn da wird ein anderer Gesang und andere Sänger sein."

143. *Geystlycher Lieder* (Leipzig, 1545), fol. Y[iii]ᵛ.

144. LW 11:393; WA 4:259-260: "*Exitus autem iste spiritualis est, qui fit pedibus animae, scilicet intellectu et affectu. Cui enim incipit cognosci et amari spiritus, ipse vere exit de Egypto, et eo magis, quo clarius intelligit et ferventius amat. Sic exit et intrat in terram promissionis, id*

est Ecclesiam. Exit, dum odit et nescire incipit mundum, cui et dorsum vertit et faciem ad coelestia."

145. *Etwas vom Liede Mosis, des Knechts GOttes, un dem Leide des Lammes, Das ist: Alt- und neuer Brüder-Gesang . . .* (London: Haberkorn, 1753; repr. Hildesheim: Olms, 1980), 1-73.

146. LW 49:68; WA BR 3:220. The original text is cited above, Chapter 9, note 6.

Notes to Chapter 17

1. WLS, No. 3092; [Johann Aurifaber], *Tischreden Oder Colloqvia Doct. Mart: Luthers/ So er in vielen Jaren/gegen gelarten Leuten/auch frembden Gesten/vnd seinen Tischgesellen gefüret/Nach den Heubstücken unserer Christlichen Lere/zusammen getragen* (Eisleben: Gaubisch, 1566; facsimile repr., Berlin: Nationales Druckhaus, 1967), 577^v: "Musicam hab ich allzeit lieb gehabt/Wer diese Kunst kan/der ist guter art/zu allem geschickt. Man mus Musicam von not wegen in Schulen behalten. Ein Schulmeister mus singen können/Sonst sehe ich ni nicht an/Man sol auch junge Gesselen zum Predigampt nicht verordnen/sei haben sich denn zuuor in der Schule wol versucht vnd geübet" (= WA TR No. 6248); see also Luther's comment in his lectures on Titus of 1527 (on Titus 1:10): "They want to be teachers but they cannot even sing," WA 25:30: "*Docere volunt, qui non novit canere.*"

While it is important from a scholarly point of view to cite the Weimar edition of the *Tischreden,* when dealing with how Luther's thinking was received and perceived in the seventeenth through eighteenth centuries there is the need to refer to Aurifaber's anthology.

2. By the early eighteenth century the connection between music and theology in the education of clergy began to break down, as is confirmed by the following observation of Johann Mattheson (echoing Martin Luther, see note 1 above), published in 1739: "But how is a clergyman to judge these matters [of music and theology] if he knows nothing of music himself? . . . one might even say it would be a political duty that no servant of the Holy Word would be admitted who is inexperienced in music; especially those who are not at all ashamed to admit this in writings, but who rather pride themselves of their ignorance. For on the authority of St. Augustine, ignorance of music is an obstacle to true comprehension in interpretation of the Holy Writ; a well-read pastor who is well known through his writings once did not believe me when I told him, in a public library, that Augustine had written three books on music; but he, as well as a librarian standing near, laughed at me; until I presented them with proof. Perhaps there are not a few like these gentlemen, one of whom is a master but the other is a doctor"; Johann Mattheson's *Der vollkommene Capellmeister: A Revised Translation with Critical Commentary,* trans. and ed. Ernest C. Harriss (Ann Arbor: University of Michigan Research Press, 1981), 127-128.

3. See Johannes Rautenstrauch, *Luther und die Pflege der kirchlichen Musik in Sachsen* (Leipzig, 1907; reprint Hildesheim: Olms, 1970). Luther provided the theological principles for these parish schools; Melanchthon the basic curriculum; the composer Johann Walter, the polyphonic settings of liturgical music to be learned in the schools and sung in the churches; and Georg Rhau published anthologies of music for school and church.

4. The three publications are given in facsimile in *Die Thomasschule Leipzig zur Zeit Johann Sebastian Bachs: Ordnungen und Gesetze 1634, 1723, 1733,* ed. Hans-Joachim Schulze (Leipzig: Zentraal Antiquariat der Deutschen Demokratischen Republik, 1987). For example,

under the heading "Von der Musik," the 1733 *Ordnungen* states (p. 22): "Es haben unsere Vorvahren angeordnet, daß die Musik auf der *Thomas*-Schule getrieben, und von den dasigen *Alumnis* in allen Stadt-Kirchen besorget werden soll" (Our forefathers ordered that music should be studied in the Thomasschule so that the alumni should serve the musical needs of all the town churches [in Leipzig]).

5. See *Oxford Composer Companions: J. S. Bach*, ed. Malcolm Boyd (Oxford: Oxford University Press, 1999), 258; see also Hans Löffler, "Johann Ludwig Krebs: Mitteilungen über sein Leben und Wirken," *Bach-Jahrbuch* 30 (1930): 100-129, and Hans Löffler, "Johann Tobias Krebs und Matthias Sojka, zwei Schüler Joh. Seb. Bachs," *Bach-Jahrbuch* 37 (1940-1948): 136-145.

6. The published writings of Johann Tobias Krebs, the younger, include: *De vsv et praestantia romanae historiae in Novi Testamenti interpretatione libellvs* (Lipsiae: Langenhemiana, 1745); *Decretum Atheniensium in honorem Hyrcani Pontificis M. Iudaeorum factum: commentario historico grammatico critico illustratum* (Lipsiae: Langenhemiana, 1751); *Commentatio historico philologica de provocatione d. Pauli ad Caesarem* (Lipsiae: Langenhemiana, 1753); *Observationes in Novum Testamentum e Flavio Josepho* (Lipsiae: Wendlerum, 1755); *Decreta Romanorum pro Judaeis facta e Josepho collecta et commentario historico-grammatico-critico illustrata* (Lipsiae: Fritsch, 1768); *De ratione Novi Testamenti e moribus antiquis illustrandi minus caute instituta prolusio declamationibus IIII . . .* (Lipsiae: Iacobaeer, 1777); *Illustris Moldani rectoris Opuscula academica et scholastica* (Lipsiae: Iacobaeer, 1778).

7. These texts and melodies were published in Selnecker's *Christliche Psalmen, Lieder, und Kirchengesang* (Leipzig: Beyer, 1587).

8. Stenger's text book, *Manuducto ad musicam theoreticam, das ist Kurtze Anleitung der Singekunst* (Erfurt, 1635), was expanded in 1659 and reached a fourth edition by 1666; see Johann Nikolaus Forkel, *Allgemeine Literatur der Musik* (Leipzig, 1792; repr. Hildesheim: Olms, 2001), 308. The hymnal Stenger edited was issued as *Christlich neuvermehrt und gebessertes Gesangbuch* (Erfurt: Brand, 1663). Copies of two of Stenger's collections of sermons — his church year sermons, *Credendorum et faciendorum Postilla* (Erfurt, 1661), and his substantial series of sermons on the Augsburg Confession, *Grund-Feste Der Augspurgischer Confession* (Jena & Erfurt: Kempf & Birckner, 1649-1654) — were in J. S. Bach's personal library; see Robin A. Leaver, *Bachs theologische Bibliothek: Eine kritische Bibliographie* (Stuttgart: Hänssler, 1983), Nos. 23 and 24.

9. Johannes Olearius, *Biblische Erklärung Darinnen/nechst dem allgemeinen Haupt-Schlüssel Der gantzen heiligen Schrifft*, 5 vols. (Leipzig: Tarnoven, 1678-1681). This Bible commentary was also in Bach's personal library; see Leaver, *Bachs theologische Bibliothek*, No. 12.

10. This was included in his hymnal, *Geistliche Singe-Kunst und ordentlich verfaßtes vollständiges Gesangbuch* (Leipzig: Gross, 1671), issued as the second part of his *Exemplarische Betkunst der Kinder Gottes*, published the previous year.

11. See, for example, *The Journals of Henry Melchior Muhlenberg*, trans. Theodore G. Tappert and John W. Doberstein, Vol. 1 (Philadelphia: Muhlenberg, 1942), 85.

12. See Leonard Hutter, *Compendium Locorum Theologicorum*, ed. Wolfgang Trillhaas (Berlin: Gruyter, 1961); Leonard Hutter, *Compend of Lutheran Theology*, trans. Henry E. Jacobs and G. F. Spieker (Philadelphia: Lutheran Book Store, 1868). The answer to Hutter's first question, "Quid est Scriptura sacra" (What is Holy Scripture?), was based on

Martin Chemnitz's *Examen concilii tridentini*, originally published in Frankfurt, 1566-73; see *Compendium*, ed. Trillhaas, 1, and *Compend*, ed. Jacobs and Spieker, 2. J. S. Bach owned a copy of this substantial theological work by Chemnitz; see Leaver, *Bachs theologische Bibliothek*, No. 5.

13. See the 1634 Thomasschule *Ordnung*, sig. H4^r in *Thomasschule Leipzig . . . : Ordnungen und Gesetze*, ed. Hans-Joachim Schulze. There is a Thomasschule manuscript headed "Catologus Lectionum," also dated 1634 (now in the Bach-Archiv, Leipzig). It presents the weekly schedule in a different format and some of the details are at variance with the printed version, such as the information that the cantor taught Luther's catechism on Fridays at 2:00 p.m., whereas the printed *Ordnung* gives Saturdays at 7:00 a.m. as the day and time for this duty. It is possible, therefore, that the manuscript represents the pre-1643 practice and the published form the minor modifications that were introduced that year.

14. Günther Stiller, *Johann Sebastian Bach and Liturgical Life in Leipzig*, trans. Herbert J. A. Bouman, Daniel F. Poellot, Hilton C. Oswald, and ed. Robin A. Leaver (St. Louis: Concordia, 1984), 50.

15. The settings were of the Ten Commandments, Apostles' Creed, Lord's Prayer (which employs the traditional *Pater noster* chant), Christ's baptismal command (Matt. 28:19 and Mark 16:16), *Verba testamenti*, and table blessings and thanksgivings (mostly psalm verses); see *Mattheus Le Maistre Catechesis and Gesenge*, ed. Donald Gresch (Madison: A-R Editions, 1982), viii-xi, xv, xix-xx.

16. Luther's catechism hymns are: *Dies sind die heiligen zehn Gebot* [Commandments], *Wir glauben all an einen Gott* [Creed], *Vater unser im Himmelreich* [Lord's Prayer], *Christ unser Herr zum Jordan kam* [Baptism], *Aus tiefer Not schrei ich zu dir* [Confession], *Jesus Christus, unser Heiland, der von uns den Gotteszorn* [Lord's Supper]; on these hymns see Chapters 5-10 above.

17. See Robin A. Leaver, "Bach's 'Clavierübung III': Some Historical and Theological Considerations, *The Organ Yearbook* 6 (1975): 17-32; Albert A. Clement, *Der dritte Teil der Clavierübung von Johann Sebastian Bach: Musik-Text-Theologie* (Middelburg: Almares, 1999).

18. See Michael Praetorius, *Syntagma Musicum: Tomus tertius* (Wolfenbüttel: Holwein, 1619), 258; see also C. L. Hilgenfeldt, *Johann Sebastian Bachs Leben, Wirken und Werke* (Leipzig, 1850; repr. Hilversum: Knuf, 1965), tab. 1, at the end of the volume.

19. *Bach-Dokumente: Supplement zu Johann Sebastian Bach Neue Ausgabe Sämtlicher Werke*, ed. Werner Neuman and Han-Joachim Schulze (Kassel: Bärenreiter, 1963-1972), 2:99-100 (a facsimile of the document is given facing page 177); *The New Bach Reader: A Life of Johann Sebastian Bach in Letters and Documents*, ed. Hans T. David, Arthur Mendel and Christoph Wolff (New York: Norton, 1998), 105.

20. For the background, see Martin Petzoldt, "Bachs Prüfung vor dem Kurfürstlichen Konsistorium zu Leipzig," *Bach-Jahrbuch* 84 (1998): 19-30, esp. 24-27.

21. Cited in Petzoldt, "Bachs Prüfung," 25.

22. Cited in Petzoldt, "Bachs Prüfung," 27.

23. *Bach-Dokumente*, 2:101.

24. *Bach-Dokumente*, 3:630-631.

25. See, for example, Joyce Irwin, *Neither Voice nor Heart Alone: German Lutheran Theology of Music in the Age of the Baroque* (New York: Lang, 1993), 143.

26. See Valentin Ernst Loescher, *The Complete Timotheus Verinus or A Statement of the*

Truth and a Call for Peace in the Present Pietistic Controversy . . . [1718-1721], trans. James L. Langebartels and Robert J. Koester (Milwaukee: Northwestern, 1998), 1:191-195.

27. See Oswald Bill, *Das Frankfurter Gesangbuch von 1689 und seine späteren Ausgaben* (Marburg: Görich & Weierhäuser, 1969), 39-42. The first edition noted its relevance for "Pfarrherrn, Schulmeistern und Cantoribus" (pastors, schoolmasters and cantors), that the hymns should be sung by their congregations and choirs ("den Chor mit singen"); from 1584 they are referred to as "Kirchen und Schuldienern" (church and school officials/servants). It is interesting to note that a copy of the 1584 edition of the Frankfurt *Kirchen Gesang* was owned by Elias Herda (1674-1728), who became Cantor in Ohrdruf in 1698. He was therefore Johann Sebastian Bach's teacher for two years, since the young Bach was then living with his older brother, Johann Christoph, after the deaths of their parents; see Martin Petzoldt and Joachim Petri, *Johann Sebastian Bach, Ehre sei dir Gott gesungen: Bilder und Texte zu Bachs Leben als Christ und seinem Wirken für die Kirche* (Göttingen: Vandenhoeck & Ruprecht, 1988), 41.

28. BC-W/K, 43; BSLK, 61: "*Est autem ecclesia congregatio sanctorum, in quae evangelium pure docetur et rechte administrantur sacramenta.*"

29. LW 11:275; WA 4:123: "*Psallere in Tubis ductilibus est predicare mysterium regni coelorum et ad bona spiritualia exhorti. Psallere in Voce tube cornee est predicare, arguere peccata et malia nostra.*"

30. LW 15:273-274; WA 54:33-34: "Denn er meinet nicht allein die lieblikeit und sussigkeit der Psalmen, nach der Grammatica und Musica, da die wort zierlich und künstlich gestellet sind, und der gesang oder dohn süsse und lieblich lautet, das da heisst, Schöner text und Schöne noten. Sondern viel mehr nach der Theologia, nach dem geistlichen verstand. . . . Solchen hertzen ist der Psalter, weil er den Messia singet und predigt, ein süsser, tröstlicher, lieblicher gesang, wenn man gleich die blossen wort, on noten daher lieset oder saget. Doch hilfft die Musica, oder noten, als ein wunderliche Creatur und gabe Gottes seer wol dazu, sonderlich wo der hauffe mit singet, und fein ernstlich zu gehet."

31. WA TR No. 1258: "*Sic Deus pradicavit euangelium etiam per musicam*"; and WA TR No. 4441: "*Musica optimum Dei donum. Saepius ita me incitavit et acuit*, das zu predigen gewonne habe."

32. LW 53:323-324; WA 50:371-372: "*Vnde non frustra Patres et Prophetae verbo Dei nihil voluerunt esse coniunctius quam Musicam. Inde enim tot Cantica et Psalmi, in quibus simul agunt et sermo et vox in animo auditoris. . . . Denique homini soli prae caeteris sermo voci copulatus donatus est, vt sciret, se Deum laudare oportere verbo et Musica, scilicet sonora praedicatione et mistis verbis suaui melodiae.*"

33. LW 49:428; WA BR 5:639: "*Et plane iudico, nec pudet asserere, post theologiam esse nullam artem, quae musicae possit aequari, cum ipsa sola post theologiam id praestet, quod alioqui sola theologia praestat, scilicet quietem et animum laetum. . . . Hinc factum est, ut prophetae nulla sic arte sint usi ut musica, dum suam theologiam non in geometriam, non in arithmeticam, non in astronomiam, sed in musicam digesserunt, ut theologiam et musicam haberent coniunctissimas, veritatem psalmi et canticis dicentes.*"

34. Sie ist mit der Theologie
Zugleich von Gott gegeben hie.
Gott die Music fein bedeckt
In der Theologie versteckt.
Er hat sie beid im Fried geschückt

Daß kein andern Ehr verrückt.
Sie sind in Freundschaft nahe verwandt,
Daß sie für Schwestern werdn erkannt. (Lines 41-44)

Die Music mit Gott ewig bleibt,
Die andern Künst sie all vertreibt.
Im Himmel nach den Jüngsten Tag
Wird sie erst gehn in rechter Wag. . . .
Im Himmel gar man nicht bedarf
Der Kunst, Grammatik, Logik scharf,
Geometrie, Astronomei,
Kein Medizin, Juresterei,
Philosophei, Rhetorika.
Allein die schöne Musica.
Da werden all cantores sein,
Gebrauchen dieser Kunst allein. (lines 145-151)

Johann Walter sämtliche Werke, ed. Otto Schroeder and Joachim Stalmann, 6 vols. (Kassel: Bärenreiter and St. Louis: Concordia, 1953-1970), 6:154, 156; F. Samuel Janzow's rhymed translation of the whole poem is found in Carl Schalk, *Johann Walter: First Cantor of the Lutheran Church* (St. Louis: Concordia, 1992), 14-22.

35. Johann Mattheson, *Grundlage einer Ehren-Pforte* (Hamburg: Mattheson, 1740; repr. ed. Max Schneider, Berlin: Liepmannssohn, 1910), 304: "Die Musika ist eine edle Kunst und ein grosses *Ornamentum* eines edlen *Ingenii*. Alle andre Künste und Wissenschafften sterben mit uns. Ein Jurist kann seine Procurator-Stücklein im Himmel nicht anbringen: denn da führet man keine Processe, wie zu Speier und anderswo. Ein Medicus wird im Himmel niemand antreffen, der von ihm begehren wird, daß er ihm ein *Reicpe [sic]* schreiben, und eine Purgation eingeben solle. Aber, was ein Theologus und ein Musikus auf Erden gelernet hat, das practisirt er auch im Himmel, nemlich, er lobet und preiset Gott"; trans. in Oskar Söhngen, "Fundamental Considerations for a Theology of Music," *Musical Heritage of the Church*, Vol. 7, ed. Theodore Hoelty-Nickel (St. Louis: Concordia, 1963), 7.

36. Some years earlier Mattheson had drawn attention to this sermon, that it had stated that "vocal and instrumental music, as gifts of God, must be given back to God in his service" ("daß die Vocal- und Instrumental-Music, als eine Gabe GOTTES, GOTT, in seinem Dienst, müsse wieder gegeben werden"); Johann Mattheson, *Der Musikalische Patriot, Welcher seine gründliche Betrachtungen, über Geist- und Weltl. Harmonien* (Hamburg: Mattheson, 1728; facsimile, Leipzig: Zentralantiquariat der DDR, 1978), 13.

37. Mattheson, *Der Musikalische Patriot*, 9: "Alle Bemühungen unsrer Componisten, Sänger und Instrumentisten ist von keiner Dauer; dafern sie nicht, ohne die geringste Heucherley, mit Davidischen recht Ernst, die Ehre und Lob Gottes zum Zweck hat: es sey nun mittelbahr, oder unmittelbahr. Singet und spielet in den Opern, infomirt und componirt so lange, als ihr wollet, endlich muss doch die Kirche einen festen Sitz geben"; trans. based on Beekman C. Cannon, *Johann Mattheson Spectator in Music* (New Haven: Yale University Press, 1947), 86.

38. Johann Mattheson, *Die neueste untersuchung der Singspiele, nebst beyfügter musikalischen Geschmacksprobe* (Hamburg: Herold, 1744; facsimile, Leipzig: Zentralanti-

quariat der DDR, 1975), 103-104: "Die Opern sind der Musik Academien: so wie die Concerte ihre Gymnasien; in der Kirche aber findet sie den rechten Beruf, und im Himmel ewigen Sitz, ja, so zu reden, Sitz und Stimme."

39. He read a chapter of the Bible and a Psalm every evening (see Cannon, *Mattheson*, 100). In his unpublished autobiography he reports that in 1759 he began reading through the Bible for the 22nd time; in 1760 that much of his time was spent in Bible reading; and by 1762 he had read through the Bible 24 times (see Cannon, *Mattheson*, 219, 220 and 224).

40. WA TR No. 2545b: "Die Noten machen den Text lebendig"; Mattheson, *Die neueste Untersuchung der Singspiele*, titlepage and 78, where the citation is identified: "Tom. VIII. Altenb. pag. 411. sqq."

41. Mattheson, *Singspiele*, 18, 40, 52, 56, 78, etc.

42. Veritophilus, *Beweis-Gründe/Worauf der rechte Gebrauch der MUSIC, beydes in der Kirchen/als ausser denselben/beruhet. . . . Samt einer Vorrede heraus gegeben Von Mattheson* (Hamburg: Schiller, 1717), a3^r; facsimile in Friedrich Erhard Niedt, *Musikalische Handleitung Teil I-III* (Hildesheim: Olms, 2003).

43. Veritophilus, *Beweis-Gründe*, a4^r; see WA BR 5:639; LW 49:427-29.

44. Veritophilus, *Beweis-Gründe*, 9, 24-26, 29, 40, 51 and 56.

45. Mattheson, *Der Musikalische Patriot*, 50: "Frage deinen Vater Lutherum, du Lutheraner! der wird dir verkundigen, was für ein herrliches, Göttliches Geschenck du an der Music habest! Seine reine Lehre lautet so: 'Die Music ist eine schöne, und herrliche Gabe Gottes, und nahe der Theologia. Ich gebe, nach der Theologia, der Music den nächsten *locum* und die höchste Ehre . . .'"; see Isabella van Elferen, "'Sie creutzigen alle sinn des liebes!' Multi-mediality, Consolatio Tragoediae and Lutheran Pedagogy in the German Baroque Passion Meditation," *Multi-Media Compositions from the Middle Ages to the Early Modern Period*, ed. Margriet Hoogvliet (Leuven: Peeters, 2004), 134-135.

46. See Cannon, *Mattheson*, 53, 168.

47. Irwin, *Neither Voice nor Heart Alone*, 146.

48. Some of this is found in *Der Musikalische Patriot* (1728), but he regarded it only as a partial discussion. At the end of the volume he wrote: "The gentle reader will gather at a glance . . . the following facts. . . . In my dissertation on *Divine demands* concerning the *musica figuralis* [polyphonic, contrapuntal music] I have not treated even half of the material, because all of the Prophets, all the Apocrypha, and all of the New Testament remained untouched . . ." ("Der geneigte Leser wird heraus . . . in einem Anblick ersehen . . . dass ich von der Dissertation über die Göttlichen Gebote, wegen der Figural-Music, lange nicht die Helffte abgehandelt habe, indem alle Propheten, Apochryphische Bücher und das gantze N.T. noch unberührt geblieben . . ."); *Der Musikalische Patriot*, 357; trans. Cannon, *Mattheson*, 86-87. Many of Mattheson's books published between 1745 and 1752 were devoted to exploring a Biblical understanding of music and the connections between theology and music; see Cannon, *Mattheson*, 204-211.

49. See, for example, George J. Buelow and Hans Joachim Marx, eds., *New Mattheson Studies* (Cambridge: Cambridge University Press, 1983).

50. See Chapter 2, notes 83 and 162.

51. Daniel Vetter, *Musikalischer Kirch- und Hauß-Ergötzlicheit* (Leipzig: Vetter, 1709-1713; facsimile Hildesheim: Olms, 1985), II, sig. C1^v-C2^r. Vetter cites Seckendorf as "L.1.S.8. § 8 . . . p. 21." This is a reference to the original Latin version of 1692 rather than the German

translation issued the year after Vetter wrote his preface: *Herrn Veit Ludewigs von Seckendorff Ausführliche Historie des Lutherthums und der heilsame Reformation . . . aus dem Lateinischen* [von Elias Frick] (Leipzig: Gleditsch, 1714).

52. Vetter, *Musikalischer . . . Ergötzlicheit,* II, sig. C2^r.

53. Vetter, *Musikalischer . . . Ergötzlicheit,* II, 91-92.

54. See Kirsten Beißwenger, *Johann Sebastian Bachs Notenbibliothek* (Kassel: Bärenreiter, 1992), 321.

55. Vetter's collection was in vogue with the middle-class intelligentsia of Leipzig, and Bach's use of his setting of *Liebster Gott, wenn werd ich Sterben?* may have been influenced by one of them, most likely a member of the Bose family, who were close to the Bachs; one member of the family was a dedicatee of Vetter's collection, and another had specifically voted for Bach as Thomaskantor in 1723; see Stephen Rose, "Daniel Vetter and the Domestic Keyboard Chorale in Bach's Leipzig," *Early Music* 33 (2005): 47.

56. See Appendix 5 below.

57. Salomon Gesner, *Commentationes in Psalmos Davidis . . . Editio tertia* (Wittenberg: Berger, 1616), 885-[937].

58. Gesner, *Commentationes in Psalmos Davidis,* 935.

59. *Gesamtausgabe der musikalische Werke von Michael Praetorius,* ed. Friedrich Blume, 21 vols. (Wolfenbüttel: Kallmeyer & Möseler, 1928-1960), 17: vii: "Demnach nun volnkommenheit und bestand des Kirchen Regiments, auch völligem Gottes Dienst, nicht allein gehörig ist Concio, Eine gute Predigt: Sondern auch dazu erförderlich Cantio, Eine gute Music und Gesang. Sintemahl recht und war ist des Justini Meinung: . . . 'Es ist und bleibet Gottes Wort, auch das da im Gemüth gedacht, mit der Stimme gesungen, auch auff Instrumenten geschlagen und gespielet wird.'" Praetorius had made the same point earlier in the first version of his *Syntagma musicum* (1614/15); see Appendix 5. It is possible that Bach knew of this preface by Praetorius. According to the inventory drawn up in 1679 the *Polyhymnia Caduceatrix et Panegyrica* (1619) was accessible in the music library of the Thomasschule; see Arnold Schering, *Musikgeschichte Leipzigs, II: Von 1650 bis 1723* (Leipzig: Kistner & Siegel, 1926), 54.

60. *Limpurgische Kirchenordnung, wie es beedes mit der Lehr und Cermenien bei allen und jeder christlichen Pfarrgemeinden der Herrschaft Limburg Speckfelder Linie soll gehalten werden* (Schwäbische Hall: Laidigen, 1666).

61. "Und nachdem Gottes Wort, wie der alte Lehrer Justinus fein davon redet, auf dreierlei Art gehandelt wird: 1. Lehr- und Predigtweise, 2. Gebet- und Gesangsweise und dann 3. Orgelweise oder durch Saitenspiel und Instrumentalmusik"; cited in Adolf Strube, *Spielleute Gottes: Ein Buch vom deutschen Kantor* (Berlin-Steglitz: Eckart, 1935), 59.

62. Söhngen, *Theologie der Musik,* 333: ". . . Johann Mattheson kann noch im Jahre 1725 in seiner *Critica Musica* Prediger und Kantor auf einer Ebene stellen."

63. Johann Mattheson, *Critica Musica* (Hamburg: Mattheson, 1722-1725; facsimile Amsterdam: Knuf, 1964), 2:313-314.

64. The particular suggestion made by Irwin (*Neither Voice nor Heart Alone,* 147) that Luther's understanding of vocation can have little significance for Bach (or, by implication, Mattheson) is not borne out by the evidence. In Bach's own copy of Abraham Calov's *Deutsche Bibel* — essentially an edition of Luther's writings arranged in Biblical order — there are significant manuscript underlinings and markings made by the composer in passages from Luther that deal specifically with "Amt" (vocation); see Robin A. Leaver, *J. S. Bach and Scrip-*

ture: Glosses from the Calov Bible Commentary (St. Louis: Concordia, 1985), 121-122 and 149; see also the discussion in Renate Steiger, "Bach und die Bibel: Einige Anstreichungen Bachs in seiner Calov-Bibel als Selbstzeugnisse gelesen," *Musik und Kirche* 57 (1987): 119-126.

65. Mattheson, *Critica Musica*, 2:316: ". . . einem rectschaffenen *Cantori*, bey Verrichtung seines heiligen Amts, Einrede zu thun, als einem Prediger auf der Kanzel zu wiedersprechen: denn sie treiben beyde Gottes Wort. *Verbum Dei est, sive mente cogitetir, sive canatur, sive pulsu edatur*, sind Ausdrückungen, die dem *Justino Martyre* zugeschrieben werden. *Vid. Gesneri Medit. super Psalter. cap. 27.*" The reference is to the appendix to Gesner's Psalm commentary; see notes 57 and 58 above.

66. Veritophilus, *Beweis-Gründe*, 5 (repeated almost verbatim on page 9).

67. Mattheson, *Ehren-Pforte*, 304-305: ". . . denn fein eigener Auspruche p. 12 lautet, aus dem Märtyrer Justin, *Quaest. 107. ad Orthod.* also: *Verbum Dei est, sive mente cogitetur, sive canatur, sive pulsu edatur.* Es ist und bleibt Gottes Wort: es mag im Hertzen bedacht; oder gesungen; oder gespielet werden: ist also kein Neben-sondern allemahl ein Hauptwerck. Das mag ein jeder Christ sicherlich glauben. Denn Gottes Wort kan kein Nebenwerck seyn."

68. Irwin, *Neither Voice nor Heart Alone*, 147.

69. In addition to the much-quoted sayings of Luther there are many other seemingly incidental statements that have a similar import, such as in a sermon preached in 1525 in which he declared that the Word of God is "to be preached and sung" (will gepredigt und gesungen sein); WA 17^{II}:120.

70. See, for example, the statement in the Limburg *Kirchenordnung* (1666): "Der Heilige Geist als der himmlische Sing-Meister wirket nicht durch gepredigte oder gelesene Worte, sondern auch durchs Gebet und Gesang . . ." (The Holy Spirit, as the heavenly singing-master, operates not only through the preached or read Word but also through prayer and song . . .); cited in Strube, *Spielleute Gottes*, 59.

71. See for example, Steven M. Oberhelman, *Rhetoric and Homiletics in Fourth-Century Christian Literature: Prose Rhythm, Oratorical Style, and Preaching in the Works of Ambrose, Jerome, and Augustine* (Atlanta: Scholars Press, 1991).

72. See Hans-Heinrich Unger, *Die Beziehungen zwischen Musik und Rhetorik im 16.-18. Jahrhundert* (Würzburg: Triltsch, 1941; repr. Hildesheim: Olms, 2000).

73. See further Robin A. Leaver, "The Liturgical Place and Homiletic Purpose of Bach's Cantatas," *Worship* 59 (1985): 194-202.

74. For a bibliography of discussions of the theological significance of Bach's compositions, see *Theologische Bachforschung heute: Dokumentation und Bibliographie der Internationalen Arbeitsgemeinschaft für theologische Bachforschung 1976-1996*, ed. Renate Steiger (Berlin: Galda & Wilch, 1998).

75. See Leaver, *Bachs theologische Bibliothek, passim.*

76. See Leaver, *Bachs theologische Bibliothek*, Nos. 2-4, 6, 7, and 28.

77. See Friedhelm Krummacher, "Luthers Musikbegriff und die Kirchenmusik Bachs," *Luther: Zeitschrift der Luther-Gesellschaft* 56 (1985): 136-151. For the background of Bach's understanding of theology, see Robin A. Leaver, "Music and Lutheranism," *The Cambridge Bach Companion*, ed. John Butt (Cambridge: Cambridge University Press, 1997), 35-45, 253-256, and Robin A. Leaver, "Religion and Religious Currents in Bach's World," in *Bach and His World*, ed. Raymond Erikson (New Haven: Yale University Press, forthcoming).

78. Aurifaber, *Tischreden*, 172ᵛ; WA TR No. 816; see also the discussion in Chapter 3 above.

79. Sermon on Law and Gospel, 1532; WA 36:25.

Notes to Chapter 18

1. LW 53:61; WA 19:72: "Vor allen dingen wil ich gar freundlich gebeten haben, auch umb Gottis willen, alle die jenigen, so diese unser ordnunge ym Gottis dienst sehen odder nach folgen wollen, das sie ja keyn nöttig gesetz draus machen noch yemands gewissen damit verstricken odder fahen, sondern der Christlichen freyheyt nach yhres gefallens brauchen, wie, wu, wenn und wie lange es die sachen schicken und foddern."

2. LW 53:63; WA 19:73-74: ". . . eyne latinsche [Messe], wilche wyr zuvor haben lassen ausgehen, und heyst Formula Misse. Dise wil ich hie mit nicht auffgehaben odder verendert haben, sondern wie wyr sie bis her bey uns gehalten haben, so sol sie noch frey seyn, der selbigen zu gebrauchen, wo und wenn es uns gefellet odder ursachen bewegt. Denn ich ynn keynen weg wil die latinische sprache aus dem Gottis deinst lassen gar weg komen, denn es ist myr alles umb die jugent zu thun. . . . Ich halte es gar nichts mit denen, die nur auff eyne sprache sich so gar geben und alle andere verachten. . . . Aber dise zwo weyse [*Formula missæ* und *Deutsche Messe*] mussen wyr also gehen und geschehen lassen, das sie offentlich ynn den kirchen fur allem volck gehalten werden. . . ."

3. LW 40:141; WA 18:123: "Ich wolt heute gerne eine deutsche Messe haben, Ich gehe auch damit umbe, Aber ich wolt ja gerne, das sie eine rechte deutsche art hette, Denn das man den lateinisch text verdolmetscht und lateinisch ton odder noten behellt, las ich geschehen, Aber es laut nicht ertig noch rechtschaffen. Es mus beide text und noten, accent, weise und geperde aus rechter mutter sprach und stimme komen, sonst ists alles ein nachomen, wie die affen thun."

4. Hans Lietzmann, *Martin Luthers Deutsche Messe, 1526* (Bonn: Marcus & Weber, 1909); Joachim Beckmann, *Quellen zur Geschichte des Christlichen Gottesdeinstes* (Gütersloh: Bertelsmann, 1956), 127-133; Wolfgang Herbst, *Quellen zur Geschichte des evangelischen Gottesdienstes* (Göttingen: Vandenhoeck & Ruprecht, 1968), 55-70; however, the second, revised edition, issued under the title *Evangelische Gottesdienst: Quellen zu seiner Geschichte* (Göttingen: Vandenhoeck & Ruprecht, 1992), 69-87, does include musical notation.

5. *The Works of Martin Luther*, 6 vols. (Philadelphia: Holman, 1915-1932), 6 (ed. Paul Zeller Strodach): 170-186; Bard Thompson, *Liturgies of the Western Church* (Cleveland: World Books, 1961), 93-137.

6. WA TR No. 968: "Die Musica ist eine schöne herrliche Gabe Gottes, und nahe der Theologie"; see also WA TR No. 3815.

7. LW 53:316; WA 35:474-475: "Und sind dazu auch ynn vier [bis fünf] stymme bracht, nicht aus anderer ursach, denn das ich gerne wollte, die iugend, die doch sonst soll und mus ynn der Musica und andern rechten künsten erzogen werden. . . . Auch das ich nicht der meynung byn, das durchs Euangelion sollten alle künste zu boden geschlagen werden und vergehen, wie ettliche abergeystlichen fur geben, Sondern ich wollt alle künste, sonderlich die Musica gerne sehen ym dienst, des, der sie geben und geschaffen hat."

8. WA TR No. 6248: "Ein schulmeister muß singen können, sonst sehe ich ihn nicht an."

Man soll auch junge Gesellen zum Predigamt nicht verordnen, sie haben sich denn in der Schule wohl versucht und geübet."

9. LW 53:69: WA 19:80: "Fur die knaben und schuler ynn der Biblia zu uben gehets also zu. Die wochen uber teglich, fur der lection/singen sie ettliche psalmen latinisch, wie bis her zur metten gewonet, denn, wie gesagt ist, wyr wollen die jugend bey der latinschen sprachen ynn der Biblia behalten und uben. Nach den psalmen lesen die knaben eyner vmb den andern zween odder drey eyn Capitel latinsch aus dem newen testament, darnachs lang ist. Darauff liset eyn ander knabe dasselbige capitel zu deudsch, sie zu ubenu und ob yemands von leyen da were und zu horet. Darnach gehen sie mit eyner antiphen zur deudschen lection, davon droben gesagt ist. Nach der lection singet der gantze hauffe eyn deudsch lied, darauff spricht man heymlich eyn vater unser. Darnach der pfarherr odder Capplan eyne Collecten und beschliessen mit dem benedicamus domino, wie gewonet ist.

"Desselbigen gleychen zur vesper singen sie etliche der vesper psalmen, wie sie bis her gesungen sind, auch latinsch mit eyner antiphen, darauff eynen hymnus, so er fur handen ist. Darnach lesen sie abermal eyner umb den andern, zween odder drey, latinsch aus dem alten testament eyn gantzes odder halbes Capitel, darnachs lang ist. Darnach lieset eyn knabe dasselbige Capitel zu deudsch. Darauff das magnificat zu latein mit eyner antiphen odder lied. Darnach eyn vater unser heymlich und die Collecten mit dem Benedicamus. Das ist der Gottis dienst teglich durch die wochen ynn stedten, da man schulen hat."

10. Günther Stiller, *Johann Sebastian Bach and Liturgical Life in Leipzig*, trans. Herbert J. A. Bouman, Daniel Poellot, and Hilton C. Oswald (St. Louis: Concordia, 1984), 48-55.

11. *E. E. Hochw. Raths der Stadt Leipzig Ordnung Der Schule zu S. Thomæ* (Leipzig: Tietzen, 1723), 32-37; facsimile in *Die Thomasschule Leipzig zur Zeit Johann Sebastian Bachs: Ordnungen und Gesetze, 1634, 1723, 1733,* hrsg. Hans-Joachim Schulze (Leipzig: Zentralantiquariat, 1987).

12. The leading ideas of the following paragraphs are based on material found in Robin A. Leaver, *Elisabeth Creutziger, the Magdeburg Enchiridion, 1536, and Reformation Theology: The Kessler Reformation Lecture, Pitts Theology Library, October 18, 1994* (Atlanta: Pitts Theology Library, Emory University, 1995).

13. LW 53:64-65; WA 19:76: "Ist auffs erste ym deudschen Gottis dienst eyn grober, schlechter, eynfeltiger guter Catechismus von nöten. Catechismus aber heyst eyne unterricht. . . . Dise unterricht odder vnterweysunge weys ich nicht schlechter besser zu stellen, denn sie bereyt ist gestellet von anfang der Christenheyt, und bis her blieben, nemlich die drey stuck, die zehen gebot, der glaube und das vater unser. Inn disen dreyen stucken steht es schlecht und kurtz fast alles, was eym Christen zu wissen not ist."

14. See Chapters 5-10 above.

15. *Leges et statuta Scholæ senatoriæ ad D. Thom.* (Leipzig: Roler, 1634), fol. H4^r; see also *E. E. Hochw. Raths der Stadt Leipzig Ordnung Der Schule zu S. Thomæ* (Leipzig: Tietzen, 1723), 20-21.

16. LW 53:69; WA 19:80: "Zum anfang aber singen wyr eyn geystlich lied odder eynen deudschen Psalmen."

17. See Robin A. Leaver, "Bach's 'Clavierübung III': Some Historical and Theological Considerations," *The Organ Yearbook* 6 (1975): 20-21.

18. LW 53:74; WA 19:90: "Auff die Epistel singet man eyn deudsch lied . . . mit den gantzen Chor."

19. LW 53:81-82; WA 19:99: "Und die weyl singe das deudsche sanctus, odder das lied, Gott sey globet, oder Johans Hussen lied, Jhesus Christus unser heyland . . . oder das deudsche Agnus Dei." This was in essence a repetition of Luther's call for Communion hymns in his *Formula missæ*.

20. *Bach Dokumente*, ed. Bach-Archiv Leipzig [Supplement zu Neue Bach Ausgabe] (Kassel: Bärenreiter, 1963-), 1:248 (Nr. 178): "Prælud[ieret] auf die Music. Und nach selbiger wechselweise prælud[ieret] und Choräle gesungen, biß die Communion zu Ende."

21. See Chapter 12 above.

22. See further Robin A. Leaver, "Liturgical Chant Forms in Bach's Compositions for Lutheran Worship: A Preliminary Survey," in *Die Quellen Johann Sebastian Bachs: Bachs Musik im Gottesdienst*, ed. Renate Steiger (Heidelberg: Manutius, 1998), 417-428.

Notes to Appendix 2

1. *Scriptores ecclesiastici de musica sacra potissimum*, ed. Martin Gerbert (St. Blaise: Typis San-Blasianus, 1784; repr. Hildesheim: Olms, 1963), 3:335-339.

2. Literally "heart," classically the seat of thought; LH-S sought a word that should combine both "mind" and "feeling."

3. An allusion to the saying *comes facundus in via pro vehiculo* — "an outgoing companion on the road is as good as a carriage" — "outgoing" rather than "chatty" and "talkative" which sound pejorative in English.

4. The meter suggests *psallentum* rather than *psallentium*.

5. 1 Kings (Vulgate) = 1 Samuel (KJV) 10:5-6.

6. *Cithara* is the Vulgate word (1 Kgs. = 1 Sam. 16:16, 23), a far better rendering of *kinnôr* than "harp."

7. *Numeri* may be variously "meter," "rhythm," or "melody."

8. See 4 = 2 Kings 3:15.

9. The Latin word also means "poets."

10. For *organa* and *chorus*, and how they might have been understood, see LH-S's notes in Margaret Bent and Andrew Wathey, eds., *Fauvel Studies: Allegory, Chronicle, Music, and Image in Paris, Bibliothèque nationale de France, MS français 146* (Oxford: Clarendon, 1998), 266-267. For *nabla* (Phoenician harps) see 1 Paral. = 1 Chron. 15:16, 20, 28, 1 Macc. 13:51.

11. Reading *est* for *et*.

12. The construction is *Heu, te deprecor, fuge, fuge tali tenore esse*.

13. Loosely used for "arteries."

14. In the Golden Legend it was her sighs; here the story has been assimilated to that of Antiochus I's passion for his stepmother Stratonice, for whose sources see Lucian of Samosata, *On the Syrian Goddess (De dea Syria)*, trans. and ed. Jane Lucy Lightfoot (Oxford: Oxford University Press, 2003), 373-374 note 1.

15. *Carmen* may also mean a magic spell as well as song.

16. Or possibly "person."

17. Reading *caput omnes*.

18. A legend concerning the martyr-bishop of Antioch.

19. The text is badly corrupt, but this must be the sense.

20. Neither *vociferando* nor *jocatur* necessarily implies music; but that is what the reader is expected to call to mind.

21. Augustine, *Confessiones*, 10. 33. 50.

22. Latin idiom says "sang."

23. See Ephesians 5:19.

24. Transcribed with corrections from Jean Gerson, *Oeuvres Complètes*, ed. Palémon Glorieux (Paris: Desclée, 1961-), 4:135-137 (No. 160).

Notes to Appendix 3

1. Walter Blankenburg, "Überlieferung und Textgeschichte von Martin Luthers 'Encomion musices,'" L-J 39 (1972): 80-104.

2. Blankenburg, "Martin Luthers 'Encomion musices,'" 90-94; the Latin text is also found in WA 50:368-374.

3. LW 53:321-324.

Notes to Appendix 4

1. See Joachim Stalmann, "Johann Walters Versuch einer Reform des gregorianischen Chorals," *Festschrift Walter Gerstenberg zum 60. Geburtstag: Im Namen seiner Schüler*, ed. Georg von Dadelsen & Andreas Holschneider (Wolfenbüttel: Möseler, 1964), 166. The first volume of the *Syntagma* was in many respects an expansion of the *Leiturgodia*.

2. Michael Praetorius, *Syntagma musicum* I (Wittenberg: Richter, 1615; facsimile Kassel: Bärenreiter, 1974), 447: "*Quia in prima Tomi parte prima, membri primi capite quarto pag. 15. Johannis Waltheri mentio facta, & ipsius conatus & industria in vitiositate cantus choralis emendanda commendata suit, & ex iis de mente ejus cognoscere: et cum praetermissa ibidem fuerunt, potius quam plane omitterentur hic in calce appendicis quasi loco ea annectere placuit, quorum lectionem benevolus lector facile cum loco supra allegato conjungere potest*"; "Since Johann Walter was mentioned in the first volume, first part, first section, fourth chapter, on page 15, and [since] his effort and industry in emending faulty choral song were commended, it would have been fitting, then, to supply that reverend old man's own words at once, and from them, to get to know [him] from his own mind. But since they were omitted in that place, it has been pleasing to add them here in this concluding appendix, as if in their proper place, rather than omit them altogether; the benevolent reader may easily join them in reading to the place mentioned above"; Michael David Fleming, "Michael Praetorius, Music Historian: An Annotated Translation of 'Syntagma musicum I, Part I'" (Ph.D. diss., Washington University, 1979), 308.

3. Fleming, "Annotated Translation," 308 (slightly modified); Praetorius, *Syntagma* I: 447.

4. Fleming, "Annotated Translation," 309-310; Praetorius, *Syntagma* I: 448: "*Etsi vero hujusmodi tam frequentia occurrant, ut illis omnibus medicinam adhibere, atq; hoc Augiae stabulum perpurgare, impossibile pene sit, & non unum Herculem requirat: tamen nonnihil tentavit ante annos plus minus octoginta Johannes Waltherus, Electoris Saxonici tum temporis*

chori Musici Magister. Is distinctis primo accurate notis, quae quibus deinde verbis conjungenda essent demonstravit, nec non potissima in pronunciationem Latinam commissa vitia, Barbarismos insuper etiam, quibus scatebant Psalmodiae vetustiores, quantum ejus fieri potuit, correxit & sustulit. Quod vero restare videbatur, in quantitatis syllabarum ratione exacte subducenda, necessario sibi relinquendum putavit: ne antiquae & consuetae clausulae, disruptae, plane novum quid & peregrinum sonarent, auresque offenderent."

5. Virtually all the church orders drawn up with significant input from Wittenberg Reformers around this time — such as Brunswick 1528, Hamburg 1529, Lübeck 1531, Herford 1532, Wittenberg 1533, Bremen 1535, Zerbst 1538, Duke Henry of Saxony 1539/40, Halle 1541, and Brunswick-Wolfenbüttel, 1543 — either included examples of traditional chants and/or made significant reference to their continuance within the reformed liturgies.

6. Fleming, "Annotated Translation," 310-11; Praetorius, *Syntagma* I: 448: *"Et sane optanum fuisset, illos Waltheri labores, tum plus successus habuisse, tum lucem adspexisse publicam. Verum tamen eam lampada, quam inextinctam ad metam usq; optatam perferre non potuit Waltherus, suscepit Lucas Lossius. Ejus Psalmodiae, non minus correctae & emaculatae, paulo post in publicum prodierunt, & incredibili applausu exceptae sunt. Quippe quo opere non tantum iis, qui in scholis & templis Musicae sacrae vacant, quos plurimis fastidiosisque transcriptionum laboribus sublevavit; sed omnibus simil piis, quibus cultus divini curae cordique sunt, succursum est."*

7. For the background, see Werner Merten, "Die *Psalmodia* des Lucas Lossius," JbLH 19 (1975): 1-18; 20 (1976): 63-90; 21 (1977): 39-67.

8. See Chapter 14 above.

9. Matthäus Ratzeberger, *Die handschriftliche Geschichte Ratzeberger's über Luther und seine Zeit,* ed. Christian Gotthold Neudecker (Jena: Mauke, 1850), 59.

10. Walter's continuing close connection to Wittenberg throughout this period is demonstrated in the publication of his *Geystliche gesangk Buchlein* (the so-called *Chorgesangbuch*) in Wittenberg in 1524, and all subsequent editions between 1528 and 1551 were similarly published in Wittenberg. But there were other Wittenberg imprints containing his music, such as Georg Rhau's *Newe Deudsche Geistliche Gesange* (1544) and *Ein Schöner Geistlicher und Christlicher newer Berckreyen* (1552).

11. Emil Sehling, ed., *Die evangelischen Kirchenordnungen des 16. Jahrhunderts* (Leipzig: 1902-1913), 1/2 : 61-190; see W. Lucke, "Die Naumberger Kirchenordnung Nikolaus Medlers," WA 35:56-69.

12. See Sehling, *Die evangelischen Kirchenordnungen,* 1/2:71-84 (without musical notation); Konrad Ameln, "'All Ehr und Lob soll Gottes sein,' Ein deutsches Gloria — von Martin Luther," JbLH 31 (1987/88): 38-52. Spangenberg also included it in the German section of his *Cantiones ecclesiasticae/Kirchengesenge Deutsch* of 1545; see 44 & 52, and Chapter 14 above.

13. See also Walter Sources in note 17 below.

14. Johannes Keuchenthal, *KirchenGesenge Lateinisch und Deudsch* (Wittenberg: Seelfisch, 1573); see Konrad Ameln, "Johannes Keuchenthal," JbLH 3 (1958): 121-124.

15. Franz Eler, *Cantica sacra* (Hamburg: Wolff, 1588; facsimile Hildesheim: Olms, 2003).

16. Fleming, "Annotated Translation," 311; Praetorius, *Syntagma* I: 449: *"Mihi equidem tantopere placuit ille liber, ut eum totum, Dei beneficio & auxilio, harmonicis numeris includere in animum induxerium. Praeterquam enim quod a primis unguiculis incredibili & singulari*

studio hujusmodi cantilenarum ductus sim; rationibus etiam & argumentis tum aliis, tum ijs praesertim, quae in manuscripto praedicti Dn. Johannis Waltheri, vir pij & sauvissimi Musici habentur, inductus: & in eo proposito magis magisq; confirmatus sum."

17. Walter Sources = polyphonic settings of chants found in the manuscripts that Walter complied for use in Torgau, many of which were his own; see Carl Gerhardt, *Die Torgauer Walter Handschiften: Eine Studie zur Quellenkunde der Musikgeschichte der deutschen Reformationszeit* (Kassel: Bärenreiter, 1949). One of the manuscripts — a tenor part-book, the so-called "Luther-Codex" — bears the inscription on the title page: "Hat myr verehret mayn guter freund | herr Johann Walther | Componist Musicie | zu Torgaw | 1530 | dem Gott gnade | Martinus Luther" (My respects to my good friend Herr Johann Walter, music composer at Torgau, 1530, by God's grace. Martin Luther), 8; settings of the German texted chants appeared in the various editions of Walter's *Chorgesangbuch*, first issued in Wittenberg in 1524.

Wittenberg = Wittenberg manuscript, dated 1543/44; see Chapter 14, note 12.

Spangenberg = monodic chants in his *Cantiones/Kirchengsenge*.

Lossius = monodic chants in his *Psalmodia*.

Praetorius = polyphonic settings of chants found in Praetorius's many volumes of church music published between 1605 and 1621; see Michael Praetorius, *Gesamtausgabe der musikalischen Werke*, ed. Friedrich Blume (Wolfenbüttel: Kallmeyer, 1928-1960), Band 21: *Generalregister*.

18. *"Et cur minus ipsa Waltheri verba vulgari lingua referam caussae nihil video"*; Praetorius, *Syntagma* I: 449. "And I see no reason not to reproduce Walther's own words in the vulgar tongue"; Fleming, "Annotated Translation," 311.

19. Fleming, "Annotated Translation," 311-316. The German can be found in Praetorius, *Syntagma* I: 449-453; and partially in WA 35:82-83.

20. Praetorius's heading: "Verba | Des alten Johan Walthers"; Praetorius, *Syntagma* I: 449.

21. In his preface to the funeral hymns of 1542, Luther made the opposite point, that in the case of funeral Responsories the melodies were pure but their associated texts corrupt; see WA 35:479; LW 53:327-28.

22. *Ein Kindelein so löbelich* is the German version of the previous item, *Dies est laetitiae*.

23. This is part of the Easter *Alleluia* beginning *Dicant nunc redempti sunt a Domino*.

24. *O adoranda Trinitas* and *O veneranda Unitas* are different parts of the Trinity Sequence *Benedicta semper sit Trinitas*.

25. Here Walter echoes Luther in the *Deutsche Messe:* "For in no wise would I want to discontinue the service in the Latin language, because the young are my chief concern" ("Denn ich ynn keynen weg wil die lateinsiches sprache aus dem Gottis deinst lassen gar weg komen/denn es ist myr alles vmb die iugent zu thun"); LW 53:63; WA 19:74. By "German Christian songs" Walter means pre-Reformation vernacular *Leisen*, such as *Christ ist erstanden* and *Nun bitten wir den heiligen Geist.*

26. Lossius's chant anthology contained a few German items; the first part of Spangenberg is devoted to Latin chants and the second to vernacular chant; Keuchenthal's collection contains both Latin and German chants; and Eler's collection of Latin chants includes a substantial appendix of German hymns.

27. What Walter means is that Luther was equally skilled in creating liturgical chants (*concentus*) and lectionary tones (*accentus*); see Andreas Ornithoparchus, *Musicae activae*

micrologus libris (Leipzig: Schumann, 1517; facsimile Hildesheim: Olms, 1977), Lib. 3, cap. 1, esp. Sig. Iij^r-Iiij^v.

28. Without the original manuscript there is no way of knowing whether this is where Walter concluded or where Praetorius decided to end his citation.

Notes to Appendix 5

1. Composite trans. based on James McKinnon, *Music in Early Christian Literature* (Cambridge: Cambridge University Press, 1987), 107 (No. 232), and Johannes Quasten, *Music and Worship in Pagan and Christian Antiquity*, trans. Boniface Ramsey (Washington, D.C.: National Association of Pastoral Musicians, 1983), 75. *Patrologiae cursus completus, series graeca*, ed. Jacques-Paul Migne (Paris: Migne, 1857-1887), 6: cols. 1353-1356: "Εἰ ὑπὸ τῶν ἀπίστων πρὸς ἀπάτην εὑρέθη τὰ ᾄσματα τοῖς δὲ ἐν νόμῳ εἰσηγήθη διὰ φρενῶν νηπιότητα, οἱ τῆς χάριτος τέλεια καὶ τῶν ῥηθέντων τρόπων ἀλλότρια παρειληφότες μαθήματα, διὰ τί ταῖς Ἐκκλησίαις κατὰ τοὺς ἐν τῷ νόμῳ νηπίους τοῖς κέχρηνται; ΑΠΟΚΡΙΣΙΣ. Οὐ τὸ ᾆσαι ἁπλῶς ἐστι τοῖς νηπίοις ἁρμόδιον, ἀλλὰ τὸ μετὰ τῶν ἀψύχων ὀργάνων ᾆσαι, καὶ μετὰ ὀρχήσεως καὶ κροτάλων· διὸ ἐν ταῖς Ἐκκλησίαις προαίρεται ἐκ τῶν ᾀσμάτων ἡ χρῆσις τῶν τοιούτων ὀργάνων καὶ τῶν ἄλλων τῶν νηπίοις ὄντων ἁρμοδίων, καὶ ὑπολέλειπται τὸ ᾆσαι ἁπλῶς. . . . Μάχαιραν τοῦ Πνεύματος τοῦτο ὁ Παῦλος ὀνομάζει, ἐν ᾧ κατὰ τῶν ἀοράτων πολεμίων ὁπλίζει τοὺς ὁπλίτας τῆς εὐσεβείας. Ῥῆμα γὰρ ἐστι θεοῦ τὸ καὶ ἐνθυμούμενον καὶ ἀδόμενον, καὶ ἀναχρουόμενον, δαιμόνων γίνεται ἀπελατικὸν"; see also Quasten, *Music and Worship*, 106, note 106.

2. In the first volume of his *Syntagma musicam*, issued a few years earlier, Praetorius identifies his source. He cites in full a Latin version of "Question 107" with its "Response" of the Pseudo-Justin document, but also gives the key sentence in the same Greek form that occurs in his introduction to the *Polyhymnia* of 1619; see Michael Praetorius, *Syntagma musicum* I (Wittenberg, 1614/15; facsimile Kassel: Bärenreiter, 1959), 138; Michael David Fleming, *Michael Praetorius, Music Historian: An Annotated Translation of* Syntagma musicum I, *Part I* (Ph.D. diss., Washington University, 1979), 286-287.

3. McKinnon, *Music in Early Christian Literature*, 160 (No. 368); *Patrologiae cursus completus, series latina*, ed. Jacques-Paul Migne, 221 vols. (Paris: Migne, 1844-1891) 37: col. 1965: ". . . tri esse genera sonorum; voce, flatu, pulsu: voce. Ut est per fauces et arterias, sine organo aliquo cantantis hominis; flatu, sicut per tibiam, vel quid ejusmodi; pulsu, sicut per citharam, vel quid ejusmodi."

4. McKinnon, *Music in Early Christian Literature*, 165 (No. 382); Migne, *Patrologiae . . . latina* 34: col. 49: ". . . sed quia facile erat animadvertere omnium sonum, quae materies cantilenarum est, triformem esse natura. Aut enim voce editur, sicuti corum est qui faucibus sine organo canunt; aut flatu, sicut tubarum et tibiarum; aut pulsu, sicut in citharis et tympanis, et quibuslibet aliis quae percutiendo canore sunt."

5. Both Hans-Joachim Moser, *Die evangelische Kirchenmusik in Deutschland* (Berlin: Merseburger, 1955), 313, and Oskar Söhngen, *Theologie der Musik* (Kassel: Stauda, 1967), 183, cite Praetorius's word-play between *concio* and *cantio*, with reference to Justin; and both refer to the material in the Limburg *Kirchenordnung* (1666), which they cite from Adolf Strube, *Spielleute Gottes: Ein Buch vom deutschen Kantor* (Berlin-Steglitz: Eckart, 1935): Moser, 315-316, and Söhngen, 333.

Bibliography

Aaburg, Ursula. "Zu den Lutherliedern im jonischen Oktavraum." JbLH 5 (1960): 125-131.

Aber, Adolf. "Das musikalische Studienheft des Wittenberger Studenten Georg Donat um 1543." *Sammelbände der Internationalen Musik-Gesellschaft* 15 (1913): 68-98.

Abert, Hermann. *Luther und die Musik.* Wittenberg: Verlag der Luther-Gesellschaft, 1924. Reprint in Hermann Abert, *Gesammelte Schriften und Vorträge,* ed. Friedrich Blume (Halle: Niemeyer, 1929).

————. *Die Musikanschauung des Mittelalters und ihre Grundlagen.* Halle: Niemeyer, 1905. Reprint Tutzing: Schneider, 1964.

Agricola, Martin. *Musica figaralis deudsch* 1532. *Musica instrumentalis deudsch* 1529. *Music choralis deudsch* 1533. *Rudimenta musices* 1539. Wittenburg: Rhau, 1532, 1529, 1533 and 1539; facsimile, Hildesheim: Olms, 1985.

————. *Musica instrumentalis deudsch 1528 und 1545.* Wittenberg: Rhau. Facsimile edited by Robert Eitner (Leipzig: Breitkopf & Härtel, 1896; repr. New York: Broude, 1966).

————. *The "Musica instrumentalis deudsche" of Martin Agricola: A Treatise on Musical Instruments, 1528 and 1545.* Translated and edited by William E. Hettrick. Cambridge: Cambridge University Press, 1994.

Aland, Kurt. *Hilfsbuch zum Lutherstudium.* 4th ed. Wittenburg: Luther-Verlag, 1996.

Alber, Erasmus. *Wider die verkehrte Lehre der Carlstader, und alle fürnemste Häupter der Sacramentirer: Rottengeister, Widerteuffer, Sacramentlsterer, Eheschender, Musica Verächter, Bildstürmer, und Verwüster aller guten Ordnung.* Neubrandenburg, 1594.

Allwohn, Adolf. *Gottesdienst und Rechtfertigungsglaube: Luthers Grundlegung evangelischer Liturgik bis zum Jahre 1523.* Göttingen: Vandenhoeck & Ruprecht, 1926.

Alpers, Paul. "'Nun freut euch, lieben Christen gmein' im Liederbuch der Anna von Köln [ca. 1500]." JbLH 5 (1960): 132-133.

Ameln, Konrad. "'All Ehr und Lob soll Gottes sein': Ein deutsches Gloria — von Martin Luther?" JbLH 31 (1987/88): 38-52.

————. "Lateinischer Hymnus und deutsche Kirchenlied." *Musik und Kirche* 6 (1934): 138-48.

————. "Luthers Anteil an dem Liede 'Nun laßt uns den Leib begraben.'" JbLH 3 (1957): 108-112.

————. "Nochmals zu 'Gib userm Fürsten und aller Obrigkeit.'" JbLH 25 (1981): 103-104.

————. "Psalmus Jn exitu Jsrael verdeutscht." JbLH 28 (1984): 65-67.

————. *The Roots of German Hymnody of the Reformation Era.* St. Louis: Concordia, 1964.

Ameln, Konrad, Christhard Mahrenholz, Wilhelm Thomas, & Carl Gerhardt, eds. *Handbuch der deutschen evangelischen Kirchenmusik nach den Quellen.* Göttingen: Vandenhoeck & Ruprecht, 1932-.

Anders, Charles. "Luther and the Composers of His Time." *The Musical Heritage of the Church* 7 (1970): 41-50.

Anton, Karl. *Luther und die Musik.* 1916. Fourth edition Berlin: Evangelische Verlagsanstalt, 1957.

Asper, Ulrich. "Musikanschauung in der Reformationszeit: zwei Lobgedichte über die Musik von Luthers musikalischem Mitarbeiter Johann Walter 1496-1570." *Musik und Gottesdienst* 37 (1983): 229-235.

Atlas, Allan A. *Renaissance Music: Music in Western Europe, 1400-1600.* New York: Norton, 1998.

Avis, Paul D. L. *The Church in the Theology of the Reformers.* London: Marshall Morgan and Scott, 1981.

Barge, Hermann. *Andreas Bodenstein von Karlstadt.* Leipzig: Brandsetter, 1905. Reprint, Nieukoop: de Graaf, 1968.

Barker, John Wesley. "Sociological Influences upon the Emergence of Lutheran Music." *Miscellanea musicologica: Adelaide Studies in Musicology* 4 (1969): 157-198.

Bartel, Dietrich. *Musica Poetica: Musical-Rhetorical Figures in German Baroque Music.* Lincoln: University of Nebraska Press, 1997.

Bäumker, Wilhelm. *Das katholische deutsche Kirchenlied in seinen Singweisen von den frühesten Zeiten.* Freiburg: Herder, 1883-1911. Reprint, Hildesheim: Olms, 1962.

Bayer, Oswald. *Living by Faith: Justification and Sanctification.* Translated by Geoffrey W. Bromiley. Grand Rapids: Eerdmans, 2003.

————. "Poetological Doctrine of the Trinity." *Lutheran Quarterly* 5 (2001): 43-58.

Beatis, Antonio de. *The Travel Journal of Antonio De Beatis: Germany, Switzerland, The Low Countries, France and Italy 1517-1518.* Translated and edited by J. R. Hale and J. M. A. Lindon. London: Hakluyt Society, 1979.

Beck, Friedrich Adolf. *Dr. Martin Luther's Gedanken über die Musik.* Berlin: Mittler, 1825.

Beißwenger, Kirsten. *Johann Sebastian Bachs Notenbibliothek.* Kassel: Bärenreiter, 1992.

Bente, Martin. *Neue Wege der Quellenkritik und die Biographie Ludwig Senfls: Ein Beitrag zur Musikgeschichte der Reformationszeitalters.* Wiesbaden: Breitkopf & Härtel, 1968.

Benzing, Josef. *Die Buchdrucker des 16. und 17. Jahrhunderts in deutschen Sprachgebiet.* Wiesbaden: Harrassowitz, 1963.

Bergsma, Johannes H. *Die Reform der Messliturgie durch Johannes Bugenhagen.* Hildesheim: Bernward, 1966.

Beutel, Albrecht, ed. *Luther Handbuch.* Tübingen: Mohr Siebeck, 2005.

Blankenburg, Walter. "Geschichte der Melodien des Evangelischen Kirchengesangbuchs: Ein Abriß." In *Handbuch zum Evangelischen Kirchengesangbuch,* edited by

Christhard Mahrenholz and Oskar Söhngen. Berlin: Evangelische Verlagsanstalt, 1954-1990.

————. *Johann Walter: Leben und Werk.* Edited by Friedhelm Brusniak. Tutzing: Schneider, 1991.

————. "Luther und die Musik." *Luther: Mitteilungen der Luther-Gesellschaft* 28 (1957): 14-27. Reprinted in *Kirche und Musik: Gesammelte Aufsätze zur Geschichte der gottesdienstlichen Musik, zu seinem 75. Geburtstag,* edited by Erich Hübner and Renate Steiger (Göttingen: Vandenhoeck & Ruprecht, 1979).

————. "Überlieferung und Textgeschichte von Martin Luthers 'Encomion musices.'" L-J 39 (1972): 80-104.

————. "Wer schuf den Gesang 'Gib unserm Fürsten und aller Obrigkeit'?" JbLH 25 (1981): 102-103.

————. "Zu Karl Honemeyers Thomas Müntzer-Buch." JbLH 19 (1975): 228-231.

Block, Johannes. *Verstehen durch Musik: Das gesungene Wort in der Theologie: Ein hermeneutischer Beitrag zur Hymnologie am Beispiel Martin Luthers.* Tübingen: Francke, 2002.

Blume, Friedrich. *Die evangelische Kirchenmusik.* Potsdam: Academische Verlagsgesellschaft Athenaion, 1931. Reprint, New York: Musurgia, 1949. Second, expanded edition, *Geschichte der evangelischen Kirchenmusik* (Kassel: Bärenreiter, 1965). Translated as *Protestant Church Music: A History* (New York: Norton, 1974).

Boës, Adolf. "Die reformatorischen Gottesdienste in der Wittenberger Pfarrkirche von 1523 an und die 'Ordenung der gesenge der Wittembergischen Kirchen' von 1543/44." JbLH 4 (1958/59): 1-40.

Böhme, Franz M. *Altdeutsche Liederbuch: Volkslieder der Deutschen nach Wort und Weise aus dem 12. bis zum 17. Jahrhundert.* 3rd ed. Leipzig: Breitkopf & Härtel, 1925.

Bornkamm, Heinrich. *Luther and the Old Testament.* Translated by Eric W. and Ruth C. Gritsch and edited by Victor I. Gruhn. Philadelphia: Fortress, 1969.

————. *Martin Luther in der Mitte seines Lebens: das Jahrzehnt zwischen dem Wormser und dem Augsburger Reichstag.* Göttingen: Vandenhoeck & Ruprecht 1979. Translated as *Luther in Mid-Career, 1521-1530* (Philadelphia: Fortress, 1983).

Bosinski, Gerhard. *Das Schrifttum des Rostocker Reformators Joachim Slüter.* Berlin: Evangelischen Verlagsanstalt, 1971.

Brady, Thomas A., Heiko Oberman, and James D. Tracy, eds. *Handbook of European History 1400-1600: Late Middle Ages, Renaissance, and Reformation.* Grand Rapids: Eerdmans, 1996.

Brecht, Martin. *Martin Luther.* 3 vols. Stuttgart: Calwer, 1981-1987. Translated by James L. Schaaf (Philadelphia: Fortress, 1985-1993).

Brilioth, Yngve T. *Nattvarden i evangeliskt gudstjänstliv.* Stockholm: Svenska Kyrkans Diakonistyrelses Bokförlag, 1926. Translated by A. G. Herbert as *Eucharistic Faith and Practice: Evangelical and Catholic* (New York: Macmillan, 1930; abbreviated and revised edition, London: SPCK, 1965).

Brodde, Otto. "'Ein neues Lied wir heben an': Martin Luther als 'Phonascus.'" *Luther: Zeitschrift der Luther-Gesellschaft* 34 (1963): 72-82.

————. "Evangelische Choralkunde: Der gregorianische Choral in evangelischen Gottesdienst." In *Leiturgia: Handbuch des evangelischen Gottesdiensts.* Vol. IV: *Die*

Musik des evangelischen Gottesdienst, edited by Karl Ferdinand Müller & Walter Blankenburg. Kassel: Stauda, 1961.

Buelow, George J. *A History of Baroque Music.* Bloomington: Indiana University Press, 2004.

Bugenhagen, Johannes. *Eine Christliche Predigt/über der Leich und begrebnis/des Ehrwirdigen D. Martini Luthers . . .* Wittenberg: Rhau, 1546.

———. *Katechismuspredigten gehalten 1525 und 1532.* Edited by Georg Buchwald. Leipzig: Heinsius, 1909.

Burmeister, Joachim. *Musical Poetics.* Edited and translated by Benito V. Rivera. New Haven: Yale University Press, 1993.

Buszin, Walter E. "Luther on Music." *Musical Quarterly* 32 (1946): 80-97. Reprint St. Paul: North Central, 1958.

Butler, Bartlett Russell. "Liturgical Music in Sixteenth-Century Nürnberg: A Socio-Musical Study." Ph.D. diss., University of Illinois at Urbana-Champaign, 1971.

Butt, John. *Music Education and the Art of Performance in the German Baroque.* Cambridge: Cambridge University Press, 1994.

The Cambridge Songs Carmina cantabrigiensia. Edited and translated by Jan M. Ziolkowski. New York: Garland, 1994.

Carpenter, Nan Cooke. *Music in the Medieval and Renaissance Universities.* Norman: University of Oklahoma Press, 1958.

Casey, Paul F. "'Start Spreading the News': Martin Luther's First Published Song." In *In laudem Caroli: Renaissance and Reformation Studies for Charles G. Nauert,* edited by James V. Mehl. Kirksville: Thomas Jefferson University Press, 1998.

Chytraeus, David. *In Leviticum, seu teritum librum Mosis.* Wittenberg, 1569. *Prolegomena* translated by John Warwick Montgomery as *Chytraeus on Sacrifice: A Reformation Treatise in Biblical Theology* (St. Louis: Concordia, 1962).

Cochlaeus, Johannes. *Commentaria de actis et scriptis Martini Lutheri Saxonis.* Maintz: Behem, 1549. Translation in Elizabeth Vandiver, Ralph Klein, and Thomas D. Frazel, eds., *Luther's Lives: Two Contemporary Accounts of Martin Luther* (Manchester: Manchester University Press, 2002).

———. *Tetrachordis Musices.* Nuremberg: Stuchsen, 1512. Reprint Hildesheim: Olms, 1971.

Coclico, Adrianus Petit. *Compendium musicis.* Nuremberg: Montan & Neuber, 1552. Facsimile Kassel: Bärenreiter, 1954. Translated by Albert Seay as *Musical Compendium* (Colorado Springs: Colorado College Music Press, 1973).

Coussemaker, Edmond de, ed. *Scriptorum de musica medii aevi nova series a Gerbertina altera.* Paris: Durand, 1864-76. Reprint Hildesheim: Olms, 1963.

Crevel, Marcus van. *Adrianus Petit Coclico: Leben und Beziehungen eines nach Deutschland emigrierten Josquinschülers.* The Hague: Nijhoff, 1940.

Degering, Herman. "Aus Luthers Frühzeit: Briefe aus dem Eisenacher und Erfurter Lutherkreis." *Zentralblatt für Bibliothekwesen* 33 (1916): 69-95.

Dix, Gregory. *The Shape of the Liturgy.* London: Dacre 1945.

Dowden, John. *Further Studies in the Prayer Book.* London: Methuen, 1908.

Dress, Walter. "Gerson und Luther." *Zeitschrift für Kirchengeschichte* 52 (1933): 122-161.

Duffy, Kathryn Ann P. "The Jena Choirbooks: Music and Liturgy at the Castle Church in

Wittenberg under Frederick the Wise, Elector of Saxony." Ph.D. diss., University of Chicago, 1995.

Eger, Karl. "Luthers Gottesdienstreform 1523-1526." *Luther: Mitteilungen der Luther-Gesellschaft* 9 (1927): 2-11.

Eler, Franz. *Cantica sacra.* Hamburg: Wolff, 1588. Facsimile Hildesheim: Olms, 2002.

Elferen, Isabella van. "'Sie creutzigen alle sinn des liebes!' Multi-mediality, Consolatio Tragoediae and Lutheran Pedagogy in the German Baroque Passion Meditation." In *Multi-Media Compositions from the Middle Ages to the Early Modern Period,* edited by Margriet Hoogvliet. Leuven: Peeters, 2004.

Endermann, Heinz. "Martin Luther in Erfurt: Student, Mönch und Wissenschaftler." *Luther: Zeitschrift der Luther-Gesellschaft* 72 (2001): 83-95.

Fendt, Leonhard. *Der lutherische Gottesdienst des 16. Jahrhunderts.* Munich: Reinhardt, 1923.

Finck, Herman. *Practica Musica.* Wittenberg: Rhau, 1556. Reprint Bologna: Forni, 1969.

Fleming, Michael David. *Michael Praetorius, Music Historian: An Annotated Translation of* Syntagma musicum *I, Part I.* Ph.D. diss., Washington University, 1979.

Flynn, William T. *Medieval Music as Medieval Exegesis.* Lanham: Scarecrow, 1999.

Foley, Edward. "Martin Luther: A Model Pastoral Musician." *Currents in Theology and Mission* 54 (1987): 405-418. Reprinted in Edward Foley, *Ritual Music: Studies in Liturgical Musicology* (Beltsville: Pastoral Press, 1995).

Follmi, Beat A. *Das Weiterwirken der Musikanschauung Augustins im 16. Jahrhundert.* Frankfurt: Lang, 1994.

Fornaçon, Siegfried. "Matthäus Lüdtke Ludecus." JbLH 12 (1967): 167-170.

———. "Wolfgang Dachstein, der erste evangelische Organist." *Der Kirchenmusiker* 7 (1956): 37-40.

Forrell, George W. "Luther and Culture." L-J 52 (1985): 152-163.

Förstemann, Karl Eduard, Otto Hartwig, and Karl Gerhard, eds. *Album academiae Vitebergensis 1502-1602.* Leipzig & Halle, 1841-1905. Reprint Tübingen: Niemeyer, 1976.

Förster, Uwe. "Lateinschule und Gymnasium zwischen Reformation und Neuhumanismus." In *Struktur, Funktion und Bedeutung des deutschen protestantischen Kantorats im 16. bis 18. Jahrhundert,* edited by Wolf Hobohm, Carsten Lange, and Brit Riepsch. Oschersleben: Ziethen, 1997.

Frederichs, Henning. "Zur Wort-Ton-Beziehung in Thomas Müntzers Deutschen Messen und Kirchenämtern." In *Thomas Müntzer Leben und Werk,* 3rd ed., edited by Walter Elliger. Göttingen: Vandenhoeck & Ruprecht, 1976.

Funck, Heinz. *Martin Agricola: Ein frühprotestantischer Schulmusiker.* Wolfenbüttel: Kallmeyer, 1933.

Gable, Frederick K. "The *Institutionum musicarum* of Erasmus Sartorius and the Rhythm of Plainsong in Seventeenth-century Germany." In *Music in Performance and Society: Essays in Honor of Roland Jackson,* edited by Malcolm S. Cole and John Koegel. Warren: Harmonie Park Press, 1997.

———. "Rhythm in 17th-Century German Chant." In *Proceedings of the Göteborg International Organ Academy, 1994.* Göteborg: University of Göteborg, 1995.

Garside, Charles. *Zwingli and the Arts.* New Haven: Yale University Press, 1966.

Gebauer, August. D. *Martin Luther und seine Zeitgenossen als Kirchenliederdichter: nebst Luthers Gedanken über die Musik und einigen poetischen Reliquien.* Leipzig: Klein, 1828.

Gebhardt, Friedrich. "Die musikalischen Grundlagen zu Luthers Deutscher Messe." L-J 10 (1928): 56-169.

Gerbert, Martin, ed. *Scriptores ecclesiastici de musica sacra potissimum.* St. Blaise: Typis San-Blasianis, 1784. Reprint Hildesheim: Olms, 1963.

Gerhardt, Carl. *Die Torgauer Walter Handschriften: Eine Studie zur Quellenkunde der Musickgeschichte der deutschen Reformationszeit.* Kassel: Bärenreiter, 1949.

Glover, Raymond, ed. *The Hymnal 1982 Companion.* Edited by Raymond Glover. New York: Church Hymnal Corporation, 1990-95.

Gojowy, Detlef. "Kirchenlieder im Umkreis von J. S. Bach." JbLH 22 (1978): 79-123.

Gotsch, Herbert. "The Organ in the Lutheran Service of the 16th Century." *Church Music* 67/1 (1967): 7-12.

Gottwald, Clytus. "Von der babylonischen Gefangenschaft der Musik: Josquin und Luthers Encomion." In *Ursprung der Biblia deutsch von Martin Luther: Ausstellung in der Wurrtembergische Landesbibliothek Stuttgart, 21. September bis 19. November 1983,* edited by Stefan Strohm and Eberhard Zwink. Stuttgart: Wurttembergische Landesbibliothek & Quell-Verlag, 1983.

Gould, Ronald Lee. "The Latin Lutheran Mass at Wittenberg 1523-1545: A Survey of the Early Reformation Mass and the Lutheran Theology of Music, as Evidenced in the Liturgical Writings of Martin Luther, the Relevant Kirchenordnungen, and the Georg Rhau Musikdrucke for the Hauptgottesdienst." S.M.D. diss., Union Theological Seminary, 1970.

Green, Lowell C. "The Chorales of Martin Luther: How Have They Fared in the *Lutheran Book of Worship?*" *Church Music* 79 (1979): 60-65.

Grimm, Harold J. *The Reformation Era 1500-1650.* 2nd ed. New York: Macmillan, 1973.

Grimm, Jürgen. *Das Neu Leipziger Gesangbuch des Gottfried Vopelius Leipzig (1682): Untersuchung zur Klärung seiner geschichtlichen Stellung.* Berlin: Merseburger, 1969.

Grohmann, Johann Christian August. *Annalen der Universität zu Wittenberg.* Meissen: Erbstein, 1801-02.

Guicharrousse, Hubert. *Les musiques de Luther.* Geneva: Labor et Fides, 1995.

Gurlitt, Wilibald. "Johannes Walter und die Musik der Reformationszeit." L-J 15 (1933): 1-112.

Hahn, Gerhard. *Evangelium als literarische Anweisung: Zu Luthers Stellung in der Geschichte des deutschen kirchlichen Liedes.* Munich: Artemis, 1981.

Heidrich, Jürgen. *Die deutschen Chorbücher aus der Hofkapelle Friedrichs des Weisen: Ein Beitrag zur mitteldeutschen geistlichen Musikpraxis um 1500.* Baden-Baden: Koerner, 1993.

Hennig, Kurt. *Die geistliche Kontrafaktur im Jahrhundert der Reformation: Ein Beitrag zur Geschichte des deutschen Volks- und Kirchenliedes im XVI. Jahrhundert.* Halle: Niemeyer, 1909. Reprint Hildesheim: Olms, 1974.

Henning, Friedrich. "Martin Luther als Lateinschüler in Eisenach." *Luther: Zeitschrift der Luther-Gesellschaft* 67 (1996): 109-113.

Herl, Joseph. *Worship Wars in Early Lutheranism: Choir, Congregation, and Three Centuries of Conflict.* Oxford: Oxford University Press, 2004.

Hiley, David. *Western Plainchant: A Handbook.* Oxford: Clarendon, 1993.

Hoelty-Nickel, Theodore. "Luther and Music." In *Luther and Culture* [Martin Luther Lectures 4]. Decorah: Luther College Press, 1960.

Holtheuser, Johann. *Encomium musicae, artis antiquiae: et divinae carmine elegiaco scriptum.* Erfurt: Dolgen, 1551.

Honemeyer, Karl. *Luther's Musikanschauung: Studien zur Fragen ihrer geschichtlichen Grundlagen.* Diss., University of Münster, 1941.

————. *Thomas Müntzer und Martin Luther, ihr Ringen um die Musik des Gottesdienstes: Untersuchungen zum "Deutzsch Kirchenampt" 1523.* Berlin: Merseburger, 1974.

Hoppin, Richard, ed. *Anthology of Medieval Music.* New York: Norton, 1978.

Horne, B. L. "A Civitas of Sound: On Luther and Music." *Theology* 88 (1985): 21-28.

Huchzermeyer, Helmut. "Luther an die Musik." *Luther: Zeitschrift der Luther-Gesellschaft* 39 (1968): 14-25.

Ihlenfeld, Kurt. "Die himmlische Kunst Musica: ein Blick in Luthers Briefe." *Luther: Zeitschrift der Luther-Gesellschaft* 34 (1963): 83-90.

Irwin, Joyce L. "The Mystical Music of Jean Gerson." *Early Music History* 1 (1981): 187-201.

————. *Neither Voice nor Heart Alone: German Lutheran Theology of Music in the Age of the Baroque.* New York: Lang, 1993.

————. "The Theological and Social Dimensions of Thomas Müntzer's Liturgical Reform." Ph.D. diss., Yale University, 1972.

Jenny, Markus. "Ein brief von Sixt Dietrich über Luther und die Kirchengemeinde in Wittenberg." JbLH 5 (1960): 134-135.

————. "Eine Korrektur Luthers an einer von seiner eigenen Melodien." JbLH 33 (1990/91): 204-205.

————. "Luthers Gesangbuch." In *Leben und Werk Martin Luthers von 1526 bis 1546: Festgabe zu seinem 500. Geburtstag,* edited by Helmar Junghans. Berlin: Evangelische Verlagsanstalt, 1983.

————. *Luther, Zwingli, Calvin in ihren Liedern.* Zurich: Theologischer Verlag, 1983.

————. "Sieben biblische Begräbnisgesänge: Ein unbekanntes und unediertes Werk Martin Luthers." In *Lutheriana: Zum 500. Geburtstag Martin Luthers von den Mitarbeitern der Weimarer Ausgabe,* edited by Gerhard Hammer and Karl-Heinz zur Mühlen. Cologne: Böhlau, 1985.

Jenny, Markus, ed. *Luther's Geistliche Lieder und Kirchen gesänge: Vollständige Neuedition in Ergänzung zu Band der Weimarer Ausgabe* [= AWA 4]. Cologne: Böhlau, 1985.

Judd, Cristle Collins. *Reading Renaissance Music Theory: Hearing with the Eyes.* Cambridge: Cambridge University Press, 2000.

Jung, Alfred. "'Nun freut euch, lieben Christen gmein': Eine theologische Untersuchung des Lutherliedes." JbLH 19 (1975): 200-209.

Junghans, Helmar. "Luther on the Reform of Worship." *Lutheran Quarterly* 13 (1999): 315-333.

Junghans, Helmar, ed. *Leben und Werk Martin Luthers von 1526 bis 1546: Festgabe zu seinem 500. Geburtstag.* Berlin: Evangelische Verlagsanstalt, 1983.

Just, Martin. "Josquins Chanson 'Niphen, napées' als Bearbeitung des Invitatoriums

'Circumdederunt me' und als Grundlage für Kontrafaktur, Zitat und Nachahmung." *Die Musikforschung* 43 (1990): 305-335.

Kalb, Friedrich. "Luther und die Musik des Gottesdienst." *Gottesdienst und Kirchenmusik* 6 (1983): 144-150.

Kappner, Gerhard. "Luther und die Musik." In *Singet und spielet dem Herrn: Bremer Beiträge zur Kirchenmusik,* edited by Gerhard Kappner. Bremen: Schünemann, 1987.

Kind, Helmut. *Die Lutherdrucke des 16. Jahrhunderts und die Lutherschriften der Niedersächsischen Staats- und Universitätsbibliothek Göttingen.* Göttingen: Vandenhoeck & Ruprecht, 1967.

Kirby, F. E. "Herman Finck on Methods of Performance." *Music & Letters* 42 (1961): 212-220.

Knecht, Justin Heinrich. *Luthers Verdienste um Musik und Poesie.* Ulm: Wohler, 1817.

Knolle, Theodor. "Luthers Deutsche Messe und die Rechtfertigungslehre." L-J 10 (1928): 170-203.

Köstlin, Julian. *The Theology of Martin Luther.* Translated by Charles E. Hay. Philadelphia: Lutheran Publication Society, 1897. Reprint St. Louis: Concordia, 1986.

Kooiman, Willem Jan. *Luther and the Bible.* Translated by John Schmidt. Philadelphia: Muhlenberg, 1961.

Kongsted, Ole. "Ludwig Senfl's 'Luther-Motetter': En forskningsberetning." *Fund og Forskning* 39 (2000): 7-41.

Korrick, Leslie. "Instrumental Music in the Early 16th-century Mass: New Evidence." *Early Music* 18 (1990): 359-370.

Kraege, Jean-Denis. "Luther théologien de la musique." *Etudes Théologiques et Religieuses* 58 (1983): 449-463.

Kramer, Joachim. "Change and Continuity in the Reformation Period: Church Music in North German Towns, 1500-1600." In *Music and Musicians in Renaissance Cities and Towns,* edited by Fiona Kisby. Cambridge: Cambridge University Press, 2001.

Krummacher, Christoph. *Musik als Praxis pietatis: Zum selbstverständnis evangelischer Kirchenmusik.* Göttingen: Vandenhoeck & Ruprecht, 1994.

Krummacher, Friedhelm. "Luthers Musikbegriff und die Kirchenmusik Bachs." *Luther: Zeitschrift der Luther-Gesellschaft* 56 (1985): 136-151.

Kümmerle, Salomon. *Encyklopädie der evangelischen Kirchenmusik.* Gütersloh: Bertelsmann, 1888-1895. Reprint Hildesheim: Olms, 1974.

Kurzschenkel, Winfried. *Die theologische Bestimmung der Musik.* Trier: Paulinus, 1971.

Lang, Paul Henry. *Music in Western Civilization.* New York: Norton, 1941.

Lausten, Martin Schwarz. "Luther and the Reformation in Denmark." L-J 71 (2004): 115-130.

Leaver, Robin A. "*Agnus dei* Compositions of J. S. Bach: Some Liturgical and Theological Perspectives." In *Das Blut Jesu und die Lehre von der Versöhnung im Werk Johann Sebastian Bach,* edited by Albert A. Clement. Amsterdam: Koninklijke Nederlandse Akadamie van Wetenschappen, 1995.

―――. "Bach and the German *Agnus Dei.*" In *A Bach Tribute: Essays in Honor of William H. Scheide,* edited by Paul Brainard and Ray Robinson. Kassel: Bärenreiter 1993.

―――. "Bach's 'Clavierübung III': Some Historical and Theological Considerations." *The Organ Yearbook* 6 (1975): 17-32.

————. *Bachs theologische Bibliothek: Eine kritische Bibliographie* [Beiträge zur theologischen Bachforschung 1]. Stuttgart: Hänssler, 1983.

————. "The Chorale: Transcending Time and Culture." *Concordia Theological Quarterly* 56 (1992): 123-144.

————. "Christian Liturgical Music in the Wake of the Protestant Reformation." In *Sacred Sound and Social Change: Liturgical Music in Jewish and Christian Experience*, edited by Lawrence A. Hofmann and Janet R. Walton. Notre Dame: University of Notre Dame Press, 1992.

————. *Elisabeth Creutziger, the Magdeburg Enchiridion, 1536, & Reformation Theology: The Kessler Reformation Lecture, Pitts Theology Library, October 18, 1994*. Atlanta: Pitts Theology Library, Emory University, 1995.

————. "Liturgical Chant Forms in Bach's Compositions for Lutheran Worship: A Preliminary Survey." In *Die Quellen Johann Sebastian Bachs: Bachs Musik im Gottesdeinst*, edited by Renate Steiger. Heidelberg: Manutius, 1998.

————. "The Liturgical Place and Homiletic Purpose of Bach's Cantatas." *Worship* 59 (1985): 194-202.

————. "Luther, Martin." New Grove 2, 15:364-369.

————. *Luther on Justification*. St. Louis: Concordia, 1975.

————. "The Lutheran Reformation." In *The Renaissance from the 1470s to the End of the 16th Century* [Music & Society 2], edited by Ian Fenlon. Englewood Cliffs: Prentice Hall, 1989.

————. "Lutheran Vespers as a Context for Music." In *Church, Stage, and Studio: Music and Its Contexts in Seventeenth-Century Germany*, edited by Paul Walker. Ann Arbor: University of Michigan Research Press, 1990.

————. "Music and Lutheranism." In *The Cambridge Bach Companion*, edited by John Butt. Cambridge: Cambridge University Press, 1997.

————. "Religion and Religious Currents in Bach's World." In *Bach and His World*, edited by Raymond Erikson. New Haven: Yale University Press, forthcoming.

Leder, Hans-Günther. "Luthers Beziehungen zu seinen Wittenberger Freunden." In *Leben und Werk Martin Luthers von 1526 bis 1546: Festgabe zu seinem 500. Geburtstag*, edited by Helmar Junghans. Berlin: Evangelische Verlagsanstalt, 1983.

Leupold, Ulrich S. *Die liturgischen Gesänge der evangelischen Kirche im Zeitalter der Aufklärung und der Romantik*. Kassel: Bärenreiter, 1933.

————. "Luther's Conception of Music in Worship." *The Lutheran Church Quarterly* 13 (1940): 66-69.

————. "Luther's Musical Education and Activities." *The Lutheran Church Quarterly* 12 (1939): 423-428.

Liebner, Johann Adolf. *Ueber D. Martin Luthers Dichtkunst und Lieder*. Wittenberg: Kühne, 1791.

Liliencron, Rochus, Freiherrn von. *Liturgisch-musikalische Geschichte der evangelischen Gottesdienste von 1523 bis 1700*. Schleswig: Bergas, 1893. Reprint Hildesheim: Olms, 1970.

Lindner, Andreas. "Non moriar sed vivam: Luther, Senfl und die Reformation des Hochstifts Naumburg-Zeitz." JbLH 36 (1996-97): 208-217.

Linke, Johannes. "Die Melodie: 'Ein feste Burg ist unser Gott' und die Bäumker'sche Analyse." *Blätter für Hymnologie* 2 (1884): 82-88, 101-105.

Lipphardt, Walther. "Die älteste Quelle des deutschen "Media vita," eine Salzburger Handschrift vom Jahre 1456." JbLH 11 (1966): 161-162.

————. "Deutsche Antiphonenlieder des Spätmittelalters in eine Salzburger Handschrift." JbLH 27 (1983): 40-82.

————. "Das wiedergefundene Gesangbuch-Autograph von Adam Reißner aus dem Jahre 1554." JbLH 10 (1965): 54-86.

Listenius, Nicolaus. *Rudimenta musicae in gratiam studeiosae iuventutis . . . comportata.* Wittenberg: Rhau, 1533. Facsimile of the 1549 Nuremberg imprint, *Musica Nicolai Listenii,* edited by Georg Schünemann (Berlin: Breslauer, 1927). Translated by Albert Seay as *Music Musica* (Colorado Springs: Colorado College Music Press, 1975).

Livingstone, Ernest F. "The Place of Music in German Education from the Beginnings through the 16th Century." *Journal of Research in Music Education* 15 (1967): 243-277.

Loersch, Heinz von. *Der Werkbegriff in der protestantischen Musiktheorie des 16. und 17. Jahrhunderts: Ein Mißverständnis.* Hildesheim: Olms, 2001.

Loescher, Valentin Ernst. *The Complete Timotheus Verinus or A Statement of the Truth and a Call for Peace in the Present Pietistic Controversy . . .* [1718-1721]. Translated by James L. Langebartels and Robert J. Koester. Milwaukee: Northwestern, 1998.

Lorenz, Ralph. "Pedagogical Implications of *music practica* in Sixteenth-century Wittenberg." Ph.D. diss., Indiana University, 1995.

Lossius, Lucas. *Erotemata musicae practicae.* Nuremberg: Gerlach, 1563. Facsimile Bologna: Forni, 1980.

Lowinsky, Edward E., ed. *Josquin des Prez: Proceedings of the International Conference held at the Juilliard School at Lincoln Center in New York City, June 1971.* Oxford: Oxford University Press, 1976.

Luther, Johannes. "Die Nachkommenschaft Martin Luthers des Reformators." L-J 7 (1925): 126-127.

Macey, Patrick. "An Expressive Detail in Josquin's *Nimphes, nappés.*" *Early Music* 31 (2003): 400-411.

McKim, Donald K., ed. *The Cambridge Companion to Martin Luther.* Cambridge: Cambridge University Press, 2003.

McKinnon, James. "Jubal vel Pythagoras, quis sit inventor musicae?" *Musical Quarterly* 64 (1978): 1-28.

————. *Music in Early Christian Literature.* Cambridge: Cambridge University Press, 1987.

Mager, Inge. "Nikolaus Selneckers Katechismusbereimung." JbLH 34 (1992/93): 57-67.

Mahrenholz, Christhard. "Auswahl und Einordnung der Katechismus lieder in den Wittenberger Gesangbüchern seit 1529." In *Gestalt und Glaube: Festschrift für Oskar Söhngen.* Berlin: Merseburger, 1960.

————. *Luther an die Kirchenmusik.* Kassel: Bärenreiter, 1937. Reprinted in *Musicologica et Liturgica: Gesammelte Aufsätze vom Christhard Mahrenholz zu siner 60. Geburtstag,* edited by Karl Ferdinand Müller (Kassel: Bärenreiter, 1960).

————. "Zur musicalischen Gestaltung von Luthers deutscher Litanie." L-J 29 (1937): 1-31. Reprinted in *Musicologica et Liturgica: Gesammelte Aufsätze vom Christhard*

Mahrenholz zu seiner 60. Geburtstag, edited by Karl Ferdinand Müller (Kassel: Bärenreiter, 1960).

―――. "Zur musicalischen Gestaltung von Luthers Gottesdienstreform." *Musik und Kirche* 5 (1933): 281-296. Reprinted in *Musicologica et Liturgica: Gesammelte Aufsätze vom Christhard Mahrenholz zu seiner 60. Geburtstag*, edited by Karl Ferdinand Müller (Kassel: Bärenreiter, 1960).

Manlius, Johannes. *Locorum communium . . . Schöne ordentliche Gattierung allerley alten und newen Exempel, Gleichniß, Sprüche, Rathschläge.* Frankfurt am Main: Feyerabend & Hüter, 1574.

Massie, Richard. *Martin Luther's Spiritual Songs.* London: Hatchard, 1854.

Mathesius, Johann. *Historien, Von des Ehrwirdigen inn Gott seligen theuren Manns Gottes, D. Martin Luthers. . .* Nuremberg: Berg, 1576. Reprint. *Dr. Martin Luthers Leben.* St. Louis: Concordia, 1883.

Mattheson, Johann. *Critica Musica.* Hamburg: Mattheson, 1722-1725. Facsimile Amsterdam: Knuf, 1964.

―――. *Grundlage einer Ehren-Pforte.* Hamburg: Mattheson, 1740. Reprint Berlin: Liepmannssohn, 1910.

―――. *Der Musikalische Patriot, Welcher seine gründliche Betrachtungen, über Geist- und Weltl. Harmonien.* Hamburg: Mattheson, 1728. Facsimile Leipzig: Zentralantiquariat der DDR, 1978.

―――. *Die neueste untersuchung der Singspiele, nebst beyfügter musikalischen Geschmacksprobe.* Hamburg: Herold, 1744. Facsimile Leipzig: Zentralantiquariat der DDR, 1975.

―――. *Der vollkommene Capellmeister.* Hamburg: Herold, 1739. Facsimile Kassel: Bärenreiter, 1954. Translated and edited by Ernest C. Harriss as *Johann Mattheson's Der vollkommene Capellmeister: A Revised Translation with Critical Commentary* (Ann Arbor: University of Michigan Research Press, 1981).

Mattfeld, Victor H. *Georg Rhaw's Publications for Vespers.* Brooklyn: Institute of Mediaeval Music, 1966.

Maxwell, William D. *An Outline of Christian Worship: Its Development and Forms.* Oxford: Oxford University Press, 1936. Reprint London: Faith, 1960.

Meconi, Honey. *Pierre de la Rue and the Musical Life at the Hapsburg-Burgundian Court.* Oxford: Oxford University Press, 2003.

Meding, Wichman von. *Luthers Gesangbuch: Die gesungene Theologie eines christlichen Psalters.* Hamburg: Lovač, 1998.

―――. "Luthers Katechismuslieder." *Kerygma und Dogma* 40 (1994): 250-271.

―――. "Luthers Lied vom Vaterunser: Waffe aus Weise und Wort." *Zeitschrift für Theologie und Kirche* 93 (1996): 500-537.

Mehl, Oskar Johannes. "Das 'Vesperale et Matutinale' des Matthaeus Ludecus (1589)." *Theologische Literaturzeitung* 80 (1955), cols. 265-270.

Merten, Werner. "Die *Psalmodia* des Lucas Lossius." JbLH 19 (1975): 1-18; 20 (1976): 63-90; 21 (1977): 39-67.

Meßner, Reinard. *Die Meßreform Martin Luthers und die Eucharistie der Alten Kirche: Ein Beitrag zu einer systematischen Liturgiewissenschaft.* Innsbruck: Tyrolia, 1989.

Micus, Rosa. "Zum Katechismusbild in der Wittenberg-Leipzig Gesangbuchfamilie." JbLH 35 (1994/95): 210-215.

Milsom, John. "*Circumdederunt*: A Favourite cantus firmus of Josquin's'?" *Soundings* 9 (1982): 2-10.

Moser, Hans Joachim. *Die Evangelische Kirchenmusik in Deutschland*. Berlin: Merseberger, 1954.

————. "Die Wittenbergisch Nachtigal." L-J 7 (1925): 87-91.

————. "Luther als Musiker." *Speculum musicae artis: Festgabe für Heinrich Husmann zum 60. Geburtstag*. Munich: Fink, 1970.

————. "Nun freut euch, lieben Christen gmein." *Gestalt und Glaube: Festschrift für Vizepräsident Professor D. Dr. Oskar Söhngen zum 60. Geburtstag am 5. Dezember 1960*. Witten: Luther-Verlag, 1960.

Müller-Blattau, Josef. "Die musikalischen Schätze der Staats- und Universitätsbibliothek zu Königsburg in Preußen." *Zeitschrift für Musikwissenschaft* 6 (1923/24): 215-239.

Müntzer, Thomas. *Deutsche Evangelische Messe 1524*. Facsimile Berlin: Evangelische Verlagsanstalt, 1988.

————. *Schriften und Briefe: Kritische Gesamtausgabe*. Edited by Günther Franz. Gütersloh: Mohn, 1968.

Nettl, Paul. *Luther and Music*. Translated by Frida Best and Ralph Wood. Philadelphia: Muhlenberg, 1948. Reprint New York: Russel & Russel, 1967.

Nirmal, A. P. "Faith's Provocations — Luther's Liturgical Reforms." *Gurukul Journal of Theological Studies* 3 (1992): 1-17.

Novak, Louis. "The Liturgical Contributions of Martin Luther." *The Iliff Review* 32 (1975): 43-50.

Oberhelman, Steven M. *Rhetoric and Homiletics in Fourth-century Christian Literature: Prose Rhythm, Oratorical Style, and Preaching in the Works of Ambrose, Jerome, and Augustine*. Atlanta: Scholars Press, 1991.

Oberman, Heiko A. *Luther: Man between God and the Devil*. Translated by Eileen Walliser-Schwarzbart. New Haven: Yale University Press, 1989.

Oettinger, Rebecca Wagner. "Ludwig Senfl and the Judas Trope: Composition and Religious Tolerance at the Bavarian Court." *Early Music History* 20 (2001): 199-225.

————. *Music as Propaganda in the German Reformation*. Aldershot: Ashgate, 2001.

Olearius, Johann Christoph. *Evangelischer Lieder-Schatz*. Jena: Bielke, 1707.

Ornithoparchus, Andreas. *Musicae activae micrologus*. Leipzig: Schumann, 1517. Facsimile Hildesheim: Olms, 1977. Translated by John Dowland as *Micrologus, or Introduction* (London: Adams, 1609).

Osthoff, Helmuth. "Vergils Aeneis in der Musik von Josquin des Prez bis Orlando di Lasso." *Archiv für Musikwissenschaft* 11 (1954): 85-102.

Østrem, Eyolf. "Luther, Josquin and *des fincken gesang*." In *The Arts and the Cultural Heritage of Martin Luther*, edited by Eyolf Østrem, Jens Fleischer and Nils Holger Peterson. Copenhagen: Museum Tusculanum Press, 2003.

Østrem, Eyolf, Jens Fleischer, and Nils Holger Peterson, eds. *The Arts and the Cultural Heritage of Martin Luther*. Copenhagen: Museum Tusculanum Press, 2003.

Ozment, Steven E. *Homo Spiritualis: A Comparative Study of the Anthropology of Johannes*

Tauler, Jean Gerson, and Martin Luther (1509-16) in the Context of Their Theological Thought. Leiden: Brill, 1969.

Padberg, Rudolf. "Luther und der Canon missae." *Catholica* 37 (1983): 288-305.

Page, Christopher. "Reading and Reminiscence: Tinctoris on the Beauty of Music." *Journal of the American Musicological Society* 49 (1996): 1-31.

Pankratz, Herbert R. "Luther's Utilization of Music in School and Town in the Early Reformation." In *A Tribute to Martin Luther: In Celebration of the Quincentennial of His Birth and the 450th Anniversary of His First Complete German Bible.* Berrien Springs: Andrews University Press, 1984.

Parrish, Carl. "A Renaissance Music Manual for Choirboys." In *Aspects of Medieval and Renaissance Music: A Birthday Offering to Gustave Reese,* edited by Jan La Rue. New York: Norton, 1966.

Peterson, Nils Holger. "Lutheran Tradition and the Medieval Mass." In *The Arts and the Cultural Heritage of Martin Luther,* edited by Eyolf Østrem, Jens Fleischer, and Nils Holger Peterson. Copenhagen: Museum Tusculanum Press, 2003.

Petzoldt, Martin. *Bach und die Bibel: Ausstellung der Leipziger Bibelgesellschaft.* Leipzig: Bibelgesellschaft, 1997.

————. "Bachs Prüfung vor dem Kurfürstlichen Konsistorium zu Leipzig." *Bach-Jahrbuch* 84 (1998): 19-30.

Pietsch, Helen. "On Luther's Understanding of Music." *Lutheran Theological Journal* 26 (1992): 160-168.

Pietzsch, Gerhard. *Die klassifikation der musik von Boetius bis Vgolino von Orvieto.* Halle: Niemeyer, 1929.

————. *Zur Pflege der Musik an den deutschen Universitäten.* Hildesheim: Olms, 1971.

Polack, William Gustave. *The Handbook to the Lutheran Hymnal.* 3rd ed. St. Louis: Concordia, 1958.

Praetorius, Michael. *Syntagma musicum.* Wittenberg and Wolfenbüttel: Richter & Holwein, 1615-1619. Facsimile Kassel: Bärenreiter, 1959.

Rambach, August Jakob. *Über D. Martin Luthers Verdienst um den Kirchengesang.* Hamburg: Bohn, 1813. Reprint Hildesheim: Olms, 1972.

Ratzeberger, Matthäus. *Die handschriftliche Geschichte Ratzeberger's Über Luther und seine Zeit.* Edited by Christian Gotthold Neudecker. Jena: Mauke, 1850.

Rautenstrauch, Johannes. *Luther und die Pflege der Kirchen Musik in Sachsen.* Leipzig: Breitkopf & Härtel, 1907. Reprint Hildesheim: Olms, 1970.

Reckziegel, Walter. *Das Cantional von Johann Herman Schein: Seine geschichtlichen Grundlagen.* Berlin: Merseburger, 1963.

Reed, Luther D. *The Lutheran Liturgy.* 2nd ed. Philadelphia: Fortress Press, 1959.

Reichert, Otto. "Der Deudsche Psalter D. Luthers zu Wittenberg 1531-1931." *L-J* 13 (1931): 29-68.

Reinitzer, Heimo. *Biblia deutsch: Luthers Bibelübersetzung und ihre Tradition.* Exhibition catalog. Wolfenbüttel: Herzog August Bibliothek, 1983.

Reu, Johann Michael. *Dr. Martin Luther's Small Catechism: A History of Its Origin, Its Distribution, and Its Use.* Chicago: Wartburg, 1929.

————. *Quellen zur Geschichte des kirchlichen Unterrichts in der evangelischen Kirche*

Deutschland zwischen 1530 und 1600. 4 vols. in 9. Güterloh: Bertelsmann, 1904-1935. Reprint Hildesheim: Olms, 1976.

Reuning, Daniel. "Luther and Music." *Concordia Theological Quarterly* 48 (1984): 17-21.

Richter, Aemilius L. *Die evangelischen Kirchenordnungen des sechsehnten Jahrhunderts.* Weimar: Verlag des Landes-Industriecomptoirs, 1846. Reprint Nieuwkoop: De Graaf, 1967.

Riederer, Johann Bartholomäus. *Abhandlung von Einführung des teutschen Gesangs in die evangelischlutherische Kirche überhaupts und in die nürnbergische besonders: wobey auch von den ältesten Gesangbüchern und Liedern so bis zum Tode Lutheri herausgegeben und verfertigt worden gehandelt wird.* Nürnberg: Endter, 1759. Facsimile Leipzig: Zentralantiquariat, 1975.

Rietschel, Georg. *Die Aufgabe der Orgel im Gottesdienste bis in das 18. Jahrhundert.* Leipzig: Dürr, 1893. Reprint Buren: Knuf, 1979.

Rivera, Benito V. *German Music Theory in the Early 17th Century: The Treatises of Johannes Lippius.* Ann Arbor: University of Michigan Research Press, 1980.

————. "The 'Isagoge' (1581) of Johannes Avianius: An Early Formulation of Triadic Theory." *Journal of Music Theory* 22 (1978): 43-64.

Robinson-Hammerstein, Helga. "The Lutheran Reformation and Its Music." In *The Transmission of Ideas in the Lutheran Reformation,* edited by Helga Robinson-Hammerstein. Dublin: Irish Academic Press, 1989.

Rorem, Paul. "Luther's Objection to a Eucharistic Prayer." *The Cresset* 38 (1978): 12-16.

Rössler, Martin. *Bibliographie der Liedpredigt.* Nieuwkoop: de Graaf, 1976.

————. "'Ein neues Lied wir heben an': Protestsong Martin Luthers." In *Reformation und Praktische Theologie: Festschrift für W. Jetter,* edited by Hans Martin Müller, Dietrich Rössler, and Martin Brecht. Göttingen: Vandenhoeck & Ruprecht, 1983.

————. "Die Frühzeit hymnologischer Forschung." JbLH 19 (1975): 123-186.

————. *Die Liedpredigt: Geschichte einer Predigtgattung.* Göttingen: Vandenhoeck & Ruprecht, 1976.

Rose, Stephen. "Daniel Vetter and the Domestic Keyboard Chorale in Bach's Leipzig." *Early Music* 33 (2005): 39-53.

Rupprecht, Oliver C. "From Exalted Precept to Pattern of Excellence: Luther's Psalm Hymns." *The Hymn* 33 (1982): 89-93.

Schalk, Carl. *Johann Walter: First Cantor of the Lutheran Church.* St. Louis: Concordia, 1992.

————. *Luther on Musik: Paradigms of Praise.* St. Louis: Concordia, 1988.

————. *Music in Early Lutheranism: Shaping the Tradition (1524-1672).* St. Louis: Concordia, 2001.

Scheel, Otto. "Luther und die Schule seiner Zeit." L-J 7 (1925): 141-175.

Schlagel, Stephanie P. "The *Liber selectarum cantionum* and the 'German Josquin Renaissance.'" *The Journal of Musicology* 19 (2002): 564-615.

Schmidt, Günther. *Die Eucharistie als Entfaltung der Verba Testamenti.* Kassel: Stauda, 1957.

————. "Über den Fauxbourdon." JbLH 4 (1958/59): 146-151.

Schmidt-Lauber, Hans-Christoph. "Das Gottesdienstverständnis Martin Luthers im ökumenischen Kontext." *Theologische Literaturzeitung* 114 (1989): 321-338.

Schmidt-Rost, Reinhard. "Martin Luthers Gedanken über die Orgel im Gottesdienst." *Württembergische Blätter für Kirchenmusik* 52 (1985): 40-45.

Schneider, Charles. *Luther Poète et Musicien et les Enchiridien de 1524.* Geneva: Henn, 1942.

Schröder, Otto, et al., eds. *Johann Walter Sämtliche Werke.* Kassel: Bärenreiter, 1953-1973.

Schueller, Herbert M. *The Idea of Music: An Introduction to Musical Aesthetics in Antiquity and the Middle Ages.* Kalamazoo: Medieval Institute Publications, 1988.

Schuhmacher, Gerhard. "Aspekte de Choralbearbeitung in der Geschichte des Liedes 'Vater unser im Himmelreich.'" *Sagittarius* 4 (1973): 111-136.

Schulz, Frieder. "Der Gottesdienst bei Luther." *Leben und Werk Martin Luthers von 1526 bis 1546: Festgabe zu seinem 500. Geburtstag,* edited by Helmar Junghans. Berlin: Evangelische Verlaganstalt, 1983.

————. "Luthers liturgische Reformen: Kontinuität und Innovation." *Archiv für Liturgiewissenschaft* 25 (1983): 249-275.

Schwiebert, Ernest G. *Luther and His Times: The Reformation from a New Perspective.* St. Louis: Concordia, 1950.

Schwier, Helmut. "Lehren, Züristen und Gedenken: Bugenhagens Abendmahls-vermahnung in ihren theologischen und liturgischen Dimensionen." JbLH 36 (1996/97): 11-50.

Sehling, Emil. *Die evangelischen Kirchenordnungen des 16. Jahrhunderts.* Leipzig: Riesland, 1902-1913. Reprint Tübingen: Mohr, 1955.

Selnecker, Nicolaus. *Historia Oratio. Vom Leben und Wandel des Ehrwirdigen Herrn/und theuren Mannes Gottes/D. Martini Lutheri.* Leipzig: Rhambaw, 1576. Facsimile, with the title *Lebenschreibung Martin Luthers,* Fürth: Flacius-Verlag, 1992.

Senn, Frank C. "Liturgia Svecanae Ecclesiae: An Attempt at Eucharistic Restoration During the Swedish Reformation." *Studia Liturgica* 14 (1980/81): 20-36.

————. "Martin Luther's Revision of the Eucharistic Canon in the *Formula Missae* of 1523." *Concordia Theological Monthly* 44 (1973): 101-118.

Serauky, Walter. *Musikgeschichte der Stadt Halle.* Halle: Buchhandlung des Waisenhauses, 1935-1942. Reprint Hildesheim: Olms, 1971.

Sessions, Kyle C. "Hymns and School Music in the Reformation." *Illinois State University Journal* 31 (1968): 21-31.

————. "Luther in Music and Verse." In *Pietas et societas: New Trends in Reformation Social History. Essays in Memory of Harold J. Grimm,* edited by Kyle C. Sessions and Phillip N. Bebb. Kirksville: Sixteenth Century Journal Publishers, 1985.

————. "Luther's Hymns in the Spread of the Reformation." Ph.D. diss., Ohio State University, 1963.

Sherr, Richard, ed. *The Josquin Companion.* Oxford: Oxford University Press, 2000.

Smend, Julius. "Luther der Liturg und Musicant." L-J 6 (1924): 21-37.

Söhngen, Oskar. "Theologische Grundlagen der Kirchenmusik." In *Leiturgia: Handbuch des evangelischen Gottesdienstes,* edited by Karl Ferdinand Müller and Walter Blankenburg, Bd. 4: *Die Musik des evangelischen Gottesdienst.* Kassel: Stauda, 1961. Revised and reissued as *Theologie der Musik* (Kassel: Stauda, 1967).

Spangenburg, Cyriacus. *Cythera Lutheri.* Erfurt: Bauman, 1569-70.

————. *Von der Musica und den Meistersängern.* Edited by Adelbert von Keller. Stuttgart: Hiersemann, 1861. Reprint Hildesheim: Olms, 1966.

Spangenberg, Johann. *Cantiones ecclesiasticae/ Kirchengesenge Deudsche.* Magdeburg: Lotter, 1545. Facsimile, with an introduction by Robin A. Leaver, Hildesheim: Olms, forthcoming.

Spangenberg, Wolfhart. *Sämtliche Werke.* Edited by Andor Tarnai and András Vizkelety. Berlin: de Gruyter, 1971- .

Spener, Philipp Jacob. *Kurtze Catechismus-Predigten, Darinnen Die fünff Haupt-Stück, aus dem Catechismo . . . einfältig erkläret werden.* Berlin: Rüdiger, 1727.

Spinks, Bryan. *Luther's Liturgical Criteria and His Reform of the Canon of the Mass.* Bramcote: Grove, 1982.

———. *From the Lord and "The Best Reformed Churches: A Study of the Eucharistic Liturgy of the English Puritan and Separatist Traditions 1550-1633."* Rome: Edizioni Liturgiche, 1984.

Stäblein, Brune, ed. *Monumenta monodica medii aevi, I: Die mittelalterlichen Hymnen des Abendlandes.* 2nd ed. Kassel: Bärenreiter, 1995.

Stähelin, Martin. "Luther über Josquin." In *Festschrift für Martin Ruhnke zum 65. Geburtstag.* Edited by Mitarbeitern des Instituts für Musikwissenschaft der Universtität Erlangen-Nürnberg. Stuttgart: Hänssler, 1986.

Stapel, Wilhelm. *Luthers Lieder und Gedichte: Mit Einleitung und Erläuterungen.* Stuttgart: Evangelisches Verlagswerk, 1950.

Sternfeld, Frederick W. "Music in the Schools of the Reformation." *Musica Disciplina* 2 (1948): 99-122.

Steude, Wolfrum. *Untersuchungen zur mitteldeutschen Musiküberlieferung und Musikpflege im 16. Jahrhundert.* Leipzig: Peters, 1978.

Stevenson, Robert M. "Luther's Musical Achievement." *Lutheran Quarterly* first series 3 (1951): 255-262. Reprinted in Robert M. Stevenson, *Patterns of Protestant Church Music* (Durham: Duke University Press, 1953).

Strunk, Oliver W. "Vergil and Music." *Musical Quarterly* 16 (1930): 482-497.

Strunk, Oliver W., ed. *Source Readings in Music History.* Revised and expanded by Leo Treitler. New York: Norton, 1998.

Suppan, Wolfgang. *Deutsches Liedleben zwischen Renaissance and Barock: Die Schichtung des deutschen Liedgutes in der zweiten Hälfte des 16. Jahrhunderts.* Tutzing: Schneider, 1973.

Tappert, Theodore G., trans. & ed. *Luther: Letters of Spiritual Counsel.* Philadelphia: Westminster, 1965.

Tarry, Joe Eugene. "Music in the Educational Philosophy of Martin Luther." *Journal of Research in Education* 21 (1973): 355-365.

Thompson, Bard. *Liturgies of the Western Church.* Philadelphia: Fortress, 1980.

Tinctoris, Johannes. *Johannes Tinctoris (1445-1511) und sein unbekannter Traktat "De inventione et usu musicae."* Edited by Karl Weinmann. Regensburg: Pustet, 1917.

Tschackert, Paul. "Justus Jonas' Bericht aus dem Jahre 1538 über Martin Luthers Eintritt in das Kloster 1505. Aus dem handschriftlichen Zusatz zu einem Urdruck der Confessio Augustana." *Theologische Studien und Kritiken* 70 (1897): 577-580.

Unger, Hans-Heinrich. *Die Beziehungen zwischen Musik und Rhetorik im 16.-18. Jahrhundert.* Würzburg: Triltsch, 1941. Reprint Hildesheim: Olms, 2000.

Uptrup, Klaus Meyer zu. "Liturgie und Katechese." *JbLH* 26 (1982): 1-19.

Vajta, Vilmos. "Martin Luther's Concept of Worship." *The Musical Heritage of the Church* 5 (1959): 18-33.

———. *Die Theologie des Gottesdiensts bei Luther.* Göttingen: Vandenhoeck & Ruprecht, 1954. Abridged translation, *Luther on Worship*, by Ulrich Leupold (Philadelphia: Fortress, 1958).

Vandiver, Elizabeth, Ralph Klein, and Thomas D. Frazel. *Luther's Lives: Two Contemporary Accounts of Martin Luther.* Manchester: Manchester University Press, 2002.

Veit, Patrice. *Das Kirchenlied in der Reformation Martin Luthers: Eine thematische und semantische Untersuchung.* Stuttgart: Steiner, 1986.

Viertel, Matthias Silesius. "Kirchenmusik zwischen Kerygma und Charisma: Anmerkungen zu einer protestantischen Theologie der Musik." JbLH 29 (1985): 111-123.

Wackernagel, Philipp. *Bibliographie zur Geschichte des deutschen Kirchenliedes im XVI. Jahrhundert.* Frankfurt: 1855. Reprint Hildesheim: Olms, 1961.

———. *Das deutsche Kirchenlied von der ältesten Zeit bis zu Anfang des XVII. Jahrhunderts.* Leipzig: Teubner, 1864-1877. Reprint Hildesheim: Olms, 1964.

Weber, Édith. *Musique et théâtre dans les pays rhénans.* Paris: Klincksieck, 1974.

Weiss, Piero, and Richard Taruskin, eds. *Music in the Western World: A History in Documents.* New York: Schirmer, 1984.

Wengert, Timothy J. "Wittenberg's Earliest Catechism." *Lutheran Quarterly* 7 (1993): 247-260.

Wetzel, Christoph. "Studie zur Musikanschauung Martin Luthers." *Musik und Kirche* 33 (1955): 238-245, 274-279.

———. *Die theologische Bedeutung der Musik im Leben und Denken Martin Luthers.* Diss., University of Münster, 1954.

Wiora, Walter. *Historische und systematische Musikwissenschaft: Ausgewählte Aufsätze.* Tutzing: Schneider, 1972.

Wissemann-Garbe. "Neue Weisen zu alten Lieder: Die Ersatzmelodien im Klugschen Gesangbuch." JbLH 37 (1998): 118-138.

Wolf, Johannes. "Luther und die musikalische Liturgie des evangelischen Hauptgottesdienstes." *Sammelbände der Internationalen Musikgesellschaft* 3 (1902): 647-670.

Wolff, Ludwig. "Zu Luthers Lied: 'Nun freut euch, lieben Christen gmein.'" JbLH 7 (1962): 99-102.

Woodley, Ronald. "The Printing and Scope of Tinctoris's Fragmentary Treatise *De inventione et vsv mvsicae.*" *Early Music History* 5 (1985): 239-268.

Wustmann, Rudolf. *Musikgeschichte Leipzigs I: Bis zur mitte de 17. Jahrhunderts.* Leipzig: Teubner, 1909.

Zager, Daniel. "Music for the Lutheran Liturgy: Johannes Spangenberg's *Cantiones ecclesiasticae/Kirchengesenge Deudsche* (1545)." In *This Is the Feast: A Festschrift for Richard Hillert at 80.* St. Louis: Morning Star, 2004.

Index